The Cistercian Evolution

The Middle Ages Series

Ruth Mazo Karras, Series Editor

Edward Peters, Founding Editor

A complete list of books in the series is available from the publisher.

The Cistercian Evolution

The Invention of a Religious
Order in Twelfth-Century Europe

Constance Hoffman Berman

PENN

University of Pennsylvania Press
Philadelphia • Oxford

Copyright © 2000, 2010 University of Pennsylvania Press

All rights reserved. Except for brief quotations used for purposes of review or scholarly citation, none of this book may be reproduced in any form by any means without written permission from the publisher.

Published by
University of Pennsylvania Press
Philadelphia, Pennsylvania 19104-4112

Printed in the United States of America on acid-free paper
10 9 8 7 6 5 4 3 2 1

Library of Congress Cataloging-in-Publication Data
Berman, Constance H.
   The Cistercian evolution: the invention of a religious order in twelfth-century Europe / Constance Hoffman Berman
      p. cm.—(The Middle Ages Series)
   Includes bibliographical references and index
   ISBN 978-0-8122-2102-8
   1. Cistercians—France, Southern-History. 2. Monasticism and religious orders—France, Southern—History—Middle Ages, 600–1500. I. Title.
BX3431 .B46 1999
271'.12—dc21   99-048399

To David and Benjamin

Contents

List of Tables and Illustrations	ix
Preface	xi
1. Twelfth-Century Narratives and Cistercian Mythology	1
2. Charters, "Primitive Documents," and Papal Confirmations	46
3. From Cîteaux to the Invention of a Cistercian Order	93
4. Charters, Patrons, and Communities	161
5. Rewriting the History of Cistercians and Twelfth-Century Religious Reform	221
Appendix One: Chronological Summary	237
Appendix Two: "Primitive Documents" Manuscripts: Relevant Contents	242
Appendix Three: Southern-French Cistercian Abbeys by Province and Diocese	246
Appendix Four: Calixtus II Documents from 1119 and 1120	251
Appendix Five: Restored 1170 Letter from Alexander III	255
List of Abbreviations	258
Notes	261
Bibliography	323
Index	359

Tables and Illustrations

Tables
1. Sequencing "primitive document" manuscripts   60
2. References to "Cistercians" or *ordo*: Silvanès, Valmagne,
   Grandselve, Berdoues   72
3. Expenditures: Gimont, Silvanès, Nonenque, Valmagne   192

Illustrations
Le Vignogoul at a distance   Frontispiece
1. "Primitive documents" in context   4
2. Sénanque, Silvacane, and le Thoronet, plans   25
3. Sénanque, exterior from distance   26
4. Sénanque, nave looking east   27
5. Sénanque, south aisle   28
6. Locations of southern-French architectural remains   29
7. Fontfroide, plan   30
8. Fontfroide, exterior from east   31
9. Fontfroide, cloister from northwest roof   32
10. Fontfroide, cloister capitals   33
11. Saint-Félix, exterior from north   34
12. Saint-Félix, plan   34
13. Saint-Félix, southern portal and earlier church   35
14. Saint-Félix, nave   36
15. Fabas, exterior, portal   37
16. Fabas, exterior, north side   37
17. Goujon, exterior, portal   38
18. Goujon, exterior, north side   38
19. Relationship of "primitive document" manuscripts   57

20. Earliest *Exordium Cistercii* without rubricated titles	64
21. Earliest lay-brother treatise and General Chapter statutes	65
22. Rota for Lucius III	82
23. Peace Charter	84
24. Privilege from Alexander III	90
25. Genealogical tree engraving from Dijon	105
26. Silvanès, exterior, east end	113
27. Silvanès, plan	114
28. Silvanès, south transept and nave wall	115
29. Silvanès, interior, nave and sanctuary	116
30. Mazan and Bonnevaux daughter-abbeys	119
31. Houses with ties to western-French congregations	125
32. Fontfroide, granges and dependent priories	132
33. Les Olieux, exterior, south door	134
34. Les Olieux, exterior, north side	135
35. Congregations in Gascony attached to Morimond	139
36. Gimont holdings with Maurencs properties	182
37. Maurencs family tree	186
38. Nonenque, Silvanès, and Valmagne granges	194
39. Valmagne, plan	197
40. Valmagne, interior, choir and south transept	198
41. Valmagne, exterior, west end	199
42. Valmagne, exterior, south side	200
43. Le Vignogoul, plan	201
44. Le Vignogoul, nave	202
45. Le Vignogoul, south interior wall, triforium	203
46. Le Vignogoul, choir vault	204
47. Trencavel and Montpellier family tree	206
48. Cistercian nuns in Provence	232
49. Southern-French abbeys listed in this study	247

Preface

When I began this book, I intended it to be a study of the institutional history of the Cistercians in southern France. My primary goal was to incorporate the evidence, fragmentary as it often is, for houses of Cistercian nuns that had been excluded from my earlier study of Cistercian agriculture.[1] I soon had to consider why, despite much local evidence to the contrary, historians had denied that women were part of the twelfth-century reform movement. In so doing, I became aware of a series of dissonances in our traditional understanding of the early Cistercians that have led me step by step to a reconceptualization of early Cistercian history. I discovered that historians employed a "double standard" of proof with regard to Cistercian nuns. For women's houses to be deemed Cistercian, they had to be mentioned in the published statutes of the Order, but the same tests were not applied to men's houses.[2] When I applied the same standards of proof to women's and men's houses, the required references in the early Cistercian records were found *neither* for houses of Cistercian monks *nor* for those of Cistercian nuns for any years before 1190. Such findings suggested that there was no Cistercian Order at all for much of the twelfth century.

This assertion turns out to be only a slight exaggeration of the main point of this book, namely that a Cistercian Order was only invented in the third quarter of the twelfth century. That Order as we usually think of it, an administrative institution that united more than five hundred abbeys by 1215 (when its organization was held up by the Fourth Lateran Council as a model to be emulated), did not appear in 1119 or 1113 or 1098, the dates usually asserted.[3] There was no General Chapter or set of dated statutes or way of affiliation with such an Order until sometime after 1150. There *could not* have been, because these administrative institutions had not yet been invented. Just as the process of founding a new abbey is a gradual one, events in the creation of a religious order did not happen all at once, but were gradual developments.[4] Only in the 1160s was a constitution written. Surviving statutes show order-building to have occurred over much of the 1180s. The five filiations to which abbeys were tied as mothers and daughters began to be devised in the 1190s and later. Moreover, the concept of a religious order itself only appeared in the second half of the twelfth century.

These conclusions are notably different from the conventional wisdom, which has dated the promulgation of the Cistercian constitution, the Charter of Charity, to the decade of the 1110s and all the rest of the Cistercian Order's administrative institutions (General Chapter, statutes, internal visitation, etc.) to shortly thereafter. My findings about the Cistercian invention of the religious order and of the gradual creation of the Cistercian Order itself draw on my increasing understanding of the rapid expansion in wealth and numbers of Cistercian communities in the twelfth century.

Before I had any sense of where this book was leading, I had begun to realize that the process of incorporation was more important to Cistercian expansion than earlier historians had thought.[5] The foundation of abbeys whose agricultural practices I had investigated earlier had not occurred by colonization from Burgundy, but by incorporation of already-established local reformers, their communities, and their properties. Moreover, such evidence of the widespread incorporation by Cistercians of existing reform communities in southern France cannot be considered aberrant. That region represents about a tenth of all twelfth-century houses for men and a similar number of houses for women, thus a significant part of all Cistercian growth. Indeed, conclusions drawn from southern-French evidence and from other regions outside Burgundy about how the concept of an order grew, as well as about how the Cistercian Order itself grew, are probably more relevant than those from any study of Burgundy alone. In the latter region, the heartland of early Cistercian practice, most growth until 1153 was in the time-honored manner of congregations under the personal control of charismatic leaders. I have learned in this study to distinguish Burgundy from other regions.

My investigation of Cistercians and incorporation has also now extended beyond the already considerable Cistercian territory of southern France to which I had confined my earlier monograph. Extensive reading of published primary materials and secondary works on Cistercians in a variety of places beyond Burgundy and southern France shows that Cistercian expansion by incorporation was widespread in the twelfth century. But what I found for southern France is typical. It is now possible to assert that the old model of "apostolic gestation" in which a mother-house in Burgundy sent out twelve monks and an abbot, or twelve nuns and an abbess, which is still found in many accounts of individual Cistercian foundations, misrepresents the facts.

In beginning to rethink what we are usually told about the early Cistercian Order, I turned first to the charters, the documents of practice, which preserve records of land conveyances to individual houses. From these sources I traced an evolution in the notion of a religious order over the twelfth century by tabulating all references to the Cistercians and their *ordo*, its practices, and the General Chapter. Lists of dates for the appearance of the term *ordo* show significant changes in its usage over this period. With a few exceptions, no references to the Cistercian General Chapter, or to an *ordo cisterciensis*, come from before the mid-twelfth century. More precisely, they first appear in cartulary versions of a handful of charters, one dated 1146, another dated 1148, and two dated 1149. These are the earliest references to *ordo* (and they mean a way of life rather than a group to which one is attached) among the 8,000 or so southern-French charters I collected for my earlier study. Even for Burgundy, with the exception of several frequently cited texts purportedly coming from the early twelfth century (every one of which has turned out to be either a forgery or misdated), the charters show that meetings of abbots that could be called annual, universal General Chapters, like the references to the Order as a group, appear only from the 1150s.

As my new findings began to challenge the standard versions of Cistercian origins, I sought the origins of those textbook accounts. I discovered that much of what we constantly repeat about early Cistercian history derives from a group of twelfth-century texts called the "primitive Cistercian documents" written by the Cistercians themselves.[6] These "primitive documents" became very contested texts in the 1950s. I soon found it impossible to sort out their sequence or dating from published editions, which are often faulty, or articles that are often polemical. Fortunately I was able to return to Europe in spring 1997 and look at all the manuscripts in question; they are fewer in number than I had realized, but I was still extraordinarily lucky to have access to all of them during a single trip. That research trip allowed me to establish a sequence of the manuscripts containing those twelfth-century "primitive" texts and to date those manuscripts to the third quarter of the twelfth century. My findings about them confirm that the Cistercian Order, as well as the *exordia* texts about its earliest history, did not appear until after the mid-twelfth century.

Despite a change in the date of its invention, the Cistercian Order probably remains the best example of an institution that could transform a group of loosely affiliated monasteries into an international organization. By the thirteenth century — indeed, by as early as the 1180s — the Cistercians would use this organization to aim at a unified practice of "customs." Nevertheless, what we frequently assume to have been a well-organized Cistercian Order dating from circa 1120 did not exist so early. For much of the twelfth century, we find a conglomeration of reform religious houses beginning to adopt practices thought to be those of Cîteaux. Up to about 1150, when Cistercians began to establish written customs, there is absolutely no basis for discussion of any centralized control of those monastic communities later to be identified as Cistercian, and certainly no reason to expect any unanimity of practice among them. Even circa 1150 there were large numbers of such independently founded houses of monks and nuns (who might at that point be called proto-Cistercians because they had begun to borrow Cistercian customs) who were still adopting Cistercian customs in a fashion that can at best be called haphazard.

Monastic communities adopted such Cistercian practices because they provided effective solutions to real and nearly universal problems for the new twelfth-century reform monastic houses. What these reformers sought were more circumscribed liturgical practices that would allow for the practice of daily manual labor by all members of the community. They also needed guidelines for how to integrate adult converts into their communities as monks and lay-brothers. The problem of truncating the liturgy to accommodate more manual labor and "converts" who had often not been educated in the monastic life in their youth was of considerably higher priority than any other issues on which historians of the Cistercians often focus. Issues such as consistency about distances between agricultural units owned, ownership of churches and tithes, or even about how abbeys should be founded remained secondary. Similarly the need to guarantee that lay-brothers would receive equitable treatment was pressing because it was quite central to recruiting new members. As I argue in Chapter 4, the charters show that recruits wanted to be assured that the community they were about to enter followed Cistercian practices.

That Cistercian customs were adopted voluntarily and selectively by individual houses to solve specific problems suggests that adherence to the *ordo cisterciensis* as a way of life at mid-twelfth century was still viewed as entailing neither an attachment to a larger entity nor any sense that conformity to an entire set of practices would be required. Indeed, this lack of concern about conformity remained true even in the earliest Cistercian constitutional documents, dating to 1165. These documents discuss mutual support (even economic support), affection, and noninterference in most local affairs, but not uniformity.

Once its institutions were invented in the third quarter of the twelfth century, the Cistercian Order probably took shape quite quickly. Still, its component parts would evolve considerably over the rest of the twelfth century. For instance, the newly invented General Chapter of the 1150s and 1160s had entirely different responsibilities from those it would undertake in the 1190s and thereafter. There was considerable difference between what it meant for an abbey in the late 1140s to adopt Cistercian practices — something that occurred without any sense of having "signed on" to an institution — and what adopting those customs meant in the thirteenth century, when it had become virtually equivalent to (and almost inevitably accompanied by) a request for affiliation addressed to the governing body of abbots, the General Chapter. Thus, in studying the twelfth-century Cistercian Order and its evolution, it is important to distinguish between dates when incorporated houses were founded, when those houses (particularly those from beyond Burgundy) began to adopt Cistercian practices, when such communities coalesced with a Burgundian congregation into an Order, and when abbeys began to be formally attached to filiation trees. These dates were rarely simultaneous. Each was a separate event in the development of Cistercian institutions. Moreover, with the exception of the foundations themselves (mostly made by independent pre-Cistercian reformers), such events date to after the mid-twelfth century.

Only after papal approval of the Cistercian constitution, which I date to 1165, did anonymous Cistercians write the narrative accounts of Cistercian origins, the *exordia*. These were promotional statements. They avoided mentioning both the women's houses in the Cistercian movement and the abbot Bernard himself. Indeed, only in the *Exordium Magnum*, written by a former monk of Clairvaux circa 1200, would Bernard and Clairvaux be written back into the story of the early Cistercians. The earlier *exordia* attributed the recently created administrative institutions of their own time to the relatively neutral figure of Stephen Harding, second abbot of Cîteaux, who had died in 1134. In attributing recent innovations to an earlier generation, the authors of the *exordia* sought to ensure that their novel and innovative institutions would endure. Their claims that these new institutions had been in existence for some time, although false, were no different from their similar claims that Cistercian innovations were simply a renewal of the original practices of the Rule of Saint Benedict. But while their method of collapsing the creation of this religious Order into a single moment in time and attaching it to Stephen Harding was a useful strategy for getting their program widely accepted at the time, historians at the end of the twentieth century should not take their assertions about how the Cistercian Order developed as the literal truth. To do so is to distort important evidence about twelfth-century institutional development that has consequences far beyond the history of religious reform.

Indeed, the Cistercian invention of an Order was part of that larger transformation in twelfth-century Christendom that was once called the twelfth-century Renaissance. These changes are now more accurately described as a shift from ad hoc to routine, from memory to written record, from gift society to exchange economy, from epic to romance, or from customary to written law.[7] Because the Cistercian invention of the religious order was part of this shift, and because our understanding of the intricacies of that Order's development has significance for the larger history of twelfth-century change, it is worthwhile to get the dates right in an otherwise obscure debate within monastic history.

If we deny, as I do here, that the *exordia* written circa 1165 and slightly later provide the "sincere truth" about the invention of the Order as they claim to do, what then becomes of the earliest Cistercians? If Cistercian administrative structures appeared only sometime after the mid-twelfth century, can we still describe a "conversation" about monastic *caritas* taking place among early reformers at Clairvaux and Cîteaux, and call that discussion of mutual concerns about monastic life a "textual community"?[8] Perhaps the discussion by those reformers about monastic charity was more confined to Burgundy until mid-century than we have thought, but an intense discussion of such issues did occur there under the aegis of Bernard of Clairvaux. This conversation about monastic charity, however, did not require the existence of the administrative Order the Cistercians later created for themselves — an international grouping of many monastic houses with written legislation, internal visitation, or an annual, universal General Chapter that would take on dispute resolution and visitation responsibilities that had earlier rested with the local bishop or the pope.

What seems most useful for our understanding is to underline the difference between the early textual community and the later Cistercian Order, to distinguish between an early discussion of the internal workings of individual monastic communities on the one hand and the later creation of administrative institutions overseeing large numbers of religious houses on the other. The earlier issues about the internal workings of such communities were eventually codified, but primarily in texts we do not often look at. These are the volumes called liturgical *ordines*, the standard Cistercian version of which is the *Ecclesiastica Officia*. Early practices were also written up in lay-brother treatises that were probably originally attached to those liturgical order-books. Such customs about practice internal to a single abbey could be used in conjunction with the Rule of Saint Benedict to administer almost any new reform house of the twelfth century. What have been presented as "primitive Cistercian documents" do not consider most of the issues found in the *Ecclesiastica Officia* or the lay-brother treatises. What are, in fact, the slightly later "primitive" texts — the *exordia*, Charter of Charity, and Cistercian statutes — are those used to organize individual reform houses into a larger umbrella group of communities. That larger group was, of course, the Cistercian Order as we think of it today.

Obviously, the findings of this book about dating when an administrative Order appeared among the Cistercians challenge traditional understandings of the impact of Bernard of Clairvaux on the eventual creation of a religious order.[9] Nonetheless, if Cistercian growth came about by local reform communities' adoption of Cistercian practices, much of those reformers' knowledge of and initial attraction to Cistercian practices must have been the result of Bernard's preaching in the 1130s and 1140s. Bernard's personal intervention in the local affairs of many independent groups gradually led to the creation of a group of houses subject to him and to Clairvaux. This group of Clarevallian abbeys was indistinguishable from other religious congregations of the time. It was wholly dependent on Bernard's charismatic personality for its cohesion, and it is distinct from the later Order. While Bernard held Clairvaux's congregation together during his own lifetime, problems arose with his passing. It seems likely that, while some abbots in the 1150s and 1160s began to collect the reports of Bernard's miracles for the promotion of his canonization, others, particularly from non-Clarevallian houses, worked to establish regulations to curb the power of Clairvaux. It was probably the activities of the latter group that led to the invention of an Order. If so, the creation of the Cistercian Order might be described as a reaction to Bernard's legacy, a response to the continued dominance of Clairvaux after Bernard's death, when his personal charisma no longer made it acceptable.

Since the Cistercian Order emerged considerably later than has generally been thought, it is possible that the invention of the religious order as a generic twelfth-century innovation was not entirely done by the Cistercians. They may have derived much from the experiments of other contemporary, non-Cistercian reform groups, whose contributions have been overlooked because of the traditional dating of Cistercian institutions to very early in the twelfth century. We now need to examine the relationship between specific components of Cistercian institutions and those of other twelfth-century religious groups in further studies. It is clear that all twelfth-century reform groups faced pressures from lawyerly popes like Alexander III to initiate better control of attached houses and to take on self-governance in the form of internal arbitration of disputes and visitation.[10] These monastic reformers were often led to invent new institutions, which could perform those tasks, by expectations of exemption from local episcopal visitation; such concessions, of course, suited very well the centralizing purposes of the papacy. Finally, it may be possible to find parallels for the rise of a General Chapter as a governing institution for twelfth- and thirteenth-century monastic groups in institutions beyond those of monasticism itself, for instance in the rise of communal governments in the twelfth-century revival of urban life, industry, and commerce. Indeed, while the Charter of Charity is frequently seen as reflecting the concerns of the earliest Cistercians in Burgundy about monastic love or charity, it may be more significant that the Cistercian constitution is called a "charter," the term used for most urban constitutions of the time.

This study has attempted to use the evidence from the medieval Midi or Occitania as supplemented by additional materials from Burgundy, England, and other parts of northern Europe to trace the history of the Cistercian

Order's creation in a way that may be generalized for all of Europe. My characterization of the development of the Cistercian Order out of two distinct components—one a tiny congregation in Burgundy itself, the other a proto-Order of independent reform houses whose widespread adoption of Cistercian practices eventually led to the creation of that religious Order—makes it possible to argue that the region to which this study was originally limited is one particularly well suited to the investigation this book has become.[11] The true story of twelfth-century monastic reform communities may only be extracted from a careful examination of local administrative charters from specific regions outside the Burgundian heartland in which a congregation developed. Indeed our understanding of the articulation of the administrative components of the Cistercian Order may best be understood from the evidence of a region such as southern France, clearly part of "old Europe," but at some distance from Burgundy.[12]

Such a study requires that the unique qualities of southern France as a medieval region be noted while its typicalness is underlined as well. It is too easy to point to southern France as being different, as having nothing in common with the cold, northern realm of Ile-de-France, or Champagne, Blois, or Normandy. In so doing we probably exaggerate the differences of medieval regions among which considerable communication actually occurred. The south of France was less off the beaten track in the Middle Ages than today, because it was a region constantly being traversed by elites, whether knights or monks, great ladies or merchants, en route to pilgrimage, Crusade, or trade in Spain, Italy, or the Levant.[13]

In the post-Carolingian age, southern France saw itself as part of the Frankish kingdom, but its twelfth-century leaders often acted virtually independently of Capetian kings, as is true of all other provinces at that time as well.[14] The peace and prosperity found in southern France and in nearly all of "old Europe" by the year 1000 had been based on an expansion of settlement and cultivation. That expansion brought much more new land under cultivation by the end of the eleventh century than economic historians have thought. They have often taken literally the assertions of monastic founders about having undertaken "pioneering" activities. In fact, by the twelfth century much of "old Europe" was rich and prosperous but becoming a bit overcrowded. It was more practical for knights of such regions to allow sons and daughters to enter religious communities than to have them marry, build castles, and control territory. The new monastic communities were often a source of desperately needed cash for those knightly families as they sent sons and brothers on Crusade or to Paris to be educated.

By the twelfth century the Midi had become almost excessively urbanized, monetized, and contractual, and both Cistercians and those who had preceded them were well tied into urban exchange networks.[15] The Midi was but one region of the "old Europe" in which such rapid urbanization was occurring.[16] Such growth in the Midi of cities and industry, as well as new monastic congregations, was mirrored in Flanders, in the Po valley of northern Italy, in the towns of Champagne that hosted the great trading fairs, and in areas of Burgundy, Poitou, and the Paris basin.

While in the older version of the twelfth-century story of the Cistercians their coming to the Midi of France might have been seen as the intrusion of unwanted hordes of new northern monastic reformers, in fact, if Burgundy transferred anything to southern France it was ideas about monastic practice, not personnel. The expansion of the Cistercian Order into the Midi of France was almost entirely by incorporation of pre- and proto-Cistercian communities already there. Some of these communities were parts of emerging congregations linking monastic groups south of the Pyrénées to those to the north (as seen in the map in Figure 35). Moreover, there are hints that some of the organizational principles of the Cistercians may have come not from Burgundy but from elsewhere, possibly even southern France. Such principles were probably being devised by abbots like Alexander of Cologne, who went from being a monk at Bernard's Clairvaux to being abbot of the house of monks at Grandselve near Toulouse (1150–58), then abbot of Savigny (1158–68), before becoming abbot of Cîteaux (1168–78). But Alexander and his co-abbots may have been aided in the formulation of a religious Order by such adult converts to the monastic life as William VI, lord of Montpellier, who retired to Grandselve circa 1150. William's years at Grandselve overlapped not only with those of abbot Alexander, but with those of another southerner, Pons of Polignac, abbot of Grandselve (1158–65), who became abbot of Clairvaux (1165–70) and then bishop of Clermont (1170–89).[17] These were individuals who had to have been in the thick of Cistercian order-making.

The conclusion that the Cistercian Order was not invented until the second half of the twelfth century has not been easily or hastily reached. The chapters that follow present the interlocking arguments for making that case as follows:

Chapter 1 discusses traditional narratives and the differences between two twelfth-century accounts written by anonymous Cistercians. Those accounts describe how Robert of Molesme and his followers left the abbey of Molesme to establish Cîteaux. Both represent Cistercian myths about the Order's foundation, but the differences between the two, the *Exordium Cistercii* and the *Exordium Parvum*, provide clues about the accuracy and the motivations of their authors. I consider other Cistercian myths as well: whether images of sites and architecture can uphold the truth of the early narratives and whether there were no women in the early Order.

Chapter 2 turns to the debate over the Cistercian "primitive documents" and the evidence of the manuscripts that contain them, as well as that of the charters and of papal confirmations of Cistercian constitutions. I argue that the Montpellier H322 manuscript, which dates to after 1161, is a key to dating the "primitive documents" manuscripts. This argument depends as well on a careful reevaluation of just what parts of another manuscript, Trent 1711, contain the "primitive documents."

Chapter 3 looks at the phenomenon of incorporation and the adoption of Cistercian customs as part of the invention of the Cistercian Order, distinguishing concerns about monastic love in a tiny congregation in Burgundy from activities of independent reform houses in other parts of Europe. It traces the evolution of a group of congregations in southern France and elsewhere that, having adopted some Cistercian customs, eventually coalesced with the Burgundian congregation into the Cistercian Order. It attempts to disentangle the history of individual communities from inferences about the Order's early growth that are based on the filiation tables created in the early thirteenth century. These filiation trees were ideal for later administrative purposes, but they are useless as evidence about foundations. Finally, it traces the evolution of some of the constituent parts of the Order in the later twelfth century.

Chapter 4 evaluates how charter evidence reflects relationships between monastic founders and donors. This evidence suggests that Cistercians were not everywhere welcome in the communities in which they settled, but also that they often entered into agreements with donors that appear contrary to Cistercian norms. It shows the extensive contributions of women in southern France as patrons, donors, and recruits to the reform houses of that region. It suggests, moreover, that women in that region were not as mesmerized by the preaching of Cathar heretics as has been averred. There were considerable opportunities for women as well as men in the reform movement of the early twelfth century in southern France, but (irrational and puzzling as it seems) the presence of women in such reform movements there and elsewhere began to be denied at almost the same moment that preaching against heresy began in earnest. I can only document, and cannot explain, this situation.

Chapter 5 presents conclusions about how the picture of Cistercians I have developed is both specific to southern France and applicable to Cistercians throughout all parts of Europe. It contends that my conclusions can be generalized to all of the "old Europe" of the twelfth-century Cistercian expansion, to all those regions that had long been settled and Christianized.

There has been considerable development in my ideas since the first version of this manuscript was submitted to publishers in the fall of 1993. My ability to work through its various drafts owes a great deal to the patience of editors, readers, and colleagues for whom other commitments have often been delayed. It is a testimony to the security of academic tenure that a significant rethinking of a major twelfth-century institution was possible in the face of the increasing dismay of current-day Trappists and Cistercians, who have found this study both puzzling and threatening. I am grateful to my department and university, which have provided me the opportunity to do so.

That writing such a history against the grain of an embedded foundation myth can be difficult is attested to by a recent acquaintance, the current librarian at Maredsous Abbey in Belgium, J.-A. Lefèvre, who began much of this discussion of the "primitive documents" as a young graduate student in the 1950s. I had the great pleasure of meeting Father Lefèvre at a conference in Dijon in fall 1998 after this book was essentially complete. Although I have been keenly aware of his work while writing (and include it in my bibliography), the polemical context in which Lefèvre's publications were received made many of his conclusions difficult to decipher; it seemed better to begin again with the manuscripts and not attempt to tie my points to his. Thus my dating and sequencing of manuscripts and texts have been established independently of Lefèvre's, although my conclusions may replicate some of what he published earlier. I thank him for his recent words of encouragement and for his earlier incursion into the thorny wilderness of the "primitive documents," which obviously made mine easier.

David Herlihy pointed me to the cartulary of Silvanès for a master's thesis and suggested that I continue with the Cistercians for a Ph.D.; he would have encouraged the whirlwind trip to look at manuscripts in spring 1997. I remember him with thanks for always encouraging me to return to the sources. Father Louis J. Lekai bears responsibility for years of encouragement; I have long thought that he designed his "Ideal and Reality" model as a way to protect young scholars like me from attacks like those made on Lefèvre. It was my colleague Katherine Tachau who enjoined me never to leave a library with a codicological puzzle unresolved; her advice on how to count manuscript quires was invaluable in resolving the mystery of Trent 1711. Richard Sundt read the manuscript at one point and discussed Cistercian architecture with me, persuading me that it could not bear the weight I was attempting to place on it. Marjorie Chibnall taught me better how to weigh authorities and continues to provide an example of untiring energy. Anne Thompson asked an obvious question much in need of being asked and was willing to read my lengthy answer during precious time in Cambridge. All deserve special thanks.

I owe much to my graduate students who have lived with this book; to William Duba's cynical comments on *ordo* and to Pat Conyer's suggestion that I read Stephen Jay Gould's *Wonderful Life*; to colleagues at the University of Iowa, Judith Aikin, Helen and Jonathan Goldstein, Carin and Peter Green, David Arkush and Hélène Lesage, and Deirdre McCloskey (who told me about alligators' tails); to students Kurt Boughan; Karen Christianson, Heather Martin, and Pam Stucky; Russ Friedman, who provided some photographs; Andrea Gayoso; Jim Halverson; Lisa Harkey; Erin Jordan; Erika Lindgren; Christine McOmber, who helped with architectural language; Chris Schabel; Jennifer Peters; and Christopher Pouliot, who made the maps. I also owe much to a Ph.D. student at the Catholic University of America, Cicely d'Autremont Angleton, who introduced me to the notion of Bernard of Clairvaux as the "Big Enchilada" in the course of writing her dissertation.

I am particularly grateful to audiences in Copenhagen, Cambridge, Oxford, Iowa City, Kalamazoo, Houston, Seattle, Leeds, Dijon, and Ithaca, who listened to and queried ideas. I must thank as well a series of longtime supporters who may not agree with the conclusions of this text and some of whose advice I have deliberately ignored. Nonetheless Bernard and Segolène Barbiche, Nicole Bériou, Uta-Renate Blumenthal, Caroline Bynum, Giles Constable, Barbara Kreutz, Brian Patrick McGuire, Jo Ann McNamara, Martha Newman, Joel Rosenthal, Miri Rubin, Wendy Pfeffer, and Jane Schulenburg have all given me encouragement and practical help. A number of other scholars, among them Janet Burton, E. Rozanne Elder, Brian Golding, Michael Gervers, Maria Hillebrandt, Carol Neel, Marcel Pacaut, Barbara Rosenwein, Robert Somerville, and Chrysogonus Waddell, all replied with care to specific queries; to all I owe thanks, but none should bear responsibility.

Institutional support during the past years has come from a variety of sources: the University of Iowa, MUCIA, the American Philosophical Society Penrose Fund, an American Council of Learned Societies Grant-in-Aid, and the National Endowment for the Humanities in the form of both a fellowship for College Teachers and several Travel to Collections grants. I thank David Skorton, University of Iowa vice president for research, for support for this book in the form of a subvention, as well as for his outstanding advocacy of funding for the humanities. Betsy Altmaier and Jay Semel also provided monies and space. The University of Iowa Center for Advanced Studies at the Oakdale campus (now the Obermann Center) provided an escape and solace from the duties of departmental administration and from the dark days of November 1991, as well as during the courageous dying of our colleague and friend, Sydney James. Clare Hall, Cambridge, and the history faculty of Cambridge University welcomed me as a visiting fellow and visiting scholar for the academic year 1994–95; there at the University Library I used the same copies of Canivez and Grundmann from which had come earlier versions of Cistercian history. In our year in Cambridge, I profited from numerous discussions with British and North American scholars; forays to France added any number of debts there as well.

I would like to thank Russ Friedman, the Archives départementales de Marne in Chaumont, the Bibliothèque municipale de Dijon, the Bibliothèque Sainte-Geneviève in Paris, and the Bibliothèque de l'école de médecine in Montpellier for permission to use photographs. Parts of Chapters 1 and 4 respectively appear in "Were There Twelfth-Century Cistercian Nuns?" *Church History* 68 (December 1999) and "Cistercian Women and Tithes," *Cîteaux* 49 (1998). Permission has kindly been granted for that material to be used here as well.

Finally, an invitation issued by Bernard Bachrach and Paul Hyams to be a plenary speaker at the Haskins Society annual meeting at Cornell in the fall of 1998, one issued by Barbara Rosenwein to speak on the intersections of Cistercian and Cluniac history in summer 1998 at Leeds, and one by Pierrette Paravy and Nicole Bouter for a paper at a C.E.R.C.O.R. conference in the fall of 1998 all gave me much-needed boosts in these last months, as well as introducing me to new colleagues. Editors at Penn, Ruth Karras and Jerome Singerman, have been invaluable supporters, but the entire staff at the University of Pennsylvania Press has made completing this book a pleasure.

This study is tied to images of place. Looking at manuscripts recently has reminded me of the help provided by many European scholars, librarians, and archivists not even named here. I cannot even begin to list all of them, but since 1997 alone I have benefited from consultation of manuscript collections in Montpellier, Trent, Ljubljana, Dijon, Paris, Metz, Laon, London, Oxford, and Cambridge. I am often inspired by a visual sense of the Cistercian landscape as it once was, and sometimes still is. When I think of those early nuns and monks, I picture them against the landscape of dry garrigues near Narbonne, the lush hillsides of the Rouergue, or facing the formidable cathedral of Rodez. I think of the abbey of Fontfroide and a kind librarian taking me there from Narbonne, of walking and hitchhiking to get to Valmagne, of bus trips to Saint-Gilles and Aigues-Mortes, of walking through the medieval city of Nîmes, of the canal in front of the archives in Toulouse, of the abbey of Silvanès and villages like Saint-Véran along the edge of the *causses*, of a memorable drive to Carcassonne, and of my vertigo when going up on the roof of le Vignogoul to take photographs.

In that world of memory there is never a rainy day or flooding. It is always late summer, early fall, or an exceptionally beautiful spring. There is never a charter that remains unseen or when seen unreadable. The dating and relationship of manuscripts is obvious and the intentions of their makers always clear. Old place-names pop out from new maps. Granges and monastic buildings can always be located. Keys for entry are always available, one always has the right film and enough light, and no monastic sites have been wantonly destroyed. The reality is different. I manage to have the wrong film, dates on manuscripts have sometimes been effaced beyond recovery, reserve rooms of libraries turn out to be closed on Tuesday mornings, and the degradation of the medieval landscape of the Midi and elsewhere continues apace. I too, like the monks and nuns about whom I write, see a Golden Age receding into the past, but I have had at least an opportunity to sample the crumbs of that disappearing medieval world.

I dedicate this book to the two men in my life, David and Benjamin, who have traveled with me to many Cistercian sites to return home puzzled about who took which photograph. Except where otherwise noted, figures were printed from our negatives.

Unless otherwise noted, all translations are my own.

I
Twelfth-Century Narratives and Cistercian Mythology

A traditional picture of the twelfth-century Cistercians and their early expansion is found in *The Cistercians: Ideals and Reality*, published in 1977 by Father Louis J. Lekai:

The amazing fact that the Cistercian Order virtually exploded and by the middle of the twelfth century possessed nearly 350 houses in every country in Europe, can be explained, however, only by the dynamic character of the "man of the century," Saint Bernard of Clairvaux.[1]

After an entire chapter entitled "Saint Bernard and the Cistercian Expansion," Lekai concludes:

The astounding rise of the Cistercian Order, within the lifespan of Saint Bernard, from a small community of humble hermit-monks to an international network of hundreds of abbeys can scarcely be explained by the consideration of natural, historical factors alone. Not even the genius of the abbot of Clairvaux can give adequate account for this unique and specifically religious phenomenon. The secret must lie in the loud and spontaneous echo Cîteaux's spirituality evoked among the congenial members of that devout generation, a spirituality exemplified to rich and poor, erudite and illiterate alike, by the austere and prayerful life of the White Monks.[2]

Although Lekai suggests that Cistercian growth was not the accomplishment solely of Bernard of Clairvaux, his description of the Order's miraculous expansion is still based on the spiritual appeal of Cîteaux. Such analyses as Lekai's have downplayed the role of incorporation in spreading Cistercian religiosity. Such studies instead see the success of the Cistercians as almost entirely a result of colonization from Burgundy, and mysterious only insofar as how it would have been possible to recruit and train so many monks in that region.[3]

This is the traditional tale, told since the end of the twelfth century, of a growing "network of hundreds of abbeys" in an Order established during Bernard's lifetime. It is one in which growth derived almost entirely from

Burgundy. It turns out to be inaccurate.[4] Cistercian growth in fact occurred through incorporating dozens of existing reform houses, rather than through founding new abbeys by colonization. Incorporation explains almost entirely the rapid Cistercian success — a point to which I return in Chapter 3. Bernard's contribution to Cistercian success was important, but it consisted much more of his publicizing early Cistercian notions of *caritas* than of any contribution to creating permanent institutions within an order. Such Cistercian notions as charity within monastic communities, manual labor shared among all members, regulations about management of lay-brothers, and reducing the liturgy inspired many independent monastic reformers of the twelfth century to adopt them. This adoption of Cistercian customs was often locally generated, coming at the initiative of independent reformers who looked to regulations from Cîteaux to solve problems specific to their own monasteries.

Investigation of early Cistercian mythology about that Order's inception and growth begins in this chapter with an analysis of the origins of such descriptions as Lekai's, which derive ultimately from the narrative accounts of early Cistercian history written by members of the Order in the twelfth century. These narratives, the Cistercian *exordia*, present a series of Cistercian myths so pervasive in our descriptions of twelfth-century monasticism that we often no longer recognize their source. Here I examine the two earliest versions of the Cistercian *exordia* as well as their influence on other Cistercian myths: one about the isolation and austerity of the Order's sites and the other about a "Golden Age" in the early Order wholly without women — a notion obviated by the many examples of twelfth-century Cistercian women's houses discussed in this study and elsewhere. Chapter 2 will present the arguments for why such *exordia* are given the sequence and new dating employed here.

The Cistercian *exordia* comprise three main texts. The earliest is the very short *Exordium Cistercii*, which was only rediscovered in the twentieth century; it was written between 1160 and 1165. A second version was written ten to fifteen years later — the often-cited "Little Exordium," or *Exordium Parvum*. Despite its name, it is a longer text than the *Exordium Cistercii*. Combining narration and documents, the *Exordium Parvum* supports a pro-Cîteaux, anti-Molesme stance, but like the earlier document it does not mention Bernard or Clairvaux. Finally there is the *Exordium Magnum*, the "Great Exordium," which covers every aspect of Cistercian history up to its own day. It includes much detail about Clairvaux, being written circa 1200 by a former monk of that abbey, Conrad, who became abbot of Eberbach.[5]

The *Exordium Cistercii* and the *Exordium Parvum* are anonymous accounts, although clearly written from within the Order. The *Exordium Parvum* was incorporated by Conrad into the first of his six books of the *Exordium*

Magnum. He uses the entire text of the *Exordium Parvum* in an account of monasticism, mostly in Gaul, from early Christian times. The other five books of the *Exordium Magnum* are about Clairvaux, incorporating many passages from twelfth-century Clarevallian authors. To the extent that later descriptions of the Cistercians incorporate Bernard into their account and contrast the white monks of Cîteaux with the decadence of Cluny and Molesme, they were most often derived from the *Exordium Magnum*. This fact gives much later Cistercian history its distinctly Clarevallian flavor.

The *Exordium Cistercii*

The earliest of the three accounts of the exodus from Molesme, the *Exordium Cistercii*, had disappeared by the time Cistercian accounts were printed. Since its rediscovery it has sometimes been treated as an abridged version of the *Exordium Parvum*. In fact, it never appears on its own, but forms a two-paragraph preface to the earliest version of the Cistercian Charter of Charity, the *Summa Cartae Caritatis*. Examination of its contents reveals clearly that this is not simply a summary of the *Exordium Parvum* but a carefully crafted account in its own right, with its own stylistic elegance. As discussed in Chapter 2, the manuscript evidence, in particular the evidence from sequencing the liturgical *ordines* manuscripts, for which marginal glosses added to earlier manuscripts are incorporated into the body of the texts of subsequent ones, shows that the *Exordium Cistercii* is the earlier text.

Certain texts are always found together and are copied into the manuscripts in the same order; Figure 1 shows that the *Exordium Cistercii* and *Summa Cartae Caritatis* are accompanied, in the one complete twelfth-century manuscript of the "primitive documents" containing them, by additional chapters on such issues as "How new abbeys should be founded," then by the liturgical *ordines*, and finally by a treatise on the handling of lay-brothers. The series of questions and answers that follow the *exordium* and Charter of Charity in all the various manuscripts of "primitive documents" are called the *Capitula* or *Instituta* and are often treated as statutes attributed to 1134 and published under that date.[6]

This early textual grouping, *Exordium Cistercii*, *Summa Cartae Caritatis*, and *Instituta*, provides basic regulations for a Cistercian administration that at the time of its composition was still relatively unarticulated. Its description of Cistercian origins, found in the opening text, the *Exordium Cistercii*, is a limited one. The language, of mother-abbeys and daughter-houses, father-abbots and sons who are abbots of daughter-houses, reflects a component of the early

"Primitive documents" in intact twelfth-century manuscripts are always found grouped in one of three ways:[1]

a: *Exordium Cistercii* + *Summa Cartae Caritatis*[2] + *Instituta*[3] + *E. Officia*[4] + Lay-Br. Treatise.

or

b: + *Carta Caritatis Prior*

or *Exordium Parvum* or + Calixtus II Bull + *Instituta* + *E. Officia* + Lay-Br. Treatise.

c: + *C. Caritatis Posterior*

---

[1] The sequence given here (with top version earliest) is derived from analysis of the liturgical order-book; see Table 1.
[2] These two texts always come together; the *Exordium Cistercii* comprises the first two paragraphs.
[3] Statutes.
[4] *Ecclesiastica Officia*, the Cistercian liturgical order-book.

Figure 1. "Primitive Cistercian document" texts in context.

Cistercian sense of community.[7] Its poetic evocation of family is done with such stylistic balance, and even elegance, that it is very hard to understand how such a text could ever have been dismissed as a summary of later ones. The *Exordium Cistercii* presents a straightforward account of Robert's return to Molesme and is considerably less antagonistic toward Molesme and other monastic communities than the later, more rhetorical *Exordium Parvum* or the earliest versions of the *Exordium Magnum*.

Chapter 1 of the *Exordium Cistercii* describes the departure from Molesme and the founding of Cîteaux. In this version of the Cistercian foundation myth, Molesme, the mother-house from which the monks of Cîteaux had fled, is described as a monastery that had become so famous that it had many riches and had fallen away from the strict observance of the Rule of Saint Benedict. Molesme's dilemma was that of all reform monastic houses; it was caught in a crisis of accumulated wealth derived from its reputation as a house of great austerity and saintliness:

In episcopatu Lingonensi situm noscitur esse coenobium nomine Molismus, fama celeberrimum, religione conspicuum. Hoc a sui exordio magnis sub brevi tempore divina clementia suae gratiae muneribus illustravit, viris illustribus nobilitavit, nec minus amplum possessionibus quam clarum virtutibus reddidit.

In the diocese of Langres there was located a monastery called Molesme of the most outstanding reputation, known for its religious practices. From only a short time after its foundation, it was shown to be protected by the grace of divine clemency, ennobled by illustrious men, and granted not only a sufficiency of possessions, but distinguished for its virtues.[8]

As a result of Molesme's growing wealth, some of its members found themselves too involved in mundane affairs and wished instead to pursue heavenly goals. These "lovers of poverty," a group of twenty-one monks, with their abbot Robert (described as of blessed memory, which is suggestive of the date of the *Exordium Cistercii*'s composition), departed from Molesme to go to a new site at Cîteaux. That place is then described in biblical terms as *locu[s] tunc scilicet horroris et vastae solitudinis*. But for these *milites Christi* such a harsh place was exactly what they sought.[9]

Chapter 2 of the *Exordium Cistercii* begins by telling us that this foundation by Robert at the *heremus* of Cîteaux had been approved in 1098 (the text's only date) by Hugh, papal legate and archbishop of Lyons, by bishop Walter of Châlons, and by duke Eudes of Burgundy, who provided much of its material support.[10] The text makes very little of the return of Robert to Molesme and his replacement by Alberic:

At vero post non multum temporis factum est ut idem abbas Robertus requirentibus eum monachis Molismensibus, Papae Urbani secundi jussu, Walterii cabilonensis episcopi licentia et assensu, Molismum reduceretur, et Albericus, vir religiosus et sanctus, in ipsius loco sustitueretur.

But after a short while, abbot Robert was needed by the monks of Molesme. At the order of pope Urban II and with the agreement of Walter, bishop of Châlons, Robert returned to Molesme. Alberic, a religious and holy man, replaced him at that place.[11]

Alberic is then described as the new father of this new monastery. In the earliest surviving version of the *Exordium Cistercii*, however, the repeated word "new" in the phrase *novum monasterium novi patris* is used only once, to modify "father," not "monastery." This may be no more than a scribal error in not copying a repeated adjective that is itself a stylistic detail in the text. But this detail in turn has probably been overinterpreted by scholars who place too much emphasis on the presence of the words "new monastery" as a means to argue for this text's very early date.[12] The *Exordium Cistercii* is earlier than the *Exordium Parvum*, but the manuscript evidence dates both to after the mid-twelfth century, as I argue in Chapter 2.

Alberic ruled for nine years and then was succeeded by Stephen Harding. Stephen is described as

homo natione anglicus, religionis paupertatis disciplinaeque regularis ardentissimus amator, fidelissimus aemulator.

An Englishman, a most ardent lover and faithful proponent of religious poverty and the discipline of the Rule.[13]

During Stephen's early reign the abbey of Cîteaux almost failed, but it was rescued by new recruits. Indeed, thirty clerics and nobles and men of power who were laymen entered Cîteaux. There is no mention that one of these recruits was probably Bernard, the later abbot of Clairvaux.[14]

Chapter 2 continues with a description of the multiplication of houses, again in familial language. There were apparently twenty offspring within twelve years, as we are told:

Donec tam de suis quam de filiis filiorum suorum viginti infra annos circiter duodecim de solis patribus monasteriorum tamquam novella olivarum in circuitu mensae suae laeta mater conspiceret.

So that within about twelve years there were twenty not only of these offspring, but of the sons of these sons from a single father monastery, like new olive trees surrounding the estate of their happy mother.[15]

Finally, Stephen's writing of a constitution is asserted:

Unde et scriptum illud cartam caritatis competenter voluit nominari, quod ea tantum quae sunt caritatis tota ejus series redoleat.

Hence he wished to call that text a Charter of Charity, appropriately enough because its whole contents concerned such love.[16]

That the text says that these customs are about to be "briefly" described in the *Summa Cartae Caritatis* of the next chapters does not mean that this is a later summary of the *Exordium Parvum*; *breviter* here echoes the opening of the text with its *sub brevi tempora*.[17]

The familial imagery of the *Exordium Cistercii* is continued in the *Summa Cartae Caritatis*. The latter constitutes Chapter 3 of this grouping and is the earliest recorded Cistercian constitution, or Charter of Charity. It is significant that the manuscripts of the *Exordium Cistercii* refer to the *Summa Cartae Caritatis* as Chapter 3; only modern scholars have separated the two parts. The *Summa Cartae Caritatis*, the earliest surviving form of the Cistercian constitution, promises the independence of affiliates. There will be no exactions by mother-abbeys from daughter-houses and only limited (once a year) visitation by father-abbots of daughter-houses:

Igitur juxta cartae illius tenorem, inter omnes cisterciensis ordinis abbatias statutum est, matres filiabus nullam posse temporalis commodi exactionem imponere, abbatem patrem abbatis filii monasterium visitantem non ejus novicium in monachum benedicere, non ejus monachum ipso invito inde abducere, non alium ad habitandum introducere, nihil denique ibidem praeter illius voluntatem constituere, aut ordinare, excepto quod ad curam pertinet animarum.

Therefore, in conformity with the tenor of that charter, it was established that among all abbeys of the *ordo cisterciensis*, mother-houses should not impose any exactions of a temporal sort on their daughters. Furthermore, father abbots should not visit monasteries which are their sons to bless novices becoming monks, to entice away monks there, to introduce new members to those communities, or to order or establish anything against the will of those communities, unless it concerns the care of souls.[18]

Father-abbots should neither bless novices as monks, nor entice away the most promising ones, nor force monks on daughter-houses, but be concerned solely with spiritual things. These are not injunctions to introduce uniformity of economic practices or to describe the proper method for the admission of monks or nuns or the foundation and incorporation of new houses, as are usually attributed to the Order's earliest constitution. This is instead a constitutional guarantee of minimal interference.

Much of the rest of the textual grouping found with the *Exordium Cistercii* concerns an incipient leadership by committee. Chapter 4, the second of the *Summa Cartae Caritatis*, declares that abbots should assemble once a year at Cîteaux, *omnium mater ecclesia cisterciensis*, to tend to the affairs of the group of abbeys, *ordinis reparandi*, and to review the activities of the abbot of Cîteaux.[19] In addition, this chapter tells us that abbots who did not attend the General Chapter meetings were to send their priors as representatives; abbots who absented themselves without cause were to be punished.[20]

Significantly, this early text promises that if the poverty of any individual house becomes known, that community will be provided for from the wealth of other houses, each giving according to its ability:

Sed et hoc bonum de conventu illo provisum fuit, ut si cujus abbatum nimia forte paupertas in communi innotuerit, fratris penuriam prout singulis caritas dictaverit, et facultas permiserit, omnes relevare procurent.

But for the good of the group, it was provided that, if it came to their attention that any abbot was in poverty, as love dictated and resources permitted, they should provide him relief.[21]

Clearly here is a notion of "charity" extending beyond a single abbey to all those in need; this clause does not appear in later versions of the Charter of Charity. Indeed, it may be a vestige of a practice probably already gone by the time this textual grouping was written in the 1150s or 1160s. Only within a small and closed congregation of abbeys, such as that attached to Cîteaux in Burgundy in the earliest part of the twelfth century, could such a practice have been contemplated or put into effect.

Chapter 5 describes the process by which a negligent abbot of any house should be deposed by the father-abbot in concert with the bishop and clergy of the diocese in which the transgressor's abbey was located.[22] In the case of Cîteaux, deposition was entrusted to the abbots of la Ferté, Pontigny, and Clairvaux. Election of a new abbot of Cîteaux was limited to someone from within the congregation, but electors would include all abbots who could assemble at Cîteaux within fifteen days. Meanwhile, the abbot of la Ferté was in charge.[23] There is no mention yet of Morimond as the fourth daughter.

The last chapters of the *Summa Cartae Caritatis* consist of a brief summary of practices with regard to acceptance and transfer of monks and lay-brothers, the material resources needed to found a new abbey, and a description of the process by which six or twelve monks and an abbot were sent forth to found a new community. There are also limited injunctions concerning uniformity in liturgical books, clothing, and food, which persons may or may not live within the monastic compound, how lay-brothers and granges should be managed, income, burial, luxury goods, and decoration.[24]

It was through establishing a sequence of the liturgical manuscripts in which this and the succeeding text are found (as described in Chapter 2), that I have established the chronological priority of the *Exordium Cistercii* and texts accompanying it over the *Exordium Parvum* and its grouping. As I argue in that chapter, the *Exordium Cistercii* textual grouping is that found in the earliest manuscripts, but even those manuscripts postdate 1160. So it is probably this Charter of Charity, possibly with the *Exordium Cistercii* as preface, that Alexander III confirmed in 1165 (see below).

The *Exordium Parvum*

The earliest textual grouping described above was soon replaced by an expanded version of the foundation account, the *Exordium Parvum*, which was accompanied in the manuscripts by one of two revised versions of the Charter of Charity, the earlier called the *Carta Caritatis Prior* and the later the *Carta Caritatis Posterior*. The *Exordium Parvum* with the earlier *Carta Caritatis Prior* (essentially the middle version of the Charter of Charity) is found in the series that begins with Ljubljana 31. It must thus date to about 1170 (although the manuscript from Ljubljana is often dated as late as 1178–82). The *Carta Caritatis Posterior*, in which Morimond's abbot joins three other daughter-houses already assigned to oversight by Cîteaux's abbot, dates to about 1175; it is found in several Paris manuscript versions of the "primitive documents" dated to slightly earlier than the Cîteaux exemplar manuscript Dijon 114 (dated to between 1182 and 1188). The numbering of chapters is inconsistent between the two expanded versions of the Charter of Charity, but basic points remain much the same.[25] The major difference is the *Carta Caritatis Prior*'s consistent use of the term *Novum Monasterium* for Cîteaux, which is dropped in the *Carta Caritatis Posterior*.[26]

The text of the *Carta Caritatis Prior* opens by telling us that "it is itself called a Charter of Charity because it does not allow exactions, but only charity, and what is useful for souls":

Hoc etiam decretum cartam caritatis vocari censebant, quia ejus statutum omnis exactionis gravamen propulsans, solam caritatem et animarum utilitatem in divinis et humanis exequitur.

This decree they have agreed to call a Charter of Charity, because this statute establishes no burden of exactions either human or divine, but only love and what is useful for souls.[27]

Both the *Carta Caritatis Prior* and the *Carta Caritatis Posterior* incorporate increasingly complex regulations for visitation, correction, and deposition of abbots, including oversight of the abbot of Cîteaux. Efforts are enjoined to enforce uniformity in the observance of the Rule of Saint Benedict and according to the customs of the new monastery. The first inklings of Cistercian conformity are found here, in paragraphs that maintain that all liturgical books should be identical to those at Cîteaux.[28] Precedence in seating and dining is given to abbot visitors, but limits on their power are still emphasized — they should correct spiritual faults only and not become involved in local affairs.[29] Visitation by a church's abbot "of all the coenobia which he has founded" should be done annually, but more frequent visitation should be gladly welcomed.[30]

The *Exordium Parvum* is much expanded from the *Exordium Cistercii*. A few details of the earlier narrative have been retained and are given considerable elaboration in this much longer text, which consists of a preface followed directly by a listing of chapter titles and then by eighteen chapters. The *Exordium Parvum* would continue to have small accretions added to it, particularly in chapter titles and rubrication, throughout the later Middle Ages. Thus, in a thirteenth-century manuscript now in Zurich from the Cistercian house of Wettingen, the *Exordium Parvum* is entitled *Epistola primitivorum cisterciensium ad omnes futuros successores eiusdem Ordinis super exordium cisterciensis coenobii*.[31] Many published versions of this text call it "The letter of the first Cistercians to all their successors about the origins of the monastery of Cîteaux."[32] Such accretions as this assert even more than does the original account of the 1170s that the *Exordium Parvum* contains the very words of the founders of Cîteaux and provides the "true facts" about the abbey's creation. But such assertions are borne out neither by the dates of the manuscripts nor by the text itself, which alternates between the voice of the founders and that of their anonymous successors. Indeed, to speak in the voice of the founders is itself an innovation. There were no such claims made in the earlier *Exordium Cistercii*.

The *Exordium Parvum* is a mixed genre. It is in part a narrative account, but this account is supported by what are purported to be documents that serve to elaborate its story. It may, moreover, have been composed in response to growing criticism of the Cistercians, particularly a letter of Alexander III dated 1170, as discussed below. This new text turns the simple familial language of the earlier *Exordium Cistercii* into a piece of rhetoric, a legal brief arguing for the legality of Cîteaux's secession from Molesme. It is accompanied in the manuscripts by an expanded Charter of Charity. Most manuscripts containing the *Exordium Parvum* also contain a series of statutes, roughly equivalent to those published by Canivez under the year 1134, starting with "How our houses are founded."

The text of the *Exordium Parvum* provides the most commonly cited version of Cistercian origins, that incorporated almost wholly without change into Book One of the *Exordium Magnum*. It is also the account that continued to be copied for distribution throughout the Order, from the early thirteenth century onward, in manuscripts containing the Cistercian liturgical *ordines* and statutes.[33]

The preface to the *Exordium Parvum* begins on an apologetic note, telling us that "we Cistercians" had founded the new abbey "canonically," but also with "what authority" and by "what persons" and at "what time" those who founded Cîteaux had left Molesme:

Nos cistercienses, primi hujus ecclesiae fundatores, successoribus nostris stilo praesenti notificamus, quam canonice, quanta auctoritate, a quibus etiam personis, quibusque temporibus, coenobium et tenor vitae illorum exordium sumpserit.

We Cistercians, first founders of this church, notify our successors with these words, how canonically, with what authority, by what persons, and at what time those founding this monastery established its way of life.[34]

Their account is the "sincere truth," *ut hujus rei propalata sincera veritate*.[35] Such a rhetorical statement suggests that there was more than one truth about the foundation at Cîteaux. The *Exordium Parvum* protests too much that "We Cistercians" tell only the true facts about a past that is also somehow still present.

Chapter 1 of the *Exordium Parvum* expands on the earlier *Exordium Cistercii* story, telling us that, even before departing from Molesme and going to the wilderness at Cîteaux, Robert and his followers had gone to ask for permission from Hugh, archbishop of Lyons and apostolic legate.[36] This statement is followed by documentation of that fact, in the form of a purported charter from Hugh that constitutes Chapter 2 of the *Exordium Parvum* text. It maintains that Hugh "joyfully" confirmed their foundation and their lives "under the authority of the holy Rule of the Father Benedict."[37]

This first embedded "document" in the *Exordium Parvum* is a letter very much in the form of a charter, opening with the *Notum sit omnibus* so familiar to those reading charters, and closing by mentioning the placement of a seal.[38] It tells us that Robert and his followers have come before Hugh, who then issued a charter describing their ambitions and the failings of Molesme:

Notum sit omnibus de sanctae matris ecclesiae profectu gaudentibus, vos et quosdam filios vestros Molismensis coenobii fratres, Lugduni in nostra praesentia astitisse, ac regulae beatissimi Benedicti quam illuc huc usque tepide ac negligenter in eodem monasterio tenueratis, artius deinceps atque perfectius inhaerere velle professos fuisse.

> Let it be known to all who are pleased by the moral progress of the mother church, that you and certain of your sons, who are brothers of the monastery of Molesme, having come to stand in our presence in Lyons, contended that you wished henceforth to live more strictly and perfectly according to the Rule of the most blessed Benedict which has been only tepidly and negligently followed at the monastery of Molesme.[39]

The letter complains of the lukewarm monastic life at Molesme and tells us that, in their desire to live "more strictly and perfectly according to the Rule of the most blessed Benedict," Robert and his group requested permission to leave that house. Hugh, papal legate and archbishop, confirms that he has permitted this, allowing Robert and his followers to leave Molesme for a new place that God would provide, but that he has also allowed others to remain at Molesme. The foundation of Cîteaux is given apostolic authority by Hugh's having impressed this charter with his seal.[40]

This charter from Hugh acts as support for the *Exordium Parvum*'s narrative assertions. Cîteaux's case is presented by the highest ecclesiastical authority in the vicinity, but it is also the testimony of a presumably neutral outsider, an independent witness, to the legality of the foundation of Cîteaux. In this and every other "document" embedded in the *Exordium Parvum*, the purpose is to assure the reader of the veracity of the statements and to put accusations against Molesme into the archbishop's mouth rather than those of Robert and his followers.

Like the other documents included in this account, however, this charter is not found outside the *Exordium Parvum* itself. It contains no language by which it can be authenticated as an original act—there is no place given, no dating clause, no witnesses, no description of the seal, except to say that it gives apostolic authority. While its contents are unusual, its form is similar to that of most charters monastic scribes wrote and copied every day. Its rhetorical function is crucial in this context, however. Like the other charters included as documentation in this tract, Hugh's charter allows the anonymous authors of the *Exordium Parvum* to make the case for the legality of having abandoned one monastery for the foundation of another. Indeed, it transfers responsibility for the decision to leave Molesme to the highest ecclesiastical authority to be found, Hugh, archbishop of Lyons and papal legate.

That the *Exordium Parvum* acted as a legal brief, that a real issue was being argued, can only be surmised, but the dates of surviving manuscripts for the *Exordium Parvum* suggest its composition shortly after 1170. If so, it would have been necessary to make the case to the highest authority, pope Alexander III. Indeed, in the *Exordium Parvum* we probably see the Cistercian response to a letter written by that pope in 1170, a letter that was critical of the Cistercians' activities. Although that papal letter had begun with praise of the

Order's support for Alexander during the recent schism, later parts of it (suppressed from official publications and forgotten until rediscovery by Jean Leclercq in 1952) criticized the emerging Order's recent behavior.[41] The charters in the *Exordium Parvum* thus constitute the documents collected (indeed created) in response to the letter from Alexander III dated 1170.

Considering that the documents in the *Exordium Parvum* are found nowhere else except in the manuscripts of the *Exordium Parvum* itself, it is surprising that charters such as that purported to come from Hugh, existing only because they are embedded in the text of this Cistercian-authored *Exordium Parvum*, have been so little questioned. By detaching the text of the *Exordium Parvum* itself from its authentic date and manuscript context, historians of the Cistercians have lost track of the circumstances in which that narrative account and polemic, the *Exordium Parvum* and its documentation, were themselves constructed. They assume the authenticity of its incorporated letters rather than querying them as possible inventions, and this despite the fact that many chroniclers of the time wrote speeches for the protagonists of their histories.[42]

Yet reasons for questioning these documents abound. The *Exordium Parvum* does not provide complete documents, only easily concocted portions of documents, often in nonstandard forms. Some have imprecation clauses, none have dating or signation. Among reasons for skepticism is the way they all speak from a single side of the debate, as outside witnesses to the legality of Cîteaux's foundation, rather than as part of an authentic correspondence between Cistercians and others.[43] No alternate contemporary manuscript evidence exists for even a single one of the documents found in the narrative account of the *Exordium Parvum*.[44] To witness to the events described in the *Exordium Parvum*, such documents should have existed independently of the manuscript context in which they are found, or be cited in other manuscripts of independent origin, or survive as originals or original copies containing all the proper diplomatic paraphernalia of seals, dating clauses, or formulae found in authenticated papal bulls or episcopal letters, or be cited in papal or episcopal registers.[45] At the very least such texts should have been demonstrated to conform to well-studied diplomatic norms for similar documents of the same date and context — their language and style should parallel that of other well-authenticated documents from the same chanceries, dates, and reigns. There is no available argument to be put forth that they do.[46]

Moreover, in making their case, the *Exordium Parvum*'s authors have left out certain facts. The *Exordium Parvum* implicitly attacks Robert of Molesme, but does not mention either Bernard of Clairvaux or Cistercian women, such as those at le Tart. Perhaps this omission is more understandable if the text is viewed as primarily a rhetorical response to papal criticisms of the Order found in Alexander III's letter of 1170. To leave Bernard unmentioned may be desirable in a tract that insists that the new monastery at Cîteaux had been legally founded, a tract in which Robert of Molesme is dramatically changed from hero to villain when he abandons the austerity of the *heremus* at Cîteaux to return to Molesme. Robert may have exhibited great instability of purpose in his role as founder of Cîteaux, but for Cistercian authors in the 1170s to have both praised Bernard and attacked Robert for returning to Molesme at the advice of the papal legate (as the *Exordium Parvum* itself tells us was the case) would have been difficult.[47] It is not easy to exonerate Bernard's own failure to maintain monastic stability, a failure to stay home to attend to his duties as abbot of Clairvaux.[48] It was better simply to leave him out of the story completely.

As for the *Exordium Parvum*'s leaving out the women who were founders, patrons, and early recruits of houses later identified as Cistercian, that too shows the text to be rhetoric, not history. There is considerable charter and narrative evidence to contradict the *Exordium Cistercii* and the *Exordium Parvum* in their silence about women in the early Cistercian movement. Such evidence is found, for instance, in the mid-twelfth-century tract by the canon of Laon, Herman of Tournai, which includes a description of some of those reform nuns at Montreuil-les-Dames in the diocese of Laon.[49] That there were women from early in the Order's history is also shown in much surviving charter evidence such as that which was published for le Tart in 1954.[50] It was a common tendency among third-quarter-of-the-twelfth-century reformers to begin ignoring the women who were part of their earlier reform activities. Modern theories about the development of religious movements, such as those of Max Weber, would explain that, whereas women are often welcome in the most primitive moments of such religious reform, they are shunned as institutionalization progresses. The *Exordium Parvum* appears to be a case in point.[51]

Historians have often limited their understanding of the *Exordium Parvum* by approaching it without the context that could be provided by the early Molesme documents, which are much richer than those from Cîteaux's archives. These documents from Molesme are very relevant to our understanding of the foundation at Cîteaux, in showing, for instance, that Robert of Molesme had made a number of new priory foundations like that at Cîteaux.[52] The Molesme documents also reveal a close association between Bernard of Clairvaux and the nuns at Jully that belies most assertions that Bernard was opposed to women's communities.[53] Records about Jully's foundation, moreover, reveal that the women were sent to that place from what was essentially a double community of religious men and women living together at Molesme.[54] This is something left wholly unmentioned in any of the accounts of Cistercian origins. It remains to be seen whether historians will be able to link the increasingly anti-Molesme stance of the *Exordium Parvum* to specific events after 1170, now that the text is more accurately dated. Certainly its tenor should be considered within the larger anti-Benedictine, anti-Cluniac, and possibly also anti-syneisactic "groundswell" of the time.[55]

Chapter 3 of the *Exordium Parvum* returns to the narrative line, and chapters thereafter alternate between narration and citing "documents" that serve as rhetorical vehicles for criticizing Molesme and praising Cîteaux. Chapter 3 tells us that Robert (at this point still a hero), having been given permission for the move, went back to Molesme to collect his twenty-one followers; with them he then departed for the *heremus* of Cîteaux. That place is described twice in a few lines as being full of dense woods and thickets, inhabited only by beasts, not men.[56] Efforts to build a monastery there of wood (rather than stone) were completed by Eudes, duke of Burgundy. Eudes is described as having given abundantly of land and livestock to supply their needs:

Tunc domnus Odo, dux Burgundiae, sancto fervore eorum delectus sanctaeque romanae ecclesiae praescripti legati litteris rogatus, monasterium ligneum quod inceperunt de suis totum consummavit, illosque inibi in omnibus necessariis diu procuravit, et terris et peccoribus abunde sublevavit.

The Lord Eudes, duke of Burgundy, informed of their sanctity by letters sent by the said legate of the holy Roman church, completed the entire wooden monastery which they had begun, provided them with all their necessities for a long time, and generously gave them lands and flocks.[57]

Again despite the implication of later manuscripts that the authors of this *Exordium Parvum* with its incipit, *Nos Cistercienses*, are the abbey's founders, what is being recited here is the mythical origin of a monastic observance in which all present Cistercians still partake. Yet its authors are at some points clearly describing something that had happened in the past, at a time when the abbey of Cîteaux was still made of wood, or even before, when they had just begun to build that *monasterium ligneum*. Indeed, to mention the wooden structure suggests that by the time of composition those wooden structures had already been replaced by stone.[58]

Chapter 4 further affirms the apostolic and canonical authorization for the foundation by Robert who received the *virga*, the abbot's staff, from the bishop of the diocese:

Eodem tempore abbas qui advenerat ab episcopo illius dioecesis virgam pastoralem cum cura monachorum, jussu praedicti legati suscepit, fratresque qui secum advenerant, in eodem loco stabilitatem regulariter, firmare fecit; sicque ecclesia illa in abbatiam canonice apostolica auctoritate crescendo surrexit.

At that time the abbot who had come there at the command of said legate, received the pastoral staff and the care of the monks from the bishop of that diocese. He made sure that the brothers who came with him conformed to monastic stability at that place, and thus was that church elevated into a canonical abbey by ever-increasing apostolic authority.[59]

This is the entire chapter. In the next we learn that despite such affirmations, Robert was called back to Molesme. According to the heading for Chapter 5 of the *Exordium Parvum*, the monks of Molesme "bothered or harassed (*inquietaverint*)" the pope to have Robert returned to them.[60]

Chapter 6 is the letter from Urban II to the legate. It is written in the form of a private charter rather than a papal bull and contains none of the usual authenticating signs for such a papal document as it purports to be. Its text (which I reproduce here in full as it appears in the *Exordium Parvum*, its only source) contrasts the monastery of Molesme with the desert of Cîteaux:

Urbanus episcopus, servus servorum Dei, venerabili fratri et coepiscopo Hugoni apostolicae sedis vicario, salutem et apostolicam benedictionem. Molismensium fratrum magnum in concilio clamorem accepimus, abbatis sui reditum vehementius postulantium. Dicebant enim religionem in suo loco eversam, seque pro abbatis illius absentia odio apud principes et ceteros vicinos haberi. Coacti tandem a fratribus nostris, dilectioni tuae per praesentia scripta mandamus, significantes gratum nobis existere, ut si fieri posset, abbas ille ab heremo ad monasterium reducatur. Quod si implere nequiveris, curae tibi sit, ut et qui heremum diligunt conquiescant, et qui in coenobio sunt regularibus disciplinis inserviant.

Bishop Urban, servant of the servants of God, to his venerable brother and fellow bishop Hugh, vicar of the Apostolic See, greetings and apostolic blessings. We have heard the complaint of the brothers of Molesme who are very insistently demanding the return of their abbot. Indeed, they have said that regular life at Molesme has been overturned and that because of the absence of their abbot they are treated with scorn by princes and other neighbors. Urged by our brothers, we inform you by this letter how much it would please us if you could return that abbot from the desert to the monastery. But if you cannot do that, that you take care that those who love the desert be left to their quiet and those who are in the monastery follow their Rule.[61]

Chapter 6 ends by telling us that the legate, Hugh of Lyons, had read this papal letter, consulted with those who had power or piety, *viros authenticos et religiosos convocavit*, and made a decision as recounted in the following chapters.[62]

Chapter 7 includes more correspondence attributed to Hugh of Lyons instructing Robert to return to Molesme and telling Gaufredus, erstwhile abbot of Molesme, to step down; it also assured the return of books to Molesme.[63] In Chapter 8, bishop Walter of Châlons transferred Robert of Molesme back to the jurisdiction of bishop Robert of Langres. Robert was absolved of his earlier obedience to the bishop of Châlons, but those monks remaining at the new monastery were also absolved from their obedience to Robert.[64]

Chapter 9 describes how Cîteaux was deprived of its founder — "became a church widowed of its shepherd" — and had to elect a new abbot, Alberic:

Viduata igitur suo pastore, cisterciensis ecclesia convenit, ac regulari electione quemdam fratrem Albericum nomine in abbatem sibi promovit.

The church of Cîteaux found itself widowed of its shepherd, and by canonical election promoted a certain brother named Alberic to be abbot.[65]

Alberic rather than Robert is described in the rubric as the first abbot of Cîteaux.[66]

Chapter 10 tells us with what admirable forethought Alberic had sent two monks, carrying letters from a series of supporters, to Pascal II in Rome to obtain papal approval.[67] The letters they carried comprise Chapters 11, 12, and 13. The first, from two cardinals, describes the need for peace between the new abbey and Molesme, from which Cîteaux had seceded for religious reasons, *a qua religionis causa discesserant*.[68] The second, in Chapter 12, is yet another letter from Hugh of Lyons explaining that the move from Molesme occurred because certain monks wished to lead a stricter and more holy (or more retired) life at the new place, following the Rule of the Blessed Benedict:

Propter artiorem et sanctiorem (alt. secretiorem) vitam secundam regulam beati Benedicti.

Because they wished to live more strictly and religiously (or secretly) according to the Rule of the blessed Benedict.[69]

Hugh's letter attacks all other monks but those of Cîteaux. He requests the apostolic blessing for Cîteaux because its *pauperes Christi* had no defense except in God and in the pope.[70] He argues that the monks at the new monastery would be denounced by those from Molesme and elsewhere because those attackers could not be seen as anything but despicable in comparison to the reformers at Cîteaux. This statement implies not only that anyone criticizing the Cistercians was merely jealous of their famous austerity, but also that such criticism was rife at the time of composition—something more likely in the third than in the first quarter of the century.[71]

In a third letter, bishop Walter of Châlons explains that the monks at Cîteaux had departed from Molesme because of its laxity, but they had only made their move with the advice of pious men. He pleads for their freedom from all authorities except himself, his successors, and the pope.[72]

Chapter 14 is the "Roman privilege" of Pascal II, seemingly a confirmation of Cîteaux's site and foundation. It is incorrect in its protocol in addressing Alberic as venerable, a title reserved by the pope for fellow bishops and their equivalents or for institutions.[73] Further niggles about diplomatic formulae in it might be made, such as the *vos igitur* and *sane si quis* clauses found here, instead of the more usual *si qua igitur* of normal imprecation clauses of this date.[74] More important, there is no independent document to witness this act. It is found in no other twelfth-century manuscript except those containing the *Exordium Parvum*. In fact, it is found in no other manuscript earlier than the *Liber Privilegiorum Cistercii*, Dijon MS 69 (598), of the late Middle Ages.[75] Finally, even if this were an authentic papal confirmation, most of it has little to do with the issue of Cîteaux's secession from Molesme and does not address either a General Chapter or a religious Order, but only Cîteaux itself. Its confirmation of earlier settlements with Molesme (which I have marked in italics in the full text below), could easily be interpolated. Despite having a fuller text than other purported documents found in the *Exordium Parvum*, it is still lacking a dating clause, seal, and attestation.

The letter (for which the *Exordium Parvum* is the only source) reads as follows,

Paschalis, episcopus, servus servorum Dei: venerabili Alberico abbati novi monasterii, quod in cabilonensi parrochia situm est, ejusque successoribus regulariter substituendis in perpetuum: Desiderium quod ad religiosum propositum et animarum salutem pertinere monstratur, auctore Deo sine aliqua dilatione est complendum. Unde nos, o filii in Domino dilectissimi, circa difficultatem omnem vestrarum precum petitionem admittimus, quia religioni vestrae paterno congratulamur affectu. Locum igitur illum quem inhabitandum pro quiete monastica elegistis, ab omnium mortalium molestiis tutum ac liberum fore sanctimus, et abbatiam illic perpetuo haberi, ac sub apostolicae sedis tutela specialiter protegi, salva cabilonensis ecclesiae canonica reverentia. Praesentis itaque decreti pagina interdicimus, ne cuiquam omnino personae liceat statum vestrae conversationis immutare, neque vestri, quod novum dicitur coenobii monachos sine regulari commendatione suscipere, neque congregationem vestram astutiis quibuslibet aut violentiis perturbare. *Eam sane controversiae decisionem, quam inter vos et molismensis claustri monachos, frater noster lugdunensis archiepiscopus tunc apostolicae sedis vicarius, cum provinciae suae episcopis aliisque viris religiosis ex praecepto predecessoris nostri apostolicae memoriae Urbani secundi perpetravit, nos tanquam rationabilem ac laudabilem confirmamus.*

Vos igitur, filii in christo dilectissimi ac desiderantissimi, meminisse debetis, quia pars vestri saeculares latitudines, pars ipsas etiam monasterii laxioris minus austeras angustias reliquistis. Ut ergo hac semper gratia digniores censeamini, Dei semper timorem et amorem in cordibus vestris habere satagite, ut quanto a saecularibus tumultibus et deliciis liberiores estis, tanto amplius placere Deo totis mentis et animae virtutibus anheletis. Sane si quis in crastinum archiepiscopus aut episcopus, imperator aut rex, princeps aut dux, comes aut vicecomes, judex aut ecclesia, quaelibet saecularisve persona hanc nostrae constitutionis paginam sciens, contra eam venire temptaverit, secundo tertiove commonita, si non satisfactione congrua emendaverit, potestatis honorisque sui dignitate careat, reumque se divino judicio existere de perpetrata iniquitate cognoscat, et a sacratissimo corpore et sanguine Dei ac Domini nostri Jhesu Christi aliena fiat, atque in extremo examine districtae ultioni subjaceat. Cunctis autem eidem loco justa servantibus, sit pax Domini nostri Jhesu Christi, quatinus et hic fructum bonae actionis percipiant, et apud districtum judicem praemia aeternae pacis inveniant.

Bishop Paschal, servant of the servants of God to the venerable Alberic, abbot of the New Monastery, located in the realm of Châlons and all his successors who are canonically elected there, in perpetuum. Something desired for religious purposes and the health of souls ought to be fulfilled by the will of God without delay. Hence, oh dearest sons in the Lord, we listen to the requests of your petition without difficulty because we examine your religious practices with the concern of a father. We sanctify that place where you have chosen to live in the wilderness in monastic quiet, so that it be free of all molestation by mortals, and that you have there in perpetuity an abbey protected under the special tutelage of the Apostolic See, saving only the canonical reverence owed to the church of Châlons. We forbid by this decree that any person be allowed to change the status of your abode or of your selves, or that you should have to accept monks at your new monastery except in a canonical way, or that anyone perturb your monastic family by guile or violence. *We confirm as both reasonable and praiseworthy the decision ending the controversy between you and the monks of the cloister of Molesme that was made by our brother the archbishop of Lyons, then vicar of the Apostolic See, with the bishops of his province and other religious men, undertaken at the request of our predecessor of apostolic memory, Urban II.* (my emphasis)
You therefore, most dear and most beloved sons in Christ, must keep in mind that a part of you have departed directly from the wide spaces of the world, and that others of you have left the less austere paths of a more lax monastery. Therefore to assure that you be esteemed, you must strive very carefully that you always have both the fear and the love of God in your hearts, and that in all the strength of your minds and souls you have as large a place for pleasing God as you have freedom from the tumult and temptations of the world. If hereafter any archbishop or bishop, emperor or king, prince or duke, count or viscount, judge or church, or any sort of secular person knowing of this letter is tempted to contravene what we have established here, and after being warned several times does not make adequate satisfaction, let him be denied the power and honor of his position and be aware that he is subject to divine judgment for the crime he has done and that he will be excluded from the sacrament of the body and blood of God and our Lord Jesus Christ, and subjected to strict judgment at the end of time. But may those who serve this place receive the Peace of our Lord Jesus Christ, so that they may realize that good actions bear fruit here on earth and bring the reward of eternal peace from the strict judge.[76]

This privilege quoted ends with an imprecation against all who would try to overturn the reformed life at this new monastery, and a papal blessing of peace, but contains no subscriptions or dating clause.[77] This confirmation, *Desiderium quod*, opens by stating: "Something desired for religious purposes ought to be fulfilled by the will of God without delay." But even if it is authentic this is at best a commonplace confirmation addressed to any number of new monastic houses by Pascal and his successors.[78] For instance, we find a text opening with the same words addressed to the nuns of le Tart by pope Eugenius III in 1147.[79]

Chapter 15, entitled *Instituta monachorum*, paraphrases the *Instituta* found with the earlier *Exordium Cistercii*.[80] It affirms that Cistercians live by the Rule of Saint Benedict, rejecting anything contrary to that Rule or to the Life of Benedict, such as full mantles and furs or diverse foods in the refectory. Also rejected because they are not attested to in the Rule are ownership of churches, altars, oblations, burial payments, tithes on the labor of others, ovens, mills, villas, and peasants.[81] Also included is a limitation on women entering or being buried in Cistercian houses, with an oblique reference to the exception found in the Life of Benedict, Scholastica, Benedict's sister.[82] This limitation on interaction with women appears to be an innovation of the 1170s documents. In versions of the *Instituta* associated with the earlier *Exordium Cistercii*, only live-in women servants are forbidden, not the burial of women who were presumably the Order's women patrons.[83]

Chapter 15 also describes what constituted perhaps the most important innovations of Cistercians and other reformers of the twelfth century, their allowing "bearded" lay-brothers to enter Cistercian communities, where those conversi would help the monks produce food for their communities and guests. It describes Cistercians accepting land to make into granges for that purpose:

Tunc diffinierunt se conversos laicos [barbatos] licentia episcopi sui suscepturos, eosque in vita et morte, excepto monachatu, ut semetipsos tractaturos, et homines mercenarios; quia sine amminiculo istorum non intelligebant se plenarie die seu nocte praecepta regulae posse servare; suscepturos quoque terras ab habitatione hominum remotas, et vineas et prata et silvas, aquasque ad facienda molendina, ad proprios tamen usus.

Then they decided to use hired laborers and to accept lay-brothers with the permission of their bishop, treating the latter in life and death like any of themselves except for their vows as monks, because without the support of such laborers they did not think they could possibly observe day and night all the precepts of the Rule. They accepted land located at some distance from settlements and vineyards, meadows and woodlands, and watercourses for making mills for their own use.[84]

This section also describes the organization of estates under the control of those lay-brothers. The latter are given control so that monks may remain, as is asserted to be most appropriate, within the confines of their monasteries,

> Et cum alicubi curtes ad agriculturas exercendas instituissent, decreverunt ut praedicti conversi domos illas regerent, non monachi, quia habitatio monachorum secundum regulam debet esse in claustro eorum.

> And when they had established farmsteads for the practice of agriculture, they decreed that said lay-brothers rather than the monks ought to be in charge of such houses, because according to the Rule the residence of monks ought to be in their enclosure or cloister.[85]

Such a description of the management of Cistercian estates found here suggests the relatively late date of the *Exordium Parvum* text, for the institution of such grange agriculture on Cistercian lands using lay-brothers cannot be documented using the administrative records for earlier than the late 1140s and was not widespread until several decades later.[86] As for the protests about enclosure and stability, they deserve more attention.[87]

Chapter 16 describes the sorrow that was felt at Cîteaux because there were no new recruits to its way of life in the early years. The earlier text, the *Exordium Cistercii*, had assigned this problem to the early part of Stephen's reign (1108–33), but in the *Exordium Parvum* it is shifted back into Alberic's (1099–1108). Chapter 17 describes the death of Alberic, the election of Stephen, the increase in properties, and the entrance of many new recruits; again Bernard of Clairvaux is not specifically mentioned.[88]

Chapter 18 of the *Exordium Parvum* describes the establishment of abbeys in many dioceses, saying that within eight years (possibly this is counting only from when the first houses were established outside the diocese of Châlons or the ecclesiastical province of Lyons) twelve houses had been founded:

> Abhinc abbatias in diversis episcopatibus ordinaverunt, quae tam larga potentique Domini benedictione in dies crescebant, ut infra octo annos, inter illos qui de cisterciensi coenobio specialiter fuerant egressi, et caeteros qui ex eisdem fuerant exorti, XII coenobia constructa fuerint inventa.

> Henceforth they established abbeys in various dioceses, which increased daily by the great and powerful blessings of the Lord. Thus, within eight years, out of those who had gone forth from the monastery of Cîteaux in particular and of the rest who would spring forth from it, twelve new monasteries were founded.[89]

This number is smaller, but covers a shorter period, than that given in the earlier *Exordium Cistercii*, which cited twenty houses in twelve years. Both statements may be correct, with twelve houses (or three a year) in the first eight years and another eight houses (or two a year) over the next four. Neither number can in itself, however, be used to date these accounts or to argue for when the Charter of Charity was issued. The numbers twelve and twenty may have been chosen for their mystical significance.[90] Probably merely indicative of a perceived rate of expansion, they could not possibly have represented a census of abbeys, at least not one beyond a tiny Burgundian congregation, which had no need of such institutions as are proposed in the Charter of Charity.

Efforts by earlier scholars to date these two *exordia* to very early in the twelfth century by reference to these numbers have caused intense scrutiny of early local archives. Those scholars have attempted to correlate the foundation dates of the first twelve or the first twenty abbeys in the Order to the early composition of the Charter of Charity and these *exordia*.[91] But this is not possible. Such experts on the early Cistercians have assumed that these texts are those of eyewitnesses to the foundation at Cîteaux, as well as that the numbers contained in them are accurate. But we should question the accuracy of these numbers, just as we should query the authenticity of documents embedded in the *Exordium Parvum* account. These same scholars cite as independent confirmation of the *Exordium Parvum* the papal bull purported to have been written by Calixtus II in 1119 confirming the Cistercian constitution.[92] But, as discussed in Chapter 2, it is easy to show that the Calixtus II bull is a forgery. The only possible shred of authentic documentation even within the *Exordium Parvum* is the "Roman privilege" of Pascal II, with all its problems.

The numbers in the earlier *Exordium Cistercii* (written circa 1165) may in fact be derived from what I shall argue is the roughly contemporary 1165 papal confirmation by Alexander III for Cîteaux. It lists sixteen daughter-houses as if they were Cîteaux's own properties:

In quibus hec propriis duximus exprimendi vocabulis, locum ipsum de Cistercio cum terris, pratis, aquis, silvis, pascuis, et omnibus pertinenciis suis, abbatiam de Firmitate, abbatiam de Pontiniaco, abbatiam de Claravalle, abbatiam de Morimundo, abbatiam de Pruliaco, abbatiam de Curia Dei, abbatiam de Bonavalle, abbatiam de Helemosina, abbatiam de Oratorio, abbatiam de Buxeria, abbatiam de Miratorio, abbatiam de Sancto Andrea, abbatiam de Balanciis, abbatiam de Personia, abbatiam de Erivado, abbatiam de Obezinna.

Which properties included the site of Cîteaux with lands, meadows, watercourses, woodlands, pasture lands, and all its appurtenances, the abbey of la Ferté, that of

Pontigny, that of Clairvaux, that of Morimond, that of Preuilly, that of la Cour Dieu, that of Bonnevaux, that of l'Aumone, that of le Leroux, that of les Bussières, that of le Miroir, that of Saint-Andrew-de-Gouffern in Normandy, that of Balerne, that of Perseigne, that of Arrivour, that of Obazine.[93]

The *Exordium Parvum* and accompanying Charter of Charity and *Instituta* continued to be influential after the twelfth century because they serve as the introduction to the Cistercian liturgical order-books. The *Exordium Parvum* was also incorporated into the first book of Conrad of Eberbach's *Exordium Magnum*, where it is detached even more from the context in which it was originally composed. As argued in the next chapter, analysis of the manuscripts for the *Exordium Cistercii* and the *Exordium Parvum* and associated texts shows that neither of them was an eyewitness account. The *Exordium Cistercii* and the slightly later *Exordium Parvum* were both written by anonymous Cistercians in the third quarter of the twelfth century. These texts were constructed by authors whose interest was to explain Cistercian origins to a later generation of monks (and nuns) who had not been there at the outset. Increasingly, however, Cistercians of the later twelfth century were coming under criticism, a fact that may explain the particularly strident tone of the *Exordium Parvum*. Its language of isolated sites and pioneering activities and the clear insinuation in the attached *Instituta* that the gestation of the Order came entirely from Burgundy turn out to be more rhetorical than true.

Yet this is an account that has been repeated by generations of historians. It has remained popular in part because there has been a tendency to think that independent affirmation of the mythical events described in one text can be found in other parts of the "primitive document" groupings, or are authenticated by the documents incorporated into the *Exordium Parvum* or the Calixtus II bull attached to it. Such purported verification by citing parallels between different texts all found in the same manuscript is obviously false, but it has been made convincing by separately denoting texts, such as *Exordium*, Charter of Charity, or *Instituta*, which in fact are part of a single larger account. The same fuzzy thinking is used in attempts at verification of the myths of Cistercian foundations using arguments from material remains.

Buildings and Sites

Cistercian historians have frequently pointed to buildings and sites as proof of the "facts" of early Cistercian history found in the two *exordia* just outlined. Pioneering activities described in the early texts just discussed are said to be confirmed by the sites and remains of Cistercian abbeys that may still be seen in places like southern France. These sites seem to confirm descriptions of Cistercian foundations "in horrid deserts and vast solitudes" and wildernesses "occupied only by savage beasts." But such sites, although they appear to conform to descriptions found in the twelfth-century accounts of the Order's origins, are sometimes more isolated today than they were in the Middle Ages.[94] Our conclusions about them, moreover, are often based on vague memories evoked by the black-and-white photographs with which studies such as this are illustrated. These lead to discussion of the "aura" or "spirit" of such buildings and the "effect of their light," or about "isolated valley sites" chosen by Bernard of Clairvaux. Such talk lends credence to assertions of early Cistercian isolation and austerity, but such impressions are usually totally false. In fact, few Cistercian sites in southern France or anywhere else were ever more than superficially the "deserts" of which Bernard and his companions dreamed.

Moreover, although historians of monastic architecture have known for decades that there is considerable diversity in detail even in those Cistercian churches most often cited as being identical, nonspecialists to architectural history continue to see evidence of Cistercian unanimity in what they perceive as the "nearly identical" early Cistercian churches found in regions like southern France.[95] Closer examination, however, contradicts assertions of any identity in plan, construction methods, or austerity in southern French Cistercian architecture. Like any other medieval construction, that associated with the Cistercians throughout Europe was influenced by climate, available materials and local building techniques, changes in secular style, and available funds. Yet advocates of Cistercian mythology assert that Cistercian churches in their pristine simplicity reflect the spirituality of early Cistercians, whose unanimous brotherhood of Burgundy's colonizing monks conformed to a single model of monastic practice, even for the construction of their buildings. They also use such notions of a purported universal Cistercian architecture to argue that communities that do not conform to such architectural prejudices, like that of Valmagne with its thirteenth-century cathedral-Gothic church discussed in Chapter 4, could not possibly be Cistercian — because Cistercians did not build cathedral-Gothic.[96]

Favored examples, such as the "three sisters of Provence," the Cistercian churches of le Thoronet, Sénanque, and Silvacane, when examined in depth, do not provide the much-vaunted evidence of unanimity of early Cistercian architectural style that they are said to display. A survey of the plans of these three churches may demonstrate this point. Although all three churches have similar cruciform plans with simple east ends, in other details, even in the plans

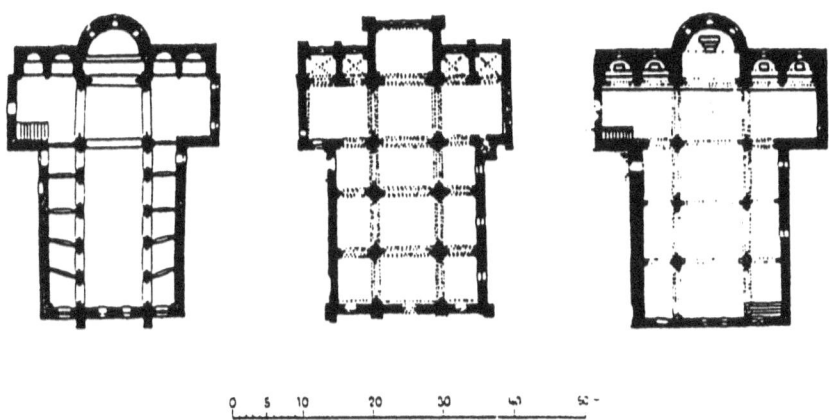

Figure 2. Plans of the Cistercian churches for monks at Sénanque, Silvacane, and le Thoronet. (Berman, after Dimier).

of these churches (see Figure 2), there is sufficient diversity to belie any claims about monolithic organization and uniform architecture among such houses. Of these three, only Sénanque (see Figure 3), had an octagonal crossing tower, for instance. Le Thoronet and Sénanque both have two chapels built on each side of a rounded main apse (see Figure 4), but those apsidal chapels are so tiny that they are built into the interior of a flat wall. Silvacane in contrast has a square apse and very obvious side chapels.

Aisles also vary. Le Thoronet has aisles with quarter-round barrel vaults that allow a thin arcade wall between nave and aisle; these had to be supported by thick exterior walls. At Sénanque and Silvacane, the aisle vaults were stilted three-eighth round vaults. Silvacane has complex piers supporting a thinner wall. Silvacane and le Thoronet have definite bays in nave and aisles. Sénanque did not, but at Sénanque the arcade wall was so thick that its pier-supports appear as deep as they are wide; see Figures 4 and 5 for Sénanque.

Light at the east ends of all these churches was the more striking because of the lack of side lighting, but solutions differed as to how the fenestration at each of them was organized. Le Thoronet has only three aisle windows and was dark, but, as we see from Figure 5, Sénanque had light from the crossing tower as well as clerestory window openings necessitating the use of exterior applied buttresses and heavy piers for support.[97]

The argument that these three churches should exhibit any unanimity in their construction becomes totally absurd if we consider their early history. They were all, in fact, incorporated houses, created at different times, occupy-

Figure 3. Cistercian church for monks at Sénanque, exterior. (Friedman)

ing different places even on the filiation trees from the thirteenth century, and having in common not much more than the fragmentary nature of their early documentation and their survival in relatively close proximity in Provence.

Art historians working on these churches have tended to project patronage relationships of the thirteenth century back onto the twelfth. Thus the church of Silvacane in the diocese of Aix-en-Provence is sometimes said to have been built between 1175 and 1230 by the lords of les Baux.[98] Although thirteenth-century documents may address the lords of les Baux as founders, this was an honorific granted to allow them burial rights there. Attributions of a date for this church to 1147, moreover, confuse the purported date at which Cistercian practices are first found for this house with that of its construction.[99]

Silvacane appears in fact to have originated a century earlier, when (in 1048) it was a cell belonging to the abbey of Saint-Victor of Marseilles; attachment to the Cistercians is only demonstrated from the 1190s.[100] Silvacane did have a daughter-house for monks founded at Valsainte in the diocese of Apt; it was probably founded under pressure from the lords of Forqualquier about 1188, perhaps at about the same time both became Cistercian.[101] Similarly, both le Thoronet and Sénanque were houses founded before Cistercian affiliation and were totally independent of each other at the outset. They were only

Figure 4. Sénanque, nave looking east. (Friedman)

later attached to the Cistercian practices by way of the hermits of Mazan and the filiation of Bonnevaux, an affiliation that may have taken place in the 1160s or later. The two houses were not necessarily affiliated simultaneously.

Inferences about the architecture of all three churches, moreover, are based on misdating of Cistercian statutes about architecture to 1134 and 1152. In fact the dates of both the statutes and the construction of these churches need reexamination.

That conflicts rather than ties among these houses were more common in the Middle Ages is suggested by a document drawn up in 1193 to settle a controversy between Silvacane and Sénanque over granges, a document from which much of our early information about both is derived.[102] For Silvacane this document may be much closer to the time of its attachment to the Cistercians than was once thought. Silvacane seems to have been particularly recalcitrant in face of efforts to enforce unanimity by the early Order. Complaints about discipline at Silvacane were made to the General Chapter in 1236, and again in the 1280s Silvacane's monks and conversi were said to be wearing black habits in contradiction to the Order's regulations.[103]

Cistercians and other new reformers of the twelfth century built their first churches in wood and then replaced those cruciform churches built on a series

Figure 5. Sénanque, south aisle. (Friedman)

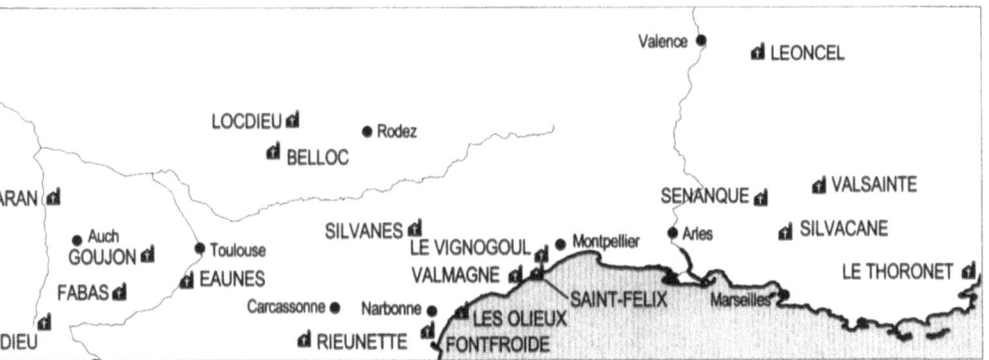

Figure 6. Locations of southern-French Cistercian abbeys and architectural remains.

of easily reproducible rectangular modules; similar churches were later constructed of stone using local construction practices. That Cistercian churches appear somewhat similar in type may be the result of retaining long-used building types that were limited by the wooden parts originally employed. But abundant remains of twelfth- and even thirteenth-century architecture for Cistercians in southern France (see Figure 6) are more a witness to the poverty of monastic communities in that region than anything else. If twelfth- and thirteenth-century churches and buildings are still standing, it is because communities were too poor to have replaced them later. Similarly, poverty is the primary explanation for the austere churches constructed for Cistercian women in this region.

Specialists on Cistercian architecture would probably now suggest that the special qualities distinguishing such Cistercian architecture from that of other twelfth-century buildings are its old-fashioned or conservative elements. These twelfth-century Cistercian churches look austere and similar primarily in comparison to newer building types being constructed in the more fashionable cathedral-Gothic style. What really determined the austerity of a Cistercian church was in general not the dictates of style but lack of wealth, for no poor house could update its architecture in later centuries.

But austerity in style and lack of substance are not always correlated in Cistercian building, because wealthy communities could also build and keep churches in an austere style. What at first glance seems a poor and isolated church may have only been disguising its assets. Nowhere is this more true than at Fontfroide, where differences between the monastic architecture in its austere setting and the realities of Cistercian wealth are extreme.[104]

The desolation of the site and monastic complex of the abbey for monks

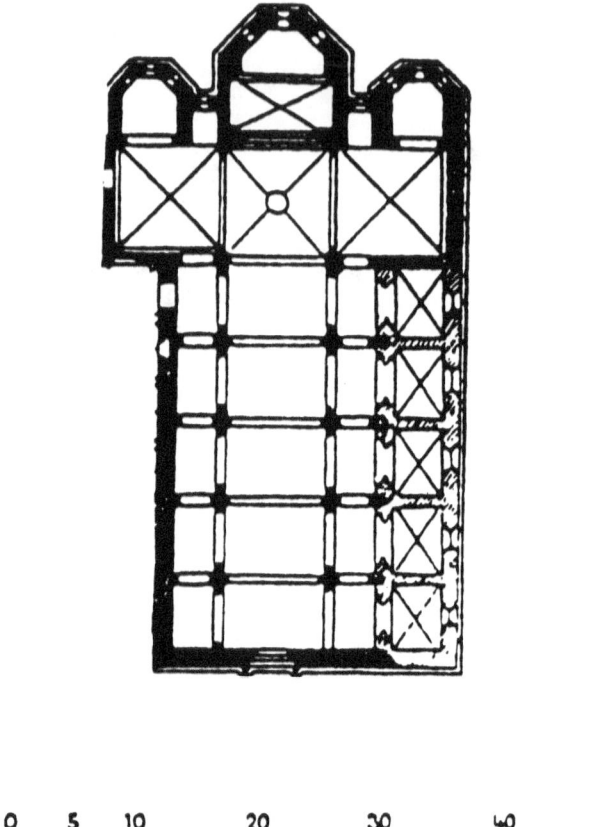

Figure 7. Plan of Cistercian church for monks at Fontfroide.

at Fontfroide (see Figures 7 and 8), located in a valley near Narbonne that is surrounded on three sides by the rugged garrigues, makes it a striking oasis of monastic solitude. Whether in the bright, blinding southern light or on a windy, rainy day, Fontfroide's church and site appear on first inspection to epitomize the "Cistercian spirit" of poverty, isolation, and rough simplicity. Much of the simplicity of Fontfroide's church and monastic buildings is deceptive. They are neither small nor humble.

The church of Fontfroide with its flat east end may look from its plan (see Figure 7) like a modest early Cistercian church. But that east wall with polygonal apse and round windows has five-sided chapels on each side and contains a complex tracery window of Gothic design higher on the end wall; see Figure 8. Fontfroide's church is not Gothic in a classic sense, having its height supported

Figure 8. Fontfroide church and abbey from garrigues to the east.

primarily by thick walls and applied buttresses. These contribute to the austere effect, but the church is both longer and much higher than it appears at first. The three-quarter vaults with pointed ribs of its north aisles rise to fourteen meters; these are heights found only at the center of the nave in other Cistercian churches in the region. Austere too is the effect of its having (like other churches in the Midi) flat roofs, although these are topped by an octagonal crossing tower and another bell tower; see Figure 9. Fontfroide's cloister is on the north side of the church for protection from the heat. Ornate elements of the arcade and columns of the cloister (seen in Figures 9 and 10) are usually explained as deriving from Fontfroide's pre-Cistercian past. Certainly the cloister's architecture is difficult to categorize, possibly because of the incorporation of materials such as capitals (see Figure 10) from earlier buildings.

Fontfroide was clearly an early incorporated house that was at first very poor. Its obscurity in the early twelfth century is confirmed by the fact that, when Bernard of Clairvaux came to Toulouse and began the process that ended in Grandselve's becoming a daughter-house of Clairvaux, Fontfroide was a mere annex to Grandselve. Yet from such obscurity Fontfroide rose to become one of the most powerful Cistercian monasteries in the Mediterranean region.[105] Fontfroide's monks, abbots, and lay-brothers were far from poor or powerless. The abbey site was not as isolated or uncomfortable as has

Figure 9. Fontfroide, cloister from northwest roof.

been contended; it was in fact protected from the diseases associated with the coastal swamps and its monks had adequate water for milling. The valley was the hub of a huge monastic estate surrounded by numerous granges, as seen in any map of its possessions; see Chapter 3, Figure 32. Fontfroide's massive monastic complex was built with a late twelfth-century confidence that the space would be needed for large numbers of monks and conversi. Whatever poverty Fontfroide may have experienced before the mid-twelfth century had disappeared in a managerial explosion of the second half of the century. Its buildings must be read as evidence not of poverty, but of the enormous wealth Fontfroide had acquired after it had adopted Cistercian practices, as is argued further in other parts of this book.

More austere in fact were the church and site of another independently founded, probably originally eremitical community in the diocese of Maguelonne. This community became a house for Cistercian nuns, the abbey at Saint-Félix-de-Montseau. Located near Gigean, the abbey sits like a fortress on an outcropping in the garrigues looking south toward the Mediterranean; see Figure 11. There are remains of two successive churches at this site. The earlier stone church may be a reflection of still earlier reform churches of the eleventh or twelfth century. Such churches were usually built in wood; here on the

Figure 10. Fontfroide, cloister capitals.

rocky outcropping where it was sited, wood, not stone, was the scarce commodity; see Figure 12. The tiny original church of Saint-Félix measured only four by eight meters; it was built directly on the rock; see Figures 12 and 13. That tiny edifice was later incorporated as a passageway from the nuns' courtyard into the second church. The northern wall was extended and incorporated into the southern wall of the new church; see Figure 13.

The newer, twelfth-century church at Saint-Félix was much larger, measuring 8 meters by 24.5 meters. It was not excessively elaborate but resembles other churches for Cistercian women in this region. Its single nave of three rib-vaulted bays and choir has ribs extending upward from corbels halfway up the walls; see Figure 14. Narrow lancet windows in its side walls and a polygonal apse with three double lancets and quatrefoil *oculi* oppose a moderate rose window on its west wall. Access for the priest or public from outside the cloister was by a north portal, which has a plain tympanum, rolled arches, and simple colonettes.[106]

Saint-Félix was a priory associated with Cistercian practices probably from 1167. Marthe Moreau has suggested that it was founded certainly before 1104 and possibly even before 1053. It was elevated to abbey status only in 1252, when Innocent IV moved its nuns from their obedience to the local

Figure 11. Church for Cistercian nuns at Saint-Félix, exterior from north.

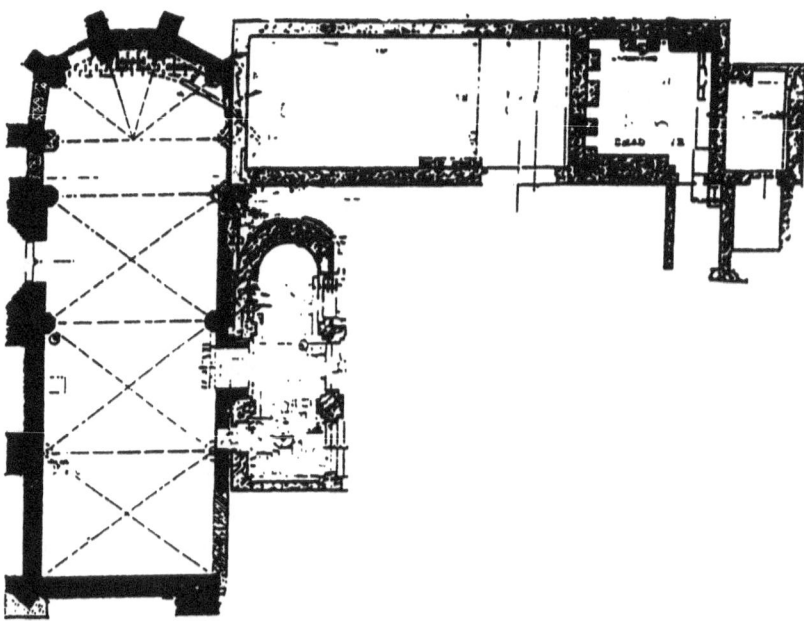

Figure 12. Plan of Saint-Félix.

Figure 13. Saint-Félix, southern portal and earlier church.

bishop to visitation by Valmagne. That pope's insistence on such regularization for many houses of Cistercian nuns suggests that the move had little to do with specific conditions at Saint-Félix. In any case, the nuns of Saint-Félix successfully left the Cistercian Order in 1332, presumably disaffected with the increasingly hostile attitudes of the Cistercian General Chapter to the Order's women.[107] We know nothing of the abbey's granges or properties and have only the remains of church and monastic buildings, and lists of prioresses and abbesses from the *Gallia Christiana*, to suggest, nonetheless, a community of women with wealth enough to build a larger second church to replace their smaller one, frugality enough to incorporate the older structure into a newer monastic complex, and a community of sufficient size to need more space.[108]

Such treatment of Saint-Félix as a twelfth-century house of Cistercian women requires an answer to the frequently heard question, "But were there twelfth-century Cistercian nuns?" While architectural historians have been unusual in their ability simply to study the remains of Cistercian women's houses without getting involved in such debate, even some of these historians have occasionally used the powerful image of an early Cistercian Order without women to argue that such stunning architectural remains as those for le Vignogoul (see the frontispiece and discussion in Chapter 4) were construc-

Figure 14. Saint-Félix, nave.

tions based on mere imitation of the Cistercians. Yet often such buildings in southern France are the strongest evidence for the very existence of such communities of early Cistercian nuns whose archives are often in disarray, if documents have survived at all. Several houses for nuns in the twelfth-century Midi are documented almost only by the remains of their churches. Thus in the diocese of Comminges a house of nuns reputed to have been associated with le Tart in Burgundy was founded at Fabas or Lumen-Dei in 1145. It would in turn found a community of nuns at Oraison-Dieu near Muret in 1167. The abbey of Fabas is also associated with other houses of women, including fourteenth-century foundations at Saint-Sigismond and Salenques, although Salenques is sometimes attributed to Beaulieu-en-Mirepoix.[109] Remains of a church built in the thirteenth century can be seen at Fabas on the boundary of the Ariège; see Figures 15 and 16. The building is now used as a barn; although the current owners acknowledge that their house was the convent, they assert that the abbey church was a quarter mile away.[110]

Similarly, not far east of Gimont another women's abbey was reportedly founded between 1135 and 1148 at Goujon on the edge of the diocese of Toulouse between Gimont and Muret. It was elevated from priory status to an

Figure 15. Church for Cistercian nuns at Fabas, exterior, portal.

Figure 16. Fabas, exterior, north side.

Figure 17. Church for Cistercian nuns at Goujon, exterior, portal.

Figure 18. Goujon, exterior, north side.

abbey in 1178, and it may have founded a bastide in the thirteenth century.[111] One can locate the church at Goujon (see Figure 17) because the abbey's valley site is marked on maps today by references to the forest of Goujon. This church too has now become a barn. Details of Gothic portals and windows are still readily apparent in its brick walls, even where they are shored up with rubble; see Figure 18. Other examples of such architectural remains of women's houses may be cited; they include those at les Olieux (Figures 33 and 34) and le Vignogoul (Figures 43–46), both discussed in later chapters.

The Illusion of an Order Without Women

Were there Cistercian women in the twelfth century?[112] The archaeological record preserves evidence of houses of Cistercian nuns in the Middle Ages, and documents suggest that they were there from as early as there was an Order.

In Burgundy, starting with the foundation at le Tart by Stephen Harding in the 1120s, and probably even earlier for nuns at Jully who had been associated with Molesme from 1113 or so and had been encouraged by Bernard of Clairvaux, nuns looked like and thought of themselves as part of the Cistercian reform movement.[113] In other parts of Europe, houses of nuns were also an important part of the monastic reforms of the early twelfth century, including that which would become the Cistercian Order. Sometimes such houses of nuns became Cistercian when the earlier congregation to which they belonged decided to adopt Cistercian practices and gradually became affiliated with the Order. Others predate the houses of monks to which they would eventually become subject, particularly as part of the movement of double houses or family monasteries, from which derived so many houses of reformers, monks and nuns alike, in the twelfth century.[114] Other houses of women were founded independently; they decided on their own to follow Cistercian practices, and they eventually became attached to the Order.

Although le Tart's daughters are often described as genuine foundations made by colonies of women sent out from Burgundy from 1120 onward, such references to colonization in groups of six or twelve nuns and an abbess may turn out to reflect the same mythology of apostolic gestation seen for Cistercian men and may be equally contrary to fact.[115] Certainly many houses among the so-called daughters of le Tart in southern France — Fabas in the Ariège and Rieunette in Languedoc, for instance, or the nunnery at Marrenz or Marrenx said to have been founded in 1157 by Count Raymond V of Toulouse — were local independent foundations that were not made by colonization from Burgundy.[116] Indeed, such houses of nuns thinking themselves Cistercian often had their earliest ties to one another, like those between nuns at Bellecombe in the Auvergne and their daughters at the house of Nonenque in the Rouergue.[117]

Why have illusions been so pervasive of a Cistercian Order free of women, of a Golden Age before the deluge of women into the Order, of women eager to become Cistercians, working on the land as hard as the monks of Clairvaux, but said to "only imitate" Cistercian practices? Why has there been so much confusion about Cistercian nuns despite the considerable local administrative evidence and architectural remains that document their existence? Telling the story of these women within that of the Cistercians in southern France and beyond has necessitated confronting the Order's myth of a Golden Age without nuns. Overturning arguments that before the introduction of a "female branch" there was no Cistercian decadence contributes to a better understanding of the history of the twelfth-century reform movement generally as well as of the history of Cistercian women.

Assertions that there were no Cistercian women are possibly based on the increasing misogyny within the religious orders of the later Middle Ages, misogyny that takes a definite upward turn in the late twelfth and early thirteenth centuries, as discussed below. But these assertions are also supported by a false image of a Cistercian Order of great uniformity closely controlled by a General Chapter that from the early twelfth century could have decided to exclude women. This excessively juridical definition of Cistercians has begun to be challenged by some of the foremost historians of the Cistercians themselves. Thus, toward the end of his life, Father Jean Leclercq would suggest:

If we consider the definition of Cistercian not in a juridical way, but as a way of life, then the women inspired by Bernard at Jully, or those fostered by Stephen Harding at le Tart, were Cistercians just as much as were the men at Cîteaux or Pontigny or Poblet.[118]

Such reevaluations of the role of women within the movement that eventually became the Cistercian Order reveal much about the diversity of religious practice out of which the early Cistercians developed as well as the slowness with which they coalesced into an Order.

Maintaining a "no women" myth has led to increasingly tortuous explanations of the entire history of the early Cistercians.[119] Indeed, not only is there considerable evidence of women's houses participating in the Order from its creation, but evidence is also being uncovered that many of the Order's earliest houses derived from double communities consisting of both religious women and religious men, such as that at Obazine and Coyroux.[120] In these double houses the religious women may have originally had the leading role, as seems to have been the case at Nonenque and Silvanès, as discussed in Chapter 4. A revised reading of the history of such early Cistercian women, like that of Cistercian sites and architecture or of the early *exordia* accounts themselves, demonstrates the flaws in traditional myths of early Cistercian unanimity, apostolic gestation, or single-gendered (masculine) monasteries "far from cities, castles, and human habitations."

Yet historians of the Cistercians have been able to argue successfully for only limited participation by women within the early Cistercian Order. Recent denials that there were twelfth-century Cistercian women may be traced to the 1935 thesis by Herbert Grundmann in which he had concluded (quite wrongly, as it turns out) that Cistercian women's houses date only to the thirteenth century.[121] Although Grundmann's treatment of religious women is usually deemed enlightened (he wrote when much women's history was simply ignored), he followed traditional explanations in his erroneous contentions about Cistercian women. He did so in part because of his reliance on local documentation coming almost entirely from German and eastern-European areas — where the Cistercians often had arrived relatively late — but his conclusions about Cistercian women upheld as well a schematization of the history of religious reform that supported his theories about heresy and mysticism. Thus, in Grundmann's thinking, the twelfth century was characterized by women's participation in heretical groups or their entry into women's religious houses that were part of double monasteries founded by Robert of Arbrissel at Fontevrault, Norbert of Xanten at Prémontré, and Gilbert at Sempringham.[122] Grundmann also saw the decisions of the early thirteenth-century Dominicans and Franciscans (and, in his view, Cistercians) to found women's abbeys as constituting a direct response to the threat of heresy and necessitated by that threat.[123] Although this may have been the case, that view does not preclude the existence of twelfth-century houses for Cistercian nuns.

Grundmann's comments on Cistercian women directly influenced the work of Ernst Krenig, whose dissertation on Cistercian nuns appeared in 1954 and soon stood as the official treatment.[124] Krenig employed Grundmann's description of the eventual admission of nuns into the Cistercian Order, one that presents monastic women in an extremely negative way. Nuns are described as "an overwhelming flood which the Order was unable to stem," and the "admission" of such women is presented as "forced on" the Order's reluctant abbots. Moreover, the Order's growing decadence is related to this addition of women.[125] Such a view ignores the considerable local evidence for the foundation of individual abbeys of women even before there was an Order — houses of nuns eventually recognized as Cistercian. The official denial that there were Cistercian women in the twelfth-century Order, moreover, has often caused historians to date the affiliation of individual houses of Cistercian nuns to the thirteenth century and deny the significance of twelfth-century evidence for such communities. This was particularly so if those twelfth-century houses of women were called priories rather than abbeys; in fact, twelfth-century priories of Cistercian nuns often existed.[126]

New evidence for twelfth-century nuns at le Tart, which was presented in France at the time of the 1953 celebrations of the octocentenary of Bernard's death, appeared just before the publication of Krenig's work.[127] Krenig incorporated it as evidence of an *imitatio cisterciensis* by women "wearing the habit of the Order and following the practices of the brothers at Cîteaux, but not officially part of the Order and not entitled to its privileges."[128] This notion of women "only imitating" the Cistercian Order, which Krenig borrowed from earlier studies, has enabled traditional histories to dismiss evidence found in local administrative records for such houses of Cistercian nuns. Even when women's participation in the Order has been acknowledged, it has been qualified by assertions based on references to Grundmann and Krenig. By treating every case as the sole exception to a more general rule, women's presence was denied or treated as aberrant.[129]

Such treatment of twelfth-century and later Cistercian women as "only imitating" the Order's practice generalizes from the example of the recluse, Yvette of Huy, who may have lived *in imitatione cisterciensi* as an anchoress.[130] But this makes an aberrant case into the rule. Yvette was clearly exceptional; most Cistercian nuns lived in communities thinking of themselves as Cistercian, following Cistercian practices, arguing for a share in the privileges of the Order (such as its tithe exemption), and seeking papal confirmation of such privileges.[131] Indeed, historians have often failed to notice that the wording found in papal confirmations of Cistercian practices by women's houses like le Tart—that they "followed the Rule of Saint Benedict and the customs of Cîteaux" (wording that when applied to nuns is used to argue that they were "imitation Cistercians")—is the same language used in twelfth-century confirmations for houses of monks as part of the Cistercian Order.[132]

In the face of such ideologies denying the existence of early Cistercian nuns, historians of women at first responded to such misconceptions by proposing that there were several stages in the early Order's treatment of women: at first totally ignoring them, then allowing women on a limited basis in the early thirteenth century, but soon attempting to exclude them again. These views, formulated primarily by Brigitte Degler-Spengler and deriving from her work on the houses of nuns in what is today Switzerland, see a brief moment between 1190 and 1250 when there were Cistercian nuns.[133] But in this perspective the brief stage of tolerance for women was already nearing an end in 1228 when the General Chapter tried to discourage abbots from further incorporations of nuns. Incorporation at that time occurred because these religious women, with the help of patrons and popes, successfully pressured the Cistercian Order's General Chapter for incorporation of women's houses. Indeed, the presence of Blanche of Castile in France from 1200 to her death in 1252, as wife of a future king, queen, and queen-regent, may have been instrumental in forcing official support of Cistercian nuns at the General Chapter. Agreements in 1251 that papal recommendations of houses of nuns to the Order would be limited henceforth may mark the end of an era of support, but they are not evidence that the Order's incorporation of new houses of nuns had ceased. In fact, the addition of women's communities after that date slowed but did not halt.[134]

In Degler-Spengler's view and those of many before her, houses of Cistercian nuns appeared only after there was an official procedure for their incorporation established by the express decision of abbots in General Chapters. She extracted from the thirteenth-century *Statuta* a list of criteria for identifying "authentically incorporated" houses of Cistercian nuns. These included notices of incorporation in the Order's *Statuta* or of inspection of resources by commissioned abbots, papal recommendations, documents mentioning the *ordo cisterciensis*, and concessions of freedom from episcopal visitation.[135] Obviously such criteria are increasingly valid ones for identifying any house, whether of monks or of nuns, added to the Order after 1190 or so. Nonetheless, given the frequent lacunae in the documents even for the thirteenth century and particularly for women's houses, the absence of such proofs means nothing. Moreover, such criteria cannot be applied to either men's or women's houses in the twelfth century, because for most of the century a fully functioning Order did not yet exist, as the next chapters of this study will argue.

But was it in any case a question of women forcing themselves on the Order? In grappling with such views of a limited admission of nuns to an Order controlled by men who did not want them, we tend to view abbots within the Cistercian Order as struggling to maintain their monastic solitude by denying or carefully controlling the incorporation of women. Yet local evidence suggests that it was sometimes the nuns themselves who actively opposed being incorporated into the Order, particularly if such incorporation would lead to their dependence on father-visitors who were the abbots of neighboring abbeys of monks, their natural rivals for property and patronage.[136] Such houses of nuns may have preferred adopting Cistercian practices informally and maintaining the practice of visitation by the bishops who had often founded their communities.[137]

Certainly some abbots' willingness to "accommodate" such pious women stemmed not from a generosity of spirit but from the temptations presented by the property belonging to those religious women. We see this, for instance, in the abbot of Staffarda's attempts to acquire property from the nuns at its daughter-houses of Rifreddo in late thirteenth-century Italy, and other such examples may also be cited.[138] Finally, even if women's houses had been attracted to Cistercian practices in the twelfth century, the growth of a more uniform Order would not necessarily have encouraged them to continue to seek such affiliation. Thirteenth-century Cistercian statutes about women's communities suggest increasingly harsh and inequitable treatment of the Order's nuns.[139] The only possibly favorable legislation declared that members of men's houses were not to demand hospitality from women's communities. (On the other hand, lay-brothers and chaplains attached to nuns' communities and who took vows directly from abbesses could still request hospitality at men's houses when they traveled.)[140] Otherwise, stern legislation mandated that nuns were to be strictly enclosed and sufficiently endowed so as not to prove a burden on neighboring men's houses. The numbers of women in these communities of nuns were to be carefully controlled. Internal visitation would only be by father-abbots, not by founding abbesses as well. Neighboring abbeys of Cistercian monks should not be required to provide chaplains or lay-brothers to the nuns, although they might choose to do so. Abbesses were not to attend the General Chapter at Cîteaux but were allowed an annual meeting at le Tart presided over by the abbot of Cîteaux. He would announce to the assembled abbesses decisions made by the General Chapter of abbots that had just met, but nuns were apparently allowed no legislative capacity. Indeed, the le Tart assembly would be disbanded by the end of the thirteenth century.[141]

The long denial of the presence of women in the twelfth-century reform movement that became the Cistercian Order, along with a tendency by other groups to cut off or limit acknowledgment of women's participation, both seem to date from the third quarter of the twelfth century, a fact deserving additional attention from historians of medieval religion. What happened in the 1160s and 1170s that made Cistercian abbots, and those of other groups as well, so anxious to distance themselves from women? Much of the documentation is not yet in. We cannot yet even count the number of women's religious houses in Europe, and guesses based on published materials from their archives are often wholly incorrect, for there is much evidence yet to be uncovered. Local archival depositories, from which all the materials on men's houses have long been available, can often not provide access to materials on religious women who would now be called Cistercian nuns. Those materials have not yet been organized and catalogued, in part because of what has remained an ambiguous status for such women's reform communities. We are finding evidence as well for many more ephemeral communities of these religious women in the late eleventh and twelfth centuries than was believed possible only a few years ago. The existence of these nursing and caregiving sisters is only now beginning to be noted because it occurs in peripheral references to such women in documents preserved for other branches of the Church.[142] Getting right the sequencing of Cistercian texts and the dating the Order's invention to the third quarter of the twelfth century, and disabusing monastic historians of their notions that there were no Cistercian nuns, will facilitate additional research on religious women, those who were part of the movement that became the Cistercian Order and those much more ephemeral women of communities of sisters that derived from similar circumstances.

2
Charters, "Primitive Documents," and Papal Confirmations

In this chapter, I argue that the work of "Order-building" by the early Cistercians must be dated to shortly after the mid-twelfth century and thus after the first generation of leaders had passed away. Indeed, there are indications, discussed in the next chapter, that the creation of a Cistercian Order was in part a reaction to the continued dominance of Clairvaux after Bernard of Clairvaux's death in 1153. The conclusion that a Cistercian Order was invented only in the 1160s, and not in the 1110s as is usually thought, is based on an analysis of just when the institutions we associate with the Cistercian Order first begin to appear in surviving documents of practice, or charters, from southern France and elsewhere. The earliest references in the charters to the Cistercians as a group to which one could belong or whose practices could be adopted, as well as their earliest references to a General Chapter, are found only in the mid-twelfth-century charters. All these indicators of the presence of a Cistercian Order appear sporadically in documents from the last years of the 1140s (in fact only in later cartulary copies of documents from 1146, 1148, and 1149); these indicators appear occasionally in the 1150s, and in the 1160s more consistently in more significant numbers.

I also describe in this chapter my examination of the authenticity and dating of the manuscripts containing the "primitive Cistercian documents," which are normally cited as eyewitness accounts to the foundation events. These have often been used to argue for an early development of the Order, but I have found that the manuscripts and the texts of these constitutional documents do not date from earlier than the 1160s. They represent the description that a later generation provided about the Order's origins. Finally, I show that the first papal confirmation of the Cistercian Charter of Charity was the papal bull, *Sacrosancta*, which appears in a form not found until the time of Alexander III (and dated to 1163 or 1165). My analysis of the early manuscripts shows that what had been thought to be the very early confirmation of the Order's constitution, *Ad hoc in Apostolicae*, attributed to Calixtus II in 1119, is a forgery. Indeed, evidence in papal documents for an Order dated earlier than the late 1140s is nonexistent. All evidence points to the 1150s as the era of the first General Chapters and to 1165 as the date of the first Cistercian constitution. The situation is clarified considerably once the evidence of the so-called "primitive documents" of the Cistercians is carefully weighed and dated.

The problem of the "primitive documents" has long been a vexing one, even in terms of definitions. There are several issues. First, these "primitive documents" were not created nearly as early as once thought. They are not "primitive" in the sense of being extremely early records, as has been implied. They were written or collected in the course of "Order-building," an activity that happened in the second part of the twelfth century. Moreover, these texts are not really "documents" at all, but a variety of legislative records and narratives. In fact, the term "primitive documents" is retained here only because it has become the standard designation for a certain group of problematic narrative and constitutional texts that have been the subject of debate over the last forty years.

The texts of these "primitive documents" include an early narrative account of the foundation of the new monastery at Cîteaux, either the *Exordium Cistercii* or the *Exordium Parvum*, each accompanied by characteristic versions of the Charter of Charity as well as by collected statutes often called the Cistercian *Instituta*. These "primitive" texts are usually accompanied in the manuscripts by a lay-brother treatise and sometimes by a papal confirmation, the latter found immediately following the *Exordium Parvum* and the Charter of Charity. The entire group of "primitive documents" is usually found in manuscript codices whose major component is the little-discussed Cistercian liturgical order-book, the *Ecclesiastica Officia*. Such collections of liturgical *ordines* are a neglected source for the earliest Cistercian practices, but in fact they include far more than what we would consider the practice of liturgy, including much detail on the internal organization of monasteries, such as the duties of various officials.[1] Much more so than the texts found with either the *Exordium Cistercii* or the *Exordium Parvum*, it is these liturgical *ordines* that comprise the earliest Cistercian regulations.

It is perhaps significant that such liturgical order-books, which concern the internal administration of individual abbeys, were more fully developed, and at an earlier date, than were such constitutional documents for the Order as its Charter of Charity. Obviously such liturgical *ordines*, as well as the lay-brother treatises that soon came to accompany them, provided the most necessary supplements to the Rule of Saint Benedict for any twelfth-century reform community wishing to adopt the reform practices associated with the brothers of Cîteaux. Only after many such houses had adopted such Cistercian practices was an Order, in the sense of an "umbrella group" of abbeys, actually needed. Many reform communities could have adopted the customs found in the *Ecclesiastica Officia* or the treatises on lay-brothers before any of the issues about relationships between houses, which are often considered central to the Cistercian constitution, would have arisen.

Thus a primary flaw in traditional accounts of the very early development of the Cistercians has been that these standard descriptions fail to make distinctions between the adoption of a new model for the internal organization of individual monasteries (such as a reformed liturgy that allowed time for field work on the part of monks and lay-brothers, or customaries for the management of lay-brothers) and regulations for a "supra-monastic" organization (that is, for an order and its governance). The failure to make such a distinction arises primarily because the full-blown Cistercian Order was assumed to have existed from such an early date. But assuming an early Order, and making no distinction between internal and extramural regulations, causes much confusion. There is in fact a difference between those issues that fall under the purview of the earlier liturgical order-books and those proper to the so-called "primitive documents," which concerned the later creation of an Order.

Most published versions of the early Cistercian documents have been based on texts drawn from a manuscript created at the abbey of Cîteaux in the 1180s: Dijon, Bibliothèque municipale MS 114. This large, lavishly-made folio codex was designed to be the exemplar manuscript for later manuscript copies of such handbooks of Cistercian practice; it is dated to between 1182 and 1188 on the basis of the commemoration in its pages of certain new saints.[2] Dijon 114 is not only an elegant manuscript by Cistercian standards, it is invaluable for understanding Cistercian practice of the 1180s and thereafter. But the practices it reflects are those of what was by then an almost fully articulated religious Order.[3] As a consequence, Dijon 114 is less useful as a source for the Order's earlier history. Yet it served until the middle of the twentieth century as the base manuscript for frequently-consulted publications of Cistercian "primitive documents," including statutes, the *Exordium Parvum*, and the Charter of Charity. Other manuscripts, however, now provide earlier versions of these texts that are the component parts of these constitutional documents, as discussed below.

Statutes Attributed to 1134 and 1152

Any discussion of dating the "primitive documents" of the Cistercians must begin with a brief consideration of a group of legislative compilations that have been published as the earliest compilations of statutes of the Cistercian Order and dated to the years 1134 and 1152. It must be stressed immediately that the dates usually given to these statutes in published editions (1134 and 1152) have no basis in the manuscript evidence, but derive instead from a series of inferences that are in fact untenable. Particularly because such statutes have often been used as justifications for how institutions are dated, this misdating of "statutes" to 1134 and 1152 has caused considerable confusion among Cistercian historians. Indeed, the amount of circularity in their arguments is often not realized by historians who have trusted that the dates of published statutes are secure and had been subject to careful source criticism before being published in such editions as that of Jean-Marie Canivez, *Statuta Capitulorum Generalium Ordinis Cisterciensis ab Anno 1116 ad Annum 1786* (Louvain, 1933). These texts, unfortunately, are not dated reliably.

While Canivez's edition of the Cistercian statutes publishes groups of statutes for the years 1134 and 1152, his dating turns out to be based on traditional hypotheses about when the Order was created, rather than on the internal evidence of the twelfth-century manuscripts, which give these statutes no dates at all.[4] The statutes published under the dates 1134 and 1152 appear undated in the twelfth-century manuscripts under the heading *Instituta* or *Capitula*. Such statutes cannot justifiably be attributed to either 1134 or 1152, which are both too early for them.

Canivez's collection provides other illusions about the early Cistercians that are equally unfounded. First, the volume suggests by its title that it is a complete transcript of all meetings of the Cistercian General Chapter between 1116 and 1786. It is often treated as if it were. Indeed, lacunae in its pages are treated by many historians as proof that nothing occurred in certain years, rather than as evidence that there are no surviving records, or that there was as yet simply no General Chapter or Order. For instance, the undated entry preceding that dated 1116 is the standard text of the Charter of Charity. The version used is not the earliest now known. Yet its placement implies that this is a document from before 1116. As I shall show, however, the Charter of Charity was probably written in the 1160s and certainly not before the second half of the century.

A perusal of Volume 1 of Canivez's edition shows that for many of the years before 1180 he included no authentic statute material. There are no surviving statutes for the years 1117–31, 1133, 1135–50, 1155–56, 1162, 1169, 1171–72, 1176, or 1178–79. That is, for 32 of the 64 years from 1116 to 1180, half of all these years, there are no statute entries at all. Texts found at some of the listed dates, moreover, starting with that for 1116, are later materials, often taken from a seventeenth-century Cistercian history by Angel Manrique. In fact, Canivez acknowledges in his introduction that he has inserted such more recent texts to fill in some of the blanks in the statute series, but one must read the introduction very carefully to discover this.[5]

A brief series of dated statutes do survive from the years 1157–61. They were published by Canivez from the Montpellier H322 manuscript discussed below. Otherwise, only for after 1179 does he give a regular series of surviving dated annual statutes. Moreover, no surviving *Statuta* dating to before 1190 concern individual houses of monks or nuns whose affairs were brought before the General Chapter. Only daughters of Cîteaux whose abbots are later designated as "proto-abbots" are mentioned once or twice in the 1180s.[6] The 1180s statutes do not yet concern the arbitration of disputes between Cistercian houses, which became regular business in the Order's later General Chapter. They only concern Order-building itself.[7]

Recently historians have noted that statutes published under the year 1134 are not consistent with one another. Attempts have consequently been made to show that some statutes published under 1134 are earlier than others.[8] But such attempts have treated 1134 as the latest possible date for any of them — an inference that is clearly incorrect, given the manuscript evidence. The manuscript evidence suggests that statutes published by Canivez for 1134 must have been gathered together fifteen or twenty years later in preparation for writing the Cistercian constitution, the Charter of Charity. That collection was presumably done just before the earliest version of that constitution, the *Summa Cartae Caritatis*, was prepared in the 1160s. Early lists of such statutes, often called *Instituta* (nearly identical to those published under 1134), were incorporated into the twelfth-century "primitive documents" manuscripts following their *exordia* and Charter of Charity. It is not clear, however, that these "statutes" found in the manuscripts as *Instituta* are really the decrees of annual General Chapters of abbots. They may be lists of ideals about practice drawn from such monastic texts as the Rule of Saint Benedict that were collected by abbots involved in the creation of the Cistercian constitution circa 1160. The gathering together of disparate lists of such ideals explains the incoherence noted with regard to those usually published (albeit incorrectly) as statutes for the year 1134.

Exceptional in the twelfth-century manuscripts containing such "statutes" is a single reference to an item found in the 1180s manuscripts in Dijon. Those manuscripts retrospectively date to the year 1152 a single item in a list of such early "statutes."[9] The statute in question is that published by Canivez as the first item for 1152, a much-cited statute concerning limiting the further affiliation of houses to the Order.[10] It seems unlikely, however, that the 1180s attribution of this statute to a General Chapter in 1152 is correct. Indeed, a

General Chapter had probably not been held as early as 1152, at least not in the annual, universal form we associate with the issuance of such detailed statutes. If the dating of this item to 1152 reflects any reality at all, it might possibly be the date of a decision made by a Burgundian congregation that existed before the Order had been invented.

More important, whether or not the attribution from the 1180s for this item to the 1150s is accurate, the retrospective dating of this single item does not provide any date for the rest of the materials published under the year 1152. In particular, it cannot date Canivez's item number six under 1152, a statute concerning a liturgical innovation for Marian feast days. This regulation can at best be bracketed to the years 1152–85, and then only if we are willing to assume that such statutes were collected in some sort of chronological order and that the 1152 date of item number one is correct. Statute number six definitely cannot be used to argue that manuscripts that lack the Marian liturgical innovation must necessarily be earlier than 1152.[11]

The fact that Canivez's edition has few reliable entries for the years before 1180, and almost none mentioning individual houses before 1190, means that lack of references in twelfth-century *Statuta* cannot be used to argue for the existence or nonexistence within the Order of specific houses of either nuns or monks. Moreover, the hypothetical dates for the early statutes cannot be used to date manuscripts or texts of "primitive documents" like the *exordia*. Indeed, the undated statutes reproduced by Canivez under the years 1134 and 1152 are preserved as *Instituta* in the very same twelfth-century manuscripts as the "primitive documents," and to argue that they can be used to date the manuscripts from which they come is absurd.

There are considerable repercussions for our understanding of all twelfth-century religious reform in knowing that these statutes so long believed to be firmly dated to 1134 and 1152 are later and perhaps are not even statutes at all. What is found under 1134 and 1152 in Canivez is neither a set of ideals agreed upon by an Order, nor precepts representative of general opinion among those monastic communities beginning to embrace the practices of Cîteaux. Yet these problems about dating the early statutes have almost entirely escaped notice in the debate over the so-called "primitive documents."

The Debate over the "Primitive Documents"

What then is the relationship between such texts and the early history of the Cistercians? Until recently few historians questioned the historical veracity of the traditional version of Cistercian history extracted from the *Exordium Par-*

vum, which promises us the "sincere truth" of early Cistercian history. Historians also did not question the early thirteenth-century *Exordium Magnum*, which incorporates the entire earlier text of the *Exordium Parvum*. Indeed, medievalists in general have given added validity to such texts, claiming that they speak in the "authentic voice" of the past. We do this often without exploring sufficiently whose "authentic voice" we are listening to and what issues that voice is addressing.

As discussed in the previous chapter, the "primitive documents" attempt to present the Cistercian Order as having been founded and having its administrative institutions all in place by the second decade of the twelfth century. Their narrative has been pervasive in most history writing up to the middle of the twentieth century. They bring with them many corollary conclusions about Cistercian singlemindedness and unanimity that depend on arguments for the early date of the creation of the Order. Indeed, despite the fact that new manuscript finds had begun to appear, it was still plausible in the 1940s for J.-B. Mahn to open his *L'ordre cistercien* by asserting:

One of the unique things about the Cistercian Order is that it represented at the very start of the twelfth century a willfully-designed organization, well-aware of its aims.[12]

Such treatment has continued in works that describe the Cistercians as "the first truly international Order," its General Chapter as a precursor of all later democratic assemblies, and its centralized annual General Chapter organization as one of the earliest modern communications systems.[13] Because of such assumptions, we have treated the Cistercians as the foremost early twelfth-century inventors, the leading creators of a religious order with a General Chapter as its head. This has also led us to explain the extraordinary wealth and power of the early Cistercians (or at least of the Cistercians by the end of the twelfth century) as the result of centralized planning, rationalization of agriculture, and other managerial feats diffused by the interactions of abbots at annual General Chapter meetings.[14]

Although considerable scholarly attention since World War II has been given to the Cistercians, much of that progress has been in studies of individual abbeys, drawing on the local administrative records produced in great abundance by twelfth- and thirteenth-century Cistercians, as well as studies of the architecture of their churches, abbey complexes, and tithe barns or on Cistercian spirituality and biblical commentary. Led by the noted Benedictine Jean Leclercq, who spent a lifetime publishing prodigiously on the Cistercians, historians of Cistercian intellectual history and theology have sorted out the authentic works of Bernard of Clairvaux from those of the pseudo-Bernards. They have also published catalogues of collections of Cistercian manuscripts in many countries and made new editions of Bernard's and other Cistercian works. It was during their forays into the libraries of Europe in the 1930s and shortly after, looking for additional manuscripts by Cistercian writers, that these scholars began to uncover variants on the Cistercian "primitive documents," including the rediscovered *Exordium Cistercii* text.[15] Circulation of publications about these finds was slow during the war years, and little discussion occurred until the 1950s.

When it came to the attention of monastic scholars that there were manuscripts earlier than the exemplar from Cîteaux, Dijon 114, and earlier versions of some of the "primitive" Cistercian texts such as the Charter of Charity and the *Exordium Parvum*, there was astonishment and disbelief. It turned out that many medievalists, not only monastic historians, had and still have a considerable intellectual investment in the authenticity and accuracy of the dating of accounts such as the *Exordium Parvum* and the early statutes. Secular historians have found it hard to believe that the published texts on which they had built sometimes substantial scholarly edifices had been published from single sources, and that such central texts had never been subjected to the rigorous source criticism assumed to have been standard in the nineteenth century.[16] Monastic scholars have felt bereft in even more dramatic ways, since they have been convinced that the very sources of their personal spiritual inspiration are being called into question by any discussion of the dating of the "primitive" texts.

Indeed most historians of the Middle Ages (not just modern members of religious orders) have found it hard to abandon the traditional Cistercian narrative about the early creation of a monolithic religious Order, apparently because this narrative has provided us with so many explanations for our views of the twelfth-century world. Economic historians have used the twelfth-century polemical attacks on Cistercian avarice as evidence for the managerial prowess of Cistercian entrepreneurs and have described Cistercian economic successes as deriving from the exchange of economic ideas and managerial strategies at General Chapter meetings in Burgundy; Cistercians viewed as being at the forefront of economic growth are used to explain the economic take-off of the High Middle Ages.[17] In North America, the Cistercians have often been seen in economic terms as the twelfth-century predecessors of doughty American frontiersmen, pulling themselves up by hard labor and becoming wealthy by abandoning cities for the frontiers where they installed a primitive egalitarian society. Even the twelfth-century history of the Cistercians' major rivals, the Cluniacs, has been written (very much in the style of the Cistercian *Exordium Magnum*) as the antithesis of everything that was happening at Cîteaux.[18]

Debate as to the dating and authenticity of the *Exordium Parvum* as an eyewitness account to the beginnings of Cistercian history arose first in Europe. It centered on the differences between the two accounts summarized in the previous chapter, the *Exordium Cistercii* and the *Exordium Parvum*. Monastic historians initially rejected the shorter version of early Cistercian history (the *Exordium Cistercii*) as nothing but a later précis of the *Exordium Parvum*. But the length of the *Exordium Cistercii* alone (comprising as it does only two short paragraphs) might suggest its composition prior to that of the much longer *Exordium Parvum*. Moreover, the *Exordium Cistercii* is always found with the *Summa Cartae Caritatis*. Confirmation that the textual grouping that contains the *Exordium Cistercii* and the *Summa Cartae Caritatis* is early is found in the fact that the abbot of Morimond is not listed as being among that special group of "proto-abbots" having oversight of Cîteaux. The abbot of Morimond is also not found in that role in the *Carta Caritatis Prior* that accompanies the earliest versions of the *Exordium Parvum*, such as that in Ljubljana (Laibach) 31; he appears only in the *Carta Caritatis Posterior*.

In Europe the attack on the authenticity of an early date for the "primitive documents" soon became a generational dispute between an entrenched intellectual establishment arguing that Calixtus II had confirmed the Charter of Charity as the Cistercian constitution in 1119 and ambitious young scholars who perceived their new manuscript findings as irrefutable evidence for their reinterpretations.[19] Medievalists of the younger generation who survived best in this climate did so by carefully sidestepping the issues of the "primitive documents"; they turned to editing Cistercian charters, describing Cistercian economic expansion, and making lists of Cistercian library holdings.[20] Those who, like J.-A. Lefèvre, were brash enough in that 1950s debate to attempt to resolve issues about the "primitive documents" were vilified.[21] Indeed, one can still be attacked for relying on Lefèvre.

In North America, criticism of traditional versions of early Cistercian history came at a slightly later date and with less generational conflict. The opening up of academic opportunities after World War II was accompanied, however, by a political climate stressing local history rather than bold general syntheses (the latter were considered too potentially dangerous as Marxism) and a new stress on social history based on the quantitative analysis of local records (among which the charters produced by twelfth- and thirteenth-century Cistercians were ideal). It was a period when the justification of American imperialism by American exceptionalism made it easy for every schoolchild to identify with a myth of Cistercian pioneers bringing light to the uncivilized parts of Europe in the twelfth century.[22] Moreover scholars from North America, often at one remove from the local context of the documents, were surprised to find contradictions between standard versions of early Cistercian history in the "primitive document texts" and the local administrative records. They often found traditional explanations so compelling that they tried to dismiss the evidence they were finding as somehow aberrant, rather than asking whether it was the traditional narratives that were incorrect.[23]

By the early 1970s, historians of monasticism in North America were pointing to the problem of the early Cistercian documents as the outstanding issue needing resolution.[24] But they also described how much dust had been raised by young scholars in Europe attempting to do so — this did not encourage younger scholars. New interpretations also arose among medievalists in North America and Britain as a generation of women academics were trained; their investigations soon turned to monastic women and uses of feminine imagery in monastic writing.[25] The question of the "primitive documents" began to be seriously raised in North America as it had in Europe, but its resolution was deferred for nearly a generation by a paper presented in 1974 at a Cistercian studies conference in Kalamazoo by Father Louis Lekai, who proposed a new methodology. That method has allowed many younger scholars to sidestep the issues of the "primitive documents" rather than resolving them.[26] His proposal was to treat the Cistercian Order's early history as a perfectly normal confrontation between idealistic institutions and local practice, between what he called "Cistercian Ideals" and "Cistercian Reality." His method has provided a context within which younger scholars can publish their findings that often have turned out to be contrary to the models, and to do so while avoiding the perils of the debate over the "primitive documents," but it has also meant that attention was diverted for some time from issues that are central to the reevaluation undertaken here.[27]

In fact, there were unacknowledged problems underlying Lekai's "Ideals and Reality in Early Cistercian History." His proposal was premised on the accuracy of the dating in Canivez's publication of the Cistercian statutes, from which he extracted "Cistercian ideals." Indeed, "ideals" were extracted particularly from the "statutes" for the years 1134 and 1152 — those which, as I have noted, cannot be dated to before the third quarter of the century. While deferring acrimonious debate, Lekai's method has over the long term allowed the publication of much more evidence of variation between local practices and ideals than he had already cited as the reason for his proposal of a divergence between ideals and actuality. Eventually, that accumulated evidence of the divergence of early practice from the purported ideals of the early Cistercians became so overwhelming that it was beginning to undermine all confidence one might have placed in the Ideals and Reality model. This study is a result of that accumulated evidence, which has come to show that divergence from the model is the norm. So many divergences from ideals can only now prove that we have assumed too early a development of any notion of uniformity and too early an articulation of Cistercian ideals themselves. Both ideals and attempts to impose uniformity developed later than has been assumed. This is confirmed once we resolve the issue of dating the "primitive documents" manuscripts and the related issue of dating the "primitive" texts that they contain.

Dating the "Primitive Documents" Manuscripts

Surviving manuscripts containing the "primitive documents" texts are very limited, as are the textual variants among the texts themselves.[28] There are five basic texts to be discussed, including the Charter of Charity. Generally, the "primitive documents" manuscripts contain one version of each of the five; the order of placement in the complete early manuscripts we discuss here is usually *Exordium*, Charter of Charity, *Instituta*, *Ecclesiastica Officia*, and lay-brother treatise. For how these texts are combined as a slightly different unit in various manuscripts, see Figure 19. A brief description of them follows.

The Charter of Charity is perhaps the best-known early Cistercian text. Three variants exist:

1. *The Summa Cartae Caritatis* is the earliest Charter of Charity with a two-paragraph prologue called the *Exordium Cistercii*. The *Exordium Cistercii* and *Summa Cartae Caritatis* are found only as a single continuous text, never existing in twelfth-century manuscripts as separate parts.
2. The *Carta Caritatis Prior*, with its references to Cîteaux as the "New Monastery"; it lists only three abbots with oversight of Cîteaux.[29]
3. The *Carta Caritatis Posterior*, which drops references to a "New Monastery" but adds the abbot of Morimond to those of la Ferté, Clairvaux, and Pontigny, making four abbots with oversight of Cîteaux.[30]

Usually one of these last two versions of the Charters of Charity follows immediately after the *Exordium Parvum*.

A second text is the *Exordium Parvum*, a long text filled with embedded documents, mostly concocted by its authors; along with but following the *Exordium Parvum* and the Charter of Charity is the forged privilege from Calixtus II, first found in the Ljubljana 31 manuscript.

A third component is the *Instituta* or *Capitula*, a collection of legislative statements about the administration of the Order and the common practices to be adopted by member houses. These look like Cistercian statutes and in

Trent MS 1711, version 1
(circa 1135)
early *Ecclesiastica Officia* only

Montpellier MS H322   Paris, Sainte-Geneviève MS 1207
(1161 or later)   (before Trent MS 1711, version II)
Extracts of early *Ecclesiastica Officia*,   *Exordium Cist.*, *Summa C. Caritatis*,
earliest Lay-Br. Treatise, 1157–61 statuta   beginning of *Instituta*

Trent MS 1711, version 2
(later than 1161)
*Exordium Cistercii, Summa Cartae Caritatis,
Instituta, E. Officia,* Lay-Brother Treatise

Paris, B.N. MS 4346A (fragment)
(circa 1170)
Exordium Parvum ONLY immediately followed by older group:
Exordium Cistercii, Summa C. Caritatis — breaks off

Ljubljana MS 31 (missing pages at end)
(dated 1178–82 by art historians)
Exordium Parvum, Carta Caritatis Prior, Calixtus II Bull,
Super Instituta, E. Officia (incomplete), Lay-Brother Treatise missing

Paris, B.N. MS 4346B
(1178–82 or later)
Exordium Parvum, C. Caritatis Posterior, Calixtus II Bull,
Super Instituta, E. Officia, Lay-Brother Treatise

Paris, B.N. MSS 4221 and N.A. 430
(1182?, identical to 4346B)

Figure 19. Relationship of "primitive Cistercian document" manuscripts, in order by new dating.

fact are identical to the so-called "statutes" Canivez published under the years 1134 and 1152, but this collection of "ideals" was not dated in any twelfth-century manuscript.

A fourth, much more substantial part is the collection of liturgical *ordines* called the *Ecclesiastica Officia*. This much-neglected liturgical handbook establishes the major customs concerning both the liturgy and office-holding in the monastery. It consists of a collection of more than a hundred, often lengthy chapters. The slight variants from one version to the next provide the material from which chronological sequencing of all the "primitive documents" manuscripts up to Dijon 114 may be established. It is the largest item in any "primitive documents" manuscript.

Finally, Cistercian "primitive documents" collections often contain a lay-brother treatise (of which there are several variants). It sometimes has a preface describing the reasons for providing such texts.

Such "primitive documents" have rarely been discussed as a unit, as texts always found together. Moreover, different parts of the collection are often treated by different Cistercian specialists—those who concentrate on liturgy, institutional history, or law, for example.[31] Yet in considering the texts of the "primitive documents" and their dating the most important point is that they usually survive together.

All the earliest complete manuscripts, those listed in Figure 19, once contained, like Dijon 114, the entire collection of "primitive" texts including the *Ecclesiastica Officia*. All contain material in their liturgical *ordines* that can easily be used to establish them in a chronological sequence in which the Dijon 114 exemplar is last. Each of the "complete" surviving manuscripts of Cistercian customs earlier than Dijon 114 that contain these documents is devoted uniquely to these five texts, although by the 1180s the Benedictine Rule and tables of commemoration dates are included, as they are as well in Dijon 114.[32] Moreover, these texts are almost never found except in such manuscripts. The Charter of Charity, *Exordia*, and *Instituta* were not detached to circulate in other types of manuscripts, such as those containing Cistercian sermons or letters, although the lay-brother treatise and extracts of the *Ecclesiastica Officia* are found in at least one manuscript, that from Montpellier, H322.[33] Moreover, the manuscripts are not histories of the Cistercian order, but liturgical books with prefaces that make reference to the Order's early growth in what are still brief introductions, like the *Exordium Parvum*. Only circa 1206 does a real history of the Order come to be written, the *Exordium Magnum*, composed by Conrad of Eberbach, which has a separate manuscript tradition.[34] In addition to the five complete manuscripts, portions of the "primitive" texts are also found in three manuscript fragments described in Figure 19 and Appendix 2.

There has been a tendency in the past to detach various texts of the Cistercian "primitive documents" from the manuscripts in which they survive and to make arguments about their dating on the basis of the content of individual texts found in those manuscripts. But such manuscripts are not really composite in the sense usually meant by that term; in fact, the entire contents of these manuscripts comprise a single unit. Such splitting apart of documents that in the twelfth-century manuscripts always occur together and the separate study of each part have made the problem of their dating more difficult. Discussion of the evidence one text at a time has also exaggerated the scope of the entire problem of the "primitive documents."

In the following pages, I establish a chronological sequence for all the manuscripts up to and including the exemplar manuscript from Cîteaux, Dijon 114, by considering all the texts within a manuscript as a single unit. The *Ecclesiastica Officia*, the often-ignored liturgical part of the "primitive documents" manuscripts, is used both to establish a chronological sequence for the entire group of manuscripts and to show that there is a small group of such manuscripts that definitely date to before the Dijon 114 exemplar manuscript (that is, before 1185). All these manuscripts, however, are also later than a twelfth-century manuscript from Clairvaux, now found in Montpellier, Bibliothèque de l'école de médecine, MS H322, that contains the earliest dated series of Cistercian statutes, those from 1157–61. Montpellier H322 thus dates the entire group of manuscripts to 1161 or later. Only one of the texts in the group of manuscripts discussed here, the *Exordium Cistercii*, and that only in one manuscript fragment, might possibly date to slightly earlier than Montpellier H322 and 1161. None of the manuscripts or texts can be dated to before 1150.

In contrast, the most recent survey of previous scholarly opinion seems to indicate that it is widely held that the *Summa Cartae Caritatis* and the two-paragraph prologue to it, the *Exordium Cistercii*, date to circa 1136. Moreover, the *Summa Cartae Caritatis* is believed to be based on an even earlier text, now lost, of the Charter of Charity, that confirmed by Calixtus II in 1119. The *Exordium Parvum* in these discussions is still much under dispute; most recently it has been dated to anywhere between 1134 and 1147. Such opinion maintains that the *Carta Caritatis Prior* comes from circa 1152 and the *Carta Caritatis Posterior* from even later.[35]

Although my chronological sequence for the group of "primitive" texts found in the "primitive documents" manuscripts derived from the evidence of the liturgical texts discussed here parallels the sequence of texts suggested by such recent scholarly opinion, my dating adds approximately thirty years to the date of each text just mentioned. I argue in this chapter that the *Exordium Cistercii* and *Summa Cartae Caritatis* date to 1163–65, the *Exordium Parvum* and the *Carta Caritatis Prior* to about 1170, and the newer *Carta Caritatis Posterior* to about 1175. Moreover, I shall contend that the Charter of Charity of the 1160s is the original Cistercian constitution by showing that the purported confirmation of an earlier constitution for the Order in 1119 by Calixtus II is a forged papal bull.

By analysis of their *Ecclesiastica Officia* the manuscripts may be placed in a chronological sequence as follows: Trent 1711 version 2; Ljubljana 31 (although it lacks its lay-brother treatise); and Paris manuscripts, B.N. Latin

TABLE 1. Sequencing the Liturgical Manuscripts

EO1:3	T and L < D, D adds *ieiuniorum*, and *quarum . . . sunt*
EO3:2	T < L; L and D have *presens defunctus*
EO3:18	T and L < D; T and L have same variant *omelia . . . terminantur*
EO4:9	T and L < D; because both T and L omit *Ad quam missam*
EO5:13–38	T < L, L and D have parallel added text
EO9:3–4	T and L < D; items 3–4 not in T and L
EO9:7–11	T < L, L and D have parallel texts not in T . . . etc. . . .
EO38:4	T and L < P1 = D; T does not have this chapter; not in L
EO39:7–9	T and L < P1 = D; items different in T, but not in L
EO41:10–13	P1 = D
EO41:14	P1 < D; last item under 41 is not in P1
EO42:7–10	P1 = D
EO46:18–28	P1 = D
EO48:2	T and L < P1 = D; "*Nisi aliud festum celebretur*" in P1 and D only
EO38:2	T < L; L and all later MSS have "*et pentecostes*"
EO51:3	T < L = P1 = P3 = P2 = D; T missing "*Post Generale capitulum*"
EO51:3	T has unique text concerning mothers, sisters
EO51:10	T omits; Exists in L = P1 = D, which all have *ordinis nostri defunctis*
EO51:12	Not in T, marginal in L, exists in P1 = P3 = D
EO51:13	Not in T or L or P1 or P2, marginal in P3, exists in D
EO60:21	*Sancti Bernardi abbatis* not in T, marginal addition in L
EO60:21	Interlineal in P1, exists in P3 and D
EO92:24	T < L
EO92:25	Missing in T or L; exists in P1 and D
EO92:26–28	Not in T or L or P1, exists in D
EO93:1–2	Not in T or L; stet in P3 and D
EO93:37	Not in T or L or P1, marginal in P3, exists in D
EO93:38	Not in T or L, exists in P3 (slight var.), P1, and D
EO98:52	Marginal in P3
EO98:55	Interlineal in P3
EO98:57	Not in T, exists in L, P3, P1, and D
EO102:1–4	Exists in M, T, L, P4 frag, P1, D
EO102:6	Not in M or T, exists in L, P1, P4, D
EO102:49	Not in L or in P1, marginal in P3, exists in D
EO110:25	Not in L; exists in L, P1, P2, and D
EO110:26	Not in T, L, P1, or P2, exists in D
EO111:19–21	Not in T; exists in L, P2, and D
EO112:13	Not in T or L; marginal in P2; exists in D
EO116:21–22	Not in T or L or P1 or P2, exists in D

Manuscripts are thus seen to be in the following sequence:
  M = Montpellier H322 (dates to 1161 or later)
  T = Trent 1711, version II
  L = Ljubljana 31
  P1 = Paris 4346B
  P2 = Paris NA 430
  P3 = Paris 4221
  P4 = Paris 12169, 115v-124v (fragment)
  D = Dijon 114 (dates to circa 1185)

EO = *Ecclesiastica Officia*, ed. Choisselet and Vernet
< indicates "earlier than"

4346B, Latin 4221, and Latin NA. 430, these last three very close together in date. All are earlier than Dijon 114. The sequencing of these manuscripts to before Dijon 114 is established by exploiting the presence of tiny changes from one to the next in their ecclesiastical *ordines*, the *Ecclesiastica Officia*. Such changes may appear negligible and unimportant — by and large they are slight elaborations on how to perform a particular liturgy on a specific feast-day — nonetheless such analysis makes it possible both to establish the sequence for all five manuscripts and then to assert which variants of texts like the Charter of Charity come first. Table 1 shows the method employed; its references (EO1, etc.) are to specific chapters of the *Ecclesiastica Officia* as numbered in the recent edition by Choisselet and Vernet.[36] The sequencing derived from the *Ecclesiastica Officia* is confirmed by the increasing articulation of regulations in the lay-brother treatises found in the same manuscripts.[37]

Dating the Texts

Much of the debate about dating both manuscripts and texts has centered on the assumption by earlier scholars that the earliest of the texts, the *Exordium Cistercii*, *Summa Cartae Caritatis*, *Instituta*, and a lay-brother treatise, can be dated to 1135 because they are all found in version 1 of the Trent 1711 manuscript of that date. My conclusions about the dating of the "primitive documents" manuscripts and their texts to thirty years later is based on a reconsideration of how the "primitive" texts fit into Trent MS 1711. Close examination shows that they are not dated by the liturgical order-book to 1135; indeed, they are not dated by version 1 at all because they are part of version 2.

Trent MS 1711 contains the usual collection of related Cistercian texts, but it is in fact a manuscript that has existed in two different versions. As it exists today, Trent MS 1711 constitutes version 2 of that manuscript, which is a recycled liturgical manuscript to which other parts have been added. The underlying liturgical manuscript, Trent 1711, version 1, has been dated by Griesser and others to 1135.[38] The earlier version of Trent 1711 is thus a palimpsest, with its text (the earlier liturgical manuscript) occasionally apparent beneath the considerable emendations, scrapings, replacements, marginal balloons, interlineal corrections, renumbering of passages, and insertions of new sections, which were used to update Trent 1711 version 1, creating Trent 1711, version 2. I do not question the dating of the earlier version of the liturgical text of version 1 of Trent 1711 to 1135. Its date, however, is irrelevant to the dating of the *Exordium Cistercii*, *Summa Cartae Caritatis*, *Instituta*, and lay-brother treatise, which are part of version 2. The "primitive" texts have been incorrectly attributed to version 1.

Certain codicological complexities, found during my examination of Trent 1711 in May 1997, had apparently been missed by earlier scholars. They became clear to me as I traced how the rubricated Roman numerals used in numbering chapters in the liturgical parts of the manuscript had been transformed by a very few penstrokes into a different numbering system.[39] I found that, in addition to revisions of its liturgical text, the makers of version 2 of Trent 1711 had added all the accompanying materials, those which constitute the "primitive" texts, to the earlier liturgical order-book.

What makes this addition difficult to see is that the remade manuscript gathered together a new first quire containing the *Exordium Cistercii, Summa Cartae Caritatis*, and *Instituta* and added it to the older but recycled liturgical manuscript, to which the lay-brother treatise was added at the end. Thus texts of "primitive documents" were placed in what became their normal position and relationship to one another in the slightly later manuscripts in which such "primitive" texts also form a unit, such as Paris, B.N., Latin 4221, or Dijon 114. But the scribes making version 2 of Trent 1711 must have found that the new texts for Quire 1 did not quite fit into that added first quire, and they had to add a new sheet to the outside of Quire 2 in order to incorporate all the additions.[40] The subtle blending of earlier and later manuscript pages within that single second quire of version 2 of Trent 1711, intended to save effort in recopying, is an irregularity in the codicology of Trent MS 1711 that has caused earlier scholars to conclude that the "primitive documents" were part of the earlier version of the manuscript. But they are not.

In considering the entire series of manuscripts containing the "primitive" texts, we see an obvious break between version 2 of Trent 1711 and Ljubljana 31.[41] I will argue below that this break reflects a reaction to specific criticism of the Cistercians, which led to the composition of the *Exordium Parvum* circa 1170 and to the eventual replacement of the *Exordium Cistercii* by the *Exordium Parvum*.[42] Ljubljana 31 thus has a new configuration of materials that replace the older *Exordium Cistercii* and *Summa Cartae Caritatis*. In Ljubljana 31, the *Exordium Parvum* is followed by the *Carta Caritatis Prior* and then by the forged Calixtus II bull dated to 1119. This is the earliest appearance of this forgery. This configuration of texts in Ljubljana 31 is the beginning of a separate branch of later "primitive documents" manuscripts, including Metz 1247, that continue to include the *Carta Caritatis Prior* rather than the *Carta Caritatis Posterior*, but both branches after Ljubljana 31 do usually contain the forged Calixtus II bull. The more known branch is that found in the three Paris, B.N. Latin manuscripts and in Dijon 114, all of which include the *Carta Caritatis Posterior* (with its shift from three to four proto-abbots). The latter became the standard grouping of these texts until the twentieth century.[43]

Several surviving fragments, also in libraries in Paris, add some details about changes from one text to the next. The earliest such fragment is one bound into another manuscript as folios 139r–140v of Paris, Bibliothèque Sainte-Geneviève, MS 1207.[44] It contains the *Exordium Cistercii* and the opening parts of the *Summa Cartae Caritatis*. This fragment cannot be dated by the manuscript into which it is bound. Given that the Paris, Sainte-Geneviève MS 1207 fragment is unusual in not having any chapter divisions and rubrication (see Figure 20), elements that are found in Trent 1711 version 2, we must conclude that Sainte-Geneviève 1207's fragment containing the *Exordium Cistercii* is earlier, but probably only slightly earlier, than the *Exordium Cistercii* found in Trent 1711.[45] That would make it roughly contemporary with Montpellier H322, the manuscript from Clairvaux discussed below.

A second manuscript fragment contains the earliest text we have of the *Exordium Parvum* bound as the first two quires of Paris, B.N. Latin 4346. These first two quires constitute a separate fragment later bound in with what is also a "primitive documents" manuscript. I refer to this fragment as Paris, B.N. Latin 4346A to distinguish it from the entire "primitive documents" codex, Paris, B.N. Latin 4346B, with which it has been bound. Again the fragment is undatable, but it can be placed in sequence with other manuscripts; see Figure 19.

Paris, B.N. Latin 4346A contains what must be the earliest *Exordium Parvum*. This is so because the fragment is not followed by one of the two versions of the Charter of Charity usually accompanying the *Exordium Parvum* (either the *Carta Caritatis Prior* or the *Carta Caritatis Posterior*), but by the older *Summa Cartae Caritatis* along with its prologue, the *Exordium Cistercii*. The order of materials in this fragment, Paris, B.N. Latin 4346A, suggests that the *Carta Caritatis Prior* had not yet been written. Paris, B.N. Latin 4346A thus appears to mark the transformative moment just after the *Exordium Parvum* had been composed, but before a revised Charter of Charity had been added to it, and before the Calixtus II forgery had been made. This fragment is thus earlier than Ljubljana 31.[46]

In order to date these manuscripts, as opposed to only sequencing them, I turn to a manuscript from the abbey of Clairvaux, now in Montpellier, Bibliothèque de l'école de médecine, MS H322. It is a slightly different type of manuscript, apparently one of a kind. This manuscript was probably taken to Montpellier in a division of manuscripts from Clairvaux in the nineteenth century because of its "scientific" content.[47] In addition to an Isagogus, a *Compotus* of Gerlandus, and a treatise on how accentuation of Latin was practiced at Cîteaux, all of little use to the discussion here, Montpellier H322 contains excerpts from an early liturgical customary or order-book described

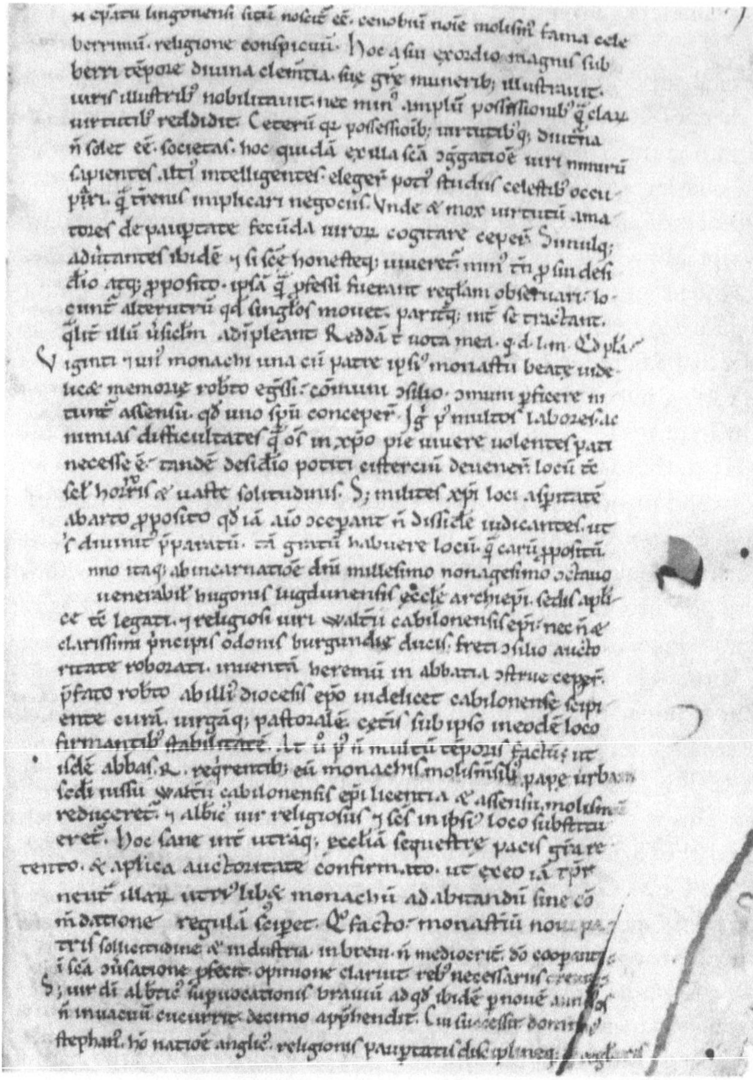

Figure 20. Earliest surviving *Exordium Cistercii* without rubricated titles. (Paris, Bibl. Sainte-Geneviève MS 1207. fol. 139r, by permission)

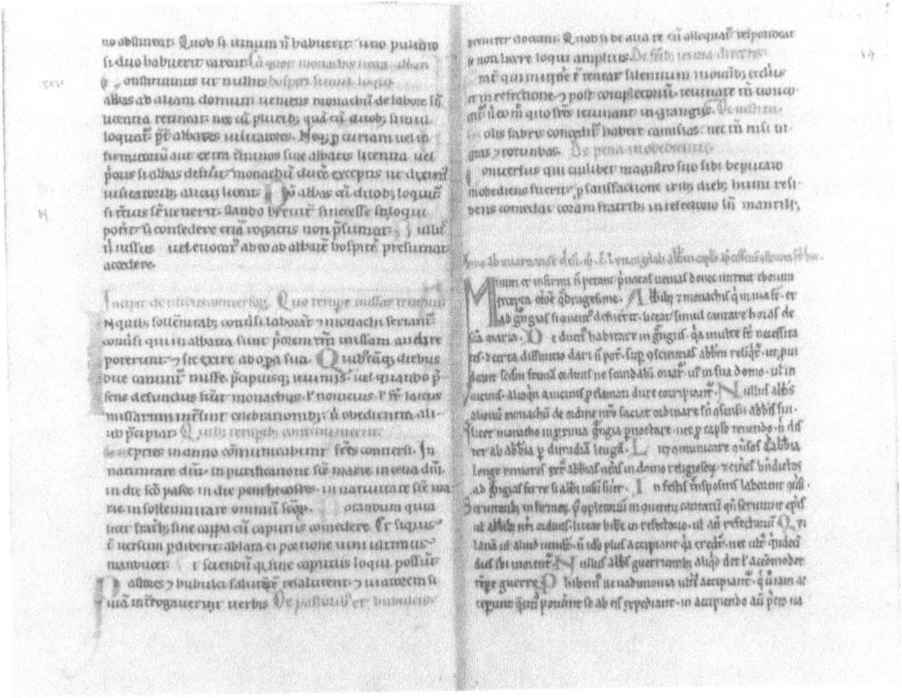

Figure 21. Earliest lay-brother treatise and earliest General Chapter statutes (1157–61). (Montpellier, Bibl. de l'Ecole de Médicine, MS H322, fol. 83v–84r, by permission)

in its rubrication as "abbreviated," as well as a lay-brother treatise and the earliest series of dated statutes from the Cistercian General Chapter, those for the years 1157–61, which date it to 1161 or later. This manuscript is critical for the dating of the "primitive documents" manuscripts because it contains several components of the "primitive" texts in a form earlier than those of Trent 1711 version 2. Thus it provides an earliest possible date for the entire series of twelfth-century "primitive documents" manuscripts.

Montpellier H322 contains the simplest and earliest of all the surviving Cistercian lay-brother treatises; this was noted by Lefèvre in the 1950s.[48] Such treatises were among the Cistercian usages most attractive to those wishing to adopt the Cistercian way of life at this time, because the Rule of Saint Benedict provided no guidance on managing lay-brothers.[49]

Montpellier H322 also contains excerpts from the Cistercian liturgical order-book, the *Ecclesiastica Officia*. These excerpts are described in its rubrications as "abbreviated," a term that has allowed earlier scholars to argue that these excerpts are only a summary of a late Cistercian order-book.[50] In fact, careful analysis of the contents of the liturgical sections of Montpellier H322 suggests that this is not a late abbreviation at all, but instead excerpts from a very early order-book. Comparison of passages published by Duval-Arnould to the edition of Choisselet and Vernet shows that those from Montpellier H322 are very like, but not quite identical to, passages on the same topics in Trent 1711 version 2. Montpellier H322 is not quite so elaborated and occasionally lacks first sentences or final phrases found in Trent version 2 — both things that are gradually attached to existing chapters. Clearly not as early as Trent 1711 version 1, which has been dated to 1135, the Clairvaux manuscript, Montpellier H322 has excerpts from a liturgical order-book, probably now lost, that falls somewhere between versions 1 and 2 of Trent 1711.

The statute material in Montpellier H322 is also less complex than are the *Instituta* found in Trent 1711 version 2. In the former, the rubrics only identify the year and are followed by very brief texts (all fewer than two dozen words), with no more than a handful of texts per year.[51] There is no explanation for why a statute was discussed or decreed, and no elaborated title precedes the text of the statute. There is no particular ordering of material; it deals with everything from commemorating the dead to selling wool on advance contracts. It is clearly the most primitive statute material that has survived.

It has been suggested that there must have been a significant lapse in time between the copying of the lay-brother treatise that ends on the upper part of folio 84r and the insertion of the dated statutes, which begin almost immediately on the same folio.[52] Examination of the manuscript, however, shows only minor variations in hand, suggesting that it was copied all at once. It appears that the scribe found himself running out of space and thus in a similar situation to that of the maker of Trent 1711 version 2. Rather than adding an additional sheet, as we see happening for the latter, the scribe of Montpellier H322 simply squeezed his letters on folio 84 into the available space, in order to include all the statute material. This in itself suggests that it was early and that there was not a clear, well-organized manuscript already in existence from which to work. As may be seen from Figure 21, which reproduces folios 83v and 84r of Montpellier H322, there was no change in the number of lines per page. More significant, since they extend into the inside margin of the page, is that the initials had to have been inserted before the manuscript was bound. This is not conclusive, for medieval manuscripts did circulate unbound, but it suggests that very little time elapsed before the statutes were copied onto folio 84r. If the last section, which contains the statutes for 1157–61, was copied immediately, this dates the entire manuscript to 1161 when the rubrication of those statutes was finished.[53]

Montpellier H322, from Clairvaux's library, does not set a precedent. It is a dead end in terms of manuscript type, because it contains neither an *exordium* nor any version of the Charter of Charity, perhaps not included because these texts had not yet been composed. We can be content, however, that those texts, the *Exordium Cistercii* and the *Summa Cartae Caritatis*, were composed shortly thereafter, thus at the earliest in 1161. Montpellier H322 thus provides an earliest possible date, 1161, for Trent 1711 version 2 and all the other "primitive documents" manuscripts that are earlier than Dijon 114.

If version 2 of Trent 1711, with its *Exordium Cistercii*, *Summa Cartae Caritatis*, and *Instituta*, comes from the early to mid-1160s at the earliest, this suggests a reason for the composition of the new texts first included in it and in the Sainte-Geneviève 1207 manuscript, the *Exordium Cistercii* and the *Summa Cartae Caritatis*. It was probably these "primitive documents," possibly with the *Instituta* attached, that were the constitutional documents confirmed by Alexander III in 1163 or 1165.[54] This confirmation by Alexander of the Cistercian constitution of 1163–65 must therefore be considered the first papal confirmation of any Cistercian constitution. This corresponds with my findings from the charters discussed in the next section, that the Order appeared in the third quarter of the twelfth century.

Between the *Exordium Cistercii* and related texts of the 1160s found in Trent 1711 version 2, there must been have a rapid development of texts in manuscripts (before Dijon 114, circa 1185), starting with Paris, B.N. Latin 4346A, which contains the earliest text of the *Exordium Parvum*. The number of surviving texts between Trent 1711 version 2 and Dijon 114, if we date them respectively to circa 1165 and circa 1185, suggests that the innovation of the *Exordium Parvum* cannot have been much later than about 1170, for it is found in most of the manuscripts under discussion here.[55] If so, then the new text, the *Exordium Parvum*, was probably written in response to criticism of the Cistercians which is epitomized in a papal letter of that year.[56]

The letter of 1170 from Alexander III was addressed to:

Venerabilibus fratribus archiepiscopis, episcopis, et dilectis filiis universis abbatibus *in cisterciensi Capitulo congregatis*. (my emphasis)

To the venerable brothers, archbishops, and bishops, and to the beloved sons, all abbots meeting *in the Cistercian Chapter*.

The letter (for which the entire Latin text is in Appendix 5) begins: "Inter innumeras mundani turbinis tempestates," that is, "Among the innumerable storms of this upsetting world." Its text casts considerable light on the issue of the Order's evolution. Often treated as a letter of wholehearted praise, it begins by thanking Cistercians for support during the schism. But parts of it were left out in most Cistercian compendia of documents, and were only restored by Jean Leclercq in the early 1950s from early manuscripts containing the complete text. In the deleted sections, pope Alexander III denounced the Cistercians for having acquired churches and altars, vassals and tenants, and for spending too much of their time in litigation and law courts, all contrary to their avowed practices. According to the pope, the Cistercian General Chapter should be able to enforce more appropriate practices on its member abbots.[57]

The response to Alexander III's letter was probably the *Exordium Parvum*, with its confection of a number of papal, apostolic, and episcopal texts praising the Cistercians, the writing of a new and more lengthy *Carta Caritatis* called *Prior*, and the forging of a confirmation of the Cistercian constitution in the purported 1119 bull of Calixtus II. That forgery is discussed in more detail at the end of this chapter. It is noticeable as well that Alexander III's 1170 letter nowhere mentions a General Chapter, but addresses abbots and monks gathered together, and specifically the abbots of Clairvaux and Cîteaux only (treating them as equals), and it uses *ordo* in the earlier sense discussed below.

Such findings suggest that the administrative Order which must have preceded the creation of an *Exordium Cistercii* or a *Summa Cartae Caritatis* or the more contentious *Exordium Parvum* appeared only after the mid-twelfth century. My conclusions about the date of the composition of the *Exordium Parvum* may be confirmed by recourse to other evidence as well. In the next section I show that local administrative records confirm that the concept of a religious order and the Cistercian Order itself were only beginning to appear by the mid-twelfth century.

From *Ordo Monasticus* to *Ordo Cisterciensis* in the Charters

At the beginning of the twelfth century, the term *ordo* to mean "a religious group" was not in regular usage.[58] Early twelfth-century reformers referred to themselves as belonging to congregations, but they did not refer to themselves as part of orders. While there is considerable discussion in pre-1150 documents, as well as in letters, treatises, and sermons from the early twelfth century, about the "*ordo monasticus*," there are few if any references to this word before the late 1140s to mean a specific group. A famous mortuary roll for Vidal of Savigny dated 1122–23 and published by Léopold Delisle, for instance, makes at least two references to the *ordo monasticus*.[59] We also see the term used in various discussions of the orders of society, of the *ordo clericus* and *ordo laicus*.[60] The anonymous treatise *On the Diverse Orders* or *Libellus de diversis ordinibus et professionibus qui sunt in aecclesia*, dated to circa 1140, is about the various "ways of monastic life" rather than about specific religious orders.

Praising religious groups, "laudo secundum ordinem uniuscuiusque monasterii viventes," it discusses "ways of life" specific to different monasteries. But these are still lifestyles, not groups to be joined.[61]

Documents for the first half of the twelfth century show the Cistercians or other reformers referring to themselves as *fratres* of a particular place or as members of a congregation following the Rule of Saint Benedict. They usually follow as well the customs or institutes of a particular abbey, not as part of a larger religious Order but as a way of life, an *ordo*. For monks and nuns alike, references to Cistercian practices from mid-century on speak at first only of abbeys *secundum formum cisterciensium fratrum*.[62] References to an *ordo cisterciensis* or phrases such as being admitted *in nostro ordine*, or to its benefits, begin to appear in the charters only circa 1150. Similarly, a number of early references that appear to be about the Cistercian Order turn out to be about the monastery of Cîteaux or Clairvaux alone. William of Malmesbury, writing about Cîteaux circa 1130, talks not of an Order but of the *religio cistellensis*, that of the abbey of Cîteaux alone.[63] Orderic Vitalis speaks of the foundation at Cîteaux, but not of an order.[64] Herman of Tournai writing at mid-century is ambiguous about the *ordo cistellensis*, which he mentions; it is not clear that it is anything other than a way of life to be professed.[65] By running searches through CD-ROM data bases such as that prepared from the *Corpus Christianorum*, I have found only a single place in Bernard of Clairvaux's collected writings where *ordo* and any form of the place name Cîteaux are even found in proximity; similar results are obtained from the *Patrologiae Latina* database.[66] I can only conclude that *ordo* was not a word used frequently by early twelfth-century Cistercians. In contrast, a Goliardic text from the 1180s cited in a recent textbook of medieval Latin uses *ordo* to distinguish different groups — White Monks from Grandmontines or Gilbertines and so on.[67]

A more systematic sifting of the charters produced by the early Cistercians provides an apt means for tracing the evolution of concepts of an Order among the Cistercians outside the vexed context of the "primitive Cistercian documents." As a source for tracing such usage, the charters are a fairly reliable index of peripheral references, although rhetorical aspects of such charters exist and are discussed further in Chapter 4. Tracing the meanings of the term *ordo* through such documents reveals that the invention of a religious Order by the Cistercians appears to have occurred only from the late 1150s or 1160s. That is considerably later than once thought.[68]

The local administrative evidence I have consulted for this purpose consists primarily of the Cistercian charters surviving for southern France, Burgundy, Britain, and elsewhere. These documents were created to record real-estate transactions, not to tell the history of the Cistercian Order. Consequently they provide fairly unbiased evidence as to the date of the introduction of a centralized government, the General Chapter, and a system of internal visitation and correction, as well as for the promulgation of written legislation about Cistercian practices. Such charters for individual houses of Cistercians are abundant. Yet their uniform lack of references to Cistercian administrative institutions before mid-century suggests that the Cistercians did not invent a religious Order until at least 1150.

This shift in the use of the terms to describe the reform movement over the course of the twelfth century is shown clearly by my review of approximately 8,000 southern-French charters dated from the 1130s to the 1250s. Notable first is that in the twelfth century there is a total absence of the words *ordo cisterciensis* to identify religious houses. There is nothing comparable to references found from the mid-thirteenth century to "the abbey of Maubuisson near Pontoise, *ordo cisterciensis*, diocese of Paris." This absence is not just apparent in twelfth-century Cistercian records; it is paralleled in the evidence for other reform groups as well. Authentic twelfth-century documents *do not* use the terms *ordo praemonstratensis* or *ordo cartusiensis* as modifiers to the name of an abbey; the same seems to be the case for documents produced by the military-religious orders.[69] Foundation accounts or foundation charters that do make reference to such abbeys as belonging to an *ordo cisterciensis* turn out to be retrospective, not authentic charters.[70] Such systematic analysis confirms that the word *ordo* changed its meaning, or at least added a new meaning, after circa 1150. From that time *ordo* began sometimes to mean a group, rather than a way of life, although the earlier meaning remained. This shift signals the events leading to the invention of the religious order as a new type of institution by the Cistercians and other reformers in the later parts of the century.

Twelfth-century southern-French Cistercian charters use the term *ordo* almost entirely in clauses about entry into monastic communities or their prayers. References to such religious benefits are frequent, but those that mention the Cistercians are limited almost entirely to after 1150.[71] Thus, in Chevalier's edition of the cartulary for the monks of Léoncel, an abbey said to be founded by Bonnevaux in the 1130s, the term *ordo* appears only three times among forty twelfth-century acts, and not before the 1170s. Thus, a confirmation by pope Alexander III circa 1176 for Léoncel includes *secundum formam ordinis cisterciensis*. In another charter, dated 1178, Léoncel was promised freedom from the competition of other *ordines*. A donor whose gift is bracketed between 1178 and 1182 was promised "part in life and death of the benefits of the Cistercian Order."[72] There are no other references to *ordo* or the Cistercians in Léoncel's twelfth-century charters. After the year 1200, when documents for Léoncel increased substantially, there is still only one reference to the Cistercians for 1202, and others in 1204, 1209, 1212, and 1213 in which patrons were promised participation "in all the benefits of the whole Cistercian Order." A charter for 1204 was addressed to Léoncel and to all the Cistercians. One for 1214 mentioning Cistercians was made by a female donor who was received as a sister "in all the benefits of the Cistercian Order" and promised burial "as if a *fundatrix*."[73]

In the Gimont cartulary, there are no references to a Cistercian Order earlier than one each for 1147 and 1158; in both cases the term *ordo* remains ambiguous as an indicator of the articulation of an administrative order. In these contexts, particularly in the 1147 charter, it could still mean "the way of life of the Cistercians," a specific form of the *ordo monasticus*.[74] This is also true in the charter from 1158 in which a donor was admitted to the "congregation" of Gimont and "vestitum habitum cisterciensis ordinis."[75] For the 1160s, there are seven more references to the benefits or customs of the Cistercians; there are seven for the 1170s, eight for the 1180s, one for the 1190s, and two for the first decade of the thirteenth century.[76] Nonetheless, among the nearly 800 charters preserved in this cartulary for Gimont containing acts dating from the 1140s to the early thirteenth century, the word "Cistercian" occurs in only a tiny number of cases. In such examples from Gimont and Léoncel, the evidence for the transformation of individual houses into members of a religious Order is most evident only in the 1160s and later.

A similarly thorough search through charters for the four houses of Berdoues, Valmagne, Silvanès, and Grandselve is presented here in tabulated form. Table 2 notes all dated occurrences of such phrases as "secundum formam ordinis nostri," as well as references to the Cistercians and to a General Chapter for these four abbeys individually, and with combined totals.[77] It shows that earliest references to Cistercians, to the General Chapter, and to the *ordo cisterciensis* begin only in 1149. Many of these early references, moreover, come from sightly later cartulary copies, which may have introduced errors or interpolations, and are thus not totally secure references for the dates that are on the charters themselves.

Only starting in the late 1150s does the evidence unambiguously suggest that Cistercian administrative institutions were coming to fruition. Although there were many entrances of monks and conversi to these houses, not until mid-century do charters refer to entrances as *secundum formam* or *secundum morem*, or *secundum instituta ordinis nostri*. The last of these phrases only appears late in the twelfth century. Then suddenly such references become the normal promise granted by monks in charters to donors seeking privileges to enter these communities. The summaries in Table 2 show that for these four houses of monks — chosen partly because their documentation was most complete, but

TABLE 2. References to "Cistercians" or *ordo* for Silvanès, Valmagne, Grandselve, Berdoues

	Mentions Cistercian Order (or its benefits)	Promises entrance secundum formam ordinis nostri	
Silvanès (from SL: 451 documents examined)			
1140s	2	0	
1150s	1	12	
1160s	0	8	
1170s	1	0	
1180s	0	2	
1190s	0	0	
totals	4 (<1% of total docs.)	22 (5 % of total docs.)	
Valmagne (from "VM": 515 documents examined)			
1140s	0	0	
1150s	4	0	
1160s	8	0	
1170s	4	1	
1180s	10	3	
1190s	3	5	
totals	29 (6% of total docs.)	9 (2% of total docs.)	
Grandselve (see Paris BN: 1295 documents examined)			
1140s	0	0	
1150s	0	0	
1160s	8	10	
1170s	0	15	
1180s	0	42	
1190s	0	6	
totals	8 (<1% of total docs.)	73 (6% of total docs.)	
Berdoues (from BD, 254 documents examined)			
1140s	0	0	
1150s	0	0	
1160s	0	0	
1170s	2	0	
1180s	1	6	
1190s	0	2	
totals	3 (1% of total docs.)	8 (3 % of total docs.)	
Combined totals		(3rd column = total of both indicators)	
1140s	2	0	2
1150s	5	12	17
1160s	16	18	34
1170s	7	16	23
1180s	11	53	64
1190s	3	13	16
totals	44 (2% of total docs.)	112 (4% of total docs.)	156 (6% of total docs.)

Appearances of variants of the word "Cistercian" or references to "our order" from four representative abbeys for monks in the Midi, for which all 2515 charters dating to before 1200 AD were examined. 1st column = references to Cistercians; 2nd column = references to "customs of our order" that do not also mention Cistercians.

also because they represent a cross-section of all possible men's abbeys to be considered — admission to abbeys "following the customs of our Order" had become frequent by the 1160s but had never occurred earlier than 1149.

The Valmagne cartulary's charters include some of the earliest references to the Cistercians. Already in the 1150s charters for the grange of Canvern express worries about whether the monks of Valmagne would continue to practice the Cistercian *ordo*; otherwise donors want their gifts to revert to Silvanès. This concern about whether Valmagne will remain Cistercian is also the occasion for references to an *ordo* and to the General Chapter in a pair of charters from 1161, which establish a hospice outside the gates of Montpellier for Cistercian monks and brothers traveling to General Chapter meetings.[78] These properties at Canvern and in Montpellier were confirmed to Valmagne in the papal confirmation by Alexander III made in 1162 when he was in Montpellier, and are discussed in Chapter 4.[79]

Charters from Grandselve probably exhibit most clearly the growing trends toward mentioning the Order as a group, but they are confusing about the moment of Grandselve's actual adoption of the *ordo cisterciensis*. The introduction of Cistercian practices at Grandselve may have been first as a daughter of Clairvaux in about 1150, but at a moment when a Cistercian Order was not yet in existence. Among the Grandselve documents, we see gifts made to this house at mid-century, which include, for instance, an 1151 charter for abbot Alexander (1150–58) that does not mention Cistercians.[80] But the abbey's charters only mention the Cistercians a few times under abbot Pons (1158–65). During Pons's rule at Grandselve, Cistercians are mentioned in charters only once in 1161, twice in 1162, twice in 1163, once in 1164, and once in 1165.[81] These references to the Cistercians in the Grandselve charters began to increase in the 1160s at the same moment that there was a burgeoning of references to *ordo* and to the General Chapter elsewhere. The bulk of the references in the Grandselve documents in Table 2 are for the 1160s in both the column counting references to the Cistercians and in that counting references to an *ordo*. References indicating a Cistercian Order peak in the Grandselve documents in the 1180s.

Charters for Berdoues share trends with those for other abbeys included in Table 2, but suggest as well that Cistercian influence came somewhat later than Berdoues's traditional foundation date in the 1130s or 1140s. Berdoues's ties to the Cistercians have been associated with an abbot Walter of Morimond, said to have attached the hermitage there as a daughter-house.[82] Given that charters for Berdoues mention the Cistercians only beginning in the 1170s and 1180s, it is likely that the Walter of Morimond who did so was Walter II (1161–62), as discussed in Chapter 3. The evidence for Gimont and its "congregation" indeed suggests that although that abbey is later treated as a daughter-house of Berdoues, Gimont itself may have adopted Cistercian practices earlier than did Berdoues.

In the Silvanès data, two charters from 1149 are found that not only mention an *ordo* but in identical terms grant entrance into the abbey to the donors, who can enter: "Si tamen secundum consuetudinem cisterciensis ordinis venire poterimus," that is, if they wished to enter according to the customs of the Cistercian *ordo*.[83] But does this really mean an Order, or only Silvanès's adoption of certain customs from the Cistercians? Such evidence for the early use of the phrase *secundum consuetudinem cisterciensis ordinis*, whatever it meant exactly, is not absolutely firmly dated to 1149, moreover, in that it comes from the Silvanès cartulary, the book of charters produced by the abbey's monks circa 1170. Such phrases redolent of the practices of an emerging Order become abundant in the 1160s and 1170s. They may have been inadvertently inserted into the text of these two charters when these charters were copied into the Silvanès cartulary in the 1170s.[84]

It is worth noting that the only other reference in the Silvanès documents to the Cistercians from so early is that for the 1150s found in a part of an undated papal bull of Eugenius III that was copied into the pages of the Silvanès cartulary considerably after it was made. This reference to Cistercians (if it is authentic) must date to no later than the year of Eugenius's death in 1153, but it also probably dates to not long before then.[85] Thus, barring the three documents just mentioned, the Silvanès evidence is similar to that found for the other three abbeys for which I have provided tabulated data. It also matches evidence for Léoncel and Gimont, described above, which both had references to "our Order" concentrated in the 1150s and 1160s. As discussed in the next chapter, the chronicle from Silvanès does introduce discussion of orders as groups at about the same time, for it was written circa 1170.[86]

The only other reference to the Cistercians I have found in southern-French charters dating to the 1140s comes from the family cartulary for the Williams of Montpellier, the untitled rulers of that city. There a reference to the Cistercians is found in the testament of William VI, which is attributed to 1146. It survives only in an early thirteenth-century cartulary copy. William VI, in fact, did not die until 1161 or 1162, but he retired from Montpellier's rulership before 1150, and soon entered the house of Cistercian or proto-Cistercian monks at Grandselve near Toulouse. There is a possibility that the terminology of William VI's will had been updated when it was copied into the cartulary, or sometime before his death in 1161–61, because William VI's gift is repeated in virtually the same words in the will of his son, William VII, who in 1172 also gave market and passage privileges to the *ordo de Cistel*. Even if these references from the late 1140s are genuine ones to the Cistercians, the charter evidence cannot be pushed back any farther than 1146.[87]

Such trends are seen beyond southern France as well. In charters from Burgundy, for instance, circumlocutions rather than references to an Order are found in documents from before 1150. A charter from 1135 for Cîteaux records that Louis VI, his son, and the queen granted exemption from customary levies to "religiosis cisterciensi, pontiniacensi, clarevallensi ceterisque omnibus ex omnibus prodeuntibus."[88] A charter addressed to Clairvaux in 1154 by Henry, count of Troyes, refers to its community as "servis Dei in Claravalle et in abbatiis pertinentibus ad eam."[89] In contrast, in 1172 for the first time Cîteaux granted to donors "fraternitate et beneficiis *cisterciensis ordinis*."[90] These suggest that new meanings for *ordo* in fact may appear later in Burgundy than in southern France.

For these same Burgundian abbeys, there are also only three references to a General Chapter before the 1170s. Each is from the 1150s, and each is open to question. The first, from circa 1156, is found in a retrospective foundation account for the abbey of Ré included in the Pontigny cartulary.[91] The counter-evidence in that same cartulary to such an early reference to the General Chapter is an arbitrated settlement between Vauluisant and Pontigny dated to 1155, which was resolved by the abbot of Cîteaux without recourse to a General Chapter.[92] A second early reference to a General Chapter is found among charters for Cîteaux published by Marilier, in a testament that he extracted from the published cartulary of Sainte-Croix d'Orléans, dated by its editors of the latter to 1153 or earlier. It may refer to a General Chapter meeting, saying that the donor is conveying

[unam?] marcam argenti monachis de Cistello ad emendum pisces toti conventui, quando tenebunt capitulum.

a mark of silver for the monks of Cîteaux to use to buy fish for the entire assembly, when they hold the chapter.[93]

But such extraordinary bequests for General Chapter meetings only became common in the 1180s, as is discussed in the next chapter.

A third possible early reference to the Cistercian General Chapter in the Burgundian documents is in an act found among the la Ferté pancartes, which includes the extravagant concession:

Sepulturam ibi haberent et quicquid agitur pro monachis ageretur pro illis per totum cisterciensem ordinem, quo et consecuti sunt in capitulo generali Cistercii, laudantibus abbatibus tocius ordinis Cistercii.

They will be buried there and have done for them whatever is done for a monk throughout the Cistercian *ordo*, and this will be confirmed by the abbots of the entire Cistercian *ordo* at the next General Chapter.[94]

While it retrospectively relates events of a gift of circa 1140, the text itself could be as late as this specific pancarte, dated by Duby to circa 1158.[95] The latter date is not at odds with other trends, but the act is still suspect because the concession seems unusually generous. In comparison a transaction done in the chapter of la Ferté circa 1175 granted only entrance as a lay-brother, not burial:

Pro hoc concesserunt mihi societatem ordinis in morte et in vita et si ordinate ad conversionem venire voluero et potero ut me recipiant.

For this they conceded to me the fellowship of the *ordo* in death and in life. It if happens that I wish to and can come *ad conversionem*, they will receive me.[96]

The confirmation by all the abbots of the Cistercian Order at a General Chapter meeting, asserted in the earlier text for la Ferté, although possible in the late 1150s, seems unlikely. It could not have happened in the 1140s.

For Cîteaux itself we find in Marilier's collection a similar gift to the General Chapter by the count of Macon, but only for the 1170s:

Cupiens fieri particeps orationum et spiritualium benefitiorum fratrum ordinis Cistercii, pro remedio anime mee et parentum meorum in generali capitulo abbatum ordinis Cistercii, dedi et concessi.

Wishing to be made a participant in the prayers and spiritual benefits of the brothers of the *ordo* of Cîteaux, for the relief of my soul and those of my parents, I gave and conceded this at the General Chapter of abbots of the Cistercian *ordo*.

This document is dated to before 1173.[97] Another Cîteaux document, for 1175, refers to the "command" of the General Chapter.[98]

The published Clairvaux documents (which appear in print only up to 1173) contain no references to the General Chapter for the years before 1173. Tithe confirmations from Alexander III in 1163 and 1165 found among documents published for Clairvaux contain references to an *ordo monasticus* of Cîteaux and to the *universus ordo cisterciensis*.[99] In the Preuilly documents the first reference to the General Chapter appears in 1201.[100] Among the earliest charters for Vauluisant is one for 1176 that provides the first instance I have found of an abbot of Morimond acting in the General Chapter as a "proto-abbot."[101] All these documents point to a date no earlier than the 1150s for a Cistercian General Chapter, and to the 1170s as the decade when the earliest genuine references to a Cistercian Order appear in Burgundy. This evidence basically parallels that for southern France.

A survey of published charters and cartularies from Cistercian abbeys in Normandy and Britain also shows that genuine acts or confirmations mentioning Cistercians come at the earliest only from the late 1140s or 1150s.[102] Anglo-Norman charters for what would become Cistercian houses are much less likely to be dated than those from the Continent, and the dates assigned to such confirmations must be established by lists of witnesses. Most of the earliest references to the Cistercians are found in cartulary copies and are confirmations made by king Henry II (1154–89). These are confirmations of earlier foundations, which may not yet have been Cistercian at the earlier dates, and suggest a certain anxiety among reform religious houses in Britain at the mid-twelfth century to be associated with the Cistercians rather than with the Savigniacs. Such worries would arise at these houses as Stephen's claims deteriorated, particularly because his family, that of Mortain, had concentrated its patronage on the Savigniacs.[103] There is also a certain amount of evidence of rivalry between Stephen's and Matilda's parties (hers including her husband Geoffrey of Anjou and their son Henry) in granting safeguards and freedom from tolls to both Cistercians and Savigniacs in these years.[104] Such grants to monastic houses were as important for asserting who was in control of royal rights as they are evidence of growing interest in the Cistercians among reform houses not necessarily founded from Cîteaux or Clairvaux.[105]

This is not to discount some genuine interest by Matilda, her spouse, her son, and her siblings in Bernard and Clairvaux. Matilda seems to have founded the abbey of Margam in 1147 with Bernard's assistance, and her monastic endowments may have been a major concern for her after 1154.[106] Similarly, her husband, Geoffrey of Anjou, made gifts for the foundation of what would become the Cistercian house of Mortemer for the soul of his father, Fulk of Anjou:

Sciatis quod ego dedi ecclesie Beate Marie Virginis de Mortuomari et fratribus ordinis Cisterciensis ibidem deo servientibus in ipsa valle Mortuimaris XXX acras terre pro salute anime Fulchonis regis Jerusalem patris mei et Erkenburgis comitisse matris mee, et pro salute anime mee et Matildis uxoris mee filiorumque meorum, et pro anima regis Henrici atque omnium amicorum meorum, ad libitum suum excolendas.

You know that I gave to the church of the Blessed Virgin Mary of Mortemer and to the brothers of the *ordo cisterciensis* serving God there in that valley of Mortemer 30 acres of land for the health of the soul of Fulk, king of Jerusalem my father and Erkenburgis countess my mother, for myself and Matilda my wife and my sons, and for the soul of king Henry and all my friends, to be freely cultivated.[107]

Geoffrey's gift is paralleled by an act by Duke Henry, which must be dated to 1151–53.[108] If this gift for Fulk is indeed an authentic charter dating to October 11, 1147, the Anjou charters parallel those from southern France, insofar as their references to an *ordo cisterciensis* are slightly earlier than such references in charters from Burgundy. In contrast, an earlier act by Stephen, assigned to 1137 by when Stephen was in Normandy, does not mention Cistercians.[109]

In general, what appear to be original royal or quasi-royal charters for the Anglo-Normans pose a different problem. A few original charters with dates assigned to them for the early 1140s mention either an *ordo* or that of the Cistercians.[110] These charters come from the hands of only one or two royal scribes — men who are suspected by the editors of the Anglo-Norman charter collections to have lost employment as Stephen's powers declined, but, having royal seal matrices still in their possession, were able to create forgeries. The hands of several of them have also been identified as making both some probably authentic charters and some forgeries from as early as the late reign of Henry I.[111] Among the suspect charters must probably be placed one from Stephen attributed to 1136 granting Buckfast in Devon to Savigny: "ad ponendum in ea abbatem secundum ordinem suum," that is, for Savigny to found an abbey following its *ordo*.[112] Suspect as well is one also dated 1136 for Rievaulx using Stephen's name, in which the same scribe says:

Sciatis me concessisse deo et ecclesie Sancte Marie et abbati et monachis de Rievallibus pro dei amore et salute anime mee et antecessorum meorum, et pro statu regni mei novem carrucatas terre quas Walterus Espec eis dedit et concessit in elemosinam perpetuam.

You know that I have conceded to God and the church of Saint Mary and the abbot and monks of Rievaulx for love of God and the health of my soul and of my ancestors and for the good of my kingdom, nine carrucates of land which Walter Espec gave and conceded to you in perpetual alms.

This charter, however, does not mention an order.[113] Also suspect is a charter from a Fountains cartulary dated February 1136 at York:

Sciatis me concessisse deo et ecclesie Sancte Marie et abbati et monachis de Fontibus qui sunt de ordine Cisterciensi pro dei amore et salute anime mee.

You know that I have conceded to God and to the church of Saint Mary and to the abbot and monks of Fountains who are of the *ordo cisterciensis* for the love of God and the health of my soul.[114]

This cartulary copy is dated by the identity of its witnesses to those for an original from Beverly Minster, but the latter was one of the charters made by a suspect scribe, thus casting some doubt on the authenticity of both "original" and cartulary copy.[115]

Such forged acts may explain copies of royal acts deriving from late medieval monastic cartularies claiming to be grants to the Cistercians from Henry I.

That granted to the entire Cistercian Order and assigned to 1128–33 and comes from a Fountains cartulary now in the Bodleian Library, on the other hand, is likely to be an authentic act from very early in the reign of Henry II, which has been interpolated into one for Henry I.[116] If such interpolation is what is going on here, the copying of royal charters in such a way as to make them appear to be from Henry I rather than Henry II may parallel the phenomenon of seeking ever-earlier Carolingian kings as founders, as has been described by Amy Remensnyder for foundation charters of rival Benedictine houses in southern France.[117]

Changing meanings of the word *ordo* over the twelfth century trace the gradual invention of a new meaning and a new institution. They also mean that words must be translated with great care. Thus a papal letter from Alexander III to the abbots of Swineshead and Furness (bracketed to 1166–79) saying "Relatum est nobis quod vos religionis intuitu Cisterciensium fratrum ordinem suscepistis" must be construed as "We are informed that you have adopted the way of life inspired by the brothers at Cîteaux," rather than as it has earlier been translated: "We have heard that you have joined the Cistercian Order"[118] Although at this late date "joining" the Order may have been an option, that is not what the document says.

This reconsideration of terminology shows that in the earliest years, Cistercian *ordo* had more to do with how people lived within communities and with regulating social conditions within monasteries than with conformity to the administrative decrees of a larger group.[119] Early Cistercian ideals about monastic *ordo* centered on notions of charity with little concern for administrative conformity or unanimity. Such evidence, which is drawn from a variety of sources, shows that up to at least the middle of the twelfth century Cistercians rarely employed language describing themselves as a religious order. References to the *ordo cisterciensis* as a group to which they belong come into common usage only in the thirteenth century. They are never found in the 1110s and 1120s, and only occasionally in the late 1140s and 1150s. They become much more frequent in the 1160s and 1170s, but even at that time they do not altogether replace older usages.[120] Indeed, even in the 1215 Lateran IV canons, in the chapter decreeing that no new religious groups were to be formed, the text uses the word *religio*, not *ordo*.[121]

Exceptional Cases

If we turn to the "primitive documents" and associated liturgical *ordines*, or to several other very famous charters often cited to document the early invention of the Order, the same evolution in the use of the word *ordo* is uncovered once those documents are correctly dated and authenticated. But at first glance several cases appear to be exceptions to the general trends regarding the term *ordo* or references to the General Chapter. All these, in fact, turn out to date after 1150 and *not* to the early twelfth century. In the earliest liturgical texts, those that date to the early twelfth century, or even those from Montpellier and Ljubljana, there are almost no references even to the practices of "our Order." Such references had become frequent by the time of the liturgical *ordines* in Dijon 114, which is dated to the 1180s. An examination of the texts of these liturgical manuscripts, or even their printed editions, also reveals that only late in the twelfth century were references to the General Chapter introduced.[122]

Yet the language of *ordo* and references to a General Chapter are found both in the papal bull of tithe exemption for Cîteaux, *Habitantes in Domo*, dated to 1132, and in the Charter of Peace with the Praemonstratensians usually dated to 1142. Reference to an Order in these two exceptional cases seems inappropriate to those dates, given all the other evidence cited here. In fact, neither text stands up to any scrutiny as evidence for the early introduction of those terms. Neither provides proof of the existence of either an Order or General Chapter at such early dates.

The tithe privilege for Cîteaux dated 1132, *Habitantes in Domo*, is possibly the most frequently cited papal bull of the twelfth century. Its references to "our Order," when read in context, clearly refer to an *ordo* in the sense of a group to which Cistercian houses belonged. But this privilege for Cîteaux in 1132 is a forgery. In it, Innocent II in 1132 was purported to grant tithe exemption to the entire Cistercian Order.[123] It attempts to make the case that Innocent II granted to Cîteaux and to the entire Order a privilege parallel to the authentic privilege issued by Innocent II to Bernard of Clairvaux and all abbeys subject to him in 1132 that marked the end of the Anacletian schism. Such a forgery reflects the thinking of a later era, however, one in which it would have been inconceivable that Clairvaux could have been granted a privilege which had not also been granted to Cîteaux.

The purported tithe exemption by Innocent II to Cîteaux in 1132 and "its order" is dated to a week earlier than that for Clairvaux. Both exist only in late medieval copies. The earliest surviving single copy of the Cîteaux privilege is from the sixteenth century. It is found in Dijon in the Côte-d'Or archives in liasse 11H4, where accompanying notes from the time indicate that it was already questioned by abbots within the Order in the late Middle Ages. This privilege for Cîteaux is also found in a collection of Cistercian papal bulls, the

Liber Privilegiorum Cistercii created by Jean of Cirey, abbot of Cîteaux (1476–1501), where it may in fact have appeared for the first time. This copy of the purported papal privilege for Cîteaux, which mentions "our Order," is a forgery that was probably based on a genuine privilege for Cîteaux from Lucius III (1181–85).[124] This does not mean that the forgery was made in the 1180s (it may well date to the late fifteenth century) but only that the forgery used a privilege from the 1180s as a model.

The text of this forged version, which is published by Marilier, includes early references to an order, such as "Ceteris vero vestri Ordinis abbatiis" and "Prohibemus ne aliquis archiepiscopus aut episcopus et vel successores tuos seu aliquem abbatem cisterciensis ordinis," appropriate to the 1180s. These are interspersed with circumlocutions which might have been used earlier: "De sibi subjectis abbatibus vel quemlibet monachum de omnibus congregationibus cisterciensibus," or "Quemlibet monachum de omnibus prefate religionis congregationibus cum consilio et deliberatione cisterciensis abbatis." Its tithe privilege, "Statuimus ut de laboribus vos et totius vestre congregationis fratres propriis manibus et sumptibus colitis et de animalibus vestris, a vobis decimas expetere vel recipere nemo presumat," is clearly one which more nearly parallels 1180s examples than those from the 1130s. Finally, as may be seen on the page from the *Liber Privilegiorum Cistercii* reproduced in Figure 22, this purported copy of an 1132 document bears the rota inscription not for Innocent II, or even for his successor Lucius II, but that for Lucius III (1181–85).

The genuine Clairvaux privilege contains no such language of "our Order," is more limited in scope, and provides a forthright explanation for its issuance, the fervent support by Bernard of Clairvaux for Innocent II at the time of the Anacletian schism (when Innocent II's rival was a member of the Pierleoni family):

Ceterum quam firma perservantique constantia causam beati Petri et sancte matris tue Romane Ecclesie dilecte in Domino filii Bernarde abbas, incandescente Petri Leonis scismate, fervor tue religionis et discretionis susceperit defensandam.

Also because of the firmness, constancy, and perseverance in the cause of blessed Peter and your holy mother the Roman church, by which our dear in the Lord son Bernard abbot, in the conflagration of the schism of the Pierleoni, took up the defense of religion and discretion.

This authentic papal privilege is directed to Bernard of Clairvaux himself, not to a Cistercian Order — an issue to which I shall return in Chapter 3. It was this group of houses subject to Clairvaux that received the tithe exemption:

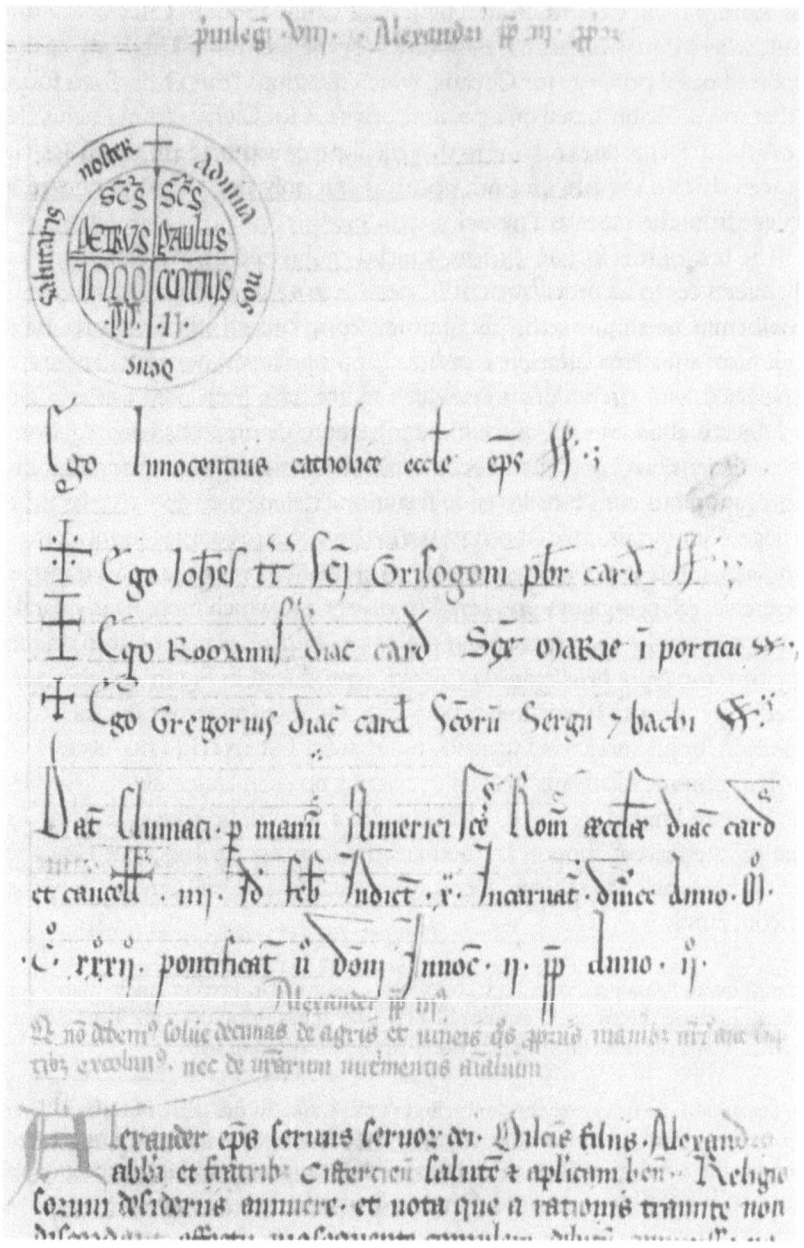

Figure 22. Rota for Lucius III found on copy of Innocent II bull for Cîteaux in *Liber Privilegiorum Cistercii*. (Dijon, Bibl. Mun. MS 69 [598], fol. 138, by permission)

Porro laborum vestrorum decimas quos propriis manibus aut sumptibus colitis, seu etiam de animalibus vestris, a vobis vel ab aliquo monasterio clarevallensi subjecto exigere vel suscipere nemo presumat.

Hereafter, no one should presume to extract or collect from you or from any monastery subject to Clairvaux, the tithes on what you cultivate by the your labor with your own hands or at your expense, or those over your animals.[125]

Only Clairvaux's privilege is authentic, and the fact that the 1132 papal privilege for Cîteaux is first found preserved in Jean of Cirey's *Liber privilegiorum Cistercii* casts further question on the authenticity of other papal privileges found nowhere else but there and with the *Exordium Parvum*.

There are similar issues with regard to the Charter of Peace between Cistercians and Praemonstratensians, which is dated to 1142 in Canivez's edition of the *Statuta* but similarly cannot be attributed to that date. It provides evidence neither for a Cistercian Order nor for a General Chapter in 1142. This Peace Charter, which has been central in arguments for the early emergence of the General Chapters of both the Praemonstratensians and Cîteaux, exists only as a subtle interpolation of what may possibly have been an authentic agreement of circa 1150, but one for which we have a surviving text only from a later date. The earliest surviving copy of this Peace Charter must date to between 1165 and 1175, a significant difference in date when we are tracing the twelfth-century emergence of religious orders.[126] Unfortunately, we cannot tell anything about an earlier Charter of Peace out of which this copy grew or the precise contents of such an agreement. It is clear that there are problems about the existing copy that make attribution to 1142 of this "chirograph" implausible.

First, neither the surviving manuscript of this text from Chaumont (see Figure 23) nor any document in Paris is the original Canivez claimed in his edition.[127] The Paris "parchment" discussed by Gerits is a *vidimus* copy of 1259 found there along with notes made by the archivist who organized the liasse. The Paris text is identical to that published in Canivez with the exception of the obvious clauses describing the copying done at the time the *vidimus* was made, so it is of little use to the discussion here.[128] Moreover, the original described by Canivez as found in the archives in Chaumont describes itself as a chirograph, but it is clearly not one in this copy. It lacks the characteristic *alphabetum* or *chirographum* written in large letters down the middle of the document to divide it into two parts, which would have defined it as an original copy. That the copy we have has two distinct attestation clauses, of which only the second is dated, suggests that the earlier document, a now-lost chirograph, had only the first attestation clause, which is not dated.

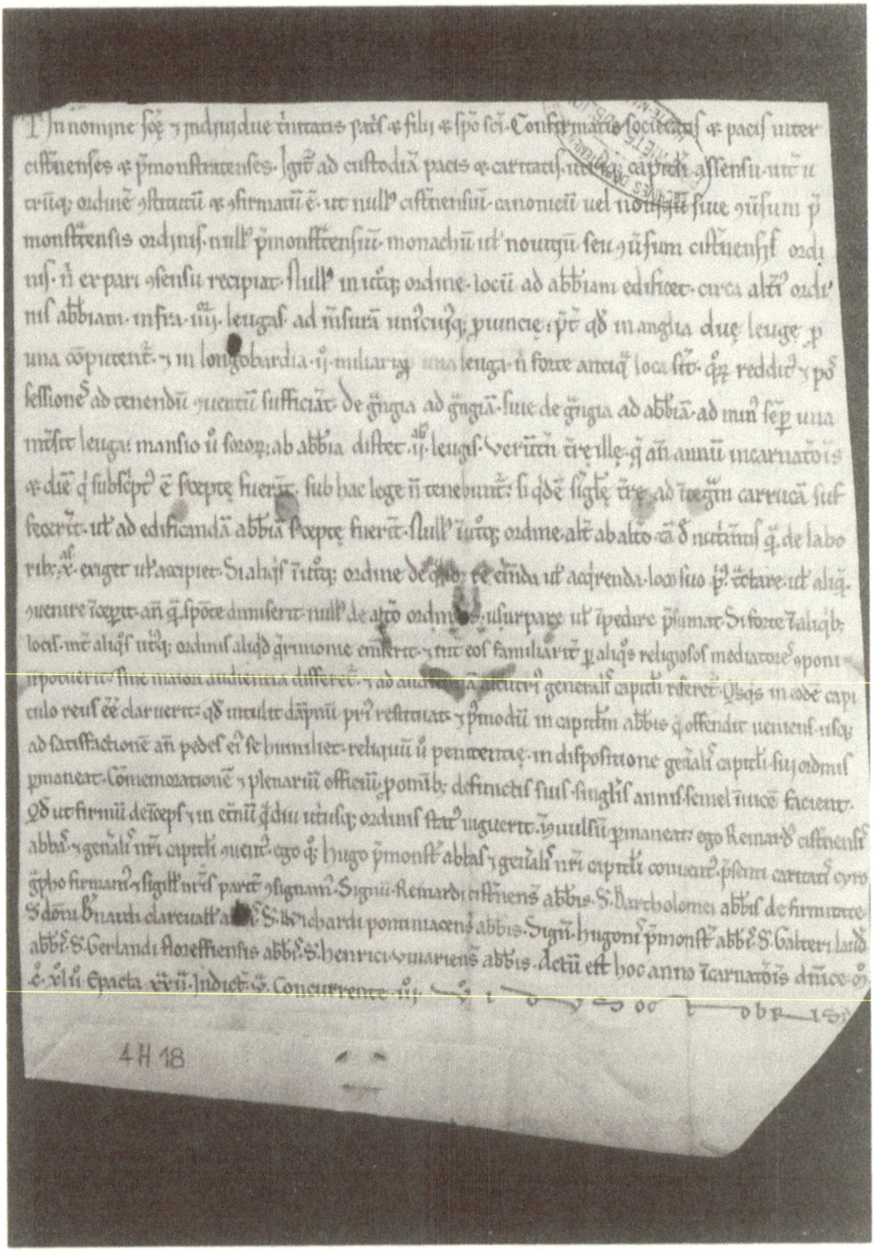

Figure 23. Peace Charter between Praemonstratensians and Cistercians. (Chaumont, A.D. Haute-Marne, 4H18, by permission)

The first attestation clause from the Chaumont Charter of Peace describes the text as a "Chirograph of Charity" and lists two abbots, one for each group, acting with the respective chapters of their communities. But those chapters are called general (possibly an interpolation at the time of copying):

Quod ut firmum deinceps, et in aeternum quamdiu utriusque ordinis status viguerit, inconvulsum permaneat, ego Rainardus Cisterciensis abbas et generalis nostri capituli conventus, et ego quoque Hugo Praemonstratensis abbas et generalis nostri capituli conventus praesenti charitatis chirographo firmamus, et sigillis nostris pariter consignamus.

So that this be firm in the future and through eternity and that it remain unchanged as long as either of these *ordines* remains strong, I, Rainard, abbot and the assembly of our general chapter, and I, Hugh abbot of Prémontrée and the assembly of our general chapter, confirm this chirograph of charity. We both affix our seals.[129]

This document must be dated by the reference to abbot Raynard of Cîteaux (1134–51) and the Praemonstratensian, Hugh of Fosse (1128–64) and if it had only this first attestation clause it would be dated to not later than 1151, but probably somewhat later than 1134, its earliest possible date. It would contain the very earliest references to general chapters and to the two orders becoming administrative units.

The second attestation clause, which includes the date 1142, is obviously archaizing, and is incorrect in its details. The dating clause attributes this text to the fifth ides of October (October 9), the feast of Saint-Denis, the day on which the general chapter of the Praemonstratensians would eventually meet. It was probably not written in 1142 because the scribes got the indiction incorrect for an October date, although correct for earlier in the year.[130] Such a calendar error is more likely in any year other than the current one. Moreover, the list of four abbots in this Charter of Peace for Cîteaux that correspond to Cîteaux and the three eldest daughters that were its "proto-abbots," as listed in the *Carta Caritatis Prior*, suggest that it was written before 1176 or so when Morimond's abbot was added to the oversight of Cîteaux by "proto-abbots."[131] References to Bernard of Clairvaux as *Dominus* but not yet as *Sanctus*, on the other hand, suggest a certain respect for him that would be most likely found after Bernard's death in 1153, but before 1174 when he was canonized.[132] The parchment from Chaumont is a copy of the chirograph with components that date it to circa 1170, but it also has archaizing features, including its attribution to 1142.

The topics covered in this Charter of Peace are also more appropriate to circa 1170. Complex issues about "Order-building" and "Order-differentiation" for both groups are included. This Charter of Peace records that the Cistercians and the Praemonstratensians will commemorate one another's dead annually. Moreover, it is agreed that the two should respect one another's tithe privileges of exemption for the work of their lay-brothers and on their animal husbandry—a privilege which also suggests a date after mid-century when grange agriculture was underway. Even more revealing is the recognition that disputes may have to be arbitrated; infringements of the agreement were to be adjudicated by either General Chapter: "Ad audientiam alterutrius generalis capituli referentur" (They will be referred to the hearing of either General Chapter).

But such referral of disputes among the Cistercians to a General Chapter did not usually happen before the 1170s, as is discussed in Chapter 3. Penance was imposed on the guilty person by his own chapter: "Reliquum vero poenitentiae in dispositione generalis capituli sui ordinis permaneat" (The punishment will be left to the decision of the General Chapter of his own Order). The charter further promised that abbots of one group would not accept members from the other's abbeys; this is something found among the Cistercians from the time of their *Summa Cartae Caritatis* of circa 1165.

The Charter of Peace also established minimum distances to be maintained between abbeys and granges, as well as between abbeys and houses for sisters: "Mansio vero sororum ab abbatia distet duabus leucis" (Houses of sisters ought to be distanced two leagues from abbeys [presumably for men]). This may reflect efforts by both Cistercians and Praemonstratensians to eliminate remaining double houses. That the topic is not one exclusively applied to houses of Praemonstratensian sisters is perhaps deserving of further investigation.

Similar promises were made in the emerging Cistercian Order; see the *Instituta* of the 1160s. Limits on foundations in proximity to established houses, or in which abbeys or groups of abbeys promise one another exclusive rights within certain territories, are increasingly present from the late twelfth century.[133] Thus findings on examination of these two exceptional cases, which appear at first glance to show an early use of terms like "our Order" but turn out not to do so at all, are similar to what can be learned about the incidence of the term *ordo* in the charters.

Papal Confirmations of the Cistercian Constitution

A reconsideration of several other papal privileges for Cîteaux with early dates reveals both archaizing of authentic documents and outright forgery. Such a finding cannot be altogether surprising, since I have already shown that the purported papal tithe privilege for Cîteaux for 1132 is a forgery.

The precocity of the papal confirmation of the Cistercian constitution by Calixtus II that implies an exemption and protection by the papacy for the Cistercians from 1119, much earlier than that for other monastic groups, has been remarked on recently by Ludwig Falkenstein. In his survey of all such privileges dating to the eleventh and twelfth centuries for all French abbeys, he states that Calixtus II's bull for 1119, *Ad hoc in Apostolicae*, predated by some decades anything comparable.[134] His observations suggest the need to investigate *Ad hoc in Apostolicae* more closely. So do its contents, which refer to institutions not otherwise documented for the Cistercians at such an early date.

Ad hoc in Apostolicae has been in many senses the lynch-pin in the whole argument for an early Cistercian Order. This purported confirmation from Calixtus II for 1119 is frequently cited not only as a confirmation of the early Cistercian constitution, but as the sole evidence that such a constitution existed at that date. That it is a forgery produced circa 1170, soon after the first appearance of the *Exordium Parvum*, is suggested by a number of internal inconsistencies. These are seen quite easily by comparison of its text to a genuine confirmation by Calixtus II from 1120 for the abbey of Bonnevaux, the house of Cistercian monks in the diocese of Vienne that was founded by Calixtus II in 1118 while he was still archbishop of that province. Both are found in Robert's collection of Calixtus II's bulls, but both are listed there as papal bulls for which we have only copies and no originals; Robert does not attempt to authenticate any but the small number of "originals" he collected for the *Bullaire* that he published.[135]

As may be seen by comparison of the texts included in Appendix 4, it is likely that it was the Bonnevaux document on which the forgery *Ad hoc in Apostolicae* was based. A number of errors in diplomatic formulae in this Cîteaux document show it to be faulty, while that for Bonnevaux is more often correct on such points.[136] The dating clause of the Cîteaux document is incorrect. Also it is said to have been done at Sediloci or Saulier, but this place is not otherwise found on the papal itinerary for that year.[137] According to Robert's collation of information from the collected original bulls of Calixtus II, papal bulls at this time did not address abbots as "venerable"; only bishops or abbeys or other institutions were so addressed. The salutation of the Cîteaux bull to the abbot of Cîteaux (who would be more properly called "beloved son") is therefore also incorrect, suggesting an interpolation from the Bonnevaux document in which a different type of institution was being addressed.[138] Similarly, *confirmamus* is a term used to protect property, as it is in the Bonnevaux privilege; it is nowhere else among Calixtus's privileges used to confirm a set of customs. *Constitutio* is not used elsewhere at this time with our sense of constitution as a law code; the more likely term in 1120 or even later would have been *forma, norma, mos, consuetudo, instituta*, or even *carta*. Only in this forgery is a Cistercian *constitutio* mentioned for this date.[139] The Bonnevaux document never uses the term *ordo*, but refers only to the *fratres* of Cîteaux sent there to found a new house; *Ad hoc in Apostolicae* refers to an *ordo* approximately thirty years before the term is used elsewhere.[140] Yet even the fact that this papal privilege, although not technically part of the *Exordium Parvum*, only appears in its context has been missed by earlier scholars.[141] All this confirms that the Calixtus II *Ad hoc in Apostolicae* is a forgery.

It is likely that this forged Calixtus II privilege is related in date to an early foundation narrative for Pontigny that has been cited as one more piece of evidence for an early foundation of an Order. This account of Pontigny's foundation, which mentions the Charter of Charity, has been dated on the basis of its witnesses to after 1147. This is an earliest date; there is no reason that it could not be several decades later.[142] It begins:

Cum Dei misericordia sua gratuita bonitate *novum monasterium*, id est Cistercium, in Burgundia constructum et regulari disciplina dotaret et copiosa monachorum multitudine adaugeret.

When by the mercy of God and the grace of his goodness the *new monastery*, that is Cîteaux, was built in Burgundy and endowed by the discipline of the Rule and it increased by an overflowing multitude of monks. (my emphasis)[143]

Because of its references to a "new monastery," which are characteristic of the *Carta Caritatis Prior* text, it most likely dates to the years from 1170 to 1175 when the *Carta Caritatis Prior* was first written. After describing the founding of Pontigny, it goes on to say that Stephen Harding then gave the Charter of Charity to that abbey:

Cartam vero caritatis et unanimitatis inter *novum monasterium* et abbatias ab eo propagatas compositam et corroboratam idem pontifex et canonicorum conventus ratam per omnia habuerunt.

The Charter of Charity and unanimity between the *new monastery* and the abbeys derived from it having been written and having been confirmed in all its contents by the bishop and his assembled canons (my emphasis).[144]

This text has been used to argue that the Charter of Charity must date to Pontigny's foundation in 1113, but obviously it shows no such thing. It is a text composed between 1147 and 1170 that can do no more than assert that

Pontigny had received such a Charter of Charity at the time of its foundation. Such an account provides no proof.

As for later papal confirmations, the assumption that the 1119 Calixtus II confirmation *Ad hoc in Apostolicae* is authentic has meant that Cistercian historians have given only limited attention to later papal confirmations of the Charter of Charity. But since the Calixtus II privilege turns out to be a forgery, there is no reason to believe that the Charter of Charity was confirmed in 1119. Hence it is worth investigating later papal confirmations of the Cistercian constitution, the Charter of Charity. Certainly the constitution was confirmed in 1165 by Alexander III's issuing of *Sacrosancta*; that confirmation may possibly even date to 1163. But could earlier popes have confirmed a version of the Cistercian Charter of Charity earlier than the *Summa Cartae Caritatis* text that I date to circa 1165?

Unfortunately, there are no published collections of all the copies and originals of papal bulls for later twelfth-century popes like the compendium for Calixtus II made by Robert. Within the morass of papal privileges needing further examination and investigations, Cistercian scholars have pointed to earlier versions of *Sacrosancta* by Eugenius III (1145–53) in 1152, Anastasius (1153–54) in 1153, and Adrian IV (1154–59) in 1157, as well as those by Alexander III (1159–81) in 1163 or 1165. These purported confirmations of the Charter of Charity cannot be checked against an entire corpus of papal privileges for any of these popes. At present they may only be verified by locating the earliest manuscript versions and checking them for such things as consistency of dating clauses. This turns out to be very difficult.

Although parts of *Sacrosancta* are attributed to Eugenius III, the earliest complete text of *Sacrosancta* I have found in any manuscript appears to be that dated to 1163 for Alexander III, found as an addition in a later hand to a partially blank page of Dijon, B.M. MS 87; see Figure 24.[145] There may be a problem with the date in this copy. The text is that usually attributed to 1165, and for this copy the indiction is certainly incorrect. It would have changed after September 1163 from 11 to 12. While this may not be sufficient evidence to discount the text of this Alexander III bull, the attribution to 1163 is questionable. Dijon 87 contains both this copy of *Sacrosancta* dated 1163 and a partial copy of one for Adrian IV, but that copy refers to the 1163 text rather than providing a complete text for the year 1157. Finally, dating just when the copies of the 1157 and 1163 documents were copied into this manuscript is impossible except to say that it must be later than the first quarter of the thirteenth century because that is the date of the manuscript in which they are found as obvious insertions.[146]

A conservative reading of the evidence about *Sacrosancta* is that Eugenius

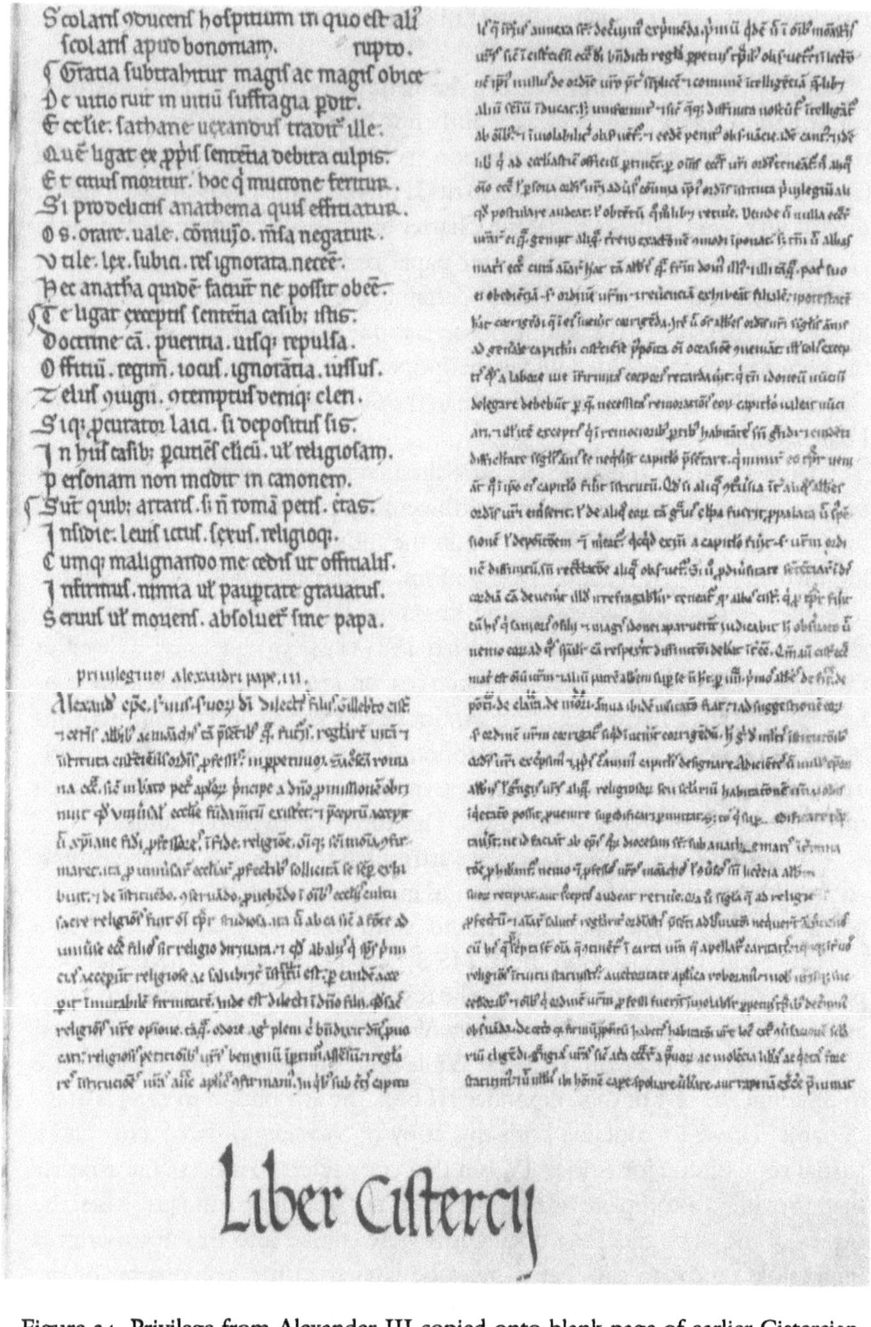

Figure 24. Privilege from Alexander III copied onto blank page of earlier Cistercian manuscript. (Dijon, Bibl. Mun. MS 87, fol. 168v, by permission)

III may have confirmed something in a bull called *Sacrosancta*, but if he did we have no authentic manuscript evidence from which to tell what it said.[147] Eugenius III's name is sometimes attached in rubrication to later versions of *Sacrosancta*, for instance in Metz 1247, possibly because Cistercians assumed that Eugenius must have been the pope to have issued a confirmation of the Cistercian constitution that Calixtus II had already confirmed. But even if Eugenius did issue a bull *Sacrosancta* for Cîteaux, it is absurd to argue that the *Sacrosancta* confirmed by Alexander III in 1165 is identical to one issued by Eugenius III; clear changes can be seen from one pope to the next, as we see in the 1157 and 1163 texts found in Dijon 87.[148] If Eugenius issued a bull called *Sacrosancta* for Cîteaux, we do not know what it said or whether it confirmed a Cistercian constitution.[149]

What can be reported is that the text of *Sacrosancta* as it has been published for Alexander III has been carefully analyzed by Van Damme, who shows by citing parallel passages that it has significant parallels to the Cistercian Charter of Charity in its earliest extant form, the *Summa Cartae Caritatis*. Parallels are found, for instance, about the Order disallowing exactions by one house of another, about life in imitation of the apostles, and about oversight of the mother abbey.[150] The two must be close in date.

Sacrosancta in its 1165 version has references to a General Chapter and to the practice of the *ordo cisterciensis* that are just beginning to suggest a group to which one belonged. It should be noted, moreover, that the 1170 letter from this same pope (reproduced in Appendix 5), used *ordo* in a more conservative way and does not mention the General Chapter at all. In its addressing clause, Alexander's *Sacrosancta* says:

Alexander episcopus, servus servorum Dei, dilectis filiis Gisleberto Cisterciensi, et caeteris abbatibus et monachis, tam praesentibus quam futuris regularem vitam et instituta cisterciensis ordinis professis in perpetuum

Alexander, bishop, servant of God's servants, to my dear son Gilbert of Cîteaux and all the other abbots and monks, who now or in the future profess the regular life and institutes of the *ordo cisterciensis* perpetually.[151]

Van Damme has argued that the close parallels with Alexander III's 1165 version of *Sacrosancta* confirm "the primordial clause about equality among abbeys found in the opening of the Charter of Charity." In its words:

Quia vero singula, quae ad religionis profectum et animarum salutem regulariter ordinastis, praesenti abbreviationi nequiverunt annecti, nos cum his quae praescripta sunt, omnia quae continentur in charta vestra, quae appellatur charitatis, et quaecunque inter vos religionis intuitu regulariter statuistis, auctoritate apostolica roboramus.

Because each one of you, having chosen to practice the religious life and because the health of souls is assured by such regular practice, but because this letter [that is the papal one] is only an abstract of everything contained in your charter that is called a Charter of Charity, whatever you establish by it among you who have adopted that religious practice, we confirm by apostolic authority.[152]

But despite the fact that what Alexander III seems to have before his eyes is the earliest extant version of the Charter of Charity (the *Summa Cartae Caritatis*), Van Damme insists that Alexander III is here confirming a "revised constitution." It seems more likely that Alexander III's scribes used the text of the *Summa Cartae Caritatis* in composing the 1165 papal privilege *Sacrosancta*. The 1165 privilege is most likely to be the original papal confirmation of the Cistercian constitution. No wonder Alexander III in 1170 should have been so concerned that the Cistercian constitution, written and confirmed only within the last decade, was not being upheld; see Appendix 5.

In my view, the similarity of language between the *Summa Cartae Caritatis* and the 1165 confirmation of the Cistercian constitution issued in *Sacrosancta* by Alexander III suggests that this is the initial confirmation of regulations for the new Order. If so, Alexander's confirmation may be the closest we can come to dating the original creation of a Cistercian Order.

3
From Cîteaux to the Invention of a Cistercian Order

Descriptions of twelfth-century monastic growth have often attached the term "religious order" or "monastic order" to communities associated with a particular reformer of that age, even when speaking of the early twelfth century.[1] But, as I showed in the previous chapter, the term *ordo* did not begin to be used in the sense of a group of monasteries until at least the mid-twelfth century. A more appropriate term for such early twelfth-century groups of abbeys, one used at the time, is "congregation." Such a religious congregation might be characterized as a group of abbeys following and inspired by a single charismatic leader. Because he or she left behind a rule or had a faithful follower who devised one, the congregation was able to maintain its existence after its founder's death.[2] Such religious congregations were familial units, each organized by a single reformer; that founder was always held in esteem. Not surprisingly, such congregations are most often imagined to be created by growth and division, by sending out new colonies of monks and nuns in groups of six or twelve and an abbess or abbot, by an imagined process that I call "apostolic gestation." In contrast, the Order created by the Cistercians, although only invented between the late 1150s and 1190, was an administrative institution for the oversight of a number of religious houses no longer dependent on a single charismatic leader. It was headed by an assembly, an annual, universal General Chapter, in which all heads of houses (or at least all male heads of houses) had in theory an equal share in governance.

Once the religious order had been invented in the third quarter of the twelfth century, many houses of religious men and women sought to be associated with such orders and in particular with the Cistercian Order. They did so at the outset because such orders made promises about equitable treatment, little interference in internal affairs, a share in privileges, and, as is seen in the Cistercian *Summa Cartae Caritatis* discussed in Chapter 1, even mutual economic support. Gradually an enforcement aspect evolved as well, especially when the secular church put pressure on monastic organizations to control their member abbeys.³ This new institution—the religious order, particularly as devised by the Cistercians—would be so successful in attracting and overseeing individual reform communities and their religious practices that in 1215 the Fourth Lateran Council would enjoin all religious communities to organize themselves into such orders, and it would hold up the Cistercian Order as the model for emulation.⁴

When the Cistercians came to tell the story of their own family of monasteries, they tended to conflate the history of the early congregation in Burgundy with that of the invention of a religious order that was only happening as they wrote. In Chapter 1, I outlined the traditional picture of the twelfth-century Cistercians as derived from their two early texts, the *Exordium Cistercii* and the *Exordium Parvum*, the stories that were invented to regularize the foundation of Cîteaux into a typical twelfth-century religious foundation. In Chapter 2, I argued for dating these accounts to the third quarter of the twelfth century. That such accounts of Cistercian origins became necessary at that time may be in part because Cistercians needed to explain away two anomalies about their early development. First, their charismatic founder, Robert of Molesme, however much he may have wanted to remain, had been forced to abandon Cîteaux and return to Molesme. Second, Bernard of Clairvaux, while clearly the most charismatic leader of the century, presented problems for their account. He was not a founder at all, but had arrived as a young recruit fifteen years after Cîteaux's foundation. While Bernard would found a new house at Clairvaux, it was clearly a colony of monks sent out from Cîteaux. Moreover, although Bernard resembled the charismatic wandering preacher-founders of an earlier generation, his extensive travels were not universally esteemed in a world in which monastic stability was becoming more important. Cistercians certainly must have been made to feel that this was a problem after their first efforts to have Bernard canonized were turned down.⁵ Indeed, abbot Stephen Harding of Cîteaux (died 1134), who had turned his attention to issues of how abbots should rule, what liturgy was most authentic, and how to administer property, but had never been a great international preacher like Bernard, may have seemed to authors of *exordia* writing in the 1160s a more promising founder for the Cistercian Order than Bernard. So it is perhaps not surprising that the *Exordium Cistercii* and the *Exordium Parvum* left Bernard out altogether and marginalized Robert of Molesme, while turning Stephen Harding into the founder and inventor of the Order. This may explain the attribution of the composition of the Charter of Charity to Stephen. It was in such a climate, in which it was deemed necessary to make decisions about whom to promote as a founder of the movement, that the Cistercian Order was devised.

The usual explanation for Cistercian success is that found in the traditional meta-texts, the *Exordium Cistercii* of circa 1165 and the *Exordium Parvum* of 1170–75, which both provide an account of the Order's origins. Growth by colonization from Burgundy is made explicit in the first item in the attached *Instituta* about how new churches are to be created,

Quomodo novella ecclesia abbate et monachis et ceteris necessariis ordinetur. Duodecim monachi cum abbate terciodecimo ad coenobia nova transmittantur. [The first phrase usually rubricated in the texts.]

How a new church is to be provided with abbot and monks. Twelve monks with the abbot as the thirteenth should be sent to the new *coenobia*.[6]

This model of growth by sending out from Burgundy a colony of twelve monks and an abbot to make the thirteenth may be described as "apostolic gestation," foundation imitating the lives of Jesus and his disciples. It is a potent image, for even when no evidence for such apostolic gestation is found in surviving local documents, it has often been assumed in descriptions of early Cistercian foundations. As this chapter argues, this image is rarely a correct version of actual events, particularly for the first half of the twelfth century.

While in the early twelfth century a tiny congregation in Burgundy grew from Cîteaux in ways similar to the way other religious congregations at the time were expanding, we must distinguish between that congregation's growth in Burgundy up to the mid-twelfth century and the growth of an Order that numbered more than 500 houses of monks and a considerable number of communities of nuns by the end of the twelfth century. That the invention of the Cistercian Order occurred later than has previously been thought calls for some explanation for both the events that preceded the Order and the process of that invention and growth during the years from after midcentury. In separating the invention of a Cistercian Order from the activities of an earlier congregation in Burgundy, however, we must still acknowledge the extraordinary growth in the influence and visibility of the abbeys of Cîteaux, Clairvaux, and their leaders.

The Cistercian expansion into an order of immense size was primarily by incorporation, by the gradual attachment of religious communities and congregations with similar goals. It was such independent communities that allowed the Cistercians to achieve the remarkable expansion in numbers of religious communities in the 1130s and 1140s throughout Europe. These houses only eventually came to be part of the Cistercian Order, through a process of incorporation in the 1160s and later. There is, moreover, considerable evidence to suggest that the initiative for affiliation came from those independent houses, rather than from abbeys in Burgundy. Attachment of such houses to the new religious Order of the Cistercians occurred because those independent religious communities sought rules and guidance for particular aspects of their organizational lives and began to adopt Cistercian practices. This process, disregarded in traditional accounts of the Order's expansion, makes sense of what is otherwise a contradiction between the poverty and simplicity of the early Cistercians in Burgundy and their extraordinary twelfth-century growth, which would lead by the end of the twelfth century to frequent denunciations of their wealth. The growth came later than is usually asserted. Moreover, it was as not as miraculous as has been thought, because it was growth by the incorporation of such existing communities. This understanding of how incorporation contributes to Cistercian growth, however, has only recently become apparent to historians.[7] It is in taking account of growth of this sort that a new history of the twelfth-century Cistercians can be constructed.

The bare bones around which such a new story must be fleshed out consist of those things that we know to be true of Cîteaux and Clairvaux despite such revisionism. Thus, we know that there was considerable discussion at early Cîteaux and Clairvaux about the internal life of the monastic community. We know that Bernard of Clairvaux spread the ideas of monastic *caritas* as practiced at his own monastery at Clairvaux by his traveling, preaching, and writing. Bernard had preached in support of Innocent II during the Anacletian schism and as a result had received a papal privilege of tithe exemption in 1132 for his abbey of Clairvaux and abbeys subject to him. As discussed in Chapter 2, that tithe privilege was granted only to Bernard and those subject to him, not to Cîteaux and the Cistercian Order as is often claimed. Other communities received tithe privileges individually because of their reform status in this period, but not as part of a Cistercian Order, an institution not yet invented in the 1130s.

There are hints that for Bernard's lifetime much Cistercian growth might be called that of an *ordo clarevallensis*. Bernard himself, however, seems not to have promoted this idea, although he did not hesitate to accommodate individuals and abbeys wishing to tie themselves to Clairvaux. To Bernard, it was Cîteaux, the house he had entered as a young man, that was the head of the reform movement, not his own abbey of Clairvaux. Indeed, Bernard's insistence that Cîteaux (and neither Molesme nor Clairvaux) was the head of the emerging new religious Order is apparent in certain events of the year 1145 that are documented in the Molesme cartulary. In that year the abbey of nuns at Jully, who had been closely associated with Bernard, were placed by Pope Eugenius III directly under the control of Molesme; Bernard's close supervision of that women's community ended. Such a concession to Molesme of control over Jully was probably given in return for Molesme's agreement to give up any lingering claims it may have had to the monastic foundation at Cîteaux itself. This arrangement (behind which we probably see Bernard at work) laid the groundwork for a congregation at Cîteaux unambiguously independent of Molesme. It also implied the primacy of Cîteaux rather than Clairvaux.[8]

The Early Textual Community in Burgundy

In tracing the invention of this religious Order, this chapter attempts to distinguish between the growth of a monastic congregation in Burgundy and that of independent reform houses elsewhere in Europe. It tracks the obscure stages by which that Burgundian congregation coalesced with independent reform communities in southern France and elsewhere into a Cistercian Order. The expansion of pre-Cistercian communities in that wider sphere will be investigated by concentrating on the evidence for development in southern France of separate communities and congregations before the Order's birth.

Perhaps already in the late 1140s certain independent reform communities founded in the twelfth century were attracted to the Cistercians. Inspired by Bernard's preaching, their first actions would have been to imitate those Burgundian reformers by adopting what they thought were the practices of Cîteaux or of Clairvaux.[9] Such actions on the part of independent religious groups would be a first step in the creation of a religious order. Only after Bernard's death, and in part because of the loss of Bernard as the charismatic leader of what up to then had resembled other early twelfth-century congregations, would further actions in its creation occur.

I have already made careful chronological distinctions between the early twelfth-century discussion of an *ordo monasticus* and later twelfth-century concern with an *ordo cisterciensis*; they are tabulated in Table 2, Chapter 2. Such evidence that the appearance of an *ordo cisterciensis* came only after mid-century suggests that there were two kinds of contributions by the Cistercians to the more general cultural developments that we might call the twelfth-century Renaissance. While the more obvious of these contributions was the somewhat later invention of a fully-formed religious Order in the second half of the century, an earlier Cistercian contribution involved the internal running and reform of individual monastic communities. This was an initial discussion around Cistercians—at Cîteaux and then at Clairvaux as well—which Brian Stock has called a "textual community."[10]

This early Cistercian conversation about *ordo*, as in *ordo monasticus*, was a discussion about spiritual concerns among the very early Cistercians; it soon may have centered on Bernard of Clairvaux. That textual community was characterized by Cistercian notions of *caritas* as discussed by such scholars as Stock, Caroline Walker Bynum, and Martha Newman.[11] This spiritual awakening, or conversation about monastic *caritas*, at Cîteaux was underway even before Bernard of Clairvaux entered Cîteaux; indeed it must have been what attracted Bernard and his followers to that new monastery. This textual community was intent on reforming the monastic world and its practice by new and inspired readings of ancient texts, from the Benedictine Rule to the Song of Songs. Many kinds of written texts emanated from those Burgundian monastic communities. Such letters, treatises, and commentaries circulated ideas about monastic *caritas* and also about the behavior of monks and abbots in reform communities.[12]

The textual community included educational innovations stemming in part from the growing need to indoctrinate adult converts into the practices of the new reform monasticism, as well as to pass on monastic customs to the enormous numbers of independently founded religious houses that began to adopt Cistercian customs after the 1140s. But it is important not to date this use of written materials too early in the twelfth century or to identify the activities of Stock's textual society with the Order's later invention. Training in the reform monastic life for adult converts, even those who were often illiterate like the many knights and peasants who became Cistercian lay-brothers or monks, or their sisters and mothers who became Cistercian lay-sisters and nuns, could be conducted more easily using liturgical order-books and written customaries about lay-brothers in conjunction with Saint Benedict's Rule. Surviving manuscripts of such written materials begin to appear from the 1160s, but it is possible that at least one early liturgical customary, that of Trent 1711, version 1, was available from 1135.[13] By the 1150s there were probably separate lay-brother customaries such as that found in a manuscript from Clairvaux, Montpellier H322.[14]

The Cistercian textual community in Burgundy has been much studied recently and its members are often split into two groups with slightly different interests. One was led by Bernard of Clairvaux, whose concern was with a return to the spirituality of the Desert Fathers; he was more interested in mystical commentary on biblical texts than on monastic administration. The other was that developing around Stephen Harding, who wanted correct texts of the Bible and of the liturgical *ordines* and gave considerable thought to internal monastic administration, for instance to the role of the abbot in the monastic family.[15] Auberger has suggested that Stephen and Cîteaux seemed to have made significantly different choices about monastic expansion than did Bernard.[16] These distinctions lapsed somewhat after the death of Stephen Harding in 1134 because followers of Bernard soon came to hold key posts in

Burgundy, even at houses founded by Stephen. In the 1130s the Burgundian Cistercian congregation was still most actively a congregation centering on Clairvaux, held together by the concepts of monastic love espoused by Bernard. That congregation was controlled almost entirely by Bernard himself, who in the 1140s not only appears to have dictated the first episcopal appointments of Cistercians, but also the movement of abbots from one community to another.[17] There was little democracy within this early congregation and little necessity for the type of administrative organization found in the religious Order which the Cistercians invented after Bernard's death. This congregation of the 1130s and 1140s remained small, with close-knit relationships, and all its houses had similar aims; its discussion about charity differed from the later Cistercian Order and its constitution, although the latter was called a Charter of Charity. The later Cistercian administrative Order was an "umbrella-organization" of independent reform houses that came into existence only considerably later than the initial discussion about the application of *caritas* to internal monastic practices.[18]

Contrasting Burgundy and the Rest of Old Europe

Cistercian growth in Burgundy up to the mid-twelfth century resembled that of other congregations of the time, with the occasional foundation or incorporation of a daughter-house, often at a site where hermits had already settled. Such hermits sought out Cistercian affiliation by applying to Cîteaux or Clairvaux. Both abbeys sent small groups of additional monks to settle at a few of these places or sent out monks to new sites at the request of patrons. We know the first process was true for la Ferté and Pontigny, where hermits preceded the Cistercians.[19] The second process of responding to donors was true for the founding of new communities of nuns, who were sent from the houses of Jully and le Tart; this was also how foundations were made by the charismatic abbess Heloise at the Paraclete, whose congregation was not Cistercian but resembled the Cistercians in many ways.[20] The Burgundian congregation's expansion from Cîteaux and Clairvaux remained very limited during the first third of the twelfth century, rarely extending beyond Burgundy.

In early Burgundy there were considerable differences of wealth and property among houses of the congregation. The high visibility of Cîteaux and Clairvaux meant that, despite an ideology of apostolic poverty, gifts of property from many benefactors came almost effortlessly to the abbots of those two communities. The charters and pancartes of la Ferté, as well as the cartularies of Pontigny, show the need for more careful husbanding of resources by abbots at the latter two houses, but those abbeys had early abbots who were competent and concerned to endow their communities with property. This was probably slightly different at Morimond, fourth daughter of Cîteaux, where early twelfth-century conditions were less secure, possibly because it neither received great beneficence nor was blessed with abbots of great managerial skill in its early years. After Bernard had squelched the proposal by Morimond's first abbot Arnold to lead his followers to Jerusalem, the prior of Clairvaux, Walter, became Morimond's abbot. Perhaps Walter took more seriously than did other abbots Bernard's injunctions about apostolic poverty and life in emulation of the Desert Fathers. Much more than abbots trained by Stephen Harding, Walter seems to have disregarded the implications of the Rule of Saint Benedict about an abbot's responsibility to create sufficient endowment for the monks dependent on him. Morimond's continued poverty up to the third quarter of the twelfth century has been remarked on by scholars of Burgundian Cistercians.[21] Such poverty may explain why, in the newly emerging Order of the 1160s, Morimond's abbot was not initially designated as being one of the "proto-abbots" having visitation obligations and oversight of Cîteaux.[22] That Morimond later gained that status says much about the strong administrative abilities of its abbots in the second half of the twelfth century, as discussed below.

The total number of abbeys in the Burgundian congregation remained low, at least until the 1130s. Indeed the immense popularity of Bernard and Clairvaux attracted many individual recruits to Clairvaux, but most would have wanted to stay there rather than leave to found new abbeys. Communities that wanted to attach themselves directly to Clairvaux remained few. Moreover, except those with exceptional ties to Burgundy, few independent religious communities outside the region could have known about the Cistercians or have adopted their monastic customs before the 1140s. A few foundations were made by patrons with family ties to Burgundy. Such is the community of monks sent to the diocese of Vienne from Cîteaux in 1118 to found Bonnevaux at the request of Guy of Burgundy, archbishop of Vienne, who would become Pope Calixtus II in 1119.[23] Exceptional as well was the foundation of a house in Yorkshire at Fountains, possibly as early as 1132, that received some encouragement in letters circa 1135 from Bernard of Clairvaux. But it has been suggested that the early history of Fountains and account of its attachment to Clairvaux that we have was one rewritten after mid-century. Fountains may not have been created as a result of any personal intervention by Bernard of Clairvaux, but was simply a secession from Saint-Mary's, York, in which reform monks, very like those at Cîteaux or Clairvaux, independently decided to seek a different life, less devoted to an endless liturgy.[24]

Information on the Cistercians and their practices only gradually trickled out of Burgundy. In the 1130s, both Orderic Vitalis and William of Malmesbury wrote about the reform monks at the abbey of Cîteaux.[25] Orderic probably learned about Cîteaux when he attended the great chapter meeting at Cluny in 1132.[26] But neither Orderic nor William makes reference to any grouping of Cistercians larger than the community of monks at Cîteaux itself, and neither of them mentions Clairvaux. They had no specific information on Cistercian practices beyond a general description of the austere conditions at Cîteaux under the leadership of the Englishman, Stephen Harding.

If Cistercian growth did not occur by emanation of religious reform from Burgundy, but was initiated by local reform groups from throughout Europe who were attracted by Cîteaux and its practices, as I argue here, it is imperative to explain how such dispersed reformers came to hear of the Cistercians. The appeal of Cistercian customs, once they were heard of, probably derived from the hope that these customs could solve such internal organizational problems as how to integrate lay-brothers or shorten the liturgy. Undoubtedly Bernard of Clairvaux's preaching was a primary vehicle for relaying information on such Cistercian customs, but that information began to be relayed at later dates than when William and Orderic had written.

The other thing we can assert about religious reform in twelfth-century Europe is the importance of adult conversion to the religious life. Among such converts was not only Bernard of la Fontaine, who came with thirty followers to Cîteaux, whence he was soon sent to be abbot of Clairvaux (1115–53), but another Bernard, a cleric, Bernardo Pignatelli, a native of Pisa who entered Clairvaux after being inspired by Bernard of Clairvaux's preaching. He was soon sent back to Italy to be head of a monastery near Rome and then was elected pope in 1145 as Eugenius III. This phenomenon of adult conversion found in the lives of both abbot Bernard of Clairvaux and Eugenius III was widespread in the twelfth century. In Burgundy and beyond, such converts were responsible for many of the new foundations of independent religious communities that would eventually become part of the Cistercian Order. Many local charismatic figures attracted followers, founded monasteries (often without the intermediate stage of having entered another one first), and created their own local reform centers. They are figures like Pons of Léras, who founded Silvanès, or Peter of Lerce, who founded a short-lived hermitage near Fontfroide (both discussed later in this chapter), many of whose names and careers have nearly escaped the notice of historians. Some of these adult converts would retire with their entire families to newly created religious centers whose cores were syneisactic (literally communities of men and women living together under the same roof). These family monasteries often eventually gave birth to twin reform communities, one for women and one for men. Sometimes both were eventually affiliated with the Cistercians. Such communities of both men and women may loosely be called "double communities," although they lack some of the elements of those great aristocratic communities under the leadership of abbesses of the early Middle Ages. In them, some of the religious women were undoubtedly those whose careers as priests' wives were being ended following active campaigns of Church legislation against clerical marriage in the early twelfth century. As widows or abandoned wives, those women sought honorable retirement, but also responded to a vocation to nurse and care for the sick and poor, for orphans, lepers, and the elderly, work that had often been undertaken by priests' wives in earlier centuries.[27]

While it has traditionally been assumed that the creation of the Cistercian Order took place before 1150 and in one step, the evidence suggests a more gradual evolution. For many abbots and abbesses and their communities a definitive attachment to mother-abbeys and to the filiation trees established for internal visitation came only in the 1180s or later.

It is useful to describe the many dispersed communities of this independent reform movement, in regions beyond Burgundy, those that eventually became incorporated into a Cistercian Order, as houses of "pre-Cistercians" up to the time when they began to adopt Cistercian customs; thereafter, they might be described as "proto-Cistercians." The terms "pre-Cistercian" and "proto-Cistercian" (which I introduce here) are used to refer to two different stages in the expansion of the twelfth-century reform movement, while such houses were not yet formally linked to the small congregation in Burgundy or to the Order which eventually appeared. Both stages probably extended in some places well into the second half of the twelfth century.

To describe the Cistercian Order as deriving from pre-Cistercian and proto-Cistercian reform communities that were eventually amalgamated into a newly invented Order, which would establish General Chapters, legislation, visitation, and filiations over a number of years, helps explain Cistercian success. Thus, by moving our definition of the earliest Cistercians away from a rigid picture of filiations, visitation, annual General Chapter meetings, uniformity of practice, and legislation about being located "far from cities, castles, and human habitations," we can make more sense of the evidence of local and central administrative records.[28] But much confusion about this progression from independent communities to an Order has arisen because the story line deriving from the early Cistercian *exordia* has interwoven two completely different types of Cistercian activity. On the one hand, there was an early twelfth-century movement of spiritual reform of monasticism within Burgundy, instigated by tiny congregations associated with Cîteaux and Clairvaux. On the other, there was the creation of an administrative Order in the 1160s and later.

Different communities developed ties with Cistercians at different rates, but until about 1150 most independent reform houses of monks and nuns in southern France were pre-Cistercian. They would eventually become part of the Cistercian Order but had not as yet experienced any direct influence from Cîteaux or Clairvaux. At least until the late 1140s they had not heard of or adopted the *ordo cisterciensis* as a set of practices spread by word of mouth, by written customaries, or in the form of liturgical *ordines* and lay-brother treatises. Indeed, it was only in the mid-1140s that pre-Cistercian houses in southern France began to hear about Cistercian customs through Bernard's preaching and to adopt practices they may have viewed as Cistercian. But the gradual transformation of these independently founded pre-Cistercian houses of reformed monks and nuns into proto-Cistercians in southern France and elsewhere laid the groundwork for what eventually was a much more rapid affiliation of those proto-Cistercians into an Order in the 1160s and thereafter.

While we must distinguish between twelfth-century developments in Burgundy and in other regions, both that Burgundian heartland and the other regions into which Cistercians spread in the twelfth century were centered on parts of Christendom that might be called "old Europe," where conditions of agricultural practice, settlement, and weather had varied little since the Roman period. These regions experienced a different sort of Cistercian growth in the twelfth century from that on the new margins of Christendom in the thirteenth century. In the thirteenth century, with a few exceptions such as the royal foundation for monks at Royaumont, created north of Paris by Queen Blanche of Castile for the soul of her husband Louis VIII, most of the Order's thirteenth-century growth occurred on the fringes of what has been called "new Europe" or involved the creation or incorporation in "old Europe" of women's houses.[29] Many of these women's houses had actually been founded slightly earlier but had evolved into Cistercian abbeys from tiny hospitals, which were taking over many of the social service roles that had earlier been performed by the wives of priests.[30]

Later accounts of Cistercian growth often describe it as having occurred on a model of "apostolic gestation" derived from the "primitive documents" and the early Cistercian statutes. But that growth tends also to be described in a colonial mode. Thus, much in the style of modern westerners characterizing their own superiority over the nonwestern world, Cistercians in their self-descriptions declared themselves superior to those "others" in the communities into which they came.[31] Indeed, the more powerful abbeys of the twelfth century justified both absorbing less powerful communities and depopulating villages in language that proclaimed the rightness of their cause in bringing light to the unconverted. We see this, for instance, in the expansion of Cistercian settlements into only recently converted Scandinavia.[32] Such Cistercian accounts of their own actions, however, seem particularly compelling because they have a small grain of truth in them. However exaggerated in general, there were a few early cases, primarily from Burgundy, of new abbeys being created by sending out colonies of monks or nuns. Such colonization, however, constituted only a very few cases.

Part of what has traditionally supported these descriptions of widespread apostolic gestation for the Order's founding has been the practice of tracing Cistercian expansion by five filiations or families of monasteries. This is how all men's houses in the Order were tied to one another in the organizational charts (filiation trees) for visitation established in the early thirteenth century. These charts (for an eighteenth-century example, see Figure 25) link mother, daughter, and granddaughter houses in tree-like models. They suggest by their very structure an organic growth of the Cistercians, but one that is contrary to the reality of Cistercian expansion.[33] Like medieval representations of the biblical tree of Jesse, such filiation trees reflect a frequent medieval image, showing the medieval fascination with noble and even biblical genealogies. But such Cistercian "genealogical" trees misrepresent the truth about the twelfth-century Cistercian Order.[34] Not only are the implications of such trees about the Order's growth by apostolic gestation incorrect, but the dates they contain and the relationships they imply between abbeys are wrong for the earliest years; moreover, they leave out Cistercian women altogether. In fact, such trees imply an organization that could not actually have worked very well for visitation. For how could Clairvaux's abbot have possibly visited all the daughter-abbeys on its tree? This difficulty was apparent from the time of the *Carta Caritatis Posterior*, which allowed a delegate to act for the father abbot.

Yet at least the illusion of systematic visitation was very important to late twelfth-century Cistercians. Not only did efficient internal control justify their exemption from episcopal oversight, but that exemption from annual bishops' visits was often conflated, by them and by their peers, with the important economic privilege of tithe exemption. The surviving documents suggest that the Cistercians only began to create such filiation trees once internal visitation had been enjoined on them in 1184; indeed, there was no reason for the trees at earlier dates. Moreover, organizational trees for visitation were still in the process of being devised in the early thirteenth century.[35]

Because such trees attempted to portray current relationships within the Order at the time they were made, they often provide very imperfect informa-

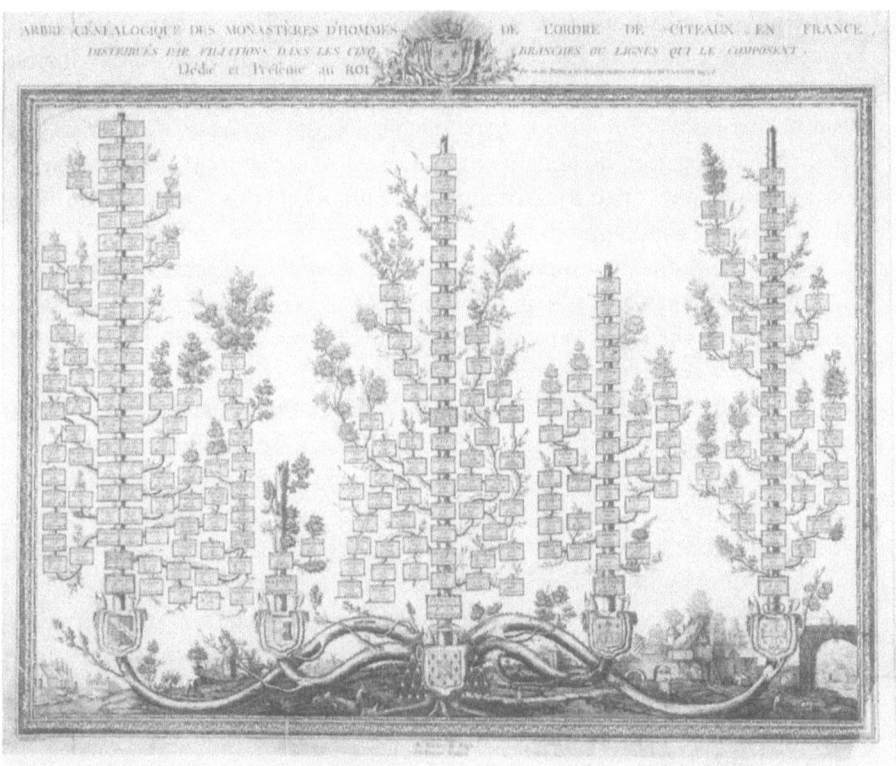

Figure 25. Engraving of an eighteenth-century genealogical tree for monasteries for men of the Cistercian Order. (Dijon, Bibl. Mun. 90-098, by permission)

tion about earlier events. Obviously those who made them were more familiar with the assumptions of the Order's *Instituta* about how early growth should occur than with the events of actual foundations and affiliations, which had often occurred a generation or more earlier. By the early thirteenth century, moreover, the dates of incorporation and foundation of a new house were often identical; that these events had been distinct in earlier times was beyond the ken of those who were constructing the filiation trees.[36] Furthermore, the use of filiation tables for establishing precedence at General Chapter meetings must have led to widespread falsification.[37]

The filiation trees made in the thirteenth century tended to blur such distinctions about foundations, for such trees required that multiple events be condensed into a single date and the place of an individual abbey be located on a particular branch. Such trees are often a hodgepodge of arbitrarily established dates and relationships mixed in with reliable ones. We can observe individual daughter-houses being moved from one filiation to another, often for no apparent reason. For instance, the abbey of Valmagne, which was attached to the mother-house of Bonnevaux and the filiation of Cîteaux on those trees, has early twelfth-century documents in its cartulary that show its foundation by Ardorel, which was tied to Cadouin and Pontigny; in this case, the claim was that Valmagne's affiliation to the Cistercians was rather by Bonnevaux.[38]

Clearly, principles employed in placing houses on such trees were not always about foundation or incorporation. It is possible, in fact, that placement close to the trunk on a filiation tree had more to do with numbers of daughter-houses than with any absolute chronology of growth.[39] Thus debate could arise in the early thirteenth century between Preuilly and Savigny about which should be treated as the fifth daughter of Cîteaux. Preuilly had been founded fifth by Cîteaux. Savigny was incorporated, as argued below, probably only in the late 1150s; but Savigny's abbot argued (unsuccessfully) that its foundation date at the opening of the twelfth century, and the many daughter-houses brought with it when its congregation was attached to Cîteaux, should give it precedence over Preuilly. Clearly what was at stake was whether strict chronological order of attachment to Cistercian mother-houses was more important in placement on such filiation charts than the numerical strength of congregations added. This appears to have been an issue with some of Morimond's daughters as well.[40]

The Profits of Incorporation Beyond Burgundy

Incorporation of existing abbeys in southern France and elsewhere continued to be the usual way in which the Cistercians expanded right up to the time of the creation of an Order in the 1160s and 1170s, but there was also variation in that pattern. During the lifetime of Bernard of Clairvaux, a number of existing houses were attached to Cistercian practices through affiliation with that abbot and the community of Clairvaux; Clairvaux tended to attach communities directly to itself.[41] Mother-abbeys elsewhere, whether or not they were future heads of filiations like Burgundian Clairvaux and Morimond, often attached whole congregations at once and consequently had a more vertically extended family tree than had Clairvaux. In most cases, moreover, attachment to the Cistercians was usually later than is implied on the filiation trees. Thus, in southern France locally founded abbeys became parts of autochthonous networks that had been in existence longer than the Order itself. Such pre-Cistercian houses had often created local networks or congregations long before Cistercian affiliation, so that when affiliation with the Cistercians did occur, it was often very rapid, because what was attached were not single houses but whole congregations.

The importance of such incorporations to Cistercian success was not only to add abbeys or even whole networks of abbeys to the Cistercian trees. Incorporated communities or congregations brought with them the accumulated economic assets of established religious houses as well as their social ties to local families of benefactors and recruits. Such houses had already recruited a membership, some of whom were monks and nuns, others lay-sisters and lay-brothers; none of these assets existed for abbeys founded de novo. We can only guess at how large a proportion of total Cistercian wealth and recruits came from these annexations that provided both landed assets and trained personnel. The incorporation of such pre-Cistercian houses and all their assets, rather than the miraculous growth often cited by historians of monasticism, is what makes sense out of an otherwise numerically impossible expansion of twelfth-century Cistercians. It is incorporation that explains numbers such as nearly 350 houses of monks at mid-century (even if many of them are redated slightly later), or 500 houses by 1200.

How many new abbeys were created by incorporation? Without querying here how many of the purported dates of "foundation" in standard tables derived from Janauschek's *Originum* are correct, we can nonetheless estimate that, of the 326 houses of monks said to have been founded by the Cistercians throughout Europe by the year 1152, all but perhaps 40 were incorporated houses.[42] Indeed, in southern France all but one or two of the houses for men traditionally dated to before 1152 were clearly incorporated houses. Only in the second half of the twelfth century were more genuine foundations made. Such new foundations, where they occur, were made locally, not by colonization from Burgundy. After 1150 mother-abbeys had consolidated their endowments. Of the nearly 200 additional men's houses added to the Cistercian Order in the second half of the century, this may mean that a few were actually created by sending out colonies of monks to new sites. Thus, although the apparent rate of increase in houses for monks was considerably slower in the second half of the century, there was probably a slightly larger proportion of real foundations being made from scratch at that time. Indeed, such authentic colonization by proto-Cistercian and Cistercian houses probably reached its peak circa 1175, coincident with the date of composition of the *Exordium Parvum*. Perhaps this is an additional reason why authors of that text and the *Instituta* associated with it described colonization as the normal means of Cistercian growth.[43]

Annexation did not always mean new abbeys. Also important to the accumulation of Cistercian property and personnel was the hidden side of incorporation occurring whenever it was decided *not* to create a new daughter-abbey but to absorb an existing priory or groups of hermits. Often such groups were attached to existing reform communities with properties, churches, and buildings taken over along with religious obligations. The personnel became monks and lay-brothers, or nuns and lay-sisters, of the more powerful annexing houses. An example is Berdoues's appropriation in 1152 of a church and community of hermits at Artigues after the founder of that community, Sanche of las Comères, entered Berdoues with his followers, all of them as lay-brothers. The owners of the property on which those hermits lived had sold their rights to Berdoues for cash, and one of the former land-owners then entered Berdoues as a monk. That hermitage with its church of Saint-Sernin of Artigues had three other dependent churches that came under Berdoues's control at that time, including one that had been brought to the hermits by a woman named Bona of Toncens when she entered that eremitical community.[44]

In a period when many reform communities in southern France were beginning to adopt Cistercian practices, we can estimate that on average two or three such smaller houses were annexed by every house of monks that itself came to be part of the Cistercian Order. As discussed in Chapter 4, even the abbey for women at Nonenque may have absorbed the hermitages it attached in the late twelfth century, rather than making daughter-abbeys of them. But Nonenque is exceptional; few other women's houses in southern France either founded daughter-houses or undertook such annexation in the twelfth century.

What happened to women like Bona of Toncens who had been members of the earlier eremitical group at Artigues that was taken over by Berdoues? Were such women transferred to communities of women already in existence, or were new separate communities created for them? Were they attached as nuns or lay-sisters to a church dependent on Berdoues where we know that thirteenth-century female patrons would be promised burial?[45] When such double communities like that at Artigues were absorbed, it was most likely to have been by a more powerful abbey, almost inevitably one of monks. It was easy for the men of earlier syneisactic communities to be admitted into men's houses that had absorbed their earlier establishments, but women of such family monasteries faced a different outcome. Their communities often retained a semi-independent existence as dependent priories attached to the powerful men's houses. Some priories in the thirteenth century became abbeys for nuns.

Even when the issue was whether to incorporate or to found a new community of monks or nuns, the decision to take on responsibility for another daughter-house could never have been easy. Abbesses and abbots were only too aware of their responsibility to provide for the material needs of the communities they ruled. The needs of an existing community for recruits and endowment had to be weighed against demands of patrons who offered land and support, but who wanted to make new foundations. Once the General Chapter and an Order were established, an issue to be addressed would be when and how often expansion should happen, as well as whether it would be by increasing the endowment of existing abbeys or by founding new communities.[46] It appears that soon after the mid-twelfth century the incorporation of new daughter-abbeys was often being discouraged in favor of converting small independent reform communities into granges. Obviously the political dimensions of this were very complex, but certain abbeys like Fontfroide profited considerably from the absorption of a number of small communities of monks and nuns after 1150.[47]

In part, such discouragement of new foundations made administrative sense not only because of the added administrative costs of visitation, or of having additional members traveling to General Chapter meetings, but because new abbeys were competitors for patronage and recruits. In contrast, to incorporate an existing house as a grange had almost nothing but benefits. It was after mid-century that injunctions to establish a reasonable distance between both abbeys and granges of different communities began to be noted, for instance in the Charter of Peace with the Praemonstratensians. Such regulations must have encouraged the increasing absorption of existing independent communities as granges, rather than the creation of new daughter-abbeys. But limiting competition in this way was possibly the primary motivation behind such agreements and legislation.

During the earliest period, which is usually thought to have encompassed the highest levels of Cistercian "growth," what we actually find expanding were those independent pre-Cistercian houses of monks and nuns that would later adopt Cistercian practices and eventually coalesce into an Order. Because so many accumulated resources came along with the independent reform houses when they were incorporated, by the time these communities became recognizably part of a Cistercian Order, most of them were no longer the impoverished and marginal communities that they may once have been and as they are often described in Cistercian mythology. From the third and last quarters of the twelfth century, the affiliation of large numbers of existing communities as new Cistercian houses must have contributed to late twelfth-century views that an astonishing accumulation of wealth by the Order had come from its aggressive consolidation of land and assertion of tithe privileges. The reputation for having become wealthy coincided, in fact, very closely with the invention of an Order in the third quarter of the twelfth century. This meant that almost immediately after it was conceived, the Cistercian Order had to struggle with the perception of having too much wealth.

Whether houses were transformed into new communities, or appropriated as endowment and granges, such incorporation brought with it members, endowment, and well-established patronage, which contributed considerably to the rapid growth of Cistercian monasticism in this region. Dating all this is difficult. What we can easily say is that such expansion was rarely by apostolic gestation, that incorporation was a central fact, and that incorporation brought many already well-established and wealthy communities into the growing Order. Not all houses of the Order can be thought to have been starving colonies of eremitical pioneers at the time of their affiliation.

The Silvanès Account

The literary sources are not altogether silent on incorporation as a factor in the growth of the Cistercian Order. Indeed, we have at least one alternative account dating to the 1170s for the success of Cistercian expansion in the twelfth century. This alternative to the story of the Cistercian *exordia* is the southern-French narrative of the foundation of Silvanès, or the *Vita* of its founder, Pons of Léras, whose eremitical foundation was eventually attached to the Cistercians.[48] The modern editor of both cartulary and chronicle for Silvanès, P.-A. Verlaguet, has identified the chronicle's author as Hugh Francigena, a monk at Silvanès who also wrote several letters on theological subjects to the bishop of Lodève.[49] Despite the early date of the account, Hugh himself had not witnessed the foundation. His knowledge of many events described is secondhand, although he tells us that his abbot had instructed him to consult those who had been present in order to write the narrative.[50] Preserving an account of the foundation of Silvanès and possibly attempting to establish a local cult for Pons, the Silvanès chronicle was also a defensive tract written in response to competition for patronage from other new reform houses nearby, like Valmagne and Bonnecombe, which were also adopting Cistercian practices at that time.[51]

The Silvanès story confirms the most striking finding of many recent studies of Cistercians in the twelfth century, the importance of incorporation. It also emphasizes the importance of the adult convert. Nonetheless, this account of such an incorporated house and adult convert is the account of events in the 1130s seen through the eyes of an author writing just before 1170. It was within thirty years of the events he describes, but thirty years of rapid change and development. During these years, a small congregation in Burgundy had blossomed into an international Order. Expectations of circa 1170, as reflected in this chronicle, thus were different on a number of points from what is found in Silvanès's charters written in earlier decades.

The narrative recounts the conversion of Pons of Léras, a knight from the vicinity of Lodève who adopted the religious life as a result of his wife's tearful pleading. According to the author, on his conversion to the life of penance, Pons placed family members in religious communities, gave up his worldly position, and gave his goods to the poor. Following visits to pilgrimage sites at Mont-Saint-Michel and Saint-Jacques of Compostela, Pons and the followers who had joined him decided to found a religious community. They arrived at Saint-Guilhelm-du-Désert near Montpellier during Holy Week, encountering storms and other difficulties that paralleled the events of the Passion. With encouragement from the bishop of Rodez, they then founded a hermitage in the southern Rouergue not far from Camarès.[52]

The account begins with an elaborate play on the words *silva, silvaniensis,* and *salva nos* in its description of the role of "salvation" at Silvanès.[53] Such literary conceits about monastic growth describe Silvanès as a tree in a heavenly forest and *arboris generosa radice cognita,* a tree known for its generous roots.[54] Ironically enough, of course, this tree was one grafted onto the later filiation trees. According to this hagiographical account, the eremitical settlement was in a wilderness solitude where the men living in the society of beasts built their little huts and created a habitable space:

In quo casulas propriis manibus fabricantes manserunt, bestiis sociati, quotidiano tamen labori insistentes, dumeta falcibus resecantes, terram ligonibus proscindentes, locum habitabilem ex inhabitabili reddiderunt.

They remained living in their little huts built by their own hands, in the society of beasts, insisting on practicing daily manual labor, cutting down with their knives or axes, uprooting the land with their hoes, they transformed an uninhabited place into a habitable one.[55]

The charters from the Silvanès cartulary tell us that Pons of Léras was granted land for building a religious house in the *mansus* of Terundo by Arnold of Pont, who was castellan at the nearby castle of Pont-de-Camarès. The cartulary shows that the land acquired by Silvanès was virtually all already under cultivation.[56]

After describing the struggles of the early years, the text turns to the regularization of the eremitical settlement and its transformation into a monastic one. As has been pointed out by Ludo Milis, hermitages and monasteries have standard developmental story lines in which groups of anonymous holy men and women go off into the wilderness where "living in the society of beasts" they attract followers. But as membership grows, the need for permanent leadership and regulations leads such houses to search for a rule and customs.[57] It seems to me that another commonplace in such hagiography is that such a search for a rule and guidance often began with the consultation of a more austere group than that with which they eventually found themselves.[58] As the Silvanès chronicle makes clear, such hermits' transformation into cenobites was a natural one, at least in hagiographical expectations.[59]

After the decision to adopt a rule, controversy arose as to the most appropriate monastic *ordo* to follow,

Facta est ergo contentio inter eos quis ordinum videretur major? Aliis laudantibus ordinem Cisterciensium, aliis vero ordinem Cartusiensium, quibusdam etiam sanctimonialium virginum monasterium construere dignum dicentibus.

Thus there arose dispute over which *ordo* was most important. While some praised the Cistercian *ordo* and others the Carthusian *ordo*, certain of them also said that it would be best to build a monastery for sanctified virgins.[60]

The use of the term *ordo* here suggests that what was being discussed was which variant form of the *ordo monasticus* — that of the Cistercians or of the Carthusians — should be adopted. *Ordo* here remains a way of life, rather than meaning "order" as a group. The oblique reference to nuns must be to the long-established relationship with nearby Nonenque.

Hugh tells us that the community sent an envoy to *la Grande Chartreuse* to consult its hermits about which *ordo* should be followed.[61] The Carthusians suggested that these men apply to the nearest Cistercian house. Pons of Léras then went to Mazan, and there handed over his community to Mazan's abbot, Peter. Here the newer usage — *ordo cisterciensis* — is apparent, for adopting the Cistercian *ordo* appears to mean attaching one's community to a mother-house of a particular monastic practice. In the thinking of the 1170s, then, the process was one in flux, both adopting a way of life and attaching the hermitage to the Cistercian Order. The novitiate was fulfilled by members going from the eremitical community of Silvanès to Mazan for training. When Silvanès became an abbey, Pons "out of humility" did not become abbot but remained a conversus.[62] Eventually, many people gathered at the original monastic site, and the monks sought more solitude by moving farther up the valley. There in 1157 they began building a church at their permanent site on land purchased in part from Nonenque, land from which the peasants would be removed.[63]

The church dated by this chronicle to 1157 still stands; see Figure 26. It has been treated by art historians as an unusual Cistercian edifice, comparable

Figure 26. Church for the Cistercian monks at Silvanès, exterior, east end. (Friedman)

only to that of the abbey of l'Escaledieu in the middle Pyrenees. The latter had originally been a hermitage like Silvanès but was eventually attached to Morimond, possibly after it had developed a congregation of affiliated houses on either side of the Pyrenees. There is no evidence for any tie between these two hermitages, but churches at Silvanès and l'Escaledieu share an exceptional feature in their construction: fairly high naves in both cases are flanked not by the usual aisles, but by a series of barrel vaults constructed slightly lower than and at right angles to the nave; see the plan of Silvanès, Figure 27. At l'Escaledieu these barrel vaults were pierced to create aisles. At Silvanès there are no aisles but barrel-vaulted side-chapels. These side-chapels have windows that provide most of the light, but there is another higher level of window-like openings in what might be described as a blind gallery; see Figure 28.

Construction at Silvanès made the exterior wall sufficiently solid to allow the nave of this church to be both wider and higher than most naves of twelfth-century southern-French Cistercian churches. The east end at Silvanès has three rounded windows in the nave wall above a flat-ended choir or sanctuary attached like a narrower and lower vaulted box to the end of the nave; see Figure 29. That choir has rounded windows with rose and oculi above. There is a small bell tower on the roof of the church; as seen in Figure 26. But there is

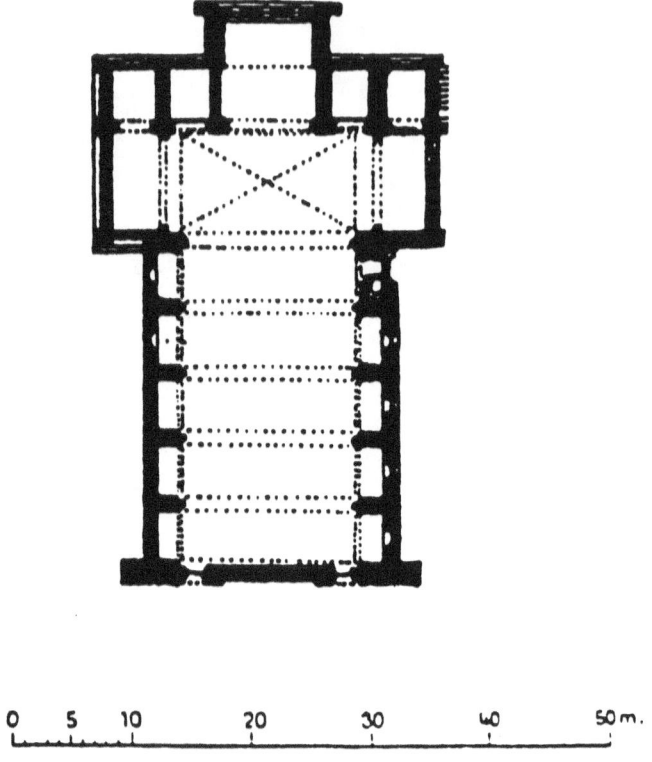

Figure 27. Plan of Silvanès.

no corresponding structure in the interior.[64] While Silvanès's church is infused with a light from its windows that corresponds to that "aura" or "spirit" often associated with what have been called "Bernardine" churches, its details differ considerably from what are usually identified as typical twelfth-century Cistercian buildings; compare its plan to those of Sénanque, Silvacane, and le Thoronet in Figure 2, or that of Fontfroide in Figure 7.

Silvanès's foundation text is also both typical and atypical. It reflects stories about saints that must have circulated widely at the time and were adopted by every hagiographer, such as how the community nearly starved like the Israelites in the desert until food miraculously appeared.[65] But the author of this account of circa 1170 also provides an alternate view of charismatic leadership, adult conversion, and the transformation of a hermitage into a monastery that was gradually affiliated with a religious Order.

Explanations for both its unusual church and the events surrounding the

Figure 28. Silvanès, interior, south transept and nave wall. (Friedman)

foundation of this community have caused Silvanès to be seen as "out of step" with how things usually happened in the Cistercian Order.[66] Indeed, even though we have the twelfth-century account of this foundation of a locally initiated attachment to the Order, that account has been treated as the aberrant one by Cistercian historians who have preferred the model of "apostolic gestation." At the very least, the chronicle is read to indicate that once the local reformers decided to adopt an *ordo*, they sought attachment to a wholly formed, centralized institution, one that had existed from early in the twelfth century. In fact, attachment to the abbey of Mazan was one thing, attachment to a Cistercian Order was something else, and the two did not take place at the same time.

While the chronicle includes a number of purely conventional elements and shows some relationship to the *Vita Prima* of Bernard of Clairvaux, its assertions often vary from what we can know from Silvanès's charters.[67] In addition to underlining the foundation of a new community by an adult convert, it provides an explanation for Cistercian success that is based on local initiative rather than apostolic gestation. As is discussed in the next chapter, Silvanès probably had its origins in a double-community with Nonenque. The monks' choice of the *ordo cisterciensis* as described in the 1170s chronicle was

Figure 29. Silvanès, interior, nave and sanctuary. (Friedman)

clearly an interpolation of earlier events. But we can document the practice of the Cistercian *ordo* in the sense of a set of practices at Silvanès by its charter evidence and date that practice's introduction there to between 1149 and 1157. We also know that Valmagne's donors mentioned Cistercian practices at Silvanès between 1158 and 1161.[68]

Mazan and Its Congregation of Hermitages

The Silvanès account written in 1170 told of the decision to adopt an *ordo*, describing how in the late 1130s Pons went to Mazan and its abbot Peter established Silvanès as an abbey. Mazan is described as the nearest Cistercian house. But this is an explanation of the 1170s about the 1130s. In the 1130s, not only was Silvanès not yet Cistercian, but neither was Mazan; it was a community of hermits at Mazan to which monks at Silvanès, and possibly nuns from Nonenque even earlier, had affiliated themselves. By the 1170s, Mazan was no longer the closest house following Cistercian practices.[69]

Mazan itself originated as an eremitical community in the Vivarais, possibly as early as 1119 or 1120. But circa 1120 was definitely not the date of its affiliation to Bonnevaux or its becoming Cistercian, as has been claimed. Indeed, there are indications that the community at Mazan itself may only have appeared somewhat later than 1120.[70] Between the 1130s and 1160s Mazan had gathered together a diverse group of daughter-houses, including Silvanès, Nonenque, Bonneval in the Rouergue (not to be confused with Bonnevaux), Sénanque and its daughter at les Chambons, and le Thoronet (which may not yet have begun to attach houses for nuns as it did at the opening of the thirteenth century), as well as houses of nuns at Nonenque, Bellecombe, Mercoire, and les Fonts.[71] Some of these communities, like Nonenque and Silvanès, had origins as double communities, as is discussed further in Chapter 4. By the 1160s or slightly earlier, this group had begun to adopt Cistercian practices, but there are hints that a congregation had been brought together earlier by a reformer of hermits at Mazan, a certain Peter Itier, who appears in the records for Mazan and for related houses.[72] Mazan was thus a prolific mother-abbey, attaching to itself at least six abbeys of monks and four of nuns, but its congregation was created by the incorporation of existing eremitical foundations.[73] By the time it was in turn attached to Cistercian Bonnevaux, Mazan had already collected a substantial congregation around itself.

Initial links within this congregation may have been as much about animal husbandry as about what kinds of monastic practices to adopt. It is indeed Mazan's location that is pivotal to our understanding of this early congregation of independent reform houses, which were all located between the Rhône valley and the Rouergue with its center in the high mountains of the Vivarais. Mazan's congregation is easily recognizable as one in which active transhumance joined the Rhône delta and coast of Languedoc to the high summer pastures of the central massif. That such pastoralism made considerable economic sense for eremitical groups in general is undoubtedly true. Particularly, sensible were the ties within such a congregation between houses at both ends of such an economic system. Mazan's congregation made pastoralism profitable because it linked houses like Sénanque and le Thoronet on the coast to houses closer to the high summer pastures of the Rouergue and Vivarais, like Nonenque, Mazan, les Chambons, and Bonneval; see Figure 30.

Silvanès's very early attachment to Mazan may have been primarily a result of such a desire to share pasture rights. Long before any of them had any thought of adopting Cistercian customs, Mazan and its daughter-abbeys like Silvanès, Sénanque, and Nonenque were probably attached to one another by the ties of a common pastoral economy in which rights to graze in pasture were shared among these religious communities of men or women. By the 1170s when the Silvanès account was written, however, Mazan had clearly become Cistercian, and the Silvanès chronicle's author had notions about how Silvanès's attachment to Mazan meant being attached to the Cistercian Order. But a generation or so earlier, such communities of adult converts to the religious life, sometimes syneisactic ones, may have found the low labor demands of a pastoral economy the most acceptable way to support their eremitical communities. Before Cistercian practices ever became an issue for any of them, the ties linking these reformers may have been the expanded possibilities of pastoralism when resources were shared in a common network of transhumance.

Such links through a common practice of pastoralism may be seen by reference not just to Silvanès and Nonenque, but to the monks of Bonneval as well.[74] Bonneval's traditional foundation date is usually given as 1147; like Silvanès it was probably originally a hermitage. Bonneval was certainly in existence by 1154, when its first abbot, Ademar, appeared among witnesses to a charter now preserved in the Silvanès cartulary.[75] Bonneval has several surviving foundation accounts, all contradictory, and at least one of which was rejected by the abbey's monks before the end of the Middle Ages. The most plausible recounts the foundation being made after the near-drowning of the bishop of Cahors, who had become lord of the local castle of Calmont-sur-Olt, but even this story is one repeated elsewhere.[76]

There is considerable information about Bonneval and its practice of pastoralism both in the Rouergue and on the high pasture lands of the Aubrac plateau. The routes still used today to move animals up to the Aubrac's summer-

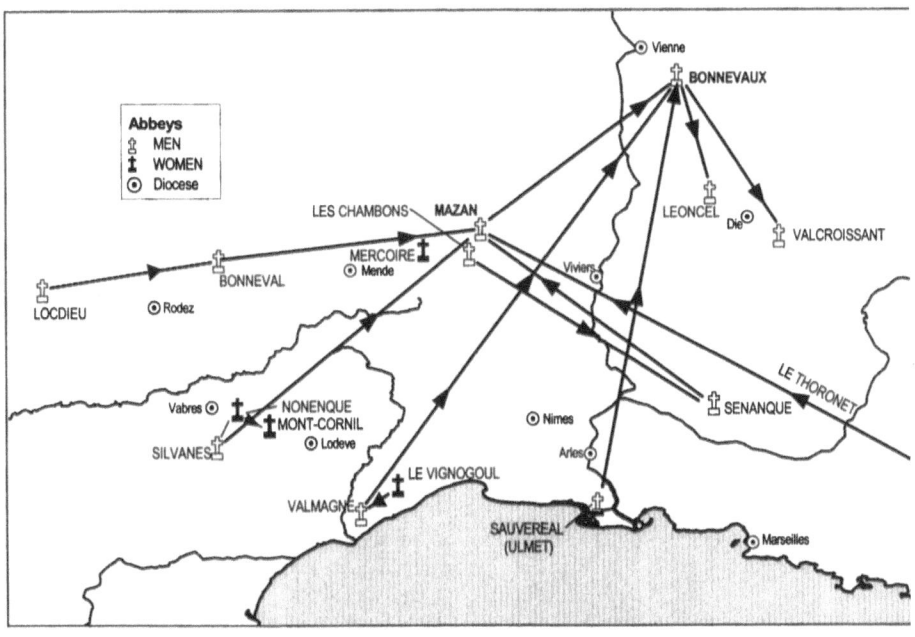

Figure 30. Mazan and Bonnevaux daughter-abbeys in the Midi.

pasture areas, the walled sheep- and cattle-roads known as the *drayas*, pass along the valley in which Bonneval is located. Gradually Bonneval divided up rights to pasture lands in that region with its rivals, houses of the military religious orders. Although a fire in its archives means that the documentation is fragmentary, a surviving inventory suggests ties to lords of Anduze in the Cévennes. Moreover, until 1178 Bonneval had a substantial grange at la Serre in the central Rouergue near the lands of the abbey of Cistercian monks at Bonnecombe, to which that grange was eventually sold.[77] Its ties to lower pasture areas providing food for its animals in winter would eventually more often represent ties to the Quercy to the west than to the Rhône valley in the east. Bonneval's creation of areas of exclusive pasture rights for its animals was accomplished in the last years of the twelfth century, in part through trading away what had formerly been granges belonging to the monks of Locdieu, as discussed below.

In addition to Bonneval, Silvanès, and Nonenque in the Rouergue, Mazan also founded or incorporated two houses of monks in Provence, at Sénanque and le Thoronet; churches for both were discussed in Chapter 1. Sénanque is usually said to have been founded or incorporated by Mazan in

1148, but gifts that may pertain to its abbey site were still being received during the next few years. Moreover, that Sénanque is said to have founded or incorporated a house for monks at les Chambons in the Vivarais by 1152 suggests that Sénanque itself had been in existence somewhat longer than since 1148 when it was attached to Mazan.[78] Although les Chambons may have been originally a grange or cell attached to Sénanque, it too became part of a growing network of interdependent quasi-eremitical religious communities associated with Mazan whose economic basis was primarily animal husbandry.[79]

Mazan also had a daughter-house for monks at le Thoronet located in the diocese of Fréjus; the date 1136 must be that of its foundation sometime before its attachment to Mazan. Le Thoronet would later develop a filiation of houses of nuns, as discussed in Chapter 5. Because of a lack of documents, little can be said about le Thoronet's economic activities except to point out that it too was located in a prime region for wintering animals that were sent in the summers to pasture areas, such as those closer to Mazan and les Chambons.

What Mazan and houses attached to it were developing in the middle third of the twelfth century may thus have been an economic alternative to that of the earliest Cistercians in Burgundy. While Burgundian Cistercians organized the economic life of reform monasticism by reemphasizing manual labor and reducing the time spent in the liturgy, as well as by introducing lay-brothers and granges, Mazan's congregation relied on pastoralism to reduce its labor needs. Mazan's pastoralism could have been equally effective as a system of support for a group of monastic communities intent on avoiding dependence on manorial assets, such as villages, tithes, and rents.

Many studies suggest that the new independent reform communities of the twelfth century could have made economic sense of their ideological goal of reduced dependence on the manorial economy not only by using lay-brothers and granges, but perhaps equally effectively by a newly emphasized pastoralism such as that practiced by Mazan.[80] In this emphasis on pastoralism, the congregation growing up around Mazan may have resembled less the Burgundian Cistercians than the Grandmontines or Carthusians, who also seem to have emphasized the less labor-intensive activities of animal husbandry. But Mazan did not combine this intensive care of animals with a fierce dread of religious women as was apparently the case for Grandmont, whose founder Stephen of Muret moved his hermitage because of the proximity of women.[81] Instead, Mazan seems to have exploited the possibilities offered by pastoralism to serve the special needs of women's houses, which often had too few laborers and usually more strict enclosure.[82] This point is discussed in Chapter 4 with regard to Nonenque.

While pastoralism was something taken up in combination with agriculture by such new reformers as the Cistercians even in Burgundy, the idea was apparently pushed much further in the Midi, because of the suitability of the terrain there. In the case of the daughters of Mazan the possibilities provided by the landscape for short-distance transhumance appear to have been the organizing principle around which Mazan's congregation was built.[83] Moreover, whereas "Cistercian" economic systems that introduced lay-brothers and granges may have been ultimately more successful, or at least served as an alternative to sole dependence on pastoralism, such pastoral activities as are suggested here are important because the initial cash needed for Cistercian consolidation of land on which to establish grange agriculture often must have come from the sale of animals and animal production.[84] By the late twelfth century, the most successful Cistercian houses of this region were those which, like Valmagne or Fontfroide, had mixed the transhumant pastoralism for which this region offered such important potential with the more traditionally "Cistercian" exploitation of granges worked by lay-brothers.

While it is likely that pastoralism provided the cash that fueled the later acquisition of granges, what is rarely discussed is whether the fact of their extensive pastoralism, often supplemented at first only by gardening in the immediate vicinity of their sites, does not also explain the extensive papal grants of exemption from tithes made to so many new religious communities in the twelfth century. Exemption from tithes on animals was personal, granted to the owner of those animals; tithes on the cultivation of fields, gardens, and vines were predial, that is, based on specific land-holdings, often land-holdings whose tithes were intended to support parish churches.[85] If those papal grants were made because such new groups were primarily practicing pastoralism rather than agriculture, the grants were much less of a threat to established tithe-holders and other landed interests.

We cannot date precisely the attachment of Mazan's congregation to the Cistercian abbey of Bonnevaux in the diocese of Vienne, but it was probably only sometime in the third quarter of the twelfth century. But Bonnevaux's creation of a congregation of houses parallels and confirms in many ways the view of the creation of networks within the early Cistercian Order that has been presented here in discussing Mazan and its congregation. Bonnevaux, which it will be recalled was founded by Guy of Burgundy, archbishop of Vienne, just before he became Pope Calixtus II (1119–24), was in many senses still a Burgundian house, although it was created just beyond the boundaries of Burgundy. When it began attaching a network of daughter-houses to itself, Bonnevaux did so by attaching proto-Cistercian houses and congregations like those at Mazan or Valmagne in southern France and others further north.

In southern France, the earliest of its daughters was possibly a genuine foundation made at Léoncel in 1137. Located in an elevated valley used for summer pasture that is reached even today only with some difficulty, Léoncel may at first glance seem to wholly confirm traditional notions of the Cistercian "desert" site. Its granges, however, were located in previously settled and considerably more accessible locations. The monks of Léoncel, moreover, like their pastoralists and the animals that created their wealth, would themselves practice a type of transhumance. After 1194 when they absorbed the priory of Pardieu, Léoncel's monks and their animals descended from the high valley where their abbey was located to spend the winter months at their second, and more clement, site at Pardieu in the Rhône valley.[86] It is likely that Léoncel was founded before the incorporation of Mazan, despite the early dates for the latter on the filiation trees.

There are indications that Bonnevaux, once having attached houses like Léoncel, acted very similarly to the congregation of Mazan in using its daughter-houses like Léoncel as part of a network of transhumance by which animals and pasture rights were moved seasonally from one region to another.[87] In such a network, Bonnevaux's attachment of Valmagne may be because of the latter's site near major urban centers on the Languedoc plain. The abbey of Valmagne was attached to Bonnevaux's filiation sometime in the 1160s or later. As discussed in more detail in Chapter 4, Valmagne was originally part of a double-community that included a women's house at le Vignogoul, both on the Languedoc coast near Montpellier. Both were probably founded by Ardorel's abbot. Ardorel's ties to Valmagne gradually faded, but were still in evidence in the 1150s. This makes the traditional dates for Valmagne's incorporation by Bonnevaux, 1152 or 1155, too early. They do not accord with the Valmagne cartulary evidence, which shows that its donors still perceived Valmagne as wavering about being Cistercian right up to at least 1161. This is discussed in the next chapter with regard to Valmagne's grange at Canvern and its hospice in Montpellier.[88] Bonnevaux may have been tempted by Valmagne as a daughter-house because Valmagne was becoming one of the richest Cistercian houses in the entire south of France.[89]

Besides Valmagne and its associated women's houses, and Mazan and its congregation, two other southern-French houses of monks came to be attached to Bonnevaux in the late twelfth century. Both these attachments to Bonnevaux, like some of those to Mazan, are explained by the context of transhumant pastoralism in this region. Except as centers for pastoralism, these daughter-houses cannot have offered great advantages to the monks of Bonnevaux. One, the house of monks originally located in the diocese of Arles at Ulmet in the Camargue, was either founded or attached in 1173. Its original site was poor and by 1240 its monks had moved to a new site at Sauveréal in the Camargue, the more usual name for the community.[90] A second house for monks, Valcroissant in the diocese of Die, was founded or attached to Bonnevaux in 1188. Valcroissant too was a community whose late foundation provided it with little endowment or even rights to pasture that could have led to its success. Ironically enough, the church and parts of other conventual buildings still stand and are described by Dimier.[91] The power of its mother-abbey at Bonnevaux within the General Chapter undoubtedly explains the later appropriation of properties belonging to a community of Cistercian nuns at Bonlieu nearby, who were suppressed and their endowment given for Valcroissant's economic support.[92]

Bonnevaux attached and founded other abbeys farther north, making of its daughters a virtual filiation, as has been remarked recently in discussions of Cistercian networks.[93] In addition to its strong emphasis on pastoralism as a component of its economic life, seen particularly in the attachment of the congregation of Mazan, Bonnevaux's "filiation" would come to include a large number of women's houses.[94]

Western-French Congregations

We can also trace ties of incorporation between what would become southern-French Cistercian houses in the later twelfth century and eremitical congregations founded in the Midi by western-French reformers like Gerald of Salles or Vidal of Savigny. There were no Savigniac houses in the Midi, but a number of foundations there claimed foundation or early affiliation by Gerald of Salles, usually identified as an early companion of Robert of Arbrissel. Such foundations in the Midi by this western-French reform movement were often communities for both men and women created by wandering preacher-hermits like Robert of Arbrissel, who had founded Fontevrault, and Stephen of Obazine, whose monastery was entered by entire families but would eventually become an abbey for monks at Obazine and an associated one for nuns at nearby Coyroux.[95] A number of such women's houses in southern France, like Lespinasse, which seems to have been paired with Grandselve at the outset, would be attached not to the Cistercians but to Fontevrault.[96] The history of such double-houses or family monasteries in this region has often been lost because of our tendency to observe the reform movement from the viewpoint of the particular order to which individual communities were ultimately attached. Men's and women's houses of what was originally a double-house often ended up entering different orders, and a recognition of their earlier relationship is lost because it seems to have been purposely covered up in narratives such as that for Silvanès, which denied its equality with Nonenque.[97]

The story of southern-French reform houses that had been attached to western-French congregations before being attached to the Cistercians usually begins with the wandering preacher, Gerald of Salles.[98] Gerald founded the abbey of Cadouin in the Dordogne in 1113 and that of Dalon in the Corrèze in the next year. These foundations were gradually followed by his foundation or affiliation of other reform houses in western France and the southwest. The evidence for what happened after Gerald's death in 1120 is extreme fragmentary. Cadouin and Dalon each seem to have created a congregation, all of whose members were in the 1140s, 1150s, and 1160s drifting toward the adoption of Cistercian practices. The Dalon cartulary suggests that the distinction between its congregation and that of Cadouin may be that Dalon and its daughters had been attached at some point after 1120 to Obazine.[99] The disorganization of their early archives, typical of such early eremitical foundations, however, means there are few secure dates. We know little about either the foundation of houses within these congregations, or how they came to be affiliated first to Cadouin and Dalon, and later to the Cistercians.

Daughters of Dalon and Cadouin in the Midi (see Figure 31) were eventually attached to either Pontigny or Clairvaux. These included the pre-Cistercian abbey for monks at Locdieu that had been founded in the western Rouergue in 1124. It was created with the cooperation of the bishop of Rodez, who gave a group of churches for its support.[100] Locdieu has a surviving church in Gothic style, which suggests that by the thirteenth century it had become somewhat more successful than it appears to have been earlier.[101] But sometime around 1177 Locdieu was suppressed by Bonneval and its granges used in an elaborate exchange of pastoral lands on the Aubrac plateau, by which Bonneval created one area of sole control and the military-religious orders another. Only in 1212 was Dalon able to reinstate Locdieu as an independent daughter-house.[102]

An even more obscure daughter-house of Dalon in the Midi was les Feuillants, located south of Toulouse. Eventually it was assigned as a daughter-house for visitation by Locdieu's abbots, but there is no reason to think that it had been founded by Locdieu.[103] That Locdieu and les Feuillants were both given incorporation dates of 1162 on the Pontigny filiation tree suggests how arbitrary are such dates; all Dalon's daughters were given 1162 as the date at which they, apparently as an entire congregation, were attached to Pontigny. This merely parallels Cadouin's claim that 1147 was the date when its daughter-houses were all attached to Pontigny. As for such claims by Cadouin, we have mentioned already that at least one of its daughters in southern France, Ar-

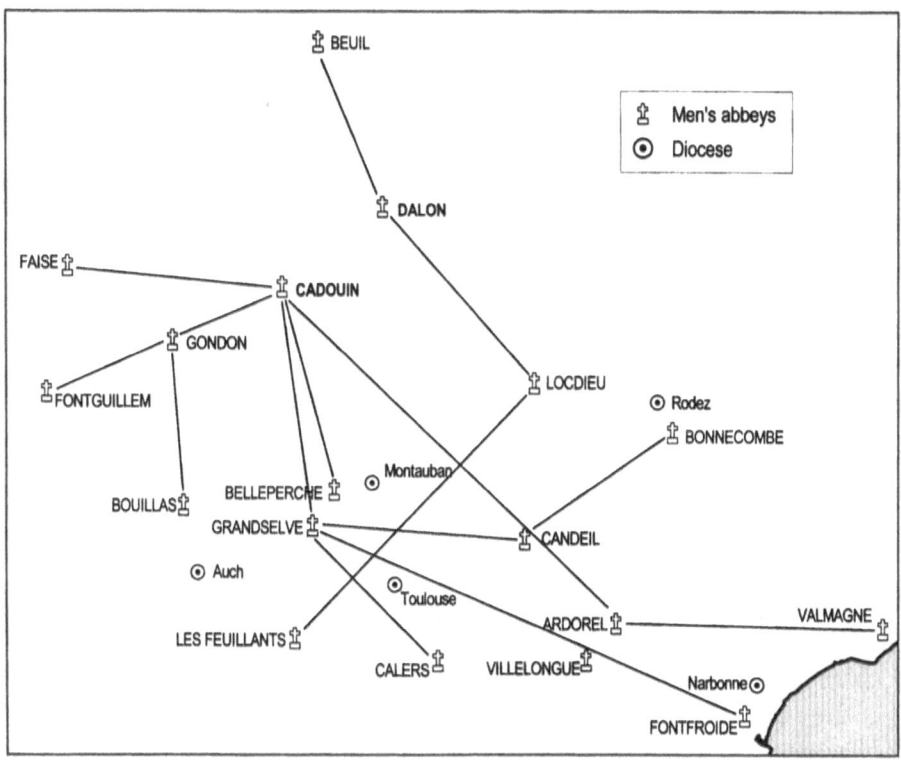

Figure 31. Cistercian houses with ties to western-French congregations in the Midi.

dorel, was not yet Cistercian even in 1157—as is shown by charters from its daughter-house at Valmagne.[104] In 1147, moreover, there was, as yet, no Order to which to be attached. The year seems to have been a particularly important one for papal confirmations, which later may have been seen as evidence for such attachments.[105]

Also tied to Pontigny by the intermediaries of Dalon and Cadouin were Fontguilhem and le Rivet, both founded in the 1120s in the diocese of Bordeaux; their incorporation by the Cistercians dated to 1147.[106] Pontaut in the diocese of Adour of the western Pyrenees claimed attachment to Cadouin between 1115 and 1125, and to the Cistercians from 1150.[107] An abbey of monks at Vielle or Divielle in the diocese of Dax may have had a similar eremitical origin and attachment to Cadouin; its Cistercian ties were shed in 1209 when it became Praemonstratensian.[108] Clariana or le Jau in the diocese of Elne was associated with Cadouin and is treated in filiation trees as a daughter of Ardorel, but other facts are unknown.[109] Ardorel had been founded about 1124 as a hermitage on the northern slopes of the Montagne Noire in the Albigeois; it was eventually attached to the filiation of Pontigny by the intermediary of Cadouin, but the date of 1147 is incorrect.[110]

Most of the houses mentioned in the preceding paragraph were small communities, marginal as to endowment and packed too tightly into the landscape, as Barrière discusses at length.[111] This was a region where overcrowding of pre-Cistercian reform houses was rife. These houses for monks were all located in an area in southwestern France that was nearly devoid of Cistercian women's houses, perhaps because many of its houses of nuns became associated with Fontevrault. For many of these houses of pre-Cistercian monks and hermits, records are all but nonexistent; if there are any for the women's houses, they have not often been consulted. None were rich or powerful, and few have left enough records about their early history to tell us how they came to be attached to the western French reformers. Yet each of these pre-Cistercian abbeys for monks and nuns had a history as a place of local reform and recruitment. Many of the men's houses were associated at the outset as double communities with houses of nuns, like that at Boulaur, which was tied to Fontevrault but today has been refounded as a house of Cistercian nuns. For Boulaur we find references in the medieval cartulary for nearby Gimont.[112] In addition to abbeys associated with western French reformers and hence to Pontigny or Clairvaux, there were those eventually attached to Morimond; see below, Figure 35.

Three houses in this region split away from those western-French reformers at an early date; they claimed to have attached themselves directly to Bernard of Clairvaux during his preaching tour to the south in 1145. These houses at Grandselve, Belloc, and Belleperche have some claim to having adopted Cistercian practices or been attached to Clairvaux from a very early date, although probably not 1145. Of these, Grandselve and its daughter-abbey at Fontfroide had considerably more economic success than other houses having ties to western-French reformers; it is more difficult to tell whether that was so for Belloc and Belleperche as well.

The association with Bernard of Clairvaux may explain a slightly different pattern of ties to women's houses than among other western French reform houses. As we have shown earlier in this chapter, there is considerable evidence that Bernard of Clairvaux was supportive of women's communities. But it is notable that, when his successors came to affiliate houses of monks in this region, abbots of Clairvaux (unlike those of Bonnevaux or possibly even those of Morimond) seem to have avoided attaching those pre-Cistercian houses associated with women. The idea that Bernard did not support monastic women (however untrue) may in fact have begun to be developed quite quickly by his successors at Clairvaux, who seem to have expanded any negative comments he had made about women into a reputation for him of misogyny.[113] While Belloc and Belleperche apparently had no early association with women's communities in the region, Grandselve is noteworthy in that, having broken away from a double community in the first place, that of Lespinasse, it did not subsequently have ties to women's communities. Even when donors attempted to get it to found a house for nuns and gave it gifts for that purpose, it did not do so.[114] That Grandselve's daughter-house at Fontfroide did annex priories of women was more an artifact of its "imperialistic" annexation of every priory in sight; more important is that it founded no houses for women itself. Did rejection of women's houses somehow get tied in with the reputations of Grandselve and Fontfroide as centers in the fight against heresy?[115]

Belloc is said to have originally been founded in the western reaches of the Rouergue with the support of a bishop of Rodez who gave it a number of churches, but bishops giving churches to support the Cistercians is a cliché with regard to that diocese. As elsewhere, those bishops were probably assenting to the transfer by lay owners of parish churches long out of episcopal control to a new monastic foundation.[116] Belloc claims to have been attached to the Cistercian practices by Bernard of Clairvaux himself, but few documents survive to support this assertion.[117] That this abbey was fairly successful in its economic adoption to conditions in the region between the massif central and Toulouse, however, is suggested by its surviving church, which is a significant example of transitional Gothic.[118]

Belleperche was a similar community north of Toulouse with ties to western-French reformers. It probably originated as a hermitage at a site called Belleperticula, which may be that of the bastide of Larrazet, and later moved closer to the Garonne River.[119] Belleperche's original foundation is attributed to Gerald of Salles, but the abbey also claimed to have been attached to Cistercian practices by Bernard of Clairvaux in the 1140s. Belleperche's records, which survive almost only in copies made by the Doat Commission, mention permission from Bernard of Clairvaux for a site change, but this is a misreading of its early documents — those that concern transfers of property for the site change are dated to 1164; Bernard of Clairvaux had of course died in 1153.[120] That a later abbot of Clairvaux, the mother-house for Belleperche, may have approved the site change, and even that Bernard himself may have visited Belleperche on his famous preaching mission to the Midi, are both more likely, but undocumented.[121]

Only for Grandselve have we positive evidence to show that this pre-Cistercian foundation made by Gerald of Salles, or possibly by Robert of Arbrissel himself, had come to the attention of Bernard of Clairvaux. Documents for Grandselve's earliest years are few, but a wealth of charters from the mid- and late twelfth century have survived. Some of these provide clues about when Grandselve became attached to Clairvaux and eventually to the Cistercian Order—probably two distinct events. The *Vita* of Gerald of Salles claims that Gerald founded Grandselve in 1114, but references in southern-French manuscripts suggest a foundation dating to 1117, describing it as a hermitage dedicated to the Virgin Mary and to Saint-Mary-Magdalene.[122] These dedications suggest its ties to Robert of Arbrissel and Fontevrault, a suggestion that is strengthened when we observe that Grandselve's foundation date in 1117 coincided with that for the nearby house of nuns at Lespinasse, later attached to the Order of Fontevrault.[123] It is likely that a double community at Lespinasse was the source from which priests and monks departed to found a separate abbey for monks at Grandselve. Lespinasse and Grandselve were distinct communities by 1130 when the bishop of Toulouse granted Grandselve two churches.[124] Papal confirmation of Grandselve's possessions in 1142, including the churches and parishes of Riquersella, Beaumont, Bouillac, and Saint-Germain, as well as granges at Comberoger, Coubirac, and Banols, did not yet mention Cistercians.[125] A document for 1143 suggests that Grandselve's abbot Bertrand had by then affiliated the house of monks at Fontfroide, but again there is no mention of the Cistercians.[126]

The affiliation of Grandselve to Clairvaux is usually attributed to Bernard's preaching mission in 1145 and documented by his letters.[127] Dated charters for Grandselve that mention the Cistercian Order first appear in 1161, but undated ones mentioning Cistercians and the abbot Pons (1158–65) may come from as early as 1158.[128] Affiliation of Grandselve to Clairvaux probably dates to abbot Alexander (1150–58), or to the late 1140s under abbot Bertrand, who was a local reformer of some renown.[129] The mid-century abbot Alexander of Grandselve has been identified as Alexander of Cologne, one of Bernard's associates who may have been a student with Bernard and have entered Cîteaux at the same time. Alexander was apparently sent to Grandselve by Bernard of Clairvaux on the reformer Bertrand's death. From there he moved on become abbot of Savigny (1158–68); he was then elected abbot of Cîteaux in 1168, where he apparently served until his death in 1175.

We see epitomized in Alexander's career as abbot the gradual transformation of this reform movement from a congregation of abbeys focusing primarily on Clairvaux and its abbot Bernard into an international Order. Indeed, whereas it may have been normal for a monk to be sent from Clairvaux to be abbot of a reformed house, and for an abbot to move laterally from one daughter-house of an abbey like Clairvaux to another—as we see in Alexander's move from Grandselve to Savigny—more significant was the shift in the curriculum vitae of this abbot with his election to the abbacy of Cîteaux itself. This election might be construed as evidence that the religious movement of which Alexander was a part was no longer an exclusively Clarevallian congregation. Alexander's leadership of important incorporated houses such as Grandselve and Savigny, and then of Cîteaux itself, at the very least suggests that he was one of the possible inventors of the Cistercian Order and of its constitution in the 1160s—an invention that, although attributed to Stephen Harding and to the first decades of the twelfth century, was indeed carried out in the third quarter of the century.[130]

Early gifts for Grandselve suggest that its support came both from local bourgeois and from knightly families gaining power in the Midi. For instance, grants to this abbey to create and endow a hospice in Toulouse are found in the cartulary of the Capdenier family, important members of the city patriciate of Toulouse.[131] More significant is the mid-twelfth-century retirement to Grandselve of the powerful lord William VI of Montpellier. Bernard of Clairvaux seems to have been William's inspiration for the latter's adult conversion to the religious life, and comments about William in the *Vita Prima* tradition confirm Grandselve's links to Clairvaux.[132]

Both bourgeois and knightly patrons must have aided Grandselve's early economic success. Grandselve soon outstripped the abbeys of Belloc and Belleperche not only in its accumulation of endowment and political power within the Order, but also in the creation of copies of charters, which have helped to assure their survival in some form. The massive surviving archives for Grandselve have allowed a description of its granges in great detail by Mireille Mousnier.[133] My own analysis elsewhere of this abbey suggests that the diversity of its granges allowed it to survive agricultural risk in ways that smaller abbeys and peasant farmers could not. It also obviously profited from the growth of demand in nearby towns not only for wheat, wine, and meat, but for raw materials needed in growing industries.[134]

By the end of the twelfth century, Grandselve had attracted the patronage of the Angevin dukes of Aquitaine and kings of England, who granted it important rights along the Garonne River, allowing Grandselve's wine to be shipped toll-free to the port of Bordeaux, as well as allowing salt granted by those kings from their own salt-pans at Bordeaux to be transported up the Garonne valley without toll.[135] Its links to the city of Toulouse, close ties to the leadership of the emerging Cistercian Order, an active campaign of foundation of new towns called bastides in the thirteenth century, and exemptions from tolls for its newly emphasized viticulture, all added to Grandselve's power.

Grandselve had several daughter-houses nearby in Gascony and also attached the monks of Sanctas Cruces in Spain.[136] By 1147 or 1148, Grandselve had a daughter-house at Calers, in the Ariège south of Toulouse, which may have been a genuine foundation. But Calers would be unlucky in its location and never really accumulated the resources with which to compete with the granges and other properties of other reform houses in the vicinity. Indeed, the most substantial documentation for the early history of Calers comes from the *convenientiae* that survive recording agreements about the division of pasture rights between Calers and other nearby religious houses. They reveal its participation in a transhumant pastoralism in the Pyrenees similar to that already discussed with regard to Mazan and its congregation further to the east; Grandselve's animals may have shared with those of Calers in such seasonal pastoralism.[137] For Calers, however, this activity was often hedged in by its more aggressive neighbors. Like Grandselve, Calers would found bastides on some of its grange lands in the thirteenth century, but whereas Grandselve's efforts seem to have been motivated by a desire to profit from increased local demand for labor-intensive viticultural products, Calers apparently founded bastides because it could not recruit sufficient laborers to work its granges.

More successful was Grandselve's daughter founded in 1152 in the forest of Candeil in the Albigeois, the abbey of Candeil. The abbey and church of Candeil no longer stand, but they were restored for the first time following the Albigensian Crusade. The Peace of Paris in 1229 enjoined on Raymond VII the rebuilding of Candeil's church, destroyed in that war, so this count has been mistakenly identified as Candeil's founder.[138] Candeil quickly established itself in a niche of the Albigeois where reform competitors were few. At the end of the twelfth century it received a gift from Eleanor of Aquitaine intended for the foundation of a house in memory of her son Richard the Lionhearted.[139] The house was apparently never founded, although somewhat earlier, in 1162, Candeil had created a daughter-house at Bonnecombe in the Rouergue.[140]

Bonnecombe itself was very adept at land acquisition as well as local politics, creating a network of granges in the central Rouergue and eastern Albigeois, participating in the region's transhumance, and maintaining close ties to urban markets.[141] The virtual suppression in 1177 of the abbey of Locdieu by neighboring Bonneval could have done no harm in the central Rouergue to Bonnecombe's shepherds, either. In addition, in 1178 Bonnecombe purchased rights to pasture in the central Rouergue from Bonneval and Mazan.[142]

At the outset, Bonnecombe had profited from the heavy indebtedness of the family of the counts of Rodez, who had apparently purchased their position from the counts of Toulouse and the Rouergue with cash borrowed against mortgages held by their knights and castle-holders. Many properties held under mortgage by local lords from those twelfth-century counts of Rodez came into the hands of Bonnecombe's monks.[143] The friendship of Bonnecombe's abbot with the counts of Toulouse at the time of the Albigensian Crusade in the thirteenth century may have caused trouble for that abbot in the Order's General Chapter when the count was excommunicated, but it yielded Bonnecombe handsome grants of pasture rights and livestock in Raymond VI's will.[144] It may have also been through friendships with the counts of Toulouse that a grange at Bernac in the Albigeois was established by Bonnecombe in close cooperation with Sicard Alaman, chief officer of that count.[145]

Grandselve's most important daughter-house was Fontfroide. In its earliest guise, Fontfroide is described as a tiny struggling house of monks founded in 1093 on lands given by Viscount Aimeric of Narbonne. The abbey had to be virtually refounded by Ermengardis, viscountess and ruler of Narbonne, in the mid-twelfth century. The dating of Fontfroide's attachment to Cistercian practices is difficult to determine, but, as discussed above, the abbey was probably attached to Grandselve in 1143 just before Bernard of Clairvaux's visit to Toulouse in 1145.[146]

Despite its isolated site, Fontfroide grew to become one of the most powerful Cistercian houses in the Mediterranean world, willing to dispute the claims of the archbishop of Narbonne when it so chose.[147] Fontfroide's affiliation in 1155 of a community of hermits at Poblet in the diocese of Tarragona linked it to a group of other Spanish houses that eventually became Cistercian.[148] It was probably very important to the success of both Fontfroide and Grandselve that their ties to Cistercian practice came at a time when existing eremitical houses beyond the Pyrenees were beginning to seek attachment to the Cistercians. But we are only beginning to evaluate the ways twelfth-century Cistercians expanded by incorporations beyond the Pyrenees. Fontfroide's site was close to rich viticultural lands, and (as seen in Figure 32) its diverse granges allowed considerable agricultural production. Many were created by the annexation of earlier groups. Indeed, Fontfroide may stand as the epitome of self-aggrandizing Cistercian houses where decisions to create additional granges rather than found new abbeys seem to have been based on self-interest rather than prudence alone.

Annexations by Fontfroide included two priories that housed both men and women, at Sainte-Eugénie and Montlaurès, which had been associated with an earlier Italian Piedmont community at Saint-Michel-de-Cluse. The first of these, the priory of Sainte-Eugénie, had begun as a community of lay-brothers and lay-sisters near Narbonne but then moved to Sainte-Eugénie near Peyriac-sur-Mer. As I discuss in Chapter 5, in 1189 the personnel were incorporated into Fontfroide and their properties converted into a series of

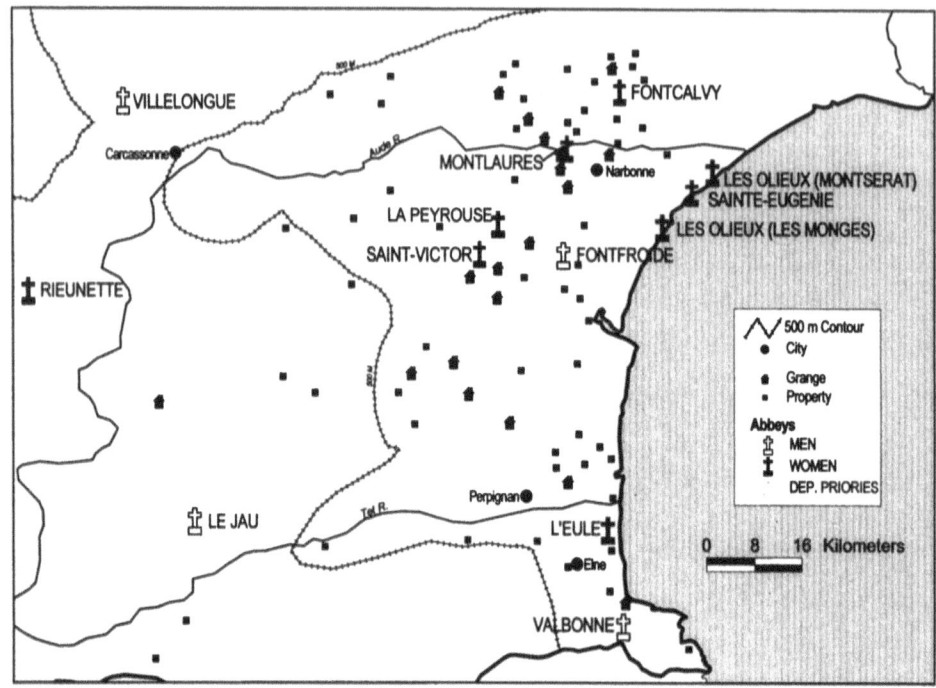

Figure 32. Granges and absorbed priories of the Cistercian house for monks at Fontfroide.

granges. The lay-sisters were established at a dependent priory of nuns at les Olieux-de-Montsérat.[149] The second priory, Montlaurès, was located just north of Fontfroide itself; its church and abbey were absorbed as a grange in 1211.[150] The house of nuns at la Peyrouse or Levrettes associated with Montlaurès — a community that had been there for more than a century — were transformed into a dependent priory; eventually its nuns seceded from the Cistercian Order in 1254 to become regular canonesses.[151] A third reform house annexed by Fontfroide, one for which there are still notable remains, was the attempted foundation of Templar-knights made at Fontcalvy north of Narbonne in the early 1180s. That property was sold by local knights and the archbishop of Narbonne to Fontfroide between 1199 and 1203.[152]

Fontfroide also seems to have attached a series of houses of nuns with ties to local bourgeois founders, founders who reflect perhaps another source of otherwise hidden patronage for both Fontfroide and its female dependencies. These priories of nuns included a house at l'Eule or Aula in the diocese of Elne near Perpignan, close to Fontfroide's olive-producing properties shared with

Grandselve and Gimont. That house had been founded by Jean Homme-de-Dieu, bourgeois of Perpignan in 1174. In 1264 it became an abbey and *filia* of Fontfroide. By 1567 it had been suppressed and its properties transformed into a priory of men dependent on Grandselve's daughter-house of Sanctas Cruces in Spain.[153]

A second community of women attached to Fontfroide, called les Olieux, was sometimes confused with the priory of les Olieux at Montsérat that had once belonged to Sainte-Eugénie. This Sainte-Marie-des-Olieux was founded in 1204 at a place called les Monges near the coastal lagoons outside the city of Narbonne on land given by Jean Bistan, a bourgeois of Narbonne. What we know about the nuns of this and other priories of women attached to Fontfroide is mostly limited to the remains of their churches. At les Monges, les Olieux's church still stands, although it is now used as a barn. It has a rectangular single nave measuring 13 by 27 meters and is divided into three identical rib-vaulted bays separated by engaged arches. In addition to a doorway on the west side, les Olieux has the characteristic southern doorway for access from the nuns' courtyard into the church found at other such churches for nuns in this region; see Figure 33. There is a single window on each side and the flat east end has three lancet windows, but no articulation of chapels. The roof made of tiles lies directly on the vault; see Figure 34.[154] Its tiny size stands in obvious contrast to the buildings at Fontfroide, as discussed in Chapter 1.

Fontfroide's abbots clearly had little tolerance for competition from even the tiniest reform community in their vicinity, attempting to swallow up every possible rival to their increasingly exclusive religious rights in the countryside around Narbonne. Fontfroide's annexation of rival houses into its extensive system of granges and other properties is particularly obvious from the abbey's own account of its annexation of the hermitage at Saint-Victor of Montveyre — a tiny cell located in the valley next to and parallel to Fontfroide's near the castle of Fontjoncouse. This hermitage had probably once been a cell of Saint-Victor of Marseilles.[155] Abandoned, it was refounded in the 1190s with the approval of both viscount and archbishop of Narbonne as well as of Pope Innocent III, but apparently without notifying Fontfroide. A dispute soon arose between Fontfroide and Peter of Lerce, founder of Montveyre, who was described as a renegade monk or lay-brother of Fontfroide. "Although under the censure of the abbot of Fontfroide," as a document produced by Fontfroide tells us, this Peter was finally readmitted to the abbey of nearby Fontfroide. Whether Peter had simply left Fontfroide with the support of the powerful, or with his followers had founded Montveyre independently, is not clear. By 1203, Peter and his followers had been incorporated by Fontfroide, and Montveyre was reduced to a grange.[156]

Figure 33. Church for Cistercian nuns at les Olieux, exterior, south door.

Figure 34. Les Olieux, exterior, north side.

In this fashion the abbey of Fontfroide in the late twelfth century became extremely powerful, as it gradually engulfed all the smaller independent reform communities of the entire Narbonnais. By reducing men's houses to granges and women's houses to dependent priories, Fontfroide soon became the sole Cistercian house in the region.[157] Its rapid absorption of property and religious obligations, and also of new personnel from incorporated priories, must have led to internal conflict such as is seen in this "secession" by Peter of Lerce, or in the many conversi revolts documented in the General Chapter statutes from the thirteenth century.[158]

Fontfroide's later medieval success can probably only be understood with regard to its contributions to preaching against heretics in southern France. Although it is unlikely that Fontfroide provided any good answer to criticisms by such heretics about the Church's excessive wealth, even before the Albigensian Crusade the abbey had provided monks, including the papal legate Peter of Castelnau, to preach against what was perceived as an increased threat of Cathar heresy. Fontfroide, like other local houses of Cistercians in this region, profited from donations from local families concerned to prove their orthodoxy by support of the Cistercians, as well as by acquiring confiscated Cathar properties at later dates.[159] Given the arrogance and litigiousness of its abbeys when dealing with old and new monastic neighbors, we should not be too surprised that Peter might have been so uncompromising as to have provoked his own murder—the event that set off the Albigensian Crusade the next year, in 1209.[160]

Fontfroide, like other Cistercian houses in this region, engaged in extensive animal husbandry. Its shepherds moved large numbers of sheep up to summer pastures in the heights of the Pyrenees. These pastures were often within sight of the Cathar strongholds still visible on the high crags today. One must wonder whether some of the conversi revolts at Fontfroide were precipitated by contact between the abbey's lay-brothers, who would have been away from the abbey for long periods of time as shepherds, and Cathar preachers in that area.[161]

Of all houses with ties linking them back to western-French reformers, this daughter of Grandselve was most economically and politically successful. Whether some of the qualities that led to the success of Fontfroide and that of its mother-house at Grandselve were what led to their being attached to Clairvaux from an early date is more difficult to discern. What is clear is that Fontfroide exemplifies, if perhaps in exaggerated style, the benefits of incorporation, of the Order's political position in preaching against Cathar heretics, and of the careful adaptation of a mixed pastoral and agricultural economy for the economic and political success of the Cistercians. But such activities must also have led to increasing denunciations of Cistercian wealth and avarice.

Walter of Morimond in Gascony

Morimond's "foundations" in southern France provide evidence of a different aspect of Cistercian growth by incorporation. Given the characterization of Morimond as a poor monastery with almost no resources in the early twelfth century, I should have been surprised to have been able to argue, as I did in an earlier publication, that three communities in Gascony, at Berdoues, Bonnefont, and l'Escaledieu, had all been attached to Morimond by the early 1140s as the result of a preaching mission (similar to that later undertaken by Bernard of Clairvaux) by Walter, second abbot of Morimond, who had earlier been prior at Clairvaux.[162] These three houses were probably all hermitages incorporated by the Cistercians; they have similar dates on the filiation trees, and references in the documents for Berdoues and Bonnefont mention Walter, abbot of Morimond. This association still suggests to me an active program of attachment. But looked at from the viewpoint not only of southern France but of Burgundy, it is likely that if there was a preaching tour by an abbot of Morimond to attach abbeys in southern France, that mission was undertaken not in the second quarter of the century but in the third, and by a second abbot Walter of Morimond during the 1160s or 1170s.[163] Early Morimond was apparently so impoverished that it was virtually a dependency of Clairvaux. Its situation was so weak that the framers of the first Cistercian constitution of 1165, the *Summa Cartae Caritatis*, and even those who revised it into the *Carta Caritatis Prior*, did not include Morimond's abbot as one of the abbots of the earliest daughter-houses of Cîteaux designated as proto-abbots in charge of oversight of Cîteaux itself.[164] Could Morimond have sent its abbot in the 1130s or 1140s on such a mission to incorporate houses in the Midi? Particularly after an earlier abbot had been censured and deposed by Bernard for attempting to go off to found a new house in the Levant? And could the secular authorities really have been so thick on the ground at Berdoues's foundation as the charters suggest? Or is the implication that they were all there at the same time a later reconstruction of events?

The Morimond evidence for the early twelfth century is fragmentary. But in addition to Walter, the former prior of Clairvaux (1126–31), sent to Morimond from Clairvaux in the 1130s after the first abbot Arnold was deposed by Bernard, there was another abbot Walter in 1161–62.[165]

The bulk of the evidence for the attachments of proto-Cistercian houses and their congregations at Berdoues, l'Escaledieu, and Bonnefont to the Cistercians in the 1130s or 1140s rather than later is found in three acts (probably not original charters, but actes-notices) in the Berdoues cartulary. These actes-notices describe foundation events at Berdoues from what is probably the viewpoint of at least a generation later. They tell us that Bernard, count of Astarac, and his son Sanche made a gift for the construction of an abbey to Walter, abbot of Morimond, "of land at Berdoues and the church in that *casale*."[166] In a second document Walter, abbot of Morimond, and William, archbishop of Auch, again appear with Bernard, count of Astarac, but without Sanche.[167] In a third act Raymond Senex, who is called "abbot of Berdoues" (of an existing community there?), gave the site of the new abbey of Berdoues to Walter of Morimond.[168] Such documents thus list an earlier leader of the eremitical community, as well as William, archbishop of Auch, who was papal legate; the count of Astarac and his son; and all the knights of the region appearing together; the last to grant pasture rights in "all their lands" by acclaim. It is likely that these documents collapse into one moment the events of a longer period. In comparison to the usual gifts for the foundation of a new abbey Berdoues's contracts seem to have collected considerably more witnesses, both ecclesiastical and secular, than would have been normal in the creation of a new abbey in the 1140s.

In these documents from the Berdoues cartulary purporting to have been made at the time of the foundation at Berdoues, we also find Forton of Vic, usually cited as the lay-founder of neighboring l'Escaledieu, and Bernard of la Barthe, usually cited as the first abbot of l'Escaledieu. Whether or not they were present at the foundation of Berdoues, this suggests that there was a tradition that l'Escaledieu had been incorporated by Morimond slightly earlier than was Berdoues. The bare crumbs that can be gathered about l'Escaledieu are almost entirely unsusceptible of any proof. It is said to have begun as a hermitage founded by Centullus, count of Bigorre, and his daughter Beatrix, for a hermit named Bernard at a place called Cabadour in the valley of Campan in the high Pyrénées; this hermitage was given to Forton of Vic in 1137. The hermits then moved north in 1142 from the original site at Cabadour to settle in the lower, more suitable valley of Bonnemazan on land donated by the prior of Saint-Christophe.[169]

The coincidence of location on the filiation trees for Morimond's daughters Berdoues and l'Escaledieu also encompasses Bonnefont-en-Comminges. Bonnefont originated as a hermitage founded on land where a Hospitaller foundation had been attempted in 1122, but failed.[170] Two acts dated to 1136 and 1137 purport to be the twelfth-century donations for the Cistercian foundation of Bonnefont, but these are obviously later confections. They tell us that Flandrina of Montpezat and her sons, castellans of the fortress of Montpezat, "gave the site for Bonnefont" and mention "brothers sent by the abbot Walter of Morimond."[171] Neither piece of information is true: there was no colonization from Burgundy, no attachment to Cistercians in 1136–37. The family name Montpezat may be a local one, but it may also be borrowed from among patron names for Gimont.[172] Although there was possibly an attachment to Morimond by an abbot Walter of Morimond, it is not likely to have been in the 1130s.[173] While pre-Cistercian hermitages may have been founded at those places in the 1130s, Berdoues, Bonnefont, and l'Escaledieu are more likely to have been attached to Morimond somewhat later.

That these houses were listed close to one another and given an early date on the filiation trees of the thirteenth century probably has more to do with the large congregations they brought to Morimond than with such an early incorporation — as I suggested above with regard to the attachment of Mazan to Bonnevaux and Cadouin to Pontigny. Indeed, substantial congregations of abbeys located both in Gascony and beyond the Pyrenees would have been added if these three houses were incorporated in the 1170s or 1180s; see Figure 35, which shows what these three congregations would have looked like in 1175. That these were eremitical attachments made to Morimond is without doubt; only the date of attachment is in question. That the congregations came into existence before their attachment to Morimond, however, seems most likely.

From Cîteaux to the Invention of a Cistercian Order

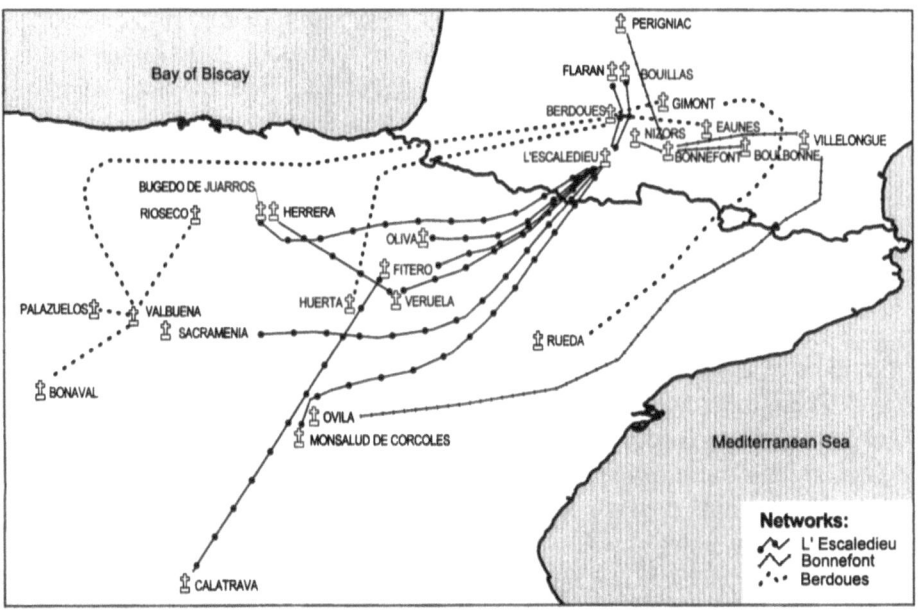

Figure 35. Congregations in Gascony and beyond the Pyrénées attached to Morimond.

Indeed, the attraction for Morimond in attaching these three houses was precisely because they brought with them whole congregations — a total of twenty-six houses for monks and an uncounted number of houses of nuns (uncountable because their history, if recoverable, has still to be noted in the compendia that list houses of Cistercians). These were not simply three communities of monks attached by Morimond at the end of the third quarter of the twelfth century, but a substantial increase to its filiation. The addition of these, if in 1175, came at a critical moment in what must have been a campaign for Morimond's abbot to be elevated to "proto-abbot" status with oversight of Cîteaux. As has been suggested, only the incorporation of considerable numbers of existing communities and congregations could have allowed the abbot of Morimond to transform himself into the fourth proto-abbot of the emerging Order. This happened after the composition of the *Summa Cartae Caritatis* (circa 1165) and the *Carta Caritatis Prior* and the *Exordium Parvum* (circa 1170–75), but before that of the *Carta Caritatis Posterior*. Morimond's efforts to build up a filiation of houses as a power base to support such a claim may have inspired other communities, such as Bonnevaux or Cadouin, to begin building such bases of support as well.[174]

Attachment of these houses in Gascony and beyond to Morimond was thus probably in the decade beginning in 1175, but adoption of Cistercian customs at some of these communities may have been slightly earlier. For instance, Cistercian customs had probably been adopted by Berdoues's daughter at Gimont by circa 1150; by 1161 Gimont was recognized as practicing the *ordo cisterciensis*, but was not yet clearly attached to Berdoues or to a filiation of Morimond. Cistercian practices were probably taken from Gimont to Berdoues by Arnold of Saint-Just, abbot of Gimont, in 1153 when he was elected abbot at Berdoues, but affiliation of either Gimont or Berdoues to Morimond was probably later than 1161, as is indicated in a document, discussed below, that concerns Gimont's sharing of an olive-producing grange near Elne with Grandselve and Fontfroide.

These three houses in Gascony, if attached in the third quarter of the twelfth century, brought with them substantial congregations not only in Gascony but south of the Pyrenees. But in some ways the incorporation of these houses further over-populated a region of Gascony that already had a number of pre- and proto-Cistercian houses, many of which would have later financial difficulties.[175] Although obviously important in providing for local religious needs, many of these abbeys were relatively small, with few surviving records and no great impact on the historical record. The daughter-houses in Gascony are mentioned only briefly here; others beyond the Pyrénées await further study.

In 1150 Berdoues incorporated an independent community of monks at Eaunes that had been established in the Ariège in 1120.[176] Further west, in Gascony proper, the abbey for monks at Flaran, which had been originally located at a place called Artigaberd, was also founded in the 1150s north of Berdoues in the Baise valley, probably not by Berdoues but by l'Escaledieu. Its site was near its own thirteenth-century bastide called Fleurance.[177] The abbey of Bouillas was located in the valley of the Gers River and had also been founded or incorporated circa 1150, probably by Bonnefont, although it was eventually controlled by l'Escaledieu.[178] Bonnefont founded yet another abbey at Nizors or la Bénédiction-Dieu on land given by the knight Bertrand of l'Isle and his family in 1184.[179]

More significant within these congregations were Gimont, Villelongue, and Boulbonne. Gimont was eventually identified as a daughter-house of Berdoues; as mentioned, it may have been earlier than Berdoues to adopt Cistercian customs.[180] As indicated in further discussion of Gimont in the next chapter, this abbey was more accessible to Toulouse and Auch because it was located virtually on the Roman road between them; its incorporation of many tiny hermitages is witness to an independent reform movement in its vicinity and to the efficacy of incorporation as a means for even pre- and proto-Cistercian growth. There is little indication of any interaction between Gimont and abbeys in Burgundy until at least the mid-1160s; and only eventually was Gimont clearly identified as associated with Morimond. Until midcentury it was friendly with Grandselve, but its cordial relationship with the reformer Bertrand, abbot of Grandselve, who died in 1150, was replaced by rivalry between Gimont and abbot Pons of Grandselve (1158–65), who quarreled with Gimont about pasture rights and grange sites. Pons later left Grandselve to become abbot of Clairvaux (1165–70), where it may have been his unfortunate personality that led to his being proposed as bishop of Clermont, where he ended his career. Given Pons's controversies with Gimont over granges, it is likely that his specific contributions to Cistercian legislation were those concerning minimum distances between granges.[181]

The abbey of Villelongue had ties to Bonnefont that date to 1150, when Bonnefont incorporated a community of hermits at Campagnes on the Montagne Noire north of Carcassonne that would form the core of the later abbey of Villelongue.[182] Buildings at the original site at Campagnes became a grange in the 1160s, when the monks moved to the lower and more commodious site at the village or *villa* of Villelongue from which they took their permanent name. That village was depopulated to create a place of solitude for their new abbey, and a new village for the existing cultivators was built just outside one of the boundaries of the *villa*. Even before the transfer to the new site had been completed, what became an associated women's house had been founded in 1162 at Rieunette by Regina, widow of Bernard of Castellione, who had earlier made gifts to Villelongue for her husband's soul.[183] But Villelongue's association with a house of nuns at Rieunette, located at a considerable distance away and in a much higher and less desirable spot than Villelongue's verdant valley, did not prevent requests from local women for their own burial at the Cistercian abbey for monks at Villelongue itself. Thus a charter for 1244 shows three daughters joining their father Hugh of Durfort in a gift to Villelongue for the soul of their mother Rica of Roque, "because it is at Villelongue that she had elected to be buried and therefore they made a donation for her soul to that abbey."[184]

Another daughter-house of Bonnefont was Boulbonne. Despite its relatively late creation circa 1162, it became a major player in the monastic politics of this region, one of the "imperialistic" abbeys, powerful perhaps in part because it was soon identified with the counts of Foix and their families. Boulbonne began as a hermitage founded by Augerius of Calmont circa 1150; it was probably attached to Bonnefont by 1163.[185] The early history of this house is as confused as that of many other such independent eremitical communities, but what we can discern about its patronage is that the Foix family's interest came relatively late and that those counts never made as extensive gifts of land to this abbey as did men and women of a slightly lower rank, although it became the family's burial place.[186]

Boulbonne was like Fontfroide in that it incorporated a number of neighboring religious communities by reducing them to granges. These included in 1196 the priory of Vajal, also called both *domus Aimerici* and Garnicia. Although much of Vajal's property came under the control of Boulbonne in that year, monks at Vajal resisted the incorporation until 1225.[187] Similarly, in 1209 Boulbonne also began incorporation of a priory at Tramesaigues or *Interambasaquas*, again with considerable contention because Tramesaigues had been independent since the late tenth century (although loosely attached to Saint-Michel-de-Cuxa in 1129).[188] Boulbonne was later associated with a group of communities of Cistercian nuns.[189] By the beginning of the thirteenth century, it had already established an abbey for women at Valnègre created by a certain Pons William, who gave Boulbonne his lordship over the *villa* of Valnègre so that his daughter Clare could become a nun there. Unlike other houses for nuns in this region, the community at Saint-Martin of Valnègre apparently had its properties administered directly by Boulbonne from the time of foundation.[190] Gimont, Villelongue, and Boulbonne would all be strong houses within the filiation of Morimond in later centuries.

Chances are that, despite early dates on the filiation trees for the motherabbeys of Berdoues, Bonnefont, and l'Escaledieu, these abbeys and their daughters were only incorporated as entire congregations in the 1170s as part of a burst of activity on the part of Morimond's abbot, intent on creating a large congregation of affiliated houses that would allow him to claim a place as fourth "proto-abbot" for visitation of Cîteaux. How Morimond came to attach two other houses of monks, possibly slightly earlier, is unclear. That at Aiguebelle in the Rhône valley claims a foundation date in 1137, but for that house there are no documents before the 1160s.[191] The other abbey under Morimond was at Franquevaux, which was located south of Nîmes in the Camargue; we know more about it in the early thirteenth century, when it established a hospice in Nîmes, than in the twelfth.[192]

But What About 1147?

If creation of a Cistercian Order and much affiliation of new communities by incorporation only happened in the 1160s or so, what about the famous instances of Cistercian incorporation that are attributed in traditional accounts to 1147? What happened to the incorporation of the entire congregation of

Savigny attributed to that year in standard accounts of the Cistercians? Or that of Obazine? Or the Cistercians's refusal to incorporate the Gilbertines?

It has been mentioned already that Cadouin's claims to have had its daughters attached to Pontigny from 1147 are refuted by evidence about two houses in that branch of the tree, Ardorel and Valmagne, both shown by documents in the Valmagne cartulary to be not yet Cistercian in the early 1150s.[193] It is possible that the preaching tour by Bernard of Clairvaux to southern France may have included a stop at Cadouin, which was certainly in existence at this time. Indeed, Cadouin and its daughters may have been inspired by Bernard to adopt Cistercian customs practiced at Clairvaux, and independent adoption of such practices by many houses could have begun to occur by 1147, but there was no affiliation to an Order in 1147 because such an Order did not as yet even exist.

The claims by Cadouin that its daughters were attached to an Order in 1147 are false, but in fact, in its claims for early affiliation with the Cistercians, Cadouin went even further, claiming a place for itself as a daughter of Pontigny since 1119. This was to claim to be as senior within the Order as Cîteaux's daughter of Bonnevaux, which had been founded by the future Calixtus II. Cadouin's argument for 1119 was that in that year it had brought a monk named Henry from Pontigny to be its new abbot. But while a monk coming from Pontigny to Cadouin in 1119 can neither be proven or disproved, affiliation to the Cistercians in that year, a date even before the death of Gerald of Salles, is impossible. As with its claims that daughters were affiliated not only to it but to the Cistercians in 1147, Cadouin was elaborating on claims about the Order's expansion that were beginning to be made in the Order's narratives from as early as the composition of the *Vita Prima* of Bernard of Clairvaux, which was complete before Bernard's canonization in 1174. In the official view of such accounts, such incorporation was limited almost entirely to a series of extraordinary decisions made at a General Chapter meeting at Cîteaux presided over by Eugenius III in 1147. This meeting in which such extraordinary incorporations took place was part of the official mythology, which argued that, although incorporation occasionally happened, it was unusual. The Order's miraculous growth was actually almost entirely by apostolic gestation in this official view, as can be seen already in statements about growth like those of the early *exordia*.

In fact, there is no evidence that any of the houses attributed to that year, Savigny, Obazine, or Cadouin, were attached to a Cistercian Order in 1147, or even that Gilbert's request for affiliation was rejected in that year. Cadouin would eventually be affiliated, although it is hard to say at what date. Savigny was affiliated at least a decade later than 1147 and Obazine probably not much before 1165. Gilbert's proposal was probably also entertained and rejected somewhat later than that year. But official mythology from an early date would push such incorporations of congregations by Clairvaux, Cîteaux, and Pontigny which occurred in the 1150s and 1160s, back a decade to the time of Eugenius and Bernard; that careful discussions had taken place about such incorporations seems to be an assertion of the dossier for Bernard's canonization.[194]

Modern historians have tended to accept this mythology and give it varying interpretations. Many recent historians have pointed to decisions to incorporate Obazine and Savigny in 1147 as mistakes made by the Order's General Chapter. In that view those incorporations brought about an almost immediate decline in Cistercian spirituality and introduced an intolerable diversity of practice leading to the gradual ruin of Cistercian monasticism altogether. The investigation by such modern historians of the incorporation of Savigny's congregation has pointed to many instances of practices contrary to the assumed ideals of the early Cistercians. But rather than using this evidence to question whether the early Cistercians were quite as monolithic in their practice or quite so early in their creation of their Order as was assumed, they have presented Savigny as the contaminating incorporation that introduced Cluny-like practices including the ownership of churches and tithes into the Cistercian Order.[195]

Such historians have also looked askance at 1147 for Obazine's being added. They treat Obazine's affiliation, which had brought with it the community of nuns at Coyroux, as the first breach in the dam against a later flood of women Cistercians.[196] Even historians who have recognized that there were early houses of Cistercian nuns nonetheless point to 1147 as a decisive moment with regard to the Order's limiting the total number of women's houses. They depict the General Chapter as having drawn the line at a request by Gilbert of Sempringham for the admission of the communities of nuns and canons, usually called Gilbertines, which he was founding in Lincolnshire and Yorkshire. This request to the General Chapter was denied.

Given traditional historians' insistence that almost no incorporation took place by the Cistercians except in 1147, it is ironic that, in fact, there is no contemporary evidence for any of these decisions having taken place in that year. Indeed, there is no evidence that a General Chapter meeting was held in 1147, whether under the presidency of Eugenius III or not. There is little evidence, none of it absolutely unquestionable, that Eugenius was at Cîteaux in that year at all. While decisions to incorporate Savigniacs and communities attached to Obazine, and not to attach Gilbertines, would all eventually be made, those decisions were not made simultaneously and were only made in the late 1150s and early 1160s after both Eugenius's and Bernard of Clairvaux's deaths. Thus the archetypical case of the incorporation of entire congregations by the Cistercians, a case presented as the exception proving the rule that otherwise houses were founded by colonization from Burgundy, has been significantly misremembered in the history of the Order.

What documentation is usually cited? We think we know of such an 1147 meeting of the General Chapter because of assertions in *The Book of Gilbert*, written circa 1202.[197] There are similar assertions in the *Vita Prima* written for the canonization of Bernard of Clairvaux. The latter, however, although based on Geoffrey of Auxerre's description of events, which he may have started to write before Bernard's death, survives as a revised version written by committee circa 1170. Few parts of it can definitely be said to have been written by Geoffrey or before 1153.[198] There are also a handful of papal bulls cited in standard lists of such documents that are asserted to have been issued from Cîteaux in September 1147, but they exist only as copies rather than originals; any or all of them could be forgeries.[199] What is most immediately striking about these privileges cited as coming from the 1147 General Chapter meeting is that not one of them is for a Cistercian house. Yet presumably a pope in attendance during such General Chapter meetings would not have taken up non-Cistercian business. Even if some of these papal bulls turn out to be authentically dated to September 1147, or even if they were also done at Cîteaux, Eugenius's presence at that abbey at that date does not mean that a General Chapter was also being held. In fact, authentic papal bulls issued from that place to non-Cistercian houses would suggest that there was no General Chapter at the time they were issued. As discussed in Chapter 2, surviving Burgundian charters do not document any such meetings of a General Chapter until a decade later, and there is no contemporary evidence from inside the Order, such as statutes enacted for such a meeting at that time.

Furthermore, there are no references to an 1147 meeting at Cîteaux, to the issue of incorporation, or to being part of the Cistercian Order in surviving dated authentic charters for Savigny, Obazine, Sempringham, or even Cadouin. In fact what evidence exists for these abbeys about that year definitely contradicts contentions that such a meeting occurred in 1147.[200] With regard to Gilbert, the surviving sources suggest that the request made by Gilbert of Sempringham for affiliation with the Cistercians was made neither to a General Chapter nor in 1147, but in 1164 and to Geoffrey of Auxerre, abbot of Clairvaux, when he visited Sempringham during that year. When Geoffrey was involved in the preparation of the *Vita Prima* later in the 1160s he may have misspoken on this point.[201] Whether he did so deliberately or inadvertently is harder to tell. It must be recalled that in 1170 Geoffrey was deposed as abbot of Clairvaux, apparently for his intransigence in opposing Thomas Becket's being sheltered at Pontigny, and that the Becket affair was inextricably linked to Gilbert and the Gilbertines.[202]

For Obazine, the only reference to the Cistercians in its documents for those years is in a charter dated circa 1148 that mentions the abbot of Cîteaux. This charter appears only in a later cartulary copy. Moreover, the group of individuals listed in it could not all have appeared at the same date. In fact, this charter is probably the conflation of two documents, one slightly later.[203] On the other hand, Obazine was definitely affiliated by the 1160s, for it is the last on a list of Cîteaux's daughters found in a papal confirmation of 1165.[204]

As for Savigny, the best evidence I have found to date regarding its affiliation to the Cistercians comes from the Gilbertine records. An undated document from the correspondence concerning the Gilbertine lay-brothers' revolt at Sempringham, dated by Raymonde Foreville to 1166, sheds some light on Savigny. This text suggests that in the 1160s Gilbertine lay-brothers were complaining that, after having taken their profession according to the practices of Cîteaux, *secundum formam ordinis Cistercie*, they had now begun to be subjected instead to those of Savigny.[205] This complaint suggests three things. First, that Savigny's practices were still distinct from those of Cîteaux in the 1160s, and hence that Savigny had not in fact yet been incorporated by the Cistercians, or at least not so completely as to have removed any distinction in practices. Second, that Savigniac practices, although usually presented as being less austere and even decadent in comparison to those of the Cistercians, were perceived by these Gilbertine lay-brothers as being more harsh.[206] Third, that such communities as that at Sempringham were unilaterally adopting Cistercian practices for the organization of their lay-brothers, without in any way committing themselves to an Order that may not yet have existed, or having had that Order commit itself to them. The complaint suggests that the Gilbertines had been adopting Cistercian practices concerning lay-brothers for some time, moreover, before the lay-brothers' revolt in the 1160s.

While such a reinterpretation about 1147 has considerable consequences for our understanding of the Savigniacs and Cistercians, it will have less for the Gilbertines, because Golding in his recent treatment of Gilbert was explicit about the lack of documents for 1147.[207] The redating presented here, on the other hand, may prove the need for some additional rethinking of the reports about the Gilbertine nun of Watton made by the abbot of the neighboring Cistercian house, Aelred of Rievaulx; these and his comments on Savigny suggest Aelred's propensity for passing on tales of scandal that reflected badly on neighboring, and rival, religious communities.[208]

Anglo-Norman charters also provide some evidence about Savigny. The

1151 grant of passage rights to the Savigniac congregation by the future Henry II, still only count of Anjou at this point, may have been a ploy to attach the Savigniacs to his and his mother Matilda's side of the dispute with Stephen, as discussed in Chapter 2. That such a grant was made in 1151 to Savigny without any reference to the Cistercians again suggests that the Savigniacs had not yet been attached to the Cistercians.[209] Indeed, there is no indication in any of the royal charters for Savigny in the third volume of the *Regesta Regum Anglo-Normannorum* that Savigny had become Cistercian before 1154 when Henry became king of England.[210] Other charters record a number of disputes regarding English Savigniacs in Yorkshire in the 1150s and 1160s, which have been interpreted by historians as showing the laxity with which those in the north of England responded to the supposed conversion in 1147 from Savigniac to Cistercian customs.[211] For many of those incidents, a simpler and more satisfactory explanation is that Cistercian attachment of Savigniacs did not occur until late in the 1150s.[212] The most likely date for attachment of Savigny to Clairvaux is when Alexander of Cologne went from being abbot of Clairvaux's daughter-house of Grandselve near Toulouse to become abbot of Savigny in 1158.[213] Dates for Obazine, Cadouin, and the rejection of the Gilbertines may have been even later. Savigny's incorporation has been in the past conflated with the attempt in 1152 by Serlo, abbot of Savigny, to resign and retire to Clairvaux, a decision countermanded by Bernard. While it has been assumed that Bernard spoke to Serlo as father-visitor in refusing this request, there is no reason to assume that Bernard would not have spoken out on the issue even if Savigny was not yet attached to Clairvaux. Serlo's retirement to Clairvaux did not occur until 1158, a much more likely date for the affiliation.[214]

The abbey of Savigny and its congregation would eventually be incorporated, as would Obazine and Cadouin with theirs. But none of these incorporations were quite so extraordinary as they have been presented in the traditional accounts. This and other recent studies have shown that there were many more incorporations of houses by the Cistercians in the twelfth century than there were genuine foundations.[215]

Thus not only did Cistercians not expand from Burgundy in the mode of apostolic gestation usually attributed to them, but the earliest Cistercian growth beyond Burgundy, except for a few abbeys with patronage ties to families from that region, was considerably later than has been thought. Bernard's preaching mission to the south of France in the mid-1140s probably brought the independent reform abbey of Grandselve near Toulouse to the attention of Clairvaux, but just when during the next decade Grandselve was attached to Clairvaux is more difficult to tell. Grandselve itself seems to have had its own charismatic abbot in the 1140s, a certain Bertrand of Grandselve, who may have been as much inspired by Greek ideas of monasticism as by those of northern France.[216] References to him are only in hagiography and in about a dozen charters from Grandselve, mentioning him as participating as abbot. Grandselve's ties to Clairvaux probably came in 1150, when Alexander of Cologne became abbot there following Bertrand's death.[217] Alexander's move to Savigny in 1158 may mark its affiliation to Clairvaux in parallel fashion to that of Grandselve earlier; his move to become abbot of Cîteaux (and not of Clairvaux) in 1168 probably marks something even more significant, the merger of the Clarevallian congregation into the Cistercian Order that was being formed.

Why then was 1147 later seen as the date of affiliation of these houses? Perhaps the fact that all these houses were located in England or western France may be relevant here. There may be specific reasons for a retrospective choice of 1147 as their affiliation date that have more to do with politics in the Anglo-Norman realm than with the Cistercians. If in the 1160s Anglo-Norman houses claimed to have been attached to the Cistercians in 1147 rather than somewhat later, such claims about attachment to Cîteaux, or even discussion of attachment to Cîteaux as in the case of Gilbert, may have served to place their creation firmly during the anarchy of the last years of Stephen's power in England (1135–54), rather than during that of the first years of Henry II's (1154–89). Obviously, further investigation is needed on this point.[218]

A Crisis After Bernard's Death?

What happened after 1153 when Bernard of Clairvaux and Eugenius III both died has been little studied by Cistercian historians, perhaps because of their assumption that the Order was already in place by that time, but also possibly because those were years of criticism for Cistercians from many quarters of the Church.[219] Other external realities also increasingly imposed themselves on the internal politics of Burgundian Cistercians. The bid for Bernard's canonization did not run smoothly.[220] The papal schism between Victor IV and Alexander III forced religious communities to choose sides and placed Alexander III for extended periods in northern France.[221] There he seems to have interfered (perhaps at the request of the parties involved) in power struggles within many reform groups, possibly contributing to a crisis of reform monasticism at this juncture.[222] Threats to its tithe privilege (which was nearly as central to Cistercian success as were the assets that were being acquired by systematic incorporation and annexation) and criticisms such as those by Alexander III in 1170 must have stimulated the Order's efforts toward achieving uniformity, and possibly even the replacement of *una caritas* with *unanimitas* by the 1180s or so.[223] Such concerns about criticism and efforts to present a unified and dignified face to the outside world were the context within which "primitive documents" like the *Exordium Parvum* and the *Summa Cartae Caritatis* were written.

Part of the crisis stemmed from growth, the need to regularize what had once been a small congregation that had suddenly become much larger. It seems likely as well that Clairvaux itself had become a source of difficulty, in part because it lacked any real comprehension of many issues faced by other houses. There are hints already in the 1140s of the increased dominance within the Burgundian congregation of Clairvaux and the congregation attached to it. Most of the growth in the 1140s was attachment to what would later be the filiation of Clairvaux. Moreover, Clairvaux attracted so many gifts of land that it did not have to purchase property during Bernard's lifetime; this may have made it less than sympathetic to houses that incurred debts in order to consolidate their endowments.[224] The earliest Cistercian abbots appointed as bishops or other officials within the secular church hierarchy, including Eugenius III, came from Clairvaux, and their appointments were very much a product of Bernard's personal influence.[225] During Bernard's lifetime, Clairvaux had become the dominant force in the pre-Order in Burgundy, and Bernard's preaching spread that congregation's monastic practices to other parts of Europe. Bernard's successors at Clairvaux must have tried to maintain such predominance immediately after his death, but with less charisma and sanctity, and possibly less skill.

A crisis with regard to Clairvaux and the legacy of Bernard's charisma is suggested as well by the fact that, when the *exordia* and Charter of Charity began to be composed in the 1160s, they do not mention Bernard at all and give Clairvaux no special mention. Given Bernard's prestige, such omissions cannot be deemed inadvertent. Moreover, the *exordia* and the Charter of Charity are first and foremost statements that no single abbot or abbey was to rule the emerging Order, that no father-abbot had excessive control over the houses under his control, no matter how many they might number. Is this not quite explicitly to reject the situation that had prevailed during Bernard's lifetime? One might also suggest that by consistently employing the language of *caritas* the authors of the *Exordium Cistercii* and *Summa Cartae Caritatis* made it more difficult for Bernard's successors at Clairvaux to resist precepts about equality, which were built into such documents. Thus the federation of abbeys that would become the Order may, in the aftermath of Bernard's death, have been attempting to shear Clairvaux of its excessive power. Close readings of the history of composition of the *Vita Prima* suggest that there began to be efforts to resist the continued dominance of Bernard's successors at Clairvaux over the Cistercian movement. This crisis has been little discussed or studied except by Adriaan Bredero in his work on the revisions of the *Vita Prima* of Bernard.[226]

We can thus infer that at least one aim in the constitutional efforts of abbots in the 1150s and 1160s was to counter the power of Clairvaux by the creation of a General Chapter that was an annual, universal assembly of all abbots. The disempowering of Clairvaux was achieved, not by dismantling the congregation of houses attached to Clairvaux but by dividing the authority over Cîteaux among three and later four proto-abbots and by vesting authority in a General Chapter of all abbots. Once the *Summa Cartae Caritatis* is dated to 1165, we can read it as the administrative response to a crisis in which the practice of *caritas* among members of a congregation of Burgundian houses had become strained. It became necessary to replace informal agreements with a written constitution. Assertions in the texts of the "primitive documents" that there would be no exactions, that abbot-visitors should not involve themselves in internal affairs, and under what conditions new houses should be founded, suggest some of the sources of conflict.[227] The texts tell us that issues of concern were who had control over what assets within communities and the sharing of rights over such resources as pastures between mother- and daughter-houses. If we read the silences about Clairvaux and Bernard in the "primitive documents" as reflecting concern to bring the overwhelming dominance of Clairvaux under control, then it may be that an *ordo cisterciensis* in some senses only emerged in response to the threat of a possible *ordo clarevallensis*.[228]

There were in the 1150s and thereafter many new problems to be faced both within and outside the Burgundian congregation. It is noticeable, for example, that the average term of service of abbots at many Burgundian communities was noticeably shorter after 1150 than before. There were also several notorious depositions of abbots as well as the first elections of non-Burgundians to rule Cîteaux and Clairvaux.[229] As already mentioned as an example of rapidly changing politics within the Order after 1150, and of a reconfiguration of power in which Cîteaux and other houses eventually seized some power back from Clairvaux, we can see that the career of Bernard's friend Alexander of Cologne is significant. From being abbot of Grandselve (1150–58), where his arrival signaled that this abbey and its daughters had become attached to Clairvaux, and again when his election in 1158 took Alexander to be abbot of Savigny (1158–68), Alexander's return to become abbot of Cîteaux in 1168–80 allowed him to collaborate more closely in the creation of an Order.[230] But there were other participants. Alexander's successor as abbot of Grandselve,

Pons of Polignac (1158–65), was also an important new influence in Burgundy after he became abbot of Clairvaux (1165–70) on the deposition of Geoffrey of Auxerre (1162–65). Geoffrey, on the other hand, had perhaps resisted the decline in Clairvaux's power following the promulgation of the *Exordium Cistercii* and the *Summa Cartae Caritatis* in 1165.[231]

Pons was not popular, and when in 1170 there was further criticism from Alexander III he was pushed out of the abbacy of Clairvaux to become bishop of Clermont (1170–89). Pons was the first in a series of non-Burgundian abbots at Clairvaux. He was followed by Girard (1170–75), who had previously been abbot of Italian Fossanova, and then by the former abbot of Hautecombe in Savoy, Henry of Marcy (1176–79) and the Italian abbot Peter Monocule (1179–86). Henry of Marcy would be an international figure; he was elevated in 1179 to cardinal, a position he held until his death in 1189, and in 1182 he started a mini-Crusade against the southern heretics.[232] Thus the influence of non-Burgundians on the center of the developing Order was very strong after Bernard's death. They were perhaps bringing new ideas about organization to Burgundy.[233]

Inventing the Order

In the 1140s, inspired by Bernard, getting information by example or written tracts about Cistercian practices, many pre-Cistercian reform communities took the step of adopting at least some Cistercian customs. This did not yet constitute their affiliation to an Order. Moreover, in the 1140s and 1150s such an Order did not yet exist; there was only a congregation in Burgundy vaguely tied together by precepts about love. Whereas later adoption of Cistercian customs would be tantamount to entering the Cistercian Order, this was not yet the perception in the mid-twelfth century. Only sometime after the deaths of Eugenius III and Bernard, both in 1153, did Burgundian houses begin to coalesce with proto-Cistercian houses from other regions of Europe into what we think of today as the Cistercian Order. The process of creating the Order out of these two distinct components would be a complex one; it has been oversimplified in earlier discussions that lump together what can be seen as different and successive stages in this transformation. Dating these stages, even for a single house, is even more difficult than establishing a foundation date for a single religious house.

Such evidence as has been collected here about how proto-Cistercian congregations were established before Cistercian incorporation of them suggests not only the importance of the property and personnel that such groups would bring to the Order, but the difficulties that would be encountered in creating what was still in the 1160s primarily an umbrella group of abbeys as outlined in the earliest version of the Charter of Charity. These difficulties would be even greater as the Order's General Chapter, probably in response to papal pressures, began to attempt the nearly impossible task of enforcing uniformity of practice on houses that had voluntarily adopted whichever Cistercian practices they had wanted, adapting Cistercian *ordo* to their own needs. Yet rather quickly such houses in the 1160s and 1170s began to be swept up into an Order that had not even been envisioned earlier. But this transformation from the first interest in Cistercian customs to the invention of the Cistercian Order was not one easily envisioned — at least not before the notion of a religious order itself had been thought of.

In southern France the beginning of ties to Burgundy, to Cistercian practices, and eventually to an Order can be documented for Silvanès, Grandselve, and Gimont, all of which were recognized as living according to Cistercian practices by the late 1150s. If Silvanès was doing so, this may mean that Mazan had adopted some Cistercian practices as well. We can add Valmagne and Fontfroide to that list by 1161, when both are documented as practicing the Cistercian *ordo*. Even for the houses just mentioned, however, relationships and later ties reflected in the filiation trees and the practice of internal visitation would happen only later, probably in the 1180s. Thus, for example, although the Silvanès chronicle mentions Mazan as a Cistercian house, it does not note any tie to Bonnevaux at the time it was written (circa 1170). The early adoption of such customs by houses like Valmagne and Grandselve with established granges and lay-brothers and the fact that these were houses that remained wealthy suggest the efficacy (at least in economic terms) of the new Cistercian formula for monastic practice. In adopting the *ordo* of the Cistercians, however, such reformers did not take on a whole program, but must have been selective, trying out practices on a voluntary basis and only adopting those they found fit real needs. All this was certainly done without any thought that their use of such customs tied them to any larger institution.

What did adopting the *ordo* of the Cistercians mean for such already established reform houses that were inspired by Bernard in the 1140s? And what could Bernard of Clairvaux, whose reputation for vagueness and unreliability about practical matters has been recognized for centuries, have actually told them about internal monastic practice? The written customs are our best clue to what pre-Cistercians actually knew about Cîteaux's practices and when they came to know it. Certain practices concerning internal administration began to be committed to writing in liturgical customaries that survive in their earliest manuscript versions from about 1135, if we can date them by assuming that version 1 of Trent 1711 was indeed a Cistercian order-book.[234] These liturgical customaries had much to say, not just about how much liturgy to undertake and what to cut, but about the duties of monastic officials. Similarly, customs about lay-brothers were certainly developing into separate lay-brother customaries by the 1150s, as is evidenced by the manuscript from Clairvaux containing what appears to be the earliest surviving Cistercian lay-brother customary, Montpellier H322.[235]

It seems logical that the earliest practices to be adopted by pre-Cistercian houses had to do with newly created problems about the internal administration of monasteries, those associated with reformers's aims about extricating the support of monastic life from dependence on the manorial economy. They concerned management of lay-brothers and granges and abbreviations to the liturgy. That lay-brother management was central to the needs of many such new reform houses is suggested not only because treatises on lay-brothers or conversi are among the earliest customs to be treated separately, but because the introductions to several such treatises (Metz 1247 and London, Add. MS 18, 148, for example) state that they were needed "Because some abbots are too harsh and others too lenient in their treatment of the lay-brothers."[236] Moreover, certain charters from circa 1160 among Valmagne's documents, as discussed in the next chapter, suggest that Cistercian practice with regard to lay-brothers was what donors and potential recruits wanted to be assured about before deciding to give land and enter such reform houses as monks or lay-brothers; this seems to be confirmed by the evidence regarding the lay-brother revolt at Sempringham as well, discussed above.

Going from adopting Cistercian practices to the process of inventing the Cistercian Order probably began with the institution of General Chapters in the 1150s. These transformed earlier ad hoc meetings of abbots in Burgundy, for instance that in 1135 addressed by Louis VI, into more formal ones to which all those following Cistercian customs were at first invited and in later decades constrained to attend. In my view it is likely that the General Chapters of the Cistercians had their origins in invitations to abbots of all houses that had adopted or wished to adopt Cistercian customs to attend meetings in the aftermath of Bernard of Clairvaux's and Eugenius III's deaths. These assemblies were primarily called in order to collect materials necessary for the promotion of Bernard of Clairvaux's canonization, but they apparently gradually moved beyond concern with that canonization to the collection of ideals (which became the later *Instituta*) and the creation of a short series of statutes during the years 1157–61. By 1165, possibly at the request of Alexander III, they had written a constitution, a "Charter of Charity and Unanimity," for papal confirmation with a short two-paragraph introduction, the *Exordium*

Cistercii. Such first steps led eventually to an Order in which centralized control would increase, universal attendance at annual General Chapters would be construed as mandatory, written statutes would be considered binding on all practitioners of Cistercian customs, and uniformity of practice would be enjoined as a means of averting complaints from outsiders.

The widespread incorporations of the 1160s and 1170s not only added large numbers of new abbeys to the Order, but turned the Cistercians into a large and rich Order virtually overnight. Administrative problems inevitably arose with such size, and earlier vague concepts of both *caritas* and *unanimitas* had to have been strained, particularly because these were also years in which endowment was consolidated. It was the consolidation of Cistercian endowment by active recourse to the real estate market in those years that allowed the great economic success of their grange agriculture. The decades from 1150 to 1180 or slightly later saw the consolidation of land holdings for all reform houses, incorporated yet or not, as is clear from a glance through nearly any cartulary for a twelfth-century reform community. That such acquisitions were undertaken by knights and peasants who had been inspired to adult conversion to the Cistercian life, and who had local knowledge of land-holding and cultivation, made these efforts particularly effective; this made the new reformers unpopular, as discussed in the next chapter.

Clearly in those years disputes over tithes became frequent because Cistercians were so active in asserting their rights to their tithe exemption, not only on animal husbandry, which was relatively painless for all concerned, but on their granges.[237] While tithe exemption may have been granted to all houses of the emerging Order by the 1180s, among the earliest issues taken up by Cistercian General Chapters in that decade would be how to respond to increasing criticisms from outsiders about that exemption.[238]

Regulation of who might enter as conversi or conversae had also varied before the 1180s when the General Chapter instructed its abbots that knights could not be admitted as lay-brothers but only as choir-monks.[239] Up until and to some extent beyond that date, in southern France both knights and peasants could become lay-brothers, and there was a certain equality among all members of monastic communities that was later lost.[240]

When did the Order happen? Southern-French evidence from several places from the 1160s and 1170s shows how fluid the notion of filiation was in this period. Charters for the foundation of a hospice in Montpellier in 1161 show that it was created for monks and conversi of the *ordo cisterciensis* traveling to Burgundy. Its foundation under the control of Valmagne with the assistance of the abbot of Silvanès suggests that Valmagne and Silvanès saw themselves as equivalent houses, at least with regard to the administration of this hospice in 1161. Relationships on thirteenth-century filiation trees are often not applicable to those events of the 1160s, and Bonnevaux and Mazan, the respective mother-houses, were not even mentioned in these negotiations. The situation would be different when a hospice in Nîmes was founded in 1210.[241]

A second charter for 1161 found among documents for Grandselve suggests the same, that relationships had not yet settled into place in an Order only beginning to coalesce. That charter records the gift in 1161 of rights of the entire garrigue of "Haute de Vescleran," where olives were to be planted and olive oil produced, *ad plantandum olivetum olivarium*. This gift was made by Richard of Saint-Laurent and his brother William, Gausbert of Saint-Hyppolyte and his brother Seguerius, and Bernard Alcherius. Recipients were listed as Grandselve and its abbot Pons William, Gimont and its abbot Bernard, and Fontfroide and its abbot Vidal; the recipients were to own and administer this grange jointly for olive production at Saint-Hyppolyte near Elne. The donors were promised the spiritual benefits of the *ordo cisterciensis* and to be received "in all the benefits" (possibly code for more formal confraternity) of Grandselve, Gimont, and Fontfroide. Furthermore, any of them who chose to enter the religious life could do so at any of these three abbeys.[242] That these three abbeys were considered equivalent in their practice of the *ordo* at this point is clear. Their later placement, however, would not even be on the same filiation trees: Grandselve and Fontfroide were attached to Clairvaux, with Fontfroide the daughter-house of Grandselve; Gimont was tied to Berdoues and through it to Morimond.

Similarly, documents for 1177 and later reveal a lack of equitable treatment of the abbey of Locdieu in the Rouergue that would seem to have been precluded by the guarantees of the Charter of Charity. In that year the neighboring Rouergat abbey of monks at Bonneval had apparently paid off the debts and taken over the properties of the monks of Locdieu. What happened is not clear, but Locdieu was somehow incorporated by Bonneval. Either its members were left at Locdieu as a dependent priory, or its monks moved to Bonneval in 1177 and the lay-brothers remained at Locdieu, which was reduced to a grange.[243] What is clear is that in 1177 Bonneval actually annexed Locdieu's properties and exchanged them with the Hospitallers for better pasture rights on the Aubrac plateau.[244] In its pre-Cistercian stage, Locdieu had had ties to the western-French reform house of Dalon; these ties apparently only resurfaced in concern on behalf of Locdieu by Dalon at the moment of making filiation trees in the thirteenth century.[245]

At the General Chapter in 1212 the abbot of Dalon raised complaints against Bonneval for suppressing Locdieu. Eventually Locdieu was reinstated as an abbey; it was then placed on the filiation trees as a daughter of Dalon, with its date on the filiation tree given as 1162.[246] It did not, however, recover important pastoral granges on the Aubrac north of Bonneval that Bonneval had annexed and traded away. The important point here is that, in 1177 Dalon and its mother-abbey of Pontigny on the one hand, and Cîteaux, Bonnevaux, and Mazan, to which Bonneval was linked on the other, apparently had no stake in what happened between abbeys like Locdieu or Bonneval as part of their respective filiations. By the thirteenth century, Locdieu received some protection and transactions of forty years earlier were reversed. In a similar case, Mazan in 1178 seems to have assumed that it could treat as its own whatever pasture rights in the Rouergue had been granted to its daughter-houses there.[247]

Thus, at the end of the third quarter of the twelfth century, relationships were still being worked out as to the properties and rights belonging to related or neighboring Cistercian abbeys. Notions of mutual aid, such as those found in the *Summa Cartae Caritatis*, which could have allowed smaller and weaker houses to remain independent, were still not widespread, if they ever became so. Certainly the support of the powerful for the weak was not apparent in these actions of abbeys in southern France.

There was much ambiguity at this time about the meanings of various institutions and terminology at specific moments. It is important to realize that the institutions that were created in the 1160s were not yet the institutions of the 1190s. The Order being invented had many structures that were only gradually transformed into the articulated forms we generally assume them to have. The process of inventing the Order had caused a shift in terminology, as has already been explored with regard to the word *ordo* itself, that reflected the gradually occurring institutional change.

The same may be said about the General Chapter. In the 1150s the General Chapter was involved in collecting ideals and material for the canonization of Bernard, as well as in writing a constitution and building an institution. But such a General Chapter, which must have often acted in very ad hoc ways in the 1150s or 1160s, was not the same General Chapter it would become in the 1190s. When did it become annual and universal? Was it only in the 1190s that efforts were made to enforce attendance at the General Chapter? Certainly it was then that complaints such as "it is impossible to come; Ireland is too far" are first documented.[248] Probably only then does universal attendance become an issue. Read in the past as marking a threat to the earlier universality of the General Chapter, such plaints may in fact reflect responses of individual abbots to the General Chapter's earliest efforts to enforce annual and universal attendance.

As the General Chapter became established as a functioning corporate body, its existence posed logistical problems in addition to those about precedence and voting within the meetings which seem to be related to the urgency with which claims were made to places on filiation trees. Who should attend and with how many attendants were issues treated in the 1180s statutes. The costs of funding such an assembly every year at Cîteaux and of providing facilities for abbots traveling to it were large, considerable enough to warrant the solicitation of bequests earmarked for its support. Such bequests include that made by Henry, count of Troyes in 1179, and that by Richard I of England in 1187.[249] The foundation of hospices for Cistercians en route to General Chapter meetings also helps to date the introduction of such annual, universal assemblies. The earliest that I know of is that already mentioned, the hospice established in Montpellier in 1161 probably with the encouragement of William VI of Montpellier, who was by that time a monk at Grandselve.[250]

Similarly, the judicial and arbitrating activities of the General Chapter did not arise all at once. It did not become the universal court of last appeal for all disputes within the Order or even the place of arbitration between the Order's houses and neighbors until the 1170s. This may be traced in records of dispute settlement. From Giles Constable's description of the early dispute between Gigny and le Miroir in Burgundy, we know that in the later years of Innocent II's reign (1139–43) Cistercians still had recourse to the papal court.[251] But appeals to Rome would not continue to be standard Cistercian practice. It became the policy of the more bureaucratized papacy of the late twelfth century to encourage reform monastic groups to devise internal mechanisms to resolve internal disputes; this somewhat contradictory papal effort appears to be an attempt to avoid overloading the papal court with monastic business, at the same time that the pope was increasing papal claims as the court of last appeal in other cases.[252]

Although among the Cistercians it was the General Chapter which took on this judicial role, in the earliest years resolution of disputes was usually by recourse to local arbitration. A dispute between Gimont and Grandselve over granges in 1158 was handled not by the General Chapter but by local arbitrators.[253] Conflict between Valmagne and Silvanès in 1161 over pasture rights was similarly not referred to the General Chapter.[254] In 1171 a papal legate was sent to oversee resolution of one dispute regarding Valmagne.[255] A 1174 controversy over pasture rights between Clairvaux's daughters in southern France, Grandselve and Belleperche, is probably that over which the abbot of Clairvaux arbitrated during a visit to the region the next year. There is no indication that this dispute reached the General Chapter.[256] Even in the early 1190s local arbitration remained an option, but the General Chapter was taking up this business. A dispute from 1191 over pasture rights between Cistercian monks of Grandselve and Boulbonne was settled locally, but another between Grandselve and Gimont in 1194 was taken to the General Chapter.[257] In 1194 as well, the General Chapter was called upon to regulate a dispute between Mazan and Bonneval.[258] In 1197 a dispute is recorded as being heard there between Bonnefont and les Feuillants.[259] There was a dispute noted in the 1204 *Statuta* between Flaran and Bouillas and that discussed above between Dalon and Bonneval dated to 1212 and 1214.[260]

Two charters of peace between Gilbertines and Cistercians in Lincolnshire may clarify the dating of this evolution. That of 1164 between Gilbertines at Sempringham and Cistercians at Kirkstead makes no mention of the General Chapter but designates local adjudicators if there were further difficulties. The charter between Gilbertines at Alvingham and Cistercians at Louth Park in 1174, however, included an enforcement clause for arbitration by the Cistercian General Chapter and the bishop and chapter of Lincoln.[261] This change coincides with the time of the writing of the earliest Charter of Charity in the mid-1160s.

Such evolution is seen as well with regard to filiations. Indeed, for networks of houses beyond those closely linked to the early Burgundian congregation, many ties were beginning to be established only in the 1170s. The way Morimond seems to have created a much more extensive filiation at that time, allowing it to make its bid circa 1175 to have the fourth proto-abbot, has already been discussed.[262] At that moment, being a "proto-abbot" was not equivalent to being head of a filiation, but the size of its filiation might nonetheless have helped Morimond's abbot make his successful bid to become a proto-abbot.

If Morimond's example established that authority in the Order might be claimed as the result of the creation of a network of dependent houses, this may have led to a race among other abbeys, not only by Cîteaux, Pontigny, and la Ferté, but by other daughters of Cîteaux like Savigny and Bonnevaux, to also increase the size of their filiations. But although the abbot of Morimond may have created a filiation as the argument for becoming the fourth proto-abbot called on to inspect Cîteaux, there was no other reason for such filiations to exist until episcopal visitation had been replaced by internal visitation by papal privileges, an exemption dated by Mahn to the 1180s.[263] (Final placement on filiation trees was still under contention in the early thirteenth century.)[264]

Filiation was related to the allocation of power and precedence within the emerging Order. Voting in General Chapter meetings must have become more explicitly tied to such filiations once the exemption from episcopal visitation was granted in 1184. Questions about equality and inequality in the emerging Order arose quite forcefully on issues such as how much power a mother-abbey could have over daughter-houses. To what extent were the assets of one the assets of the other? Historians have usually thought these questions were resolved from an early date, because the *Summa Cartae Caritatis* told father-abbots that their interference in the affairs of daughter-houses was to be limited. That the *Summa Cartae Caritatis* was only written circa 1165, as I contend, explains why in that year the abbey of Bonnefont still listed for papal confirmation all its daughter-abbeys and their properties as if they were part of its own endowment.[265] Indeed, Cîteaux itself in 1165 still listed its daughter-houses as its dependencies.[266]

Such a new interpretation of the history of twelfth-century Cistercians can best be seen from the vantage point of regions beyond Burgundy. For the first half of the twelfth century, Burgundy had its own specific development as a pre-order or congregation. After Bernard's death pressures mounted for that Burgundian congregation to take control of all the independently founded houses of proto-Cistercians that were borrowing Cistercian customs. The outlines of an Order began to be formed. The evolution of such communities already following Cistercian practices into a Cistercian Order is similar to that of other increasingly bureaucratized religious groups at this time, and the Cistercians were only one of many new reform groups who became more routinized. As elsewhere, moreover, the creation of an Order by the Cistercians was not the work of a single reformer and should not be attached to either Stephen Harding or Bernard of Clairvaux. Instead, the Cistercian evolution happened more gradually, probably with considerable borrowing from other reform groups' practices. Indeed, the administrative evolution at Cîteaux has more in common with the model for Fontevrault described by Penny Shine Gold than she realized.[267]

Earlier descriptions of the Cistercians and their creation of an Order have been based on assumptions about the Cistercians' exceptional leadership among twelfth-century reform groups in developing new institutions. To date their creation of an Order to the very beginning of the twelfth century is to treat the Cistercians as the sole inventors of the religious order among twelfth-century monastic reformers, and to describe all other reformers in Cistercian terms. This happened because by the thirteenth century Cistercian institutions would be held up as exemplary for other reform groups. But there is little reason to believe that Cistercians being the winners by 1215 was inevitable, any more than that their institutions had been created soon after reformers set out from Molesme in 1098 or even at the moment when the first daughter-houses were established in 1113.

Such revised notions about the invention of the Cistercian Order in the 1150s or later, rather than in the teens of the twelfth century, have consequences not just for Cistercian history, but for the standard narrative of growth among all new twelfth-century monastic groups. Until now that narrative has been heavily dependent on official Cistercian accounts such as the *Exordium Cistercii* and the *Exordium Parvum*, which were assumed to have been eyewitness accounts. But their authors were members of the Cistercian Order of the 1160s and 1170s. While such texts may imply much about the pressing concerns for Cistercians at the time of their composition, their narrations of earlier events are faulty. It has been necessary to begin again, to amass a different kind of evidence for describing the Order's earliest development and dating its structures. In rewriting this Cistercian history, there is much that can eventually be known about the Order's institutions that has still not been reconstructed, because the piecing together of that story must be built from often fragmentary references in documents really about other things. To further refine the revised dates for institutions set forth here will require a rereading of many additional archival sources from the 1150s and later from a wide area of Europe looking for fragmentary references to changes in the use of terms such as *ordo cisterciensis*, and in the introduction of the institutions of the Cistercian Order.

4
Charters, Patrons, and Communities

Many treatments of benefaction attempt to identify the sources of monastic support, pointing to the social classes who were most interested in the advent of a new monastic community and showing how beneficence to monastic communities served to legitimize the power of such patrons. Studies of medieval monasticism often compare levels of bequests to various abbeys in regional studies or trace benefactors who became members of the monastic communities in life or at death.[1] Given the arrangement and tenor of the documents recording such bequests (discussed below), historians have tended to ascribe agency in patronage relationships to the outsiders rather than to members of monastic communities. In concentrating on the patrons' needs for social legitimation and religious salvation, such considerations often forget the monks and nuns who were also involved in these transactions. Yet many patrons crossed the invisible divide between secular and religious life to become members of monastic houses. Relationships between patrons and monastic personnel were often those of brothers and sisters by blood, and monastic administrators often had to balance the demands and needs of their monastic communities with those of their families of birth living nearby. Careful study of the monastic charters can clarify some of these issues.

Idealized versions of early Cistercian history such as the *Exordium Parvum* have contaminated not only historians' portrayals of how the Cistercian Order grew, but our views of Cistercian interaction with their patrons. Our views of patronage have been distorted as well by inferences from the thirteenth-century filiation trees about single foundation dates, single founders, or "apostolic gestation" of religious communities, as well as by the assertions of charters and cartularies about who were the most important founders and patrons. This chapter's analysis of pre-Cistercian and Cistercian relationships with patrons will attempt to go beyond earlier pious quantification of donors and their gifts. It examines how monks and nuns actively sought to create an endowment by interactions with secular neighbors in areas into which they came or where their houses were located, although the active roles of members of religious communities in such land acquisition are often muted or masked in the monastic charters.

Charter-Making and Southern-French Society

The reality of Cistercian relationships with their neighbors may be discovered by looking very closely at the charters produced by specific houses of these reformed monks and nuns. Here I undertake a detailed consideration of the records of three such communities: the scattered surviving charters for nuns at Nonenque in the Rouergue, who seem never to have made a cartulary, and charters found in the cartularies for two houses of Cistercian monks, Gimont in Gascony and Valmagne near Montpellier. All three abbeys had adopted Cistercian practices by sometime in the third quarter of the twelfth century. The charter evidence confirms that their benefactors came primarily from the knightly class and cooperated in the foundation of new religious houses in which their daughters and sons could take religious garb. It was also to these abbeys that such patrons themselves might retire before death. While it appears that the social level of donors and recruits to the nuns of Nonenque was slightly higher than was that of patrons for Gimont and Valmagne, all three received little patronage from those at the level of titled lords such as the Raymonds, counts of Toulouse, at least not before the end of the twelfth century.

Such charters convey more than land alone, for they both illuminate and obscure our understanding of social relationships. For example, a Valmagne charter for 1185 tells us that Adelaide, wife of the late Bernard of Saint-Pons, gave to Valmagne and to abbot Amedeus the entire honor or property that her son, Peter Raymond, had relinquished to that abbey in the last days of his life. The charter depicts this widow, undoubtedly grief-stricken at having lost her son, pressing the monks of Valmagne to accept a gift made by him on his deathbed. But is this really how the scene had played out? The poignant drama of a son's death and his mother's confirmation of a gift for his burial are part of what lies behind such a charter, in which Adelaide's gift comes to resemble all other gifts. What totally disappears from view in this case is the spectacle of the monks of Valmagne rushing to the deathbed of Peter Raymond to receive his gift, after which Adelaide may have had little choice except to confirm this gift for his soul and his burial.[2] Such a situation is not mentioned in the Valmagne charter, but in a charter for Bonnecombe concerning Lady Alazais, wife of the knight William Gac, we do read the description of the monks at

Bonnecombe gathering around her deathbed in 1228, promising her burial at their abbey in return for a much desired concession of property.[3] Would such a scene have been exceptional? Particularly when such deaths occurred in monastic infirmaries?

The Valmagne cartularies confirm women's roles. We see in one charter the wife of Jacob of Minzano confirming a transfer of land to Valmagne that he had made "during the illness from which he died" and, in another, Raymonda, wife of Pons Constantine, consenting to a gift allowing her husband to become a monk at Valmagne "to serve God there," while she still lived.[4] Another Adelaide, wife of Raymond Peter, seems to have demanded even more in her exchanges with Valmagne. In 1191 she "gave her body as well as her soul" to those monks and asked for prayers for her soul, her husband's, of her sons who had died, her parents', and the souls of all the faithful dead. Adelaide received significant concessions, and her property must have been important real estate. It was described as lying on the old Roman road from Montpellier to Narbonne that passed not far from Valmagne. She had persuaded Valmagne's monks to accept her as a member of their community, as a lay-sister or at death—the charter says *pro sorore et pro sepultura*. The monks promised that they would say as many prayers for her after her death as they would have for any monk of the community.[5] Such concessions were not unusual at Valmagne, and they are found elsewhere as well.[6] The importance of women as both patrons and recruits to such houses of proto-Cistercians and Cistercians is apparent from such examples in this and other cartularies.

Conveyances like those just described were made by women of property in return for religious benefits for themselves and their families. They also confirm several things not necessarily apparent in the earlier historiography on medieval women. First, whatever the appeal of heretics in southern France to a few women in its ruling families, women of the knightly classes there more often supported orthodox forms of the apostolic poverty movement.[7] Such women were founders of monasteries for women and were recruited into them, but they were also patrons for houses of monks or double houses from which abbeys of either monks or nuns originated. Mothers and wives made gifts to monasteries that promised to provide for the souls and retirement of sons and husbands; many of these were abbeys that eventually adopted Cistercian practices.[8] Other women demanded religious benefits for themselves. Thus Guillelma, daughter of William of Montpesat, "gave herself to God and to the monastery of Bonnefont-en-Comminges."[9] Even before such communities were clearly Cistercian, the wealthiest women of the region, like Ermengardis, viscountess of Narbonne, made bequests to reform monks such as those of Silvanès, Fontfroide, and Grandselve.[10] Gifts also came from slightly less lofty but still important women like the widow of Humbert of Capraria, who arranged for her husband's burial at Valmagne "with as many benefits as if he had been a monk."[11]

Second, southern-French women continued to have a hand in the control of family property. Such women donors acting with family members are indeed seen throughout this chapter. Even at the end of the twelfth century, the importance of women as donors remained unabated. Women most often acted as part of larger family groups in charters in which gifts were mixed with outright sales, making it difficult to characterize these transactions. Determining how much individual as opposed to familial power was being exercised by women participating in the such confirmations is often a futile exercise.[12]

Third, documents securing places for men in Cistercian monasteries suggest that women were entering religious communities in similar high numbers. Despite the lack of documentation bearing directly on the history of such women's communities (there are few archival collections for such communities and their early contents are scanty), such women's monasteries are often documented on the margins of the evidence for men's houses. They are literally on the margins, moreover, when such houses of nuns or their properties are mentioned as being locations on the peripheries or perambulations of property conveyed to monks. Often this is the only documentation we have for them.

We also know that women became sisters at such men's houses, for instance, after consenting to the entrance of their menfolk into communities like Valmagne while both were still alive.[13] Demographic arguments suggest that many women must have entered twelfth-century religious houses because the twelfth century probably saw higher death rates for men than for women, given the perils of warfare in a region close to conflict in Spain and the Crusades in the Levant. But if men were dying on such military adventures, the women who stayed home may have been living longer. A declining female mortality from childbirth is probable at this time given improvements in European diet. In addition, although pregnancy and childbirth remained perilous, those risks were reduced to the extent that the campaign against clerical marriage was effective, leading to fewer pregnancies and fewer deaths in childbirth. This too must have added to women's relative longevity (as well as to the population of spinsters and abandoned wives wanting to enter religious communities) in the twelfth century.[14] Finally, the growth of women's religious houses at this time may have been spurred by new marriage practices among the nobility, such as that described below for the Maurencs family. Only one son was allowed to marry in this and many other families, so eventually fewer daughters could have married. Thus, in addition to those women retiring with their husbands to such reformed religious communities, there were many other potential female entrants to women's communities, not only widows but unmarried women whose potential husbands had converted to the religious life, were now living as celibate priests, had died in battle or at tournaments as unmarried youths, or were kept from marrying by the new familial strategies of property management associated with theories of primogeniture.

When we consider the actual size of twelfth-century communities for Cistercian or pre-Cistercian women, however, the women's houses were consistently smaller than those for Cistercian men. Women's houses also probably housed a relatively lower proportion of lay-sisters to nuns than there were lay-brothers to monks in men's houses. The women's houses themselves, moreover, provided places for a certain number of male Cistercians — those priests and lay-brothers who took their monastic vows directly from abbesses.[15] As may be seen in the discussion of Nonenque below, Cistercian communities of nuns may have served a slightly higher social class than those for monks. This, too, would have prevented women of the same social level as the men entering Cistercian houses from entering Cistercian houses for nuns. Such women may have ended up in the more ephemeral recluse houses and hospital communities of nursing sisters and religious women, which we know of only from oblique references in the charters. Indeed, we cannot ignore the possibility that they actively chose these alternatives. Fragmentary references to such communities as the hospital founded by Guillelma of Montpellier (discussed later in this chapter), for which there are only two charters that happen to be found in the Valmagne cartulary, suggest that someone like Guillelma, who undoubtedly could have entered the house of Cistercian nuns of her choice, preferred to found and manage a hospice.

The surviving documents of practice produced by Cistercians in southern France are the most reliable source from which such conclusions may be drawn about the distribution of religious houses, their size, the gender of their occupants, and the approximate dates of their foundation and incorporation into the Cistercian practice. These documents consist primarily of charters recording real estate contracts: the gifts, sales, and other conveyances of property to religious communities or agreements reached in settlement of disputes about the use of their property. They bear witness to an active land market and a strong local tradition of recourse to written records. The great value of these charters is that they were written for the purposes of monastic land administration without having any external audience in mind. Charters, unlike the Order's early *exordia* or the lives of Cistercian founders and saints, did not attempt to promote or sell the Order and its benefits but simply recorded the transactions by which those abbeys gained endowment. Their evidence is usually reliably dated and often earlier, as well as closer in date to the events, than such accounts as the *Exordium Parvum* or even the *Exordium Cistercii*. Such charters thus represent the most accurate sources from which to reconstruct the history of the early Cistercians.

Surviving collections of such charters, or documents of practice, particularly those preserved in monastic cartularies, are very rich for southern France.[16] Most southern-French cartularies date to the period 1150–1250, when that region's monasteries, bishops, and great families copied charters into their private charter-books at about the same time that we begin to see contracts preserved in urban notarial registers.[17] While cartularies have been used primarily for the purposes of social history during the past half century, recently concern has arisen about the authenticity of the earliest charters in medieval cartularies and about how our vision of the Middle Ages is refracted through the lens of such collections.[18]

Such charters must obviously be used with care. They frequently omit any mention of the long negotiations undertaken before conveyances occurred or what discussions about promised religious benefits had prefaced them. Thus, for example, when in 1191 William of Montbazin, the descendant of an early patron of Valmagne, gave "everything I seek justly or unjustly in the field above Valmagne," this was more than simply an abbey's consolidation of property. The implication is of the resolution of a long conflict. William was not only being transformed into a donor, he was also received into "all the benefits of the *ordo*."[19] Such charters and testamentary bequests—not necessarily made at the very end of a donor's lifetime—can thus reveal the liminal state of donors who were about to leave the secular world and enter the monastic one.

We can also tell something about lay-brothers from such charters. In 1193, Bernard Sicard, describing himself as in sound mind and making his last testament, left his body and soul to Valmagne, in death and in life, to become a "conversus" there. Here the rhetoric of gift may be important to avoid charges of simony, but the contract gives an interesting glimpse at social standing as well. Bernard's conveyances of a house in the parish of Saint-Peter of Pabiran, his rights in the castle of Montigniac, and his rights over a family of peasants—Salvarius with his wife, sons, and daughters—reveal that this donor, who was about to be transformed into a lay-brother or conversus at Valmagne, was not a peasant but was probably of the knightly class.[20] That in 1193 such a member of the knightly class should have entered Valmagne as a lay-brother, possibly out of humility (as is explicit in the case of Silvanès' founder, Pons of Léras, discussed in Chapter 3), suggests a continued equality between monks and lay-brothers, as well as the limited impact of the 1188 General Chapter statute forbidding admission of knights as lay-brothers.[21] Indeed, there are indications in charters from elsewhere in southern France that monks in the 1160s and even later were still working in the fields alongside lay-brothers; distinctions between the two had not yet become rigid.[22] Knights might choose to become lay-brothers at the reform houses they had helped to found because they preferred a more balanced life of physical labor and prayer. There are indications that such men opted for houses following Cistercian customs because they were assured an equitable treatment as conversi—something beginning to be codified in the lay-brother treatises being composed at Cîteaux and Clairvaux from the 1150s onward.[23]

Most Cistercian transactions were recorded as charters close to the date at which the events had taken place, and a remarkable number of charter texts have been preserved in excellent twelfth- and thirteenth-century cartulary copies made by monastic communities. In most cases, charters in such collections are unquestionably authentic, for Cistercians had much less reason to create ancient deeds to justify current ownership than had earlier monastic communities claiming Carolingian or even Merovingian roots.[24] Because Cistercian cartularies were made at most only several generations (rather than several centuries) after the contracts they contain, fewer inaccuracies were introduced deriving from misunderstood or misidentified personal and place names, or changed legal concepts.

Cartularies and the charters in them survive more easily than individual parchments, but cartulary-making was expensive in both materials and labor. Cartularies were thus more likely to have been made by wealthier houses or those that had members with writing skills willing to undertake the physical work of copying. They were also more likely to have been written by religious houses heavily involved in the reconsolidation of fragmented holdings, something we see happening, for instance, at Silvanès, as discussed below. Land consolidation appears to have been more actively pursued by men's houses than by women's, if we can judge from the limited comparison of Silvanès and Nonenque. This fact skews the surviving evidence heavily in the direction of the better-endowed, more administratively successful religious communities and toward houses of monks rather than of nuns. This is not because nuns were not literate or able to copy charters but because they were richer and able to buy land in larger blocks, and thus possibly less willing to take on the labor of copying and the expense of materials when it was unnecessary for their acquisition of endowment. Nuns kept archives; they simply did not so often keep them in duplicate or triplicate. Finally, survival of archives is haphazard. Even for men's houses, a fire that hit an archive directly, as happened at Bonneval, could destroy even parchments, leaving little material from which to trace the history of that extremely rich abbey.[25] In certain regions in southern France, there was also much destruction of archival materials by warfare.[26]

How cartularies were collected and arranged often varies, but creating such books out of monastic archives usually meant copying all charters for an abbey up to the date when the cartulary was complete.[27] Sometimes copying was done by a single scribe; in other cartularies several hands are found. Given the routines of monastic life, the copying of the larger cartularies may have taken only several years, but sometimes their creation was a more continuous effort over a longer period. Individual charters were usually copied in toto into a codex (rarely, a parchment roll) to which rubrication and indices were then added. The southern-French cartularies usually seem to have had their charters organized in some way before copying began. The organization of charters within such cartularies might be by types of contract, such as papal bulls, land acquisitions, and rental agreements, or by granges or other properties. Frequently all gifts from "princes," papal confirmations, royal diplomata, gifts from titled lords, or concessions of pasture rights from important authorities were placed ahead of sections on individual property groupings. Sometimes an entire volume was devoted to a single grange. Within such chapters or volumes, charters might be organized with most prestigious donors first, by subproperties or by date.[28] Dates at which cartularies were redacted can be reconstructed from the latest dates of acts copied continuously, as well as to some extent from manuscript hands.

For southern France it is obvious that most Cistercian cartularies come from the years between 1200 and 1250.[29] These cartularies appear to have considerably more internal logic than is found in the lists of donors and gifts in the Burgundian pancartes.[30] We must constantly keep in mind, however, that there were two times of production — two historical moments with different motivating forces behind them — that of charter-making and that of cartulary-making. They must be sorted out and treated separately.

As for the charters themselves, whether preserved in originals or in cartulary copies, their language and organization are conservative.[31] Such private acts were modeled on traditional royal diplomata and papal acts of confirmation. By the twelfth century, such charters included both gifts and sales, gifts and mortgages, or confirmations and gifts mixed within single contracts. This is seen in one in which a certain Beatrix tells us that she gives, confirms, and sells (*dono, laudo et vendo*) whatever she had in the mansus Embacis to Silvanès for 15 solidi of Melgueil.[32] In another early undated charter for Silvanès, we see reference to giving and confirming, but also a price:

Ego Petrus de Luganio et ego Stephana, uxor ejus, ... donamus et laudamus ... Deo et altari Sancte Marie de manso Terundi et Poncio de Leracio ... totam vicariam .... et ut hoc donum perpetuo tenore firmaretur ... accepimus ab eis XXX solidos.

I, Peter of Luganio, and I, Stephanie his wife, ... give and confirm ... to God and to the altar of Saint Mary in the mansus of Terundo and to Pons of Léras ... all the vicarial rights .... And that this gift be held firm perpetually ... we accept from them 30 solidi.[33]

In such reflections of heavenly equations, written with an eye to the Last Judgment, our distinctions between onerous conveyances and gifts in free alms are not always particularly apt.

Contracts between monastic communities and the secular world were ambiguous. Most contracts were freely given and at the same time asked responses of various sorts from a religious community, including their prayers. It was obvious even to the most hard-hearted vendor that spiritual rewards could be derived from a transaction with monks and nuns. For historians working in quantitative ways, the monastic scribes' tendency to combine gift and sale in the same contract poses methodological problems. Although a study of aggregate trends in land acquisitions as reflected in total numbers of documents, counting such as that I undertook in *Medieval Agriculture*, can use charters in large numbers to show reliable trends, counting how many contracts are designated as either donations or sales, free or onerous, can also distort the reality in which they were so often both. There are other caveats about how Cistercian charters and cartularies may be used.[34] Yet charters, when read in their cartulary context, allow us not only to understand the initial motives of the monastic community at the time when it had made a transaction but to discern something about the priorities of monastic administrators at the time of cartulary production; often these were not the same. This is seen even in the physical organization of cartulary books, in which the placement of charters reveals attitudes contemporary to the time of cartulary-making about the relative importance of certain donors or certain transactions. Confusion about motives, misdirection of the reader, interpolation, and forgery were all possible distortions, any of which might be introduced by those who were transforming archives full of charters into cartularies, just as they were also real possibilities in writing historical accounts or charters themselves. Part of the difficulty is the difference between our modern idea of what a contract means and how its invariability makes it valid and twelfth-century views of charters. Such contracts were only then beginning to take on some of the connotations we give contracts today. Fortunately, conscious efforts to hide what was really happening in charters preserved by Cistercian cartulary-making of this time appear to have been rare.[35]

Our reading of twelfth-century southern-French charters is made more complicated because of several changes underway during that century, changes that only gradually appeared. First, the donation contract traditionally used in monastic contexts was being transformed in the more commercialized world of the twelfth century and used to describe new types of transactions. There are hints as well of a confrontation between a newer market economy and the older gift economy, which was described for eleventh-century Cluny and its patrons by Rosenwein. But just as we still today occasionally operate in a gift economy, there was no clear break between the gift economy of the eleventh century and the profit economy of the twelfth.[36] Donors to new groups like the Cistercians often clearly believed that their transactions were made as temporary gifts (available to be called back from a religious community at need) in the style of conveyances to monastic houses made in earlier centuries. That Cistercians as recipients of such transfers of property treated them with a new, possibly more market-driven, attitude and as permanent conveyances to themselves sometimes caused disputes.

There are also important issues of emerging law. The making of Cistercian documents in southern France occurred at a moment when notions about the validity of private charters had begun to be transformed.[37] Most twelfth-century monastic charters from this region remained memoranda of public acts. They describe public transactions and list the witnesses to those actions. Such witnesses might be recalled later to attest to the living drama between individuals about which the charter had only noted the details. Such private acts had no legal force as documents per se and did not themselves constitute proof; instead, they were the record of witnesses to such donors and recipients interacting face-to-face. Only gradually did the texts of such transactions inscribed on parchment become dispositive, obtaining the quality of legal proof in and of themselves, becoming literally title deeds. This change in the charter's value as a legal instrument is part of a larger change from ad hoc to more formal structures throughout medieval Europe in this period. This growing sense of identity between a transaction and the document that recorded it may have appeared earlier in other regions, but in southern France it appeared only about the year 1200. When it did arrive, it was brought by outsiders and was accompanied by the practice of attaching seals to such documents.[38]

The need for the *laudatio parentum*, the requirement that a wide-ranging group of family members confirm conveyances and be offered countergifts for their acts, contributed an additional dimension to the problem of the interpretation of charters.[39] Indeed, the need for the *laudatio* explains the avid search by monastic communities for confirmations of even outright gifts, as well as their frequent payment of cash for such confirmations. In many contracts even "donors" received countergifts.[40] Donors, as well as the monks and nuns who were recipients, would have been concerned that their transfers of property to religious houses remain valid and would have wanted such token gifts made in order to assure the validity of gifts to monasteries. Certainly perpetual prayers for souls must have been viewed as depending on the perpetuity of such gifts.[41] Moreover, clear title was far from obvious in an inheritance regime in which familial claims created a morass of legitimate rights to ownership that monastic acquisition had to disentangle. As a result, even when considerable care had been taken, new contracts might have to be written up and additional sums paid for land that religious communities must have thought they already owned. For example, it was only after the monks of Valmagne took possession of the mills given them along the Hérault River by one of the sons of William VI of Montpellier that the abbey discovered that this supposedly "free gift in alms" was in fact the acquisition of a heavily mortgaged property.[42] Yet this was a conveyance from a major family of Cistercian supporters.

Despite such issues, administrative records like charters remain the best and most unbiased evidence available from which to trace the major directions of economic activities among Cistercians and pre-Cistercians in Mediterranean France. But charters must be used with great care when we turn to the less clear-cut issues of donors' intentions and relationships between the secular community and any monastery. Charters used by the Cistercians and others in the twelfth century regularly employed a "language of donation," even when such contracts were clearly not gifts but sales, and indeed even when those contracts should more properly be called purchases by the monks and nuns of those monastic communities. Even though we know that many contracts present outright sales in the language of gifts, it is very easy to take such language too literally. For instance, in a contract from the Valmagne cartulary from 1196 we see Pons-Raine, Guillelma his wife, and Bernard of Marcellian, son of the late Raymond Ravionis, all acting together to convey the lordship over the garrigue of Puy Bonenque to abbot Peter and the monks of Valmagne by gift. They received 300 solidi.[43] Despite the payment made to them, the principals were presented in the charter as if they were benefactors of the monastery; in a case that the charter makes clear was instigated by the monks, they were primarily vendors. Recent debate has raised the question whether such contracts should be called sales, "gifts and countergifts," or "disguised sales." The last term was introduced by legal scholars as a convenience to denote a type of contract not easily categorized, but it is unfortunate in its connotations of dishonesty.[44] What such discussions often do not note is that many monastic contracts should not be characterized as donations or sales at all, but are instead acquisition contracts in which the monks and nuns actively made purchases or sought gifts from patrons. Their contracts' language of donation hides this active role of the religious community, as well as reducing the range of possible interactions that may be noted between monastic houses and their neighbors. The contracts portray every single transaction as if it were only a variation on an archetypical gift: all are made by identical donors all equally in need of salvation. Yet any study of these contracts en masse soon shows that monastic communities were, and had to be, the active parties in such acquisitions, frequently initiating them.[45]

When we consider charters more specifically as reflections of an interaction between monastic communities and their donors and benefactors, what is immediately noticeable is how little had changed in the nature of the contracts as used by the new monastic groups. Although denouncing the economic regimes of older monasticism with its interactions between tenants and members of religious communities, the twelfth-century charters recording transactions undertaken by reformed monastic communities resemble very closely those made between monasteries like Cluny and its neighbors in previous centuries. Contract forms persist, despite the fact that such new monks and nuns sought to escape dependence on the manorial regime and the proprietorial church, which were the centerpieces of earlier monastic ownership.[46] Even if the properties that the new groups acquired were slightly different in kind, the charter forms employed to record monastic property acquisitions had not appreciably changed from those used by other, earlier religious groups.

Yet if anything, twelfth-century religious communities had more control over how the charters of land acquisition presented their activities. While in earlier centuries charters had often been written for monastic communities in the scriptoria of counts and kings, twelfth-century monastic charters were almost always written by scribes from within the new abbeys and priories. Earlier charters written by nonmonastic scribes mentioned the donors who employed such scribes first as part of an etiquette of power, reflecting such donors' superiority in local secular and ecclesiastical hierarchies. In the twelfth century, the charters were no longer written by scribes employed by those lay donors but increasingly on behalf of the monks and nuns who were the recipients. Benefactors were lower on the social scale than those of earlier centuries and usually did not have their own scribes, but the "donor-first" pattern continued, suggesting that the authentic voice of the conveyancer to the monastic community was being lost because he or she was no longer in control of the composition of charters written in his or her own name. This may explain a subtle dissonance in twelfth-century charters written by monastic communities, one between the outward appearance and the actual content of such charters. Outsiders to the monastic are always "donors," depicted as the actors and initiators of transactions, while monastic communities are presented as passive recipients of unsought benefits. Such a posture of monastic passivity tends to mask the active pursuit of property by monastic communities and what could be quite aggressive behavior by such monks and nuns toward secular and ecclesiastical neighbors. As a consequence, historians must take into account that within twelfth-century charters recording gifts, sales, and exchanges to the new monastic communities there is always a certain fiction, one of monastic inadvertence.

Although the terms of the charters are not fictitious — obviously donors specified certain things — the initial motivation for a transaction is often lost in the language of giving. Rhetorically speaking, monastic acquisitions were made in a larger economy of salvation because of the great spiritual neediness of the donors. Monastic acceptance of gifts was supposedly reluctant and their acquisition inadvertent. But this was not the reality. The language of donation of such charters masks monastic agency and pushes those of us discussing monastic acquisitions to speak of "donors and benefactors" acting on monastic houses. Such a language of inadvertence was often very convenient for the monastic recipients.

But such implications of purity of motives in Cistercian economic dealings with their neighbors, while present in the monastic charters, need not be naively believed by monastic historians. Such posturing and attitudes found in the Cistercian charters coincide with the rhetoric of the Cistercian *exordia* as well. The latter proclaim that the move from Molesme was forced on the monks who went to Cîteaux, that they had virtually no option but to leave, and that the move had been approved by all members of the ecclesiastical hierarchy. What became clear from the charters, when studied en masse in my earlier work on Cistercian agriculture in southern France, was that the gathering together of endowment was no accident; far from inadvertent, it was the result of conscious and careful management.[47] That this was so suggests that we read the charters' imputation of inadvertence to monks or salvational needs of donors with a certain skepticism.

That a certain aggressiveness was necessary for such new reform communities to create the necessary endowment for their survival is undoubtedly true. As I showed in *Medieval Agriculture*, the abbeys founded by Cistercians and proto-Cistercians in southern France in the twelfth century were not created in total isolation from the secular world.[48] No huge tracts of uncleared and uncultivated land were available. A lower level of wealth among typical monastic patrons meant that they could make only small gifts to most newly founded communities. This meant that the process of putting together a monastic endowment was harder in the twelfth century than it had ever been before. Moreover, Cistercian economic goals necessitated frequent interactions with previous landowners and their tenants. These new monks and nuns were not content to be supported by the economic regime used by earlier monastic groups (who had soon become lords of villages), but set out instead to create granges on which they could work themselves. To do so, they had often had to remove earlier tenants, and many reform communities were successful in doing so. Cistercians and their predecessors successfully rearranged the landscape to create their granges, but their charters reflect ideologies about what sources of support were appropriate to monastic communities. Only with an active land market, including an active market in peasant tenures, and the availability of large amounts of cash was that consolidation possible.

Such new monastic communities could turn existing tenures into new self-directed granges; however, they were less able to take account of the consequences of land acquisitions for their neighbors. Whether the fiction of inadvertence in their charters is in fact related to a seeming reluctance on their part to take responsibility for the more unpleasant consequences of their creation of endowment, such as the displacement of peasants because of the creation of new granges, is unclear. But it has certainly encouraged historians to ignore those outcomes.

Such appropriation of the moral high ground in their charters may have contributed to an arrogance with which Cistercians and proto-Cistercians conducted their land acquisitions in the twelfth century. Moreover, the rhetoric of donation in monastic charters may have hidden from their eyes, as it hides from the historian's gaze, the occasions when monks and nuns founding abbeys and granges were not welcome in new communities. That some inhabitants actively resisted the entry of such reformers into established villages and parishes is documented, for instance, in the record of a conflict in the mid-twelfth century between the monks of Berdoues and villagers at Cuelas in Gascony. The villagers resisted the reform monks' attempts to create a grange there, and resistance erupted into violence when one of the villagers killed a lay-brother who had been attempting to set out the boundaries of the Cistercian grange. This violent reaction to monastic encroachments at Cuelas, however, was only recorded because out of remorse the villagers gave up the very lands they had earlier refused to convey to Berdoues. Murder in this case set the stage for what was ultimately a monastic victory, and that victory is recorded because land acquisition needed to be documented by a charter granting land to the monks.[49]

This action by the villagers of Cuelas must be seen as part of a larger trend too often unrecorded but documented occasionally in the charters. Those documents sometimes reveal resistance to Cistercian creation of granges in their indirect discourse, noting neighbors hesitant to take up the "opportunities for giving" provided by monks and nuns. It is unlikely that the monks of Berdoues ever recognized how their insensitivity to the needs and desires of neighboring communities into which they had extended their reach provoked a murder at Cuelas. Only a careful and deep reading of many such sources can occasionally recover such reactions. A posture of monastic inadvertence in their contracts allowed twelfth-century monks and nuns to deny the consequences of their actions, but it has also infected our modern discussion of monastic relationships with their neighbors. It is difficult for the historian to resist monastic self-presentation in the charters, which leads us perhaps too often to talk about donors and benefactors rather than about monastic acquisitiveness.

Finally, although all types of charters mix authentic transactions with bits of added narrative, many so-called "foundation charters" are not really charters at all.[50] They reflect no single legal transaction or group of transactions, but are in fact retrospective narratives made to look like charters. Such memoranda share a vision of how the Order came to be with the early Cistercian *exordia* and other hagiographical literature. Despite being retrospectively drawn up, their authors and dates are almost invariably unknown. Historians too often attach such accounts to the earliest possible dates and treat them as if they recorded authentic transactions.[51]

Gimont

The abbey for monks at Gimont was sited between Toulouse and Auch at the convergence of a Roman road and the Gimone River. Despite the illusion of isolation, its location near one of the pilgrimage routes leading west from Toulouse suggests that Gimont's site was not the desert of Cistercian mythology. Its granges to the north were also located close to those associated with the house of monks for Grandselve. Gimont profited considerably from annexing a number of tiny hermitages that often consisted of family groups practicing religious lives in isolated spots where they supported themselves by animal husbandry and gardening in minor clearances.[52] The fact that these communities often consisted of men and women living together in spiritual friendship under the same roof was only one of the irregularities of such ad hoc forays into the eremitical life. Many of these groups also appear to have included married priests and their families. Bishops and patrons alike must have welcomed the opportunity to place such tiny groups under the control of a reformed monastic house like Gimont and must have urged affiliation of such hermits to such established houses.[53]

Gimont's origins were similar. The earliest charters in the Gimont cartulary, from the years 1147 and 1148, reveal a small group of hermits living with their abbot Arnold at a place along the Gimone River called l'Artigue, a common term for such recently cleared land; this site appears to be near the later site of the abbey of Gimont. Their leader appears to be Arnold of Saint-Just, who served as the first abbot of Gimont (probably 1147–53) and then became abbot for the next forty years at the community of Berdoues, located in the Baise River valley southwest of Gimont. Some relationship between Gimont and Berdoues existed from 1153, and probably earlier. There are hints of early cooperation as well between Gimont and the nearby abbey of Grandselve. Such cooperation continued at least up to 1161 when Gimont was granted a grange for olive-production along with Grandselve and Fontfroide in the diocese of Elne. But while the latter two abbeys became attached to Cistercian practices by Bernard of Clairvaux and eventually to what would become the filiation of Clairvaux, Gimont did not. It appears that, when Arnold of Saint-Just became abbot of Berdoues, he was construed as having removed Gimont from any association with Grandselve and having made it into a daughter of Berdoues; a later story was that Berdoues had founded a daughter-house at Gimont.

Arnold was still abbot of Gimont while Bertrand was abbot of Grandselve in the late 1140s; the latter died in 1150. The two houses seem to have cooperated regarding granges and pasture in these early years, and Gimont, like Grandselve, probably learned of Cistercian practices from Bernard of Clairvaux or his friend Alexander of Cologne, sent to be abbot of Grandselve (1150–58) after Bertrand's death. From Gimont, Cistercian customs were taken by Arnold to Berdoues in 1153, whence they eventually were spread to other Gascon and Spanish houses in Morimond's filiation.[54] With the election of Pons of Polignac as abbot of Grandselve (1158–69), conflict over pasture rights and granges immediately erupted between Grandselve and Gimont.[55] The abbots present at a preliminary arbitration of the dispute suggest that congregations of Spanish and Gascon proto-Cistercians were by the late 1150s developing under the control of mother-abbeys at Berdoues, Bonnefont, and l'Escaledieu, but still had no ties to Morimond.[56] The dispute with Grandselve over pasture and granges may have been what pushed Gimont firmly into the camp of the congregation associated with Berdoues. Gimont's independent origins became so transformed that it was treated as a daughter-house of Berdoues in the filiation trees. Moreover, by the last decade of the twelfth century two charters asserting Berdoues's foundation of Gimont had found their way into the Gimont archives and then into the Gimont cartulary. Such a rewriting of Gimont's foundation history probably did not occur until just after the death of abbot Arnold of Saint-Just (who had once been abbot of Gimont) at Berdoues circa 1193. Indeed, those charters probably appeared during the abbacy of Arnold of Broil (1191–94), since the new "foundation charter" attributed founder status to that current abbot's grandparents.[57]

The opening two charters of the Gimont cartulary, which assert that Gimont was founded by Berdoues and that the foundation had been made in response to a gift by Gerald of Broil and his family, provide a good example of how cartulary-makers could distort earlier events, often simply by directing our attention to certain charters within an archive as those most significant or by placing them as the opening acts of the charter-book. In this case, however, there is evidence of considerable interpolation in the opening two charters of the Gimont cartulary, and possibly outright forgery in the first.

The first charter, the Gimont foundation charter, presents the Broil family as founders. It is an account of a foundation by apostolic gestation that is obviously fictitious, given the evidence of other Gimont charters that show an eremitical settlement already there. Charter 1 presents founders going to the mother-house of Berdoues to have it found the abbey of Gimont:

In nomine Domini sciendum est quod [Giraldus dez Broil et Gasens uxor ejus], pro se et pro omnibus successoribus suis presentibus et futuris pro amore Dei et remissione peccatorum suorum donaverunt Deo et beate Marie de Berdonas, atque Alberto abbati et conventui ejusdem loci presenti et futuro, centum concadas de terra in nemore quod dicitur Planasilva, ut ibi construatur abbatia in honore Dei et beate Marie Genitricis ejus, et sancti Benedicti omniumque sanctorum, secundum consuetudinem cisterciensis ordinis.

In the name of the Lord it is understood that Gerald of Broil and Gasens his wife, for themselves and for all their successors at present and in future times, for love of God and for the remission of their sins gave to God and to the Blessed Mary of Berdoues and to Albert abbot and to the community of that place now and in the future, 100 concades of land in the woods that is called Planesylve, in order to construct an abbey there in honor of God and the blessed Mary his Mother, and of Saint Benedict and all the Saints, following the customs of the Cistercian *ordo*.[58]

For Charter 1, it is possible to argue a simple transposition of the date from an earlier act by Gerald of Broil; that is, we can argue that the makers of the cartulary transformed a charter for 1147 into one for 1142 when they copied *mcxlii v aprilis* instead of *mcxlvii aprilis*. This allows us to argue that Gimont was probably not attached to Berdoues until 1147 and that Berdoues itself was only founded in 1142 or thereabouts.⁵⁹ But other indications suggest outright forgery. The place-name Planesylve is an interpolation not used elsewhere at this time for this site. The phrase *pro amore Dei et remissione peccatorum suorum* is characteristic of charters with dates from 1190 through 1210 in the Berdoues cartulary, as is the phrase *secundum consuetudinem cisterciensis ordinis*, which does not appear elsewhere in Gimont's documents (except in Charter 2 and in one other document for 1147) until late in the twelfth century. As copied into the cartulary, this foundation charter and Charter 2, which supports it, are retrospective constructs pushing in the direction of outright forgery, although they may have interpolated acts already available at the moment of cartulary-making. The bulk of the charters in the Gimont cartulary suggest that the Broil family and that of Arnold of Bigmont (who appears in the second charter) participated in making early gifts to Gimont but that they were not alone in the monastic foundation there.⁶⁰

Charter 2 is also clearly interpolated:

Arnaldus de Bigmont et Willelmus Arnaldus filius ejus, pro amore Dei et redemptione animarum suarum, bone fide, sine omni retencione, libere et absolute jure perpetuo, pro se et pro omnibus suis successoribus, donaverunt et concesserunt et absolverunt Deo et beate Marie Gemundi et Bernardo abbati et conventui ejusdem loci presenti et futuro totum illud donum quod Geraldus des Brol, et uxor ejus Gasens, et filius ejus Trencher, et Geraldus, et Willelmus Raimundus, et Matildis uxor ejus fecerant Deo et beate Marie de Berdonas et Alberto abbati ejusdem loci de centum concadas de terra ad construendam prefatam abbatiam Gemundi.

Arnold of Bigmont and William Arnold his son for the love of God and for the redemption of their souls, in good faith and without retention, freely and absolutely in perpetual rights, for themselves and all their successors, gave and conceded and left to God and Blessed Mary of Gimont and to Bernard abbot and to the community of that place at present and in future all that gift that Gerald of Broil and his wife Gasens and their son Trencher and Gerald and William Raymond and Matilda his wife made to God and to the blessed Mary of Berdoues and to Albert abbot of that place, of 100 concades of land to build said abbey of Gimont.

Although Charter 2 is dated 1142, the abbot receiving the confirmation for Gimont is Bernard (1154–67); indeed it is likely that 1142 (*mcxlii*) is a transposition of the date of 1162 (*mclxii*) in the original.⁶¹

But did such interpolation of the early thirteenth century do anything more than present false claims about which family was responsible for the foundation? While it is obvious that some interpolation had happened in the interest of flattering the Broil family, there is also an assertion of control over Gimont by Berdoues. Perhaps this interpolation also solidified the claims about "apostolic gestation" within Gascony and for an early attachment of Berdoues and its sister-houses to Morimond. There is no evidence in the Berdoues cartulary itself for the foundation of Gimont as a daughter-house. Finally, in an earlier publication I argued for a missionary tour of Gascony by the first Walter of Morimond, but much of the support for an early date of Cistercian affiliation for Berdoues was based on the assumptions that Gimont had been created by Berdoues in 1147 and that Charter 1 of the Gimont cartulary had only a transposed date. The evolution was probably more complicated. Gimont did not found Berdoues, or vice-versa, in 1153, and both were probably independent pre-Cistercian foundations. But Cistercian customs were introduced to Berdoues by Gimont's former abbot, Arnold of Saint-Just, in 1153, and (in rather Cluniac fashion) Gimont was considered to have become Berdoues's dependency when Arnold of Saint-Just was called from Gimont to be abbot of Berdoues.

Problematic opening charters notwithstanding, the charters and cartulary for Gimont provide a reasonably accurate reflection of the process by which that abbey's monks acquired extensive lands around the abbey, at its home farm, and at its five granges. Gimont's holdings were almost all acquired in the twelfth century. They reflect typical proto-Cistercian or Cistercian reorganization of land by careful purchase and consolidation. The abbey's transformation of some of its holdings into bastides in the thirteenth century is also typical of trends in southwestern France, where the lines between the English and French were being drawn a century before the beginning of the Hundred Years War.[62]

Charters in the Gimont cartulary reveal individuals and families who worked to create Gimont's endowment and also often bridged in their own lives the gap between abbey and secular community. One group of charters that reveals these relationships for the 1160s are those in the cartulary section concerning Gimont's grange of Aiguebelle and its early monk and administrator there, William of Blancafort.[63] His activities in pursuit of properties for this grange, which would become the bastide of Saint-Lys in the thirteenth century, reflect not only Gimont's aims but some of those of the family of donors into which he had been born. William's father, Ato of Blancafort, with his wife Guillelma or Guisla and her brothers Arnold and Centullus of Gironde, had participated in the initial gifts for creating a grange at Aiguebelle. In fact, their benefactions seem to have been made with the intention that Gimont would found a new abbey at this site, although that never happened. Only in hindsight is it easy to see that the founding of new reform houses (especially for monks rather than for nuns) rarely occurred after the mid-twelfth century except by the intervention of a major political figure. Although the founding of new monasteries was not entirely past, a community like Gimont of only middling size (at this point with not yet sufficient endowment) was not likely to create a daughter-house circa 1160. Instead, it was more likely to add new granges. This was probably particularly so at a place like Aiguebelle, where there is no indication that what was at issue was the affiliation of an already-existing religious community with a church. Moreover, the region around Aiguebelle was already becoming overcrowded with houses and granges of the emerging Cistercian Order. But none of this was very apparent to donors who had seen houses of reform monks founded by their peers only a few years earlier. By the 1160s and 1170s such overcrowding would lead to negotiations within the Order and with its neighbors about minimum distances between monasteries and granges such as those found in the Charter of Peace with the Praemonstratensians discussed in Chapter 2.

After William of Blancafort became a monk at Gimont, he was dispatched with a group of conversi to the grange of Aiguebelle, where he acted in land acquisition much as an abbot or prior of a small independent house.[64] In some senses acting simultaneously as both patron and monk, William was probably as eager as his family to see this grange elevated into a new abbey; if so, he did not succeed. The charters reveal him aggressively instigating or accepting gifts on behalf of Gimont for this grange. Land with the most questionable title was that most likely to be conveyed to such new monastic communities and in part these charters reveal a playing out of older rivalries in the context of monastic land acquisition.

But William's actions also suggest his ambitions for his grange. William's forceful actions provoked negative reactions from neighbors and even from his extended family. He asserted Gimont's tithe exemption in ways that extracted tithes for Gimont without making any recompense to earlier owners for their rights — and this at a time when most Cistercians could exert tithe privileges only by repurchasing tithes from existing owners.[65] He resorted to judicial procedures and court hearings, producing charters as if they were title-deeds in support of his claims, even in conflicts with his own family. When William's brother-in-law claimed that William's widowed mother, Guisla, had made illegal sales of property to Gimont and argued that her guardianship did not allow her to alienate her children's property, William took the complaint to court and successfully overturned it when Guisla testified that she had been forced to sell some of the children's property only to provide money for their maintenance.[66] When similar claims were made by William's maternal cousin, Bernard of Bigorre, William brought out the charters of gifts from their common ancestors and displayed them; the cousin withdrew his claims.[67]

Charters for another of Gimont's granges, that at Hour, show other types of interactions between Cistercians and their neighbors, revealing how many contracts described as "gifts" to a monastic community were only grudgingly made. "Benefactors" often confirmed such transactions, moreover, only after countergifts and other concessions had been made. The cartulary section for this grange reveals the frequent tendency to flatter the rich and powerful by inflating the importance of their gifts. It opens with an act dated 1169 in which the viscounts of Mauvezin (see Figure 36 for some of these locations) were presented as if they were the most significant patrons. The charter tells us:

Willelmus Raimundus, vicecomes de Malvezein et Petrus Raimundus, frater ejus, confirmaverunt et autorgaverunt Bernardo abbati et habitatoribus Gemundi totum hoc quod conquisierunt et acaptaverunt in toto honore Dosartvila de Maria d'Escornabou et de filiis ejus et de hominibus eorum et in toto honore del Forc de Gailardo de Sirac. Et insuper concesserunt expletam et pascua et ingressum et egressum per totam terram suam, . . . et totam decimam Sancte Marie de Carambad, quantum pertinent ad totam seignoriam Gaillardi de Sirag.

William Raymond, viscount of Mauvezin, and Peter Raymond, his brother, confirmed and authorized to Bernard abbot and the inhabitants of Gimont all that which they had acquired and obtained in all the honor of Assartville (literally, the recently cleared estate) from Marie of Escornabou, at that village and over its inhabitants, as well as in all the honor of Forc obtained from Gaillard of Sirac. And in addition the viscount and his brother conceded usage rights and pasture, ingress and egress through all their lands . . . as well as all the tithes of Saint-Mary of Carambad, which pertain to the entire lordship of Gaillard of Sirac.[68]

In fact the viscounts' importance lies in their title rather than their generosity. But by placing this act at the beginning of a major section the makers of the cartulary asserted that support from the viscounts of Mauvezin was of the utmost importance. The first act only mentions in passing two of the actually significant patrons, Marie of Escornabou and Gaillard of Sirac.

A different story about this grange at Hour emerges from a more chronological survey of charters in the cartulary section. It reveals the three families who were most central as instigators in land conveyances there to Gimont. Starting in 1158, Marie, chatelaine of Escornabou (or Escornaboeuf), gave substantial gifts to Gimont. Over the years she would also secure the *laudatio* for Gimont from her sons and from her daughter and a son-in-law. She would also command dependents to make conveyances to the monks.[69] Perhaps most important was her advocacy of conveyances to Gimont by an eremitical group at Arbielle, whose members, including Peter of Carambad, priest, with Martin, Arnold, and Peter of Sotol, gave their recently made clearances to Gimont, setting out the boundaries of land conveyed. They all then entered the monas-

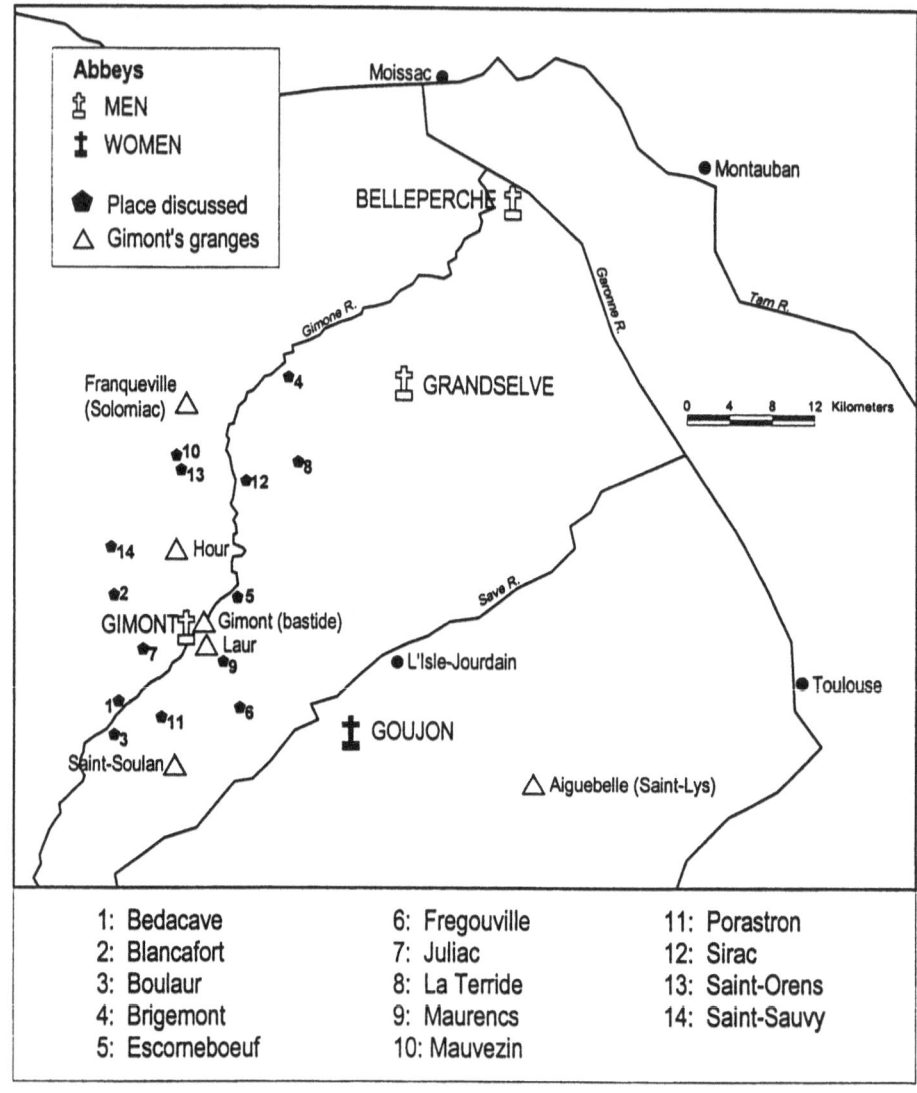

Figure 36. Gimont holdings with Maurencs family properties.

tery of Gimont—some as monks, others as lay-brothers. (Their foundation may be that referred to in the above quote as Saint-Mary of Carambad.)[70]

When she first appears in the Gimont charters, Marie was probably already a widow, but her husband, Ato of Escornabou, had been an early donor to Gimont, probably entering the community to die there within a year of its appearance in 1147.[71] Marie's charters never mention her late husband, but her close ties to the monastic community after Ato's death are revealed by a document dated 1163. It records her gift to Gimont "for love of God, for the health of her soul and those of her parents, and for love of Odo of Maurencs," the last a monk at Gimont and son of a neighboring family.[72] Marie's effusive concern for this monk and the monastic community at Gimont is striking in comparison to that of many other patrons, even those who were more generous in their conveyances. Marie was such an important advocate and supporter of Gimont that its abbot and monks promised her that when she and her son Gautier died each would have as many divine services performed at the abbey as would be done for a monk of that community.[73]

Charters written by Gimont's scribes often state directly that donors made spontaneous benefactions, but they also provide indirect evidence that the abbey was actively seeking such gifts as it consolidated its landholdings. In the case of Gaillard of Sirac, they reveal that patronage could be considerably less amiable than that of Marie of Escornabou. Gaillard's relationship to Gimont was more predatory than protective, his conveyances never gifts but always sales. Concessions of tithes by Gaillard and his nephew Odo were grudging, sticking strictly to the terms of the papal exemption granted to the Cistercians and other reform groups.[74] Gaillard's title to land conveyed to the abbey was often questionable, the land either being under mortgage or needing to be redeemed from other claimants. These two patrons even profited from exploiting the competition between Gimont and the neighboring abbey of Grandselve over land located between Gimont's granges of Forc and Franqueville and Grandselve's grange of la Terride.[75]

If Gaillard was not always truthful in his dealings with Gimont, his nephew Odo was openly hostile. Conflict arose over Odo's claims to pasture rights, which the monks asserted had not been redeemed by him along with an earlier pledge of land.[76] But Gaillard and Odo may be more typical donors than Marie of Escornabou. Enormous differences between the relationship of Marie of Escornabou to Gimont, and of Gimont with Gaillard of Sirac, are hard to see on the surface of the charters. In superficial terms, the transactions between these two families and Gimont are recorded in nearly identical terms, but the support Marie and Gaillard provided was not at all equivalent.

A third family of benefactors for this grange at Hour was that of Ademar and William of Juliac and their elder sister Gassia. Their conveyances in the 1160s to Gimont were sales initiated by Ademar and William, who also made gestures of support for Gimont by frequently acting as witnesses for monastic transactions. Although their conveyances over a period of twenty years almost inevitably required some cash in return, this family's dealings with the monks did not cause any controversy. Moreover, after twenty years of such innocuous interactions, men in the family chose Gimont as a place to retire. In 1179 Gassia's son Bernard, over thirty by that time, entered the abbey, possibly as a conversus, and he was soon followed by his uncle, Ademar of Juliac, who entered Gimont, when he must have been nearing fifty, as a monk.[77] That two members of the same family could enter Gimont circa 1180, one to become a monk and one a conversus, suggests that class lines between monks and lay-brothers had not yet emerged in abbeys in this region. This example, although it suggests possible downward mobility on the part of the younger man, also shows how often knights continued to choose the life of conversi rather than that of monks.

The three families described here supported Gimont in small ways rather than in grand gestures. They might control castles from which they protected surrounding countryside, they might grudgingly give tithes, but none of them owned or conveyed established churches or whole parishes to Gimont. They were minor benefactors in comparison to the Blancafort family, associated with the grange of Aiguebelle, or even the Broil family, whose gifts have been enshrined in Charter 1 of the cartulary's opening section as those of founders at the time when their grandson was abbot. All three families, those of Escornabou, Sirac, and Juliac, were much more involved in the creation of Gimont's grange at Hour than the viscounts of Mauvezin ever were, but the Mauvezins were presented by the cartulary-makers of the early thirteenth century as of greater importance. In most areas of southern France, such notables only rarely noticed the Cistercians and then only to assent to the gifts made by their dependents. They rarely gave or even sold or mortgaged land of their own.

In many ways Gimont's real founders, members of the family of the monk who had inspired Marie of Escornabou's gifts, Odo of Maurencs, were the most omnipresent among all Gimont's patrons.[78] The Maurencs family controlled the lordship and "castellum" at Maurencs, a castle large enough to have its own church and chaplain. A confirmation of 1167 shows that the Maurencs family was of sufficient social status to have other knights as their dependents; this family had no title but controlled considerable property in the mid-twelfth century.[79] Maurencses are described in the charters as lords, and their wives are frequently referred to with the honorific *Na*, short for *Domina*. This family, more powerful than either the Broils or the Blancaforts, stood at a level between the latter (with their one or two castles) and the titled nobles of southern France like the viscounts of Mauvezin.

The head of the Maurencs family was Yspanus. Familial strategies for property maintenance in this family apparently dictated that only one son per generation should marry; only Yspanus, probably the eldest, appears to have done so. He and his wife Alazais had at least one son, whose name may have been Esparrons, a daughter Paloma, and a daughter Alexandria, who became prioress of a nearby community of nuns.[80] The earliest charters for this family reveal Yspanus heading a group of brothers acting in concert who probably held their lands in a joint lordship or *frairesche*; see Figure 37.[81] They were sometimes joined by two men who were allied to the family by their marriages to Yspanus's two sisters, Gassia and Galdris.

After Yspanus there was a second brother, Fezac, who disappears from the Gimont records after 1151, either having died soon thereafter or possibly having departed permanently for military adventures in Spain. Another brother, Odo, made a great success as a monastic administrator at Gimont. A fourth, William, remained single, but acted frequently with Yspanus as a witness and guarantor in the Gimont charters.[82]

Transactions involving the Maurencs family began soon after Gimont's foundation in 1147. Probably the earliest encounter was in 1151 when they received 100 solidi from abbot Arnold of Gimont for the *casale* of Saint-Sernin and its honor on both sides of the Marchaona River, a conveyance that contributed to the assemblage of land for the grange of Laus or Laurs located several kilometers southeast of the abbey. All four brothers, Odo, William, Yspanus, and Fezac, appear in this contract; it is after this that Fezac disappears from further records.[83] In fact, Yspanus was the actual seller of the *casale* of Saint-Sernin to Gimont in 1151, although the conveyance was done with the assent of his brothers.[84] In the next few years the Maurencs family's ties to Gimont became closer. William of Maurencs appeared often as guarantor, co-donor, and witness, but he rarely actually gave or sold property to the monks; possibly as a younger son he had little property of his own. He seems to have died soon after 1177, when he last appeared in the records.[85]

William was predeceased by his brother Odo, who had entered Gimont as a monk before 1158 and is reported to have died in 1165, possibly at the abbey of Morimond in Burgundy.[86] An undated charter describes the ceremony in the monastic garden when Odo became a monk. At that time he made gifts of land to abbot Bernard "for the souls of his mother and father," and the abbot agreed to pay off certain debts of Odo's; the monks also gave him 114 solidi with which to pay off other debts.[87] Properties conveyed had already been pledged to Gimont against mortgages, and it is likely that Odo's entrance into Gimont solved a serious financial crisis for his family. Odo, like William of Blancafort at Aiguebelle, acted as "granger" for Gimont at its grange of Laurs. There, in 1158, he was described as acting "at the door of the grange of Laurs" and having a bailiff; in that year it was "into the hand of Odo of Maurencs"

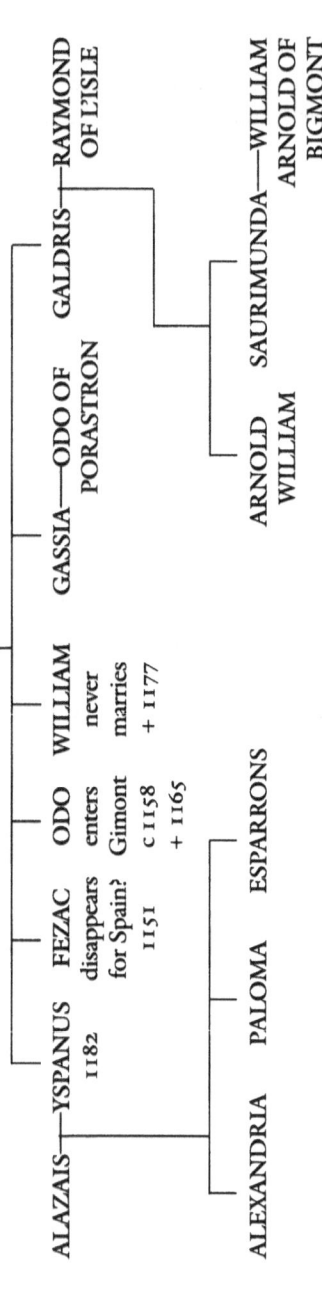

Figure 37. Family tree for the Maurencs, patrons of Gimont. (Berman)

that Bertrand of Laurs in a deathbed bequest confirmed his sale to Gimont of a mill and its site near the grange of Laurs.[88]

The relationship between the Maurencs family and the abbey of Gimont alternated from day to day depending on the circumstances. Yspanus and his brothers rarely initiated gifts to Gimont but were more often the last to consent to transactions made by their tenants. In a typical year, concessions of land in one place were made to the monks of Gimont by this family, but there might also be considerable controversy with Gimont over property elsewhere. Part of the problem lay in Gimont's accepting pledges of land (medieval mortgages) as security for money lent by its monks to the Maurencs. This was exacerbated by Gimont's acquisition of similar pledges on the family's lands from third parties. For example, in 1168, Yspanus and William transferred to Gimont all rights and lordship in the *casale* of Pin and in the church of la Mazières and confirmed to Gimont whatever their relatives and others had given, or pledged against mortgage (*impigneraverunt*), to that abbey. For this concession and promises that they would "defend all the property of Gimont and its inhabitants," Yspanus and William received 49 solidi as payment and were given the kiss of peace.[89] While the Maurencs brothers promised that they would "do no violence or injury in any way to said abbot or brothers," the charter suggests that the family saw Gimont as aggressive in its acquisition of mortgages and other rights over lands, woods, and pasture that pertained to the family, their men, their clerics, and their knights. Monastic communities like Gimont could be particularly uncompromising with regard to such pledges, having on their side both the corporate advantage of longevity and more cash, as well as the onerous terms of the medieval mortgage, in which the fruits of the pledged land did not reduce the principal at all. In the give and take of secular relationships, there was always the hope that one secular lord would be able to redeem land pledged to another lord when their fortunes had reversed. Once land fell into the hands of an abbey like Gimont, any such hope of recovering pledged land was lost.[90]

That the Maurencs family's motives in dealings with Gimont were mixed is nowhere more evident than in charters initiated circa 1167 by Yspanus's brother-in-law, Raymond of l'Isle, husband of Galdris, as Raymond prepared to leave for Jerusalem on Crusade. Raymond and Galdris gave Gimont whatever rights they had in half the tithes and first fruits over land that Gimont had acquired in the parish of Juliac, and they received 60 solidi from Gimont for what was, in legal theory at least, a return of tithes to the church.[91] Concessions in this parish were confirmed in 1168 by the couple's daughter Saurimunda and her husband William Arnold of Bigmont, possibly on the occasion of their wedding; we thus see the establishment of a kinship tie to another family of patrons of Gimont.[92] In 1169, Raymond "quando ivit ultra mare" gave abbot Bernard rights at a place called Hautmont and was absolved of the 200 solidi debt already secured by that land. He received "ad opus itineris sui" an additional 160 solidi and the loan of a mule worth 80 solidi.[93] While the Crusader Raymond of l'Isle had extracted considerable cash from Gimont for his voyage to the East, Gimont's "protection" of his property and financing of his journey by such gifts and mortgages had the potential to become the first step in monastic acquisition of those lands. The fact that these contracts are part of the cartulary of Gimont suggests that this is indeed what happened.

As brothers disappeared and Yspanus grew older, the need for peacemaking recurred, because conflict between Gimont and the Maurencs continued. In 1176, when his brother William was near death or had just died, Yspanus conveyed to Gimont all his rights and lordship in all the lands and in all the churches, tithes, and first fruits that Gimont held by gift, sale, or mortgage in a wide swath of territory "from Frégeville to Saint-Just." Yspanus is described as standing before the abbot and community at Gimont's altar, swearing over the Gospels that he would observe this concession in perpetuity. In return the abbot gave him 120 solidi and promised that the monks would fetch his body and bury him at Gimont, if Yspanus died within a certain territory.[94] Two years later, in 1178, Yspanus was still alive. Urged by a tenant who had been promised admission as a conversus "if he came to Gimont healthy and whole in all his members," Yspanus gave up his rights over that man and his tenancy.[95] Only in 1182, "in the illness from which he died," did Yspanus give to Arnold, prior of Gimont, the *casale* of Tresseira already held by Gimont as pledge for a mortgage of 45 solidi. He also confirmed all earlier conveyances to Gimont, releasing the monks from claims he had been making, and returned to them land at Volpilliac "which he had unjustly stolen."[96]

Yspanus of Maurencs exemplifies a whole class of knights who were often unable to provide castles for all their sons. The family's very survival was tied to their ability to alienate or mortgage land to Gimont when needing cash. Despite their care for family property in limiting marriages, their consumption needs meant that they gradually transferred much of their land to Gimont. They fought this tendency to lose their land at every turn. For instance, Yspanus gave dowries for his daughter to enter a nunnery and then took back the land to give elsewhere.[97] And they constantly found new reasons for getting yet another bit of money from the same house of monks at which they intended to be buried. In this society of knights, who were constantly in need of cash and with either too few or too many children and not enough land for all their needs, even the purest donor wanted prayers for his gifts, but he also wanted cash from the monks. On the other hand, with a brother who was an important administrator at Gimont, a daughter who was the prioress of a neighboring house of nuns, a brother-in-law who was a Crusader, and his own numerous actions as witness, *fidejussor*, and *mandator* for Gimont, Yspanus of Maurencs was a knight with heavenly assurances of many kinds. He must have felt confident enough about the health of his own soul to resist the demands of Gimont when he wished to do so. Someone with a less forceful personality than Yspanus might have been less resistant in the face of monastic intransigence about who owned what, which sometimes shows through from behind the facade of Gimont's charters.

Yspanus's attitude in his dealings with Gimont retained something of the older notions of "give and take" that we have come to associate with Cluny and its benefactors during the eleventh century.[98] What better example can be found of the relationships between monks and nuns of the new reform communities and patrons who would often enter those communities, retire there, or die there, but who often interacted with such new monastic communities in the same ambivalent ways as had donors of earlier centuries?

Nonenque

Charters from Nonenque also reveal the often mixed reasons for conveyances to Cistercian houses, but relationships with patrons of this small community of nuns in the southern Rouergue can only really be understood by making comparisons to the patronage found in contracts of its sister-abbey, the house of monks at Silvanès. Ties were complex between these two closely associated Cistercian communities located in parallel river valleys on the edge of the southernmost plateau or *causse* of the central massif of France, but it is clear that their activities even at pre-Cistercian or proto-Cistercian stages were often interlocked. Nonenque had been founded by or before the fourth decade of the twelfth century. Most histories assert that it had been colonized by nuns sent from the abbey of nuns at Bellecombe located at Yssingeaux near le Puy, but this may be only a variation on the standard Cistercian gestational myth. There was clearly an early attachment between Nonenque and Bellecombe.[99] Both women's houses soon became part of a wider reform group and, like Silvanès, Nonenque and Bellecombe were eventually tied to Mazan and then to the filiation of Bonnevaux. Although the chronicle of Silvanès claims that the third abbot of Silvanès founded Nonenque, the charters show otherwise.[100] Silvanès itself was only founded in the late 1130s. A charter in the Silvanès cartulary dated 1139 describes the conveyance to Silvanès of land "in the valley of Elnonenca," a place-name suggesting that the nuns were already there and had been established there for some time.[101]

The charters in other ways undermine accepted narratives about relationships between Nonenque and Silvanès. Nonenque was a house of aristocratic women who had their own lay-brothers and lay-sisters. Their charters call them *dominae*, rather than *sanctimoniales*.[102] The size of conveyance and amounts spent in the charters suggest that Nonenque was the wealthier house in the twelfth century. Silvanès may even have originated from a community of priests who undertook the "care of souls" for Nonenque's community of nuns. Probably those priests evolved into or joined the eremitical community founded by the "converted" knight, Pons of Léras, and his companions.[103] Only at the end of the thirteenth century would Nonenque become definitively subject to Silvanès's abbot as visitor.[104] Indeed, the very fact that Silvanès's control over this house of nuns was contested by Mazan at the Cistercian General Chapter meetings in the mid-thirteenth century gives credence to assertions of Nonenque's wealth as well as Nonenque's origin as an independent house of women, which was only later made dependent on Silvanès.[105]

Relationships between Nonenque and its neighbors and patrons in the twelfth century differed slightly from those of other Cistercians and proto-Cistercians in the region. The nuns seem to have had both recruits and patrons from a slightly higher social level than are found for contemporary houses of Cistercian monks.[106] Nonenque's patrons included the family of counts and bishops of Rodez and their wives. In 1170 the entire *villa* of Lioujas was granted to Nonenque by Ermengardis of Creyssels, dowager countess of Rodez, when she entered that community as a nun. Her conveyance to Nonenque was confirmed by her son, Hugh, count of Rodez.[107] In contrast, Silvanès and most other Cistercian houses for men did not attract such "land-giving" patronage from such a high social level at such an early date. Silvanès's earliest patron, Arnold of Pont, was one of a consortium of many small property-holding families granting rights to that abbey. A measure of his limited wealth in comparison to that of the counts of Rodez, patrons of Nonenque, is that his sons would hold the family castle at Pont-de-Camarès jointly as a *frairesche*.[108]

Nonenque was also more prolific than Silvanès, in both the creation of new abbeys and the attachment of existing ones. In the twelfth century, Nonenque had annexed one nearby community of nuns at Mount-Cornil near Lodève as well as a neighboring church. We know that the church was traded away in the thirteenth century for a grange, but it is not clear if a daughter-community remained at Mont-Cornil or not.[109] Nonenque also founded a priory at Saint-Sulpice near Albi in 1267, under the aegis of Sicard Alaman, an official of Alphonse of Poitiers.[110] A third daughter-house of nuns would be founded at la Falque, north of Rodez, probably in the fourteenth century.[111] Nonenque, Bellecombe, and the community at Mont-Cornil had all begun as independent, quasi-eremitical communities of women who were part of the larger movement of religious reform in the early twelfth century that included women. On the other hand, the powerful lord Sicard Alaman had helped Nonenque found Saint-Sulpice specifically so that his daughter could become a nun there.[112] In contrast to Nonenque, Silvanès had no daughter-houses.

Documents for Nonenque survive less completely than for Silvanès because Nonenque's nuns did not make a medieval cartulary. A cartulary was probably less needed because the nuns did not undertake the same types of land consolidation as did Silvanès and other houses of Cistercian monks in this region. Nonetheless, sufficient charter evidence does survive to make comparisons between the two houses. Nonenque's nuns expended considerable sums in individual transactions in twelfth-century property acquisitions, as seen in Table 3. Although we do not have as complete a collection of charters for the nuns, totals for Nonenque nonetheless were considerably larger than those expended by nearby Silvanès in the years covered by its cartulary.

The size of conveyances and a certain exclusiveness on Nonenque's part is suggested as well by two contracts. A last testament of 1182 shows a certain Ermengardis conveying 1,000 solidi to Silvanès in order that she be buried in its cemetery and have all the services performed for her as if she had been a monk there. In that same will she gave a dowry gift of 500 solidi to Nonenque for the entrance of her daughter, Sibilia, as a nun there.[113] The suggestion made by this charter that there were limited places for women at Nonenque is confirmed by another contract in which a woman named Jordana was accepted at Nonenque, *secundum ordinem nostrum*, and Maria, her mother, was promised her daughter's place if the daughter died first.[114] Did Silvanès simply have more monastic personnel to provide the religious services after death for a donor like Ermengardis? Or was Silvanès more available for providing religious benefits to women about to die than was Nonenque? There is a similar hint that burial was as likely by the monks at Villelongue as by the nuns at Rieunette, even for a female donor, as mentioned in Chapter 3. But given the limited materials available, one would not wish to refine too much based on such examples.

The charters for the two communities show equal or larger gifts being made to Nonenque than to Silvanès. Even the lay founder of Silvanès, Arnold of Pont, in his last testament in 1153, gave as large a bequest to the nuns of Nonenque as to Silvanès.[115] Similarly, in a document for 1152 Elizabeth, pri-

TABLE 3. Comparison of Cash Expenditures by Gimont, Silvanès, Nonenque, Valmagne

Years	Total charters	Cash expended (sol.)	Solidi/charter
Abbey of monks at Gimont (from GM)			
undated	27	—	
1130–49	19	250	13
1150–69	282	4,653	17
1170–89	349	3,396	10
1190–1209	83	274	3
1210–29	11	—	
1230–49	5	—	
totals:	776	8,573	11
Abbey of monks at Silvanès (from SL)			
undated	22	—	
1130–49	114	3,500.0	31
1150–69	312	21,678.0	69
1170–89	26	4,785.5	184
1190–1209	4	110.0	27
1210–29	5	60.0	12
totals:	483	30,133.5	62
Abbey of nuns at Nonenque (from NO)*			
1150–69	4	3750	938
1170–89	7	3337	477
totals:	11	7087	644
Abbey of monks at Valmagne (from "VM")			
undated	18	174.0	10
1130–49	20	3,146.5	157
1150–69	130	6,568.5	51
1170–89	251	45,687.5	182
1190–1209	228	20,866.5	92
1210–29	12	1,000.0	83
totals:	659	77,443.0	118

*These are much more fragmentary surviving records, making comparison inexact. Column 2 includes purchases only, not total charters.

oress of Bellecombe in the Auvergne, Nonenque's mother-abbey, and Lady Nazaria, prioress of Nonenque, exchanged land with the abbot of Silvanès as equal partners in a contract that implies no dependency. This conveyance in 1152 lists Nonenque's members as only ten to twelve nuns, but their community was apparently of some wealth; at the time Silvanès had about twenty members but apparently somewhat less available cash.[116] The contract in question, however, was a purchase made by the monks of Silvanès after they had decided to move to a more appropriate spot to build their permanent monastery and church. Silvanès had to purchase rights of *fevum* for its new site in the mansus of Salellis from the nuns of Nonenque. Although such a contract does not imply feudalism in this region, in fact the nuns seem to have been effectively Silvanès's superiors at the site where the abbey was eventually built. There are also implications in this contract about the original ties between the two houses.[117]

Nonenque's wealth and power are seen in the many concessions of tithes and churches it received, such as the efforts to acquire tithes in 1199 made by Lady Garsendis of Vintro, *procuratrix* for the nuns of Nonenque, who was acting along with the prioress of that house.[118] Indeed, the churches and tithes controlled by Nonenque would be equal to or greater than those held by Silvanès, at least after a gift was made to those nuns by the bishop of Rodez in 1170 of churches in the eastern Rouergue, in four parishes where the women already owned properties.[119] In contrast, Silvanès had owned only one parish church, that of Saint-Jean of Gissac, until 1164, when it was granted two more.[120] In the parishes of Saint-Paul of la Fos, Saint-Jean of Olcas, Saint-Jean of Alcapiès, and Notre-Dame of Cassanuéjouls, Nonenque developed a strong economy of tithe-free "grange" exploitation that centered on pastoralism. Its efforts in this regard were similar to those undertaken by nearby Cistercian houses of monks such as Silvanès or Valmagne; see Figure 38.[121]

That Nonenque exercised tithe privileges in identical fashion to houses of monks is seen in an early papal privilege of tithe exemption for Nonenque from Alexander III. Preserved only in the confirmation copy by the local bishop, but seemingly given in Montpellier in 1162, it reads:

Decimas siquidem et primicias animalium vestrorum cunctis generaliter clericis et laicis a vobis exigere seu accipere seu aliquas indebitas et irrationabiles consuetudines super vos imponere prohibemus.

We forbid that any tithes and first fruits be collected, exacted, or accepted on your animals by clerics or the laity or that they in any other way impose unreasonable customs on you.[122]

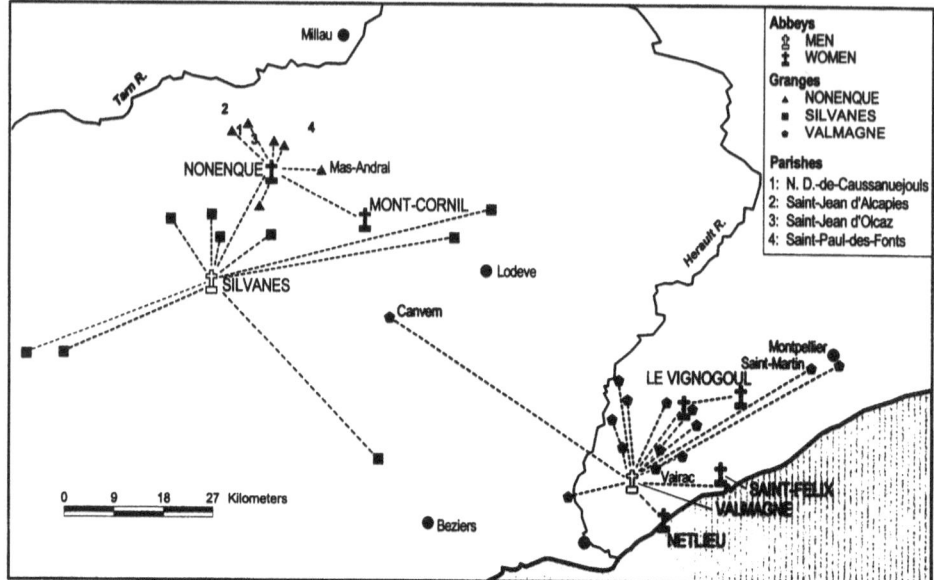

Figure 38. Locations of granges for nuns of Nonenque and monks of Silvanès and Valmagne.

The privilege of 1170 by Alexander III (again embedded in a bishop's confirmation) is more typical of such privileges for Cistercians:

Quod de laboribus quos propriis manibus aut sumptibus colitis sive de nutrimentis vestrorum animalium nullus omnino clericus vel laicus a vobis aliquid accipiat nec exigere presumat.

That no cleric or member of the laity in any way presume to accept or exact from you [tithes] from the fruits of the labor of your own hands or cultivated at your expense or from the raising of your animals.[123]

This privilege is identical to those granting exemption from tithes on the direct cultivation of granges and on animal husbandry for those houses of monks that are treated as Cistercian from the twelfth century.[124]

A number of Nonenque's twelfth-century contracts show the considerable endowment acquired by this community of women as it established a series of granges for its pastoralism on the *causses* of the eastern Rouergue.[125] Nonenque's dependence on Silvanès's good will in the exercise of these rights, however, is seen already in the actions of the latter's abbot as representative for Nonenque in a tithe dispute of 1177.[126] This public case (*placito*) arose between Raymond, abbot of Saint-Sauveur of Lodève, and Petronilla, prioress of Nonenque. It was arbitrated locally without recourse to either the papacy or the Cistercian General Chapter.[127] The terms of the dispute settlement show Nonenque practicing tithe-exempt cultivation on mansi in the parish of Saint-Beaulize, as well as keeping animals there under the care of lay-brothers and lay-sisters.[128] Nonenque's pasture rights in this region would be eroded in the thirteenth century by the competition and the possible collusion of several abbeys of Cistercian monks (Bonneval, Bonnecombe, and possibly Mazan) and Hospitaller and Templar houses who divided pasture land in the Rouergue and adjoining parts of the Auvergne among themselves, squeezing out the pastoralists of the smaller Cistercian communities of Nonenque, Silvanès, and Locdieu.

An impression of impoverished circumstances at Silvanès may in part reflect literary conceits included in its chronicle, but its relative poverty in comparison to Nonenque is borne out by its cartulary. Silvanès was forced to undertake consolidation of land by many small contracts recording acquisitions of fragments of land and rights to it for relatively small sums. This is obvious from the numbers of charters that were used in land consolidation; see Table 3. Such twelfth-century managerial feats were a necessity at Silvanès. The richer abbey of nuns at Nonenque had considerably more cash to expend on land acquisition and did not have to resort to piecing together many small holdings, a process at which Silvanès became adept. The nuns instead spent larger sums to purchase whole *villae*.

Both Nonenque and Silvanès had adopted Cistercian practices and were full-fledged members of the Cistercian Order before the end of the twelfth century. In the mid-thirteenth century, Nonenque's position within the Order was further regularized when its status as priory was raised to that of abbey and its prioress became an abbess.[129] This was a pattern of regularization of women's houses frequent in the Order at this time, but it made Nonenque more dependent than earlier on the abbot of Silvanès. Recent studies of houses of nuns in the thirteenth century have suggested that such changes in the status of women's communities in the Cistercian Order toward more consistency, including elevating them to abbey status, were often resisted by communities of religious women who did not wish to be attached to a neighboring abbot as father-visitor.[130] (In most cases that attachment put them at the mercy of the abbot of a community that was their most serious competitor for patronage.) Such resistance is seen in Nonenque's unsuccessful attempt in 1293 to leave the Cistercian Order. The surviving documents tell us that Nonenque's abbess "had rebelled" and that she had been deposed. Moreover, certain families who had supported her were refused admission into any house in the Cistercian

Order. Silvanès's abbot was reconfirmed as Nonenque's father-visitor.[131] Arguments related to establishing Silvanès's control over these women, who had probably originally been part of a double community with those monks, began to be established much earlier. Just as Jully and le Tart were left out of the history of relationships between Cîteaux and Molesme in the *Exordium Parvum*, Nonenque had already been transformed, in the chronicle of the foundation of Silvanès, written circa 1170, into a "foundation" made by the abbot of that house of monks.

Valmagne

The history of the reform house that came to be a Cistercian abbey at Valmagne must be understood in the context of the medieval reorientation of trade and rural production on the Languedoc coast towards the city of Montpellier. The thriving market and administrative center of the twelfth and thirteenth centuries at Montpellier had not existed in Roman times, but by the twelfth and thirteenth century Montpellier was beginning to replace Narbonne in controlling trade on a long stretch of the Languedoc coast. Valmagne's earliest history is obscure because historians have until recently had only very limited access to its cartulary, which is in private hands.[132] Nonetheless, it is obvious that this abbey was sited not in any great solitude, but relatively close to a major Roman road connecting the thriving new city of Montpellier to older centers at Nîmes and Marseille to the east and Agde, Béziers, and Narbonne to the west. Valmagne had origins as a double community that parallel those of Nonenque and Silvanès; its earliest history was tied to that of a community of nuns at Bonlieu or le Vignogoul. By the third quarter of the twelfth century, both le Vignogoul and Valmagne, like Nonenque and Silvanès, were acknowledged to be following Cistercian practices.[133] The abbeys of Valmagne and le Vignogoul both have surviving churches that are among the most important examples of southern-French Cistercian Gothic.

Church architecture at Valmagne and its sister-house of nuns at le Vignogoul reflects the importance of both abbeys as well as the region's growing thirteenth-century wealth. Their style, however, stands in contradiction to many stereotypes about Cistercian architecture of the late Middle Ages. Unfortunately, there is no trace of the twelfth-century churches at Valmagne or le Vignogoul.[134] We know from the archives that funds for the building of Valmagne's great Gothic church began to be collected by 1248–49 when a gift was made by the king of Aragon and another by the bishop of Béziers, Bernard of

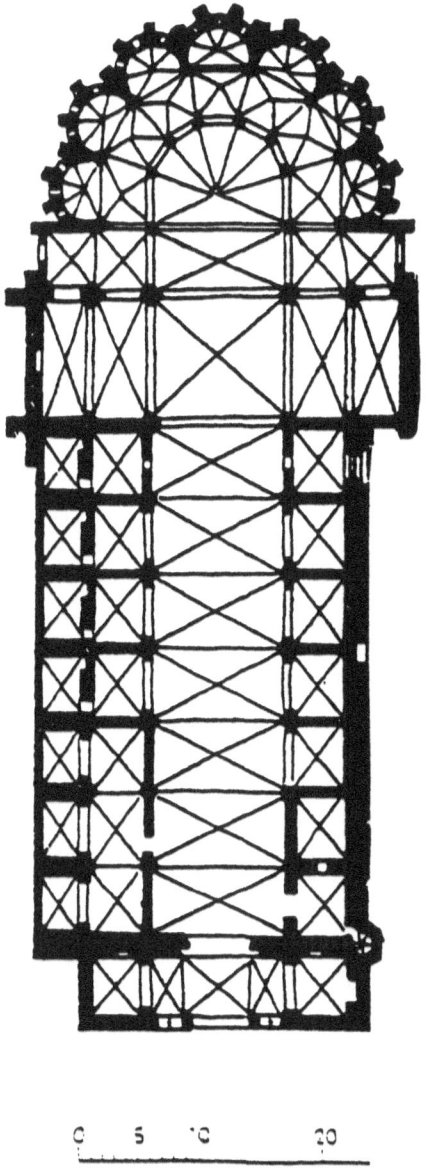

Figure 39. Plan of church for Cistercian monks at Valmagne.

Figure 40. Valmagne, interior, choir and south transept.

Cuxa. Between 1252 and 1257, permission to begin building the new church was obtained from the diocesan bishop of Agde.

Valmagne is an extraordinary two-story, cathedral-style aisled church of considerable height and length with aisleless transepts. Although the plan had probably been established by the mid-thirteenth century, construction did not occur all at once and may have continued into the fourteenth century; see Figure 39. Valmagne's choir has an ambulatory with seven radiating chapels joined by a single square chapel on each side of the transepts. Openings in that choir arcade are gradually compressed in width toward the central opening, providing an impression of even greater length and height; see Figure 40. On the north side, the walls at Valmagne were opened up for a series of chapels adjoining the north aisle. Its massive fortified front (see Figure 41) reminds us that this was a region of considerable religious disturbance in the thirteenth century. Valmagne's flat-roofed construction, customary in this region, allowed architects to the open up long clerestory windows that extend almost to the level of the roof terrace over the aisles; see Figure 42.

In contrast, le Vignogoul has a single nave of three bays extended by a square choir and heptagonal apse flanked by smaller chapels that echo that apse; see Figures 43 and 44. The austerity of its buttressed west end and

Figure 41. Valmagne exterior, west end.

Figure 42. Valmagne, exterior, south side.

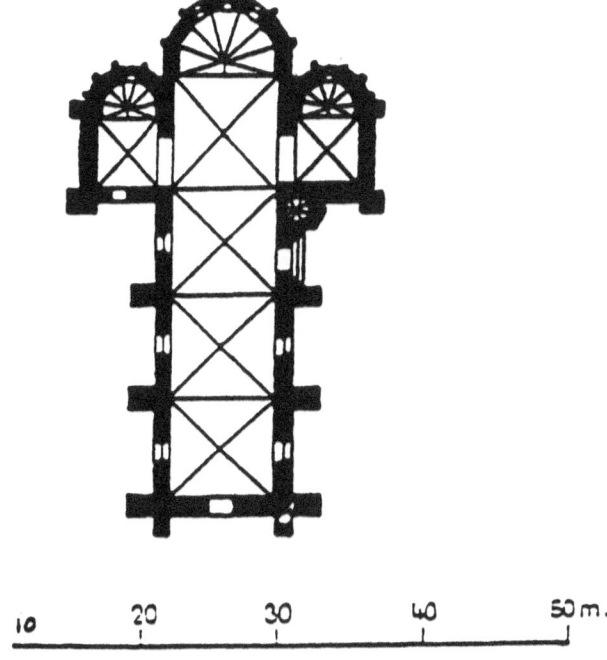

Figure 43. Plan of church for Cistercian nuns at le Vignogoul.

western facade resembles that of the earliest Cistercian churches such as Fontenay. But for the nuns at le Vignogoul such austerity appeared long after the initial period of Cistercian expansion and may be a measure of the relative poverty of most Cistercian women's communities. Measuring 37 meters by 7.75 meters without its lateral chapels, le Vignogoul is among the largest of Cistercian women's churches in the region.[135]

Inside the west end, le Vignogoul is dark and undecorated, with small, high window openings in its nave walls. These provide great contrast to the complicated and graceful long windows of the more refined and light-filled eastern end (Figure 44).[136] It is in the elegance of its eastern end and side chapels that le Vignogoul becomes an edifice of exceptional beauty. On its eastern exterior there are no severe buttresses. Thin engaged columns terminate in leafed capitals at the angle between the long windows of the apse with their slightly pointed arches and the cornices that are crowned with medallions and triangular attics pierced by oculi (frontispiece). As elsewhere in the region, le Vignogoul's roof is covered with flat stones lying directly on the fifteenth-century vaults. The entrance for the nuns from cloister to nave was

Figure 44. Le Vignogoul, nave.

Figure 45. Le Vignogoul, south interior wall, triforium.

through a southern door. The exterior of this portal consists of an undecorated tympanum surrounded by elegant rolled moldings and columns.[137]

Visible in the distance across the rich vineyards from which its name derives (frontispiece), the church of le Vignogoul was preserved because after the community left its rural site in 1683 for Montpellier, the nuns maintained their former abbey as a rural retreat.[138] Le Vignogoul has no aisles or transepts. Instead, doorways are punched through the nave wall into smaller heptagonal chapels flanking the apse; see Figures 43 and 44. Those openings are surmounted by a tiny pseudo-triforium (Figure 45) with triple trifoliate arches set on colonettes with foliated capitals. Its elegant vaults are everything that is most Gothic; see Figure 46.

Le Vignogoul was, with Valmagne, originally part of a double house on the model of Fontevrault, possibly located originally at a place called Bonlieu. It would develop as the early sister-abbey to Valmagne. Le Vignogoul is first reported as a priory of Cistercian nuns in 1178, but this only means that this is the first record surviving and that the head was referred to as prioress. Apparently only in 1245 was le Vignogoul elevated to abbey status, as one of a group of women's houses associated with Valmagne. In addition to that at le Vignogoul, with which it had been associated in its pre-Cistercian period, Val-

Figure 46. Le Vignogoul, choir vault.

magne was given oversight over the community of nuns at nearby Saint-Félix-de-Montseau or Gigean in 1252.[139] In addition, by 1490 the community of Cistercian nuns at Netlieu, which had been founded in the nearby village of Mèze in 1195, would also be placed under the oversight of Valmagne's abbot as father-visitor. Unfortunately, we know very little about these three houses of nuns.[140]

We know more about Valmagne. Valmagne's cartulary shows this abbey originating as a tiny independent reform house, one of those churches originally associated with western-French reformers, at a place called Tortoreria in 1138. The community of Valmagne adopted Cistercian customs and was attached to the abbey of Bonnevaux sometime after the mid-twelfth century. The Valmagne cartulary contains copies of five charters of gifts for the foundation of Valmagne in 1138 or the next year. They were directed to the proto-Cistercian house of Saint-Mary of Ardorel in the Albigeois and to abbot Fulk there. They include a conveyance by William Fredo and his wife Ermessendis, Berengar Rostagnus and his wife Amada, and Peter of Pradines, who conveyed to Ardorel all their rights in the district called Tortoreria:

ad construendam ecclesiam secundum instituta vestra et ordinem vestrum.

to establish a church following your practices and *ordo*.[141]

But these donors went farther than most and literally gave themselves and their children to the newly planned community, apparently intending to lead religious lives there in a family monastery.[142] It is difficult to tell for how long Valmagne continued to be a syneisactic community or family monastery of this type.

Valmagne's foundation excited some early interest, if not support, from the Trencavel family; see family tree, Figure 47. The Trencavels are mentioned peripherally in two early gifts to Valmagne, although there is no clear evidence in the form of charters of conveyances by the viscounts themselves. A donation made by Bernard William of Montbasen and his wife Adelaide to abbot Fulk of Ardorel confirmed "all that our *fevales* gave for this house in the territory of Tortoreria" and "as much as our lord Raymond Trencavel gave or will give in the future."[143] Such references have led historians to attribute the foundation of both Valmagne and Ardorel to Cecily, countess of Provence, wife of the Trencavel viscount, Bernard-Aton IV. Cecily probably gave Valmagne rights to some of her own property in the village of Mèze located on the coastal lagoon not far from Valmagne. Her daughter, Ermengardis Trencavella, seems to have inherited those rights; by 1150, Ermengardis, with her husband, the count of

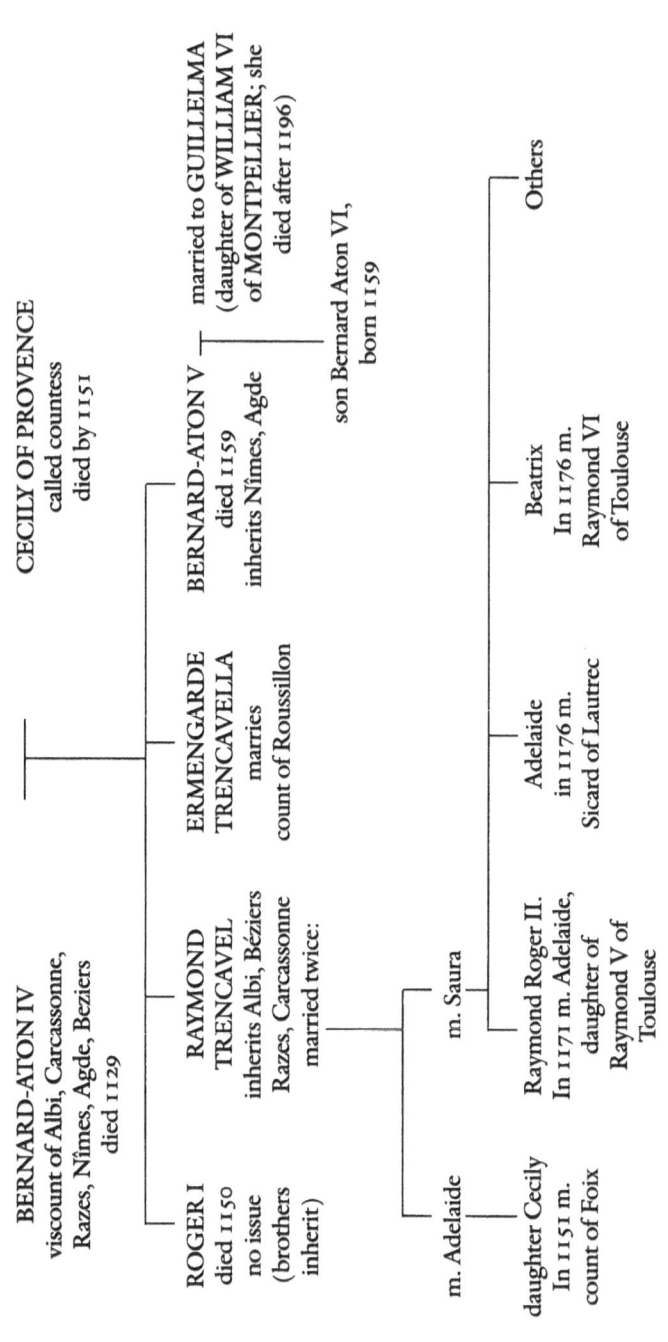

Figure 47. Trencavel family tree

Roussillon, made a concession allowing Valmagne to have a fishing boat on the lagoon near Mèze free of dues.[144]

Valmagne's importance within the thirteenth-century Cistercian Order is reflected in numerous commissions from the General Chapter mentioned in the thirteenth-century *Statuta*. Its power and properties grew slowly at first, but the charters suggest increased expansion in its landholding and recruits from the late 1140s to 1162, the period during which Cistercian practices were adopted and the monks came to be affiliated with the abbey to Bonnevaux. This period coincides with the retirement of William VI from active rule as lord of Montpellier. His daughter Guillelma, who was married to Bernard-Aton V of Nîmes and Agde, one of the sons of Cecily of Provence (see Figure 47), would be extremely active in the affairs of Valmagne, encouraging the son born to her in 1159 after her husband's demise, Bernard-Aton VI, in his support of Valmagne.

Valmagne was an independent abbey for a considerable period before it began to adopt Cistercian customs after mid-century; the traditional dating of its affiliation to Bonnevaux in the Vienne, as early as 1152 or 1155, is not confirmed by any of its charters. This abbey acted in the 1150s and before much more in a local context, interacting with abbeys such as Nonenque, Silvanès, and Ardorel. Charters for the 1140s, indeed, suggest very confused notions among donors about just what they were supporting. Gifts of that time were sometimes described as being for the building of an abbey, a grange, a hermitage, or a hospital. One gift in 1140 reads:

ad construendam domum ut habitant fratres ad laborandas terras et suscipiendos pauperes Christi.

for building a house where brothers will live for working the land and supporting the poor of Christ.[145]

This gift seems to have been made for a hospice at Creis to shelter the homeless poor; later this would be the site of one of Valmagne's granges. Valmagne had been granted tithe privileges on lands worked by its own labor by Eugenius III, who conveyed this privilege to abbot Peter and "fratribus tam presentibus quam futuris regularem vitam perfectis" in 1147.[146] That act does not mention Cistercian customs, and it is unlikely that the house had yet begun to adopt such practices.

Many of the earliest conveyances to Valmagne were essentially the return or sale of tithes to the church. For instance, tithes in the territory of Tortoreria were conveyed in 1149 and 1150 by Bernard of Capraria as he prepared "to go to Jerusalem," but a confirmation of this gift in 1150 by his two brothers, Peter

William and Frezolinus, and his sister, Adelaide, elicited a countergift of 220 solidi.[147] In that same year other rights to tithes "on their labor or land worked by their cattle," in all the honor that Valmagne had acquired "from the *fevales* of the viscount," were purchased by the abbey for 500 solidi. We find at least three other charters conveying rights to those tithes.[148] By the 1150s Valmagne had sufficient funds to begin consolidating land by purchases at prices ranging from 50 to 400 solidi. That these purchases included in 1153 a sale for 150 solidi of rights in a stone quarry "ad faciendam omnia opera vestra" suggests that construction of the first stone buildings had begun by that date. Again there is no mention in these contracts of Cistercian practices.[149]

Valmagne's independent, unaffiliated status had changed by 1162 when Pope Alexander III was present in Montpellier and mentioned Valmagne's adoption of Cistercian practices: "In ordo monasticus qui secundum Domini et Beati Benedicti regulam et normam fratrum Cisterciensium." The Cistercian tithe privilege, *Sane laborum*, was granted and the Pope confirmed Valmagne's ownership of three major properties: a grange at Valautre near the abbey, one in the parish of Beceria at Canvern, and a house in Montpellier.[150] When Lucius III again confirmed properties for Valmagne and abbot Amedeus in 1185, the tiny abbey with three properties had expanded considerably. Lucius III's privilege established:

Ut ordo monasticus secundum Domini et Beati Benedicti regulam atque institutionem Cisterciensium fratrum in eodem monasterio noscitur institutus.

That the *ordo monasticus* following God and the blessed Benedict's Rule and the institutes of the brothers of Cîteaux is understood to have been established in that monastery.[151]

He also granted the standard tithe privileges.

Properties confirmed in 1185 included the abbey site and holdings at Valautre and Canvern that had been mentioned earlier, as well as new holdings at Vairac, Ortis, Saint-Paul, Mercoire, Fontdouce, Burau, and the mills at Paollan. Although the house or hospice in Montpellier was no longer listed in the 1185 papal confirmation, the grange at Fontdouce that served as endowment for that hospice was still listed. Explicit mention of this hospice in Alexander III's confirmation of 1162, but not in that of 1185, suggests that by 1185 Cistercian notions of uniformity in practice were beginning to influence the thinking of monks at Valmagne, who had obviously drawn up lists for both papal confirmations. In 1162, Valmagne's control of an urban house or hospice was not at all problematic to this community of proto-Cistercians. But by 1185 such an urban property was seen as more unusual, and the hospice is referred to only obliquely in the privilege's references to Fontdouce. By 1185 Valmagne was probably aware of the Cistercian ideology about foundations "far from cities, castles, and human habitations" that was being articulated in collections of "statutes."[152] In 1162 an abbey might think of itself as following the practices of the brothers of Cîteaux, but by 1185 it knew the implications of such a statement and had adjusted its list of landholdings for papal approbation to conform to Cistercian ideology.

The house in Montpellier is described in detail in two documents found in both the Valmagne and the Silvanès cartularies.[153] They outline the conditions under which this hospice was established in December 1161. In the first charter, a certain Atbrandus and his wife gave to the entire Cistercian order and its members, but also to Valmagne's abbot Ermengaudis and his successors, land just outside the walls of the city of Montpellier at the Saint-Guillelm gate:

Ad fundandam et construendam ibidem quandam domum piam ad honorem Dei et beatae Mariae et ad recipiendos et hospitandos monachos et conversos ordinis Cisterciensis et pertinentes ad eos.

For the foundation and construction there of a certain pious house in honor of God and the blessed Mary and for receiving and providing hospitality for the monks and laybrothers of the Cistercian *ordo* and anyone attached to them.[154]

The hospice was to be run by a brother chosen by Valmagne's abbot with the counsel of Atbrandus or his heirs. Atbrandus would be the first administrator. The contract specified that, if Valmagne did not continue in the Cistercian practice, its control of the hospice would be transferred to another Cistercian abbot chosen by the General Chapter, although the abbot and community of Valmagne would continue to be welcomed there. Furthermore, any disagreement between Valmagne's abbot and Atbrandus or his heirs was to be arbitrated by the abbot of Silvanès, and if not by him, by an abbot appointed by the Cistercian General Chapter or by the Chapter itself. As is obvious from the discussion in Chapter 3, this document is a very early instance of the attribution of arbitrator status to the General Chapter.

The second document from the same year is the countergift made to Atbrandus by Ermengaudis, abbot of Valmagne, at the same time and place, but confirmed later before twenty monks at Valmagne's internal chapter.[155] In this charter abbot Ermengaudis conceded management of the house at Montpellier to Atbrandus, described as *consiliator* of that hospice. The abbot granted Atbrandus and the hospice property in the region of Tortoreria: "Ad edificandam unam grangiam cum fonte qui ibidem est." This property in the area called Tortoreria would become the grange of Fontdouce. Income from this grange was to be used for the construction, improvement, adornment, and provisioning of the Montpellier hospice, and any surplus was to be applied to the hospice's use. The hospice was thus operated with income from a grange. The abbot of Valmagne would provide the monks and conversi to operate the grange of Fontdouce. Moreover, the wording of his promise suggests that in 1161 monks and lay-brothers still worked together in the fields at Valmagne. That a hospice was still there later is confirmed by thirteenth-century evidence describing its transformation into a Cistercian college.[156]

What is most striking about these negotiations is this gift's stipulation that unless Valmagne adopted the Cistercian *ordo* the hospice would be given to a different abbey. By this stipulation the balance was tipped toward Valmagne's adoption of Cistercian practices.[157] It is interesting that the documents for this hospice are among the earliest to refer to General Chapters. The creation of this hospice appears to have been part of an effort to encourage abbots of newly affiliated members in Languedoc and beyond the Pyrenees to participate in such Chapter meetings. By facilitating their travel to Burgundy for such meetings, donors and administrators like Atbrandus were encouraging the emergence of that Chapter as an annual and universal assembly of abbots.[158]

The charters suggest that behind the scenes of the public transactions for the establishment of this hospice and its attachment to Valmagne and Cistercian customs was the retired lord of Montpellier, William VI. The hospice was established in 1161 under the control of a member of a family of William VI's officials in Montpellier, and William is known to have been in Montpellier earlier that year, overseeing a property settlement between his sons William VII and Guy.[159] The career of this lord after he retired from power in Montpellier in 1146 to enter the abbey of Grandselve near Toulouse by the early 1150s appears to have been the result of an adult conversion, possibly as a result of Bernard of Clairvaux's preaching.[160] After handing over the city to William VII, William VI traveled to Spain to participate in the battle of Tortosa, but possibly also to encourage Cistercian affiliations to Grandselve and Fontfroide there. He retired to Grandselve circa 1150, about the same time that Bernard of Clairvaux's close friend Alexander of Cologne was installed as abbot (1150–58).

William VI died as a monk at Grandselve probably in the early 1160s, certainly before 1172.[161] In that year his son William VII made a will giving his own son, Raymond, to become a monk at Grandselve. That document provides interesting sidelights on the family. The 1172 document recorded William VII's decision to be buried himself at Grandselve and conveyed a rent to that abbey to support prayers for his father's soul. One of William VII's daughters appears to have been sent as a nun to the Cistercian house for women at le Tart. William VII's interest in the Cistercians may have increased with his arrangements to marry Matilda of Burgundy in 1157.[162] The two Williams' enthusiasm for Cistercians may explain the eventual attachment to the *ordo cisterciensis* of the abbeys of Franquevaux and Valmagne, both in the vicinity of Montpellier. But this family's early gifts are missing from Valmagne's cartulary.

At Grandselve this William was a frequent witness to acquisition contracts in the years 1154 to 1161.[163] From the mid-1150s, William VI may have been occasionally involved in the affairs of several houses in the region that had adopted Cistercian practices; for instance, he was a witness to a contract in the Silvanès cartulary in 1156.[164] In 1162 he was described as a monk of Grandselve when he was released from a debt owed to viscountess Ermengardis of Narbonne.[165] It is possible that the entrance of men experienced in secular politics, like William VI, provided the burgeoning Order with models of how to organize its administration. It is also possible that Valmagne became interested in affiliation with Bonnevaux through William VI's advocacy, which tied its monks to a powerful house with close ties to Burgundian families.[166] It is impossible to know whether William VI was still alive and in Montpellier when Alexander III came there after fleeing Rome at the outbreak of the papal schism. But it was in Montpellier that Alexander III in that year confirmed Valmagne's early properties, as well as granting the tithe privileges to Nonenque mentioned above.

Another property of Valmagne's that was confirmed by Alexander III when he was in Montpellier in 1162 was the grange at Canvern, created in the parish of Beceria in the foothills of the Cévennes, northwest of the abbey in the direction of Albi. Canvern originated from a conveyance in 1156 by bishop William of Albi and the canons of his church of Saint-Cecilia, who gave the church of Saint-Peter of Beceria to Valmagne. The contract specified that Valmagne's abbot would name the parish priest with the counsel of the bishop. The priest at Beceria would be in charge of the care of souls, attend the bishop's synods, and exploit for his own use whatever rights pertained to that church except for tithes on the labor and animals of the household of the brothers of Valmagne: "De labore et peccoribus familie fratrum Vallismagne provenerit."[167] Extensive acquisitions in the parish of Beceria would follow. That this contract was witnessed by Peter, abbot of Ardorel, as well as by abbot Ermengaudis and other monks from Valmagne, suggests that in 1156 the relationship between Valmagne and Ardorel was still close.

Contracts from 1158 and 1159 for Canvern express concern that Valmagne adopt Cistercian practices such as those apparently already in use at Silvanès.[168] In 1158, Peter and Pons of Boisedo gave abbot Ermengaudis and "the rest of the Cistercian brethren there" a mansus their father had held at Canvern—a property Valmagne would have to redeem from a pledge of 80 solidi. The donors specified that if Valmagne did not practice the Cistercian way of life the property would be given instead to Silvanès:

et si forte quod absit monasterium Vallismagne a Cisterciensi ordine aliquo modo recesserit domus Salvaniensis teneat hunc predictum honorem donec ad eundem ordinem redeat.

and if it comes about that the monastery of Valmagne resigns in any way from the Cistercian *ordo*, the house of Silvanès will have that said honor until Valmagne returns to that Cistercian practice.[169]

Four other contracts from 1158 also specified that property conveyed would revert to Silvanès if Valmagne did not continue in its practice of the Cistercian *ordo*.[170] Hugh of Cévennes and two sons gave Valmagne, "scilicet de cisterciensi ordinis," their rights over a mansus at Canvern worked by a certain Durandus. This was done so that the souls of Hugh's late wife and deceased sons "might share in all the goods" of Valmagne and the entire *ordo cisterciensis*. On the next folio of the cartulary an act for the same year records that Durandus could enter Valmagne "as a brother" if he wished to convert: "Ut quando Dei gratia ad conversionem volueris in domo nostra pro fratre suscipiamus."[171] That this offer was not immediately taken up may be suggested by the fact that in 1163 a Durandus of Canvern is still found among parishioners acting with Bernard, priest of Beceria, to confirm tithes to Valmagne.[172]

Charters show that Raymond Beovers and his two sons conveyed rights at the mansus of Canvernet in 1158; they were promised that one of them might enter Valmagne whenever he wished to come "ad conversionem."[173] This last phrase is ambiguous; it could mean entrance as a monk as well as a lay-brother, but the rights conveyed in this contract, "allodium, fevum et beneficium," make it clear that these donors (unlike Durandus, a tenant) owed allegiance for this land to no lord. Another contract promised entry into Valmagne to Bernard Bego of Provencos and his son, who received permission in 1158 to enter Valmagne after conveying a mortgaged property.[174] In 1159 three brothers from Montlaur gave Valmagne half of the tithes of a mansus at Canvern; if one of them "wished to convert to the religious life," he could enter that house and would contribute his third of the remaining tithes over that mansus to Valmagne.[175] In 1160, following a conveyance of rights at Canvernet in which they were joined by their sister, one of another group of three brothers was promised entrance to Valmagne's community if the chosen one wished to come "secundum ordinem nostrum."[176] Bernard Boze entered Valmagne after he, his wife Petronilla, and their three children had all given rights over two mansi.[177] Raymond Amicus of Provencos "veniens ad conversionem" also gave a mansus at Beceria.[178] Given the number of such inhabitants who became lay-brothers, such concern about *ordo* had to do with Cistercian practices regarding lay-brothers.[179]

These charters also give some sense of Cistercian exploitation of the land. Two men who were peasants, Pons of Canvern and his brother Hugh, conveyed "their bodies and souls" to Valmagne and gave all their mobile goods, including rights at Canvern. They were settled at Canvern as shepherds or farmers for the abbey. One version of this charter reports that the abbot of Valmagne provided these men with three pair of oxen, three cows and two calves, sixty sheep, money to buy eleven pigs, some fleeces, two cheese, and three sets of clothing (the total investment more than 370 solidi).[180] In 1161 another newly recruited lay-brother was established at a shepherd's hut or *cabana* near Canvern, where he was to make cheese.[181] Such formerly independent owners or their tenants thus became secure members of a religious house as well as contributing to the creation of a grange where pastoralism and animal husbandry were probably more important than tilling the land.

How should we read the willingness of these inhabitants of Beceria to become monks and conversi at a grange being attached to Valmagne? Was theirs simply religious fervor, or do we have here an earlier quasi-eremitical community ripe for Cistercian incorporation? Was their eagerness to adopt the secure lives of lay-brothers the result of the economic uncertainties of living in such relatively newly founded villages in what must have been marginal locations? All are possible explanations. Whatever their reasons, the inhabitants of that parish, by their bishop's conveyance of the church of Beceria to Valmagne, suddenly faced either a challenge to their independence or an opportunity to live religious lives as monks and lay-brothers at Valmagne. For those who welcomed a change in their economic circumstances, even if they did not choose to become lay-brothers, this was an unusual opportunity to leave with a cash stake, perhaps for a thriving town like Montpellier. Normally peasants were not free to make such a change in circumstances on their own and could only leave their tenancies with permission from their lords.[182]

Such attachment of lay-brothers who were former tenants on land being transformed into a Cistercian grange was not confined for Valmagne to its grange of Canvern, nor was it a practice found exclusively at Valmagne. Indeed, it is how most Cistercian granges were founded and staffed, as I have discussed elsewhere.[183] But for Canvern and for several other places associated with Valmagne, we can see particularly clearly the links between local inhabitants and the growing numbers of lay-brothers and lay-sisters tying themselves to new religious houses. Such numerous lay-brothers and lay-sisters are also seen for Valmagne's grange at Vairac and for a hospital of lay-brothers and lay-sisters at Saint-Martin near Montpellier, which was also loosely affiliated to Valmagne. In both cases, as well, we see Guillelma, daughter of William VI of Montpellier, acting with her son Bernard-Aton VI, Trencavel lord of Nîmes and Agde, as an important patron; see the family tree in Figure 47.[184]

The more unusual case was Guillelma's founding of a community of religious women and men at the hospital at Saint-Martin near Montpellier, a hospital seemingly under Valmagne's control but definitely distinct from Valmagne's urban hospice, as has already been discussed.[185] There is no foundation document, and the fragmentary surviving references give no very clear understanding of the relationship of this hospital "near Montpellier" to either the nuns of le Vignogoul, whose priory was also located much closer to Montpellier than was Valmagne, or Valmagne itself. It was certainly founded before 1179. The Saint-Martin hospital differed from the hospice in Montpellier founded earlier. Saint-Martin had its own staff of resident lay-brothers and lay-sisters, rather than using laborers sent from the abbey. It had its own budget and endowment. This hospice is documented in only two charters in the Valmagne cartulary, although it is possibly also referred to in two of Nonenque's documents.[186]

Saint-Martin is representative of the many independent, nearly spontaneous foundations of twelfth-century hospitals founded in this period. These are a nearly undocumented phenomenon. The religious women of such hospitals, nursing the sick, the poor, and lepers as well as offering shelter to travelers, were the successors of priests' wives in that they fulfilled the same social services to the community that those wives had earlier. The eremitical and syneisactic aspects of these institutions were often forgotten by the later communities that eventually took over their holdings.

There are only two contracts that directly concern the Saint-Martin community. First is a charter from the Valmagne cartulary dated April 1192 that records the sale of the garrigue and parish of Saint-Martin of Colons for 300 solidi to abbot Amedeus of Valmagne and to Guillelma, once viscountess of Nîmes, now *procuratrix* of the hospital of Saint-Martin.[187] The second is a contract dated January 1196, in which Guillelma is described as "procuratrix domus hospitalis Sancti Martini site iuxta Montempessulanum," and acting with the consent of the brothers and sisters of this hospital (Raymond Gerald, Peter Lombard, William Reverdida, William Crispin, Pons John, Raymonda,

Guillelma Reverdida, Beatrix, and Adelina), to transfer some of the hospital property to Valmagne. All these witnesses attested that Guillelma was acting for the hospital's benefit.[188]

Guillelma's support may also be seen for a second property belonging to Valmagne, a grange located at the former village of Vairac close to the site of the abbey of Valmagne itself. Inhabitants of Vairac would either be moved to a new village or enter the abbey as members of the community, but, at Vairac as at Canvern, we see no evidence of resistance to the creation of a Cistercian grange, as was recorded for Berdoues's acquisitions at Cuelas.[189]

It was probably in conjunction with the conversion of the village of Vairac into a grange that Guillelma's son Bernard-Aton VI had in 1179 granted to abbot Amedeus of Valmagne a virtual religious monopoly in a certain territory between Montpellier and Agde. He granted to Valmagne that, in the district of Tortoreria, no other "religious," lay or clerical, men or women, of any *ordo* were to be introduced "ad edificandum sive ad habitandum" or to presume to have a church, build a grange, erect a hospital, or establish a *reclusorium* in that district. Bernard-Aton VI promised ownership as a "free allod" of whatever Valmagne acquired or would acquire from his *fevales* and other men in Tortoreria, Vairac or its *villa noveta*, Creis, or any of his other lands in the diocese of Agde.[190] He granted pasture rights for Valmagne's animals in the entire territory of Tortoreria in perpetuity, gave his protection to the abbey against any armed attack, and confirmed whatever his *fevales* gave to Valmagne to be guaranteed by him "just as if he had given it to them himself."[191]

That such a zone of exclusive religious rights was granted to Valmagne in 1179 was not unprecedented. Such a concession may derive from older notions about monastic immunities.[192] It also has parallels in the actions of the Order's General Chapter, where regulations about minimum distances between abbeys and granges were being established from the 1150s.[193] This concept of exclusive rights parallels Carthusian conceptions of having monastic properties sited entirely within a limited, enclosed zone.[194] It also echoes pacts between Cistercians and their neighbors, for instance, the agreement with the Praemonstratensians discussed in Chapter 2, limiting how close to one another their religious houses could be founded. In the thirteenth century such thinking would be seen in the establishment of areas of exclusive pasture rights by many Cistercian and other religious communities.[195]

In the next year, 1180, Bernard-Aton VI, again with the encouragement of his mother, laid the basis for the creation of a grange at Vairac that would include the removal of tenants to a newly founded village at nearby Villeveyrac. The precise reasons for Bernard-Aton VI's sale of all his rights to Vairac in 1180 are unclear, but there are several possibilities. This may have been a project long planned but timed to celebrate his becoming an adult (he would be twenty-one in that year) or a means of settling dowry issues for his mother. Another incentive may have been to establish good relations with the Cistercians, for it was a time of increased accusations of heresy in this region, particularly against his Trencavel cousins.[196]

The political importance of this sale is certainly suggested by the enormous number of important witnesses called to attend the public act of conveyance.[197] The contract states that in 1180 Bernard-Aton VI sold for 5000 solidi all his rights in the *villa* of Vairac:

... cum hominibus et feminis, fevalibus, albergis, consiliis, dominiis, dominationibus, usaticis, pasturiis, pasturalibus, arboribus, aquis, campis vineis, ortis, cultis et incultis, piscariis, molendinis.

... with the men and women, holders of feudum, of auberge, council, dominium, lordship, usage, pastoralists and pasture rights, trees, water, fields, vines, gardens, lands cultivated and fallow, fishponds, mills.

This acquisition in 1180 by Valmagne of what appears to be the highest level of lordship over a villa would seem to be wholly in contradiction to recently enunciated Cistercian principles about what kinds of holdings the Order's abbeys should acquire.[198] But a villa such as Vairac located so close to the abbey site must have been a property long desired. Moreover, the acquisition of Vairac may have been necessary to create a space of monastic solitude, that place "far from human habitation" increasingly seen as appropriate to houses that had adopted Cistercian practices.

Valmagne's eventual acquisition of nearby Vairac was probably inevitable; there are earlier hints that it would occur. A charter for 1165 reveals the presence at Vairac of a cell belonging to the monks of the abbey of Sainte-Foi of Conques in the Rouergue, which held a portion of Vairac's tithes. These were conceded by Conques for 200 solidi, but only following a year-long dispute. Only in 1189 would Conques give up its last residual rights to property there.[199] Vairac is also mentioned as part of a concession in 1174 by Sibilla, daughter of William of Mont-Ferrario, who with her husband Raymond of Castronovo made a gift to establish a house for the poor there "secundum ordinem cisterciensem"; she was promised burial in Valmagne's cemetery.[200]

After Bernard-Aton VI's conveyance in 1180, Valmagne moved quickly to consolidate property, to remove current occupants from the low-lying site up onto a rocky ridge where a new village called Villeveyrac was established, and to drain a marsh to create additional holdings and allow the monks to construct more mills.[201] In 1182, in what was probably the key contract for this grange, the abbey purchased rights at Vairac from Bernard of Capraria and three other individuals for a total of 12,500 solidi and 35 muids of wheat, to be paid over 10 years. Bernard was promised admission as a monk at Valmagne and his wife Raimunda was to get 1,000 solidi toward her entrance into a women's monastery.[202] Confirmations and additional concessions by their children and dependents in the next several years continued; Valmagne paid them an additional 4,550 solidi, several horses, various rents, and a garden.[203]

As had been true earlier for Canvern, the charters show that entrance into the religious community was an important aspect of these acquisitions at Vairac. Many donors received rights to enter the abbey as *fratres* — an ambiguous term except when explicitly contrasted to monk. For instance, in 1182 Raymond of Portale ceded rights at Vairac to Valmagne and entered the abbey as a monk, his father was promised admission "as monk or *frater*," and the donor's two brothers together received 1200 solidi and a muid of wheat for their confirmation.[204] In 1182 the area called the *stagnum de Vairaco* was sold to Valmagne for 400 solidi. In 1184 a mill and other rights at Vairac were given to Valmagne by Rostagnus of Popian and his wife for the soul of their son, William, who had died at Valmagne. Rostagnus was to be received there as a brother, and their minor son Bernard was to be boarded and taught there for the next four years until he was of age. The donors promised that another son, Arnold, would confirm this conveyance within the next year.[205] In 1185, additional rights to build mills at Vairac were granted to Valmagne in return for promises of admission as *fratres*.[206] In another contract for 1184, Senegundis, daughter of the late Peter William, with her husband Peter Lawrence, her mother Guillelma, and her sisters Ermessendis and Ricarda, confirmed a gift of land at Vairac made by her brother Peter when he was accepted as a *frater* by Valmagne; the donors received 500 solidi for Ermessendis's dowry.[207] In 1185 Raymond of Pereto gave his body and soul to Valmagne and was received as a frater *in ordinis nostri*; he confirmed earlier conveyances.[208]

Some inhabitants became peasants in the *villa noveta*, where they would hold their newly established tenancies from the monks. The Valmagne cartulary contains a *censier* of their annual "usages." Rents are listed at four solidi, a sheep, and two kegs of wine to be paid annually to Valmagne for every mansus, although it is not possible to tell how many mansi there were. In addition, six bordariae owed three solidi and three kegs of wine payable annually to Valmagne by their tenants. Each of two smaller holdings owed only two solidi and two kegs of wine. While these may appear to be newly established tenancies and rents rather than long-established ones, it is puzzling that a group of three tenants together owed hospitality dues of *albergum* for up to thirteen knights.[209]

Tenants from the earlier *villa* of Vairac ceded many different kinds of rights to Valmagne. Their rights were often purchased by Valmagne for substantial sums, such as the 450 solidi for a farmstead with courtyard and buildings, or the 800 solidi granted to Agnes, widow of Peter Blanc, and her children for property she had inherited from her mother.[210] Some tenants and owners entered or were buried at the abbey; Peter of Vairac, for example, gave his body and soul to Valmagne along with the mill he had at Vairac, his holding at Vairac, the olive trees he had there, and various other pieces of land. Other holdings he explicitly left to his wife and daughter, but with reversion of these as well to Valmagne.[211] Mention of both vines and olive trees in conveyances to Valmagne for this grange suggest its proximity to the Mediterranean, with climate mild enough for olive production as well as viticulture at Vairac.

Frequently such conveyances were made for cash, but many donors sought religious benefits, giving their bodies and souls for burial, or entered the abbey as conversi.[212] A number of charters mentioned some type of confraternity, such as participation in the benefits of the Cistercian *ordo*.[213] Some "entered" as sisters.[214] Others remained pensioners with fixed annual incomes for life.[215] Patrons even managed to have their adolescent children educated or taken in if they became orphans.[216] The entire panoply of social services were available to neighbors at Valmagne at this time, and there is no indication of any limits imposed by the General Chapter on Valmagne's interactions with the local community. Whatever the Chapter's attempts to enforce uniformity of practices (for instance, to deny women entrance to men's houses or to not offer anniversary masses), they did not filter down to Valmagne's interactions with its neighbors.

Expenditures to acquire Vairac were the largest for a single grange made by any Cistercian house in the region. In the 1160s, 350 solidi were paid out before the 5,000 solidi paid to Bernard-Aton VI in 1180. A number of additional sums of varying size were spent, totaling 23,245 solidi in the 1180s and another 3,160 solidi in the 1190s. These sums approach total expenditures for all land acquisitions for many Cistercian communities in this region.[217] What Valmagne got from Bernard-Aton VI's concessions in 1179 and 1180 was his political support to create an area of sole religious control and permission to move tenants elsewhere so that the abbey could create a grange center at the site of the former villa. That there is no hint of resistance by tenants to the transformation of Vairac into a grange or to their resettlement at Villeveyrac suggests that, given the proximity to the thriving city of Montpellier, the cash offered for tenants to give up their lands was sufficient enticement. In fact, many inhabitants stayed, either to become part of the religious community at Valmagne or to live in its new village.

We do not know the source of the enormous amounts of cash needed for such purchases of rights at Vairac. Gifts from Valmagne's most important patrons, such as the 500 solidi left by William VII of Montpellier in his will of 1172, were not sufficient for such purchases.[218] Did such large sums come from the revenues derived from agricultural, pastoral, and viticultural activities of Valmagne alone? Or were there hidden sources of income, possibly cash donations made by bourgeois recruits, which might not be recorded in charters because no land transfer was involved?[219] What is obvious is that such purchases for cash could easily have led some observers to see such abbeys as Valmagne as avaricious and land-hungry. In expending huge sums to acquire their lands at granges, did Cistercian houses like Valmagne alienate local supporters or threaten the continued privilege of tithe exemption, which had been granted initially to such reform houses because they were poor? Valmagne resembled Fontfroide in gradually taking control of nearly all the smaller reform communities in its vicinity. But in this case there was explicit permission for this activity by the secular authorities in the 1179 concession from Bernard-Aton VI. That concession laid the groundwork for Valmagne's takeover of failing religious communities located in the surrounding garrigues during the next half century.[220]

The activity of annexing such smaller communities seems to have been encouraged by older Benedictine abbeys that were ameliorating their own estates by selling off distant properties at this time. In Valmagne's documents, such sales are explained by churches like Saint-Guilhelm-du-Désert or Sainte-Foi as being done because such churches had become "unfruitful" to their mother abbeys.[221] A particularly noticeable aspect of the continued expansion of Valmagne's landholdings in the 1190s and early thirteenth century was that its monks, like those of Gimont or Fontfroide, took over many tiny rural churches, or hermitages. Contracts for such communities as the canons of Cacian, the religious women of Ferlet, or the priory of Saint-Adellan were transferred to Valmagne's archives when the land and inhabitants of such places were annexed by Valmagne.[222]

The charters discussed in this chapter show how much the newly developing Cistercian Order, and proto-Cistercians at an earlier stage, interacted in a variety of ways with donors who were not all equally committed to the ideals of these monastic communities. They also show that monks and nuns entering the new religious communities did not suddenly lose their ties to the secular world into which they were born. Such contracts also show that Cistercians and proto-Cistercians were not always loved by the local community as they settled in new places, for they upset old relationships, supported upstarts, or encouraged knights to become dependent on them for cash. Such reformers prayed for many souls and received new recruits, but they also changed the shape of the landscape of the medieval countryside into which they came.

Such houses first adopted Cistercian customs as proto-Cistercians, then gradually become part of the developing Order before century's end. As a result of their fragile early economic status and their gradual adoption of Cistercian practices, it is difficult to determine precisely when these newly founded independent reform houses began adhering to any one monastic customary. This picture could be painted again and again from the surviving records.

Close observation of monks and nuns acting in the charters cited in this chapter, however, confirms conclusions of earlier chapters that the Cistercian Order appeared only in the third quarter of the twelfth century. The period in which independent reform communities gradually became Cistercian was one in which there was little uniformity of practice because there was still no central authority in place that could have enforced any such "unanimity." The diversity of practices of monastic houses that for most of the twelfth century were at most only proto-Cistercian and had not been founded from Cîteaux or by any of its daughters, was a reality for much of the Order. Their diversity becomes more understandable in this light.

Micro-histories such as these reveal how critical to the formation of a Cistercian Order were the contributions of previously independent southern-French reformers, including patrons who never actually became members of the reform houses. Such a discussion of patronage shows that the story of how Cistercians succeeded is not only one of anonymous ascetic men creating the cells from which a later abbey's property would be derived and the Order built. If Cistercian successes in this region are attributable to the independent ascetics who preceded the Order there, it must be recognized that among them were many anonymous ascetic women as well. Those women, who have left fragmentary traces in the twelfth-century record, were increasingly written out of the Order's history after the third quarter of the twelfth century. Evidence for them remains in the charters, because those charters were preserved as important title deeds to monastic holdings.

5
Rewriting the History of Cistercians and Twelfth-Century Religious Reform

In 1241 the Cistercian General Chapter instructed the abbots of Calers and Boulbonne to inspect the site of an existing religious community at Valle de Nutibus in the diocese of Elne for its possible admission into the Order.[1] There in 1242 the abbey of Valbonne was "founded" as a daughter of Fontfroide under the aegis of the king of Majorca and with the authority of the General Chapter. In many respects this creation of a daughter-abbey by Fontfroide in the middle of the thirteenth century appears to have been done in absolute accordance with a long tradition about the expansion of the early Cistercians and their Order. The foundation charter for Valbonne is found published in the *Gallia Christiana* and comes from the collection of documents made by the Doat Commission sent to the Midi by Colbert; it offers us a view of a Cistercian foundation typical of monastic history as written since the twelfth century. The text tells us that six monks were sent from Fontfroide with the equipment needed: that is, with eighteen sets of clothing, six mattresses, six blankets, four table-covers, six hand-towels, three cauldrons, two cooking pots, a hundred cheeses, three measures of oil, fifty *émines* of wheat, a hundred sheep, a mule, 300 solidi in gold, two silver chalices, a censer and everything necessary for the altar, sixty codices (many of them listed individually), and a piece of the True Cross.[2] Presumably these material goods had been provided by the largess of the founder, the king of Majorca, rather than wholly reflecting Fontfroide's generous treatment of a daughter community. As has been seen, Fontfroide was more apt to have swallowed up whole an existing priory than to have created a new monastic community. In fact, the king of Majorca, by applying directly to the General Chapter of Cistercian abbots to have them inspect the site, had prevented Fontfroide from simply absorbing another religious community, as was its usual practice and possibly its reputation as well.[3]

Valbonne was the foundation of a new and additional abbey for monks made by a large and wealthy house nearby after careful deliberation by the Order's General Chapter. Those abbots in the General Chapter had probably been pressured into insisting on such a foundation by the king of Majorca, but they were accustomed to such pressure from Europe's rulers at this time, having responded to numerous petitions from the royal family of Castile and the kings of England for prayers for family members or for the safe delivery of heirs, or from the countesses of Flanders for everything from sponsorship of new women's foundations to providing lay-brothers to act as estate managers and administrators for the countesses.[4]

As queen of France, Blanche of Castile had just persuaded the Order's General Chapter to found a house for Cistercian monks at Royaumont in northern France for the soul of her late husband Louis VIII. She had also begun building a monastery for Cistercian nuns at Maubuisson near Pontoise, whose community would be visited by the abbot of Cîteaux himself; she retired to this monastery, but only at her death, and was buried there. She was also involved in founding a second house for Cistercian nuns at le Lys near Melun; to it she would leave her heart.[5] Valbonne's foundation by application to the Cistercian General Chapter thus fits a model of how a properly managed religious order should attach or found daughter-houses. That ideal coincided with a notion of apostolic gestation and colonization from Burgundy that had begun to be promulgated in the *Instituta* of 1165 or thereabouts found with the Order's "primitive documents." These materials were widely diffused in the Order by edict of the General Chapter after 1202, and such notions were certainly part of the administrative organization praised by the Fourth Lateran Council in 1215.[6]

This is not how the Cistercian Order began. Early twelfth-century Cistercians were at first simply the monks of a single house called Cîteaux. Later they became a small congregation in Burgundy. Later traditions would date an enormous expansion of the Order to the 1130s and 1140s, but many of the houses counted for those decades were still pre-Cistercian or proto-Cistercian until after mid-century. In 1165 Cîteaux itself had only sixteen daughter-houses, although the expansion of Clairvaux had perhaps been somewhat greater.[7] Monastic reformers beyond Burgundy in the first half of the twelfth century began to have contact with Cistercian practices only late in the 1140s.[8] Expansion of the Cistercian reform into southern France and elsewhere, when it did come, was not an outpouring of monastic personnel from Burgundy, although occasionally an abbot or an abbot and a few brothers were sent. Instead the greater part of Cistercian expansion began to be initiated in the late 1140s and 1150s, when groups of reformers from outside Burgundy started to borrow regulations and practices from Cîteaux. Only circa 1150 do documents begin to speak of customs associated with the *ordo* or practices of Cîteaux: at mid-twelfth century that word still means a way of life and not a group to which one belongs. Such independently founded, indigenous reform houses were attracted to the *ordo cisterciensis* not because they sought a group to which they could belong but because they sought customs for organizing reformed monastic lives. These reformers, like those in Burgundy, espoused a return to apostolic poverty and simplicity, the necessity of manual labor for all members of communities, and the incorporation of adult converts as both monks and lay-brothers. But the phrase *secundum consuetudinem cisterciensis ordinis* often found in thirteenth-century documents appears only occasionally in the late twelfth century; the identification of abbeys as part of an *ordo cisterciensis*, in the sense of an administrative group, also became widespread only in the thirteenth century.[9]

We have no evidence of a Cistercian Order as an administrative institution that attempted to enforce specific practices on member abbeys until after the death of Bernard of Clairvaux in 1153. Indeed, only gradually in the 1150s and 1160s were the first steps taken to create such an institution after pre-Cistercian reform communities began to adopt the Cistercian *ordo* as a way of life. At this early moment when the Order had not yet been created, what such communities sought were useful monastic practices associated with charismatic leaders like Robert of Arbrissel, Gerald of Salles, Stephen of Obazine, or Bernard of Clairvaux. Whatever the dates given on filiation trees, when such independent abbeys adopted such customs they must have had no sense of having joined an order or having signed on to a whole package of regulations. These local reform communities sought only to solve internal problems specific to their own monasteries — problems about lay-brothers, granges, and liturgy. If they sought any affiliation at all, it was to local congregations with whom they pooled certain resources, for instance, Mazan and its daughter-houses sharing pasture rights. Only later did their adoption of the *ordines* of the Cistercians lead to their attachment to a Cistercian Order as an administrative institution, to General Chapter meetings, regular internal visitation, filiation trees, and efforts to enforce statutes. When the *ordo cisterciensis* first began to be adopted by independent reform houses, the Cistercian Order had not yet been invented.

One of the frustrations of a study such as this is that it seems nearly impossible to provide specific details on precisely how the Cistercian Order as an administrative institution first appeared. In part this is because it is necessary to peel away so many layers of accumulated interpretation, but it is also because the Cistercian Order's invention was piecemeal and a matter of fits and starts, making it difficult to date. Only gradually did such an umbrella group of abbeys or heads of those houses emerge. That group was still itself being transformed over much of the late twelfth century from being practitioners of a specific *ordo monasticus* practiced in emulation of the brothers of Cîteaux or Clairvaux into a group to which one belonged, a Cistercian Order. The Cistercian Order, like the very notion of a religious order itself, was a gradually emerging result of the twelfth century's inchoate religious reform movement. It was nonetheless probably a Cistercian invention.

We can say that the invention or creation of that Order occurred circa 1165 because we know that in that year a constitution was approved, but the authors of that new institution are remarkably elusive. They tried to make their creation stand by attributing its creation to predecessors like Stephen Harding.[10] Such archaizing tendencies in the writing of the histories of the Order's individual communities would be reinforced by several of its institutions. Both the filiation charts or trees used to organize internal visitation and the systems of precedence (by date of foundation) at the annual assembly of all abbots, the General Chapter, tended to encourage monastic communities to seek earliest dates to which to attribute their own foundation, rather than to enumerate the various stages of their development. The ideology of the Order, which after 1170 was heavily invested in "apostolic gestation" as the model for growth, must have also contributed to convenient lapses of memory about origins.

Ultimately, many individual houses were attached to an Order, and this new international Order reaped the benefits of the many reform efforts sown by its predecessors, the earlier local reformers. Incorporation brought already accumulated productive lands, personnel, and other assets, including well-established relationships with patrons and promises to them of specific religious benefits, such as burial or entrance at a future date. Incorporation, whether in creating new daughter-houses or in reducing indigenous communities to granges, was the greatest factor in the huge Cistercian success of the twelfth century. But incorporation brought issues not apparent in the model of apostolic gestation; in particular, such incorporated houses included a wide variety of internal monastic practices as well as a great diversity in notions about the rights and responsibilities of monastic communities related to one another.[11]

This new religious Order as it emerged in the third quarter of the twelfth century encompassed many different styles of monastic life and management of monastic resources. Many individual abbeys came only late to what would otherwise be assumed to be a very early practice of charity and equality, particularly in concern for the financial well-being of neighboring houses, the equitable treatment of other abbeys, and a policy of noninterference by abbot visitors in the affairs of daughter-houses. These ideals are all enunciated in the "primitive documents," but those so-called documents, like the Charter of Charity, were not in fact expounded until the third quarter of the twelfth century. At that moment so much growth was occurring that ideals could not be immediately communicated with any ease to abbeys beginning to be affiliated to the emerging Order. Local communities in the proto-Cistercian movement often grew wealthy in these years by annexing additional granges or properties rather than by founding new houses, but this is hard to discern because there was so much growth — most of it, by incorporation. During the third and fourth quarters of the twelfth century particularly aggressive abbeys often swallowed up existing houses. As a consequence, affiliation did not always, or even in the majority of cases, create new Cistercian abbeys.

Thus, while the language of *caritas* may have been available in the letters and sermons of Bernard of Clairvaux and his confrères, putting principles about equality into practice throughout the emerging Order came only slowly, and often only after the diffusion of the Cistercian constitution in the early thirteenth century. Many tiny priories and hermitages, having gained Cistercian customs, disappeared from the historian's view to become mere granges. Their properties and efforts contributed to what has been called the miraculous Cistercian expansion in wealth and power of the later twelfth century, but there is little recognition of their existence after they were engulfed by the Cistercians and their predecessors. Records of these independent communities, and of the donors who had founded them, have often been almost totally eradicated.

That the Order and its legislation were only beginning to emerge toward the end of the twelfth century and that both *una caritas* and *unanimitas* still were not widely enforced is not the usual interpretation, which sees an early and rapid expansion of the Cistercian Order in the first decades of the twelfth century, widespread adherence to all its most charitable practices in the second quarter of the century, and an inexorable decline after 1153. Nonetheless, the interpretation presented here of the course of Cistercian development in the twelfth century accords more with the documents. It may, for instance, explain better the less charitable aspects of a second incorporation account also found among the Fontfroide documents, copied by the Doat Commission, and printed in the *Gallia Christiana*. This is the account of the annexation by Fontfroide in 1189 of the nearby house of monks and nuns, lay-brothers and lay-sisters, at Sainte-Eugénie. It is a document written in the style of a charter in which William of Lac, prior, and five other monks gave their priory at Sainte-Eugénie, with three churches (one of which had nuns attached) and their possessions at two other places to the Blessed Virgin Mary of Fontfroide, and to Bernard, abbot there. It tells us that they did so because they had realized that their priory had become overburdened by debt and harassed by lenders, and that affairs had reached such a crisis that they were in danger of dying of hunger. They confessed to being able to respond to their creditors only by selling the monastery, its lands, and all their goods to Fontfroide:

Ego Guillelmus de Lacu prior domus S. Eugeniae et nos fratres ejusdem loci, scilicet ego Johannes de Vitraco, et ego Guillelmus de S. Marcello, et ego Guillelmus Cornellii et ego Martinus de Mata, et ego Arnaldus Pastor, non inducti metu, vel dolo, sed bono fide, et firmo et laudabili proposito, divini numinis aspiratione, eligentes arctioris vitae viam, considerantes domui nostrae S. Eugeniae imminere graves aeris alieni molestias et importunas instare creditorum exactiones attendentes etiam predicta onera elevari non posse, vel praetaxata debita solvi, nisi praedictae domus mobilia et immobilia venderentur, ut sic in fine distractis possessionibus, alia non restaret vita, nisi nos fame perire, donamus et offerimus ac tradimus nosmetipsos per fratres Domino Deo et beatae Mariae monasterii Fontisfrigidi et tibi Bernardo, ipsius loci abbati. . . . Nos sorores domus S. Eugeniae scilicet ego Maria, que fui uxor Viduani de Bagis, et ego Garsendis de Mata, et ego Arsendis de Gatpadenis, sorores domus S. Eugeniae, et ego Arnaldus filius quondam Viduani de Bagis et ego Pontius de S. Marcello, et ego Remundus de Rabedolz, et Johannes Caragauli confratres ejusdem domus S. Eugeniae, laudamus et confirmamus.

I, William de Lac, prior of the house of Saint Eugénie and we the brothers of that place, that is, I, John of Vitrac, and I, William of Saint Marcellus, and I, William Cornellii, and I, Martin of Mata, and I, Arnold Pastor, not induced by fear but acting in good faith, firmly and laudably, inspired by the divine and having elected the more austere course in life, given the fact that our house of Saint Eugénie weighed down by debt is in imminent danger of falling prey to the exactions of our creditors, indeed, realizing that we are not able to lift that weight or to pay our debts without selling all our moveable and immobile goods, and, if we sold our possessions, we would have no way to avoid perishing from hunger, give and offer and transfer ourselves as brothers to the Lord God, to the blessed Mary of the monastery of Fontfroide and to you Bernard, abbot of that place. . . . [This act was] praised and confirmed by all the sisters of the house of Saint Eugénie as well; that is, I, Mary, widow of Viduanus of Bagis, and I, Garsendis of Mata, and I, Arsendis of Gatpendis, sisters of the house of Saint Eugénie, and I, Arnold, son of the late Viduanus of Bagis, and I, Pons of Saint Marcellus, and I, Raymond of Rabedolz, and [I], John Caragauli, *confratres* of said house of Saint Eugénie.[12]

Here at Sainte-Eugénie incorporation is not for the creation of a new community of monks or an independent community of nuns with their own assets, but for the dismantling of an existing house of monks and nuns, lay-sisters, and lay-brothers. The nuns would be set up in a dependent priory at les Olieux; it would first be independent but then rapidly impoverished. It probably had disappeared by the end of the Middle Ages. The monks and lay-brothers were absorbed directly into Fontfroide itself. Sainte-Eugénie's properties and religious obligations were taken over, including any outstanding promises for admission of patrons, who would probably have been received by Fontfroide itself. In the language of "donation" typical of Cistercian charters, this community of religious men and women is rescued from starvation by Fontfroide by becoming a gift to the abbot of Fontfroide. The entire religious community, lock, stock, and barrel, with its members and their obligations, would be taken over, and nearly all record of an independent community of monks and nuns would disappear into obscurity.

What is significant is both the date and the abbey of Cistercian monks involved in this takeover. Fontfroide appears to have been part of the earliest wave of Clarevallian houses to emerge as part of a more international movement of religious houses in the 1150s. Attached to Grandselve in 1143 just before Bernard's preaching mission to the Midi, and itself an incorporated house, Fontfroide might have been expected to have absorbed much of the Cistercian message of *caritas* in the relationships between monastic houses that Bernard was preaching at the time. Fontfroide would at mid-century attach one community of hermits in Catalonia at Poblet, which became Fontfroide's daughter-abbey in 1155.[13] But its absorption of Sainte-Eugénie epitomizes the trends toward the aggrandizement of certain Cistercian communities that I have attempted to describe in earlier chapters. Moreover, in September 1189 there is no sign that the abbot of Fontfroide is about to go off to the General Chapter meeting to get permission for such an annexation, no sign of any hesitation to take on the religious care of women, no sign of sharing resources or undertaking to set Sainte-Eugénie on its feet, but instead a forthright "takeover" by Fontfroide. In this charter, preserved because it was found by the Doat commissioners in the Fontfroide archives, Fontfroide's self-depiction is that of passive recipient of a "gift" from the prior and monks of Sainte-Eugénie. William of Lac and his associates confess that their incompetence in management has led to their near starvation, but it is likely that Fontfroide's competition with its neighbor contributed to Sainte-Eugénie's demise. Its unhesitating annexation of Sainte-Eugénie in 1189 and other examples of its appropriation of desirable nearby communities discussed in Chapter 3 suggest how much the takeover was the *modus operandi* for Fontfroide in the late twelfth century and after. Only a powerful individual like the king of Majorca could have forced Fontfroide to make a new settlement of monks as it did at Valbonne in 1242.

In reading accounts such as that of the abbey of Valbonne in light of assumptions about miraculous growth in the Cistercian Order during the previous century, historians of the Cistercians have tried to explain the Order's success as the inadvertent result of its austere practices and of foundations made whenever communities became too large or too rich, by "apostolic gestation," in which heroic monks in bands of six or twelve and an abbot went out with lay-brothers to make monastic settlements at new sites, which were inevitably located in uncleared and uncultivated wilderness. There those new foundations disrupted no existing communities and had no effect on existing arrangements for the support of parishes. They could demand tithe exemptions with impunity, for their abbeys were in places where they competed for the produce of the land only with the wild beasts. Their only encroachments were on the hunting grounds of the rich and powerful.[14]

In depicting the organization of the Order in terms of vast filiation trees and its growth as that of an organism expanding to give birth to new generations, thirteenth-century Cistercians perpetuated this image. They did so as well when they repeatedly described their sites in terms recalling the Old Testament or the sayings of the Desert Fathers.[15] As I have shown at length elsewhere, we have too closely identified the Cistercians with pioneering activities in "old Europe." Considerable rural economic growth had occurred from the year 1000 on, but Cistercians and pre-Cistercians were the beneficiaries of such growth, not its authors. In fact, those pioneering activities were already over in most places before even pre-Cistercian houses had been founded.[16] If the early Cistercians knew how many of the houses that were becoming Cistercian had origins as double-communities, a term that could certainly be applied to Molesme, this was not discussed in their later reformulating of their own past to fit the model of how things should be in the present.

In fact, Cistercian descriptions of sites, economic circumstances, and existence on noval lands and tithes may have fit the circumstances of the thirteenth century better than the twelfth. After the year 1200, expansion of Cistercian men's houses and additions to their lands were limited to the fringes of Europe, to what might be called "new Europe," or to areas of major reclamation with high capitalization costs such as the polders of Flanders.[17] Women's houses attached to the Order in the early and middle thirteenth century were more likely than were men's houses of the twelfth century to have received marginal lands on the so-called "internal frontiers" of "old Europe." What those nuns got were some of the last and least productive lands available, often because donors founding houses in the thirteenth-century had little else to give.[18]

There is thus a certain displacement of what was happening in the late twelfth and thirteenth centuries back onto the Cistercians' descriptions of what they saw as their origins in the early twelfth century. This is nowhere more clear than with regard to their exemption from tithes. When tithe privileges were granted to new reform communities in the twelfth century, these privileges stressed the typical ideology of monastic reformers of that era, a discussion about the monastic return to manual labor. Twelfth-century tithe exemptions were grants of exemption on land labored on or managed by the monks and nuns themselves, described in the typical formula *Sane laborum*. But in the early thirteenth century the Fourth Lateran Council limited Cistercian tithe privileges to a different type of criterion, exemption on *novalia*, by which were meant apparently noval lands and noval tithes alike, as well as exemption on the Order's animal husbandry, viticulture, and gardening. The 1215 exception made for all lands already in Cistercian hands meant that for most men's houses, at least, not much had changed, for most had already gained nearly all their endowment. What is interesting is how much the emphasis on noval lands as those receiving tithe exemption paralleled Cistercian circumstances in the thirteenth century, when most of the Order's new communities were being founded on the fringes of Europe, and in lands on which tithes had never before been collected.[19] Not only did the emphasis on noval lands fit Cistercian circumstances in the thirteenth century better than it would have in the twelfth, but such land-holdings and exemption from noval tithes may have reflected and been reflected in the self-depiction as frontiersmen and colonists found in Cistercian narratives of the late twelfth and thirteenth centuries.[20] Only the nuns of the Order would continue to expand in "old Europe" in the thirteenth century, and, as has been mentioned, they tended to receive extremely marginal lands, which were those most likely to become wholly unproductive.

A concern for a sufficiency of internal endowment explains discussion about how new foundations should be made and regulations about the distance between abbeys and granges; it is found in the initial collections of ideas about how the Order should operate, the Cistercian *Instituta*, as well as in the Charter of Peace with the Praemonstratensians; the two come from roughly the same period — the 1150s and 1160s.[21] But concern about whether to found houses is not usually how Cistercian expansion is discussed. Not incorporation, not annexing hermitages and reducing them to granges, but "apostolic gestation" has been the standard story of the miraculous twelfth-century Cistercian expansion.

But founding new daughters versus annexation was a critical question for every house that would become associated with the Cistercians. From the mid-twelfth century fewer independent priories became new men's communities. In fact, in southern France we see Berdoues, Fontfroide, Boulbonne, and Valmagne all involved in reducing neighboring priories to granges; chances are that this was very widespread practice even when we cannot document it. The advantages of Cistercian longevity in acquisition of land for granges and in accumulated privileges, such as passage rights for herds and flocks, for marketing of produce without tolls, and for tithe-free grange agriculture would help houses like Fontfroide gradually undercut other monastic competition, including the competition of newer houses adopting Cistercian practices.[22] Moreover, in the late twelfth century the promises discussed in the previous chapter of exclusive religious rights in certain territories, like that made by Bernard-Aton VI of Nîmes and Agde, were beginning.[23]

Thirteenth-century and later Cistercian historians would ignore the important contribution of houses like Sainte-Eugénie to the Order's growth, while viewing a foundation like that at Valbonne or Royaumont as reflecting the typical way houses were founded. They describe such foundations as explaining the success of the Order that had grown from its origins in 1098 by such colonization from Burgundy. Ironically enough, this creation of an abbey for monks at Valbonne would be one of the last foundations of a house for Cistercian men in France, and one of only a very small number of such monasteries for Cistercian monks to be founded in "old Europe" after 1215. In fact, the thirteenth century in "old Europe" saw instead the extraordinary flowering of new women's religious communities in the Cistercian Order.

In southern France the history of the thirteenth-century foundation of houses for Cistercian women, or of the denial that there were earlier women's houses, is inextricably tied up with assumptions about the spread of religious heresy in that region. Any discussion of southern France and the Cathars includes glimpses of Cistercians as preachers against such dualist heretics, because the Order was among the first to be involved in preaching missions against the Cathars and the Order's northern leaders were particularly involved in the Crusade against the "Albigensian" heretics.[24] A famous Cistercian career is that of Arnold Amalric, a monk of Catalonian Poblet who moved circa 1200 from southern France, where he had been abbot of Grandselve, to election as abbot of Cîteaux. He was sent back to the south as papal legate and leader of the Albigensian Crusade and soon became archbishop of Narbonne.[25] After the first phase of the Albigensian Crusade, it would be the abbot of the Cistercian abbey of Grandselve, Elie Guarin, who negotiated the Peace of Paris of 1229 between Louis IX's regent Blanche of Castile and the defeated count Raymond of Toulouse. That peace treaty included huge indemnities to be paid by Raymond both to Cistercian houses in the south and to the abbey of Cîteaux itself.[26] As has been discussed with regard to Fontfroide, there is no doubt that Cistercian abbeys profited from the confiscated goods of Cathar heretics. Reform houses in the region also received gifts made by secular leaders in that region attempting to avoid accusations of heresy by their support of the new and clearly orthodox monastic groups.[27]

In the thirteenth century, moreover, foundation of communities of Cistercian women was viewed as a significant prophylactic against the spread of heresy.[28] Such houses of Cistercian nuns in the Rhône Valley are especially noticeable in this trend. Le Thoronet's abbot at the turn of the thirteenth century, the reformed troubadour Fulk of Marseilles, gave significant support to houses of religious women. A number of such foundations in some way dependent on le Thoronet flourished with the support of the Porcelet family of Arles. Fulk went on to rule as bishop of Toulouse (1205–1231) and was closely associated with the foundation of the first Dominican house for friars in Toulouse as well as that for Dominican nuns at Prouille.[29] Houses of such Cistercian nuns in the Rhône valley included a community founded at Saint-Pons of Géménos in 1205. Its site on land near a sacred well above the city of Marseilles was given by the bishop and chapter of Marseilles to a woman named Garsenda and her four daughters for an abbey of Cistercian women. Between 1209 and 1213, the nuns of Saint-Pons then founded an abbey at Mollèges between 1209 or 1213 on land given by Sacristana, daughter of Raymond Sacristan, a member of the Porcelet family. In 1218 Sacristana also gave her rights in the burg of Arles and in the Camargue to Mollèges and its nuns, who by 1238 had created Notre-Dame-de-Beaulieu in Arles.[30] See Figure 48.

Other new women's houses added to the Order at this time included Saint-Pierre-du-Puy at Orange, which had originally been founded in the Gard near Uzès in 1217, and Saint-Pierre-d'Almanarre, which was founded in 1221 in the village of Hyères, apparently at the request of Honorius III.[31] The monks of Cistercian Aiguebelle were associated with an abbey for nuns at le Bouchet founded circa 1150, and tradition has it that circa 1200 another community of nuns was founded as well at nearby Bonlieu by Veronica, countess of Marsanne. It was these last nuns who were suppressed in about 1400 so that their properties could be given to the impoverished monks of Valcroissant.[32] Another church for nuns at a second site, also named Bonlieu, and a church for nuns at la Vernaisson seem also to have been associated with the monks of Aiguebelle.[33]

But while the threat of heresy may have played a role in founding what became the Dominican women's house at Prouille or in founding houses of Cistercian nuns with the assistance of le Thoronet in Provence, that is not the whole story. In fact, women actively sought to become Cistercian nuns and actively chose the life of orthodox reform monasticism; the *ordo cisterciensis* was not for women just a safe alternative to Catharism. Yet almost everything

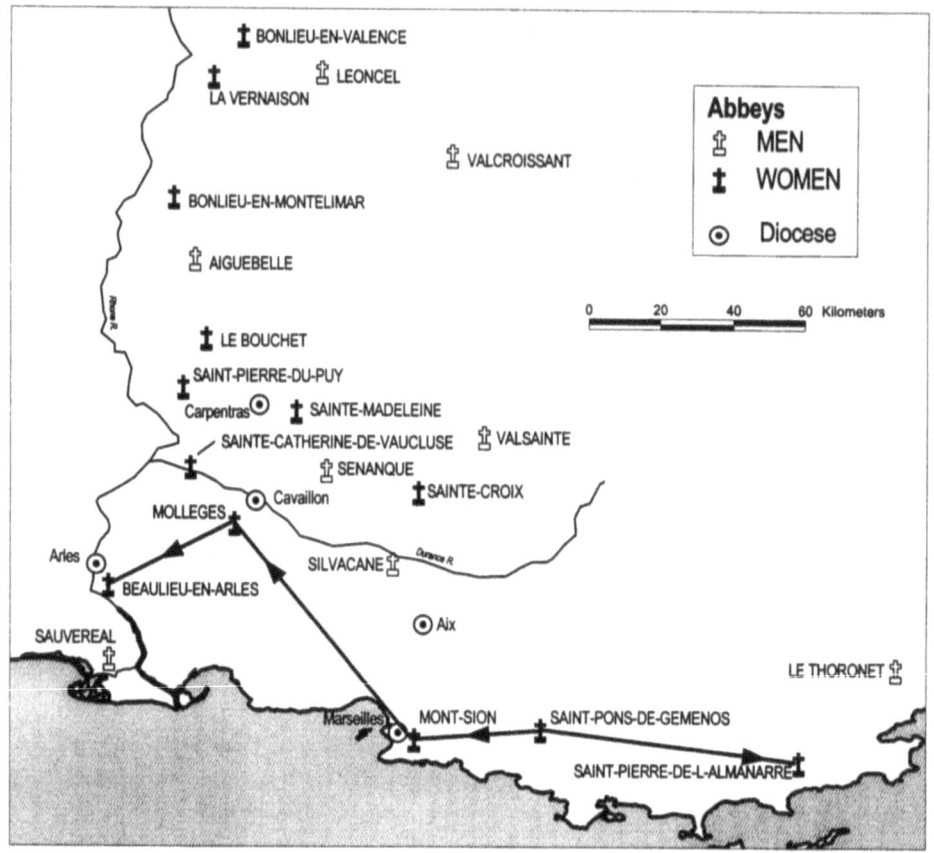

Figure 48. Houses of Cistercian nuns in Provence added in the thirteenth century.

written on southern French heresy has stressed the attractions of the Cathar heresy for women and minimized women's support for orthodox monastic reform in this region. In fact, many houses of nuns or early double communities had already been established during earlier stages of pre- and proto-Cistercian reform. Not only did they provide women with communities to enter, but they stayed well within the boundaries of orthodoxy and provided a very visible witness to the monastic *caritas* that was of such concern to religious reformers.[34] Many Cistercian nuns were already in place before Fulk of Marseilles began his foundation; women had acted as patrons of the Cistercians, requesting for themselves the prayers of Cistercian monks and nuns, and had sought entrance into those communities. The charters for Valmagne, Grandselve, and other abbeys as well show that many reform communities for women that eventually became Cistercian took an active role in the care of the sick and poor. Such women's houses as part of a nearly invisible "hospital movement" in the twelfth century may have continued the same caring roles that many women had played in earlier times as priests' wives.[35]

What is often missed in considerations of the growth of heresy in twelfth-century southern France is the extent to which orthodox religious reform was present there in the twelfth century. Preaching about the apostolic life and the growth of new groups within the nobility brought many new converts to the monastic life in the twelfth century.[36] While the search for a life of poverty in imitation of the apostles sometimes lapsed into anti-clerical and dualist heresy like that of the Cathars, it more often led to the foundation of indigenous houses of religious men and women, many of which would eventually be affiliated with the Cistercians. My reassessment shows, moreover, that the independent "ladies" of the Midi who ruled castles and handled property on their own played a large role in support of reform communities that became Cistercian. The role of women like Guillelma of Montpellier and Marie of Escornabou in promoting new monasteries has been downplayed in the history of the Cistercians. This is perhaps because sometime in the third quarter of the twelfth century association with women began to be a hallmark of heretical activity.[37] As fear of accusations of heresy grew, monastic leaders began to act as if associating with women might cause them to be seen as heretics. It was perhaps as a consequence of the increased concern over heresy that distancing oneself from women and from the care of nuns' souls, began to be seen as a necessary aspect of monastic purity; interestingly enough, this seems to have led to a reinterpretation by later Cistercians of Bernard of Clairvaux's early activities in support of women's monasticism, and to a certain amount of reinterpretation of some of his remarks.[38]

There was considerable ambivalence about women's houses among Cistercians after the 1170s and 1180s, yet this was the period of greatest expansion of women's houses within the Order. This may explain how the first half of the thirteenth century could also be a period of administrative articulation of that ambivalence.[39] As the General Chapter became stronger, so did its concern to keep women under strict control. But the concern went beyond that, to the denial of the presence of women there in the first place—as in the Silvanès chronicle, which masks Nonenque's origins, or in the denial of ties between Bernard of Clairvaux and Jully in the Order's *exordia*.

This new concern about association with women was not unique to the Cistercians; it was played out in the thirteenth century in the increased regulation of all religious women, including Cistercian nuns. Thus, at the same time that many new houses of Cistercian women were founded throughout Europe in the thirteenth century, regulation of women's communities within the Order increased dramatically. Women's communities that had initially been treated as unproblematic were subjected to limitations. In the years between 1200 and 1250 important backers of Cistercian women like Blanche of Castile and Innocent IV seem to have insisted that Cistercians continue to allow women an official part of the Order, but the Order initiated legislation that was more and more "controlling," such as that about how new foundations were to be made. Thirteenth-century popes, worried about the impoverished state of many houses of nuns, attempted to force the various orders to take more responsibility for the *cura monialium*, the care of nuns' souls that religious men seem to have been trying to avoid. Such papal concern expressed itself in papal requests that orders establish maximum sizes of women's houses; admonitions that abbesses not admit any nuns above the maxima unless property increased were paired with warnings about avoiding simony.[40] All priories of nuns in the Cistercian Order were made into abbeys from the mid-thirteenth century, and all prioresses elevated into abbesses. While this may suggest a new independence, in fact those abbeys of women were also attached directly to neighboring houses of monks, whose abbots were assigned visitation duties of such *filiae*. Few houses of nuns would profit from the mid-thirteenth-century appointment of neighboring abbots as father visitors. Such abbots were often "wolves in sheep's clothing," annexing the nuns' properties for their own abbey's uses, or crowding the nuns' animals by over-pasturing with their own.[41] The women's houses may have been more viable economically as dependent priories in the twelfth century, with more claim on the resources of the men's houses, than after they were detached in the thirteenth century. From the thirteenth century, these newly independent women's abbeys began to be treated as satellites of neighboring men's houses, and ties among women's houses began to disappear; at the same time the women lost any claim on the resources belonging to the abbeys for men—occasionally resources that had been given at first for the support of a double-house.[42]

Several other things are clear about these changes with regard to women's houses. First, the formal rules for the affiliation of Cistercian nuns developed in General Chapter meetings of the thirteenth century should not be understood to apply to twelfth-century affiliation of such women's (or men's) houses. Second, regularization of Cistercian women's houses in the thirteenth century into filia of neighboring houses of Cistercian monks meant that by circa 1300 the Order's abbots were visitors for nearly as many houses of nuns as of monks. That some abbots, particularly in Flanders, were indeed overburdened with the care of nuns, however, cannot be generalized to the entire Order. Frequently, moreover, such complaints of the burdens of caring for nuns were probably in response to complaints by the nuns about neglect. Third, all Cistercian women's houses had a more perilous future after 1250 than did men's. In what became the Order of Cîteaux, most men's houses created sufficient endowment to survive up to the French Revolution.[43] All the men's houses in the region except les Feuillants, which split off to form its own congregation, and Valbonne, Sauvelade, and Le Jau, which were Pyrenean abbeys treated at that date as not part of France, were counted in the report of the commission inspecting monasteries in 1790; as far as I can tell from Lekai's extracts, the commission did not count the houses of nuns.[44] Moreover, it was not necessarily the poorest houses of nuns that perished. The financial condition of women's houses is often cited as a reason for their suppression in this period, but there are indications that such suppressions provided houses of monks with coveted properties. Thus, at the end of the fifteenth century, for instance, a wealthier but vulnerable community of women might be more likely to be suppressed than a poorer one.[45]

Moreover, only powerful lay patrons seem to have protected these women — women might resist their own suppression, but there was no outcry among men's houses when women's houses were suppressed. Thus, protection for a men's house absorbed by a rival was given to Locdieu by a mother-abbey in the early thirteenth century, as discussed above.[46] Although in 1453 Boulbonne would suppress the monks at Calers, resistance to this move by Calers's mother-abbey, Grandselve, led to the reversal of this suppression.[47] Rather than being suppressed, the monks at Valcroissant were rescued by the addition to their lands of the confiscated properties of a nearby community of nuns whose inhabitants were sent elsewhere.[48] No such protection was accorded communities of nuns. By the late fifteenth century many houses of Cistercian women in France had been suppressed, as is well demonstrated by a recent study by Anne Bondéelle-Souchier.[49] In England, all would disappear with the first suppressions of the English Reformation.[50]

While nuns had been there from the start, the increasing organization of the Order into an international body would inevitably handicap the women's communities, whose abbesses were not allowed to participate in the deliberations of the General Chapter. Women were given, but only for a short while, a General Chapter of their own, held at le Tart, at which the abbot of Cîteaux could announce to the assembled abbesses the decisions of the abbots. Although neither charity nor equality is suggested for these Cistercian women who had no voice in either chapter, the foundation of Cistercian houses for women continued to be popular long after the men's houses were reduced in size, found it increasingly difficult to recruit lay-brothers, and began to "farm out" granges or convert them into bastides. It is not surprising that communities of nuns attempted to secede, and sometimes did successfully leave the Order.[51]

Although the documentation for Cistercian women in southern France is sparse, it is abundant for other regions, and the inclusion of the history of Cistercian women in this study has significantly shaped its conclusions. Although there is still further clarification to be done with regard to the second half of the twelfth century, the major outlines of a new picture are now clear. Understanding that a Cistercian Order was a new invention of the twelfth century, but only of the third quarter of the twelfth century, has been the major consequence of the attempt to tell the story of the early Cistercians with women in it. In seeking to verify why arguments that there were no twelfth-century Cistercian nuns could be made by recourse to the published statutes, I began to investigate carefully the contents of the first volume of published statutes by Canivez and to look at the manuscripts that lay behind them. What that revealed was that the Order would be built up gradually out of many independently founded reform houses that eventually looked to Cistercian customs for managing their internal affairs. From adopting customs for internal affairs to membership in an Order was a gradual process that occurred in the years after Bernard of Clairvaux's death. Only by 1165 was there a first Cistercian Charter of Charity, the *Summa Cartae Caritatis*, and some of its most charitable aspects were lost in the revisions of the next several years.

My conclusions about how the religious order was invented by Cistercians in the second part of the twelfth century will have considerable repercussions for the history of twelfth-century monastic reform more generally. As we look again, with the newly established dating for Cistercian documents firmly in mind, at the accumulated body of evidence for all monastic groups in the twelfth century, we may find that Cistercians can no longer be given credit for all the innovations that led to the creation of a new twelfth-century institution, the religious order. Only considerable further examination of the documents of the third quarter of the twelfth century, both those produced within the Cistercian Order and those in the archives of its competitors, will provide the documentation allowing the picture presented here to come totally into focus. What can be said definitively here is that not only was the Cistercian Order not founded in 1098, it was not even founded before the death of Bernard of Clairvaux in 1153.

Appendix 1. Chronological Summary

Traditional chronology
(after Bredero, Bernard, *282–87)*
1098 Cîteaux founded

1113 Bernard enters Cîteaux

1114 Founding of Pontigny and first version of Charter of Charity
1115 Founding of Clairvaux

1119 Archbishop of Vienne is elected as Calixtus II — confirms early Charter of Charity

c 1123 editing at Clairvaux of the *Exordium Cistercii*
c 1130 *Summa Cartae Caritatis* replaces an earlier Charter of Charity (of which no copy

New chronology
(based on findings of this study)
1098 Date attached to move to Cîteaux from Molesme in *Exordium Parvum* accounts from 1160s: no foundation charter exists — at this time Robert of Molesme founded many priories
(*Exordium Parvum* does not mention Bernard entering Cîteaux)
1114 Foundation of Pontigny is described in a retrospective charter of the 1160s

1118 Guy of Burgundy, archbishop of Vienne requests foundation of Bonnevaux by Cîteaux
1119 Guy of Burgundy is elected Calixtus II, but he does not issue a confirmation to Cistercians (it is a forgery)
1120 Bonnevaux confirmation issued by Calixtus II (on which forgery of the Cîteaux bull is based)

1130s Most foundations outside Burgundy at these dates are of pre-Cistercian communities

survives), according to Bredero	
1132 Innocent II grants a privilege to the Cistercians exempting them from paying tithes on their own labor or animal husbandry	1132 Innocent II grants a tithe privilege, but only to Bernard and abbeys subject to him; that for Cîteaux and its order is a forgery
1134 Stephen Harding dies and first collection of Statutes made	1134 "Prima collectio" of statutes is not collected at this date, but only in the 1150s; it is not dated in any twelfth-century manuscripts
	1135 c. Orderic Vitalis and William of Malmesbury both describe monks from the monastery of Cîteaux, not the members of a Cistercian Order
	1135 Earliest parts of Trent 1711, version I; this may be an early liturgical *ordo* for the Cistercians, but no "primitive documents" are dated by it
1138 Bernardo Paganelli enters Clairvaux	
	1140 c. Philip of Harvengt describes monks from the monastery of Cîteaux
1142 Charter of Peace with the Praemonstratensians	1142 No reason to date charter of Peace with Praemonstratensians to this date; surviving manuscript is clearly a recension of the 1160s
1145 Henry of France, brother of Louis VII, becomes a monk at Clairvaux; Bernardo Paganelli elected Pope as Eugenius III	1145 Bernard preaching mission to the south
1146 Bernard begins preaching Second Crusade	1146 Eugenius III definitively grants Jully to Molesme, and Bernard ceases his interventions there
1147 Bernard receives Eugenius III at Clairvaux, Eugenius pre-	1147 Papal bulls by Eugenius III are possibly issued from Cî-

sides over General Chapter at Cîteaux that incorporates Savigny and Obazine, and rejects Gilbertines

1149 Henry of France leaves Clairvaux to become bishop of Beauvais

1152 Second issue of collected statutes by General Chapter

1153 Eugenius III dies on July 8, Bernard dies on August 20
1155 Group of Cistercian abbots meet to evaluate *Vita Prima*, version A

teaux in September (all may be forgeries), but there is no General Chapter meeting. There is an 1147 papal confirmation for the Cistercian women of le Tart
1146–49 First charters for southern France and Normandy mention an *ordo cisterciensis/cistellensis*
1150 c. Herman of Tournai describes *ordo cistellensis* and practices of the brothers of Clairvaux, as undertaken by the nuns of Montreuil
Alexander of Cologne becomes abbot of Grandselve
1152 No statutes from this date; that on limiting the number of monasteries is retrospectively dated to this year only in 1180s
1152 *Sacrosancta* from this date is probably the bull of Alexander III misattributed to Eugenius III

1155–61 Liturgical usages on which the Montpellier H322 usages are based
1157 Adrian IV issued *Statuimus* only, no confirmation of a Cistercian constitution
1157–61 First General Chapter statutes, as identified in the rubrics of Montpellier H322
1158 Alexander of Cologne becomes abbot of Savigny; abbot Serlo retires to Clairvaux

Appendix 1

1158 Valmagne hesitates about Cistercian usages

1159 Alexander III's election causes schism

1160 c. First collection of statutes or ideals

1161 Hospice for Cistercians founded in Montpellier

1162 Geoffrey of Auxerre becomes abbot of Clairvaux

1163 Council of Tours chaired by Alexander III refuses to act on the request for Bernard's canonization; *Vita Prima* manuscript returned for new redaction

1164 Height of Becket affair

1165 Geoffrey of Auxerre (abbot of Clairvaux) objects to Thomas Becket being hosted at Pontigny

1165 Alexander III and Louis VII demand and receive Geoffrey's abdication as abbot of Clairvaux

1165 c. *Exordium Cistercii/Summa Cartae Caritatis*

1165 *Sacrosancta* issued by Alexander III to confirm the Cistercian Charter of Charity

1165 Pons of Polignac becomes abbot of Clairvaux

1165 Obazine listed among daughters of Cîteaux in a papal privilege

1168 Alexander of Cologne becomes abbot of Cîteaux

1170 Thomas Becket is murdered

1170 Alexander III issues stern letter to the Cistercians; see Appendix 5.

1170 c. *Exordium Parvum* written

1170 c. Calixtus II bull forged

1170 c. *Carta Caritatis Prior* written

1173 Alexander III canonizes Thomas Becket, and a new request for Bernard's canonization is submitted

1174 Bernard canonized January 18

1174 Bernard canonized
1176 Vauluisant charter mentions Morimond abbot as proto-abbot
1176 c. *Carta Caritatis Posterior*
1176 Henry of Marcy becomes abbot of Clairvaux, goes on a mission to southern France to preach against the Cathars
1184 Papal exemption from episcopal visitation
1188 Knights not to become conversi
1190 First citations of individual abbeys before the General Chapter
1200s Cistercian preaching against heresy in southern France
1202 First promulgation of a Cistercian constitution to all houses
1209 Arnold Amalric leads the Albigensian Crusade
1215 Fourth Lateran Council commends the Cistercian Order, but limits its tithe privileges

Appendix 2. "Primitive Documents" Manuscripts : Relevant Contents

Montpellier, Bibliothèque de la fatculté de l'école de médecine, MS H322, produced at Clairvaux in 1161 or slightly later. It is dated by its series of statutes from 1157–61. It was taken to Montpellier in the nineteenth century in a division of the library of Clairvaux. "In hoc volumine continentur Ysagoge in compotum lune, Componis gerlandi, Opusculum de accentibus, Abbreviario usuum, et Instituta generalis capituli," fol 1r. Among the abbreviated usages are excerpts from an early *Ecclesiastica Officia*, what appears to be the earliest Cistercian regulations *De usibus conversorum* (see fig. 21, p. 65); see Andrée Vernet, *La bibliothèque de l'abbaye de Clairvaux du XIIe au XVIIIe siècle* (Paris, 1979), vol. 1, esp. p. 280 and *La léqislation cistercienne abrégée du manuscrit de Montpellier H322*, ed. Louis Duval-Arnould (Paris, 1997), which publishes part of this manuscript.

Paris, Bibliothèque Sainte-Geneviève, MS 1207, fragment on fols. 139r–140v. It includes a complete *Exordium Cistercii* with no rubrication, followed by the *Summa Cartae Caritatis,* no rubrication, and part of the *Instituta,* again witout rubrication. See fig. 20, p. 64. They are part of a composite manuscript (ex libris S. Genovesia parisiensis 1753, 4^B:L13) which includes excerpts from the apostle James, Isidore, Jerome, and a history of the church which appears to include a life of the blessed Hugh of Cluny (if the year 1109 is indicative), letters to Adele of Chartres, and the *Exordium Cistercii*. None of the other contents can be said to help date the fragment, which is presumably earlier than Trent 1711.

Trento, Bibliotheca communale, MS 1711, recension I from circa 1135; recension II from after 1161; this manuscript may have come from Villers-Bettnach. The first version is a liturgical *ordo* which was recycled into recension II. The latter contains an *Exordium Cistercii, Summa Cartae Caritatis, Instituta* or *Capitula, Ecclesiastica Officia,* and a *Usus conversorum*; see Bruno Griesser, "Beiträge zur Beurteilung des Cod. 1711 von Trient," *Cîteaux in der Nederlanden* 6 (1955): Les 117–30; *Les "Ecclesiastica Officia" cisterciens du XIIe siècle: texte latin selon les manuscrits édités de Trente 1711, Ljubljana 31 et Dijon 114 version française, annexe liturgique, notes, index et tables*, ed. Danièle Choisselet and Placide Vernet. Documentation Cistercienne 22 (Reiningue, France, 1989).

Ljubljana, University and State Library, MS 31, part of the manuscript collection which came from the Cistercian abbey of Stiçna (or possibly Kostanjevica) in Slovenia (other remains of the Stiçna library are in the Austria National Library in Vienna). It contains the *Exordium Parvum*, the *Carta Caritatis Prior*, the first example of the Calixtus II bull, the *Super Instituta*, and much of the *Ecclesiastica Officia*, which however is incomplete; the Lay-Brother Treatise is also missing. The manuscript hand and capitals have been dated to 1178–82 by art historians; see *Stiski rokopisi iz 12. stoletja: codices Sitticenses saeculi XII*, ed. Natasia Golob (Ljubljana, 1994), p. 98, and "Codex Manuscriptus 31 Bibliothecae Universitas Labacensis," ed. Canisius Noschitzka, *ASOC* 6 (1950): 1–124, which incorporates text from *Les monuments primitifs de la règle cistercienne*, ed. Philip Guignard (Dijon, 1878), for missing portions at the end.

Paris, Bibliothèque nationale Latin MS 4346, Part A (first two quires), is a fragment containing the *Exordium Parvum* followed immediately by the *Exordium Cistercii* and *Summa Cartae Caritatis*; the later breaks off. It is undatable, but earlier than the rest of manuscript 4346, part B (and probably earlier than Ljubljana 31). Latin MS 4346, part B, contains the more usual grouping of *Exordium Parvum*, *Carta Caritatis Posterior*, the Calixtus II bull, *Super Instituta*, *Ecclesiastica Officia*, *Usus conversorum*; my estimated date for the second part of this manuscript is after Ljubljana 31 or later than 1178. A Norman origin is suggested by a number of notes from the fifteenth and sixteenth centuries, and the mention on folios IV and 139V of the city of Dreux in the Eure. It belonged to the abbot of Targny, keeper of manuscripts for the King of France; on his death in 1737 it entered the royal library along with Targny's entire library. (Private communication, Mme. Marie-François Damongeot, Conservateur en Chef, manuscript department of the Bibliothèque nationale, August 1997.)

Paris, Bibliothèque nationale, Latin MS 4221 (B), is part of a collection of holdings coming from the Benedictine Abbey of Lyre, diocese of Evreux; see Léopold Delisle, *Cabinet des Manuscripts*, 2, 251; according to the handwritten ex libris inserted in each volume, "Cl. Puteani," these belonged to the collector Claude Dupuy, who died in 1594. They were given to his sons, who left their collections to the king's library in 1656. This volume contains an *Exordium Parvum*, a *Carta Caritatis Posterior*, the Calixtus II bull, the *Super Instituta*, an

Ecclesiastica Officia, and an *Usus conversorum*, but no rule of Saint Benedict; it is slightly earlier than Dijon 114, that is, circa 1182.

Paris, Bibliothèque nationale, MS nouvelle acquisition latine 430, comes from the Cistercian abbey of Savigny; it contains an *Exordium Parvum*, *Carta Caritatis Posterior*, Calixtus II bull, *Super Instituta*, *Ecclesiastica Officia*, *Usus conversorum*, and Rule of Saint Benedict. According to my calculations, it dates to slightly earlier than Dijon 114, thus circa 1182. It came into the B.N. with the collection of Jules Desnoyers; see Léopold Delisle, *Catalogue des manuscrits anciens et des chartes de la collection de M. Jules Desnoyers* (Paris, 1888), pp. 24–25, no. XXVI. Although worn, it is almost identical to Latin MS 4221 (B).

Paris, Bibliothèque nationale, Latin MS 12169, includes fragments of "primitive documents" materials bound into a different manuscript containing parts of a commentary on Genesis by Augustine and a treatise on the instruction of novices by Hugh of Saint Victor. On folios 115ff. are found parts of the *Ecclesiastica Officia* and Lay-Brother Treatise from circa 1182. This manuscript comes from the abbey of Notre-Dame-du-Val, near Pontoise (Val d'Oise), which was united with the Feuillants of Paris in the beginning of the seventeenth century; it came into the collection of the B.N. at the time of the Revolution. See Léopold Delisle, *Cabinet des manuscripts*, 2: 251.

Dijon, Bibliothèque municipale de la ville, MS 114 (once 82), folio-sized exemplar volume from Cîteaux measuring 48 x 32 cm, with 2 or 3 columns of sixty lines on each page. "In hoc volumine continentur libri ad divinum officium pertinentes quos utique non dicet in ordine nostro diversos haberi. Sunt autem hic in unum corpus ea maxime ratione redacti ut presens liber sit exemplar invariabile ad conservendam uniformitatem et corrigendam in aliis diversitatem." It lists its contents as a breviary, epistles, text of the Evangelists, missal, collect, calendar, rule, customs, psalter, *cantica de privatis dominicis et festis diebus*, hymns, antiphon with its preface, gradual with its preface. In comparison to earlier collections, it contains the Rule of Saint Benedict. The contents of its customary section are *Exordium Parvum*, *Carta Caritatis Posterior*, the Calixtus II bull, *Instituta*, *Ecclesiastica Officia*, and *Usus conversorum* (in that order). This exemplar manuscript is usually dated to 1182–88. It contains one date attached to a statute for 1152, but comparison to other manuscripts from Cîteaux of approximately the same date in Dijon shows that a scribe probably extrapolated an item number from the series of *Instituta*, making it mistakenly into that date. For further comments, see Yolanta Zaluska, *Manuscrits enluminés de Dijon* (Paris, 1991), pp. 118–19.

Metz, Bibliothèque publique, MS 1247 (from the monastery of Beuil line of Dalon) contains an *Exordium Parvum*, the *Carta Caritatis Prior*, a Calixtus II bull, *Super Instituta*, and a copy of portions of *Sacrosancta* attributed marginally to Eugenius III but probably of Alexander III. Its Lay-Brother Treatise has a prologue similar to the London manuscript listed next. It is later than Ljubljana 31.

London, British Library Additional MS 18,148, contains an *Exordium Parvum* (but no Charter of Charity), the Calixtus bull, *Ecclesiastica Officia*, *Instituta*, and *Regulum de Disciplina Conversorum*, with its preface; it is later than Ljubljana 31.

Laon, Bibliothèque publique, MS 217, contains the first two paragraphs of the *Exordium Cistercii* with rubrications, *Super Instituta*, *Ecclesiastica Officia*. A number of pages that are modern restorations; there is no Charter of Charity in a twelfth-century hand, no Lay-Brother Treatise.

Oxford, Corpus Christi College, MS 209, from Fountains Abbey, bound in sealskin with chemise binding. Composite manuscript of Augustine, the Life of Saint Olaf, the *Exordium Parvum*, and the letter of Archbishop Thurstan concerning the foundation of Fountains Abbey.

Appendix 3. Southern-French Cistercian Abbeys by Province and Diocese

Southern-French reform houses for monks and nuns founded before 1350, totaling 81 houses, 41 for men and 40 for women. Numbers preceding names of abbeys correspond to the map in Figure 49.

Note that some twelfth-century dates are for foundation rather than Cistercian affiliation; in a few cases, both are given. To find a specific abbey, see the Index, which cites numbers in this list.

Province of Auch: 12 for men, 3 for women
Diocese of Aire
1: Pontaut — men, 1115–25/1150
Diocese of Auch
2: Berdoues — men, c. 1137/c. 1142
3: Bouillas (Portaglonium) — men, 1150
4: Flaran — men, 1151
5: Gimont — men, 1147
Diocese of Bayonne
6: Saint-Bernard-de-la-Cagnotte — women, 1168
Diocese of Bazas
7: le Rivet — men, 1120s/1147
8: Fontguilhem — men, 1124/1147
Diocese of Dax
9: Villedieu, Divielle, Vielle, 1132, left order in 1209
10: Saint-Sigismond-d'Orthez–women, 1227
Diocese of Lescar
11: Sauvelade — men, 1127/1287
Diocese of Saint-Bertrand-de-Comminges:
12: Bonnefont — men, 1122/1142
13: Fabas (Lumen Dei) — women, 1145/1150
14: Nizors la Bénédiction-Díeu — men, 1184
Diocese of Tarbes
15: l'Escaledieu — men, 1137/1142

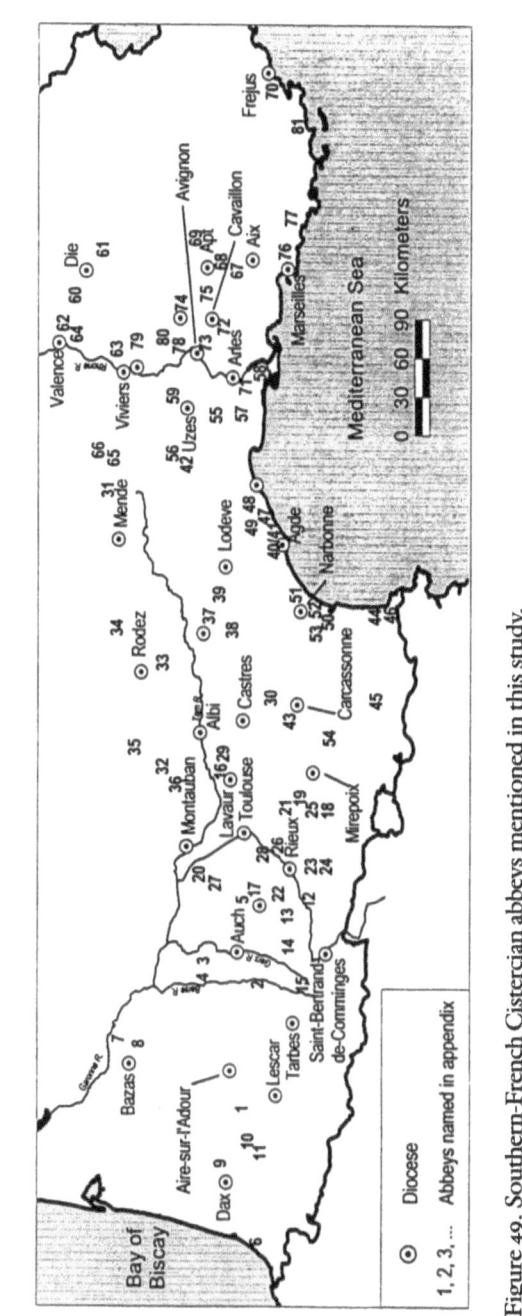

Figure 49. Southern-French Cistercian abbeys mentioned in this study.

Province of Toulouse: 6 for men, 7 for women
Diocese of Lavaur
16: Saint-Sulpice-de-la-Pointe — women, c. 1250
Diocese of Lombez
17: Goujon — women, 1154/1167
Diocese of Mirepoix
18: Beaulieu-en-Pamiers — women, 1295
19: Boulbonne — men, 1150/1163
Diocese of Montauban
20: Belleperche — men, c. 1110/c. 1145
Diocese of Rieux
21: Calers — men, 1148
22: Les Feuillants — men, 1120s/1162??
23: Marrenx — women, 1159
24: Salenques — women, 1353
25: Valnègre — women, c. 1200
Diocese of Toulouse
26: Eaunes — men, 1120/1162
27: Grandselve — men, 1114/1145
28: Oraison-Dieu (Muret) — women, 1197

Province of Bourges (southern parts only): 7 for men, 3 for women
Diocese of Albi
29: Candeil — men, 1152
Diocese of Castres
30: Ardorel — men, c. 1110/1147
Diocese of Mende
31: Mercoire — women, 1207
Diocese of Rodez
32: Belloc — men, 1133–44/c. 1144
33: Bonnecombe — men, 1162
34: Bonneval — men, 1147
35: Locdieu — men, 1124/1162
36: Oraison-Dieu-de-Costejean — women, c. 1210
Diocese of Vabres
37: Nonenque — women, 1136
38: Silvanès — men, 1132/1138

Province of Narbonne: 7 for men, 14 for women
Diocese of Lodève
39: Mont-Cornil — women, 1190

Diocese of Agde
40: Netlieu — women, 1195
41: Valmagne — men, 1138/1155
Diocese of Alès
42: Sainte-Claire — women, c. 1220/1300
Diocese of Carcassonne
43: Villelongue — men, 1148/1151
Diocese of Elne
44: l'Eule (Soler) — women, 1176
45: le Jau (Clariana) — men, 1147/1162
46: Valbonne — men, 1242
Diocese of Maguelonne (Montpellier)
47: Saint-Félix-de-Montseau (Gigean) — women, 1058/1167
48: le Vignogoul — women, 1130/1178
49: Bonlieu-en-Languedoc — women, c. 1200
Diocese of Narbonne
50: Fontfroide — men, 1093/1145
51: les Olieux (Montsérat) — women, 1153/1204
52: les Olieux (les-Monges) — women, 1205
53: la Peyrouse — women, c. 1050c/1145
54: Rieunette — women, 1162
Diocese of Nimes
55 Beaulieu-en-Gard — women, 1211
56: les Fonts-de-Rosiers, or Fonts-lès-Alais — women, c. 1220
57: Franquevaux — men, 1143
58: Sauveréal (Ulmet) — men, 1173
Diocese of Uzès
59: Valsauve-en-Gard — women, 1217

Province of Vienne (southern parts only): 4 for men, 3 for women
Diocese of Die
60: Léoncel — men, 1137
61: Valcroissant — men, 1188
Diocese of Valence
62: Bonlieu-en-Valence — women, c. 1200
63: Bonlieu-en-Montélimar — women, c. 1200
64: la Vernaison — women, 1180s
Diocese of Viviers
65: les Chambons — men, 1152
66: Mazan — men, 1120/1136

Province of Aix: 3 for men, 1 for women
Diocese of Aix
67: Silvacane—men, 1050c/1147
Diocese of Apt
68: Sainte-Croix—women, 1234
69: Valsainte—men, 1188
Diocese of Fréjus
70: le Thoronet—men, 1136

Province of Arles: 2 for men, 9 for women
Diocese of Arles
71: Beaulieu-en-Arles—women, 1238
Diocese of Avignon
72: Mollèges—women, 1207
73: Sainte-Catherine-de-Vaucluse—women, 1254
Diocese of Carpentras
74: Sainte-Madeleine-de-la-Plan—women, c. 1200
Diocese of Cavaillon
75: Sénanque—men, 1148
Diocese of Marseilles
76: Mont-Sion—women, 1245
77: Saint-Pons-de-Géménos—women, c. 1205
Diocese of Orange
78: Saint-Pierre-du-Puy—women, c. 1200
Diocese of Saint-Paul-Trois-Châteaux
79: Aiguebelle—men, 1137
80: le Bouchet (Vauluisant)—women, c. 1150
81: Saint-Pierre-de-l'Almanarre—women, 1221

Appendix 4. Calixtus II Documents from 1119 and 1120

Since on the authenticity of this bull rests the entire argument for the issuance of a Charter of Charity in 1119, I show the parallels between the texts in parallel columns, which suggest that the text on the left is a forgery.

Robert, no. 116: 23 dec, 1119
"Confirmation" of Statutes, forged privilege for Cîteaux. Quotes give usual name for this papal bull.

Robert, no. 134: 7 feb, 1120
"Confirmation" of possessions for Bonnevaux in Vienne, founded by future Calixtus. Square brackets are from Robert's edition.

Calixtus episcopus, servus servorum Dei,

Calixtus episcopus, servus servorum Dei, dilectis filiis Johanni, abbati [monasterii Sanctae Mariae] de Bonavalle, [et ejus fratribus, tam praesentibus quam futuris, in perpetuum. Etsi nos universis Ecclesiae filiis debitores ex apostolicae sedis benevolentia existimamus, vobis tamen propensiori convenit charitatis studio providere.
In Viennensis siquidem ecclesiae adhuc regimine positi, sapientium ac religiosorum virorum consilio, locum vestrum elegimus et vos assensu

carissimis in Christo filiis Stephano, venerabili Cisterciensis monasterii abbati, et

charissimi filii nostri Stephani, Cisterciensis abbatis, de ipso venerabili ac religioso Cister-

ejus fratribus, salutem et apostolicam benedictionem. "*Ad hoc in apostolice sedis*" regimen, Domino disponente, promoti conspicimur, ut ipso prestante, religionem augere et que recte atque ad salutem animarum statuta sunt, nostri debeamus auctoritate officii stabilire.

Idcirco,
filii in Christo carissimi, petitioni vestre caritate debita impertimur assensum et religioni vestre paterno congratulantes affectu, Dei operi quod cepistis manum nostre

confirmationis apponimus. Siquidem consensu et deliberatione communi abbatum et fratrum monasteriorum vestrorum et episcoporum, in quorum parrochiis eadem monasteria continentur, quedam de observatione regule beati Benedicti et de aliis nonnullis que ordini vestro et loco necessaria videbantur, capitula statuistis. Que nimirum ad majorem monasterii quietem et religionis observantiam auctoritate sedis apostolice petitis confirmari. Nos ergo vestro in Domino profectui gaudentes, capitula illa et constitutionem auctoritate apostolica confirmamus et omnia imperpetuum rata permanere

ciensi monasterio assumptos in eo.

Statuimus ut ibi deinceps religionis monasticae disciplina, protegente Domino, conservetur. Vestris

igitur,
filii in Christo charissimi, petitionibus annuentes, vos et praedictum] locum vestrum sub apostolicae sedis tutela excipimus [et vestra omnia beati Petri patrocinio communimus.

Confirmamus enim . . . usuarium . . . in silvis Sibonis, militis de Bello visu . . . ex dono ipsius Sibonis et uxoris sue ac filiorum . . . ; ex dono Garini de Pineto et uxoris sue ac filiorum . . . ; ex dono jamdicti Sibonis militis, uxoris et filiorum ejus, et Rostandi Ervuini et Brunonis consanguineorum . . . , usque ad terram Letaldi Peregrini, Guillelmi de Castellione et Silvionis, filii Berengarii . . . , et usque ad terram Sibonis Lunelli . . . et mulieris ejus Sore; ex dono Rostandi Crocelani et omnium fratrum ejus . . . ; ex dono Laetardi Peregrini et uxoris et filiorum ejus . . . ; ex dono Rostandi de Colunces, uxoris et filiorum ejus; ex dono Silvionis, filii Berengarii, uxoris ejus et filiorum . . . ; ex dono Melioris et fratris ejus Genisii, nec non ex matris eorum Adele . . . ; ex dono Jarentonis de Clavaisone et uxoris ac filiorum ejus . . . ; ex dono Guillelmi Hugonis et fratrum ejus Ademari, Lamberti . . . de proprio censu castri quod vocatur Montilium.

decernimus, illud nominatim omnimodis prohibentes ne abbatum aliquis monachos vestros sine regulari commendatione suscipiat.

Decernimus itaque ut nemini liceat vos et vestrum monasterium temere perturbare aut possessiones ejus auferre vel ablatas retinere, minuere vel temerariis vexationibus fatigare, sed omnia integra et illibata conserventur, eorum pro quorum sustentatione ac gubernatione concessa sunt, usibus omnimodis pro futura.

Si qua igitur ecclesiastica secularisve persona nostre confirmationi huic et constitutioni vestre temeritate aliqua obviare presumpserit, tanquam religionis et quietis monastice perturbatrix auctoritate beatorum Petri et Pauli et nostra, donec satisfaciant, excommunicationis gladio feriatur. Qui vero conservator extiterit, omnipotentis Dei et apostolorum ejus benedictionem et gratiam consequatur.

Interdicimus autem ne quis con-

Si qua igitur in futurum ecclesiastica saecularisve persona hanc nostrae constitutionis paginam sciens contra eam temere venire tentaverit, secundo tertiove commonita, si non congrua satisfactione emendaverit, potestatis honorisque sui dignitate careat reamque se divino judicio existere de perpetrata iniquitate cognoscat et a sacratissimo corpore ac sanguine Dei et Domini Redemptoris nostri Jesu Christi aliena fiat atque in extremo examine districtae

versos laicos vel professos vestros ad habitandum suscipiat.

Ego Calistus, catholice Ecclesie episcopus, confirmavi et s.

Datum Sedeloci per manum Grisogoni, sancte Romane Ecclesie diaconi cardinalis ac bibliothecarii, x kalendas januarii, indictione xiiii, incarnationis Dominice anno M.C. XIX, pontificatus autem domni Calixti secundi pape anno I.

ultioni subjaceat. Cunctis autem eidem loco justa servantibus sit pax Domini Jesu Christi, quatenus et hic fructum bonae actionis percipiant et apud districtum judicem praemia aeternae pacis inveniant. Amen.

Ego Calixtus, Ecclesiae catholicae epicopus.]

Data Viennae per manum Grisogoni, sanctae Romanae Ecclesiae diaconi cardinalis ac bibliothecarii, vii idus februarii, indictione xiii, incarnationis Dominicae anno m c xx, pontificatus autem domni Calixti secundi pape anno ii.

Appendix 5. Restored Text of 1170 Letter from Pope Alexander III to the Cistercians

(Reproduced from *Statuta*, ed. Canivez [Louvain, 1933], pp. 77–78, with insert of text from Jean Leclercq, "Passage supprimé dans une épitre d'Alexandre III," *Revue bénédictine* 62 [1952]: 149–51. I have left the transcription as it appears in each. Note that, in addition to addressing those congregated at Cîteaux, it directly addresses "his dear sons at Cîteaux and Clairvaux." It does not ever refer to a General Chapter; it refers to *ordo* as a rule that they serve.)

Alexander episcopus, servus servorum Dei, Venerabilibus fratribus archiepiscopis, episcopis, et dilectis filiis universis abbatibus in cisterciensi Capitulo congregatis, salutem et apostolicam benedictionem. Inter innumeras mundani turbinis tempestates, quas contra Ecclesiam Dei, et nos ipsos ferventis persecutionis procella commovit, magnum nobis est praestitum, Deo providente, remedium, cum universitatis vestrae ferventissima charitas, nec pericula timuit, nec adminicula denegavit: ex his videlicet retributionis cumulum, ex illis, authore Domino, patientiae consecutura triumphos. Meminimus plane, et cum omnium gratiarum actione recolimus, quam inviolabili firmitate fluctuantem Petri naviculam fidei vestrae anchora servavit in turbine; qualiter etiam frequens orationum instantia, quasi iterum dormientem in eadem navicula Salvatorem, ingruente suscitavit tempestate, ita ut saepenumero magnitudine stupefacti miraculi; et ipsum glorificemus; quo mari et fluctibus imperante, optata coepit arridere tranquillitas, et vos penitus venerabiles habemus, quorum nobis suffragantibus meritis coelestis creditur placata maiestas.

Accedit ad haec omnia, dilectorum filiorum nostrorum Cisterciensis et Claraevallensis abbatum sollicitudo laudabilis et devota, qui non humano instinctu, sed superni concilii spiritu provocati, pro pace universalis Ecclesiae labores maximos et pericula subierunt. Quod tanto nobis et fratribus nostris gratum est amplius et acceptum; quanto eorum studium et laborem universae Dei Ecclesiae magis confidimus profuturum. Maximeque speramus, quod pia eorum instantia, vestris orationibus incessanter adiuta, ad Ordinis honorem et commodum, et optatae pacis profectura sit incrementum. Debitores ergo vobis, pro tam multiplici charitatis vestrae munere, constituti; vos et sacrum

Ordinem quem servatis omni qua possumus affectione diligimus, et eiusdem Ordinis profectibus, et augmentis, amplissimo studio promptae sollicitudinis aspiramus; quandoquidem inutiliter videmur superni agricolae vicissitudinem gerere, si plantationem, quam plantavit dextera eius, opportunis cessaremus imbribus irrigare.

Ea propter universitatem vestram per Apostolica scripta rogamus, monemus et exhortamur in Domino: quatenus recolentes, qualiter haec plantatio sancta, haec vitis fructifera, haec denique vinea Domini Sabaoth, sub primis Ordinis patribus pullulavit et palmites suos longe lateque producens, ad mortifera circumquaque venena pellenda, flores protulit et odores effudit; pervigili custodia studeatis eorum in omnibus inhaerere vestigiis, per quos, cooperante Domino, in deserto mundi huius, flos huiuscemodi plantatus est honestatis; hi quoniam monasticae frugalitatis continentissimi professores, optimum ponentes in paupertate principium totius sufficientiae assecuti sunt complementum, Ecclesiae chari, episcopis et praelatis accepti, atque in conspectu regum et principum fama et merito gloriosi.

[*Section suppressed in Canivez follows*:] Nunc autem, quod dolentes dicimus, etsi non ab omnibus neque in omnibus, a plerisque tamen et in plerisque ab illa sancta institutione dicitur declinatum, in tantum quod aliqui ex uobis primae institutionis obliti penitus uel ignari, contra ordinis uestri gloriam et decorem, uillas et molendina, ecclesias et altaria possident, fidelitates et hominia suscipiunt, rusticos et tributarios tenent, et omne studium adhibent ut termini eorum dilatentur in terris quorum tota conuersatio esse debebat in caelis. Laeditur hinc ordo penitus et mutatur, nec est haec mutatio dexterae excelsi, quin immo de dextera potius in laeuam transeunt, qui cum relicto saeculo sub paupertatis habitu Deo militare decreuerint, negotiis denuo saecularibus implicantur. Inde est quod uobis ab his qui foris sunt contentiones et litigia suscitantur et, abbatibus in causis forensibus occupatis, plerumque in commissis domibus et tepor ordinis et dissolutio noscitur caritatis, maxime quia caritas in paupertate plus proficit et, cupiditatis dedignata consortium, nisi illa restinguitur, haec tepescit.

Ideoque sanctum et uenerabile collegium uestrum precibus et monitis quibus possumus exhortamur, quatinus domus illae quae a prima sui origine in ordine sunt fundatae constitutis et ordinariis terminis sint contentae nec uelint ad ea manus extendere quae sine laboribus et periculis multis, et demum sine magna ordinis confusione, minime poterunt retinere. Si enim, relictis originalibus ordinis institutis, ad communia volueritis aliorum monasteriorum iura diuertere, oportebit et uos communi iure censeri, quia dignum est ut qui similem cum aliis suscipiunt uitam, similem sentiant in legibus disciplinam.

Caeterum domus illae quae de aliis institutionibus ad uestrum se ordinem transtulerint, uestris omnino satagant usibus conformari, ut relictis uidelicet possessionibus uel mutatis quas institutio uestra non recipit, sic se in omnibus uestrae religioni coaptent ut quemadmodum se gaudent in societatem ordinis mutatione habitus et obseruantiae regularis assumptos, sic etiam in parcitate temporalium rerum uestris se laetentur institutionibus conformatos, quatinus inde et superno Conditori magis amabiles et nobis atque uniuersae ecclesiae Dei fieri debeant merito cariores. Sane si super possessionibus ipsis in aliquo de monasteriis uestris apostolicae sedis auctoritas dispensauit, a nullo uestrum sumendum est in exemplum, quia temerarium est penitus et indignum aliquem sibi sua auctoritate praesumere quod romana ecclesia alicui monasterio, certa ratione inspecta, singularibus uoluit beneficiis indulgere. [*end of deleted section*]

De cetero nos et totum Ecclesiae sanctae negotium vestris devotis orationibus commendamus; orantes et ipsi ut omnipotens Pater, in cuius estis nomine congregati, ordinationes et opera vestra in beneplacito suo disponat; et vos pariter, ac subditos fratres ad spiritualia iugiter incrementa promoveat. Adhuc quia praedictum Claraevallensem abbatem, pro inevitabili necessitate promovendae pacis, ab adventu Capituli duximus retinendum; eum a vobis petimus haberi excusatum, sicut et de ipso Cisterciensi, in patientia vos sustinere rogamus, si forte contigerit, ut eum pro tanta necessitate, celebrato Capitulo, revocemus. Datum Benevento, XIV kalend. Augusti.

Abbreviations

AO:	Moreau, Marthe. *L'âge d'or des religieuses: monastères féminins du Languedoc méditerranéen au Moyen Age.* Montpellier: Presses du Languedoc, 1988.
AP:	*Analecta Praemonstratensia.*
ASOC:	*Analecta Cisterciensia,* or *Analecta Sacri Ordinis Cisterciensis.*
Atlas:	Van der Meer, Frederik. *Atlas de l'Ordre cistercien.* Paris: Séquoia, 1965.
BC:	*Cartulaire de l'abbaye de Bonnecombe,* ed. P.-A. Verlaguet. Rodez: Carrère, 1918–25.
BD:	*Cartulaire de l'abbaye de Berdoues-près-Mirande,* ed. Cazaurin. The Hague: Nijhoff, 1905.
Berman, *MA:*	Berman, Constance H. *Medieval Agriculture, the Southern-French Countryside, and the Early Cistercians: A Study of Forty-Three Monasteries.* Transactions of the American Philosophical Society 76. Philadelphia: American Philosophical Society, 1986.
BF:	*Recueil des actes de l'abbaye cistercienne de Bonnefont-en-Comminges,* ed. Ch. Samaran and Ch. Higounet. Paris: Bibliothèque nationale, 1970.
Bull.:	*Bulletin*
BV:	*Cartulaire de l'abbaye de Bonneval-en-Rouergue,* ed. P.-A. Verlaguet, intro. J.-L. Rigal. Rodez: Carrère, 1938.
BX:	*Cartulaire de l'abbaye Notre-Dame de Bonnevaux au diocèse de Vienne, ordre de Cîteaux,* ed. Ulysse Chevalier. Grenoble: Allier, 1889.
CC:	*Cistercienser-Chronik.*
CCM:	*Cahiers de la civilisation médiévale.*
CF 21:	*Les Cisterciens de Languedoc (XIIIe–XIVe siècle).* Cahiers de Fanjeaux, Vol. 21. Toulouse: Privat, 1986.
CF 23:	*La femme dans la vie religieuse du Languedoc (XIIIe–XIVe siècle).* Cahiers de Fanjeaux, Vol. 23. Toulouse: Privat, 1988.
CI:	*Chartes et documents concernant l'abbaye de Cîteaux 1098–1182,* ed. J.-M. Marilier. Rome: Editions cisterciennes, 1961.
CL:	*Recueil des chartes de l'abbaye de Clairvaux, XIIe siècle,* ed. Jean Waquet. Troyes: Archives départementales de l'Aube, 1950–82.
COCR:	*Collectanea ordinis cisterciensium reformatorum.*

Cottineau:	Cottineau, L.-H. *Répertoire topo-bibliographique des abbayes et prieurés*. 3 vols. Macon, 1935–38.
CSQ:	*Cistercian Studies Quarterly*.
Desmarchelier:	Desmarchelier, Michel. "L'architecture des églises de moniales cisterciennes, essai de classement des différents types de plans (en guise de suite)." *Mélanges Dimier* 2,5: 109–21.
DHGE:	*Dictionnaire d'histoire et de géographie ecclésiastique*.
Distant Echoes:	Medieval Religious Women 1. Ed. John A. Nichols and Lillian Thomas Shank. Kalamazoo, Mich.: Cistercian Publications, 1984.
Doat 77, etc.:	Paris, B.N., Collection Doat. Vol. 77, etc.
EO:	*Les "Ecclesiastica Officia" cisterciens du XIIe siècle: texte latin selon les manuscrits édités de Trente 1711, Ljubljana 31 et Dijon 114, version française, annexe liturgique, notes, index et tables*. Documentation cistercienne 22, ed. Danièle Choisselet and Placide Vernet. Reiningue, France, 1989.
FE:	*Recueil des pancartes de l'abbaye de la Ferté-sur-Grosne: 1113–1178*, ed. Georges Duby. Aix-Marseilles, 1953.
FF:	Cauvet, E. *Etude historique sur Fonfroide* [sic]. Montpellier: Séquin, 1875.
GC:	*Gallia Christiana in Provincias Ecclesiasticas Distributa*, ed. P. Piolin. 13 vols. Paris: Imprimerie royale, 1870–78. (Ed. B. Hauréau, 3 vols. Paris: Imprimerie royale, 1856–65.)
GM:	*Cartulaire de l'abbaye de Gimont*, ed. Abbé Clergeac. Paris: Champion, 1905.
HGL:	*Histoire générale de Languedoc*. 2nd ed., ed. Claude Devic and Jean Vaissete. 18 vols. Toulouse: Privat, 1872–1904.
Hidden Springs:	2 vols. Medieval Religious Women 3, 4. Ed. John A. Nichols and Lillian Thomas Shank. Kalamazoo, Mich.: Cistercian Publications, 1995.
Jully:	*Histoire du prieuré de Jully-les-Nonnains, avec pièces justificatives*, ed. Abbé Jobin. Paris, 1881.
LC:	*Cartulaire de l'abbaye Notre-Dame de Léoncel, diocèse de Die, Ordre de Cîteaux*, ed. Ulysse Chevalier. Montélimar: Bourron, 1869.
LIM:	*Liber instrumentorum memorialium: cartulaire des Guillems de Montpellier*, ed. A. Germain. Montpellier: Jean Marel Ainé, 1884.
Les cartulaires:	Guyotjeannin, Olivier, Laurent Morelle, and Michel Parisse, eds., *Les cartulaires: actes de la table ronde organisée par l'Ecole nationale des chartes et le G.D.R. 121 du C.N.R.S., Paris, 5–7 décembre 1991*. Paris: Ecole des chartes, 1993.
Mélanges Dimier:	Chauvin, Benoît, ed. *Mélanges à la mémoire du père Anselme Dimier*. 3 vols. in 6. Pupillon: Arbois, 1982–87.

Mém.:	*Mémoire*.
MO:	*Cartulaires de l'abbaye de Molesme, ancien diocèse de Langres, 916–1250: recueil de documents sur le Nord de la Bourgogne et le Midi de la Champagne, publié avec une introduction diplomatique, historique et géographique*, ed. Jacques Laurent. 2 vols. Paris: Picard, 1907, 1911.
Moreau, *AO*:	Moreau, Marthe. *L'âge d'or des religieuses: monastères féminins du Languedoc méditerranéen au Moyen Age*. Montpellier: Presses du Languedoc, 1988.
NO:	*Cartulaire et documents de l'abbaye de Nonenque*, ed. C. Couderc and J.-L. Rigal. Rodez, Carrère 1955.
Originum:	Janauschek, Leopoldus. *Originum Cisterciensium*: Vienna, 1877. Reprint Ridgewood, N.J.: Gregg Press, 1964.
PAT:	*Les plus anciens textes de Cîteaux: sources, textes et notes historiques*, ed. Jean-de-la-Croix Bouton and Jean-Baptiste Van Damme. Cîteaux: Studia et Documenta 2. Achel: Abbaye cistercienne, 1974.
PL:	Migne, J. D., *Patrologiae Cursus Completus, Series Latina*. 221 vols. Paris: Migne, 1844–64.
PO:	*Le premier cartulaire de l'abbaye cistercienne de Pontigny (XIIe–XIIIe siècles)*, ed. Martine Garrigues. Paris: Bibliothèque nationale, 1981.
Pro.:	*Proceedings*.
R.:	*Revue*.
Regesta Regum AN:	*Regesta Regum Anglo-Normannorum 1066–1154*. Vol. 1, ed. H. W. C. Davis; Vol 2, ed. Charles Johnson and H. A. Cronne; Vols. 3 and 4, ed. H. A. Cronne and R. H. C. Davis. Oxford, 1913–70.
RHE:	*Revue d'histoire ecclésiastique*.
SL:	*Cartulaire de l'abbaye de Silvanès*, ed. P.-A. Verlaguet. Rodez: Carrère, 1910.
Statuta:	*Statuta Capitulorum Generalium Ordinis Cisterciensis ab Anno 1116 ad Annum 1786*, ed. J.-M. Canivez. 8 vols. Louvain: Bureaux de la Revue, 1933.
"*VM*":	Montpellier, A.D. Hérault, film no. 1 Mi 260–261 (private deposit), unpublished "Cartulaire de Valmagne."

Notes

Preface

1. Constance H. Berman, *Medieval Agriculture, the Southern-French Countryside, and the Early Cistercians: A Study of Forty-Three Monasteries* (Philadelphia, 1986); hereafter Berman, *MA*.

2. *Statuta Capitulorum Generalium Ordinis Cisterciensis ab Anno 1116 ad Annum 1786*, ed. J.-M. Canivez, 8 vols. (Louvain, 1933), hereafter *Statuta*. See also Brigitte Degler-Spengler, "The Incorporation of Cistercian Nuns into the Order in the Twelfth and Thirteenth Century," *Hidden Springs*, ed. John A. Nichols and Lillian Thomas Shank, 2 vols., Medieval Religious Women 3, 4 (Kalamazoo, Mich., 1995), hereafter *Hidden Springs*, vol. 1, pp. 85–134 (an adaption of Degler-Spengler's earlier "Die Zisterzienserinnen in der Schweiz," *Helvetia Sacra* [Bern] 3 [1982]: 507–74; see also *Distant Echoes* in the list of abbreviations).

3. See Louis J. Lekai, *The Cistercians: Ideals and Reality* (Kent, Ohio, 1977).

4. But while such problems with regard to individual monastic foundations and their monastic foundation charters have been explored extensively by V. H. Galbraith and others, they have not been taken up with regard to the dating of how abbeys were attached to twelfth-century orders, because foundations are assumed to have followed the invention of an Order like that of the Cistercians; on individual houses, see V. H. Galbraith, "Monastic Foundation Charters of the Eleventh and Twelfth Centuries," *Cambridge Historical Journal* 4 (1934): 205–22, 296–98.

5. This insight was confirmed by Marcel Pacaut, private communication, September 1998.

6. David Knowles, "The Primitive Cistercian Documents," *Great Historical Enterprises: Problems in Monastic History* (London, 1963), pp. 197–222.

7. Michael T. Clanchy, *From Memory to Written Record: England, 1066–1307*, 2nd ed., (Oxford, 1993); Barbara Rosenwein, *To Be the Neighbor of Saint Peter: The Social Meaning of Cluny's Property, 909–1049* (Ithaca, N.Y., 1989); Ellen E. Kittel, *From Ad Hoc to Routine: A Case Study in Medieval Bureaucracy* (Philadelphia, 1991); Charles Homer Haskins, *The Renaissance of the Twelfth Century* (Cambridge, Mass., 1922).

8. Martha G. Newman, *The Boundaries of Charity: Cistercian Culture and Ecclesiastical Reform, 1098–1180* (Palo Alto, Calif., 1996); Brian Stock, *The Implications of Literacy: Written Language and Models of Interpretation in the Eleventh and Twelfth Centuries* (Princeton, N.J., 1983).

9. Adriaan H. Bredero, *Bernard of Clairvaux: Between Cult and History* (Grand Rapids, Mich., 1997).

10. On that pressure on Cistercians, see Jean Leclercq, "Passage supprimé dans une épitre d'Alexandre III," *R. bénédictine* 62 (1952): 149–51, discussed further below; the suppressed passage is restored to the 1170 letter in my Appendix 5.

11. See *Atlas de l'Ordre cistercien*, ed. Frederik van der Meer (Paris, 1965), here-

after *Atlas*. In speaking of southern France and Cistercians there, I include the ecclesiastical provinces of Aix, Arles, Narbonne, Toulouse, Auch, and Bourges (Albi, Castres, Mende, Rodez, Vabres), and southern dioceses in the province of Vienne (Die, Valence, Viviers, but not Vienne itself). I briefly discuss the abbey of Bonnevaux in the latter diocese because it became mother-house to many southern abbeys. I leave out the diocese of Cahors in the province of Bourges and the nearby dioceses of Sarlat and Agen in the province of Bordeaux because destruction in the early modern period means that almost no documents have survived, but I mention Cadouin, mother-abbey for several southern houses. Political boundaries make little sense for limiting the region of this study; secular reigns provide better approximate endpoints than do events in church history. Church councils, including the great Fourth Lateran assembly in 1215, did not signal immediate changes in the monastic history of southern France or elsewhere. Ends of reigns did have some significance: a pair of possible endpoints are 1249, when the last male member of the Raymondine comital family of Toulouse died, and 1270, when Raymond VII's daughter Jeanne (who had inherited his political rights) and her husband, Alphonse of Poitiers (son of Louis VIII of France), both died on Crusade.

12. The treatment by Robert Bartlett, *The Making of Europe: Conquest, Colonization, and Cultural Change, 950–1350* (Princeton, N.J., 1994), pp. 255–60 and ff., suggests the need to differentiate between "old" and "new" Europe, in the twelfth century more generally and in undertaking further investigation.

Obviously, the documents from other regions, carefully dated and handled, eventually will allow other scholars to provide clarifications of the picture provided here.

13. The Midi did have a much longer history of Greek and Roman settlement and legal practices, in places a true Mediterranean polyculture of vines, olives, and wheat, and a landscape with many changes of elevation, making it suitable for the institution of transhumance. Roger Brunet, *Les campagnes toulousaines: étude géographique* (Toulouse, 1965); Charles Higounet, *Paysages et villages neufs du Moyen Age: recueil d'articles de Charles Higounet* (Bordeaux, 1975). See also *Histoire générale de Languedoc*, 2nd ed., ed. Claude Devic and Jean Vaissete (Toulouse, 1872–1904), esp. vol. 6, hereafter *HGL*; document collections such as *Liber instrumentorum memorialium: cartulaire des Guillems de Montpellier*, ed. A. Germain (Montpellier, 1884), hereafter *LIM*.

Certain aspects of the southern French juridical and legal situation stand out, including the fact that relationships between lord and follower and between military equals were often regulated by written contracts; see Elisabeth Magnou-Nortier, *La société laïque et l'église dans la province ecclésiastique de Narbonne (zone cispyrénéenne) de la fin du VIIIe à la fin du XIe siècle* (Toulouse, 1974), esp. pp. 179, 550–63; eadem, "Fidélité et féodalité méridionales d'après les serments de fidélité (Xe-debut XIIe siècle)," *Les structures sociales de l'Aquitaine, du Languedoc et de l'Espagne au premier age féodal* (Paris, 1969), pp. 115–42, 152; Pierre Bonnassie, "Les conventions féodales dans la Catalogne du XIe siècle," ibid., pp. 187–219; Archibald R. Lewis, "The Guillems of Montpellier—a Sociological Appraisal," *Viator* 2 (1971): 159–69; idem, *The Development of Southern French and Catalan Society, 718–1050* (Austin, Tex., 1965), pp. 39, 53–55, 350–52; Jean-Pierre Poly, *La Provence et la société féodale 879–1166: contribution à l'étude des structures dites féodales dans le Midi* (Paris, 1976); F. L. Cheyette, "The 'Sale' of Carcassonne to the Counts of Barcelona (1067–1070) and the Rise of the Trencavels," *Speculum* 63 (1988): 826–63.

14. Charters from the twelfth-century southwest, for instance, invariably refer to the local bishop, count, and king of the Franks by name, sometimes in place of giving any date; see, e.g., *Cartulaire de l'abbaye de Berdoues-près-Mirande*, ed. Cazaurin (The Hague, 1905), hereafter *BD*.

15. Cistercians are described by Robert Fossier as "having nearly missed the train as it pulled out of the station"; see Robert Fossier, "L'économie cistercienne dans les plaines du nord-ouest d'Europe," *L'économie cistercienne: géographie—mutations du Moyen Age aux temps modernes*, pp. 53–75, esp. 55, Flaran 3 (Auch, 1983); and Berman, *MA*, passim.

16. John Hine Mundy, *Liberty and Political Power in Toulouse, 1050–1230* (New York, 1954); Susan Reynolds, *Kingdoms and Communities in Western Europe, 900–1300* (Oxford, 1984).

17. See Chapter 3.

Chapter 1

1. Lekai, *Cistercians*, p. 34.
2. Lekai, *Cistercians*, pp. 50–51.
3. Lekai, *Cistercians*, pp. 44ff.
4. David Knowles, *The Monastic Order in England: A History of Its Development from the Times of St. Dunstan to the Fourth Lateran Council, 940–1216*, 2nd ed. (Cambridge, 1963), p. 223, describes its "system of government of unrivalled excellence . . . in a virile and unfolding society" contemporary with Bernard of Clairvaux's earliest years as abbot.
5. See *Exordium Magnum Cisterciense: sive narratio de initio cisterciensis ordinis auctore conrado monacho Clarevallensi postea ad Eberbacensi ibidemque abbate ad codicum fidem recensuit*, ed. Bruno Griesser, Series Scriptorum Sacri Ordinis Cisterciensis 2 (Rome, 1960), which has just appeared in a new edition: *Exordium Magnum Cisterciense: sive narratio de initio cisterciensis ordinis auctore conrado monacho Clarevallensi postea ad Eberbacensi ibidemque abbate ad codicum fidem recensuit*, ed. Bruno Griesser, Corpus Christianorum Continuatio Mediaevalis 138 (Turnhout, 1997); and in translation: Conrad d'Eberbach, *Le grand exorde de Cîteaux ou récit des débuts de l'Ordre cistercien*, trans. Anthelmette Piébourg, intro. Brian P. McGuire, under direction of Jacques Berlioz, Cîteaux: Studia et Documenta 7 (Turnhout, 1998).
6. On which texts are found together, see Appendix 2 and Jean-Baptiste Auberger, *L'unanimité cistercienne primitive: mythe ou réalité?* (Achel, 1986), fold-out charts. Latin texts of the *Exordium Cistercii* and *Summa Cartae Caritatis* were most recently published as separate chapters (although they always appear together in the manuscripts as a continuous unit) in *Les plus anciens textes de Cîteaux: sources, textes et notes historiques*, ed. Jean-de-la-Croix Bouton and Jean-Baptiste Van Damme, Cîteaux: Studia et Documenta 2 (Achel, 1974), hereafter *PAT*; the early *Instituta* found with the earliest complete manuscript version—that of Trent 1711—are not published in *PAT* but are roughly equivalent to the statutes published by Canivez under 1134 in *Statuta*; but see discussion in Chapter 2 questioning this date. *PAT* also includes versions of the texts of the *Exordium Parvum* and the *Carta Caritatis Prior* as found in Ljubljana 31 and in a separate chapter the Calixtus II *Ad hoc in Apostolicae* confirmation, which in fact immediately follows the *Carta Caritatis Prior* in that manuscript. Lekai, *Cistercians*, pp.

444ff., includes a translation by Bede K. Lackner of the *Exordium Cistercii*, *Summa Cartae Caritatis*, and *Instituta*, very correctly in one continuous grouping, but simplifying somewhat the transformation. The second textual grouping has an *Exordium Parvum* with the *Carta Caritatis Posterior*.

7. Caroline Walker Bynum, *Jesus as Mother: Studies in the Spirituality of the High Middle Ages* (Berkeley, Calif., 1982), esp. pp. 59ff.

8. *PAT*, p. 111.

9. *PAT*, p. 111.

10. *PAT*, p. 112.

11. *PAT*, p. 113.

12. *PAT*, p. 113: *Quo facto novum monasterium novi patris sollicitudine et industria, in brevi, non mediocriter Deo cooperante, in sancta conversatione profecit, opinione claruit, rebus necessariis crevit*. *Novum* is missing in the Paris, Sainte-Geneviève MS 1207 fragment, the earliest surviving text; on what has been seen as the significance of this terminology in the *Carta Caritatis Prior*, see discussion by Jean Marilier, "Le vocable 'Novum Monasterium,'" *CC* 57 (1950), pp. 81–84.

13. *PAT*, p. 113.

14. *PAT*, p. 113: *Ita ut in cella probandi novitiorum tam clerici quam laici et ipsi secundum saeculum nobiles atque potentes, triginta pariter cohabitarent.*

15. *PAT*, p. 113.

16. *PAT*, pp. 113–14; it is significant that the *exordia* attribute the writing of the Charter of Charity to Stephen Harding, not because it means that is so, but because it means that, as Father Jean-de-la-Croix Bouton has suggested, the *exordia* could not have been written in Harding's lifetime. Bouton points out that Stephen would not willingly have concurred in such self-glorification; see Jacques Winandy, "Les origines de Cîteaux et les travaux de M. Lefèvre," *R. bénédictine* 67 (1957): 49–76, which cites this opinion of Bouton's.

17. *PAT*, p. 113: *Quae quidem carta sicut ab eodem patre digesta et a prefatis viginti abbatibus confirmata sigilli quoque apostolici auctoritate munita est largius continet ea quae diximus sed nos summam tantum eorum hic breviter perstringemus.*

18. *PAT*, p. 117.

19. *PAT*, p. 118.

20. *PAT*, p. 118.

21. *PAT*, p. 118.

22. *PAT*, p. 118.

23. *PAT*, p. 119.

24. *PAT*, pp. 120–25.

25. *PAT*, pp. 132ff.

26. *PAT*, pp. 132ff.

27. *PAT*, pp. 89, 132; the latter is apparently from Laibach 31 and varies in spelling of "chartam" and "exsequitur."

28. *PAT*, p. 92:

Ut idem libri ecclesiastici et consuetudines sint omnibus. Et quia omnes monachos ipsorum ad nos venientes in claustro nostro recipimus, et ipsi similiter nostros in claustris suis, ideo opportunum nobis videtur et hoc etiam volumus, ut mores et cantum, et omnes libros ad horas diurnas et nocturnas et ad missas necessarios secundum formam, morum, et librorum novi monasterii possideant, quatinus in actibus nostris nulla sit discordia, sed una caritate, una regula similibusque vivamus moribus.

It is possible that in some such texts the term *unanimitas* is a corruption of *una caritas*.

29. *PAT*, p. 93.

30. *PAT*, p. 94.

31. *PAT*, p. 54, n. 2.

32. As noted in the translation by Lackner (Lekai, *Cistercians*, p. 451).

33. *PAT*, pp. 24-37, does not show which manuscripts include the *Ecclesiastica Officia*; see Appendix 2, below.

34. *PAT*, p. 54.

35. *PAT*, p. 54.

36. *PAT*, pp. 56-57.

37. *PAT*, p. 58.

38. *PAT*, p. 58; it may well be that the references in both *exordia* to the practice of sealing documents (which appears in various parts of Europe only in the twelfth century) might be used as a means of confirming the dating of these texts. Unfortunately, the dating of the regional diffusion of sealing is only beginning; see Brigitte Bedos-Rezak, "Diplomatic Sources and Medieval Documentary Practices: An Essay in Interpretive Methodology," *The Past and Future of Medieval Studies*, ed. John Van Engen (Notre Dame, Ind., 1994), pp. 313-43.

39. *PAT*, p. 58.

40. *PAT*, p. 58.

41. Leclercq, "Passage," 149-51, and Appendix 5 below, which reproduces the entire text.

42. In *The Ecclesiastical History of Orderic Vitalis*, ed. Marjorie Chibnall, 6 vols. (Oxford, 1969-80), intro. to vol. 5, p. xiv, Chibnall discusses the invention of such texts and speeches by twelfth-century historians.

43. It is notable that no Cistercian authors contribute to the documentation included in the *Exordium Parvum*, although letters of Bernard of Clairvaux and others were obviously extant; a rhetorical purpose, using outsiders to praise the Cistercians, is suggested.

44. For instance, papal bulls in *Regesta Pontificum Romanorum*, ed. Philip Jaffé (Leipzig, 1885-88), I: 6795; II: 9600.

45. The most recent survey of this kind of study is that of Olivier Guyotjeannin, Jacques Pycke, and Benoît-Michel Tock, *Diplomatique médiévale: l'atelier du médiéviste II* (Turnhout, 1993); Chrysogonus Waddell, "Prelude to a Feast of Freedom: Notes on the Roman Privilege *Desiderium Quod* of October 19, 1110," *Cîteaux* 33 (1982): 247-303, discusses the importance of such diplomatic investigation, particularly of late medieval manuscripts created for Jean of Cirey, abbot of Cîteaux (1476-1501).

46. See M. de Waha, "Aux origines de Cîteaux: rapports entre l'*Exordium Cistercii* et *Exordium Parvum*," *Latomus: R. d'études latines* 158 (1978): 152-82.

47. *PAT*, pp. 62ff.

48. Bredero, *Bernard*, pp. 81-82.

49. *De miraculis sanctae Mariae Laudunensis* of Herman of Tournai, *PL* 156: 962-1018.

50. Jean-de-la-Croix Bouton, "Saint Bernard et les moniales," in *Mélanges Saint Bernard* (Dijon, 1954), pp. 225–47, but see also Bouton, Benoît Chauvin, and Elisabeth Grosjean, "L'abbaye du Tart et ses filiales au moyen-âge," *Mélanges Dimier* 2,3 (1984): 19–61, hereafter *Mélanges Dimier*, and Bouton, *Les moniales cisterciennes* (Aiguebelle, 1986).

51. Penny Shine Gold, *The Lady and the Virgin: Image, Attitude, and Experience in Twelfth-Century France* (Chicago, 1985), pp. 80–81, discusses Weber; see Chapter 3.

52. *Cartulaires de l'abbaye de Molesme, ancien diocèse de Langres, 916–1250: recueil de documents sur le Nord de la Bourgogne et le Midi de la Champagne, publié avec une introduction diplomatique, historique et géographique*, ed. Jacques Laurent, 2 vols. (Paris, 1907, 1911), passim, hereafter *MO*.

53. *Histoire du prieuré de Jully-les-Nonnains, avec pièces justificatives*, ed. Abbé Jobin (Paris, 1881), p. 29, hereafter *Jully*, and nos. 3–10 from *MO*, nos. 3–10.

54. *MO*, nos. 126, 135, 79.

55. On anti-Cluniac polemic, see Giles Constable, *The Reformation of the Twelfth Century* (Cambridge, 1996), pp. 125ff.; on antisyneisacticism, see Jo Ann Kay McNamara, "The *Herrenfrage*: Restructuring of the Gender System, 1050–1150," *Medieval Masculinities: Regarding Men in the Middle Ages*, ed. Clare Lees, Thelma Fenster, and Jo Ann McNamara (Minneapolis, 1994), pp. 3–29.

56. *PAT*, pp. 59–60.

57. *PAT*, p. 60, gives *delectatus* (pleased); *delectus* (informed) is more likely correct.

58. Anselme Dimier, *L'art cistercien: France*, trans. Paul Veyriras (Paris, 1974), p. 47, where he suggests that the first stone structures at Cîteaux dated to between 1130 and 1150.

59. *PAT*, p. 61.

60. *PAT*, p. 62.

61. *PAT*, p. 63.

62. *PAT*, p. 63.

63. *PAT*, pp. 64–67.

64. *PAT*, p. 69.

65. *PAT*, p. 69.

66. *PAT*, p. 69.

67. *PAT*, p. 69.

68. *PAT*, p. 71, the word "religiously" is frequent in this letter.

69. *PAT*, p. 72.

70. *PAT*, p. 72, which closes this letter.

71. Earlier, *Unde molismensis ecclesiae fratres, et quidam alii adjacentes monachi, eos infestare et inquietare non desinunt, aestimantes se viliores ac despectiores haberi apud saeculum, si isti quasi singulares et novi monachi inter eos habitare videantur*, *PAT*, p. 72.

72. *PAT*, pp. 73–74.

73. On this point, see *Bullaire du Pape Calixte II, 1119–1124 Essai de Restitution*, ed. Ulysse Robert (Paris, 1891, reprint New York, 1979), pp. xviiff.

74. More normal maledictions begin *Si qua igitur*, not *Vos igitur*.

75. Chances are that this copy too came directly from the *exordia*, for there is no evidence of an original document cited elsewhere in *Chartes et documents concernant l'abbaye de Cîteaux 1098–1182*, ed. J.-M. Marilier (Rome, 1961), hereafter *CI*, no. 21; his notes on this manuscript give contradictory information. In fact, the *Liber Privilegiorum*

Cistercii is a manuscript from the late fifteenth century; Dijon, B.M. MS 69 (598), pp. 133-34; see Figure 22, which reproduces part of a page of this manuscript.

76. *PAT*, pp. 74-75.

77. Cf. Appendix 4; was this imprecation clause also copied from Bonnevaux's confirmation?

78. Original papal bulls for any Cistercian houses in the first half of the twelfth century are rare. See Benoît Chauvin, "Papauté et abbayes cisterciennes du duché de Bourgogne," *L'église de France et la papauté (Xe-XIIIe siècle)*, ed. Rolf Grosse (Bonn, 1993), pp. 326-62; Chauvin attempts to list all those for Burgundy.

79. See below, Chapter 3, n. 105.

80. *PAT*, pp. 121ff.

81. *PAT*, p. 77.

82. *PAT*, p. 77: *Et quia nec in regula, nec in vita sancti Benedicti eumdem doctorem legebant possedisse ecclesias vel altaria, seu oblationes aut sepulturas vel decimas aliorum hominum, seu furnos vel molendina, aut villas vel rusticos, nec etiam feminas monasterium ejus intrasse, nec mortuos ibidem excepta sorore sua sepelisse.*

83. *PAT*, p. 123: *XVII. Quod in ordine nostro foeminarum cohabitatio interdicta sit. Remota omni occasione sive nutrimentorum augendorum vel conservandorum sive rerum monasterii quarumlibet, ut quando necesse est, lavandarum sive denique cujuscumque necessitatis feminarum cohabitatio nobis et conversis nostris omnino interdicta est.*

84. "Bearded" is not in all versions.

85. *PAT*, p. 78.

86. See Berman, *MA*, pp. 73-76, for examples of the earliest southern-French documentation from the late 1140s for such granges; *SL*, nos. 390 (1146), 391 (1146), 392 (1147), 411 (1147). Neither Constance B. Bouchard, *Holy Entrepreneurs: Cistercians, Knights, and Economic Exchange in Twelfth-Century Burgundy* (Ithaca, N.Y., 1991), nor R. A. Donkin, *The Cistercians: Studies in the Geography of Mediaeval England and Wales* (Toronto, 1978), provides any clear evidence of such activities from documentation dating before the 1170s and 1180s.

87. The issue is discussed for a slightly earlier period in Phyllis G. Jestice, *Wayward Monks and the Religious Revolution of the Eleventh Century* (Leiden, 1997); could it be of particular concern in the late twelfth century?

88. *PAT*, pp. 81ff.

89. *PAT*, p. 84.

90. *PAT*, p. 113.

91. See Auberger, *L'unanimité*, and responses to it, for instance, in a paper by Christopher Holdsworth at the Cistercian studies conference in 1994, or Brian Patrick McGuire, "Who Founded the Order of Cîteaux?" *The Joy of Learning and the Love of God: Essays in Honor of Jean Leclercq*, ed. E. Rozanne Elder (Kalamazoo, Mich., 1995), pp. 389-414.

92. Thus their works carry a species of authentication that we recognize today as attempting to make historians' conclusions more convincing; see Alan B. Spitzer, *Historical Truth and Lies About the Past* (Chapel Hill, N.C., 1996).

93. *CI*, no. 175 (1165). These abbeys are not all identified with certainty by the editor; it is possible that Saint-Andrew is a house later attached to Savigny.

94. Auberger, *L'unanimité*, pp. 109ff., discusses manuscript illuminations and images from the Benedictine Rule in Cistercian *exordia* texts.

95. Cf. Marcel Aubert, "Existe-t-il une architecture cistercienne?" *Cahiers de la civilisation médiévale* (hereafter *CCM*) 1 (1958): 158.
96. Dimier, *L'art cistercien*, shows the importance of southern-French remains; on the nuns, see idem, "L'architecture des églises de moniales cisterciennes," *Cîteaux* 25 (1974): 8–23, and Michel Desmarchelier, "L'architecture des églises de moniales cisterciennes, essai de classement des différents types de plans (en guise de suite)," *Mélanges Dimier* 2, 5: 109–21, hereafter Desmarchelier.
97. Dimier, *L'art cistercien*.
98. Paul Pontus, *Silvacane Abbey* (Paris, 1966).
99. Anselme Dimier, *Recueil de plans d'églises cisterciennes* (Paris, 1949), vol. 1, p. 162; *Statuta*, 1249, no. 20, and *Atlas*, p. 297.
100. A. Albanès, "Notes sur l'abbaye de Silvacane et nouvelle liste de ses abbés," *R. des sociétés savantes des départements* 7 (1882): 163–200.
101. J.-B. François Porte and Alphonse Rabbe, "Notice historique sur l'abbaye de N.-D. de Silvacane et ses dépendances," *R. sextienne* 7 (1879): 104–11; 8 (1880): 112–20.
102. *Statuta*, 1190, no. 41; 1195, no. 73; 1191. no. 8: *Querela novae abbatiae Silvaecanae committitur abbatibus Vallismagnae et Liberaevallis. Terminos considerent et aptitudinem loci si possit abbatia stare et debeat et sequenti capitulo denuntient. Similiter controversia quae vertitur inter abbatias Sinanquae et Silvacanae de grangia auctoritate capituli definiant.*
103. *Statuta*, 1236, no. 43; 1289, no. 14; 1290, no. 12; that for no. 42 surely refers to a different abbey in Spain.
104. Fontfroide's charters survive in fifteenth-century inventories only: Carcassonne, A.D. Aude, H211, "Inventaire de la mense conventuelle de Fonfroide"; and Narbonne, Bibliothèque municipale, MS 259, "Inventaire de la mense abbatiale de Fonfroide." I wish to thank the municipal librarian of Narbonne who allowed me to make a microfilm of the latter.
105. Lawrence J. McCrank, "The Cistercians of Poblet as Landlords: Protection, Litigation, and Violence on the Medieval Catalan Frontier," *Cîteaux* 28 (1976): 255–83.
106. Marthe Moreau, *L'âge d'or des religieuses: monastères féminins du Languedoc méditerranéen au Moyen Age* (Montpellier, 1988), pp. 51, 60–61, 218–24; hereafter Moreau, *AO*.
107. Moreau, *AO*, pp. 17, 53, 60–61; this house may be called Garrigues in *Statuta*, 1225, no. 23; 1226, no. 21; 1227, no. 13.
108. Moreau, *AO*, pp. 52ff.
109. Bouton et al., "L'abbaye de le Tart"; L.-H. Cottineau, *Répertoire topo-bibliographique des abbayes et prieurés*, 3 vols. (Macon, 1935–38), vol. 2, col. 2133; *Atlas*, p. 290, notes that benefactors included count Raymond of Toulouse and that the house suffered in the Albigensian Crusade; see also Anselme Dimier, "Fabas," *DHGE* 16 (1967): 301–5. Salenques was founded by Fabas with the patronage of Gaston de Foix and his widow Aliénor de Comminges; its community was transferred to Montesquiu in 1574; Cottineau, vol. 2, col. 2932, and *Atlas*, p. 296.
110. Desmarchelier, pp. 83ff., is describing the parish church.
111. Pierre-Roger Gaussin, "Les communautés féminines dans l'espace languedocien de la fin du XIe à la fin du XIVe siècle," *La femme dans la vie religieuse du Languedoc*

(XIIIe-XIVe siècle), Cahiers de Fanjeaux 23 (Toulouse, 1988), hereafter *CF 23*, pp. 299–332, esp. 307–8; Paul Gabent, "Goujon, abbaye et paroisse," *R. de Gascogne* 36 (1895): 497–506, 545–59; Gratien Leblanc, "L'église de l'abbaye des moniales de Goujon: étude historique et archéologique," *Mélanges Saint Bernard* (Dijon, 1954), pp. 350–58; on its possible foundation of the *bastide* at Saint-Clar, see Victor Fons, "L'abbaye de Goujon," *Mém. Société archéologique du midi de la France* 7 (1860–1865): 335–41.

112. Constance H. Berman, "Were There Twelfth-Century Cistercian Nuns?" *Church History* 68 (1999).

113. Bouton, "L'abbaye de Tart," 19–61; *Jully*, p. 29.

114. Constance H. Berman, "Men's Houses, Women's Houses: The Relationship Between the Sexes in Twelfth-Century Monasticism," *The Medieval Monastery*, ed. Andrew MacLeish (Minneapolis, 1988), pp. 43–52.

115. Elizabeth Conner, "The Abbeys of Las Huelgas and Le Tart and Their Filiations," *Hidden Springs*, vol. 1, pp. 29–48.

116. Gaussin, "Communautés," pp. 307–8.

117. *Cartulaire et documents de l'abbaye de Nonenque*, ed. C. Couderc and J.-L. Rigal (Rodez, 1955), hereafter *NO*, no. 1 (1139), and Chapter 4 below.

118. Jean Leclercq, "Cisterciennes et filles de Saint Bernard: à propos des structures variées des monastères de moniales au Moyen Age," *Studia Monastica* 32 (1990): 139.

119. R. W. Southern, *Western Society and the Church in the Middle Ages* (Harmondsworth, 1970), p. 320, n. 24, cites the 1961 edition of Grundmann; in repeating five or six times on a single page of that survey that there were no twelfth-century Cistercian women, Southern (p. 250) suggests his own uncertainty.

120. See Bernadette Barrière, "The Cistercian Monastery of Coyroux in the Province of Limousin in Southern France, in the Twelfth-Thirteenth Centuries," *Gesta* 31, 1 (1992): 76–82; Chrysogonus Waddell, "One Day in the Life of a Savigniac Nun: Jehanne de Deniscourt," *CSQ* 26 (1991): 134–51. One unsuccessful attempt is described in Brian Golding, *Gilbert of Sempringham and the Gilbertine Order c. 1130–c. 1300* (Oxford, 1995), pp. 26ff.

121. *Religious Movements in the Middle Ages: The Historical Links Between Heresy, the Mendicant Orders, and the Women's Religious Movement in the Twelfth and Thirteenth Century, with the Historical Foundations of German Mysticism*, trans. Steven Rowan, intro. Robert E. Lerner (Notre Dame, Ind., 1995), translation of *Religiöse Bewegungen im Mittelalter* (Berlin, 1935, new ed., 1961).

122. Grundmann, *Religious Movements*, pp. 21ff.

123. This was epitomized in the foundation of Prouille as the first Dominican house; see Grundmann, *Religious Movements*, pp. 91ff.

124. Ernst Günther Krenig, "Mittelalterliche Frauenklöster nach den Konstitutionem von Cîteaux," *ASOC* 10 (1954), 1–105.

125. Grundmann, *Religious Movements*, pp. 108ff., on the "flood" of nuns.

126. Pace Micheline de Fontette, *Les religieuses à l'âge classique du droit canon: recherches sur les structures juridiques des branches féminines des ordres* (Paris, 1961), pp. 27–63. The entire concept of a feminine branch is, of course, questionable.

127. Bouton, "Saint Bernard et les moniales."

128. See *Calendar of Close Rolls 1268–72*, p. 301 (43 Henry III) and discussion in Coburn Graves, "English Cistercian Nuns in Lincolnshire," *Speculum* 54 (1979): 492–99, esp. p. 496, n. 28; on *"imitatio cisterciensis,"* see Krenig, pp. 15ff.

129. Simone Roisin, "L'efflorescence cistercienne et le courant féminin de piété au treizième siècle," *RHE* 39 (1943):342–78; Catherine E. Boyd, *A Cistercian Nunnery in Medieval Italy: The Story of Rifreddo in Saluzzo, 1220–1300* (Cambridge, Mass., 1943).

130. Jennifer Carpenter, "Juette of Huy, Recluse and Other (1158–1228): Children and Mothering in the Saintly Life," *Power of the Weak: Studies on Medieval Women*, ed. Carpenter and Sally-Beth MacLean, pp. 57–93 (Urbana, Ill., 1995).

131. *Le Chartrier de l'Abbaye-aux-Bois*, ed. Brigitte Pipon (Paris, 1996), no. 192 (1253), a papal confirmation of Cistercian privileges found in the archives for these nuns.

132. For monks at Silvanès, see the papal bull of Alexander III, *ut ordo monasticus qui secundum Deum et beati Benedicti regulam et normam fratrum Cisterciensium* in *Cartulaire de l'abbaye de Silvanès*, ed. P.-A. Verlaguet (Rodez, 1910), hereafter *SL*, no. 1 (1162). For monks of Chaalis in northern France, *ut ordo monasticus qui in eadem ecclesia secundum beati Benedicti regulam et Cisterciensium fratrum observantiam auctore Domino institutus esse dinoscitur*, in François Blary, *Le domaine de Chaalis, XIIe–XIVe siècles* (Paris, 1989), pp. 390–91. In a papal confirmation attributed to Calixtus II and 1124, an abbey, Balerne, which was transferred from Molesme to the Cistercians in 1136, is already described as following *consuetudines praeterea, quod juxta regulam beati Benedicti vel ad exemplar Cisterciensium institutae sunt*. This papal bull is found in Robert, *Bullaire Calixtus II*, no. 514 and is cited by René Locatelli, "Papauté et cisterciens du diocèse de Besançon au XIIe siècle," *L'église de France et la papauté (Xe–XIIIe siècle)*, ed. Rolf Grosse (Bonn, 1993), p. 312. For 1144, Bellevaux's charter *ut exinde vobis agere liceat secundum consilium Cisterciensis capituli* may refer to Cîteaux's internal chapter. It is likely that an act for the same abbey dated 1145 would have an interpolation in the addition of the term *ordinis* to the *facultatem disponendi ex eadem ecclesia secundum consilium Cisterciensium ordinis capituli*; again see, Locatelli, "Papauté," p. 313.

References cited by Locatelli include a papal bull dated 1185 concerning nuns at Corcelles in the diocese of Besançon who were definitely Cistercian but whose charters reproduce only the standard formula, *Ordinem monasticum qui secundum Deum et beati Benedicti regulam atque institutionem Cisterciensium fratrum*. "Papauté," p. 306. For le Tart, see Conner, "Las Huelgas," p. 40.

133. Degler-Spengler, "Incorporation," pp. 87ff.; Las Huelgas dates to 1187, but Tulebras to 1157, might be considered to have been founded independently of any men's house, as was Montreuil-les-Dames in northern France, founded in 1136; see Boyd, *Rifreddo*, pp. 78–81.

134. Degler-Spengler, "Incorporation," pp. 105ff.

135. Degler-Spengler, "Incorporation," pp. 96ff., lists all but *ordo cisterciensis*; on the last, see Graves, "English Cistercian."

136. Southern, *Western Society*, p. 317, cites instances from *Statuta*, 1242, nos. 15–18; 1243, nos. 6–8, 61–69; 1244, no. 8, of nuns rebelliously locking out new abbot visitors; he mistook this resistance to local visitors for resistance to being Cistercian.

137. On the support of such bishops, see examples in Constance H. Berman, "Abbeys for Cistercian Nuns in the Ecclesiastical Province of Sens: Foundation, Endowment, and Economic Activities of the Earlier Foundations," *R. Mabillon* 73 (1997): 83–113.

138. Boyd, *A Cistercian Nunnery*, esp. pp. 95ff., but see also Anne Bondéelle-Souchier, "Les moniales cisterciennes et leurs livres manuscrits dans la France d'ancien

régime," *Cîteaux* 45 (1994): 193–336, and Constance H. Berman, "The Labors of Hercules: The Cartulary, Church, and Abbey of La Cour-Notre-Dame-de-Michery," *Journal of Medieval History*, 26 (January 2000).

139. Size limitations for houses of nuns are listed in records such as Auxerre, A.D. Yonne, H787, fols. 21ff.; see also Paulette l'Hermite LeClercq, *Le monachisme féminin dans la société de son temps: le monastère de La Celle (XIe–début du XVIe siècle)* (Paris, 1989); Penelope D. Johnson, *Equal in Monastic Profession: Religious Women in Medieval France* (Chicago, 1991); Roberta Gilchrist, *Gender and Material Culture: The Archaeology of Religious Women* (London, 1994); Marilyn Oliva, *The Convent and the Community in Late Medieval England: Female Monasteries in the Diocese of Norwich, 1350–1450* (Woodbridge, 1998); and Constance H. Berman, *Sisters in Wealth and in Poverty: Endowment and Administration of Property of Cistercian Houses for Women in the Ecclesiastical Province of Sens, 1190–1300*, in preparation.

140. *Statuta*, 1213, nos. 3, 4; 1218, nos. 4, 84; 1219, no. 12; 1220, no. 4; 1225, no. 1; 1228, no. 16; 1233, no. 12; 1239, no. 7.

141. Anselme Dimier, "Chapitres généraux d'abbesses cisterciennes," *Cîteaux* 11 (1960): 268–75.

142. See Chapter 4's discussion of Valmagne.

Chapter 2

1. Bede K. Lackner, "Early Cistercian Life as Described in the *Ecclesiastica Officia*," *Cistercian Ideals and Reality*, ed. John R. Sommerfeldt (Kalamazoo, Mich., 1978), pp. 62–79.

2. Also consulted were Dijon, B.M. MSS 87, 597, 598, 600, 601, 611, 633.

3. Dijon 114 has been, for instance, recently used as the base manuscript for an edition of the Cistercian liturgical *ordo*. *Les "Ecclesiastica Officia" cisterciens du XIIe siècle: texte latin selon les manuscrits édités de Trente 1711, Ljubljana 31 et Dijon 114, version française, annexe liturgique, notes, index et tables*, ed. Danièle Choisselet and Placide Vernet, Documentation Cistercienne 22 (Reiningue, 1989), hereafter *EO*. The editors contend that these liturgical manuscripts can be dated to before 1152 on the basis of their lack of the Marian commemoration published by Canivez under 1152, no. 6, but this statute is only bracketed to 1152–85; see below.

4. Other problems about Canivez's publication are discussed by Chrysogonus Waddell, "The Cistercian Institutions and Their Early Evolution: Granges, Economy, Lay-Brothers," *Espace Cistercien*, ed. Léon Pressouyre (Paris, 1994), pp. 27–38; Leclercq, "Passage." On the Chirograph of Charity with the Praemonstratensians, see below.

5. *Statuta*, vol. 1, intro., pp. xi–xxv.

6. *Statuta*, 1183, no. 1, for "abbatis generalis"; exceptional also are *Statuta*, 1181, no. 7; 1182, no. 10; 1189, no. 10. The year 1180 begins the first series in which there is a collation of five manuscripts along with the printed edition from Manrique. For 1190 an announcement of the meeting and citations of individual abbeys also begin; see *Statuta*, 1180s, passim, and 1190, nos. 1, 18.

7. *Statuta*, 1181, nos. 4, 5; 1183, no. 12; 1189, no. 3; etc.

8. Auberger, *L'unanimité*, pp. 61ff., 340ff.

9. Dijon, B.M. MS 114, fol. 184v, col. 2.
10. *Statuta*, 1152, no. 1:

> Ne ulterius alicubi construatur nova abbatia nostri ordinis neque aliquis locus alterius religionis per subiectionem nostro ordini societur. Licet tamen alicui abbati pro aliqua incommoditate intolerabili, consilio et assensu patris abbatis, abbatiam suam ad locum magis idoneum transferre, qui tamen ab aliis abbatiis nostri ordinis ad minus decem leugis Burgundiae distet, et duabus a grangiis, sive ille locus ad quem fit translatio alterius ante fuerit religionis, sive non; ita quod priorem locum vel omnino deserat, vel in eo grangiam faciat, si ultra dietam inter se non distent. Nulli enim licet a modo ab abbatia sua ultra communem dietam grangiam facere. Sciendum etiam quod non licet per manum fugitivi nostri ordinis aliquem locum sive ad abbatiam, sive ad grangiam faciendam recipere. Loca tamen quae ante illud generale Capitulum aedificari coeperant, concessum est, ut si ante Capitulum generale subsequentis anni honeste et secundum instituta ordinis fieri posset, in abbatiam surgerent. Quod si ante illud Capitulum convenienter, ut dictum est, accepta loca in abbatiam surgere non possent, ex tunc remota omni dispensatione dimmitterentur, nisi grangia ibi secundum Ordinem fieri posset.

On this statute and numbers of houses, see Southern, *Western Society*, p. 254.

11. *Statuta*, 1152, no. 6:

> In vigilia Natalis Domini ad laudes commemoratio beatae Mariae intermittatur usque in crastinum Epiphaniae; et tunc ad laudes incipiatur. Similiter in Coena Domini ad laudes intermittatur usque in quintam feriam post diem Paschae, et tunc ad laudes dicatur.

Editors of *EO*, pp. 19ff., suggest that because the liturgical treatises included in early manuscripts (Trent and Ljubljana) make no reference to that Marian innovation, the manuscripts must date to earlier than 1152; this is an obvious argument *ex silentio*, based on the assumption that the innovation *"In vigilia Natalis"* was introduced in 1152. It does not appear before Dijon 114, and the statute concerning it there can at best be dated between 1152 and 1185.

12. J.-B. Mahn, *L'ordre cistercien et son gouvernement des origines au milieu du XIIIe siècle (1098–1265)* (Paris, 1945), p. 1.

13. Southern, *Western Society*, pp. 250ff.; Sophia Menache, *The Vox Dei: Communication in the Middle Ages* (New York, 1990).

14. James Westfall Thompson, *Economic and Social History of the Middle Ages*, 2 vols. (New York, 1928, reprint 1959), for example.

15. See, e.g., Leclercq, "Manuscrits cisterciens dans des bibliothèques d'Italie," *ASOC* 5 (1949): 94–119.

16. A variety of circumstances allowed early Cistercian texts to escape the earlier "source criticism" that we associate with nineteenth-century German historians like Leopold von Ranke or the expositors of "L'art de vérifier des textes" among the earlier Maurists in France; on such problems with editions, see R. Howard Bloch, *God's Plagiarist: Being an Account of the Fabulous Industry and Irregular Commerce of the Abbé*

Migne (Chicago, 1994), and *Les cartulaires: actes de la table ronde organisée par l'Ecole nationale des chartes et le G.D.R. 121 du C.N.R.S. Paris 5–7 décembre 1991*, ed. Olivier Guyotjeannin, Laurent Morelle, and Michel Parisse (Paris, 1993), hereafter *Les cartulaires*.

17. For instance, Richard Roehl, "Plan and Reality in a Medieval Monastic Economy: The Cistercians," *Studies in Medieval and Renaissance History* 9 (1972): 83–113.

18. C. H. Lawrence, *Medieval Monasticism: Forms of Religious Life in Western Europe in the Middle Ages*, 2nd ed. (London, 1989), pp. 86–110.

19. Major contributions by J.-A. Lefèvre are "A propos de la composition des *Instituta generalis capituli apud Cistercium*," *COCR* 16 (1954): 157–82; "A propos d'un nouveau texte de la *Carta Caritatis Prior* dans le Ms. Metz 1247," *R. bénédictine* 65 (1955): 90–109; "A propos des sources de la législation primitive de Prémontré," *AP* 30(1954): 12–19; "L'évolution des *Usus Conversorum* de Cîteaux," *COCR* 17 (1955): 65–97; "La bulle *Apostolicae sedis* pour Cîteaux avait-elle une souscription longue?" *R. bénédictine* 74 (1964): 111–43; "Les traditions manuscrites de l'*Exordium Parvum*," *Scriptorium* 10 (1956): 42–46; "Les traditions manuscrites des *Usus Conversorum* de Cîteaux," *COCR* 17 (1955): 11–39; "Pour une nouvelle datation des *Instituta generalis capituli apud Cistercium*," *COCR* 16 (1954): 241–66; "Que savons-nous du Cîteaux primitif?" *RHE* 51 (1956): 5–41; "Saint Robert de Molesme dans l'opinion monastique du XIIe et du XIIIe siècle," *Analecta Bollandiana* 74 (1956): 50–83; "Un texte inconnu de l'*Exordium Cistercii* et de la *Summa Cartae Caritatis* dans le Ms. Melun 55," *COCR* 17 (1955): 265–71; and "Le vrai récit primitif des origines de Cîteaux est-il l'*Exordium Parvum*?" *Le Moyen Age* 61 (1955): 79–120.

20. *Recueil des pancartes de l'abbaye de la Ferté-sur-Grosne: 1113–1178*, ed. Georges Duby (Aix-Marseilles, 1953), hereafter *FE*; Duby, *Saint Bernard: l'art cistercien* (Paris, 1979); Robert Fossier, "L'essor économique de Clairvaux,"*Bernard de Clairvaux* (Paris, 1953); pp. 95–114; Jean Leclercq, "La date du premier sermon sur le Cantique des Cantiques," *Saint Bernard mystique* (Paris, 1948), pp. 480–83; Leclercq, "Les écrits de Geoffrey d'Auxerre," *R. bénédictine* 62 (1952): 274–91; but also Leclercq, "Epitres d'Alexandre III sur les cisterciens," *R. bénédictine* 64 (1954): 68–82.

21. Knowles, *Great Historical Enterprises*, pp. 197–222.

22. Some of this is covered in Peter Novick, *That Noble Dream: The "Objectivity Question" and the American Historical Profession* (Cambridge, 1988), pp. 8off.

23. L. de Lacger, "Ardorel," *DHGE* 7 (1924): 1617–20; Bennett Hill, *English Cistercian Monasteries and Their Patrons in the Twelfth Century* (Urbana, Ill., 1968); Graves, "English Cistercian Nuns."

24. According to Giles Constable, "Most serious scholars today accept that the early documents of Cistercian history—and the institutions they describe—developed over a considerable period of time and do not reflect the nature of the Order at its beginnings"; Constable, "The Study of Monastic History Today," *Essays on the Reconstruction of Medieval History*, ed. Vaclav Mudroch and G. S. Couse (Montreal, 1974), pp. 21–51, quotation p. 38. He also describes J.-A. Lefèvre's 1954–59 publications as "a scholarly bombshell."

25. See Bynum, *Jesus as Mother*, esp. pp. 59–89, 110–69. Bynum read an earlier version of the first of these at the Cistercian Studies Conference at Kalamazoo in 1974.

26. Louis J. Lekai, "Ideals and Reality in Early Cistercian Life and Legislation,"

Cistercian Ideals and Reality, ed. John R. Sommerfeldt (Kalamazoo, Mich., 1978), pp. 4–29, from a conference session in spring 1974.

27. For a full list of publications on these issues, see François de Place, "Bibliographie raisonnée des premiers documents cisterciens (1098–1220)," *Cîteaux* 35 (1984): 7–54.

28. In comparison, there are many more manuscripts of Bernard's *Sermons*, even from the twelfth century, as evidenced by the number collated for the edition of Bernard of Clairvaux's "Sermons on the Song of Songs," *Sancti Bernardi Opera*, ed. Jean Leclercq et al. (Rome, 1957 seq.) vols. 1, 2, passim; lists of twelfth-century manuscript copies of letters or treatises by Bernard of Clairvaux confirm this; see studies by Leclercq, such as "Textes et manuscrits cisterciens à la bibliothèque Vaticane," *ASOC* 15 (1959): 79–103.

29. *PAT*, pp. 132ff., compares the two texts, the *Carta Caritatis Prior* found with Ljubljana 31 and Metz 1247, and the *Carta Caritatis Posterior* found with the slightly later Paris Latin 4346 (part B), Paris, B.N. Latin 4221, and in Dijon 114.

30. A charter from Vauluisant, dated 1176, as discussed below, shows Morimond's abbot acting as a "proto-abbot" at a General Chapter meeting for the first time.

31. Typical is the tendency to sort out all publications according to which of the specific texts is discussed, as in De Place, "Bibliographie," passim.

32. These were introduced just before Dijon 114 was compiled; at this point the ordering of the texts within the manuscripts begins to break down.

33. Ljubljana is included because it was once complete, but the last part of the manuscript is gone and so it no longer has the last parts of its *Ecclesiastica Officia* or its lay-brother treatise.

34. See Griesser's edition of the *Exordium Magnum Cisterciense* (1997), pp. 9ff, for numbers of manuscripts; Constable, *Reformation*, p. 38, n. 171, for date of Conrad's volume.

35. Constable, *Reformation*, p. 38, n. 171, presents scholarly opinion as of circa 1996.

36. Sequencing the manuscripts in this way was proposed by Father Chrysogonus Waddell in the first paper in the same 1974 session in Kalamazoo at which Lekai proposed "Cistercian Ideals and Reality"; see Waddell, "The *Exordium Cistercii* and the *Summa Cartae Caritatis*: A Discussion Continued," *Cistercian Ideals and Reality*, ed. John R. Sommerfeldt (Kalamazoo, Mich., 1978), pp. 30–61; the third paper was Constance H. Berman, "The Foundation and Early History of the Monastery of Silvanès: The Economic Reality," *Cistercian Ideals*, pp. 280–318.

37. While there are only basically five, because the Ljubljana 31 MS has lost its lay-brother treatise, those for Metz 1247 and London, Add. MS, add some interesting details.

38. Bruno Griesser, "Beiträge zur Beurteilung des Cod. 1711 von Trient," *Cîteaux in der Nederlanden* 6 (1955): 117–30; and Jean Leclercq, "Une ancienne rédaction des coutumes cisterciennes," *RHE* 47 (1952): 172–76.

39. Only careful examination in situ makes it possible to see the variation in the red ink that allows one to discern changes such as that which occurs when a Roman numeral such as XXII becomes XXXIII by careful additions of strokes before and after the numbers. Once I began to examine such changes, it became apparent that this was not just the correction of erroneous numbering but a reworking of the entire liturgical manuscript.

40. This could easily be missed by scholars who followed the usual codicological practice of verifying handwriting by checking whether the handwriting at the end of one quire continued onto the beginning of the next. In the second version of Trent 1711 there is a continuity of handwriting from Quire 1 onto the outside page of Quire 2, but that hand does not continue through Quire 2.

41. Published in Canisius Noschitzka, "Codex Manuscriptus 31 Bibliothecae Universitas Labacensis," *ASOC* 6 (1950): 1–124; it must be noted that the editor inserted text from *Les monuments primitifs de la règle cistercienne*, ed. Philip Guignard (Dijon, 1878), to replace text from missing pages at the end of this manuscript.

42. Ljubljana 31 is dated to 1178–82 by art historians who have compared its initials to other illuminated capitals in a series of manuscripts now in Ljubljana and Vienna that were all created for the Slovenian monastery of Stiçna. See *Stiski rokopisi iz 12. stoletja: codices Sitticenses saeculi XII*, ed. Natasia Golob (Ljubljana, 1994), p. 98, a description of Ljubljana MS 31, and her plate from MS 31 (misidentified as MS 35; it begins: "Nos cistercienses primi huius ecclesie fundatores, successoribus nostris stilo presenti notificamus"). The hand is identified as that of the same copyist who had copied a datable manuscript concerning Frederick I; see *Stiski*, p. 25. (I owe this citation to Dr. Jasma Hrovat in Ljubljana, to whom I am extremely grateful for help in my investigation of the manuscript details when I visited there in 1997.) Also see next note.

43. Paris, B.N. Latin 4346B has a liturgical *ordines* text that is later than Ljubljana's, followed by the *Carta Caritatis Posterior*. It contains the slightly elaborated *Super Instituta Generalis Capituli* text, which has roughly the same *Capitula* items as are in Ljubljana 31 but with a more rational table of contents and numbering. Both Paris, B.N. Latin 4346B and Ljubljana 31 have emendations to chapters on taverns, suggesting that they date close to, but not much earlier than, the regulations on taverns of *Statuta*, ed. Canivez, 1182, no. 6. It is possible that Ljubljana MS 31 is based on a slightly earlier manuscript from Burgundy, now lost, which would be dated closer to the date of the *Carta Caritatis Prior* text that I posit here probably to be before 1176. There are very limited differences between Paris, B.N. Latin 4346B and 4221, which is very close in its contents to the Dijon 114 manuscript and to Paris, Latin NA 430 (heavily used); all probably appeared only a year or two before Dijon 114.

44. Paris, Bibliothèque Sainte-Geneviève, MS 1207, is a volume of letters from Hugh de Fleury to Countess Adèle of Chartres; they have no bearing on the dating of the fragment.

45. Sainte-Geneviève MS 1207 does not include reference to both a "New Monastery" and a "New Abbot" as version 2 of Trent 1711 does. As I discussed in Chapter 1, such references to the "New Monastery" for Cîteaux have been deemed significant by some scholars; See discussion in Chapter 1, p. 6.

46. A fragment in Paris B.N. Latin 12169 found at fols. 115–24 is part of a text similar to B.N. Latin 4221, but this single quire bound into the manuscript, which has its outside folio turned inside out, is in fact only parts of the liturgical order-book.

47. Andrée Vernet, *La bibliothèque de l'abbaye de Clairvaux du XIIe au XVIIIe siècle* (Paris, 1979), vol. 1, p. 280; I am grateful to Father Chrysogonus Waddell for bringing this attribution to my attention.

48. Lefèvre, "L'évolution des *Usus Conversorum*" and "Les traditions manuscrites des *Usus Conversorum*," both of 1955. Lefèvre clearly waffles on whether Montpellier is the earliest, although his arguments that it is are sound.

I wish to thank Father Chrysogonus Waddell, who very kindly provided me typescript of an edition of these lay-brother treatises in three versions, *Usus conversorum cisterciensium saeculi duodecimi secundum tres recensiones successivas*, which gives Trent 1711 separately and collates Paris B.N. Latin 4221, 4346B, N.A. 430; Troyes 1599; San Isidro de Duenas 1; Donaueschingen, 413; and then again collates Dijon 601 and 114. I disagree with his argument that this is an excerpted text from a longer lay-brother treatise because it is entitled "Incipit *de* usibus conversorum." See Figure 21, for instance, which on the verso page includes this quote. Such use of the word "Incipit" and titles such as *De usibus conversorum* are standard in manuscripts of this date. Twelfth-century manuscripts habitually mark the beginning and end of separate texts using "Incipit" and "Explicit"; see, for example, the opening of *Grand Cartulaire de la Sauve Majeure*, ed. Charles Higounet and Arlette Higounet-Nadal (Bordeaux 1996), pp. 31, 33.

49. This is discussed in the next chapter, but see also Duane Osheim, "Conversion, *Conversi*, and Religious Life in Late Medieval Tuscany," *Speculum* 58 (1983): 368–90. Despite Isabel Alfonso, "Cistercians and Feudalism," *Past and Present* 133 (1991): 3–30, I think there was a moment when lay-brothers were treated equitably with monks.

50. Duval-Arnould, *H322*, pp. 34ff. contends that the shorter soi-disant "abbreviated" text cannot be the earlier, but comparison of the contents to those in the *Ecclesiastica Officia* for Trent 1711, version 2, belie that conclusion.

51. This is Canivez's manuscript "O" in *Statuta*. Canivez publishes the items which appear in the Montpellier manuscript under 1157 as *Statuta* 1157, nos. 1–6; for 1158 as *Statuta* 1157, nos. 7–14, 16, 17; for 1159 as *Statuta* 1157, nos. 18–21; for 1160 as *Statuta* 1157, nos. 22–27; for 1161 as *Statuta* 1157, nos. 30–32. Their simplicity can immediately be seen, even in Figure 21.

52. Auberger, *L'unanimité*, pp. 62–64.

53. *La législation cistercienne abrégée du manuscrit de Montpellier H322*, ed. Louis Duval-Arnould (Paris, 1997), publishes part of the manuscript; see p. 16 for the Latin list of contents from fol. 1r rubrics: "In hoc volumine continentur ysagoge in compotum lune, Compotus gerlandi, Opusculum de accentibus, Abbreviatio usuum, et Instituta generalis capituli."

54. See discussion of J.-B. Van Damme, "La constitution cistercienne de 1165," *ASOC* 19 (1963): 51–104, below.

55. Moreover, because the transformation from the earlier *Carta Caritatis Prior* to the later *Carta Caritatis Posterior* seems to have taken place by 1176 or so, this suggests that the *Exordium Parvum* (which accompanies both) must have appeared by 1170 or so.

56. See complete text in Appendix 5. Much discussion seems to have centered on the problem of Cistercian tithes. On such complaints, see Coburn V. Graves, "The Economic Activities of the Cistercians in Medieval England (1128–1307)," *ASOC* 13 (1957): 3–60, esp. 45–54, and Giles Constable, *Monastic Tithes from Their Origins to the Twelfth Century* (Cambridge, 1964), pp. 270ff.

57. Leclercq, "Passage supprimé," published in 1952, has been met with silence in many treatments; Lekai, *Cistercians*, pp. 66–67, implies (incorrectly) that it concerned only tithes.

58. Georges Duby, *The Three Orders: Feudal Society Imagined*, trans. Arthur Goldhammer (Chicago, 1980), reminds us how often historians have elevated the medieval

narrative text into an "authentic" voice speaking without rhetorical purpose or hidden agendas, rather than problematizing it.

59. *Rouleau mortuaire de B. Vital, abbé de Savigni contenant 207 écrits en 1122–1123 dans différentes églises et France et d'Angleterre*, ed. Léopold Delisle (Paris, 1909), titulus 56, titulus 62. I owe these references to Patrick Conyers.

60. On *ordo* to mean "way of life," see Giles Constable, "The Orders of Society," *Three Studies in Medieval Religious and Social Thought: The Interpretation of Mary and Martha; The Ideal of the Imitation of Christ; The Orders of Society* (Cambridge, 1995), pp. 249–360, esp. pp. 251ff.; and Constable, *Reformation*, pp. 20ff.

61. *Libellus de diversis ordinibus et professionibus qui sunt in aecclesia*, ed. Giles Constable and Bernard Smith (Oxford, 1972), p. 28, chap. 14, and intro., p. xxix, which discusses Martène's edition.

62. Even these phrases were not used at the time of the foundation of women's houses such as le Tart in the 1120s, Jully in 1113, or even Nonenque in 1139. See Chapter 1.

63. *De Gestis Regum Anglorum de Willelmi Malmesbiriensis Monachi*, ed. William Stubbs (London, 1887), vol. 1, p. 1.

64. *Orderic Vitalis*, ed. Chibnall, book 8, section 26, vol. 4, p. 322.

65. *De miraculis* of Herman of Tournai, *PL* 156: 962–1018. The passage about Montreuil has been cited extensively, but not always translated accurately; see Gold, *Lady*, p. 83; Lekai, *Cistercians*, p. 347; Grundmann, *Religious*, pp. 21ff; Ernst McDonnell, *Beguines and Beghards in Medieval Culture, with Special Emphasis on the Belgian Scene* (New Brunswick, N.J., 1954), pp. 105–7.

66. Cetedoc, Library of Christian Latin Texts (CLCLT-2) (Turnhout, 1996); Cetedoc, "Corpus diplomaticorum" (Nouveau Wauters) (Turnhout, 1997); *Patrologiae Latina*, Chadwick-Healy, circa 1990.

67. Nigel Whiteacre, *Speculum stultorum*, dated 1179–80, cited in Keith Sidwell, *Reading Medieval Latin* (Cambridge, 1995), pp. 357–61. A handful of references to an *ordo cisterciensis*, or to *in ordine nostro* and *de suo ordine* are found in the manuscripts of "primitive Cistercian documents"; I argue above that these postdate 1160.

68. It is too easy for William of Malmesbury's description of the early monks at the abbey of Cîteaux to become in English a description of "the Cistercians." That such descriptions of the monastery of Cîteaux continue to be read as if they were descriptions of the Order is clear from Pierre-André Burton, "Aux origines de Cîteaux d'après quelques sources écrites du XIIe siècle: enquête sur une polémique," *Cîteaux* 48 (1997): 209–28.

69. Joseph F. O'Callaghan, "The Affiliation of the Order of Calatrava with the Order of Cîteaux," *ASOC* 15 (1959): 161–93; 16 (1960): 3–59, 255–92; in 15 (1959) on pp. 183ff. O'Callaghan concludes that, although the group had "taken an order" (*ordinem receperint*) by 1158, there are no clear references to its interactions with the *ordo cisterciensis* until the 1180s. O'Callaghan, "The Foundation of the Order of Alcàntara, 1176–1218," *Catholic Historical Review* 47 (1962): 471–86, says on p. 480 that the group was not there before 1176 or more likely 1187.

My findings perhaps may also explain some of the dearth of Templar documents for the East noted by Malcolm Barber in *The New Knighthood: A History of the Order of the Temple* (Cambridge, 1994), pp. 18ff, where many of the earliest documents do not mention *ordo*, but only knights. Michael Gervers finds this as well in the Hospitaller cartularies; "The Dating of Medieval English Private Charters of the Twelfth and Thirteenth Centuries," ⟨www.utoronto.ca/deeds⟩, and private communication, 1998.

70. An example is *Cartulaire de l'abbaye de Gimont*, ed. Abbé Clergeac (Paris, 1905), *GM* I, no. 1 (1142?), hereafter *GM*, as discussed in Chapter 4.

71. Combined totals for a slightly different group of charters, those for Berdoues, Bonnecombe, Gimont, Grandselve, and Silvanès, show promises of admission to 72 individuals in 1140–59 (0.7 per year per abbey, but these are concentrated in the 1150s), to 202 individuals in 1160–79 and 210 individuals in 1180–99 (2.0 and 2.1 per year per abbey respectively).

72. *Cartulaire de l'abbaye Notre-Dame de Léoncel, diocèse de Die, Ordre de Cîteaux*, ed. Ulysse Chevalier (Montélimar, 1869), hereafter *LC*, no. 13 (circa 1170), no. 25 (1176), no. 27 (1178), no. 41 (1178–82). A similar concession to Bonnevaux, *Cartulaire de l'abbaye Notre-Dame de Bonnevaux au diocèse de Vienne, Ordre de Cîteaux*, ed. Ulysse Chevalier (Grenoble, 1889), hereafter *BX*, no. 4, came from Alexander III.

73. *LC*, nos. 67 (1202), 68 (1204), 71 (1209), 73 (1212), 75 (1213), 76 (1214).

74. *GM* IV, no. 8 (1147); there is a good possibility that this is a transcription error.

75. *GM* IV, no. 24 (1158), no. 82 (1158), no. 42 (1158).

76. *GM* I, no. 82 (1176); *GM* II, no. 3 (1163), no. 74 (1177), no. 153 (1178); *GM* III, no. 67 (1187); *GM* IV, no. 56 (1168); *GM* VI, no. 6 (1160), etc.; *GM* VI, no. 85 (1187), says *"teneat ordinem de Cistello,"* etc.

77. I depend most heavily on my collection of all possible Cistercian documents (or copies of documents) for southern France from before 1250 A.D., made for Berman, *MA*; those that lend themselves most readily to tabulation (about 2,500 documents in all from collections for Silvanès, Grandselve, Berdoues, and Valmagne) are summarized in Table 2. These charters constitute about half of all twelfth-century Cistercian charters from that region, and they are those that are the least ambiguous in their transmission. They also happen to represent a cross-section of houses with regard to origin and filiation.

78. This donation is made for the monks and conversi of the entire Cistercian Order as well as to Ermengaudis, abbot of Valmagne; see Montpellier, A.D. Hérault, film no. 1 Mi 260–61 (private deposit), "Cartulaire de Valmagne," hereafter "VM," I, fol. 151v (1159). These two charters were added to the Silvanès cartulary in the mid-thirteenth century; see *SL*, nos. 462, 463 (1161). I count them only in the Valmagne tabulations.

79. "VM," I, fol. 6r (1162).

80. P. Fournier, "Alexandre, abbé de Cîteaux," *DHGE* 2 (1914): 200–201; this is based primarily on the *Exordium Magnum* text, which does not mention Alexander going to Savigny.

81. A gift dated 1151 by Ermengardis, viscountess of Narbonne, to Grandselve's abbot Alexander is the earliest to him; it does not mention Cistercian benefits. Another dated 1161 to abbot Pons does mention them; see Paris, B.N. Latin 9994, fols. 220r (1151), 225r (1161).

82. Constance H. Berman, "Origins of the Filiation of Morimond in Southern France: Redating Foundation Charters for Gimont, Villelongue, Berdoues, l'Escaledieu, and Bonnefont," *Cîteaux* 41 (1990): 256–77; I would now revise some of its conclusions, as discussed in Chapter 3.

83. *SL*, nos. 262, 263 (both dated 1149).

84. The possibility of such updating of phraseology must be considered because it is quite plausible that in cartulary copies certain earlier phrases being expanded from abbreviations can be expanded in such a way as to reflect the usage of the moment of cartulary-making and not earlier.

85. *SL*, no. 3: no. 6 is problematic.

86. Dijon, B.M. MS 611, contains the Pons of Léras account, as discussed in Chapter 3.

87. Eugenius was a recruit to Clairvaux from Pisa; see Charles Spornik, "The Life and Reign of Pope Eugene III (1145–1153)," Ph.D. dissertation, Notre Dame University, 1988; I wish to thank Professor Katherine Tachau for bringing this dissertation to my attention.

88. *CI*, no. 109 (1135); cf. *Le premier cartulaire de l'abbaye cistercienne de Pontigny (XIIe–XIIIe siècles)*, ed. Martine Garrigues (Paris, 1981), hereafter *PO*, no. 180 (1135, before 3 August). Her citation to Marilier's edition is incorrect; further discrepancies are found in comparison to Achille Luchaire, *Etudes sur les actes de Louis VII* (Paris, 1885).

89. *Recueil des chartes de l'abbaye de Clairvaux, XIIe siècle*, ed. Jean Waquet (Troyes, 1950–82), hereafter *CL*, no. 126 (1154), comes from a thirteenth-century cartulary copy. On the other hand, *CL*, no. 23 (1144–53), says, "Concessi in manus [sic] venerabilis Bernardi Clarevallensis abbatis fratribusque Clarevallensibus et omnibus qui sunt ex ordine Cisterciensi," while *CL*, no. 24, by Louis VII "king of France and duke of Aquitaine," which addresses "fratribus Clarevallis cenobii," must date to about 1145. A sale to Cîteaux of 1151 was done at Cîteaux, but not at the General Chapter, "Item hoc donum Humbertus Arnaldus et Odo sororius ejus fecerunt in capitulo Cistercii in manu Gotsewini abbatis. Hoc pactum utriusque partis ego Odo Burgundie dux sigilli mei impressione confirmo." *CI*, no. 139 (1151).

90. *CI*, no. 208 (1172); Marilier does not distinguish between acts found in narrative sources such as the *Exordium Parvum* and authentic charter evidence, nor is there a distinction made between internal administration of Cîteaux *qua* abbey and that of the Order. Thus activities of the internal chapter of Cîteaux are thought to be those of a General Chapter meeting. See *CI*, no. 106, which may be as late as 1148, "Rainaldo Dei gratia venerabili cisterciensi abbati omnibusque ejusdem sancti ordinis abbatibus Rainaldus comes Burgundie salutem" is retrospective, recalling count Rainald's coming to the chapter of Cîteaux (not to a General Chapter) in the presence of Stephen Harding. *CI*, no. 116 (1140–63) is an ambiguous use of *ordo* in "fratribus cisterciensis ordinis."

91. *PO*, no. 114 (attributed to 1156).

92. *PO*, no. 34 (1155).

93. *CI*, no. 128 (1146–53); Marilier's note tells us that this was extracted from *Cartulaire de Sainte-Croix d'Orléans* (Paris, 1906), ed. Thillier and Jarry, no. 5 (p. 10), who cited Loiret, G 224, col. 1, ll. 48–50, a bishop's register for Manassès of Garlande (1146–53). I have not seen the original reference.

94. *FE*, no. 8.

95. *FE*, no. 8, and intro. by Georges Duby.

96. *FE*, no. 184 (circa 1175).

97. *CI*, no. 222 (1173) is problematic; cf. *CI*, no. 223 (1173), and *CL*, no. 150

(1173). All three have the same witness list, but those of 1173 are done at Losne; only the first mentions the General Chapter.

98. *CI*, no. 226 (1175).

99. *CL*, nos. 92 (1163), 97 (1165), tithe confirmations in later copies.

100. *Chartes et documents de l'abbaye cistercienne de Preuilly*, ed. Albert Catel and Maurice Lecomte (Montereau, 1927); no. 128 (1201), is extracted from a collection of statutes; Preuilly was the fifth daughter of Citeaux.

101. The earliest example from the Vauluisant cartulary of a reference to the General Chapter is the sale of an entire grange by the abbey of Arrivour to the abbey of Vauluisant done at the General Chapter in 1176 and witnessed by abbots of Cîteaux, la Ferté, Clairvaux, and Morimond, although not by that of Vauluisant's near neighbor and rival, Pontigny:

> Alexander, dei gratia abbas cistertiensis, Willelmus de Firmitate, Henricus Clare Vallis, Henricus Morimondensis, omnibus ad quos littere iste pervenerint, salutem in Domino. Noverit universitas vestra quod Arduinus abbas de Ripatorio, consilio fratrum suorum et assensu tocius capituli sui, vendidit grangiam unam que dicitur Chevreium cum omnibus appenditiis suis et quicquid ex dono Anscheri Senonis habebant Petro, abbati Vallis Lucentis, et fratribus eiusdem domus pro sescentis et .L. marcis fini argenti ad pondus trecense. Actum est hoc in generali capitulo Cisterciensi, anno ab incarnatione domini M.c.lxx..sexto. Quod ut ratum omni tempore habeatur, sigillorum nostrorum attestatione roboravimus. (Paris, A.N. AB XIX 1713, "Feuillet d'un cartulaire perdu de l'abbaye de Vauluisant, provenant des Archives départementales de l'Orne")

This is not an original but a cartulary copy described as being in a hand of circa 1183; it is from a larger edition of the charters of Vauluisant up to 1230 that has been recently edited by William O. Duba, "Cartulary of Vauluisant," master's thesis, University of Iowa, 1994. I wish to thank Mr. Duba for searching his databases for earliest references to such terms.

102. Included are *Abstracts of the Charters and Other Documents Contained in the Chartulary of the Cistercian Abbey of Fountains*, ed. William T. Lancaster, 2 vols. (Leeds, 1915); *The Beaulieu Cartulary*, ed. S. F. Hockey (Southampton, 1974); *Cartularium abbathie de Rievalle Ordinis cisterciensis*, ed. John C. Atkinson (Durham, 1889); *The Cartulary of the Abbey of Old Wardon*, ed. G. H. Fowler (Aspley Guise, Bedfordshire, 1930); *Chartularium Abbatie de Novo Monasterio Ordinis Cisterciensis*, ed. G. H. Fowler (Durham, 1878); *The Chartulary of the Cistercian Abbey of St Mary of Sallay in Craven*, ed. Joseph McNulty, 2 vols. (York, 1933–34); *Chronica monasterii de Melsa*, ed. Edward A. Bond, 3 vols. (London 1866–68); *The Coucher Book of Furness Abbey*, ed. John C. Atkinson and John Brownbill, 6 vols. (Manchester, 1886–1919); *The Coucher Book of the Cistercian Abbey of Kirkstall*, ed. William T. Lancaster (Leeds, 1904); *The Coucher Book, or Chartulary, of Whalley Abbey*, William A. Hulton, 4 vols. (Manchester, 1847–49); *Memorials of the Abbey of St. Mary of Fountains*, ed. John Richard Walbran and J. T. Fowler, 3 vols. (Durham, 1863–1918); *Monasticon Anglicanum*, ed. William Dugdale, with revisions by John Caley et al., 6 vols. (London, 1830); *Quarr Abbey and Its Lands, 1132–1631*, ed. S. F. Hockey (Leicester, 1970); *Rufford Charters*, ed. C. J. Holdsworth (Nottingham, 1972); *The Sibton Abbey Cartularies and Charters*, ed. Philippa Brown

(Woodbridge, Suffolk, 1984); *The Thame Cartulary*, ed. Herbert E. Salter (Oxford, 1947–48).

103. That nobles profited from the anarchy to found religious houses using land held from the Crown is suggested by Bennett Hill, *English Cistercian*, pp. 42–62. The observation that many Savigniac houses both in Britain and on the Continent were located on lands belonging to King Stephen and his family of Mortain is an observation I owe to Patrick Conyers. See further discussion of Savigniacs in the next chapter.

104. *Regesta Regum* AN, vol. 3, nos. 114, 115, 116.

105. See, for instance, the parallel charters of rights confirmed to Biddlesden Abbey. The first is by Stephen, published in *Regesta Regum* AN, vol. 3, no. 103 (dated by editors to circa 1149), which says: "Sciatis me concessisse et presenti carta confirmasse donationem illam quam Ernaldus de Bosco fecit deo et monachis de ordine Cisterciensi de manerio de Betlesdena cum omnibus appendiciis suis ad fundandam ibidem abbatiam Cisterciensis ordinis." The second is that in *Regesta Regum* AN, vol. 3, no. 104, granted in 1153 or 1154 by Henry, duke of Normandy and Aquitaine and count of Anjou: "Sciatis me concessisse et confirmasse donationem illam quam Ernaldus de Bosco fecit deo et monachis de ordine Cisterciensi de manerio de Betlesdena cum omnibus appendiciis suis, ad fundandam ibidem abbatiam ordinis Cisterciensis."

106. The rivalry between Stephen and Matilda even in the foundation of religious communities, seen particularly with regard to Mortemer and la Valaise, is discussed by Marjorie Chibnall, *The Empress Matilda: Queen Consort, Queen Mother, and Lady of the English* (Oxford, 1991), esp. pp. 140–41, 182–89. On p. 93, Chibnall describes the foundation of Margam in 1147 by Matilda's brother Robert and Bernard of Clairvaux's brother Nivard, apparently with Matilda's help.

107. *Regesta Regum* AN, vol. 3, no. 599.

108. *Regesta Regum* AN, vol. 3, no. 600.

109. *Regesta Regum* AN, vol. 3, no. 598.

110. *Regesta Regum* AN, vol. 3, no. 132, for Buildwas, "de ordine saviniacensi" in 1138, written by the suspect scribe xiii; no. 116, Matilda for Bordesley Abbey, "de ordine Cisterciensi" in 1141–42 (in the same hand as what some think is the spurious no. 115); no. 300 by Stephen for Faversham Abbey, "de ordine monacorum cluniacensium" in 1148; no. 321, for Flaxley Abbey from Henry, duke of Normandy and Aquitaine and count of Anjou, to "monachis ordinis cisterciensis" in 1153–54.

111. See *Regesta Regum* AN, vol. 3, intro., p. xiii, on suspect scribes, scriptor xiii, scriptor xiv.

112. *Regesta Regum* AN, vol. 3, no. 800, suspect scribe XIII.

113. *Regesta Regum* AN, vol. 3, no. 716, suspect scribe XIV.

114. *Regesta Regum* AN, vol. 3, no. 335.

115. See *Regesta Regum* AN, vol. 3, nos. 335, 99, the first is a cartulary copy, the later an "original" definitely made by scribe XIII, but they have identical witness lists.

116. But see the confirmation of rights to all Cistercians from Henry I from the Fountains cartulary; *Regesta Regum* AN, vol. 2, p. 381, CCLXXXV cal no. 1820, charter of Henry I dated 1128–33 must be for Henry II.

117. Amy G. Remensnyder, *Remembering Kings Past: Monastic Foundation Legends in Medieval Southern France* (Ithaca, N.Y., 1995).

· 118. Hill, *English Cistercian*, pp. 107–8.

119. Constance H. Berman, "Les cisterciens et le tournant économique du XIIe

siècle," *Bernard de Clairvaux (1089–1153): histoire, mentalités, spiritualité*, pp. 155–77 (Lyons, 1992).

120. Former abbots of Grandselve and Bonnevaux were instrumental in establishing a peace between Alexander III, the Emperor Frederick I, and the Cistercians of the Empire in 1177; *Statuta*, 1177, p. 85, and Timothy Reuter, "Das Edikt Friedrich Barbarossas gegen die Zisterzienser," *Mitteilungen des Institut fur österreichische Geschichtesforschung* 84 (1976): 328–36.

121. *Conciliorum oecumenicorum decreta*, ed. Josepho Alberigo et al. (Basil, 1962), p. 216, "Constitutiones of Concilium Lateranense IV-1215," where we find constitution number 12, "De communibus capitulis monachorum," saying

> Advocent autem caritative in huius novitatis primordiis duos Cisterciensis ordinis abbates vicinos, ad praestandum sibi consilium et auxilium opportunum, cum sint in huiusmodi capitulis celebrandis ex longa consuetudine plenius informati.

Such practice does not necessarily go back to 1120. Constitution 13 is on new orders, "De novis religionibus prohibitis," saying,

> Ne nimia religionum diversitas gravem in ecclesia Dei confusionem inducat, firmiter prohibemus, ne quis de caetero novam religionem inveniat, set quicumque voluerit ad religionem converti unam de approbatis assumat.

Cf. Raymonde Foreville, *Latran I, II, III, et Latran IV* (Paris, 1965), pp. 342–86, esp. 353–54.

122. One may trace the elaboration of item "CX, *De Abbate*," paragraphs 18–23, for instance, through all manuscripts; only Paris, B.N. Latin 4221 and Dijon 114 contain the reference in paragraph 23 of Item CX to *"nostri ordinis."*

123. This is a new finding. I had, however, noted an anomaly about these privileges in Constance H. Berman, "The Development of Cistercian Economic Policies During the Lifetime of Bernard of Clairvaux," *Bernardus Magister: In Celebration of the Nonacentenary of the Birth of Bernard of Clairvaux*, ed. John R. Sommerfeldt, pp. 303–13 (Kalamazoo, Mich., 1993).

124. *CI*, no. 90 (1132), in which Marilier reproduces the earliest copy of the bull *Habitantes in Domo*, is a copy dating to 1540 (Archives Côte d'Or 11 H4); it is also preserved in the late medieval Bullaire for Cîteaux, Dijon, B.M. 598, 136–38, *Liber privilegiorum Cistercii*, which has a rota (see Figure 22) with an inscription for Lucius III (1181–85), suggesting clumsy interpolation of an 1180s document. This purported document for Cîteaux says:

> Datum Cluniaci per manum Aimerici sancte romane ecclesie diaconi cardinalis et cancellarii IIII idus februarias, indictione X, incarnationis dominice M C XXXII pontificatus vero domini Innocentii II pape anno II.

In contrast, *CL*, no. 4 (1132), is a genuine 1132 bull of Innocent II for Bernard of Clairvaux and all the abbeys subject to him (which says nothing about an order); it states:

Datum Lugduni per manum Eimerici [var. Aimerici, Aymeriti], sancte Romane Ecclesie diaconi cardinalis et cancellarii, XIIII [var. XIII, XII] kalendas martii, indictione x, Incarnationis Dominice anno M C XXXII, pontificatus domini Innocentii pape secundi anno III. [var. II].

This too comes from a copy, but one dating to nearly a century earlier and authenticated by a royal official — Jacques de Roffey, lieutenant of the bailli of Troyes in 1468; its authenticity has not been questioned.

See Thomas Frenz, *Papsturkunden des Mittelalters und der Neuzeit* (Stuttgart, 1986), pp. 17ff. My thanks to Professor Bernard Barbiche for helpful discussion, as well as the Archives départementales de la Côte d'Or in Dijon, which provided me photocopies from series H of materials not available on the one day I visited; these liasses contained notes suggesting that Cistercian abbots from elsewhere than Cîteaux had already raised questions about this bull in the late Middle Ages.

125. *CL*, no. 4 (1132) contains a *"Sane conversos"* clause that is more likely to be authentic than the parallel *"Porro conversos"* clause in *CI*, no. 90 (1132).

126. This document is transcribed in *Statuta*, vol. 1, for the year 1142, as a Charter of Peace between Cistercians and Praemonstratensians; it refers to itself as a chirograph but is not. I wish to thank the Archives départementales for providing me a photograph of the so-called "original" (Chaumont, A.D. Haute-Marne 4H18) for la Chapelle-aux-Planches (see Figure 23).

127. *Statuta*, vol. 1, p. 35.

128. Kolumban Spahr, "Zum Freundschaftsbündnis zwischen Cisterciensern und Prämonstratensern," *CC* 73 (1966): 10–17; Trudo J. Gerits, "Les actes de confraternité de 1142 et de 1153 entre Cîteaux et Prémontré," *AP* 40 (1964): 192–205.

129. The echoing of the phrase "Charter of Charity" in this document, which calls itself a *"charitatis chirographum,"* is perhaps significant.

130. Thus:

Actum est hoc anno Incarnationis Domini M. CXLII, epacta XX [XXXII], indictione quinta, concurrente tertio, quinto Idus octobris. (The brackets contain my correction of Canivez's transcription from the manuscript.)

See Canivez, *Statuta*, vol. 1, p. 35 (1142, but obviously incorrectly dated).

131. The second attestation clause moves the dating of this text backward in time to 1142 by listing signatories appropriate to that date:

Sigillum Rainardi Cisterciensis abbatis, Bartholomaei abbatis de Firmitate, [Signum Domini] Bernardi Claraevallensis abbatis, Wichardi Pontigniacensis abbatis, Sigillum Hugonis Praemonstratensis abbatis, Walteri Laudeunensis abbatis, Gerlandi Floreciensis abbatis, Henrici Vivariensis abbatis.

132. The version from Chaumont refers only to Bernard as *Dominus*, suggesting the esteem after his death but before his canonization in 1174, when he would have been referred to as *Sanctus*. That names of abbots are correct for 1142 suggests that archaizing was consciously done.

133. Berman, *MA*, pp. 94ff; "VM," I, fol. 100r (1179), discussed in Chapter 4.

134. Ludwig Falkenstein, *La papauté et les abbayes françaises aux XIe et XIIe siècles* (Paris, 1997), pp. 204–5, remarks that this is exceptional, "A la différence de tous les autres ordres, les Cisterciens se sont donné très tôt une législation dont le noyau remont à 1114. Dans une privilege octroyé le 23 décembre 1119, [etc.]"

135. *Bullaire Calixte II*, no. 116 for Cîteaux's *Ad hoc in Apostolicae*; no. 134 for the Bonnevaux confirmation; both are reproduced in Appendix 4.

136. The papal year is correct in both the Cîteaux and Bonnevaux copies, but the indiction of 14 given in the Cîteaux document would be correct for December 1121, not December 1119; see Arthur Giry, *Manuel de diplomatique* (Paris, 1894), or Guyot-jeannin, *Diplomatique médiévale*.

137. That among surviving charters from Cîteaux's archives are found several acts from 1164 in which members of that community were present at Saulier in adjudication of a controversy between that abbey and the priory of Vergy that was resolved in the hand of Henry of Burgundy, bishop of Autun (who must have been a cousin of that Guy of Burgundy who became Calixtus II), suggests that Saulier was chosen because it was associated with Calixtus II's family. See *CI*, nos. 167, 168 (1164); no. 172 (1164–59); on the Burgundy family, see Constance Brittain Bouchard, *Sword, Miter, and Cloister: Nobility and the Church in Burgundy, 980–1198* (Ithaca, N.Y., 1987), appendices.

138. Robert, *Bullaire*, in his introduction gives the principles about what should be in such a bull from this time; these conclusions are quite properly based only on originals. His citation of his source for *Ad hoc in Apostolicae* (Robert, *Bullaire*, no. 116) is one that derives from the *Exordium Parvum* manuscripts. In this privilege for Cîteaux, as found in *Exordium Parvum* publications, an additional phrase, "Interdicimus autem ne quis conversos laicos vel professos vestros ad habitandum suscipiat," has been tacked on; this is surely an interpolation. In the later *Exordium Magnum*, ed. Griesser, pp. 58–59, it has been moved to a more normal location before the imprecation clause.

139. Careful checking in this edition of Robert and a search of the *PL* database confirms that neither *constitutio* nor *constitutum* was used in such privileges at this time.

140. In the earliest versions, *Ad hoc in Apostolicae* is without subscriptions; see Lefèvre, "*Apostolicae sedis*," but cf. *PAT*, p. 104, which implies that Ljubljana 31 has subscriptions and a dating clause. It does not.

141. That interpolation from the Bonnevaux charter to make *Ad hoc in Apostolicae* was done slightly later than the confection of charters for the internal text of the *Exordium Parvum* itself is suggested because the Paris B.N. Latin 4346A text of the *Exordium Parvum* does not contain the papal bull. A separate issue, worth noting, is that the last parts of the imprecation clause of the Bonnevaux charter are identical to those of the Pascal II bull in the *Exordium Parvum*, possibly suggesting that the Pascal II bull was also based on the Bonnevaux confirmation.

142. Dating by Garrigues, editor of the recently published cartularies of Pontigny; see *PO*, no. 84.

143. *PO*, no. 84.

144. *PO*, no. 84.

145. Van Damme, "Constitution de 1165," p. 59, says, "On peut s'étonner de ce que le statut primordial de la constitution ne soit approuvé explicitement qu'en 1165."

146. These texts were copied somewhat later onto a nearly blank folio of a volume of Garnerius de Ruperforti, *Distinctiones*, from Cîteaux. Dijon, B.M. MS 87, folios 168r,

v; see plate 22 for 168r. The manuscript, dated by Yolanta Zaluska, *Manuscrits enluminés de Dijon* (Paris, 1991), pp. 162–63, to the first quarter of the thirteenth century, thus dates these copies to the middle of the thirteenth century or later.

147. No papal bulls for Cîteaux before that of 1165 are found in any context outside the *Exordium Parvum* before the fifteenth-century copies found in the Dijon, B.M. MS 598 *Bullaire* for Cîteaux commissioned by Jean of Cirey, abbot of Cîteaux (1476–1501); see *CI*, passim.

148. Auberger, *L'unanimité*, pp. 340ff, uses such arguments with regard to *Sacrosancta*.

149. This is cited in Migne, *PL* 186, 1541–43, as copied from Mansi, *Concil.* XXI 669, and Jaffé I: 9600. In the manuscripts this is not necessarily a complete text for a bull for Eugenius; see Metz, B.M. MS 1247, fols. 16ff., where the text of a bull *Sacrosancta* is included and attributed in the rubrication to Eugenius III but has no salutation or other dating material. It does not mention a Charter of Charity, although it does mention a General Chapter. It refers to the Cistercians as a congregation and their way of life as an *ordo*. Only the abbots of la Ferté, Pontigny, and Clairvaux are mentioned.

150. Van Damme, "Constitution de 1165," 55–59.

151. Migne, *PL* 200, cols. 393cff. for Alexander III, cited as copied from Mansi *Concilium* XI, 959, and cited in Jaffé II: 11226; this is what Van Damme used in the article cited in the previous note.

152. *PL* 200, cols. 393cff.

Chapter 3

1. Traditional historians explain the Order's growth as resulting from the charismatic influence of Bernard of Clairvaux alone. Thus Lekai, *Cistercians*, has a chapter entitled, "Saint Bernard and the Expansion," pp. 33–51, but see also Adriaan H. Bredero, "The Conflicting Interpretations of the Relevance of Bernard of Clairvaux to the History of His Own Time," *Cîteaux* 31 (1980): 53–81.

2. See discussion of such congregations in Bede K. Lackner, *The Eleventh-Century Background to Cîteaux* (Spencer, Mass., 1972), and Henrietta Leyser, *Hermits and the New Monasticism: A Study of Religious Communities in Western Europe, 1000–1150* (London, 1984). Only one such congregation in the Midi seems to have survived without Cistercian incorporation, that of the Order of Chalais in Provence; see *Chartes de l'Ordre de Chalais: 1101–1401*, ed. Jean-Charles Roman d'Amat, 3 vols. (Paris, 1923), and Marie-Laure Crosnier Leconte, "Une cousine provinciale dans la France du sud-est: l'architecture de l'Ordre de Chalais," *Mélanges Dimier* (1984) 3, 5: 65–78. Among such congregations we must include foundations made by the abbess Heloise from the Paraclete; see Bruce Venarde, *Women's Monasticism and Medieval Society: Nunneries in France and England, 890–1215* (Ithaca, N.Y., 1997), pp. 121ff. Franz J. Felten also discusses an *ordo Paraclitensis* in "Verbandsbildung von Frauenklöstern. Le Paraclet, Prémy, Fontevraud mit einem Ausblick auf Cluny, Sempringham, und Tart," *Vom Kloster zum Klosterverband*, ed. Hagen Keller and Franz Neiske (Munich, 1997), pp. 277–341, esp. 294ff.

3. The 1170 letter from Alexander III, given in full in Appendix 5, is discussed in Chapter 2.

4. Cf. *Conciliorum*, ed. Josepho Alberigo et al. (Basil, 1962), and Foreville, *Latran*, pp. 342–86.

5. Bredero, *Bernard*, pp. 43ff.

6. *Statuta*, 1134, no. 1.

7. Marcel Pacaut, "La filiation clarevallienne dans la genèse et l'essor de l'Ordre cistercien." *Histoire de Clairvaux: actes du Colloque de Bar-sur-Aube/Clairvaux, 22–23 June, 1990* (Bar-sur-Aube, 1991), pp. 135–47.

8. In 1145, Eugenius III confirmed the gift of Jully's site made by Milon of Bar to abbot Gerald of Molesme and the brothers "professing the regular life there." He was establishing that Jully and the holy nuns of that church and their properties in the dioceses of Langres and Chalons would be under the management of Molesme. Those nuns, described as following the "institutes" established for Jully, were to be enclosed and their secular business provided for by the monks of Molesme. Bernard's earlier oversight was at an end. The text is from *Jully*, no. 10 (1145):

> Eugenius, episcopus, servus servorum Dei, dilectis filiis Geraldo, Molismensi abbati, ejusque fratribus tam presentibus quam futuris, regularem vitam professis in perpetuum. Sicut injusta poscentibus nullus est tribuendus assensus, sic legitima desiderantium non est differenda petitio, quatinus et devotionis sinceritas laudabiliter enitescat et utilitas postulata vires indubitanter assumat. Ea propter, dilecti in Domino filii, vestris justis postulationibus, placido occurentes assensu, donationem Milonis, comitis Barri, Molismensi eccelesie de Juliaco factam, et Josceranni felicis memorie, Lingonensis episcopi, canonico munimine roboratam, vobis vestrisque successoribus, inconvulso jure, concedimus obtinendam, et presentis scripti suffragio roboramus; statuentes ut ipsa Juliacensis et que, Deo favente, jam ex ea processerunt sanctimonialium ecclesie, quas propriis congruum duximus exprimendas vocabulis: in episcopatu Lingonensi, ecclesia Ose; in episcopatu Catalaunensi, ecclesia Vivifontis et ecclesia One; vel si que future sunt Juliaci propagines, arbitrio et ordinatione abbatis Molismi regulariter disposite, ad laudem et gloriam Dei, sub ditione Molismensis ecclesie jugiter perseverent. Quia vero predicte sanctimoniales, secundum Juliacensis instituti propositum, perpetua signate clausura ad secularia non declinant negotia, de monachis Molismensibus habebunt sibi spiritualium et temporalium bonorum provisores et ministros.

See also *CL*, no. 49 (1147–62), which confirms that "Guido de Bresmur dedit Deo et beate Marie Clarevallis quicquid habebat in finagio Campaniaci absque ulla retentione, pro eo quod domnus abbas Bernardus duas filias ejus fecit sanctimoniales apud Ulmetum."

9. As some mid-twelfth-century sources sometimes call them. See *De miraculis sanctae Mariae Laudunensis* of Herman of Tournai, *PL* 156: 962–1018; also *MGH* 12 (1925): 653–62.

10. Stock, *Implications*, pp. 88ff, 405ff.

11. Newman, *Boundaries*, pp. 10ff.; Bynum, *Jesus as Mother*, pp. 59ff.

12. Stock, *Implications*, pp. 403ff., discusses Bernard of Clairvaux's *Sermons on the Song of Songs*, dated according to Jean Leclercq, "La date du premier sermon," *Saint Bernard mystique*, pp. 480–83), to between 1135 and 1153. That such spiritual writings

were widely copied and read is implied by Jean Leclercq, "Les manuscrits cisterciens du Portugal," *ASOC* 6 (1950): 131–39; "Manuscrits cisterciens dans des bibliothèques d'Italie," *ASOC* 5 (1949): 94–119; "Textes et manuscrits cisterciens en Suède," *ASOC* 6 (1950): 125–30; "Recherches dans les manuscrits cisterciens d'Espagne," *ASOC* 5 (1949): 109–19; "Textes cisterciens dans des bibliothèques d'Allemagne," *ASOC* 7 (1951): 46–77; and "Textes et manuscrits cisterciens à la bibliothèque Vaticane." *ASOC* 15 (1959): 79–103.

13. Griesser, "Beiträge zur Beurteilung des Cod. 1711 von Trient."

14. Discussed in Chapter 2; see Lefèvre, "Les traditions manuscrites des *Usus Conversorum* de Cîteaux," *COCR* 17 (1955): 11–39; "L'évolution des *Usus Conversorum* de Cîteaux." *COCR* 17 (1955): 65–97.

15. Martha Newman, "Stephen Harding and the Creation of the Cistercian Community," *R. bénédictine* 107 (1997): 307–39.

16. We may need to treat the reform of the chant by Stephen Harding separately from revisions of liturgical order books like the *Ecclesiastica Officia*, which contain much more than liturgy. Stephen may have been more involved than Bernard in discussions of equality among abbots of various monasteries that harken back to Bede; Auberger, *L'unanimité*, passim, and Newman, "Stephen Harding"; McGuire, "Who Founded the Order?"; H. E. J. Cowdrey, *"Quidam Frater Stephanus Nomine, Anglicus Natione* (The English Background of Stephen Harding)," *R. bénédictine* 101 (1991): 322–40.

17. René Crozet, "L'épiscopat de France et l'Ordre de Cîteaux au XIIe siècle," *Etudes de civilisation médiévale IXe–XIIe siècles: mélanges dédiés à Edmund-René Labande*, pp. 263–68, *CCM* 18, 1975.

18. Hence much of the idea of a crisis of monasticism is based on the fiction of an early foundation of a Cistercian Order; see John van Engen, "The 'Crisis of Cenobitism' Reconsidered: Benedictine Monasticism in the Years 1050–1150," *Speculum* 61 (1986): 269–304, which is in response to Jean Leclercq, "The Monastic Crisis of the Eleventh and Twelfth Centuries," *Cluniac Monasticism in the Central Middle Ages*, ed. Noreen Hunt, pp. 215–37 (Hamden, Conn., 1971).

19. On la Ferté's origins in an eremitical group, see *FE*, intro. by Duby; on Pontigny's, see *PO*, Garrigue's intro., p. 11.

20. Bouton et al., "L'abbaye de Tart"; *Jully*, p. 29; Venarde, *Women's Monasticism*, pp. 120ff.

21. Auberger, *L'unanimité*, pp. 147, 154, 163, 165.

22. See *Carta Caritatis Prior* versus *Corta Caritatis Posterior*.

23. Bonnevaux was the eighth daughter-abbey of Cîteaux; see J.-M. Canivez, "Bonnevaux," *DHGE* 9 (1937): 1074–76, and Marie-Odile Lenglet, "Notes sur l'histoire de l'abbaye de Bonnevaux," *Mélanges Dimier* 2, 4: 700–718. In 1167, Bonnevaux was granted the Cluniac priory of Artasium located in the parish of Maceoneya and absorbed its properties; see *BX*, no. 118 (1167). We see internal visitation appearing when a gift was made at Bonnevaux in the presence of Alexander, abbot of Cîteaux (1168–78); see *BX*, nos. 44, 155 (1151). Additional documents are published in *Cartulaire de l'abbaye Notre-Dame de Bonnevaux, au diocèse de Vienne, ordre de Cîteaux*, ed. anon. [Anselme Dimier] (Notre-Dame-de-Tamié, Savoie, 1942); among these we see a charter that dates to circa 1150, in which Bernard of Clairvaux and Rainald of Cîteaux join abbots of Bonnevaux, Hautecombe, and Mazan to oversee a donation to Bonne-

vaux that must date to circa 1150. Yet it is still not clear from this document whether Mazan was actually attached to Bonnevaux in 1150.

24. Constable, *Reformation*, pp. 53–54.

25. See Chapter 2.

26. Marjorie Chibnall, private communication, November 1998.

27. Jo Ann McNamara, *Sisters in Arms: Catholic Nuns Through Two Millennia* (Cambridge, Mass., 1996), esp. pp. 241ff.; Dyan Elliott, *Spiritual Marriage: Sexual Abstinence in Medieval Wedlock* (Princeton, N.J., 1993), pp. 81ff.

28. Cf. *Statuta* vol. 1, pp. xxviff.; such paraphrases of the Rule of Saint Benedict were probably "collected" in the 1150s and 1160s.

29. Bartlett, *Making*, pp. 228ff.

30. McNamara, *Sisters in Arms*, pp. 260ff.

31. Edward W. Said, *Orientalism* (New York, 1978), offers an analysis of colonial outlooks that could easily be compared to earlier narratives of Christian monastic foundations.

32. James France, "The Coming of the Cistercians to Scandinavia—*Ad exteras et barbaras regiones*," *Cîteaux* 48 (1997): 5–14.

33. Leopoldus Janauschek, *Originum Cisterciensium*, vol. 1 (only volume produced) (Vienna, 1877; reprint Ridgewood, N.J.: Gregg Press, 1964), hereafter cited as *Originum*.

34. On problems in using such models of organic growth in general, see Stephen Jay Gould, *Wonderful Life: The Burgess Shale and the Nature of History* (New York, 1989), esp. pp. 23–52, "The Iconography of an Expectation." I would also like to thank Nicole Bériou for reminding me of the interest in genealogies within twelfth-century secular society, as discussed in Georges Duby, *The Knight, the Lady, and the Priest; The Making of Modern Marriage in Medieval France* (New York, 1983), esp. chaps. 12 and 13.

35. This is noted in Janet Burton, *Monastic and Religious Orders in Britain, 1000–1300* (Cambridge, 1994), pp. 182–83. She has also mentioned (private communication, 1998) that at one point there was a proposal that the abbot of Fountains should act as visitor for all Clairvaux's daughters in England; it came to nothing.

36. Nonetheless, adoption of Cistercian practices, the creation of an Order, and attachment to it as daughters in a filiation were for twelfth-century houses of monks and nuns most often different events, happening at different dates that were sometimes widely separated.

37. We compound the error of these filiation trees by our use of them to make graphs and tables, a use assuming that they contain firm dates when they do not; this tendency is seen in Berman, *MA*, as elsewhere.

38. "VM" I, fols. 1ff.

39. This is the case for Mazan, which added more houses than any other abbey associated with Bonnevaux. It is also true for Berdoues, l'Escaledieu, and Bonnefont; as discussed later in this chapter, their addition to the filiation of Morimond, if it occurred in 1175, would have added twenty-six more houses for monks and an uncounted number for nuns.

40. Filiation trees were still being made up in the thirteenth century, as is clear from such citations as may be seen in *Preuilly*, no. 168 (1210). Savigny's wealth allowed it to have even a stable outside the gates at Cîteaux for the use of the abbots of "its

congregation" at General Chapter meetings; Paris, A.N. L 966, no. 7. A similar dispute about where Cadouin fit on the tree for Pontigny, which Cadouin seems to have won, is described in J.-M. Canivez, "Cadouin," *DHGE* 11 (1949): 118-22.

41. Pacaut, "La filiation claravallienne," notes the difference in shape of the Clairvaux filiation as against others.

42. I have used numbers from Southern, *Western Society*, p. 254.

43. Constance H. Berman, "Diversité et unanimité des cisterciens du XIIe siècle," *Unanimité et diversité cisterciennes: filiations, réseaux, relectures du XIIe au XVIIe siècle*, ed. Nicole Bouter (Saint-Etienne, 1999).

44. *BD*, nos. 173 (1152), 189 (n.d), 190 (1212), 222 (n.d.), 229 (n.d.), 231 (n.d.), 232 (n.d.), 253 (n.d.); *BD*, no. 266 (1155) is the concession to Berdoues by the archbishop of Auch of the three churches that had belonged to the hermitage for an annual rent of thirty *concades* of wheat.

45. *BD*, nos. 17 (1210), 20 (1210), 800 (1242).

46. It was probably such changing approaches to incorporation at mid-century that were being remembered in the retrospective dating (done at circa 1185) of the statute about Cistercian growth usually attributed to 1152; see Chapter 2.

47. This is probably an even larger component of why Cistercians became wealthy than was the Cistercian management discussed by Roehl, "Plan and Reality," or Berman, *MA*, passim.

48. Berman, "Foundation of Silvanès."

49. *SL*, no. 470 is the chronicle; Verlaguet's edition is based on the Doat volume copy. That the chronicle was still in the south of France in the seventeenth century suggests that the manuscript, Dijon B.M. MS 611, "Incipit tractatus de conversione Pontii de Laracio et exordii monasterii vera narratio," which also includes letters by Hugh Francigena, was still at Silvanès when the Doat Commission made its copies. The text is translated by Beverly M. Kienzle, "The Tract on the Conversion of Pons of Léras and the True Account of the Beginning of the Monastery of Silvanès," *CSQ* 29 (1995): 219-43; see also Derek Baker, "Popular Piety in the Lodèvois in the Early Twelfth Century: The Case of Pons de Léras," *Studies in Church History* 15 (1978): 39-47.

50. Hugh writes:

Ad memoriam etiam futurorum quatenus cognoscat successionis notre posteritas omnis a qualibus quantisque patribus religio domus nostre sumpsit exordium, ut bone arboris generosa radice cognita, secundum generis sui speciem fructus afferre studeant, qui maneant semper immarcescibiles ad testimonium et laudem et gloriam arboris hujus pulcherrime, videlicet Salvaniensis ecclesie matris nostre, quam ab initio Celestis Agricole manus tanquam humile virgultum semper excoluit et excolere semper non desinit, incrementum ei tribuens et augmentum, irrigans eam plurimis beneficiis tanquam celestibus pluviis, cujus studio diligenti atque inter cetera ligna silvarum jam in tantum cacumen extulit ut operiat montes umbra ejus, etc. (*SL*, p. 372)

51. Berman, "Foundation of Silvanès," pp. 280-318. The threat Bonnecombe posed to Silvanès can be seen in Bonnecombe's acquisitions near Comps, where Silvanès had earlier attempted to acquire land. *SL* no. 218 (1161) and *Cartulaire de*

l'abbaye de Bonnecombe, ed. P.-A. Verlaguet (Rodez, 1918–1925) hereafter *BC*, nos. 72 (1220), 51 (1244). This *Vita* of Pons de Léras deserves consideration in relation to other Cistercian hagiography: see *La vie de Saint Etienne d'Obazine*, ed. Michel Aubrun (Clermont-Ferrand, 1970); Brian Golding, "The Hermit and the Hunter," *The Cloister and the World: Essays in Medieval History in Honor of Barbara Harvey*, ed. John Blais and Brian Golding (Oxford, 1996), pp. 95–117; and J.-M. Bienvenu, *L'étonnant fondateur de Fontévraud: Robert d'Arbrissel* (Paris, 1981). Later accounts are all we have for Gerald; see Lenglet, "Géraud de Salles."

52. Hugh continues:

> Fuit vir unus in Lodovensi pago, miles officio, nomine Pontius de Larasio, quod erat castrum ejus inexpugnabile. Hic secundum seculi dignitatem genere clarus, opibus dives, possessionibus felix, ingenio acer, viribus potens, armis strenuus, municipio firmus et in omni gloria seculari conspicuus, inter ceteros eminebat.... Sed quia uxorem habebat, sine cujus assensu hoc facere non valebat, consilii sui ei secretum credidit utque ipsa taliter faceret magnis precibus exoravit. Que ut erat nobilis genere, mente nobilior piis viri votis libenter annuit, pietatis tamen mota visceribus et tota perfusa lacrimis patrem pro suis liberis exoravit, filium namque et filiam habebat, quorum affectu maternum pectus pietas agitabat. Sed pater providus dum bene sibi cavere studuit, etiam filiis bene cavit; matrem enim et filiam cum magna sue portione substantie in monasterio virginum, quod Brinonia dicitur, honorifice collocavit. Filium vero in monasterio Lodovensi, quod Sancti Salvatoris dicitur, monachorum conventui sociavit. (*SL* pp. 373–74)

Compare this account with that given in *Grand Cartulaire de la Sauve Majeure*, no. 17:

> Istam vocem audiebat et implebat opere Guido comes Pictavensis dux et Aquitanie Guido dictus in baptismo Willelmus cognomine, potens armis, clarus gestis et regalis genere. Iste vir late per orbem fama celeberrimus licet esset occupatus in terrenis actibus atque bellis insudaret nimium frequentibus nunquam tamen desistebat a piis operibus. Defensor ecclesiarum plures ipse condidit ubi conventus monachorum sub abbate posuit. Aliis possessiones et honores addidit etiam Silve Maiori multa dona contulit.

53. *SL*, p. 382, "At illi elegerunt sibi quendam locum, qui antiquitus Silvanium a silvis dicebatur, quem ipse sive successores eorum Salvanium vocaverunt, i mutata in a, ut qui ante Silvanium a silvis dicebatur, Salvanium a salvatione deinceps diceretur."

54. *SL*, p. 372.
55. *SL*, p. 382.
56. Berman, "Foundation of Silvanès," passim.
57. Ludo Milis, "Ermites et chanoines réguliers au XIIe siècle," *CCM* 22 (1979): 39–80.
58. Maire Wilkinson, "The *Vita Stephani Muretensis* and the Papal Reconstitution of the Order of Grandmont in 1186 and Thereafter," *Monastic Studies: The Continuity of Tradition*, ed. Judith Loades (Bangor, Gwynned, Wales: Headstart History, 1990), suggests that there may be a hagiographical "construct" of papally approved adoption of rules.

59. On this point, the Silvanès chronicle parallels the *Vie de Saint-Etienne d'Obazine*, pp. 78ff.
60. *SL*, p. 385.
61. *SL*, p. 385:

> Tunc hanc causam ponere placuit in arbitrio Cartusiensium. Ob quam causam Pontius de Larazio pergens Cartusiam, priori ceterisque fratribus causam exposuit; qui inspecta regula veritatis, pre ceteris cunctis ordinibus Cisterciensium ordinem laudaverunt eumque potius expetendum eidem Pontio mandaverunt. Cui consilio hoc insuper addiderunt ut de illa abbatia ordinis que loco illi vicinior videretur, ordo deduceretur ne in eundo sive redeundo laborem nimium paterentur. Tunc Pontius de Larazio vale faciens illis ad Mansum Ade venit.

Compare with the account in *Vie de Saint Etienne d'Obazine*, p. 78:

> Audiens autem famam Cartusiensium monachorum, quos tunc pre ceteris religiosis fama nobilitabat, ad videndum eos gratam quidem sed laboriosam sibi peregrinationem assumpsit; in quo itinere multas famis ac frigoris injurias est perpessus. . . . Pervenientes ad Cartusiam, satis humane a fratribus illis excepti sunt. Erat enim festivitas dedicationis ecclesie ipsorum, que eos in unum omnes convexerat, Nam ceteris diebus privatis singuli. . . . Vir itaque Dei cum priore loci familiariter collocutus, erat enim discretus et religione fundatus, consilium querebat quam sibi viam religionis decerneret eligendam. . . . Ad quod ille respondens dixit Cistercienses nuper exortos regiam viam tenere.

62. *SL*, p. 387, "Illi vero qui suis laboribus locum primitus inceperunt in sanctitate vite in humilitate et obedientia permanserunt, donec terra corpora, celo animas reddiderunt. Frater autem Pontius de Larazio, qui humiliorem locum semper eligere studuit, in habitu laicorum fratrum conversus permansit."
63. *SL*, p. 387, "Postea vero procedente tempore, placuit domno abbati Guiraldo et fratribus universis ut propter insolentiam secularium hominum et alia multa incommoda monasterium mutari deberet in locum alterum, qui melior et religioni convenientior videretur et aliis abundans multis commoditatibus."
64. Dimier, *L'art cistercien*, pp. 74ff, 142ff.
65. *SL*, pp. 382–84.
66. Cf. Lekai, "Ideals."
67. Berman, "Foundation of Silvanès."
68. "VM" I, beginning on 82r (1156).
69. *SL*, p. 380.
70. Mazan has traditionally been described as affiliated in either 1120 or 1136 by Bonnevaux, Cîteaux's eighth daughter; see Marie-Odile Lenglet, "Un problème d'histoire monastique: la fondation de l'abbaye de Mazan," *Cîteaux* 21 (1970): 5–22 and eadem, "Les origines de l'abbaye de Mazan; autocritique d'une précédente étude," *Cîteaux* 37 (1986): 76–81. I do not agree with the reading by Lucien Parat, "Les origines de l'abbaye de Mazan," *Revue Région* (1987), of Bonnevaux documents such as *BX*, no. 313 (which I would date to 1131 not 1120) to argue that Mazan was founded circa 1120 by Bonnevaux.

71. *Atlas*, p. 288, incorrectly gives 1254 as the foundation date for Mercoire; this must be the date of assignment to Mazan's abbot; see Moreau, *AO*, pp. 244–48 and Desmarchelier, pp. 81, 95.

72. The Silvanès chronicle tells us that attachment to Mazan was to an abbot Peter, *SL*, p. 380. Is this the same Peter as in Regné, *Mazan*, no. 1 (which is probably a retrospective "acte-notice"), and *NO*, no. 10 (1169) which mentions Peter Itier, and *NO*, no. 27 (1181), possibly a family member, Raymond Itier, and the abbot Peter who was sent to affiliate Sénanque in 1148 mentioned in Barruol, *Sénanque*?

73. "L'abbaye de Mazan: catalogue des actes de l'abbaye de Mazan (1123–1494)," ed. Jean Regné, *R. du Vivarais* 28 (1921): 86–89, 107–12, 134–42, 169–74, 211–17, 243–46, etc.; my special thanks to the University of Iowa Interlibrary loan librarians who obtained this for me from France.

74. Jacques Bousquet, "Les origines de la transhumance en Rouergue," *L'Aubrac: étude ethnologique, linguistique, agronomique, et économique d'un établissement humain*, 4 vols. (Paris, 1971), vol. 2, pp. 217–55; Berman, *MA*, pp. 94ff.

75. *SL*, nos. 170–71 (1154).

76. *Cartulaire de l'abbaye de Bonneval-en-Rouergue*, ed. P.-A. Verlaguet, intro. J.-L. Rigal (Rodez, 1938), pp. 3, 668–78. Cf. Anselme Dimier, "Quelques légendes de fondation chez les cisterciens," *Studia Monastica* 12 (1970): 97–105; Penelope D. Johnson, "Pious Legends and Historical Realities: The Foundations of La Trinité de Vendôme, Bonport, and Holyrood," *R. bénédictine* 91 (1981): 184–93.

77. Rodez, 3H nouv. ser. 19, "Inventaire de Bonneval" for Anduze; *BC*, no. 64 (1178), and associated documents for the sale of la Serre to Bonnecombe. On Locdieu, see below.

78. A. Robert, "Les abbés du monastère cistercien des Chambons au diocèse de Viviers (1152–1791)," *R. de Vivarais* 72 (1968): 119–30; 73 (1969): 30–35; idem, "L'abbaye cistercienne de Mazan (Ardèche) et ses filles provençales: Sénanque et le Thoronet," *Fédération historique du Languedoc Mediterranean et du Roussillon 90e congrès* (1968): 77–101; and idem, "Deux documents sur les Chambons et la terre de Borne," *R. de Vivarais* 90 (1986): 215–23. In my view both Sénanque and les Chambons were probably attached to Mazan before it became Cistercian.

79. Jean Barruol, *Sénanque et le Pays du Lubéron au Ventoux* (Lyon, 1975); Martin Aurell i Cardona, *Une famille de la noblesse provençale au Moyen Age: les Porcelet* (Avignon, 1986).

80. This would have been particularly important for women; see Constance H. Berman, "Economic Practices of Cistercian Women's Communities: A Preliminary Look," *Speculum Studiosorum: Studies in Honor of Father Louis J. Lekai, OCSO*, ed. John Sommerfeldt (Kalamazoo, Mich., 1993), pp. 15–32.

81. Whether that dread of women described in hagiography concerning Stephen of Grandmont was that of the saint or of his biographer is difficult to judge; see "Vita Venerabilis Viri Stephani Muretensis," *PL* 204: 1065–72; Carole A. Hutchinson, *The Hermit Monks of Grandmont* (Kalamazoo, Mich., 1989), chap. 1; Elizabeth M. Hallam, "Henry II, Richard I, and the Order of Grandmont," *Journal of Medieval History* 1 (1975): 165–86; Maire Wilkinson, "Stephen of the Auvergne and the Foundation of the Congregation of Muret-Grandmont According to Its Primitive Traditions," *Medieval History* 2 (1992): 45–67; and Gert Melville, "Von der *Regula regularum* zur Ste-

phansregel: Der normative Sonderweg der Grandmontenser bei der Auffächerung der *Vita religiosa* im 12. Jahrhundert," *Vom Kloster zum Klosterverband*, ed. Hagen Keller and Franz Neiske, pp. 342–63 (Munich: Wilhelm Fink, 1997). I wish to thank Maria Hillebrandt for providing me with the Keller and Neiske volume.

82. Constable, *Reformation*, pp. 71ff. cites the statutes.

83. On Clairvaux, see Robert Fossier, "La puissance économique de l'abbaye de Clairvaux au XIIIe siècle," *Histoire de Clairvaux: actes du colloque de Bar-sur-Aube/Clairvaux, 22–23 June, 1990* (Bar-sur-Aube, 1991), pp. 73–83.

84. Berman, *MA*, pp. 137ff.

85. See Berman, "Development"; Constable, *Monastic Tithes*; and more recently idem, *Reformation*, pp. 225ff.

86. *LC*, no. 53 (1194); the community was to stay at Pardieu from the feast of Saint Andrew until at least Easter. See also *LC*, nos. 24 (1194), 68 (1204), 134 (1244), etc. and articles published by the modern religious community at Léoncel in *Cahiers de Léoncel*.

87. On Bonnevaux and Léoncel as pastoralists, see *BX*, nos. 429 (c. 1130), 431 (1222), 430 (1185); and *LC*, nos. 23 (1173), 24 (1174), 27 (1178), 34 (1185), 35 (1185), 42 (1191), 50 (1193), 60 (1196), etc.

88. Gifts to Ardorel that provided for the double community appear to have included land located within Cecilia of Provence's dower property near Mèze in the diocese of Agde; see Pierre de Gorsse, *L'abbaye cistercienne Sainte-Marie de Valmagne au diocèse d'Agde en Languedoc* (Toulouse, 1933), and Jean Segondy, *L'abbaye du Vignogoul* (Montpellier, 1952). The story is complicated by later claims over Valmagne from Bonnevaux; see "VM," I, fols. 1ff.

89. On Valmagne's wealth, see expenditures in Table 3, Chapter 3 and Berman, *MA*, p. 142.

90. Franquevaux (hardly a disinterested party) was commissioned to inspect the new site in the Camargue at Sauveréal. The community of Ulmet was moved there shortly after 1240; see *Statuta*, 1240, no. 61.

91. Dimier, *L'art cistercien*, p. 53.

92. Only a single document survives, see *L'abbaye de Notre-Dame-de-Valcroissant de l'Ordre de Cîteaux au diocèse de Die*, ed. Jules Chevalier (Grenoble, 1897). In *The Tax Book of the Cistercian Order*, ed. Arne Odd Johnson and Peter King (Oslo, 1979), p. 40, the first assessment for Valcroissant was only six livres while that for Valmagne was four times that. On the expropriation of the nuns of Bonlieu, see *Statuta*, 1400, no. 31.

93. On Bonnevaux's filiation, see Hélène Morin-Sauvade, "La filiation de Bonnevaux," *Unanimité et diversité cisterciennes: filiations, réseaux, relectures du XIIe au XVIIe siècle*, ed. Nicole Bouter (Sainte-Etienne, 1999).

94. On resources for pasture, as an appropriate endowment for communities of nuns, see Berman, "Economic Practices," esp. 21ff.

95. *Le cartulaire de l'abbaye cistercienne d'Obazine (XIIe–XIIIe siècle)*, ed. Bernadette Barrière (Clermont-Ferrand, 1989), p. 12, where she describes it as a double-monastery affiliated to the Cistercians. The discussion continues about whether we should use the term "double-monastery" to describe such family monasteries, or early twelfth-century eremitical and monastic communities in which men and women treat one another with equality; obviously these are different from the double-monasteries of the early Middle

Ages. Moreover, all women's communities were by their nature "double" in needing to have at least a hired priest to say mass for them. Most Cistercian communities of women had both lay-brothers and priests attached; the lay-brothers certainly took their vows directly from the abbess.

96. Toulouse, Haute-Garonne, H205 Lespinasse, liasse 12, no. 11, and discussion by Berman, "Men's Houses."

97. See discussion earlier in this chapter and in Chapter 4.

98. Bernadette Barrière, "Les abbayes issues de l'érémitisme," *CF* 21, pp. 71–106.

99. Barrière, "Les abbayes," p. 102; I rely on Barrière's quotations from the unpublished Dalon cartulary edited by Grillon, unavailable to me.

100. Locdieu was incorporated into the Order in 1162 with Dalon; see Janauschek, *Originum*, pp. 147–48, 172; Victor Lafon, "Histoire de la fondation de l'abbaye de Loc-Dieu," *Mém. Société des lettres de l'Aveyron* (Rodez) 11 (1879): 339–53.

101. Dimier, *L'art cistercien*, p. 50.

102. *Documents concernants l'abbaye de Locdieu*, ed. anon. (Villefranche, 1892) and *Les plus anciennes chartes en langue provençale*, ed. Clovis Brunel (Paris, 1926 and 1952); the latter includes many vernacular charters for Locdieu taken from the Order of Malta collection in Toulouse.

103. Les Feuillants is mentioned in the annals of the thirteenth century in connection with a short-lived military-religious confraternity called the Order of Peace and Faith founded in 1229 by bishop Fulk of Toulouse to combat heresy. See Dimier, "Feuillans," *DHGE* 16 (1967): 1334–35. A number of abbeys contended for control of les Feuillants, which was assigned to la Creste in 1217. Almost nothing is known about it until the sixteenth century, when les Feuillants became the center from which a reform of the Cistercians—the Feuillantines—was spread; see Ferrands, "Feuillants," *DHGE* 16 (1967): 1338.

104. See discussion of Valmagne's granges in Chapter 4.

105. That for le Tart in 1147, *PL* 180, cols. 1199–1200:

> Eugenius episcopus, servus servorum Dei, dilectis in Christo filiabus Elizabeth abbatissae de Tart, ejusdem sororibus, tam praesentibus quam futuris, regularem vitam professis in perpetuum. Desiderium quod ad religionis propositum et animarum salutem pertinere dignoscitur animo nos decet libenter concedere, et petentium desideriis congruum impertiri suffragium. Eapropter, dilectae in Christo filiae, vestris justis postulationibus clementer annuimus, et praefatum locum in quo divino mancipatae estis obsequio, sub beati Petri et nostra protectione suscipimus, et praesentis scripti privilegio communimus; statuentes ut quascunque possessiones, quaecunque bona idem locus in praesentiarum juste et canonice possidet, aut in futurum concessione pontificum, largitione regum vel principum, oblatione fidelium seu aliis justis modis, Deo propitio, poterit adipisci, firma vobis vestrisque succedentibus et illibata permaneant: in quibus haec propriis duximus exprimenda vocabulis: Locum ipsum de Tart, et locum qui dicitur Marmot cum appendiciis suis, et plenarium usagium totius nemoris de Villers; grangiam de Lamblento cum appendiciis suis, quam Humbertus de Bisseio vobis libere dedit cum Patro majore et haeredibus ejus, de assensu Hugonis de Bello-Monte, de cujus casamento erat grangiam de Alta-Silva cum appendiciis suis, et plenarium in campis et in silvis et in pascuis; et decimas quas possessores earum

ante dedicationem ecclesiae illius grangiae in aspectu domini praesulis Cabilonensis verpierunt. Sane laborum vestrorum, quos propriis manibus aut sumptibus colitis, sive de nutrimentis vestrorum animalium, nullus a vobis decimas exigere praesumat... [etc.]

See Chauvin, "Papauté," p. 351, which discusses the original; cf. *PL* 180, cols. 1197–98 for Bonnevaux.

106. Elizabeth Traissac, "Les abbayes cisterciennes de Fontguilhem et du Rivet et leur rôle dans le défrichement médiévale en Bazadais," *R. historique de Bordeaux* 9 (1960): 141–50.

107. *Atlas*, p. 292.

108. *Atlas*, p. 227, says it was "founded" circa 1132, and left the Order to affiliate with Casadei in 1209; just when it had been affiliated or adopted Cistercian practices is unclear.

109. B. Alart, "Monastères de l'ancien diocèse d'Elne: II: l'abbaye de Sainte-Marie de Jau ou de Clariana, Ordre de Cîteaux," *Mém. Sociétés des Pyrénées-Orientales* 11 (1872): 278–308, suggests that le Jau was placed under control of Ardorel in 1162, but that it had already been founded by then.

110. Pace L. de Lacger, "Ardorel."

111. Barrière, "L'érémitisme," speculates as to why those abbeys attached to Clairvaux became more successful.

112. There are references to Boulaur in the Gimont cartulary; see *GM* I, no. 137 (1200), which is the conveyance of the deceased Eudes Despax for burial at Gimont by his sons, one of whom is the prior of Boulaur; and *GM* I, no. 96 (1183), in which William of Batcave is mentioned as a conversus of Boulaur. Venarde, *Women's Monasticism*, pp. 100ff. has investigated some of these houses.

113. Jean Leclercq, *Women and Saint Bernard of Clairvaux*, trans. Marie-Bernard Said (Kalamazoo, Mich., 1989). That Cistercians took a middle road on this as on other things seems to be the implication of Constable, *Reformation*, pp. 71–72. I agree that Bernard's prohibitions about "double communities" or "having women and laybrothers meeting at mills" do not exclude the Order and the pre-Order having had women's houses.

114. See Paris, B.N. Latin MS 11008, nos. 65 (1164), 145 (1174), for efforts to get Grandselve to found a women's community, which did not seem to have happened.

115. Further investigation is in order on how these houses are treated in standard accounts of the Albigensian Crusade, along with discussion in their sources of women as heretics.

116. Constable, *Monastic Tithes*, is concerned with the phenomenon of tithes being returned not to bishops but to monastic communities.

117. Canivez, "Beaulieu-en-Rouergue," *DHGE* 7 (1934): 164; *Originum*, p. 79; the latter mentions the Bishop of Rodez, Vivian, whose donation of four churches to Belloc earned him the title of "founder."

118. Dimier, *L'art cistercien*, p. 57.

119. Doat 91, nos. 1 (1164), 2 (1164) 3 (1166), 4 (1166), 2bis (including a donation dated 1166); on bastides and Cistercians more generally, see Higounet, *Paysages*, pp. 266–74.

120. Victor Fons, "Les monastères cisterciens de l'ancienne province ecclésias-

tique de Toulouse," *R. de Toulouse et du Midi de la France* 25 (1867): 116, says that it was founded by Gerald of Salles. I have found no contemporary evidence for this; see *Originum*, p. 75.

121. On the preaching mission, see Cicely d'Autremont Angleton, "Two Cistercian Preaching Missions to Languedoc in the Twelfth Century: 1145, 1178," Ph.D. dissertation, Catholic University of America, 1984; R. I. Moore, "St. Bernard's Mission in Languedoc," *Bull. Institute of Historical Research* (London) 47 (1974): 1–14; Walter L. Wakefield, *Heresy, Crusade and Inquisition in Southern France, 1100–1250* (Berkeley, Calif., 1974).

122. A letter that commends the "holy men" at Grandselve was copied into a volume of the writings of John Cassian that may have belonged to the abbey. See *Originum*, p. 75; Toulouse, A.D. Haute Garonne, 108H, liasse 61; Toulouse, Bibl. Mun., MS 152.

123. For Lespinasse dedication, see Toulouse, A.D. Haute-Garonne, Lespinasse, H205 liasse 12, and discussion in Berman, "Men's Houses."

124. R. Rumeau, "Notes sur l'abbaye de Grandselve," *Bull. Société géographique de Toulouse* 19 (1900): 247–85, esp. 249–50.

125. Doat 76, no. 2 (1130); Rumeau, "Grandselve," p. 250, includes the text of the 1142 bull of Innocent II; it does not mention Cistercians.

126. Paris, B.N. Latin 9994, no. 746 (1143); Paris, A.N., Latin 1009 bis, no. 13.

127. Bernard de Clairvaux, "Epistola CCXLII: Ad Tolosanos, post reditum suum," *Sancti Bernardi Opera VIII* (Rome, 1977), pp. 128–30, which begins, "In adventu carissimi fratris et coabbatis nostri Bertrandi de Grandi Silva." For an English translation, see *The Letters of Saint Bernard of Clairvaux*, trans. Bruno Scott James (London, 1953), no. 318.

128. The earliest charter for Pons and the *ordo* is an undated fragment of a chirograph: Paris, A.N. L 1009, no. 7, in which a certain Galardus gave Pons, abbot of Grandselve, land in the parish of Saint Jorii for five solidi of Morlaas; Grandselve conceded participation and society in all the spiritual benefits of Grandselve and all the *ordo cisterciensis* to the donor, his wife and son, telling them that if they wished to come to the religious life "secundum formam ordinis," they would be received.

129. Despite Bouchard, *Holy Entrepreneurs*, p. 209, Grandselve had ties to Clairvaux before the time of Pons.

130. Fournier, "Alexandre."

131. On the Capdenier family, their documents, and a hospice founded by them in Toulouse for Grandselve, see Mundy, *Liberty in Toulouse*, pp. 62ff., and his Appendix 5 of published documents.

132. Among the earliest dated charters for Grandselve in which William of Montpellier is mentioned is Paris B.N. Latin 9994, fol. 182v (1154); it appears that he had died by 1162; Georges Passerat, "La venue de Saint Bernard à Toulouse et les débuts de l'abbaye de Grandselve," *Bull. de la littérature ecclésiastique* 93 (1992): 27–37; p. 36, cites a vision in which William was informed of Bernard's dying just as it happened.

133. Mireille Mousnier, "L'abbaye cistercienne de Grandselve du XIIe au debut du XIVe siècle," *Cîteaux* 34 (1983): 53–76, 221–44; eadem, "Les granges de l'abbaye cistercienne de Grandselve (XIIe–XIVe siècle)," *Annales du Midi* 95 (1983): 7–28; eadem, "Grandselve et la société de son temps," *Cisterciens de Languedoc CF* 21 (1986): 107–26.

134. Berman, *MA*, passim.

135. Charles Higounet, "Un mémoire sur les péages de la Garonne du début du xive siècle,"*Annales du Midi* 61 (1948–49): 32–45, which is based on Paris, B.N. Latin MS 11010.

136. *Originum*, pp. 81–82. See also Ermelindo Portela Silva, *La colonizacion cisterciense en Galicia (1142–1250)* (Compostela, 1981), esp. p. 23, for a diagrammatic account of Clairvaux's intervention there.

137. See Berman, *MA*, pp. 109–10.

138. Toulouse, A.D. Haute-Garonne, H Grandselve, nos. 5, 7, 8 (all 1150), are gifts for Candeil's foundation; J.-M. Canivez, "Candeil," *DHGE* 11 (1949): 719 and *HGL* 8, cols. 1759, no. 28 (1150), and 886, the last the treaty of Paris in which Raymond of Toulouse is to pay "abbatia Candelii CC marcas ad dicta monasteria construenda."

139. E. Rossignol, "Une charte d'Aliénor, duchesse d'Aquitaine, de l'an 1172," *R. d'Aquitaine et du Languedoc* 5–6 (1861): 224–28. Rossignol misdated the act; it must be for Richard, and thus after 1199.

140. *BC*, no. 251 (1163–66).

141. For urban properties, see Rodez, A.D. Aveyron, H. Bonnecombe, nos. 6 (1222), 7 (1245), etc.

142. *BC*, no. 64 (1178), and below for discussion of Locdieu.

143. Rodez, Société de lettres, MS "Cartulaire d'Iz," nos. 73 (1183), 121 (1194), 158 (1199), reveal that lands ceded to Bonnecombe by those knights had been mortgaged to them by the counts of Rodez for a loan of one thousand solidi, which had been part of the price of their title purchased from the counts of Toulouse.

144. *BC*, no. 51 (1244); *Statuta*, 1226, no. 18: "Abbas de Bonacumba, qui scandalizarit Venerabile in patrem dominum cardinalem Romanum, deferundo ad ipsum litteras Raymundi quondam comitis Tolosani excommunicati, in quibus continebatur quod ibidem Raymundus prohibebat domino cardinali, ne suam terram intraret, et excommunicato communicavit."

145. Rodez, A.D. Aveyron, H. "Cartulaire de Bernac"; Sicard Alaman would also create a house for nuns at Saint-Sulpice west of Albi with the aid of the Cistercian nuns of Nonenque for his daughter; see *NO*, doc. 88 (1267) and discussion in Chapter 4.

146. Paris, B.N. Latin MS 9994, no. 746 (1143).

147. E. Cauvet, *Etude historique sur Fonfroide* [sic] (Montpellier, 1875), hereafter *FF*, pp. 173–79, 226–50.

148. Charles Higounet, "Une carte des relations monastiques transpyrénéennes au Moyen âge," *R. de Comminges* 64 (1951): 129–138; much work on this issue remains to be done.

149. Moreau, *AO*, pp. 56, 209–12. The community at Montsérat may have become a community of monks by 1176, but that at les Monges survived as an independent abbey for women in the Order until the Revolution (see Desmarchelier, p. 81). It is probably les Monges that is referred to in *Statuta*, 1249, no. 24, "Inspectio domus monialium Sanctae Maria de Olivis pro quia incorporanda ordini scribit dominus Papa, de Vallemagna et de Villalonga abbatibus committitur, ut ad locum praesentialiter accedant etc., et sit filia Fontisfrigidi."

150. *FF*, pp. 227ff.

151. Montlaurès had apparently been founded as the result of a gift to the abbey of

Saint-Michel-de-la-Cluse in 1044 from Berengar, viscount of Narbonne, Garsinde his wife, and their three sons, Raymond, Peter, and Bernard; in 1211, in an act confirmed by Arnaud Amalric, abbot of Cîteaux and papal legate, it was sold to Fontfroide for 2000 solidi of Melgueil; *FF*, p. 234.

152. *FF*, pp. 333–34.

153. Gaussin, "Communautés," p. 308; Desmarchelier, p. 97.

154. Moreau, *AO*, pp. 209–12, and photographs that show simple ribbed vaults; I was not able to see the vaults in 1993 because of rotting floor boards in that loft. The neighbor reported that his adjoining farm had once been inhabited by the priests who served this community of women but that there survive no visible vestiges of the occupation on his property.

155. *FF*, pp. 173–79, 226–50; my interpretation differs slightly.

156. Cf. Remensnyder, *Remembering*, with regard to la Grasse.

157. *FF*, pp. 201–22.

158. James S. Donnelly, *The Decline of the Medieval Cistercian Laybrotherhood* (New York, 1949); revolts at Fontfroide are documented in *Statuta*, 1190, no. 75; 1212, no. 52; 1213, no. 9.

159. François Grèzes-Rueff, "L'abbaye de Fontfroide et son domaine foncier au XIIe–XIIIe siècles," *Annales du Midi* 89 (1977): 253–80, esp. pp. 268–70; Carcassonne, A.D. Aude, H211, "Inventaire de Fontfroide," fol. 16 (1217), for a gift by Simon de Montfort.

160. See Wakefield, *Heresy*, p. 92, for the murder of Peter of Castelnau in 1208.

161. McCrank, "Cistercians," passim.

162. Berman, "Origins," 256–77, where I suggested that an abbot of Morimond, named Walter, made a trip to the Midi paralleling that of Bernard of Clairvaux, but a tour by Walter II in the 1160s or 1170s is more likely.

163. The list of abbots for Morimond found in Louis Dubois, *Histoire de l'Abbaye de Morimond* (Paris, 1851) is confused; these are reproduced with corrections by Bouchard, *Holy Entrepreneurs*, pp. 217–19.

164. Only in the *Carta Caritatis Posterior* does he appear.

165. Auberger, *L'unanimité*, pp. 163ff., suggests the early poverty of Morimond and its overshadowing by Clairvaux; Bouchard, *Holy Entrepreneurs*, esp. p. 133, also suggests peculiarities in its surviving records—almost half involve quarrels with the sons, grandsons, and sons-in-law of donors, most from the 1170s and 1180s.

166. *BD*, no. 92.

167. *BD*, no. 350.

168. *BD*, 125 (1142?); the last included a grant of pasture rights to Berdoues made by Bernard, count of Astarac and all the knights of Astarac by acclaim; a confirmation of that concession by heirs of them is found in *BD*, no. 269 (1157).

169. Anselme Dimier, "L'Escaledieu," *DHGE* 15 (1963): 844; Gratien Leblanc, "La répartition géographique des abbayes cisterciennes du sud-ouest de la France," *France méridionale et pays ibériques: mélanges géographiques offerts en hommage à M. Daniel Faucher* (Toulouse, 1949), vol. 2, pp. 584–608; p. 585 cites *Bull. monumental* 92 (1933) and Marbotin, pp. 59–60. See also *Originum*, pp. 47–48; *Gallia Christiana in provincias ecclesiasticas distributa*, ed. P. Piolin, 13 vols. (Paris, 1870–78), vol. 1, col. 1260.

170. *Recueil des actes de l'abbaye cistercienne de Bonnefont-en-Comminges*, ed. Ch. Samaran and Ch. Higounet (Paris, 1970), p. 19.

171. *BF*, nos. 1, 2.
172. *GM* II, no. 13 (c. 1160).
173. *BF*, nos. 1, 2, are accounts from much later.
174. Much work on trans-Pyrenean connections remains to be done.
175. For instance, Flaran and Bouillas; see *Statuta*, 1204, no. 37.
176. Anselme Dimier, "Eaunes," *DHGE* 15 (1963): 263–64.

177. Documents from 1155, 1157, and 1158 record gifts made to the first abbot, William, by Forton del Tilh, of the woods called "Artigaberd"; this suggests a recently-cleared site. Land at le Tillet was acquired for building a grange. That donor also confirmed concessions made to Flaran by his dependents in those places; see *Originum*, p. 126, and P. Benouville and P. Lauzun, "L'abbaye de Flaran," *R. de Gascogne* 28 (1887): 575–81; 29 (1888): 291–302, 504–18; 30 (1889): 115–21, 221–33, 401–24; in 29 (1888): 511–13 the authors report a tradition regarding Berdoues as founder; in 30 (1889): 115–21 they concluded that it should be attributed to l'Escaledieu.

178. Paris, B.N. Latin MS 12752, fol. 566, mentions the 1160s, as does *Originum*, p. 121; Charles Bourgeat, *L'abbaye de Bouillas: histoire d'une ancienne abbaye cistercienne de diocèse d'Auch* (Auch, 1954), p. 150, says that the eventual filiation was with l'Escaledieu.

179. *Originum*, p. 184.
180. Gimont's foundation charter, *GM* I, no. 1, is discussed in Chapter 4.
181. See *Statuta*, 1134, the so-called "prima collectio."

182. Affiliation of Campagnes to Cistercians from 1150 is based on mis-transcriptions of dates by Doat copyists. On correct dating of the charters for Villelongue in the Doat collection, see Berman, "Origins"; my suggestions have been incorporated by Benoît Chauvin, "Quelques additions et corrections au *Recueil des actes de l'abbaye cistercienne de Bonnefont-en-Comminges* tirées des archives de l'abbaye de Villelongue (Aude), 1149–1168," *Annales du Midi* 103 (1991): 77–94. Affiliation with Bonnefont considerably predates Villelongue's site and name change. Contracts from July 1150 for Campagnes already mention Bonnefont; see Doat 70, fols. 20, 24, 26, charters for Arnold, prior "of that place" [probably Bonnefont]. See *Cartulaire et archives de l'ancien diocèse et de l'arrondissement administratif de Carcassonne*, ed. M. Mahul, 6 vols. (Paris: 1857–82), vol. 4, p. 23, publishes part of a charter from Doat 70, fol. 28, "Hoc donum factum fuit solum modo pro amore Dei et S. Mariae in manu Servati abbatis Bonifontis et Arnaldi prioris et pro participatione orationis et beneficiorum ordinis cisterciensis . . . ," dated to 1150, but possibly slightly later given some of its terminology such as "pro amore Dei," which appears only at the end of the century, for instance, in Gimont and Berdoues charters. But a date of 1150 is not problematic, unless we read the reference to *ordo cisterciensis* here, as indicating affiliation of Campagnes and Bonnefont to an administrative Order that had not yet appeared.

183. Mahul, *Carcassonne*, vol. 5, p. 22, documents from Doat 70 for Rieunette; Regine became the first prioress.

184. Doat 70, fols. 149, 159 (1244).

185. Doat 83, nos. 10 (1154), 11 (1156), 16 (1159), 17 (1160) are for the priory of Vajal, not for Boulbonne. Doat 83, no. 80, which concerns disposition of Augerius of Calmont's property must be dated to circa 1163 (despite the date 1183). Doat 83, no. 18 (1161) records Augerius of Calmont as a layman making a gift to Vajal with his brother Do. Doat 83, no. 30 (1165) records him as a novice of Boulbonne; see Berman,

MA, pp. 63ff; cf. Roger Armengaud, "Boulbonne, une abbaye aux frontières des comtés de Foix et du Languedoc (1130–1790)," *Bull. Société des études du Comminges* 97 (1984): 193–212; Jean Bayle, "L'abbaye de Boulbonne et la croisade des albigeois," *Pyrénées ariégeoises* (1983): 83–91, has construed that incorrect dating to prove that there were two men named Augerius de Calmont—that is to make too much of a common transcription error in certain Doat volumes, particularly those from the western parts of the region covered by the commission.

186. C. Cathala, "Boulbonne," *DHGE* 10 (1938): 60–70, and Doat 83, nos. 26 (1163), 96 (1188), 101 (1192), 130 (1200), 136 (1203), 137 (1209), 176 (1274) for the family of Foix.

187. Founded circa 1120 by reformers associated with Gerald of Salles; see Casimir Barrière-Flavy, *L'abbaye de Vajal dans l'ancienne comté de Foix* (Toulouse, n.d.), and Doat 83, nos. 120 (1196), 102 (1193), 105 (1195), 100 (1225).

188. Doat 83, nos. 1 (962), 138–41 (all 1209), 167 (1227), 527 (1232); *Originum*, p. 123; Cathala, "Boulbonne," cols. 67–70.

189. A house of nuns at Marrencs [sic] was founded by the counts of Toulouse in 1159; it would be suppressed in 1450 by Boulbonne. See J.-M. Canivez, "Beaulieu-à-Mirepoix," *DHGE* 7 (1134): 162–63; Gaussin, "Communautés," p. 322; Cottineau, *Répertoire*, 1745, 2932, 3289; *Atlas*, 286, 300; Cathala, "Boulbonne," p. 70; Doat 83, fol. 36r (1219); Doat 86, fols. 261, 273, 317; Casimir Barrière-Flavy, *Histoire de la Ville et de la Chatellenie de Saverdun, dans l'ancien Comté de Foix avec de nombreuses pièces justificatives et des plans* (Toulouse, n.d.).

190. Valnègre apparently sent nuns to found Beaulieu-en-Mirepoix about 1295. The latter then sent nuns to Salenques in the diocese of Rieux in 1353 (this may have been a site change). Beaulieu's community was formally suppressed in 1370 and its property divided between Boulbonne and the bishop and chapter of Mirepoix. In 1432, Valnègre was united with Boulbonne and the nuns were suppressed.

191. Aiguebelle may have been associated with an earlier Cluniac priory at Montjoyer; see J. Sautel, "Aiguebelle," *DHGE* 1 (1912): 1122–31. *Chartes et documents de l'abbaye de Notre-Dame d'Aiguebelle*, 2 vols. (Paris, 1954 and Lyon, 1969), vol. 1, no. 4 gives the text from a stone inscription, "VI Kal. iulii anno ab incarn. MCXXXVII dedit Gontardus Lupis Dominus de Rochefortis locum istum abbatie Morimundi ad abbatiam ibidem construendam in honorem beate Marie," but such a stone could have been carved at any time; cf. nos. 1, 7, 9. Aiguebelle is once more a Cistercian house today; Jean-François Holthof, "Cîteaux, XIIe–XXe siècle," *Saint Bernard et le monde cistercien*, ed. Léon Pressouyre (Paris, 1990), p. 184.

192. Nîmes, A.D. Gard, H series, has about 50 documents from the twelfth century for Franquevaux but none for its foundation. Many of the documents that do survive are recorded in an inventory of 1687 for properties in the diocese of Mende (department of the Lozère); see J. Baroot, "Les possessions territoriales de l'abbaye de Franquevaux dans le diocèse de Mende," *Bull. Société des lettres de la Lozère* 2 (1915–16): 47–72.

193. Canivez, "Cadouin," pp. 118–22; whatever early ties there were, Cadouin did not become firmly attached to the Cistercian Order before 1175 and yet was successful in claiming an early date for itself on the Order's filiation tables; see *Le cartulaire de l'abbaye de Cadouin, précédé de notes sur l'histoire économique du Perigord méridional à l'époque féodale*, ed. J.-M. Maubourguet (Cahors, 1926), p. ix, and *Originum*, pp. 7–8.

194. Golding, *Gilbert* traces these ideas into the *Vita Prima* of Bernard, etc.; see pp. 22ff.
195. Hill, *English Cistercian*, pp. 80ff.
196. Van Damme, "Constitution 1165," pp. 64–65.
197. See pp. 40ff. Golding, *Gilbert*, pp. 7ff., 27, 40–42, discusses the medieval life of Gilbert, called *The Book of Saint Gilbert*, ed. Raymonde Foreville and Gillian Keir (Oxford, 1987), which was written shortly after October 13, 1202. One wonders if the request for affiliation with a stricter group is not a trope in monastic hagiography; see discussion of Silvanès and Obazine above.
198. A narrative written after the death of Eugenius III is included as a document for 1147 in *CI*, no. 131 (1147), and in *Statuta*, vol. 1, under the year 1147; these are both later accounts. On the *Vita Prima*'s evidence, see Bredero, *Bernard*, pp. 43ff.
199. *Regesta*, ed. Jaffé, II, 9132, 9133 (false), 9134, 9135, 9136, 9137, 9138, are the seven bulls of Eugenius III dated to Cîteaux, 1147. One is well recognized as false, but they are probably all false, as is suggested by the fact that none are for Cistercian houses; *Regesta*, ed. Jaffé, II, 9139, dated at Sequanum (Barbeaux) several days later was issued for Savigny; see *PL* 180, col. 1282.
200. Golding, *Gilbert*, pp. 26ff. finds no evidence earlier than the *Vita Prima* of Bernard.
201. Marjorie Chibnall, *Anglo-Norman England: 1066–1166* (Oxford, 1986), p. 204, points out the significance of 1164 in the Becket dispute when "matters came to a head at the Council of Clarendon in January, 1164." Becket soon fled to Pontigny. One of the reasons for deposing Geoffrey of Auxerre from Clairvaux was his opposition to sheltering Becket; see Bredero, *Bernard*, pp. 49ff.
202. Golding, *Gilbert*, pp. 38ff.
203. *Cartulaire d'Obazine*, document 26 (1159–84) (and notes 5 and 6 on p. 76), mentions Cîteaux; it concerns land given by Archambald, viscount of Comborn, that he had previously given to the monastery of le Landais for the foundation of an abbey at Sourden. It tells us that the abbot of Sourden had returned to le Landais because of the poverty of the newly attempted foundation; land had thus reverted first to him and then to Obazine, "sicuti mos est Cisterciensis ordinis." The *Cartulaire d'Obazine*'s document 532 (1148–49), which the cartulary dates to 1148, was a gift of two *mansi* made to Stephen of Obazine by Aymeric of Gourdon with Boso and Ebles, the viscounts of Brassac. Witnesses listed were Raynaldus, abbot of Cîteaux; Bernard, abbot of la Cour-Dieu; William, abbot of Belleaigue; and John, abbot of Bonnaigue, all Cistercian monasteries. The problem is that while Raynaldus, abbot of Cîteaux, died in 1150 or 1151, Bonnaigue's foundation was in 1157 (see Jean-Loup Lemaître, *Bonnaigue: une abbaye cistercienne au pays d'Ussel* [Abbeville, 1993], pp. 61–62).
204. *CI*, no. 175 (1165).
205. The text of this document states:

> Assistentibus itaque in presentia nostra magistro Gileberto de Sempingham et tam canonicis quam conversis sui ordinis, conquesti sunt conversi quod magister G. compulit eos novam facere professionem abbatie de Sabaneia et juramenta prestare contra primam professionem quam dudum fecerant venerabili domui de Sempingham secundum formam ordinis Cistercie professione unquam ei fecerant, nec illi professioni quam primo apud Sempingham postea apud Sabaneiam coacti fecerant professionem contrariam sed nec aliquam.

See Raymonde Foreville, *Un procès de canonisation à l'aube du XIIIe siècle (1201–1202)* (Paris, 1943), p. x, n. 1, who cites *Statuta*, p. 37 (but Canivez at this point depends on A. Manrique, *Cisterciensium seu verius ecclesiasticorum annalium a condito Cistercio tomi IX* [Lyons, 1642–59]). This event of 1147 is more often treated simply as common knowledge; see Lawrence, *Medieval Monasticism*, pp. 156, 199, and Lekai, *Cistercians*, p. 49. Foreville, *Procès*, pp. 82ff., suggests that Alexander III insisted on well-established "institutes" for all new reform houses.

206. The account printed in Canivez is from Manrique's history, which cites the *Vita Prima* of Bernard of Clairvaux written by Geoffrey of Auxerre:

Instabat tempus capituli generalis. Igitur (ait Godefridus, qui praesens fuit) eodem anno apud Cistercium iuxta morem, abbatibus congregatis, praedictus papa venerabilis adfuit.

207. Golding, *Gilbert*, pp. 84ff.; on p. 84, with regard to a purported visit of bishop Alexander of Lincoln to the Cistercians, he states that the failure of contemporary chroniclers to mention this "is not conspiracy of silence, but rather due to the fact that there was nothing to report."

208. Giles Constable, "Aelred of Rievaulx and the Nun of Watton," *Medieval Women*, ed. Derek Baker (Oxford, 1983), pp. 205–26; it seems significant that the account of the nun of Watton is found in Cambridge, Corpus Christi College MS 139, fols. 149–51; this manuscript, probably from Durham, contains other materials concerning the foundation of Fountains, such as the letter by the archbishop Thurstan.

209. *Recueil des actes de Henri II, roi d'angleterre et duc de Normandie concernant les provinces françaises et les affaires de France*, ed. Léopold Delisle (Paris, 1909), 1: 26–27, no. 20, a charter for Savigny of November 1151; I owe this reference to Patrick Conyers.

210. See *Regesta Regum* AN, vol. 3, nos. 800–813. Confusion is also caused by a reference for Savigny found in the *GC*, vol. 2, col. 545: "Tam Savigneium, quam cetera omnia ad illud pertinentia monasteria, ordini cisterciensi contradicit et subjecit in manibus sancti Bernardi abbatis clarevallensis." This reference seems to suggest that Savigny was incorporated by Clairvaux rather than by the Cistercians. See Hill, *English Cistercian*, pp. 104–5, n. 67.

211. Janet Burton, "The Settlement of Disputes Between Byland Abbey and Newburgh Priory," *Yorkshire Archaeological Journal* 55 (1983): 67–72.

212. In my view Aelred of Rievaulx had an unfortunate tendency to pass on scandal that reflected badly on houses that were rivals to his own; cf. Constable, *Nun of Watton*; Burton, "The Abbeys of Byland," passim.

213. *GC*, vol. 11, cols. 542ff. Alexander as seventh abbot of Savigny is described as "Alexander ex monacho Clarevallensi abbas Grandissilvae de consilio Clarevallensis abbatis Fastredi a monachis Saviniacensibus electus abbas."

214. On Serlo, the standard account is Jacqueline Buhot, "L'abbaye normande de Savigny, chef d'ordre et fille de Cîteaux," *Le Moyen Age* 46 (1936): 1–19, 104–21, 178–90, 249–72, esp. pp. 178ff., which discusses Serlo's attempts to retire to Clairvaux starting in 1152, Bernard's refusal to let him do so, and then Serlo's actual retirement there in 1158 when Alexander of Cologne went from being abbot of Grandselve to being abbot of Savigny (see n. 213). The standard assumption has been that Savigny's

incorporation by the Cistercians had already taken place in 1147, but it turns out that there is no evidence for incorporation of Savigny until a decade later.

215. Pacaut, "La filiation claravallienne," passim.

216. Constable, *Reformation*, pp. 155, 308.

217. Paris, B.N. Latin 9994, passim.

218. See forthcoming work by Patrick Conyers, who has chosen the issue of Savigny's pre-Cistercian history for a doctoral dissertation.

219. In Britain, claims were being made against the Fountains tithe-exemption, Aelred of Rievaulx was composing letters to friends about the lay-sister at Watton, and Gilbertine lay-brothers had revolted, claiming subjection to increasingly onerous customs. Burton, *Monastic and Religious Orders*, passim. In France, Grandmontine monks rebelled against the lay-brothers who had control of their purse, and Praemonstratensians increasingly refused to provide religious care to women. Increasingly Cistercians were being attacked by the satirists for their wealth. Maire Wilkinson, "Laïcs et convers de l'Ordre de Grandmont au XIIe siècle; la création et la destruction d'une fraternité," *Les mouvances laïques des ordres religieux*, ed. Nicole Bouter, pp. 35–50 (Saint-Etienne, 1996). The deposition of Geoffrey of Auxerre from abbacy of Clairvaux in 1165 (because of his reprehensible life, as one source says, or because of the reprehensible telling of the *Vita Prima*, which had been unsuccessful in the first bids for Bernard's canonization in the early 1160s, or because of his attack on Pontigny's sheltering of Thomas Becket) suggests some of the internal turmoil in these years when Clairvaux's supremacy was gradually being replaced by the notion of an Order. Bredero, *Bernard*, pp. 49ff.

220. Alexander III refused to take up the issue of canonization of Bernard at the Council of Tours in 1160. Before the canonization took place in 1174, it was necessary to rewrite the *Vita Prima*; see Bredero, *Bernard*, pp. 49ff.

221. Newman, *Boundaries*, p. 215, following Martin Preiss, *Die politische Tatigkeit und Stellung der Cisterzienser im Schisma von 1159–1177*, Historische Studien 248 (Berlin, 1934), p. 79.

222. See Ludo Milis, *L'ordre des chanoines réguliers d'Arrouaise: son histoire et son organisation de la fondation de l'abbaye-mère (vers 1090) à la fin des chapitres annuels (1471)*, 2 vols. (Bruges, 1969); or Foreville, *Un procès*.

223. These efforts must have lent credence to assumptions among writers of texts in that period that an early unanimity had existed. Mahn, *L'ordre cistercien*, p. 111, n. 1, cites Mansi, *Concilium*, vol. 22, col. 329, 3rd Council of Lateran, 1179, part 13, col. 6, as an exhortation to Cistercians to not extend their tithe privileges to lands rented out. On ownership of churches, see *Conciliorum oecumenicorum decreta*, p. 194, item 13.

224. Berman, "Cisterciens et le tournant économique," passim; Jean-Baptiste Auberger, "Les cisterciens à l'époque de Saint Bernard," *Bernardo Cistercense* (Spoleto, 1990), 20–43, esp. pp. 32ff.; see also *CI*, nos. 24ff.

225. Newman, *Boundaries*, Table 1, p. 250, gives evidence that despite *Statuta*, 1134, no. 61, the fact of monks becoming bishops was not yet an issue in 1134 when only one Cistercian had become a bishop.

226. Bredero, *Bernard*, pp. 43ff.

227. See Canivez, *Primo Collectio*, vol. 1 (1134).

228. See *De miraculis* of Herman of Tournai, *PL* 156: 962–1018, for references to following Clairvaux, not Cîteaux, circa 1150.

229. Bouchard, *Sword, Miter*, pp. 407–9; Newman, *Boundaries*, pp. 250–53.

230. Fournier, "Alexandre."

231. The usual interpretation is that Pons de Polignac, abbot of Clairvaux (1165–70), was removed from leadership of Clairvaux by having him made bishop of Clermont, possibly because he was too aggressive on behalf of Clairvaux and Bernard's canonization; see Bredero, *Bernard*, pp. 53–56.

232. Yves Congar, "Henri de Marcy, abbé de Clairvaux, cardinal-évêque d'Albano et légat pontifical," *Analecta Anselmiana* 43 (1959): 1–90; Angleton, "Two Cistercian Preaching Missions."

233. Thus these abbots, and possibly abbesses as well, along with supporters like William VI of Montpellier, who were converting to the Cistercian life after careers in the secular world, began the process of creating the Cistercian Order. In so doing they invented the notion of a religious order as well.

234. Griesser, "Beitrage . . . 1711."

235. Montpellier, H322 is discussed above in Chapter 2.

236. See London, British Museum, Additional MS 18148, and Metz, Bibliothèque publique, MS 1247, which both include such comments in paragraphs preceding the lay-brother customaries.

237. Local tithe privileges document grange cultivation for the late 1140s at Silvanès, 1160s at Berdoues and Grandselve, 1170s at Bonnecombe and Nonenque, 1180s at Bonneval, 1190s or earlier at Candeil, and 1200s at Bonnefont. Moreover, almost all the Order's land acquisitions and other acquisitions of endowment—at least for its men's houses—were done between 1153 and 1215; see Berman, *MA*, passim.

238. *Statuta*, 1180ff., and see *CI*, no. 244, 1180 bull of Alexander III.

239. *Statuta*, 1188, no. 8.

240. In addition to Pons of Léras mentioned above, see the discussion of the Juliac family in Chapter 4. Monks helped harvest olives for Grandselve; see Paris, B.N. Latin 9994, fol. 224v.

241. See Berman, "Monastic Hospices," forthcoming.

242. Paris, B.N. Latin 9994, fol. 225r (1161).

243. The account is in part from *GC* 1: cols. 263–64, which mentions 20,000 solidi changing hands; see Berman, *MA*, pp. 112–13.

244. Locdieu only gained back its independence in 1217 or 1218 and never regained its granges; see Berman, *MA*, pp. 112ff.

245. The archives surviving for both Locdieu and Bonneval are fragmentary; much of what is preserved is in the Order of Malta collection in Toulouse from which *Les plus anciennes chartes* by Brunel drew heavily. This dividing up of pastoral areas is seen as well for Calers and Boulbonne in the Ariège; see Berman, *MA*, pp. 109ff.

246. *Statuta*, 1212, no. 54; 1214, no. 62.

247. *BC*, no. 64 (1178); see also *Cartulaire de la Chartreuse de Bonnefoy*, ed. Jean-Loup Lemaître (Paris, 1990), nos. 19, 135 for Mazan's conflicts with Bonnefoy over pasture.

248. See Lekai, *The Cistercians*, pp. 49–50; *Statuta*, vol. 8 indices, for instance, pp. 87ff., for such complaints. In the right column on p. 91 there appear ten "impossibilitas veniendi ad Capitulum propter guerras"; 1197, no. 34; 1215, no. 19; 1269, no. 12; 1274, no. 43; 1340, no. 7; etc. On exemptions from annual attendance for Irish houses, see *Statuta* 1190, no. 17, "Abbates de Hibernia tribus annis remaneant et quarto anno veniant. . . ."

249. *CI*, no. 234 (1179), for count Henry's twenty *librae* from bridge tolls, "ad procurandos abbates qui generali capitulo cisterciensi interfuerunt"; on Richard's gift, see Lekai, *Cistercians*, p. 75.
250. See discussion of William VI in Chapter 4, pp. 210–11.
251. Giles Constable, "Cluniac Tithes and the Controversy Between Gigny and le Miroir," *R. bénédictine* 70 (1960): 591–624, esp. p. 609, where the dispute is seen as occurring in two phases, possibly because of the assumption that a general tithe concession to the entire Order had been made already in 1132. The letter mentioned on p. 610 from Peter the Venerable to a group of Cistercian abbots "in Christi nomine congregatis" is not yet addressed to a formal General Chapter.
252. Bernhard Schimmelpfennig, *The Papacy*, trans. James Sievert (New York, 1992), pp. 151–69, esp. p. 160, gives considerable information on bureaucratic growth at the time of Alexander III; so does Ian Stuart Robinson, *The Papacy, 1073–1198: Continuity and Imagination* (Cambridge, 1990); Hill, *English Cistercian*, p. 113, which documents recourse to Rome in the dispute of 1157–60 between the abbot of Meaux and the Austin canons of Merton priory, as well as appeals to Alexander III before 1170 by Cistercian abbots in Lincolnshire and by the abbey of Rufford in 1179.
253. *GM*, III, nos. 50, 66 (circa 1158, 1163).
254. *SL*, no. 38 (1161).
255. "VM," I, fol. 57r (1171).
256. Doat 76, no. 40 (1174).
257. Doat 83, no. 99 (1191); *Statuta*, 1194, no. 14.
258. *Statuta*, 1194, no. 35.
259. *Statuta*, 1197, no. 27.
260. *Statuta*, 1204, no. 28; 1212, no. 54.
261. Golding, *Gilbert*, pp. 280–81, citing *Cartularium Abbathiae de Rievalle*, pp. 181–83; this may be the event that the abbot of Clairvaux, Geoffrey of Auxerre, attended.
262. See Vauluisant charter quoted in Chapter 2, n. 101.
263. Mahn, *L'ordre cistercien*, pp. 119ff.
264. See discussion above for Cadouin, pp. 143ff.
265. *BF*, intro., p. 32, and no. 23 (1165).
266. *CI*, no. 175 (1165).
267. Gold, *The Lady and the Virgin*, pp. 80–81, proposes a model from Max Weber's *The Sociology of Religion*, ed. Talcott Parsons (Boston, 1963); she thought her model not applicable to Cistercian nuns, but it is.

Chapter 4

1. See Joan Wardrop, *Fountains Abbey and Its Benefactors, 1132–1300* (Kalamazoo, Mich., 1987); Bouchard, *Holy Entrepreneurs*, and Bouchard, *Sword, Miter; Rufford Charters*, vol. 1, ed. C. J. Holdsworth (Nottingham, 1972); Sally Thompson, *Women Religious: The Founding of English Nunneries After the Norman Conquest* (Oxford, 1991).
2. Montpellier, A.D. Hérault, microfilm "Cartulaire de Valmagne," hereafter "VM" II, fol. 12v (1185). The cartulary is privately owned, but a microfilm was made available in 1979 under limited conditions—consultation restricted to the departmental archives, no copies to be made, etc. A grant from the American Philosophical

Society's Penrose Fund allowed me to spend nearly six weeks in summer 1981 reading and taking notes on that microfilm; I thank both the APS and archives personnel. Materials in this chapter draw on notes taken at that time.

3. Rodez, Société des lettres, sciences et arts de l'Aveyron, MS "Cartulaire de Moncan," no. 160 (1228), or Rodez, Société des lettres, MS "Cartulaire de Magrin," no. 84 (1194), or gifts by Austorga of tithes in Rodez, Société des lettres, MS "Cartulaire d'Iz et Bougaunes," no. 87 (1193).

4. "VM" I, fols. 45r (undated), 52r (1191).

5. "VM" II, fol. 10v (1191).

6. See Alamanda's gift, "Si filios legitimos habuerit unus post alium in predicta domo Berdonarum si ad ordinem venire voluerint pro fratribus debent recipi," *BD*, no. 455 (1210); that of Amada "pro hoc predicto dono Gillelmus Gassias frater eorum qui vocatur Parrabere fuit receptus pro converso in domo Berdonarum," *BD*, no. 204 (1182); or that of a certain Martha "Et pro hoc predicto dono Vitalis predicte Marthe filius fuit receptus pro converso in domo Berdonarum," *BD*, no. 25 (undated). See also Raphaela Averkorn, "Die Cistercienserabteien Berdoues und Gimont in ihren Beziehungen zum laikalen Umfeld: Gebetsgedenken, Konversion und Begräbnis," *Vinculum Societatis: Joachim Wollasch zum 60. Gebertstag*, ed. Franz Neiske, Dietrich Poeck, and Mechthild Sandmann (Sigmaringen, 1991); she describes burial of women at Berdoues on pp. 17-18.

7. On the countesses of Foix and Carcassonne, see Wakefield, *Heresy*, pp. 65-81, 83ff.; cf. Richard Abels and Ellen Harrison, "The Participation of Women in Languedocian Catharism," *Mediaeval Studies* 41 (1979): 215-51, who suggest that women's participation in heresy has been exaggerated.

8. *BD*, no. 564 (1174), "Marfavius pro converso et Johanna, mater ejus, pro sorore spirituali recepti sunt in domo Berdonarum."

9. *BF*, no. 90 (1168).

10. *SL*, no. 396 (1152); she was associated with the virtual refoundation of Fontfroide, as reported in Cauvet, *FF*, pp. 231-39. On Grandselve, see *LIM*, no. 186 (1162).

11. "VM" I, fol. 30r (1183).

12. Cf. David J. Herlihy, "Land, Family, and Women in Continental Europe, 701-1200,"*Traditio* 1 (1962): 89-120.

Paris, B.N. Latin MS 11008, nos. 65 (1164), 145 (1174); these contracts are also found in Paris, B.N. Latin MS 9994.

13. This was legitimate; see Dyan Elliott, *Spiritual Marriage: Sexual Abstinence in Medieval Wedlock* (Princeton, N.J., 1993), pp. 67ff.

14. On diet, see Georges Duby, *The Early Growth of the European Economy: Warriors and Peasants from the Seventh to the Twelfth Century* (Ithaca, N.Y., 1973,) esp. pp. 17-25; Christopher Dyer, *Standards of Living in the Late Middle Ages: Social Change in England c. 1200-1520* (Cambridge, 1989); Barbara Harvey, *Living and Dying in England, 1100-1540: The Monastic Experience* (Oxford, 1993).

15. Ljubljana (Laibach) MS 32, a collection of Cistercian customs later than MS 31.

16. On the formal characteristics of such acts see Guyotjeannin et al., *Diplomatique médiévale*, esp. pp. 115ff.; Robert Delort, *Introduction aux sciences auxiliaires de l'histoire* (Paris, 1969); *Les cartulaires*, esp. Afterword by Parisse; G. R. C. Davis, *Medieval*

Cartularies of Great Britain: A Short Catalogue (London, 1958), and Henri Stein, *Bibliographie générale des cartulaires français* (Paris, 1907 and suppl.).

17. Mireille Castaing-Sicard, *Les contrats dans le très ancien droit toulousain (Xe–XIIIe siècle)* (Toulouse, 1957).

18. Dominique Iogna-Prat, "La confection des cartulaires et l'historiographie à Cluny (XIe–XIIe siècles)," *Les cartulaires*, pp. 27–44; Patrick Geary, *Phantoms of Remembrance: Memory and Oblivion at the End of the First Millennium* (Princeton, N.J., 1994).

19. "VM" II, fol. 49v (1191).

20. "VM" II, fol. 36v (1193).

21. *Statuta*, 1188, no. 8. *Nobiles laici venientes non fiant conversi sed monachi.*

22. Paris, B.N. Latin MS 9994, fols. 224vff., and below.

23. On lay-brother-treatises, see above, Chapter 3, p. 153.

24. Remensnyder, *Remembering*; Thomas A. Waldman, "Abbot Suger and the Nuns of Argenteuil," *Traditio* 41 (1985): 239–71.

25. On damage from fire at Bonneval in 1719, see *BV*, p. ix.

26. Denifle, no. 556, p. 250.

27. Paul Ourliac, *Les pays de Garonne vers l'an mil: la société et le droit* (Toulouse, 1993); cartularies may sometimes have served as originals in cases such as at Bonnecombe, where they were made and kept at granges. Those copies (although in charter books) apparently constituted the notes from which a more formal and ornate "original" would be made. If this is so, they resemble notarial cartularies.

28. Guyotjeannin et al., *Diplomatique médiévale*, pp. 50ff.; Castaing-Sicard, *Les contrats*, pp. 476–89; *BF*, p. 18, or *Les cartulaires des Templiers de Douzens*, ed. Pierre Gérard et al. (Paris, 1965), intro., pp. xvii–xviii.

29. While it may be argued that the cartularies were made by Cistercian houses to aid in property acquisitions, the redaction of Cistercian cartularies in fact occurred at the moment when individual houses had ceased or were ending their large-scale land acquisitions. The Gimont cartulary can be dated to circa 1200, Berdoues's to no earlier than the 1260s, and Valmagne's to the 1230s, though its first volume may have been done as early as 1210 or so. Although we can still argue that the placement of charters within cartularies reflects an abbey's estate administration at the point of its greatest expansion, the impetus for cartulary compilation lies elsewhere than in the acquisition process, perhaps in growing notions that documents constituted legal proof or because of disruption of property rights caused by the Albigensian Crusade.

30. *FE*, ed. Duby, describes pancartes in the introduction; see also *CL*, pp. 8ff.

31. Guyotjeannin et al., *Diplomatique médiévale*, pp. 105ff., 115ff., 223ff.

32. *SL*, no. 22 (circa 1140). For my purposes here, the distinctions in currencies are not important, but the solidi discussed in this chapter for Gascony are those of Morlaas; elsewhere they are those of Melgueil.

33. *SL*, no. 32 (n.d.).

34. See Berman, *MA*, pp. 137ff., where I attempted to tabulate onerous versus non-onerous charters rather than categorize them as one type of conveyance.

35. But see Berman, "Labors of Hercules," which describes a cartulary used as a dossier for the suppression of nuns.

36. See Rosenwein, *Neighbor*, pp. 49ff., 202–7, for this and later references to Cluny in this chapter.

37. Clanchy, *Memory*, pp. 234ff., suggests that in England many landowners had developed enough Latin by circa 1250 to manage to read charters. See also Emily Z. Tabuteau, *Transfers of Property in Eleventh-Century Norman Law* (Chapel Hill, N.C., 1988), pp. 211–22; Castaing-Sicard, *Contrats*, passim; and Marjorie Chibnall, "'Clio's Legal Cosmetics': Law and Custom in the Work of Medieval Historians," *Anglo-Norman Studies* 20 (1997): 31–43.

38. Clanchy, *Memory*, passim; no similar study exists for all of France, but see Castaing-Sicard, *Les contrats*, passim, and Tabuteau, *Transfers*, pp. 211–22. The earliest Cistercian evidence for sealing comes from cases in which the princes of the region or of the Church were involved; see contracts for 1179 and 1180, sealed by Bernard-Aton VI and his mother, Guillelma of Montpellier, in "VM" I, fols. 100r (1179), 100v (1180), or the chirograph sealed by the abbot of Cîteaux for the foundation of a hospice for Franquevaux in Nîmes, A.D. Gard, H 74 and H 76 (1215).

39. Stephen D. White, *Custom, Kinship, and Gifts to Saints: The "Laudatio Parentum" in Western France, 1050–1150* (Chapel Hill, N.C., 1988).

40. Among the largest purchases except on the Languedoc coast is one involving sixty *librae* (1200 solidi) paid to Aicelina, widow of Raymond Talairan, and her sons and daughters for land near Saint-Hilaire in the vicinity of Bonnecombe's grange of Vareilles, *BC*, no. 299B (1225); this was only exceeded by purchases for Valmagne's grange of Vairac, discussed below. The Grandselve cartularies reveal women like the widow Sasena who lived by the gradual alienation of properties by mortgage or sale to the monks; see Paris, B.N. Latin MS 11011, fol. 171r (1182), etc.

41. Megan McLaughlin, *Consorting with Saints: Prayers for the Dead in Early Medieval France* (Ithaca, N.Y., 1994).

42. Guy Guerrier, son of William VI of Montpellier, conveyed mills on the Hérault River to Valmagne for his soul and that of his brother William of Tortosa; see *LIM*, no. 97 (1177), and "VM" I, fols. 135v–137r (1174).

43. "VM" II, fol. 2v (1196).

44. For discussion of disguised sales, see Constance H. Berman, "The Debate on Cistercian Contracts," *Cîteaux* 43 (1992): 432–40; *Rufford Charters*, i: introduction.

45. Berman, *MA*, passim.

46. This is the gist of the "prima collectio" of the Cistercians. This collection, as discussed above, does not date to 1134.

47. Berman, *MA*, pp. 43–50.

48. Berman, *MA*, pp. 18ff.

49. *BD*, no. 470 (1154).

50. Galbraith, "Monastic Foundation Charters."

51. E.g., *BF*, nos. 1, 2.

52. In 1154, Ademar Tocons or Teccos, father of Bernard, had confirmed for an additional 42 solidi the land at "la Artigua citra et ultra rivum," *GM* I, no. 13 (1154); see n. 53.

53. There are references to *servitia* owed there; see *GM* I, no. 13 (1154); on *artigue* as a term associated with hermitages and recent clearance, see Higounet, *Paysages*, pp. 83–110, and Berman, *MA*, pp. 29–30. *BD*, nos. 173–266, concern the grange, formerly the hermitage, of Artigues.

54. *GM* III, no. 66, mentions negotiations twelve years earlier between Bertrand of Grandselve (who died in 1150) and Arnold of Saint-Just, who was abbot of Gimont

from 1147 to 1153; these must have occurred between 1147 and 1150. The meeting between Pons of Grandselve (1158–65) and Bernard of Gimont (1154–67) must therefore date to between 1159 and 1162.

55. Found in the Gimont cartulary under the date 1158, *GM* III, no. 50 concerns a dispute that appears to have continued up into the 1160s as suggested by *GM* III, no. 66.

56. *GM* III, no. 50 (dated 1158); present were abbot Garsias of l'Escaledieu; abbot Augerius of Bonnefont; abbot Arnold of Berdoues; abbot Sanche of Eaunes; William-Peter Curta Sola and William Girmon, monks of Berdoues; abbot Raymond of Verula (a house in Spain attached to l'Escaledieu, but for which the earliest date given is usually 1184; perhaps that refers to its first year as a Cistercian house); abbot Bernard of Gimont; abbot Galin of Bouillas; prior Raymond Vidal of Gimont; William of Toulouse and Umbertus, monks of Gimont; abbot Pons William of Grandselve; Albert of Finna and Ugo of Mored; monks of Grandselve; and brother William of Aspa, conversus of Gimont. The year 1163 may be more likely for this contract, given dates for the abbot of Bouillas in *GC*, which are for the 1160s; in that case, records for disputes dated 1158 and 1163 may concern a single dispute.

57. Arnold of Broil is found entering Gimont as a monk between 1167 and 1173. See *GM* I, nos. 23 (1167), 24 (1173); *GM* IV, no. 10 (1194); Berman, "Origins," p. 267. If we assume that the one person who would have remembered the correct events was Arnold of Saint-Just, abbot of Berdoues, former abbot of Gimont, these charters were most likely to have been done just after his death in circa 1193.

58. *GM* I, no. 1.

59. *BD*, nos. 16 (1191), 20 (1210), 31 (1213), 107 (1204), 108 (1204), 124 (1204), etc.; the abbreviated fashion of publication of the Gimont cartulary does not allow this to be done from its documents.

60. Berman, "Origins," passim; but I would now question some of my earlier conclusions in that article, as discussed below.

61. *GM* I, nos. 1, 2; the cartulary editor asserts that William Raymond of Broil was the son of a lord of four castles. The family's position in society is also suggested by *GM* I, no. 13 (1164), in which "donors" Bernard Teccos and his brother Raymond are described as having tenants of their own but are still treated as of lower rank than the Broil family, who were among the *fidejussores* and *mandatores*, but cf. *GM* I, no. 26 (1154).

62. Two granges would later be converted into fortified market towns or bastides at Solomiac and Saint-Lys; the abbey farm itself would become the prosperous bastide called Gimont. See Constance H. Berman, "From Cistercian Granges to Cistercian Bastides: Using the Order's Records to Date Landscape Transformations," in *Espace Cistercien*, ed. Léon Pressouyre (Paris, 1994), pp. 204–15, and "Cistercian Vernacular Architecture in Southern France, the Question of Bastides," *Studies in Cistercian Art and Architecture*, ed. Meredith Parsons Lillich (Kalamazoo, Mich., 1998), vol. 5, pp. 238–69

Although having one early daughter-house in Spain at Rueda in Aragon, probably incorporated in 1153, Gimont would only in 1287 incorporate Sauvelade in the diocese of Lescour, an existing house of monks, as a second daughter-abbey; *Originum*, p. 312. *Atlas*, p. 296, suggests that Sauvelade was a Benedictine house founded in 1127 and incorporated by Cistercians in 1287.

63. *GM* VI, no. 138 (1192) and passim; cf. P. Delaux and F. Liberos, *Histoire de la bastide de Saint-Lys* (Toulouse, reprint 1980).

64. References are to a house rather than a grange; *GM* VI, no. 1 (1164) is the conveyance of an established farmstead (*casale*) in front of an enclosed area (*barriale*) also conveyed; the grant included 100 *concades* of *landes* or *yzencas*—possibly uncleared, but small in comparison to other conveyances of long-settled land for this grange. See *GM* VI, nos. 6 (1160), 7 (1160), 105 (1174), 107 (1163), 10 (1180), and for existing tenants: *GM* VI, nos. 57 (1168), 30 (1164), 66 (1163), etc. One act denies the monks the right to cut trees or to plow, *GM* VI no. 68 (1183); elsewhere charcoal makers and the smith of Saixes protect their rights, *GM* VI, no. 31 (1177).

65. See discussion of how Cistercians gained tithes almost entirely on land already in their ownership, in Constance H. Berman, "Cistercian Development and the Order's Acquisition of Churches and Tithes in Southern France," *R. bénédictine* 91 (1981): 193–203.

66. *GM* VI, nos. 2 (1164), 3 (1171), 4 (1169), 5 (1168), 27 (1167).

67. *GM* VI, no. 139 (1191).

68. *GM* III, no. 1 (1169). A Raymond of Mauvezin is found as a brother of the community, *GM* III, no. 48 (1169); this does not necessarily mean he was from the family of viscounts, simply that he came from that castle, where he may have been a dependent.

69. *GM* II, nos. 2 (1158), 2 bis (1159); *GM* III, nos. 1 (1169), 8, 9, 14.

70. *GM* II, nos. 2, 2 bis; III, nos. 1, 8, 9, 10, 14, 15 (1163), 24 (1162), 32 (1163).

71. *GM* III, no. 1 (1148).

72. *GM* II, no. 18 (n.d.).

73. *GM* II, nos. 12, 18, 24 (1162), 26 (1162–63); *GM* III, nos. 1 (1148), 2 and 32 (1158); *GM* IV, no. 27 bis.

74. Tithes on as much land as "cum aratris suis vel expenses in predicte ecclesie decimario laboraverint" were given in *GM* III, no. 64 (1187).

75. *GM* III, nos. 50, 66 (circa 1158). Paris, A.N. L1009 bis, no. 32, is a gift in that vicinity by Arnold of Syrag, son of Galard of Syrag, to Grandselve in 1163.

76. *GM* III, nos. 33 (1184), 2 bis (1159), 12 (1162), 4 (n.d.), 22 (1171), 30 (1172), 33 (1185), 59 (1171), 3 (1164), 45 (1176), and 25 (1164).

77. See *GM* III, no. 24 (1162), in which the three siblings Ademar of Juliac and William his brother, with Lady Gassia their sister (and the children of the last, Bernard of Badcaina, Na Fortona, Na Bernarda, Na Stephana, and Na Sanchia with her husband Arnold Auriolo) sold 100 *concades* of land in the *decimario* of Saint-Martin of Toget to Gimont with the tithes and first fruits for 200 solidi of Morlaas. Family members were *fidejussores* in *GM* III, nos. 13 (1161), 16 (1163), 40 and 53 (1179), 57 (1184). Bernard of Badcaina was old enough to be a guarantor in 1161, possibly sixteen; if so, that makes him at least thirty-four when he was received at Gimont in 1179, "pro monacho vel converso si tamen ante Natalem Domini secundum consuetudinem ordinis venerit." His uncle, Ademar of Juliac, entered Gimont five years later as a monk. Even if he were five or ten years younger than his sister Gassia, he still would have been about ten when his nephew Bernard of Badcaina was born. If he were five years older than his nephew, he was 44 when he entered Gimont, if ten years older, 49. Ademar appears as *fidejussor* in *GM* III, nos. 40 (1179) and 53 (1179), when the abbot promised to receive his nephew Bernard if he came before Christmas. See also *GM* II, no. 59 (1175).

78. In 214 charters for Laurs, sixty charters (28 percent) mention Maurencs family members as donors, sellers, *fidejussores*, *mandatores*, or witnesses.

79. *GM* II, no. 7 (1167).

80. Yspanus's wife Alazais appears in *GM* II, no. 162 (1182); *GM* V, no. 101 (1188). The daughter, Alexandria, is mentioned as prioress of the church of nuns of Saint-Orient and Saint-Jean located just north of Gimont, *GM* II, no. 46 (1169); her father took back land given them in *GM* II, no. 94 (1177). If Alexandria was a nun in 1169 and prioress in 1177, Yspanus was probably 25 in 1151 and the eldest of four brothers all acting to confirm and thus all of age in 1151; he died in 1182, thirty years later, when he was at least fifty-five years old. Other contracts mention Paloma, another daughter, and sons, but not by name, *GM* II, no. 162 (1182).

81. *GM* II, nos. 186 (1159), 107 (1158), 175 (1188), 176 (1188); *GM* VI, no. 27 (1167).

82. *GM* II, no. 18 (probably 1160), cf. *GM* II, nos. 29 (1160), 7 (1167).

83. Raymond of l'Isle, who married their sister Galdris, appears in *GM* II, no. 106 (1151); *GM* I, no. 17 (1169) and no. 18 (1167). A sixth sibling, a sister Gassia married to Odo of Porastron, appears in *GM* V, no. 2 (1162). Esparrons of Maurencs's relationship to them is unclear; see *GM* II, no. 117 (1170). He "ceded to the monks of Gimont all claims to any gifts, sales, or mortgages in the *casale* of Saint-Sernin" that the abbot of Gimont had received from Odo of Maurencs and from his brothers Yspanus and William.

84. *GM* II, no. 106 (1151).

85. *GM* II, nos. 142 (1162), 94 (1177).

86. *GM* II, nos. 57–61, 65, 89, 171.

87. *GM* II, no. 59 (before 1158); *GM* I, no. 33 (1165); *GM* II, no. 178 (should be 1165 as well).

88. *GM* II, nos. 107 (1158), 113 (1158); "*Hoc totum factum est in manu Odonis de Maurencs qui inde est fidejussor.*" *GM* II, nos. 114 (1159), 115 (1162); see *GM* II, nos. 116 (1159) and 119 (1171), in which a niece sells land so that a son will be received as a monk "*ad conversionem*," *GM* II, no. 33 (1165).

89. *GM* II, nos. 46 (1169), 133 (1167), 134 (1168); *GM* V, no. 10 (1168).

90. Robert Génestal, *Le rôle des monastères comme établissements de crédit: étudie en Normandie du XIe à la fin du XIIIe siècle* (Paris, 1901). Mortgage as a first step in acquisition is discussed in Constance H. Berman, "Land Acquisition and the Use of the Mortgage Contract by the Cistercians of Berdoues," *Speculum* 57 (1982):250–66.

91. *GM* I, nos. 17, 18 (both 1167).

92. *GM* I, no. 15 (1168).

93. *GM* I, no. 17 (1169).

94. *GM* II, no. 149 (1176), witnessed by the entire monastic chapter.

95. *GM* II, nos. 153 (1178), 162 (1182).

96. *GM* II, no. 162 (1182).

97. *GM* II, nos. 46 (1169), 94 (1177).

98. Rosenwein, *Neighbor*, passim.

99. *NO*, Introduction, p. xi.

100. *SL* p. 389: "*Tertius (abbas) dompnus Guiraldus fuit qui jure regiminis XVII annis strenue gubernavit monasterium . . . et domum de Annonenca fundavit et in ea religionem*

sanctimonialium propagavit." On the reliability of the chronicle in comparison to the cartulary on other issues, see Berman, "Silvanès."

101. *SL*, no. 147 (1139); also *NO*, no. 1 (1139).

102. *NO*, no. 11 (1169), "Relinquimus etiam et solvimus prefacto monasterio et dominabus et omnes servitores."

103. See Berman, "Men's Houses," for double communities; for the joining of two eremitical groups, see *Grand Cartulaire de la Sauve Majeur*, pp. 34–47.

104. *NO*, no. 102 (1296).

105. *Statuta*, 1252, no. 49; 1255, no. 31.

106. Cf. Dagmar Kroebel, "Les moniales de l'abbaye cistercienne de Nonenque: leur vie d'après le cartulaire entre 1140 et 1350," *Les religieuses dans le cloître et dans le monde des origines à nos jours* (Saint-Étienne, 1994), pp. 507–13.

107. *NO*, nos. 8 and 9 (1167–68), 17 (1170), 18 (1171); concerning the grange of Lioujas at a later date, see Constance H. Berman, "Les Granges cisterciennes fortifiées du Rouergue," *Cahiers de la Ligue Urbaine et Rurale* 109 (1990): 54–65.

108. *SL*, nos. 70 (1153), 116 (1158), 134 (1159), 145 (1164), 146 (1165), 147 (1168).

109. In 1190 the nuns of Nonenque acquired the monastery of Mont-Cornil in the diocese of Lodève and the tiny church of Saint-Etienne-de-Rogaz; the church was exchanged in 1275 with the monks of Saint-Sauveur of Lodève for rights in the church at Saint-Beaulize, *NO*, intro., pp. x–xiii. Nonenque's daughter-house at Mont-Cornil apparently continued to exist.

110. *NO*, no. 88 (1267).

111. *Atlas*, p. 275.

112. *NO*, no. 88 (1267).

113. *SL*, no. 486 (1182).

114. *NO*, no. 7 (1162).

115. *SL*, no. 60 (1153).

116. *NO*, no. 3 (1152), mentions ten members but does not claim to be complete; *SL*, no. 70 (1153), lists all twenty monks. It was a small men's house at mid-century.

117. Silvanès paid 200 solidi for *fevum* to the nuns, *NO*, no. 3 (1152), intro., p. xii, and purchased allodial rights from the "founder" Arnold of Pont and his sons for another 200 solidi, *SL*, no. 51 (1151).

118. *NO*, nos. 33 (1199), 27 (1181). A Tiburce de Vintrou would be the prioress and then abbess of Nonenque from 1233 to 1253; *NO*, p. xiv.

119. *NO*, no. 12 (1170).

120. *SL*, nos. 8 (1133–44), 231 (1164).

121. *NO*, no. 11 (1169), a sale for 1450 solidi.

122. *NO*, no. 6 (1162).

123. *NO*, no. 12 (1170).

124. See further discussion in Constance H. Berman, "Cistercian Women and Tithes," *Cîteaux* 49 (1998): 95–128; short extracts of that article, revised here, are used with permission.

125. Giselle Bourgeois, "Les granges et l'économie de l'abbaye de Nonenque au Moyen Age," *Cîteaux* 24 (1973): 139–60.

126. *NO*, nos. 26 (1177), 8 (1167–68), 21 (1173).

127. For a papal legate involved at Valmagne, see "VM" I, fol. 57r (1171).

128. The latter were presumably dairymaids at this grange on the high *causses* where the nuns raised sheep and produced cheese, practices confirmed by other records that refer to Nonenque's cheese-curing caves at Roquefort.

129. *NO*, intro, pp. xiiff.

130. See discussion of Rifreddo in Berman, "Cistercian Nuns and Tithes"; for regularization, see eadem, "Abbeys for Cistercian Nuns," which primarily treats houses in northern France.

131. *Statuta*, 1295, no. 3; *NO*, no. 6 (1162), pp. xviiff, xlviff.

132. Copying of the first volume was probably underway just as a Cistercian-led Crusade was launched against the Albigensian heretics in 1209. Redactors of the cartulary probably played down its pre-Cistercian history because of its early ties to the Trencavel family, whose orthodoxy had become suspect. Additionally, the conflict in the first years of the thirteenth century over control of Montpellier that raged between Marie, daughter of William VIII by a first marriage, and her younger half-brother, William IX, has probably infected the contents of both the Valmagne cartulary ("VM") and the William family cartulary (*LIM*). Both cartularies lack some obvious bequests to Valmagne by the William family, for instance, those at Creis, which may be inferred from related documents.

133. The earliest surviving charters for a house of nuns at this site near Pignan were not accessible to researchers when I spent an entire summer in those archives. Moreau mentions charters from 1150, 1153, 1162, 1172, and 1211, but there are possibly many more; Moreau, *AO*, pp. 53, 61, 70. This house's adoption of Cistercian customs is confirmed by her French paraphrase of a papal confirmation of 1178 by Alexander III, "De l'ordre monastique qui, selon la crainte de Dieu, le bienheureux Benoît, et les institutions des frères cisterciens a été institué," Moreau, *AO*, p. 61. This is clearly a translation of the standard papal acknowledgment of Cistercian practices at this date.

134. Vivian Paul, "The Abbey Church of Valmagne," *Mélanges Dimier* 3, 6: 639–52, who says that by the time Valmagne was rebuilt (1250–1350), two separate but parallel interpretations of Gothic architecture had developed within Cistercian architecture, single-nave Gothic and an austere cathedral rayonnant Gothic. According to Paul, the profile of the nave piers and tracery patterns is similar to those used in southern-French cathedrals of the late thirteenth century at Clermont-Ferrand, Limoges, Toulouse, and Rodez, suggesting that construction commenced in the 1280s. For northern comparisons, see Caroline A. Bruzelius, "Cistercian High Gothic: The Abbey Church of Longpont and the Architecture of the Cistercians in the Early Thirteenth Century," *ASOC* 35 (1979): 3–204, and "The Twelfth-Century Church at Ourscamp," *Speculum* 56 (1981): 28–40.

135. Moreau, *AO*, p. 231.

136. There is no documentary evidence. Aubert has dated the eastern end of le Vignogoul to circa 1250 and explains the stylistic discrepancies by positing the unusual procedure of starting the church at the west end; see Marcel Aubert, *L'architecture cistercienne en France*, 2nd ed., 2 vols. (Paris, 1947), vol. 2, pp. 181–82; Moreau, *AO*, pp. 227–34.

137. Art historians still dismiss the southern-French church for monks at Valmagne as not Cistercian because it is built in a southern version of rayonnant Gothic, the thirteenth-century cathedral Gothic style. Documents from Valmagne show that

this was an incorporated house, but that from 1155 it was as Cistercian as any other abbey for men. Its records include the two-volume medieval cartulary, "VM," which gives references to it as practicing the *ordo cisterciensis* from the late 1150s. Its abbots were active members of the General Chapter in the thirteenth century, receiving a series of commissions to carry out local investigations (see *Statuta*, passim), and it paid among the higher assessments for taxes to the Order; see *Tax Book*, ed. Johnson and King, esp. p. 40.

138. Segondy, *Vignogoul*, pp. 41ff.

139. See Chapter 1.

140. Daniel Rouquette, "Note sur la date de fondation et l'emplacement de l'abbaye de Netlieu," *Mélanges Dimier* 3, 6: 697–700. Sometimes collections in the archives are not yet available to researchers because they have not yet been catalogued, as, for instance, was the case in 1981 in the Archives départementales de l'Hérault.

141. "VM" I, fol. 26r (1138); a copy of this conveyance with all the same witnesses is dated to the Kalends of March 1138 and mentions that it is "VM" I, fol. 25v (1138 or 1139).

142. Valmagne's origins are thus similar to those of Obazine in western France, in whose charters is also found evidence of whole families entering the monastery as a group; see *Cartulaire d'Obazine*, no. 103 (1150–59).

143. "VM" I, fol. 26r (1138); Adelaide of Saint-Eulalie and sons gave rights at Tortoreria to Ardorel with the same clauses, "VM" I, fol. 26r (1138); "VM" I, fols. 26v, 27r (1138), 24v (1150).

144. Although there is no surviving document for this bequest, its confirmation by Trencavel's grandson, Gerald, count of Roussillon, is found in "VM" I, fol. 137v.

145. "VM" I, fol. 8r (1140).

146. "VM" I, fol. 1v (1147).

147. "VM" I, fol. 25r (1148).

148. "VM" I, two documents on fol. 24v (1150), and fols. 26v (1150), 27r (1150).

149. "VM" I, fols. 27v (1153), 27r (1150), 28v (1151); 2 documents at fol. 28v (1154); fol. 30v (1154).

150. "VM" I, fol. 6r (1162).

151. "VM" I, fol. 6v (1185); Lucius III's is the standard *Sane laborum*.

152. See Chapter 1 above.

153. "VM" I, fols. 146vff.; published in *SL*, nos. 462, 463 (both Dec. 1161); these texts were added to the Silvanès cartulary only at the mid-thirteenth century.

154. *SL*, no. 462 (1161).

155. *SL*, no. 463 (1161).

156. On the Cistercian college in Montpellier, see Berman, "Monastic Hospices," forthcoming.

157. Atbrandus may be the official of William found in *LIM*, no. 96 (1172); the hospice is mentioned in later charters of "VM." In one of them, dated 1166, concerning William VI's son, Guy Guiereato, Guy is described as having acted at Valmagne's house *ante portale sancti Guillelmi*; see "VM" I, fols. 56v (1166), 148r (1167).

158. Made in Montpellier in December 1161 in the presence of William VII of Montpellier, with a "founder" Atbrandus (probably coming from a family of that lord's officials), this transaction was made shortly after William VI had been in the city in October to settle a dispute between two of his sons; *LIM*, no. 159 (1161).

159. *LIM*, no. 159 (1161).

160. William VI's choice of Grandselve may actually confirm its recent attachment to Clairvaux, for William is reputed to have been in correspondence with Bernard, and early versions of the *Vita Prima* of Bernard of Clairvaux report a miracle in which Bernard appeared foretelling his own death to William in a dream. Bredero, *Bernard*, pp. 47ff.

161. Passerat, "La venue," passim; *SL*, no. 457 (1156); *LIM*, nos. 159 (1161), 186 (1162); but see next notes.

162. *LIM*, no. 129 (1157). This marriage treaty may explain references to the largess given Silvanès by the countesses of Burgundy in the Silvanès chronicle of circa 1170; *SL*, no. 470, pp. 370ff.

163. Paris, B.N. Latin, 9994, passim.

164. *SL*, no. 457 (1156).

165. *LIM*, no. 186 (1162).

166. *LIM*, nos. 159 (1161), 187 (1172).

167. "VM" I, 82r (1156).

168. Canvern's geographical proximity to Silvanès and Nonenque is seen in a later contract for 1165 in which Pons, abbot of Silvanès, and Raymond of Fraissenel, chaplain of Nonenque, were among the witnesses when a group of orphaned siblings granted rights at Canvern to Valmagne for 30 solidi plus an annuity of 10 solidi to continue until the youngest had reached adulthood; "VM" I, fol. 76r (1165).

169. "VM" I, fol. 75r (1158); a second charter, "VM" I, fol. 75r (1164), no longer makes a point of the Cistercian practice; its reference to the castle of Saint-Nazaire of Léras is suggestive of the close relationship between patrons for Valmagne's grange of Canvern and the founder of nearby Silvanès, Pons of Léras.

170. "VM" I, fol. 76r (1158); that on fol. 78v (1158) also specifies Cistercian practice.

171. "VM" I, fol. 76v (1158), fol. 77v (1158).

172. "VM" I, fol. 77v (1163).

173. "VM" I, fol. 79v (1158).

174. "VM" I, fol. 80r (1158).

175. "VM" I, fol. 78r (1159), "hoping to protect their heavenly homes" and "as a gift for their souls."

176. "VM" I, fol. 79r (1160).

177. "VM" I, fol. 80r (1160).

178. "VM" I, fol. 80r (1160).

179. See preface for the lay-brother treatise in London, B.M. Additional MS 18148.

180. "VM" I, fols. 76r, 77r (1160).

181. "VM" I, fol. 78r (1161) cf. fol. 75v (1159), a conveyance of two *borderiae* along with pasture for Valmagne's animals in all the donors' lands.

182. See Paul Ourliac, "Les villages de la région toulousaine au XIIe siècle," *Annales* 4 (1949): 268–77.

183. Berman, *MA*, pp. 31ff.

184. Guillelma's marriage to Bernard-Aton V, son of Cecily, countess of Provence, and Bernard-Aton IV, had taken place shortly before her father's "retirement" to become a monk at Grandselve in 1146. Guillelma made a career for herself as widowed guardian for Bernard-Aton VI, the son born after his father's death in 1149, and as a supporter of religious reform—an activity in which she is documented up into the

1190s. Guillelma's dowry was probably eventually given by her with family property at Creis, which is mentioned in William VI's will, but not in relation to Guillelma; see *LIM*, no. 95 (1146).

185. Two documents for Nonenque, which derive from a 1327 *vidimus*, mention this hospital; the personnel do not correspond to it but to the other hospice for travelers to the General Chapter. I suspect that these documents conflate the two hospices. They may, however, be evidence that the hospital of Saint-Martin had been in existence since 1167; see *NO*, nos. 8 and 9 (1167–68), no. 17 (1170).

186. A contract in 1178 for a "domus pauperum secundum ordinem cisterciensem" to be founded may be relevant; see "VM" I, fols. 8r. (1178), 126v (1174).

187. "VM" II, fol. 100r (1192); the hospital of Saint-Martin is mentioned again in a charter of 1195 when its land is described as adjoining that of Valmagne's earliest grange of Valautre; "VM" II, fol. 106r (1195).

188. Guillelma conveyed to Peter, abbot of Valmagne, an honor that Peter Gonterius had once given to the hospital of Saint-Martin for the sum of 240 solidi. These properties conveyed to Valmagne are described as being unfruitful and of no utility to the hospital of Saint-Martin; "VM" II, fol. 86v (1196). Witnesses included the abbot of Silvanès. Unlike the hospice in Montpellier for which Valmagne had set aside a separate grange in 1161, but for which that abbey provided the laborers, Guillelma's institution in the 1190s apparently operated on a wholly separate budget from Valmagne's.

189. See above at pp. 174–75.

190. "VM" I, fol. 100r (1179).

191. "VM" I, fol. 100r (1179).

192. Barbara H. Rosenwein, "Cluny's Immunities in the Tenth and Eleventh Centuries: Images and Narratives," *Die Cluniazenser in ihrem politisch-sozialen Umfeld*, ed. Giles Constable, Gert Melville, and Jörg Oberste (Münster, 1998), pp. 133–63.

193. *Statuta*, vol. 1, p. 20, no. 32.

194. *Cartulaire de Bonnefoy*, passim.

195. Bourgeois, "Nonenque," passim.

196. The excommunication of Bernard-Aton VI's cousin, Raymond-Roger II, in 1180 for harboring heretics must have encouraged such transactions with the Cistercians; see Alan Friedlander, "Trencavel," *Medieval France: An Encyclopedia*, ed. William W. Kibler et al. (New York, 1995), p. 925.

197. "VM" I, fol. 100v (1180); a transaction in Valmagne's hospice in Montpellier in the presence of William, lord of Montpellier, who promised to uphold it, with Hugh, count of Rodez, who served as one of many witnesses when a contract was sealed by Bernard-Aton VI, Guillelma his mother, and Peter, bishop of Agde (and later by Berengar, archbishop of Narbonne). But see also the charter in *NO*, 27 (1181), in which Hugh's mother Ermengardis is present.

198. On enunciated principles, see *Statuta*, vol. 1. pp. 12ff., "prima-collectio," which actually dates to from the 1150s or later; on the acquisition of previously occupied land elsewhere, see Berman, *MA*, passim.

199. "VM" I, fols. 129r (1189), 127v (1165); one witness in the latter was Raymond, prior of Silvanès.

200. "VM" I, fol. 126v (1174).

201. This may have been intended as a way to bring more vines under cultivation; it resembles earlier encastellation in this and other regions of the Mediterranean. See.

Monique Bourin-Derruau, *Villages médiévaux en Bas-Languedoc: genèse d'une associabilité (Xe–XIVe siècles)*, 2 vols. (Paris, 1987), esp. 87ff.; Pierre Toubert, *Les structures de Latium médiévale: le Latium méridional et la Sabine du Ixe siècle à la fin du XIIe siècle*, 2 vols. (Rome, 1973).

202. "VM" I, fol. 101r (1182). This Bernard of Capraria had conveyed land to Valmagne thirty years earlier when he was about to set off on Crusade, so it may be that his contract was the culmination of many years of preparation.

203. "VM" I, fols. 102r (1182), 103v (1182), 104r (1182), 104v (1182), 103r (1183).

204. "VM" I, fols. 102v (1182), 106v (1185), 103r (1191), 107r (1161), 107v (1184).

205. "VM" I, fols. 110r (1184); 110v (1185); see also "VM" I, fols. 110v (1184), 111r (1189).

206. "VM" I, fols. 108v (1182), 109r–v (1185).

207. "VM" I, fol. 109v (1184).

208. "VM" I, fol. 107r (1185).

209. "VM" I, fols. 128v–129r (undated).

210. "VM" I, fols. 116v (1182), 116v (1182), 117r (1188).

211. "VM" I, fols. 113r–v (1182), 114r (1184).

212. "VM" I, fols. 123v (1186), 124r (1187), 124v (1185), 125v (1183), 125v (1181), 134r (1195), 134r and 135r (1198).

213. "VM" I, fols. 111r (1180), 105v (1187), duplicate on 106r (1187).

214. On *conversae*, see "VM" II, fols. 10v, etc., or *LC*, no. 76 (1214).

215. "VM" I, fol. 38r or 47v.

216. "VM" I, fol. 101r (1182).

217. See Table 3.

218. *LIM*, no. 96 (1172).

219. On the phenomenon in northern France, see Constance H. Berman, "Cistercian Nuns and the Development of the Order: The Cistercian Abbey at Saint-Antoine-des-Champs Outside Paris," *The Joy of Learning and the Love of God: Essays in Honor of Jean Leclercq*, ed. E. Rozanne Elder, pp. 121–56 (Kalamazoo, Mich., 1995), esp. document on pp. 144–45.

220. That 1179 document does suggest, however, that the dependencies of Valmagne in that area (le Vignogoul, Netlieu, and even the hospital of Saint-Martin) were probably already in place by that date. Netlieu's earliest document appears to be from 1195; Moreau, *AO*, p. 58.

221. "VM" II, fol. 85r, rights given because *infructuosa et inutilia*.

222. "VM" II, fols. 30–84.

Chapter 5

1. *Statuta*, 1241, no. 33.

2. *FF*, pp. 223–26, which draws on a document from *GC* 6, Instrumenta, p. 487; David Bell, "*Fons Sapientiae*: une étude de la collection de livres de l'abbaye de Fontfroide du XIIe au XVIe siècle," *Cîteaux* 46 (1995): 77–108; on the Doat collection, see H. Omont, "La Collection Doat à la Bibliothèque Nationale: documents sur les re-

cherches de Doat dans les Archives du Sud-Ouest de la France de 1663 à 1670," *Bibliothèque de l'école des chartes* 77 (1916): 286–336.

3. Toulouse, 108H56, Grandselve inventory.

4. *Statuta*, 1227, no. 2; 1236, nos. 12, 60, 63; 1237, nos. 12, 27; 1238, no. 11; 1240, no. 18; 1242, no. 20; etc.; Reinhard Schneider, *Vom Klosterhaushalt zum Stadt- und Staatshaushalt der Zisterziensische Beitrag* (Stuttgart, 1994).

5. Anselme Dimier, *Saint Louis et Cîteaux* (Paris, 1954), discusses Blanche's activities at some length.

6. Lekai, *Cistercians*, pp. 75–76; Foreville, *Latran*, pp. 353–54.

7. For *CI*, no. 175 (1165) is the list of daughters contained in a papal privilege. Pacaut, "Filiation clarevallienne," p. 138, counts 55 direct daughters of Clairvaux by 1153, as listed in *Originum* by Janauschek based, of course, on thirteenth-century filiation trees. Savigny, for instance, for which 23 daughters would have been counted, was not incorporated in 1147 and probably not until after Bernard's death, probably in 1157 or 1158.

8. See discussion of the comments by Orderic Vitalis, William of Malmesbury, and Herman of Tournai in Chapter 2.

9. See Chapter 2. Exceptions turn out to be interpolated; see in *GM* I, no. 1 (discussed in Chapter 4); cf. *BD*, no. 86 (1256).

10. See Chapter 1.

11. Indeed, expansion into almost every region of "old Europe" was the result of incorporation, not foundation. J.-M. Canivez, "Cîteaux," *DHGE* 12 (1953): 852–997 provides a number of examples of such incorporation. See also Brenda Bolton, "For the See of Saint Peter: The Cistercians at Innocent III's Nearest Frontier," *Monastic Studies* (Bangor, Gwynned, 1990), pp. 146–57; Brian Patrick McGuire, *The Cistercians in Denmark: Their Attitudes, Roles, and Functions in Medieval Society* (Kalamazoo, Mich., 1982); Newman, *Boundaries*, pp. 123–40; Hill, *English Cistercian*, and Donkin, *The Cistercians*; the last also provides discussion of site changes.

12. *FF*, p. 227, from *GC* vi, "Instrumenta Ecclesiae Narbonensis," Charter 54, col. 46; Doat 59, fol. 120.

13. While gifts by Ermengardis, viscountess of Narbonne in 1157, to abbot Vidal of Fontfroide make no mention of the Cistercians, Fontfroide can definitely be identified as part of Cistercian practice from as early as a charter dated 1176 in which Aimeric of Narbonne, "cupiens orationibus Cisterciensis ordinis," "gave himself" to Fontfroide; witnesses included the prior of Poblet and Alphonse, king of Aragon, *GC* 6, Instrumenta, cols. 38ff.

14. On this theme see Golding, "Hermit and Hunter," passim.

15. On the influence of such imagery on the early Cistercians, see Auberger, *L'unanimité*, pp. 85ff.; for such images in American settlement, see Matthew Dennis, *Cultivating a Landscape of Peace: Iroquois-European Encounters in Seventeenth-Century America* (Ithaca, N.Y., 1993), pp. 15–18.

16. Berman, *MA*; Donkin, *Cistercians*, pp. 37ff.

17. See Erin Jordan's forthcoming work from a Ph.D. dissertation on the patronage of the Cistercians by the thirteenth-century countesses of Flanders.

18. Berman, "Abbeys for Cistercian Nuns," esp. pp. 108ff.

19. Berman, "Cistercian Nuns and Tithes," pp. 103ff.

20. France, "The Coming of the Cistercians," passim; Bartlett, *Making of Europe*, pp. 139ff.

21. See *Instituta*, often published under 1134, as in Canivez's *Statuta*, but collected in the 1150s and 1160s.

22. Certainly there was less of the kind of conflict between the new reformers and old monks described by Constable, "Cluniac Tithes"; but see Remensnyder, *Remembering*, passim. Most conflict was instead among new reform houses, such as the Cistercian nuns of Nonenque in the Rouergue, who suffered competition for pasture rights with Templars, Hospitallers, and Cistercians; see Bourgeois, "Les granges de Nonenque." The monks of Silvanès resolved disputes with new religious groups over tithes by concessions of fractions of land in certain parishes in lieu of tithes; *SL*, nos. 170 and 174 (1154), etc.

23. See Chapter 4, p. 215.

24. Angleton, "Two Preaching Missions," pp. 176ff., and Congar, "Henri de Marcy," passim. Cistercian popularity disappeared with their poverty; see Wakefield, *Heresy*, pp. 65–81; Christine Thouzellier, "La pauvreté, arme contre l'albigéisme, en 1206," in Thouzellier, *Catharisme et Valdeisme en Languedoc* (Paris, 1969), pp. 189–203.

25. Raymonde Foreville, "Arnaud Amalric, archévêque de Narbonne: 1196–1225," *Narbonne: archéologie et histoire* (Montpellier, 1973), pp. 129–46.

26. *HGL*, 8, 886.

27. Grèzes-Rueff, "L'abbaye de Fontfroide," passim.

28. Ties between thirteenth-century houses for Cistercian women and patrons involved in the Albigensian crusade are discussed in Berman, "Abbeys for Cistercian Nuns," and Monique Zerner-Chardavoine, "L'épouse de Simon de Montfort et la croisade albigeoise," *Femmes, mariages, lignages, XIIe–XIVe siècles: mélanges offerts à Georges Duby* (Brussels, 1992), pp. 449–70; but see also *BX*, no. 49 (1181, 1189), which suggests that the ideological fight against heresy was already well underway.

29. Fulk of Marseilles, formerly merchant and troubadour, then abbot of le Thoronet, then bishop of Toulouse (1205–31), was buried at Grandselve; *HGL* 4, 1: n. 66. His foundations of women's houses as a means of combating heresy included that in 1207 at Prouille, later treated as the first house of Dominican nuns; it is not clear that the intention at the outset was not for a house of Cistercian women. See J. Guiraud, *Cartulaire de Notre-Dame de Prouille*, 2 vols. (Paris, 1907), vol. 1, esp. no. 1 (1207). Fulk is mentioned in *The Life of Marie d'Oignies by Jacques de Vitry*, trans. Margot H. King (Toronto, 1993).

30. See Aurell i Cardonna, "Cisterciennes," passim; the houses in Arles may also be related to a hospice for Cistercian monks and lay-brothers in that city founded under the authority of Sénanque. Other studies of thirteenth-century nuns in this area include Jean-de-la-Croix Bouton and Dominique Mouret, "Convers et converses de moniales cisterciennes aux XIIIe et XIVe siècles," *CF* 21 (1985): 283–312; Yvonne Carbonell-Lamothe, "L'abbaye du Vignogoul," *CF* 21 (1985): 269–282; Moreau, *AO* and eadem, "Les moniales du diocèse de Maguelone au XIIIe siècle," *CF* 23 (1988): 241–60; and Elisabeth Magnou-Nortier, "Formes féminines de vie consacrée dans le pays du Midi jusqu'au début du XIIe siècle," *CF* 23 (1988): 193–216.

31. Aurell i Cardona, "Cisterciennes," pp. 243–46 and *Une famille de la noblesse provençale au Moyen Age: les Porcelet* (Avignon, 1986), pp. 162–69; Desmarchelier, pp. 83ff.; Cottineau, 1874, 3291; *Atlas*, pp. 288, 295, 301.

32. Cottineau, 422, 449; *Atlas*, p. 273; J.-M. Canivez, "Bonlieu," *DHGE* 9 (1937): 1007. Dimier, *Recueil*, at Bonlieu, follows the older tradition that it was a foundation of "moniales, puis hommes en 1400s." Jean-de-la-Croix Bouton, "L'abbaye de Bonlieu," *Mélanges Dimier* 2, 4: 449–61 has reopened the question, suggesting that the tradition about the countess of Marsanne cannot be upheld, but that it was once under the jurisdiction of Aiguebelle. What we do know is that in 1239 there were an abbess Ademara, a subprioress, and at least seven other nuns; conversi, a priest, and monks sent from Aiguebelle are also mentioned. In 1262 the lord of Montélimar left a chalice to each of the communities of Aiguebelle, le Bouchet, Bonlieu, and the nuns of Aleyrac. In 1275 Raymond de Bavas left a pittance to the nuns of Bonlieu and ten solidi to those of Aleyrac. In 1277 Ayar II of Poitiers elected to be buried at Bonlieu, and in 1283 Decan d'Uzes elected burial there as well. In 1283 Polite de Bourgogne, countess of Valentinois, left 20 livres to the nuns of Bonlieu for an anniversary. Bonlieu is mentioned in *Statuta* 1291 as the *filia* of Aiguebelle.

33. Jean-de-la-Croix Bouton, "La Vernaisson," *R. Drômoise* 83 (1980): 38–74.

34. See below, n. 41.

35. John Hine Mundy, "Charity and Social Work in Toulouse, 1100–1250," *Traditio* 22 (1966): 203–87.

36. Alexander Murray, *Reason and Society in the Middle Ages* (Oxford, 1978), pp. 81ff, 352ff. discusses the demography of the medieval nobility as it affected individuals.

37. Clichés about heretics' association with women were typical denunciations from early Christianity; see Abels and Harrison, "Participation," or Elliott, *Spiritual Marriage*, p. 32, who asserts that "dangerous familiarity between the sexes will from this point [late antiquity] on be consistently identified as one of the hallmarks of heretical doctrines."

38. See, e.g., the usual readings of the commentary on the Song of Songs, as discussed by McNamara, "Herrenfrage," p. 27, n. 73.

39. If they saw how important were the contributions of women as donors and founders, they still often denied the necessity of founding houses for those women's daughters or put barriers in the way of affiliating all but the most choice of such communities of nuns; see details in Degler-Spengler, "Incorporation."

40. Accusations of simony may have been particularly frequent against nuns; on the subject in general, see Joseph Lynch, *Simoniacal Entry into Religious Life from 1000 to 1260* (Columbus, Ohio, 1976).

41. Some historians have argued that medieval religious women's communities may have deliberately chosen dependency as being more in the apostolic mode; see *Cartulaire d'Obazine*, pp. 9–13, and Barrière, "The Cistercian Monastery of Coyroux."

42. Boyd, *Rifreddo*, and Bourgeois, "Nonenque," passim. Complaints were brought to the General Chapter about the annexation of granges belonging to nuns by neighboring monks; *Statuta*, 1267, no. 71; 1268, no. 66; and 1277, no. 57 concern Villelongue and Rieunette; *Statuta*, 1295, no. 3, concerning Nonenque and Silvanès.

43. Johnson and King, *Tax Book*, pp. 54, 76, provides assessment rates for Fontfroide at about 33£, Grandselve at 37£, and Poblet at 51£; these were the highest for these regions. Double assessments give slightly more information: Grandselve 76£., Fontfroide 67£., Belleperche 60£., Bonnecombe 60£., Valmagne 48£., Pontaut 48£., le Thoronet 39£., Bonneval 31£., le Rivet 30£., Sauveréal 30£., les Chambons 29£., Loc-

dieu 19£., Ardorel 18£., Silvanès 18£., Mazan 18£., Belloc 18£., Bonnevaux 17½£., Calers 17£., Berdoues 17£., Gimont 16£., etc.

44. Those for men's houses in southern France are found in Berman, *MA*, pp. 142–3.

45. See Berman, "Labors of Hercules."

46. See Chapter 3, pp. 155–156.

47. Cathala, "Boulbonne," 67.

48. *Statuta*, 1400, no. 31, says that because of the excessive poverty of Valcroissant the General Chapter united the abbey of nuns of Bonlieu in the diocese of Valence to Valcroissant. Bouton, "Bonlieu," p. 453, adds that the abbey was reduced to a grange, then sold off for stone in 1424; from 1436 the abbot of Valcroissant was called the abbot of Valcroissant and Bonlieu.

49. Bondéelle-Souchier, "Les moniales cisterciennes," contains an excellent analysis of the medieval situation.

50. Oliva, *Convent and Community*, Chapter 7.

51. See discussion of Nonenque above, Chapter 4.

Bibliography

UNPUBLISHED ARCHIVAL SOURCES

Albi: A.D. Tarn
  H1–9 Ardorel
  H38 "Répertoire de Candeil (1739–1741)"
  I/J74/3, Candeil
Cambridge: Corpus Christi College MS 139
Carcassonne: A.D. Aude, H211, "Inventaire de la mense conventuelle de Fontfroide"
Chaumont: A.D. Haute-Marne, 4H 18, for la Chapelle-aux-Planches
Dijon: Archives de la Côte d'Or, 11 H Cîteaux, 4:11
Dijon: Bibliothèque municipale, MSS 87, 114, 597, 598, 600, 601, 611, 633
Laon: Bibliothèque publique, MS 217
Ljubljana: State and University Library, MSS 31 and 32
London: British Museum, Additional MS 18148
Metz: Bibliothèque publique, MS 1247
Montauban: A.D. Tarn-et-Garonne
  H1 Belloc
  H3 Belleperche
  H59 Grandselve
Montpellier: A.D. Hérault
  Film no. 1 Mi 260–61 "Cartulaire de Valmagne"
  H series, "Villemagne copy" of Valmagne cartulary
Montpellier: Bibliothèque de l'école de Médecine, MS H322
Montpellier: Société archéologique de Montpellier
  "Cartulaire dit de Trencavel (XIe–XIIIe s.)"
Narbonne: Bibliothèque municipale
  MS 259, "Inventaire de la mense abbatiale de Fonfroide"
  MS 260, "Cauvet Notes"
  MS "Inventaire de l'archevêché de Narbonne"
Nîmes: A.D. Gard
  H33–H103, Franquevaux
Oxford: Corpus Christi College MS 209
Paris: Archives nationales
  L 966, no. 7 Savigny
  L 1009 bis, Grandselve
Paris: Bibliothèque de l'arsenal
  MS 6470, Belloc
Paris: Bibliothèque nationale,
  Collection des Bénédictins: 12751, 12752, 12756

Collection Doat
  vol. 59, Fontfroide
  vol. 70, Villelongue
  vols. 76–80, Grandselve
  vols. 83–86, Boulbonne
  vols. 91–92, Belleperche
  vols. 114–15, Candeil
  vols. 138–39, Bonnecombe
  vol. 150, Silvanès
Collection Duchesne, vol. 118
Latin MSS 4221, 4346, 12169, N.A. 430, "Primitive documents"
Latin MSS 9994, 11008, 11009, 11010, 11011, Grandselve
Latin MS 10975, Locdieu
Latin MS 11012, Eaunes
Latin MS N.A. 1698, Belloc
Latin MS 9169, Cartulaire de Royaumont
Paris: Bibliothèque Sainte-Geneviève, MS 1207
Rodez: A.D. Aveyron
  2H non côté, "Cartulaire de Bernac"
  "Inventaire de Serres" (anc. coté 267–68)
  2H liasses 9–88
  "Registre de Pousthoumy (anc. coté 198), Bonnecombe
  3H nouv. ser. 19, "Inventaire de Bonneval"
Rodez: Société de lettres, sciences et arts de l'Aveyron
  MS "Cartulaire de Magrin"
  MS "Cartulaire de Moncan"
  MS "Cartulaire d'Iz et Bougaunes"
Toulouse: A.D. Haute-Garonne
  108H Boulbonne, liasse and registres 1–3
  H Calers, liasses 4–20
  H Eaunes, liasse 5
  lo8H Grandselve, liasses 1–60
  H Nizors, liasses 1–21 and "Inventaire de Nizors"
  H205 Lespinasse, liasses 12ff.
  7D Collège de Saint Bernard, nos. 37, 41, 138, 141
  Ordre de Malte, Sainte Eulalie (Locdieu documents)
Toulouse: Archives municipales, MS 342, Belleperche
Toulouse: Bibliothèque municipale
  MS 152, Grandselve
  MS 638, Boulbonne
Trento: Bibliotheca communale, MS 1711

PUBLISHED DATABASES

Cetedoc: Library of Christian Latin Texts, CLCLT-2, published by Brepols
Cetedoc: Corpus Diplomaticorum: Belgian Latin Text, published by Brepols
Patrologiae Latina, CD-ROM index published by Chadwick-Healy

Published Documents and Texts

L'abbaye de Calers. Ed. Casimir Barrière-Flavy. Toulouse: Chauvin, 1887–89.
"L'abbaye d'Eaunes." Ed. D. Garrigues. *Bull. Société archéologique du Midi* 22 (1953): 78ff.
"L'abbaye de Mazan: catalogue des actes de l'abbaye de Mazan (1123–1494)." Ed. Jean Regné. *R. du Vivarais* 28 (1921): 86–89, 107–12, 134–42, 169–74, 211–17, 243–46, etc.
L'abbaye de Notre-Dame de Valcroissant de l'Ordre de Cîteaux au diocèse de Die. Ed. Jules Chevalier. Grenoble: Allier, 1897.
"L'abbaye de Vajal dans l'ancien comté de Foix (preuves)." Ed. Casimir Barrière-Flavy. Toulouse: n.p., n.d.
Abstracts of the Charters and Other Documents Contained in the Chartulary of the Cistercian Abbey of Fountains. Ed. William T. Lancaster. 2 vols. Leeds: J. Whitehead and Sons, 1915.
Acta pontificum romanorum inedita I Urkunden der Papste vom Jahre 748 bis zum Jahre 1198. Ed. J. v. Pflugk-Harttung. Vol. 1, Tubingen: F. Fues, 1880. Vols. 2–3, Stuttgart: Verlag von W. Kohlhammer, 1884–86.
The Beaulieu Cartulary. Ed. S. F. Hockey. Southampton: University Press, 1974.
Bernard of Clairvaux. *The Letters of Saint Bernard of Clairvaux*. Trans. Bruno Scott James. London: Burns Oates, 1953. Reprint New York: AMS Press, 1980.
———. *Opera Omnia in IV Volumes. PL*, vols. 182–85.
———. *Sancti Bernardi Opera*. Ed. J. Leclercq, C. H. Talbot, and H. M. Rochais. Rome: Editiones Cistercienses, 1957–98.
The Book of Saint Gilbert. Ed. Raymonde Foreville and Gillian Keir. Oxford: Clarendon Press, 1987.
Bullaire du Pape Calixte II, 1119–1124: essai de restitution. Ed. Ulysse Robert. Paris: Imprimerie nationale, 1891. Reprint New York: Georg Olms Verlag, 1979.
Cartulaire de l'abbaye cistercienne d'Obazine (XIIe–XIIIe siècle). Ed. Bernadette Barrière. Clermont-Ferrand: Institut d'Etudes du Massif Central, 1989.
Cartulaire de l'abbaye de Berdoues-près-Mirande. Ed. Cazaurin. The Hague: Nijhoff, 1905.
Cartulaire de l'abbaye de Bonnecombe. Ed. P.-A. Verlaguet. Rodez: Carrère, 1918–25.
Cartulaire de l'abbaye de Bonneval-en-Rouergue. Ed. P.-A. Verlaguet, intro. J.-L. Rigal. Rodez: Carrère, 1938.
Cartulaire de l'abbaye de Cadouin, précédé de notes sur l'histoire économique du Périgord Méridional à l'époque féodale. Ed. J.-M. Maubourguet. Cahors: Couselant, 1926.
Cartulaire de l'abbaye de Gimont. Ed. Abbé Clergeac. Paris: Champion, 1905.
Cartulaire de l'abbaye de Notre-Dame d'Ourscamp de l'Ordre de Cîteaux, fondée en 1129 au diocèse de Noyon, publié par M. Peigné-Delacourt. Amiens: Lemer, 1865.
Cartulaire de l'abbaye de Silvanès. Ed. P.-A. Verlaguet. Rodez: Carrère, 1910.
Cartulaire de l'abbaye Notre-Dame de Bonnevaux au diocèse de Vienne, Ordre de Cîteaux. Ed. Ulysse Chevalier. Grenoble: Allier,1889.
Cartulaire de l'abbaye Notre-Dame de Bonnevaux au diocèse de Vienne, Ordre de Cîteaux. Ed. [Anselme Dimier]. Tamié: Abbaye Notre-Dame de Tamié, 1942.
Cartulaire de l'abbaye Notre-Dame de Léoncel, diocèse de Die, Ordre de Cîteaux. Ed. Ulysse Chevalier. Montélimar: Bourron, 1869.
Cartulaire de la Chartreuse de Bonnefoy. Ed. Jean-Loup Lemaître. Paris: C.N.R.S., 1990.

Cartulaire de la Selve: la terre, les hommes, et le pouvoir en Rouergue au XIIe siècle. Ed. Paul Ourliac and Anne-Marie Magnou. Paris: C.N.R.S., 1985.
Cartulaire de Notre-Dame de Prouille. Ed. J. Guiraud, 2 vols. Paris: Picard, 1907.
Cartulaire et archives de l'ancien diocèse et de l'arrondissement administratif de Carcassonne. Ed. M. Mahul. 6 vols. Paris: V. Didron, 1857–82.
Cartulaire et documents de l'abbaye de Nonenque. Ed. C. Couderc and J.-L. Rigal. Rodez: Carrère, 1955.
Cartulaires de l'abbaye de Molesme, ancien diocèse de Langres, 916–1250: recueil de documents sur le nord de la Bourgogne et le Midi de la Champagne, publié avec une introduction diplomatique, historique et géographique. Ed. Jacques Laurent, 2 vols. Paris, Picard, 1907, 1911.
Cartulaires des Templiers de Douzens. Ed. Pierre Gérard and Elisabeth Magnou. Paris: Bibliothèque nationale, 1965.
Cartularium abbathie de Rievalle Ordinis cisterciensis. Ed. John C. Atkinson. Durham: Surtees Society, 1889.
The Cartulary of the Abbey of Old Wardon. Ed. G. H. Fowler. Aspley Guise: Bedfordshire Record Society, 1930.
Cartulary of Vauluisant. Ed. William O. Duba. Master's thesis, University of Iowa, 1994.
Catalogus Codicum Latinorum Bibliothecae Regiae Monacensis. Vol. 1, part 3. Munich, 1884.
Chartes de l'Ordre de Chalais: 1101–1401. Ed. Jean-Charles Roman d'Amat. 3 vols. Paris: Picard, 1923.
Chartes et documents concernant l'abbaye de Cîteaux 1098–1182. Ed. J.-M. Marilier. Rome: Editions cistercienses, 1961.
Chartes et documents de l'abbaye cistercienne de Preuilly. Ed. Albert Catel and Maurice Lecomte. Paris: Champion, 1927.
Chartes et documents de l'abbaye de Notre-Dame d'Aiguebelle. Ed. Commission d'histoire de l'Ordre de Cîteaux. Vol 1. Lyons: Audin, 1954. Vol. 2. Aiguebelle: Commission, 1969.
"Chartes inédites extraites des cartulaires de Molême intéressant un grand nombre de localités du département de l'Aube." Ed. Emile Socard. *Mém. Société académique de l'Aube* 28 (1864): 163–364.
Chartrier de l'Abbaye-aux-Bois. Ed. Brigitte Pipon. Paris: Ecole des chartes, 1996.
Chartularium abbatie de Novo Monasterio Ordinis cisterciensis. Ed. G. H. Fowler. Durham: Surtees Society, 1878.
The Chartulary of the Cistercian Abbey of St. Mary of Sallay in Craven. Ed. Joseph McNulty. 2 vols. York: Yorkshire Archaeological Society, 1933–34.
Chronica monasterii de Melsa. Ed. Edward A. Bond. 3 vols. London Rolls Series, 1866–68.
The Coucher Book of Furness Abbey. Ed. John C. Atkinson and John Brownbill. 6 vols. Manchester: Chetham Society, 1886–1919.
The Coucher Book of the Cistercian Abbey of Kirkstall. Ed. William T. Lancaster. Leeds: J. Whitehead and Sons, 1904.
The Coucher Book, or Chartulary, of Whalley Abbey. Ed. William A. Hulton. 4 vols. Manchester, 1847–49.
The Cistercian World: Monastic Writings of the Twelfth Century. Ed. Pauline Matarasso. New York: Penguin, 1993.

"Codex Manuscriptus 31 Bibliothecae Universitas Labacensis." Ed. Canisius Noschitzka. *ASOC* 6 (1950): 1–124.
Conciliorum oecumenicorum decreta. Ed. Josepho Alberigo et al. Basil: Herder, 1962.
De Gestis Regum Anglorum de Willelmi Malmesbiriensis Monachi. Ed. William Stubbs. 2 vols. London: Eyre and Spottiswoode, 1887.
De institutione clericorum of Philip of Harvengt. *PL* 203: 836–37.
De miraculis sanctae Mariae Laudunensis of Herman of Tournai. *PL* 156: 962–1018; also *MGH* 12 (1925): 653–62.
Documents concernant l'abbaye de Locdieu. Ed. anon. Villefranche: Société des Amis, 1892.
Documents historiques sur le Tarn-et-Garonne. Ed. François Moulenq. 4 vols. Montauban: Forestié, 1879–94.
Documents sur l'ancien hôpital d'Aubrac. Ed. J.-L. Rigal and P.-A. Verlaguet. 2 vols. Rodez: Carrère, 1913–17; Millau: Artières et Maury, 1934.
Les *"Ecclesiastica Officia" cisterciens du XIIe siècle: texte latin selon les manuscrits édités de Trente 1711, Ljubljana 31 et Dijon 114. Version française, annexe liturgique, notes, index et tables.* Ed. Danièle Choisselet and Placide Vernet. Documentation cistercienne 22. Reiningue, France: Abbaye d'OElenberg, 1989.
The Ecclesiastical History of Orderic Vitalis. Ed. Marjorie Chibnall. 6 vols. Oxford: Clarendon Press, 1969–80.
Etudes sur les actes de Louis VII. Ed. Achille Luchaire. Paris: Picard, 1885.
Exordium Magnum Cisterciense: sive narratio de initio cisterciensis ordinis auctore conrado monacho Clarevallensi postea ad Eberbacensi ibidemque abbate ad codicum fidem recensuit, ed. Bruno Griesser. Series Scriptorium Sacri Ordinis Cisterciensis II. Rome: Editiones Cistercienses, 1960. With new edition: Ed. Bruno Griesser. Corpus Christianorum Continuatio Mediaevalis 138. Turnhout: Brepols: 1997. In translation: Conrad d'Eberbach. *Le grand exorde de Cîteaux ou récit des débuts de l'Ordre cistercien.* Trans. Anthelmette Piébourg, intro. Brian P. McGuire, under direction of Jacques Berlioz. Cîteaux, Studia et documenta 7. Turnhout: Brepols, 1998.
Gallia Christiana in provincias ecclesiasticas distributa. Ed. P. Piolin. 13 vols. Paris: Impr. royale, 1870–78. Ed. B. Hauréau. 3 vols. Paris, 1856–65.
Grand Cartulaire de la Sauve Majeure. Ed. Charles Higounet and Arlette Higounet-Nadal, with Nicole de Pena. Bordeaux: La Nef Chastrusse, 1996.
Histoire du prieuré de Jully-les-Nonnains, avec pièces justificatives. Ed. Abbé Jobin. Paris, 1881.
Histoire générale de Languedoc. 2nd ed. Ed. Devic and Vaissete. 18 vols. Toulouse: Privat, 1872–1904.
Layettes du Trésor des Chartes. Ed. Alexandre Teulet et al. 5 vols. Paris: Plon, 1863–1909.
La législation cistercienne abrégée du manuscrit de Montpellier H322. Ed. Louis Duval-Arnould. Paris: Champion, 1997.
The Letters of Peter the Venerable. Ed. Giles Constable. 2 vols. Cambridge, Mass.: Harvard University Press, 1967.
Libellus de diversis ordinibus et professionibus qui sunt in aecclesia. Ed. Giles Constable and B. Smith. Oxford: Clarendon Press, 1972.
Liber instrumentorum memorialium: cartulaire des Guillems de Montpellier. Ed. A. Germain. Montpellier: Jean Marel Ainé, 1884.
The Life of Marie d'Oignies by Jacques de Vitry. Trans. Margot H. King. Toronto: Peregrina, 1993.

Le livre juratoire de Beaumont-de-Lomagne: cartulaire d'une bastide de Gascogne. Ed. Gustave Babinet de Rencogne. Montauban: Forestié, 1888.
Memorials of the Abbey of St. Mary of Fountains. Ed. John Richard Walbran and J. T. Fowler. 3 vols. Durham: Surtees Society, 1863–1918.
Migne, J. D. *Patrologiae Cursus Completus, Series Latina.* 221 vols. Paris: Migne, 1844–64.
Le moine Idung et ses deux ouvrages: "Argumentum super Quatuor Questionibus" et "Dialogus Duorum Monachorum." Ed. R. B. C. Huygens. Spoleto: Centro italiano di studi sull'alto medioevo, 1980.
Monasticon Anglicanum. Ed. William Dugdale, with revisions by John Caley et al. 6 vols. London: James Bohn, 1830.
Les monuments primitifs de la règle cistercienne. Ed. Philip Guignard. Analecta Divionensia 10. Dijon: Rabutot, 1878.
Les plus anciennes chartes en langue provençale. Ed. Clovis Brunel. Paris: Picard, 1926. Supplement, Paris: Picard, 1952.
Les plus anciens textes de Cîteaux: sources, textes et notes historiques. Ed. Jean-de-la-Croix Bouton and Jean-Baptiste Van Damme. Cîteaux, Studia et documenta 2. Achel: Abbaye cistercienne, 1974.
Le premier cartulaire de l'abbaye cistercienne de Pontigny (XIIe–XIIIe siècles). Ed. Martine Garrigues. Paris: Bibliothèque nationale, 1981.
Quarr Abbey and Its Lands, 1132–1631. Ed. S. F. Hockey. Leicester: Leicester University Press, 1970.
Recueil des actes de Henri II, roi d'Angleterre et duc de Normandie concernant les provinces françaises et les affaires de France. Ed. Elie Berger. Vol 1. Paris: Impr. nationale, 1916–27. In *Recueil des historians de Gaules et de la France.* Ed. Léopold Delisle. Paris: Impr. nationale, 1909.
Recueil des actes de l'abbaye cistercienne de Bonnefont-en-Comminges. Ed. Ch. Samaran and Ch. Higounet. Paris: Bibliothèque nationale, 1970.
Recueil des chartes de l'abbaye de Clairvaux, XIIe siècle. Ed. Jean Waquet. Troyes: Archives départementales de l'Aube, 1950–82.
Recueil des pancartes de l'abbaye de la Ferté-sur-Grosne: 1113–1178. Ed. Georges Duby. Aix-Marseilles: Faculté des lettres, 1953.
Recueil des plus ancient actes de la Grande-Chartreuse (1086–1196). Ed. Bernard Bligny. Grenoble: Allier, 1958.
Regesta Pontificum Romanorum ab condita ecclesia ad annum post Christum natum MCXCVIII. Ed. Philip Jaffé. 2 vols. Berlin and Leipzig: Veit, 1885–88.
Regesta Regum Anglo-Normannorum 1066–1154. 4 vols. Vol. 1, ed. H. W. C. Davis; vol. 2, ed. Charles Johnson and H. A. Cronne; vols. 3 and 4, ed. H. A. Cronne and R. H. C. Davis. Oxford: Clarendon Press, 1913–70.
Rouleau mortuaire de B. Vital, abbé de Savigni contenant 207 écrits en 1122–1123 dans différentes églises de France et d'Angleterre. Ed. Léopold Delisle. Paris: H. Champion, 1909.
Rufford Charters: Volume 1. Ed. C. J. Holdsworth. Nottingham: Derry and Sons, 1972.
The Sibton Abbey Cartularies and Charters. Ed. Philippa Brown. Woodbridge, Suffolk: Boydell and Brewer for the Suffolk Records Society, 1984.
Statuta capitulorum generalium ordinis cisterciensis ab anno 1116 ad annum 1786. Ed. J.-M. Canivez. 8 vols. Louvain: Bureaux de la Revue, 1933.

Statuts, chapitres généraux et visites de l'Ordre de Cluny. Ed. G. Charvin. Vol. 1. Paris: Boccard, 1965.
The Tax Book of the Cistercian Order. Ed. Arne Odd Johnson and Peter King. Oslo: Universitetsforlaget, 1979.
The Thame Cartulary. Ed. Herbert E. Salter. Oxford: Oxfordshire Record Society, 1947–48.
"Usus conversorum cisterciensium: saeculi duodecimi secundum tres recensiones successivas." Ed. Chrysogonus Waddell. Forthcoming.
La vie de Saint Etienne d'Obazine. Ed. Michel Aubrun. Clermont-Ferrand: Institut des études du Massif Central, 1970.
"Vita Venerabilis Viri Stephani Muretensis." *PL* 204: 1065–72.

SECONDARY MATERIALS

Abels, Richard and Ellen Harrison. "The Participation of Women in Languedocian Catharism." *Mediaeval Studies (Toronto)* 41 (1979): 215–51.
Acht, Peter. "Die Gesundtschaft König Konrads III. an Papst Eugen III. in Dijon." *Mitteilungen des Instituts für Österreichische Geschichtsforschung* 62 (1954): 668–73.
Alart, B. "Monastères de l'ancien diocèse d'Elne. II: L'abbaye de Sainte-Marie de Jau ou de Clariana, Ordre de Cîteaux." *Mém. Société agricole des Pyrénées-Orientales* 11 (1872): 278–308.
Albanès, A. "Notes sur l'abbaye de Silvacane et nouvelle liste de ses abbés." *R. des Sociétés savantes des départements* 7 (1882): 163–200.
Albe, E. "Notes sur l'abbaye de Leyme: contribution à l'histoire de l'abbaye, analyse et traduction de pièces." *Bull. Société des études littéraires du Lot* 27 (1902): 91–112, 141–155; 28 (1903): 3–9.
Alfonso, Isabel. "Cistercians and Feudalism." *Past and Present* 133 (1991): 3–30.
Angleton, Cicely d'Autremont. "Two Cistercian Preaching Missions to Languedoc in the Twelfth Century: 1145, 1178." Ph.D. dissertation, Catholic University of America, 1984.
Annat, J. "Première restitution de Sauvelade." *R. de Gascogne* 45 (1904): 116–22.
D'Arbois de Jubainville, Henri. *Etudes sur l'état intérieur des abbayes cisterciennes, et principalement de Clairvaux, au XIIe et au XIIIe siècle.* Paris: August Durand, 1858.
Armengaud, Roger. "Boulbonne, une abbaye aux frontières des comtés de Foix et du Languedoc (1130–1790)." *Bull. Société des études du Comminges* 97 (1984): 193–212.
Astell, Ann W. *The Song of Songs in the Middle Ages.* Ithaca, N.Y.: Cornell University Press, 1990.
Auberger, Jean-Baptiste. *L'unanimité cistercienne primitive: mythe ou réalité?* Achel, Belgium: Sine parvulos, 1986.
———. "Les cisterciens à l'époque de Saint Bernard." *Bernardo Cistercense: atti de XXVI Convegno storico internazionale Centro Italiano di Studi sull'alto medioevo* (Spoleto, 1990): 20–43.
Aubert, Marcel. "Abbaye de Fontfroide." *Congrès archéologique* (1954): 425–32.
———. *L'architecture cistercienne en France.* 2nd ed. 2 vols. Paris: Editions d'art et d'histoire, 1947.

———. "Existe-t-il une architecture cistercienne?" *CCM* 1 (1958): 153–58.
Aurell i Cardonna, Martin. "Les Cisterciennes et leurs protecteurs en Provence rhodanienne," *CF 21*, 235–68.
———. *Une famille de la noblesse provençale au Moyen Age: les Porcelet.* Avignon: Aubanel, 1986.
Averkorn, Raphaela. "Die Cistercienserabteien Berdoues und Gimont in ihren Beziehungen zum laikalen Umfeld: Gebetsgedenken, Konversion und Begräbnis." *Vinculum Societatis: Joachim Wallasch zum 60. Gebertstag*, ed. Franz Neiske, Dietrich Poeck, and Mechthild Sandmann. Sigmaringendorf: Glock and Lutz, 1991.
Avril, Joseph. "Recherches sur le politique paroissiale des établissements monastiques et canoniaux (XIe–XIIIe siècles)." *R. Mabillon* 59 (1976–80): 453–517.
Baker, Derek. "Popular Piety in the Lodèvois in the Early Twelfth Century: The Case of Pons de Léras." *Studies in Church History* 15 (1978): 39–47.
Barber, Malcolm. "The Origins of the Order of the Temple." *Studia Monastica* 12 (1970): 219–40.
———. *The New Knighthood: A History of the Order of the Temple.* Cambridge: Cambridge University Press, 1994.
———. *The Two Cities: Medieval Europe, 1050–1320.* London: Routledge, 1992.
Baroot, J. "Les possessions territoriales de l'abbaye de Franquevaux dans le diocèse de Mende." *Bull. Société des lettres de la Lozère* 2 (1915–16): 47–72.
Barrau, H. de. "Etude historique sur l'ancienne abbaye de Bonnecombe." *Mém. Société des lettres de l'Aveyron* 2 (1839–40): 193–264.
Barrière, Bernadette. *L'abbaye cistercienne d'Obazine en Bas-Limousin.* Tulle: Orfeuil, 1977.
———. "Les abbayes issues de l'érémitisme." *CF 21*, 71–106.
———. "Aubazine (Corrèze): Monastère de Coyroux." *Archéologie médiévale* 14 (1984): 311–12.
———. "The Cistercian Monastery of Coyroux in the Province of Limousin in Southern France, in the 12th–13th Centuries." *Gesta* 31 (1992): 76–82.
———. "Les cloîtres des monastères d'Obazine et de Coyroux en Bas-Limousin." *Mélanges Dimier* 3: 177–93.
———. "L'économie cistercienne du sud-ouest de la France." *L'économie cistercienne: géographie—mutations du Moyen Age aux temps modernes*, pp. 75–99. Flaran 3. Auch: Comité du tourisme du Gers, 1983.
———. "Les granges de l'abbaye cistercienne d'Obazine au XIIe et XIIIe siècles." *Bull. Société des lettres de la Corrèze* 70 (1966): 33–51.
———. "La place des monastères cisterciens dans le paysage rural des XIIe–XIIIe siècles." *Moines et monastères dans les sociétés de rite grec et latin*, ed. Jean-Loup Lemaître, Michel Dmitriev, and Pierre Gonneau, pp. 191–209. Geneva: Droz, 1996.
Barrière-Flavy, C. *Histoire de la ville et de la châtellenie de Saverdun dans l'ancien comté de Foix.* Toulouse: Edouard Privat, n.d.
Barruol, Jean. *Sénanque et le pays du Lubéron au Ventoux.* Lyon: Lescuyer, 1975.
Bartlett, Robert. *The Making of Europe: Conquest, Colonization and Cultural Change, 950–1350.* Princeton, N.J.: Princeton University Press, 1994.
Bayle, Jeanne. "L'abbaye de Boulbonne et la croisade de Albigeois." *Pyrénées ariègeoises* (1983): 83–91.
Beaunier, Dom and J.-M. Besse. *Abbayes et prieurés de l'ancienne France.* 4 vols. Paris: Poussielgue, 1910.

Becquet, Jean. "L'érémitisme clérical et laïque dans l'Ouest de la France." *Eremitismo in occidente nei secoli XI e XII*, pp. 182–211. Milan: Università Cattolica, 1965.
———. "*L'institution*: premier coutumier de l'Ordre de Grandmont." *R. Mabillon* 46 (1956): 15–32.
———. "La première crise de l'Ordre de Grandmont." *Bull. Société archéologique du Limousin* 87 (1960): 283–324.
Bedos-Rezak, Brigitte. "Diplomatic Sources and Medieval Documentary Practices: An Essay in Interpretive Methodology." *The Past and Future of Medieval Studies*, ed. John Van Engen, pp. 313–43. Notre Dame, Ind.: University of Notre Dame Press, 1994.
Bell, David N. "*Fons Sapientiae*: une étude de la collection de livres de l'abbaye de Fontfroide du XIIe au XVIe siècle." *Cîteaux* 46 (1995): 77–108.
Benouville, P. and P. Lauzun. "L'abbaye de Flaran." *R. de Gascogne* 28 (1887): 575–81; 29 (1888): 291–302, 504–18; 30 (1889): 115–21, 221–33, 401–24.
Berenguier, Raoul. *Thoronet Abbey*. Trans. John Seabourne. Paris: Monuments historiques, 1965.
Berger, Jutta Maria. "Gastfreundschaft und Gastrecht in hochmittelalterlichen Orden." *Vom Kloster zum Klosterverband*, ed. Hagen Keller and Franz Neiske, pp. 354–405. Munich: Wilhelm Fink, 1997.
Berlière, Ursmer. "Les origines de Cîteaux et l'Ordre bénédictin au XII siècle." *RHE* 1 (1900): 448–71; 2 (1901): 253–90.
Berman, Constance H. "Abbeys for Cistercian Nuns in the Ecclesiastical Province of Sens: Foundation, Endowment, and Economic Activities of the Earlier Foundations." *R. Mabillon* 73 (1997): 83–113.
———. "Les acquisitions rurales des abbayes cisterciennes féminines en l'Ile-de-France." *Paris et Ile-de-France: Mém.* 48 (1997): 113–20.
———. "Administrative Evidence for the Cistercian Grange:The Record of the Cartularies of Bonnecombe." *Cîteaux* 30 (1979): 201–20
———. "Cistercian Development and the Order's Acquisition of Churches and Tithes in Southern France." *R. bénédictine* 91 (1981): 193–203.
———. "Cistercian Nuns and the Development of the Order: The Cistercian Abbey at Saint-Antoine-des-Champs Outside Paris." *The Joy of Learning and the Love of God: Essays in Honor of Jean Leclercq*, ed. E. Rozanne Elder, pp. 121–56. Kalamazoo, Mich.: Cistercian Publications, 1995.
———. "Cistercian Vernacular Architecture in Southern France, the Question of Bastides." *Studies in Cistercian Art and Architecture*, vol. 5, ed. Meredith Parsons Lillich, pp. 238–69. Kalamazoo, Mich.: Cistercian Publications, 1998.
———. "Cistercian Women and Tithes." *Cîteaux* 49 (1998): 95–128.
———. "The Cistercians in the County of Toulouse." Ph.D. dissertation, University of Wisconsin-Madison, 1978.
———. "Les cisterciens de la province ecclésiastique de Sens: quelques exemples d'une étude comparative du patrimoine des abbayes des moines et des abbayes de moniales." *Moines et monastères dans les sociétés de rite grec et latin*, ed. Jean-Loup Lemaître, Michel Dmitriev, and Pierre Gonneau, pp. 211–21. Geneva: Droz, 1996.
———. "Les cisterciens et le tournant économique du XIIe siècle." *Bernard de Clairvaux: histoire, mentalités, spiritualité*, chap. 5, pp. 155–77. Colloque Lyon-Cîteaux-Dijon. Paris: Editions du Cerf, 1992.

———. "The Debate on Cistercian Contracts" (review article). *Cîteaux* 43 (1992): 432–40.

———. "Development of Cistercian Economic Policies During the Lifetime of Bernard of Clairvaux." *Bernardus Magister: In Celebration of the Nonacentenary of the Birth of Bernard of Clairvaux*, ed. John R. Sommerfeldt, pp. 303–13. Kalamazoo, Mich.: Cistercian Publications, 1992.

———. "Disentangling Cluniacs from Cistercian Fictions." Fifth Annual Medieval Studies Conference, University of Leeds. *American Catholic History Review*, forthcoming.

———. "Diversité et unanimité des cisterciens du XIIe siècle." *Unanimité et diversité cisterciennes: filiations, réseaux, relectures du XIIe au XVIIe siècle*, ed. Nicole Bouter. Saint-Etienne: Université de Saint-Etienne, 1999.

———. "Dowries, Private Income, and Anniversary Masses: The Nuns of St. Antoine-des-Champs (Paris)." *Pro. Western Society for French History* 20 (1993): 3–20.

———. "Early Cistercian Expansion in Provence." *Heaven on Earth*, ed. E. Rozanne Elder, pp. 43–54. Kalamazoo, Mich.: Cistercian Publications, 1983.

———. "Economic Practices of Cistercian Women's Communities: A Preliminary Look." *Speculum Studiosorum: Studies in Honor of Father Louis J. Lekai, OCSO*, ed. John R. Sommerfeldt, pp. 15–32. Kalamazoo, Mich.: Cistercian Publications, 1993.

———. "Fashions in Monastic Patronage: The Popularity of Supporting Cistercian Abbeys for Women." *Pro. Western Society for French History* 17 (1990): 36–45.

———. "Fortified Monastic Granges in the Rouergue." *The Medieval Castle: Romance and Reality*, ed. Kathryn Reyerson and Faye Powe, pp. 124–46. Medieval Studies at Minnesota 1. Dubuque, Iowa: Kendall/Hunt, 1984.

———. "The Foundation and Early History of the Monastery of Silvanès: The Economic Reality." *Cistercian Ideals and Reality*, ed. John R. Sommerfeldt, pp. 280–318. Kalamazoo, Mich.: Cistercian Publications, 1978.

———. "From Cistercian Granges to Cistercian Bastides: Using the Order's Records to Date Landscape Transformations." *L'espace cistercien*, ed. Léon Pressouyre, pp. 204–15. Paris: Comité des travaux historiques et scientifiques, 1994.

———. "From *ordo monasticus* to *ordo cisterciensis* in the Twelfth Century." Forthcoming in Festschrift for Jaroslav Pelikan.

———. "Les granges cisterciennes fortifiées du Rouergue." *Cahiers de la Ligue urbaine et rurale* 109 (1990): 54–65.

———. "The Labors of Hercules: The Cartulary, Church, and Abbey of La Cour-Notre-Dame-de-Michery." *Journal of Medieval History* 26 (2000).

———. "Land Acquisition and the Use of the Mortgage Contract by the Cistercians of Berdoues." *Speculum* 57 (1982): 50–66.

———. *Medieval Agriculture, the Southern-French Countryside, and the Early Cistercians: A Study of Forty-Three Monasteries*. Transactions of the American Philosophical Society 76, 5. Philadelphia: American Philosophical Society, 1986.

———. "Men's Houses, Women's Houses: The Relationship Between the Sexes in Twelfth-Century Monasticism." *The Medieval Monastery*, ed. Andrew MacLeish, pp. 43–52. Minneapolis: University of Minnesota Press, 1988.

———. "Monastic Hospices." Forthcoming.

———. "Origins of the Filiation of Morimond in Southern France: Redating Foundation Charters for Gimont, Villelongue, Berdoues, l'Escaledieu, and Bonnefont." *Cîteaux* 41 (1990): 256–77.

———. *Sisters in Wealth and in Poverty: Endowment and Administration of Cistercian Houses for Women in the Ecclesiastical Province of Sens, 1190–1350.* In preparation.

———. "Were There Twelfth-Century Cistercian Nuns?" *Church History* 68 (December 1999).

———. "Women as Donors and Patrons to Southern-French Monasteries in the Twelfth and Thirteenth Centuries." *Worlds of Medieval Women: Creativity, Influence, Imagination.* Papers from the Ninth Conference of the Southeastern Medieval Association, ed. Constance H. Berman, Judith Rice Rothschild, and Charles W. Connell, pp. 53–68. Morgantown: West Virginia University Press, 1985.

Bethell, Denis. "The Foundation of Fountains Abbey and the State of St. Mary's York in 1132." *Journal of Ecclesiastical History* 17 (1966): 11–27.

Bienvenu, J.-M. *L'étonnant fondateur de Fontévraud: Robert d'Arbrissel.* Paris: Nouvelle éditions latines, 1981.

Biget, Jean-Louis, Henri Pradalier, and Michèle Pradalier-Schlumberger. "L'art cistercien dans le Midi toulousain." *CF 21*, pp. 313–70.

Blary, François. *Le domaine de Chaalis: XIIe–XIVe siècles.* Paris: C.N.R.S., 1989.

Bligny, Bernard. *L'église et les ordres religieux dans le royaume de Bourgogne aux XIe et XIIe siècles.* Grenoble: Allier, 1960.

Bloch, Herbert. "The Schism of Anacletus II and the Glanfeuil Forgeries of Peter the Deacon of Monte Cassino." *Traditio* 8 (1952): 159–264.

Bloch, R. Howard. *God's Plagiarist: Being an Account of the Fabulous Industry and Irregular Commerce of the Abbé Migne.* Chicago: University of Chicago Press, 1994.

Bock, Columban. "Les cisterciens et l'étude du droit." *ASOC* 7 (1951): 3–31.

———. *Les codifications du droit cistercien.* Westmalle, Belgium: Abbaye cistercienne, n.d.

Bois, Michèle. "La Basilique Sainte Anne." *R. Drômoise* 83 (1980): 75–81.

Bolton, Brenda. "For the See of Saint-Peter: The Cistercians at Innocent III's Nearest Frontier." *Monastic Studies: The Continuity of Tradition,* ed. Judith Loades, pp. 146–57. Bangor, Gwynned, Wales: Headstart History, 1990.

Bonal, Antoine. *Comté et comtes de Rodez.* Rodez: Carrère, 1885.

Bondéelle-Souchier, Anne. "Les moniales cisterciennes et leurs livres manuscrits dans la France d'ancien régime." *Cîteaux* 45 (1994): 193–336.

Bonnassie, Pierre. "Les conventions féodales dans la Catalogne du XIe siècle." *Les structures sociales de l'Aquitaine, du Languedoc, et de l'Espagne au premier âge féodale,* pp. 187–219. Paris: C.N.R.S., 1969.

Bouchard, Constance B. *Holy Entrepreneurs: Cistercians, Knights, and Economic Exchange in Twelfth-Century Burgundy.* Ithaca, N.Y.: Cornell University Press, 1991.

———. "Noble Piety and Reformed Monasticism: The Dukes of Burgundy in the Twelfth Century." *Noble Piety and Reformed Monasticism,* ed. E. Rozanne Elder, pp. 1–9. Kalamazoo, Mich.: Cistercian Publications, 1981.

———. *Sword, Miter, and Cloister. Nobility and the Church in Burgundy, 980–1198.* Ithaca, N.Y.: Cornell University Press, 1987.

Bourgeat, Charles. *L'abbaye de Bouillas: histoire d'une ancienne abbaye cistercienne du diocèse d'Auch.* Auch: Cocharaux, 1954. Also published as "L'abbaye de Bouillas." *Bull. Société archéologique, historique et scientifique de Gers* 54 (1953): 273–82; 55 (1955): 60–90, 388–405; 56 (1956): 83–109, 180–203.

Bourgeois, Giselle. "Les granges et l'économie de l'abbaye de Nonenque au Moyen Age." *Cîteaux* 24 (1973): 139–60.
Bourin-Derruau, Monique. *Villages médiévaux en Bas-Languedoc: genèse d'une associabilité, Xe–XIVe siècle.* 2 vols. Paris: L'Harmattan, 1987.
Bousquet, l'Abbé. "Anciennes abbayes de l'Ordre de Cîteaux dans le Rouergue." *Mém. Société des lettres de l'Aveyron* 9 (1867): 9–29.
Bousquet, Jacques. "Hughes, comte de Rodez et les consuls de Millau." *Annales du Midi* 72 (1960): 24–42.
———. "Les origines de la transhumance en Rouergue." *L'Aubrac: Etude . . . d'un établissement humain.* 4 vols. Vol. 2, pp. 217–55. Paris: C.N.R.S., 1971.
Bouter, Nicole, ed. *Les mouvances laïques des ordres religieux.* Saint-Etienne, 1996.
Bouton, Jean-de-la-Croix. "L'abbaye de Bonlieu." *Mélanges Dimier* 2,4: 449–61.
———. "L'établissement des moniales cisterciennes." *Mém. Société pour l'histoire du droit (Dijon)* 19 (1953): 83–115.
———. "The Life of the Twelfth- and Thirteenth-Century Nuns of Cîteaux." *Hidden Springs*, vol. 1, pp. 11–28.
———. *Les moniales cisterciennes.* Aiguebelle: Commission pour l'histoire de l'Ordre de Cîteaux, 1986.
———. "Saint Bernard et les moniales." *Mélanges Saint Bernard*, pp. 225–47. Dijon: Assoc. bourguignonne des sociétés savantes, 1954.
———. "La Vernaisson." *R. Drômoise* 83 (1980): 38–74.
Bouton, Jean-de-la-Croix and Dominique Mouret. "Convers et converses des moniales cisterciennes aux XIIIe et XIVe siècles." *CF 21*, pp. 283–312.
Bouton, Jean-de-la-Croix, Benoît Chauvin, and Elisabeth Grosjean. "L'abbaye de Tart et ses filiales au moyen-age." *Mélanges Dimier* 2,3: 19–61.
Boyd, Catherine E. *A Cistercian Nunnery in Medieval Italy: The Story of Rifreddo in Saluzzo, 1220–1300.* Cambridge, Mass.: Harvard University Press, 1943.
———. *Tithes and Parishes in Medieval Italy: The Historical Roots of a Modern Problem.* Ithaca, N.Y.: Cornell University Press, 1952.
Boyer, Raymond. "The Companions of St. Bruno in Middle English Verses on the Foundation of the Carthusian Order." *Speculum* 53 (1978): 784–85.
Bredero, Adriaan H. *Bernard of Clairvaux: Between Cult and History.* Grand Rapids, Mich.: Eerdmans, 1997.
———. "The Canonization of Saint Bernard and the Rewriting of His Life." *Cistercian Ideals and Reality*, ed. John R. Sommerfeldt, pp. 80–105. Kalamazoo, Mich.: Cistercian Publications, 1978.
———. *Christendom and Christianity in the Middle Ages: The Relations Between Religion, Church, and Society.* Trans. Reinder Bruinsma. Grand Rapids, Mich.: Eerdmans, 1994.
———. *Cluny et Cîteaux au douzième siècle: l'histoire d'une controverse monastique.* Amsterdam: North Holland, 1985.
———. "The Conflicting Interpretations of the Relevance of Bernard of Clairvaux to the History of His Own Time." *Cîteaux* 31 (1980): 53–81.
———. *Etudes sur la "Vita Prima" de Saint Bernard.* Rome: Editiones Cistercienses, 1960.
Bru, Yves. "Les deux églises de l'abbaye de Saint-Sulpice-en-Bugey." *Mélanges Dimier* 3,5: 205–25.

Brunet, Roger. *Les campagnes Toulousaines: étude géographique*. Toulouse: Privat, 1965.
Bruzelius, Caroline. "Cistercian High Gothic: The Abbey Church of Longpont and the Architecture of the Cistercians in the Early Thirteenth Century." *ASOC* 35 (1979): 3–204.
———. "The Twelfth-Century Church at Ourscamp." *Speculum* 56 (1981): 28–40.
Buhot, Jacqueline. "L'abbaye normande de Savigny: chef d'ordre et fille de Cîteaux." *Le Moyen Age* 46 (1936): 1–19, 104–21, 178–90, 249–72.
Burton, Janet. "The Abbeys of Byland and Jervaulx and the Problems of the English Savigniacs, 1134–1156." *Monastic Studies: The Continuity of Tradition*, ed. Judith Loades. Bangor, Gwynned, Wales: Headstart History, 1991.
———. *Monastic and Religious Orders in Britain, 1000–1300*. Cambridge: Cambridge University Press, 1994.
———. "The Settlement of Disputes Between Byland Abbey and Newburgh Priory." *Yorkshire Archaeological Journal* 55 (1983): 67–72.
Burton, Pierre-André. "Aux origines de Cîteaux d'après quelques sources écrites du XIIe siècle: enquête sur une polémique." *Cîteaux* 48 (1997): 209–28.
Bynum, Caroline Walker. *Jesus as Mother: Studies in the Spirituality of the High Middle Ages*. Berkeley: University of California Press, 1982.
Cabanis, Alfred. "L'abbaye de Valmagne." *Mém: Société des lettres de l'Aveyron* 5 (1844–1845): 424–27.
Cabau, Patrice. "Foulque, marchand et troubadour de Marseille, moine et abbé du Thoronet, évêque de Toulouse (v. 1155/1160-25.12.1231)." *CF 21*, pp. 151–82.
Caille, Jacqueline. "Les seigneurs de Narbonne dans le conflit Toulouse-Barcelone au XIIe siècle." *Annales du Midi* 97 (1985): 227–44.
Calmels, Norbert. "Saint Norbert, Rome, et l'Ordre canonial de Prémontré." *AP* 49 (1973): 145–60.
Canivez, J.-M. "Beaulieu à Mirepoix." *DHGE* 7 (1134): 162–63.
———. "Beaulieu-en-Rouergue." *DHGE* 7 (1934): 164.
———. "Bellecombe." *DHGE* 8 (1936): 837–38.
———. "Bonlieu." *DHGE* 9 (1937): 1007.
———. "Bonnevaux." *DHGE* 9 (1937): 1074–76.
———. "Bouchet." *DHGE* 9 (1937): 1467.
———. "Cadouin." *DHGE* 11 (1949): 118–22.
———. "Calers." *DHGE* 11 (1949): 387–388.
———. "Candeil." *DHGE* 11 (1949): 719.
———. "Cîteaux." *DHGE* 12 (1953): 852–997.
———. "Costejean." *DHGE* 13 (1960): 935.
Carbonell-Lamothe, Yvonne. "L'abbaye du Vignogoul." *CF 21*: 269–82.
Carpenter, Jennifer. "Juette of Huy, Recluse and Other (1158–1228): Children and Mothering in the Saintly Life." *Power of the Weak*, ed. Carpenter and Sally-Beth MacLean, pp. 57–93. Urbana: University of Illinois Press, 1995.
Castaing-Sicard, Mireille. *Les contrats dans le très ancien droit toulousain (Xe–XIIIe siècle)*. Toulouse: Espic, 1957.
———. "Donations toulousaines du Xe au XIIIe siècles." *Annales du Midi* 70 (1958): 27–64.
———. *Monnaies féodales et circulation monétaire en Languedoc (Xe–XIIIe siècles)*. Toulouse: Association Marc Bloch, 1961.

Castelnau, L. de. "L'abbaye de Bonneval." *R. du Midi* 2 (1887): 65–69.
Cathala, C. "Boulbonne." *DHGE* 10 (1938): 60–70.
Cauvet, E. *Etude historique sur Fonfroide* [sic]. Montpellier: Séquin, 1875.
Cazes, Daniel. "L'abbaye de Grandselve, problèmes d'art et d'archéologie: l'église." *Bull. Société archéologique de Tarn-et-Garonne* 103 (1975): 51–64.
———. "Le chevet de l'église abbatiale de Grandselve d'après les fouilles." *Bull. Société archéologique de Tarn-et-Garonne* 107 (1979): 75–84.
———. "Recherches archéologiques sur l'abbaye de Grandselve." *Mélanges Dimier* 2,5: 227–64.
Cezérac, C. "La prieuré du Carmel-de-Lectoure et l'abbaye de Grandselve." *R. de Gascogne* 43 (1902): 318–28.
Chauvin, Benoît. "De la 'Villa Carolingienne' à la grange cistercienne: le cas de la terre de Glénon (Arbois, Jura), du milieu du Xe à la fin du XIIe siècle." *Francia* 11 (1982): 164–84.
———. "Hildegard de Bingen et les Cisterciens: note sur les *Epistolae LXX et LXXI*." *Cîteaux* 46 (1995): 159–65.
———, ed. *Mélanges à la mémoire du père Anselme Dimier*. 3 vols. in 6. Pupillon: Arbois, 1982–87.
———. "Papauté et abbayes cisterciennes du duché de Bourgogne." *L'église de France et la papauté (Xe–XIIIe siècle)*, ed. Rolf Grosse, pp. 326–62. Bonn: Bouvier, 1993.
———. *Pierres . . . pour l'abbaye de Villelongue, histoire et architecture*. 2 vols. Beernem: Windroos, 1992.
———. "Quelques additions et corrections au 'Recueil des actes de l'abbaye cistercienne de Bonnefont-en-Comminges' tirées des archives de l'abbaye de Villelongue (Aude), 1149–1168." *Annales du Midi* 103 (1991): 77–94.
Cheney, C. R. "A Letter of Pope Innocent III and the Lateran Decree on Cistercian Tithe-Paying." *Cîteaux* 13 (1962): 146–51.
Chevalier, Ulysse. "Notes historiques sur l'abbaye de Vernaison." *Bull. d'histoire ecclésiastique de Valence, Gap, Grenoble et Viviers* 2 (1881): 15–24, 45–56.
Chevrier, G. "Remarques sur la distinction de l'acte à titre onéreux et de l'acte à titre gratuit d'après les chartes du Rouergue au XIIe siècle." *Annales de la faculté de Droit de l'Université d'Aix-Marseilles* 43 (1950): 67–79.
Cheyette, Fredric L. "The 'Sale' of Carcassonne to the Counts of Barcelona (1067–1070) and the Rise of the Trencavels." *Speculum* 63 (1988): 826–63.
Chibnall, Marjorie. *Anglo-Norman England, 1066–1166*. Oxford: Blackwell, 1986.
———. "'Clio's Legal Cosmetics': Law and Custom in the Work of Medieval Historians." *Anglo-Norman Studies* 20 (1997): 31–43.
———. *The Empress Matilda: Queen Consort, Queen Mother, and Lady of the English*. Oxford: Blackwell, 1991.
Cholvy, Gerard, ed. *Le Diocèse de Montpellier*. Paris: Beauchesne, 1976.
Les Cisterciens de Languedoc (XIIIe–XIVe siècle). Cahiers de Fanjeaux 21. Toulouse: Privat, 1986.
Clanchy, Michael T. *From Memory to Written Record: England, 1066–1307*. 2nd ed. Oxford: Blackwell, 1993.
Clergeac, A. "Les abbayes de Gascogne du XIIe siècle au grand schisme d'occident." *R. de Gascogne* 47 (1906): 316–29, 530–44.
Cocheril, Maur. "Espagne cistercienne." *DHGE* 15 (1963): 944–69.

Colvin, Howard Montagu. *The White Canons in England*. Oxford: Clarendon Press, 1951.
Congar, Yves M.-J. "Henri de Marcy, abbé de Clairvaux, cardinal-évêque d'Albano et légat pontifical." *Analecta Anselmiana* 43 (1959): 1–90.
Conner, Elizabeth. "The Abbeys of Las Huelgas and Le Tart and Their Filiations." *Hidden Springs*, vol. 1, pp. 29–48.
Constable, Giles. "Aelred of Rievaulx and the Nun of Watton: An Episode in the Early History of the Gilbertine Order." *Medieval Women*, ed. Derek Baker, pp. 205–26. Oxford: Blackwell, 1978.
———. "Cluniac Tithes and the Controversy Between Gigny and Le Miroir." *R. bénédictine* 70 (1960): 591–624.
———. "The Financing of the Crusades in the Twelfth Century." *Monks, Hermits, and Crusaders in Medieval Europe*, ed. Giles Constable. London: Variorum Reprints, 1975.
———. *Letters and Letter Collections*. Turnhout: Brepols, 1976.
———. *Medieval Monasticism: A Select Bibliography*. Toronto: University of Toronto Press, 1976.
———. *Monastic Tithes from Their Origins to the Twelfth Century*. Cambridge: Cambridge University Press, 1964.
———. *The Reformation of the Twelfth Century*. Cambridge: Cambridge University Press, 1996.
———. "The Study of Monastic History Today." *Essays on the Reconstruction of Medieval History*, ed. Vaclav Mudroch and G. S. Couse, pp. 21–51. Montreal: McGill-Queen's University Press, 1974.
———. *Three Studies in Medieval Religious and Social Thought: The Interpretation of Mary and Martha; The Ideal of the Imitation of Christ; The Orders of Society*. Cambridge: Cambridge University Press, 1995.
Cortese-Esposito, R. "Analogie e contrasti fra Citeaux et Cluny." *Cîteaux* 19 (1969): 5–39.
Cottineau, L.-H. *Répertoire topo-bibliographique des abbayes et prieurés*. 3 vols. Macon: Protat, 1935–38.
Couget, Alphonse. "L'abbaye de Bonnefont-en-Comminges." *R. de Comminges* 2 (1886): 37–56.
Cowdrey, H. E. J. *The Cluniacs and the Gregorian Reform*. Oxford: Clarendon Press, 1970.
———. "*Quidam Frater Stephanus Nomine, Anglicus Natione*: The English Background of Stephen Harding." *R. bénédictine* 101 (1991): 322–40.
Crozet, René. "L'épiscopat de France et l'Ordre de Cîteaux au XIIe siècle." *Etudes de civilisation médiévale IXe–XIIe siècles: mélanges dédiés à Edmund-René Labande*, pp. 263–68. *CCM* 18, 1975.
Cuerne, Louis de. "L'abbaye cistercienne de Loc-Dieu." *Connaissance du monde* 84 (1965): 13–27.
Davis, G. R. C. *Medieval Cartularies of Great Britain: A Short Catalogue*. London: Longmans, 1958.
De Beaufort, G. "La Charte de Charité cistercienne et son évolution." *RHE* 49 (1954): 391–437.
Decap, Jean. "L'abbaye de Bonnefont au comté de Comminges, en 1667." *R. de Gascogne* 40 (1899): 188–99.

De Fontette, Micheline. *Les religieuses à l'âge classique du droit canon: recherches sur les structures juridiques des branches féminines des ordres*. Paris: Vrin, 1961.

De Ganck, Roger. "The Cistercian Nuns of Belgium in the Thirteenth Century Seen Against the Background of the Second Wave of Cistercian Spirituality." *CSQ* 5 (1970): 169–87.

———. "The Integration of Nuns in the Cistercian Order, Particularly in Belgium." *Cîteaux* 35 (1984): 235–47.

De Place, François. "Bibliographie raisonnée des premiers documents cisterciens (1098–1220)." *Cîteaux* 35 (1984): 7–54.

Degert, A. "Berdoues." *DHGE* 8 (1936): 351.

Degler-Spengler, Brigitte. "The Incorporation of Cistercian Nuns into the Order in the Twelfth and Thirteenth Century." *Hidden Springs*, vol. 1, pp. 85–134.

———. "Die Zisterzienserinnen in der Schweiz." *Helvetia Sacra* (Bern) 3 (1982): 507–74.

Delaux, P. and F. Liberos. *Histoire de la bastide de Saint-Lys*. Toulouse: Eché réédition, 1980.

Delessart, L. "Les débuts de l'abbaye de Morimond." *Mém. Société pour l'histoire du droit* 15 (1953): 65–68.

Dennis, Matthew. *Cultivating a Landscape of Peace: Iroquois-European Encounters in Seventeenth-Century America*. Ithaca, N.Y.: Cornell University Press, 1993.

Dereine, Charles. "L'élaboration du statu canonique des chanoines réguliers spécialement sous Urbain II." *RHE* 46 (1951): 534–65.

———. "Chanoines: des origins au XIIIe siècle." *DHGE* 12 (1953): 354–405.

———. "Les coutumiers de Saint-Quentin de Beauvais et de Springiersbach." *RHE* 43 (1948): 411–42.

———. "Coutumiers et ordinaires de chanoines réguliers." *Scriptorium* 5 (1951): 107–13; 12 (1957): 244–48.

———. "Enquête sur la règle de Saint Augustin." *Scriptorium* 2 (1948): 28–36.

———. "La fondation de Cîteaux d'après l'*Exordium Cistercii* et l'*Exordium Parvum*." *Cîteaux* 10 (1959): 125–39.

———. "Les origines de Prémontré." *RHE* 42 (1947): 352–78.

———. "Le premier *ordo* de Prémontré." *R. bénédictine* 58 (1948): 84–92.

Desmarchelier, Michel. "L'architecture des églises de moniales cisterciennes, essai de classement des différents types de plans (en guise de suite)." *Mélanges Dimier* 2, 5: 109–21.

Dimier, Anselme. *Amédée de Lausanne: disciple de saint Bernard*. Rotomagi: Editions de Fontenelle, 1949.

———. "L'architecture des églises de moniales cisterciennes." *Cîteaux* 25 (1974): 8–23.

———. *L'art cistercien: France*. Trans. Paul Veyriras. 2nd ed. Paris: Zodiaque, 1974.

———. "Chapitres généraux d'abbesses cisterciennes." *Cîteaux* 11 (1960): 268–75.

———. "Cîteaux et les emplacements malsains." *Cîteaux in der Nederlanden* 6 (1955): 89–97.

———. "Eaunes." *DHGE* 15 (1963): 263ff.

———. "L'Escaledieu." *DHGE* 15 (1963): 844.

———. "L'Eule." *DHGE* 15 (1963): 1386.

———. "Une évêque Cistercien oublié: Guigues, abbé de Bonnevaux 1151, évêque d'Amélia 1159." *COCR* 6 (1939): 284–88.

———. "Fabas." *DHGE* 16 (1967) 301–5.
———. "Feuillans." *DHGE* 16 (1967): 1334.
———. "Les fondations de Saint Bernard en Italie." *ASOC* 13 (1957): 63–68.
———. "Fonts-lès-Alès." *DHGE* 17 (1970): 990–91.
———. "Goujon." *DHGE* 18 (1973): 938–39.
———. "Granges, celliers, et bâtiments d'exploitation cisterciens." *Archeologia* 65 (1973): 52–63; 74 (1974): 46–57.
———. "Observances monastiques." *ASOC* 11 (1955): 149–98.
———. "Le premier monastère de Tamié." *COCR* 20 (1958): 67–71.
———. "A propos de la Charte de Charité: Cîteaux et Chalais." *COCR* 8 (1946): 241–56.
———. "Quelques légendes de fondations chez les cisterciens." *Studia Monastica* 12 (1970): 97–105.
———. *Recueil de plans d'églises cisterciennes*. 4 vols. Grignan, Drome: Abbaye Notre-Dame d'Aiguebelle, 1949 (plus updates).
———. "Saint Bernard et le recrutement de Clairvaux." *R. Mabillon* 42 (1952): 17–30, 56–68, 69–78.
———. *Saint Louis et Cîteaux*. Paris: Letouzey et Ané, 1954.
———. "Un témoin tardif peu connu du conflict entre cisterciens et clunisiens." *Analecta Anselmiana* 40 (1956): 81–94.
———. "Vita venerabilis Amedei Altaeripae (c. 1150) — Auctore monacho quodam Bonaevallensi synchrono et oculato." *Studia Monastica* 5 (1963): 265–304.
Donkin, R. A. *A Check-List of Printed Works Relating to the Cistercian Order*. Documentation cistercienne 2. Rochefort, Belgium: Abbaye N.D. de S. Remy, 1969.
———. *The Cistercians: Studies in the Geography of Mediaeval England and Wales*. Toronto: Pontifical Institute of Mediaeval Studies, 1978.
Donnelly, James S. *The Decline of the Medieval Cistercian Laybrotherhood*. New York: Fordham University Press, 1949.
Douais, M. "Le Cartulaire de Nizors." *R. de Gascogne* 28 (1887): 565–67.
Dubois, Jacques. "L'implantation monastique dans le Bugey au Moyen Age." *Journal des savants* (Jan.–Mar. 1971): 15–31.
———. "L'institution des convers au XIIe siècle: forme de vie monastique propre aux laïcs." *I laici nella "societas Christiana" dei secoli XI e XII*, pp. 183–261. Milan: Università Cattolica, 1968.
———. "Les moines dans la société du Moyen Age: 950–1350." *R. d'histoire de l'église de France* 60 (1974): 5–37.
———. "Les ordres religieux au XIIe siècle selon la curie romaine." *R. bénédictine* 78 (1968): 283–309.
———. "Quelques problèmes de l'histoire de l'Ordre des Chartreux à propos de livres récents." *RHE* 63 (1968): 27–54.
———. "Le rôle du chapitre dans le gouvernement du monastère." *Sous la règle de Saint-Benoît*, pp. 21–37. Paris: Droz, 1967.
Dubois, Louis. *Histoire de l'abbaye de Morimond*. Paris: Sagnier et Bray, 1851.
Dubord, R. "Les abbayes cisterciennes filles de Gimont." *R. de Gascogne* 27 (1876): 221–22.
———. "Essai historique sur l'abbaye de Gimont." *R. de Gascogne* 11 (1871): 427–31; 12 (1872): 93–101, 193–204, 289–302; 13 (1873): 49–67, 227–43; 14 (1874): 25–38, 69–84, 448–56, 496–505; 15 (1875): 69–80, 156–74.

———. "Foundations civiles de l'abbaye de Gimont." *R. de Gascogne* 17 (1877): 388–402, 429–37, 504–19, 559–72.
Dubourg, A. *Ordre de Malte: histoire du grand prieuré de Toulouse*. Paris: Société bibliographique, 1883.
Duby, Georges. *Saint Bernard: l'art Cistercien*. Paris: Flammarion, 1979.
——— *The Early Growth of the European Economy*. Trans. Howard B. Clarke. Ithaca, N.Y.: Cornell University Press, 1974.
———. "Un inventaire des profits de la seigneurie clunisienne à la mort de Pierre le Vénérable." *Petrus Venerabilis, 1156–1956: Studies and Texts Commemorating the Eighth Centenary of His Death*, ed. Giles Constable and James Kritzeck, pp. 128–40. Rome: Herder, 1956.
———. *The Knight, the Lady, and the Priest: The Making of Modern Marriage in Medieval France*. New York: Pantheon, 1983.
———. *Rural Economy and Country Life in the Medieval West*. Trans. Cynthia Postan. Columbia: University of South Carolina Press, 1968.
———. *La société aux XIe et XIIe siècles dans la région mâconnaise*. Paris: SEVPEN, 1971.
———. *The Three Orders: Feudal Society Imagined*. Trans. Arthur Goldhammer. Chicago: University of Chicago Press, 1980.
Duby, Georges and Armand Wallon, eds. *Histoire de la France rurale*. 5 vols. Paris: Seuil, 1975.
DuCange, Charles De Fresne. *Glossarium mediae et infimae latinitatis*. Ed. Léopold Favre. 10 vols. Paris: Librairie des sciences et des arts, 1937–38.
Durand, Geneviève. "L'abbaye cistercienne de Silvanès." *R. du Rouergue* 40 (1986): 141–172.
———. "L'église de l'abbaye cistercienne de Sylvanès (Aveyron)." *Archéologie du Midi médiéval* 2 (1984): 81–96.
Durliat, Marcel. "L'abbaye de Valmagne." *Cahiers de N.D. del Pessebre* (1956): 17–20.
———. "L'abbaye de Villelongue." *Carcassonne et sa region: fédération historique du Languedoc méditerranéen et du Roussillon par la Fédération des sociétés académiques et savantes de Languedoc-Pyrénées-Gascogne*. Carcassonne: Fédération, 1970, pp. 65–67.
Dyer, Christopher. *Standards of Living in the Late Middle Ages: Social Change in England c. 1200–1520*. Cambridge: Cambridge University Press, 1989.
Elder, E. Rozanne, ed. *The New Monastery: Texts and Studies on the Early Cistercians*. Kalamazoo, Mich.: Cistercian Publications, 1998.
Elkins, Sharon. *Holy Women of Twelfth-Century England*. Chapel Hill: University of North Carolina Press, 1988.
Elliott, Dyan. *Spiritual Marriage: Sexual Abstinence in Medieval Wedlock*. Princeton, N.J.: Princeton University Press, 1993.
Esparseil, Raymond. "Rieunette." *Mém. Société des arts de Carcassonne* 10 (1952–53): 190–98.
Falkenstein, Ludwig. "Alexandre III et Henri de France: conformités et conflits." *L'église de France et la papauté*, ed. Rolf Grosse, pp. 103–76. Bonn: Bouvier, 1993.
———. *La papauté et les abbayes françaises aux XIe et XIIe siècles*. Paris: Champion, 1997.
Felten, Franz J. "Verbandsbildung von Frauenklöstern: Le Paraclet, Prémy, Fontevraud mit einem Ausblick auf Cluny, Sempringham, und Tart." *Vom Kloster zum Klosterverband*, ed. Hagen Keller and Franz Neiske, pp. 277–341. Munich: Wilhelm Fink, 1997.

La femme dans la vie religieuse du Languedoc (XIIIe–XIVe siecle). Cahiers de Fanjeaux 23. Toulouse: Privat, 1988.
Ferrands, L. "Feuillants." *DHGE* 16 (1967): 1338.
Ferras, Vincent. *Un cistercien occitan au XIIe siècle: Pons de Léras*. Dourgne: Abbaye d'en Calcat, 1971.
———. *Documents bibliographiques concernant le rayonnement médiéval de l'Ordre de Cîteaux en pays d'Aude*. Abbaye d'en-Calcat, 1971.
Fillet, l'Abbé. "Documents relatifs au monastère de Notre-Dame du Plan, près de Bollène — rectification à la nouvelle *Gallia*." *Bull. Historique Comité des travaux historiques et scientifiques* (Paris) (1895): 84–93.
Fons, Victor. "L'abbaye de Goujon." *Mém. Société archéologique du Midi de la France* 7 (1860–65): 335–41.
———. "L'abbaye royale de Fabas." *R. de Toulouse et du Midi de la France* 23 (1866): 374–85.
———. "L'abbaye royale des Salenques." *R. de Toulouse et du Midi de la France* 32 (1875): 81–98.
———. "Les monastères cisterciens de l'ancienne province ecclésiastique de Toulouse." *R. de Toulouse et du Midi de la France* 25 (1867): 112–34.
Fonseca, Cosimo Damiano. "*Constat . . . monasterium esse tam canonicorum quam et monachorum*: le influenze monastiche sulle strutture istituzionali delle Canoniche e delle Congregazioni canonicali." *Vom Kloster zum Klosterverband*, ed. Hagen Keller and Franz Neiske, pp. 239–51. Munich: Wilhelm Fink, 1997.
Foreville, Raymonde. "Arnaud Amalric, archevêque de Narbonne: 1196–1225." *Narbonne: archéologie et histoire. Fédération historique du Languedoc méditerranéen et du Roussillon*. Montpellier: Fédération, 1973, pp. 129–146.
———. *Latran I, II, III, et Latran IV*. Paris: L'Orante, 1965.
———. *Un procès de canonisation à l'aube du XIIIe siècle (1201–1202)*. Paris: Bloud et Gay, 1943.
Fossier, Robert. "L'économie cistercienne dans les plaines du nord-ouest d'Europe." *L'économie cistercienne: géographie — mutations du Moyen Age aux temps modernes*, pp. 53–74. Flaran 3. Auch: Comité du tourisme du Gers, 1983.
———. "L'essor économique de Clairvaux." *Bernard de Clairvaux*, pp. 95–114. Paris: Alsatia, 1953
———. "La puissance économique de l'abbaye de Clairvaux au XIIIe siècle." *Histoire de Clairvaux: actes du Colloque de Bar-sur-Aube/Clairvaux, 22–23 June, 1990*, pp. 73–83. Bar-sur-Aube: Némont, 1991.
Fournier, Gabriel. "La création de la grange de Gregovie pas les Prémontrés de Saint André et sa transformation en seigneurie (XIIe–XVIe siècles). *Le Moyen Age* 56 (1950):307–55.
———. *Le peuplement rural en Basse-Auvergne durant le haut Moyen Age*. Paris: Presses Universitaires de France, 1962.
Fournier, P. "Alexandre, abbé de Cîteaux." *DHGE* 2 (1914): 200–201.
Framond, M. de. "Historique de l'abbaye de la Vernaison." *R. Drômoise* 83 (1980): 151–54.
France, James. *The Cistercians in Medieval Art*. Kalamazoo, Mich.: Cistercian Publications, 1998.
———. "The Coming of the Cistercians to Scandinavia — *Ad exteras et barbaras regiones*." *Cîteaux* 48 (1997): 5–14.

Freed, John. "Urban Development and the 'Cura Monialium' in Thirteenth-Century Germany." *Viator* 3 (1972): 311–27.
Frenz, Thomas. *Papsturkunden des Mittelalters und der Neuzeit.* Stuttgart: Steiner, 1986.
Friedlander, Alan. "Trencavel." *Medieval France: An Encyclopedia,* ed. William W. Kibler et al., p. 925. New York: Garland, 1995.
Gabent, Paul. "Goujon, abbaye et paroisse." *R. de Gascogne* 36 (1895): 497–506, 545–59.
Galabert, J.-A.-Firmin. "L'église abbatiale de Grandselve et ses reliques." *Mém: Société archéologique de Tarn-et-Garonne* 15 (1887): 212–18.
Galbraith, V. H. "Monastic Foundation Charters of the Eleventh and Twelfth Centuries." *Cambridge Historical Journal* 4 (1934): 205–22, 296–98.
Garrigues, D. "L'abbaye Notre-Dame d'Eaunes en Comminges." *R. de Comminges* 26 (1912): 133–50, 255–70; 28 (1915): 1–14.
Gaussin, Pierre-Roger. "Les communautés féminines dans l'espace languedocien de la fin du XIe à la fin du XIVe siècle." *CF 23,* pp. 299–332.
Gayne, P. "L'abbaye du Grandselve." *Bull. Société archéologique de Tarn-et-Garonne* 77 (1949): 104–27.
———. "A propos de l'abbaye de Grandselve." *Bull. Société archéologique de Tarn-et-Garonne* 82 (1957): 95–97.
Geary, Patrick. *Phantoms of Remembrance: Memory and Oblivion at the End of the First Millennium.* Princeton, N.J.: Princeton University Press, 1994.
Genest, Jean-François. "La bibliothèque de Clairvaux de Saint-Bernard à Humanisme." *Histoire de Clairvaux: actes du Colloque de Bar-sur-Aube/Clairvaux, 22–23 June, 1990,* pp. 113–33. Bar-sur-Aube: Némont, 1991.
Génestal, Robert. *Le rôle des monastères comme établissements de crédit: étudie en Normandie du XIe à la fin du XIIIe siècle.* Paris: Rousseau, 1901.
Gerits, Trudo J. "Les actes de confraternité de 1142 et de 1153 entre Cîteaux et Prémontré." *AP* 40 (1964): 192–205.
Gervers, Michael, ed. *The Second Crusade and the Cistercians.* New York: St. Martin's Press, 1992.
———. "The Dating of Medieval English Private Charters of the Twelfth and Thirteenth Centuries." At ⟨www.utoronto.ca/deeds⟩.
Gilchrist, Roberta. *Gender and Material Culture: The Archaeology of Religious Women.* London: Routledge, 1994.
Giry, Arthur. *Manuel de diplomatique.* Paris: Hachette, 1894.
Gold, Penny Schine. *The Lady and the Virgin: Image, Attitude, and Experience in Twelfth-Century France.* Chicago: University of Chicago Press, 1985.
———. "Male/Female Cooperation: The Example of Fontevrault." *Distant Echoes,* pp. 151–68.
Golding, Brian. *Gilbert of Sempringham and the Gilbertine Order, c. 1130–1300.* Oxford: Clarendon Press, 1995.
———. "The Hermit and the Hunter." *The Cloister and the World: Essays in Medieval History in Honor of Barbara Harvey,* ed. John Blais and Brian Golding, pp. 95–117. Oxford: Clarendon Press, 1996.
———. "Hermits, Monks and Women in Twelfth-Century France and England: The Experience of Obazine and Sempringham," *Monastic Studies: The Continuity of Tradition,* pp. 127–45. Bangor, Gwynned, Wales: Headstart History, 1990.

Golob, Natasa, ed. *Stiski rokopisi iz 12. stoletja: codices Sitticenses saeculi XII*. Ljubljana: Slovenska knjig, 1994.
Gorsse, Pierre de. *L'abbaye cistercienne Sainte-Marie de Valmagne au diocèse d'Agde en Languedoc*. Toulouse: Lion, 1933.
Gould, Stephen Jay. *Wonderful Life: The Burgess Shale and the Nature of History*. New York: Norton, 1989.
Grant, Lindy. *Abbot Suger of St-Denis: Church and State in Early Twelfth-Century France*. London: Longman, 1998.
Graves, Coburn V. "The Economic Activities of the Cistercians in Medieval England (1128–1307)." *ASOC* 13 (1957): 3–60.
———. "English Cistercian Nuns in Lincolnshire."*Speculum* 54 (1979): 492–99.
———. "The Organization of an English Cistercian Nunnery in Lincolnshire," *Cîteaux* 33 (1982): 333–50.
———. "Stixwould in the Market-Place." *Distant Echoes*, pp. 213–36.
Grèzes-Rueff, François. "L'abbaye de Fontfroide et son domaine foncier au XIIe–XIIIe siècles." *Annales du Midi* 89 (1977): 253–80.
Griesser, Bruno. "Beiträge zur Beurteilung des Cod. 1711 von Trient." *Cîteaux in der Nederlanden* 6 (1955): 117–30.
Grill, Léopold. "Benediktinisch-cisterziensischer Einfluss auf die Gründung des Kartäuserordens." *Die Kartäuser in Österreich* 2 (1981): 4–18.
———. "Der hl. Bernhard als bisher unerkannter Verfasser des *Exordium Cistercii* und der *Summa Cartae Caritatis*." *CC* 66 (1959): 43–57.
Grinda, A. "Sur la charte de fondation de l'abbaye de Boulbonne." *Mém. Société archéologique du Midi de la France* 11 (1884): 34–35; 12 (1885): 16–17.
Grosse, Rolf, ed. *L'église de France et la papauté (Xe–XIIIe siècle); Die Französische kirche und das Papsttum (10.–13. Jahrhundert): actes du XXVIe colloque historique franco-allemand organisé en coopération avec l'Ecole nationale des chartes part l'Institut historique allemand de Paris (Paris, 17–19 octobre 1990)*. Etudes et documents pour servir à une Gallia Pontificia. Bonn: Bouvier, 1993.
Grundmann, Herbert, *Religious Movements in the Middle Ages: The Historical Links Between Heresy, the Mendicant Orders, and the Women's Religious Movement in the Twelfth and Thirteenth Century, with the Historical Foundations of German Mysticism*. Trans. Steven Rowan, intro. Robert E. Lerner. Notre Dame, Ind.: Notre Dame University Press, 1995. Originally *Religiöse Bewegungen*. Berlin, 1935; new ed., 1961.
Guillemain, Bernard. "Les moines sur les sièges épiscopaux du sud-ouest de la France aux XIe et XIIe siècles." *Mélanges dédiés à Edmund-René Labande*. *CCM* 18 (1975): 377–84.
Guyotjeannin, Olivier. "L'influence pontificale sur les actes épiscopaux français (provinces ecclésiastiques de Reims, Sens, et Rouen, XIe–XIIe siècles)." *L'église de France et la papauté (Xe–XIIIe siècle)*, ed. Rolf Grosse, pp. 83–102. Bonn: Bouvier, 1993.
Guyotjeannin, Olivier, Laurent Morelle, and Michel Parisse, eds. *Les cartulaires: actes de la table ronde organisée par l'Ecole nationale des chartes et le G.D.R. 121 du C.N.R.S., Paris 5–7 décembre 1991*. Paris: Ecole des chartes, 1993.
Guyotjeannin, Olivier, Jacques Pycke, and Benoît-Michel Tock. *Diplomatique médiévale*. L'atelier du médiéviste 2. Turnhout: Brepols, 1993.

Hallam, Elizabeth M. "Henry II, Richard I, and the Order of Grandmont." *Journal of Medieval History* 1 (1975): 165–86.
Hallinger, Kassius. "Die Anfänge von Cîteaux." *Aus Kirche und Reich: Festschrift für Friedrich Kempf*, ed. Hubert Mordek, pp. 225–35. Sigmaringen: J. Thorbecke, 1983.
Harvey, Barbara. *Living and Dying in England 1100–1540: The Monastic Experience*. Oxford: Clarendon Press, 1993.
Haskins, Charles Homer. *The Renaissance of the Twelfth Century*. Cambridge, Mass.: Harvard University Press, 1922.
Herlihy, David. "Land, Family, and Women in Continental Europe, 701–1200." *Traditio* 1 (1962): 89–120.
Higounet, Charles. "Une carte des relations monastiques transpyrénéennes au Moyen Age." *R. de Comminges* 64 (1951): 129–38.
———. "Le chemins de Saint-Jacques et les sauvetés de Gascogne." *Annales du Midi* 63 (1951): 294–304.
———. "Cisterciens et bastides." *Le Moyen Age* 56 (1950): 69–84.
———. "La maison et les chais de l'abbaye de Grandselve à Bordeaux." *Mélanges Dimier* 2,4: 697–99.
———. "Un mémoire sur les péages de la Garonne du début du XIVe siècle."*Annales du Midi* 61 (1948–49): 32–45.
———. "Nouvelles réflexions sur les bastides 'cisterciennes.'" *CF 21*, pp. 127–38.
———. *Paysages et villages neufs du Moyen Age: recueil d'articles de Charles Higounet*. Bordeaux: Fédération historique du Sud-Ouest, 1975.
Hill, Bennett D. *English Cistercian Monasteries and Their Patrons in the Twelfth Century*. Urbana: University of Illinois Press, 1968.
Hillebrandt, Maria. "Abt und Gemeinschaft in Cluny (10.–11. Jahrhundert)." *Vom Kloster zum Klosterverband*, ed. Hagen Keller and Franz Neiske, pp. 147–72. Munich: Wilhelm Fink, 1997.
Holdsworth, Christopher. *The Piper and the Tune: Medieval Patrons and Monks*. Stenton Lecture 1990, University of Reading, 1991.
Hollier, Emile. *Histoire de l'abbaye de Gigean (Saint-Félix-de-Montseau)*. Montpellier: n.p., 1925.
Holthof, Jean-Francois. "Cîteaux, XIIe–XXe siècle." *Saint Bernard et le monde cistercien*, ed. Léon Pressouyre and Terryl N. Kinder, pp. 177–97. Paris: Monuments historiques, 1990.
Hourlier, Jacques. *Le chapitre général jusqu'au moment du Grand Schisme: origines, développement, étude juridique*. Paris: Librairie du recueil Sirey, 1936.
———. "Cluny et la notion d'ordre religieux." *A Cluny: Congrès scientifique, fêtes et cérémonies liturgiques en l'honneur des saints abbés Odon et Odilon 9–11 juillet 1949*, pp. 219–26. Dijon: Société des amis de Cluny, 1950.
Hutchinson, Carole A. *The Hermit Monks of Grandmont*. Kalamazoo, Mich.: Cistercian Publications, 1989.
Iogna-Prat, Dominique. "La confection des cartulaires et l'historiographie à Cluny (Xie–XIIe siècles)." *Les cartulaires*, ed. Olivier Guyotjeannin et al., pp. 27–44. Paris: Ecole des chartes, 1993.
———. "Coutumes et statuts clunisiens comme sources historiques (ca. 990–ca. 1200)." *R. Mabillon* n.s. 3 (1992): 23–48.

Jacqueline, Bernard. *L'episcopat et papauté chez Saint Bernard de Clairvaux*. Paris: Champion, 1975.
Janauschek, Leopoldus. *Originum Cisterciensium*. Vienna, 1877. Reprint Ridgewood, N.J.: Gregg Press, 1964.
Jestice, Phyllis G. *Wayward Monks and the Religious Revolution of the Eleventh Century*. Leiden: Brill, 1997.
Jobin, Isabelle. "Abbaye Notre-Dame de Valcroissant." *R. Drômoise* 83 (1980): 134–48.
———. "Deux caractères originaux de l'abbaye de Valcroissant." *Mélanges Dimier* 3,6: 583–600.
Johnson, Penelope D. *Equal in Monastic Profession: Religious Women in Medieval France*. Chicago: University of Chicago Press, 1991.
———. "Pious Legends and Historical Realities: The Foundations of La Trinité de Vendôme, Bonport and Holyrood." *R. bénédictine* 91 (1981): 184–93.
Jongler, M. "Monographie de l'abbaye de Grandselve." *Mém. Société archéologique du Midi* 7 (1853–60): 179–234.
Kastner, Jörg. *Historiae fundationum monasteriorum: Frühformen monastischer Institutionsgeschichtsschreibung im Mittelalter*. München: Arbeo-Gesellschaft, 1974.
Kaul, Bernardus. "De Kalendario Cisterciensi eiusque revisione instituenda." *ASOC* 5 (1949): 1–80.
Keller, Hagen and Franz Neiske. *Vom Kloster zum Klosterverband: das Werkzeug der Schriftlichkeit, akten des Internationalen Kolloquiums des Projekts L2 im SFB 231 (22–23 Februar 1996)*. Munich: Wilhelm Fink, 1997.
Kennen, Elizabeth. "The *De Consideratione* of Saint Bernard of Clairvaux and the Papacy in the Mid-Twelfth Century: A Review of Scholarship." *Traditio* 23 (1967): 73–115.
Kienzle, Beverly M. "The Tract on the Conversion of Pons of Léras and the True Account of the Beginning of the Monastery of Silvanès." *CSQ* 29 (1995): 219–43.
Kittel, Ellen E. *From Ad Hoc to Routine: A Case Study in Medieval Bureaucracy*. Philadelphia: University of Pennsylvania Press, 1991.
Knowles, David. *Cistercians and Cluniacs: The Controversy Between St. Bernard and Peter the Venerable*. London: Oxford University Press, 1955.
———. *Great Historical Enterprises: Problems in Monastic History*. London: Thomas Nelson and Sons, 1963.
———. *The Monastic Order in England: A History of Its Development from the Times of St. Dunstan to the Fourth Lateran Council: 940–1216*. 2nd ed. Cambridge: Cambridge University Press, 1966.
Knowles, David and Richard Neville Hadcock. *Medieval Religious Houses: England and Wales*. 2nd ed. London: Longmans, 1971.
Kovács, François. "A propos de la date de la redaction des *Instituta Generalis Capituli apud Cistercium*." *ASOC* 7 (1951): 85–90.
———. "Relation entre l'officium defunctorum fériale et la liturgie cistercienne primitive." *ASOC* 7 (1951): 78–84.
Krenig, Ernst Günther. "Mittelalterliche Frauenklöster nach de Konstitutionen von Cîteaux." *ASOC* 10 (1954): 1–105.
Kroebel, Dagmar. "Les moniales de l'abbaye cistercienne de Nonenque: leur vie d'après le cartulaire entre 1140 et 1350." *Les religieuses dans le cloître et dans le monde des origines à nos jours*, pp. 507–13. Saint-Etienne: C.E.R.C.O.R., 1994.

Kuhn-Rehfus, Maren. "Cistercian Nuns in Germany in the Thirteenth Century: Upper-Swabian Cistercian Abbeys Under the Paternity of Salem." *Distant Echoes*, pp. 135–58.

La Hitte, Odet de. "L'abbaye de Lum-Dieu (Lumen Dei) de Fabas au diocèse de Comminges." *R. de Gascogne* 22 (1881): 400–23.

Lacger, L. de. "Ardorel." *DHGE* 7 (1934): 1617–20.

Lackner, Bede K. "Cistercian Nuns in Medieval Hungary." *Hidden Springs*, vol. 1, pp. 159–70.

———. "Early Cistercian Life as Described in the *Ecclesiastica officia*." *Cistercian Ideals and Reality*, ed. John R. Sommerfeldt, pp. 62–79. Kalamazoo, Mich.: Cistercian Publications, 1978.

———. *The Eleventh-Century Background to Cîteaux*. Spencer, Mass.: Cistercian Publications, 1972.

Lafon, Victor. "Histoire de la fondation de l'abbaye de Loc-Dieu." *Mém. Société des lettres de l'Aveyron* 11 (1879): 339–53.

Lagneau, Jean-François. "L'abbaye de Flaran." *Monuments historiques* 115 (1981): 22–26.

Lambert, Elie. "L'ancienne abbaye de Saint-Bernard de Bayonne." *Gure Herria* 1 (1958): 53–59.

———. "L'ancienne abbaye de Saint-Bernard de Bayonne." *Société des sciences, lettres et arts de Bayonne* 86 (1958): 167–72.

Lapart, J. "Quelques découvertes archéologiques récentes dans le département du Gers." *Bull. Société archéologique du Gers* 83 (1982): 127–43.

———. "Valence sur Baïse: Villa gallo-romaine et grange cistercienne sur le site du Mian." *Archéologie du Midi médiéval* 3 (1985): 176–79.

Laporte, M. P. "Monographie de la commune d'Auradé." *Bull. Société archéologique du Gers* 16 (1915): 13–58.

Laurent, J. "Les noms des monastères cisterciens dans la toponymie européenne." *Saint Bernard et son temps*, pp. 168–204. Dijon: n.p., 1928.

———. "La prière pour les défunts et les obituaires dans l'Ordre de Cîteaux." *Mélanges Saint Bernard*, pp. 383–96. Dijon: Assoc. bourguignonne des sociétés savantes, 1954.

Lavergne, Adrien. "Les chemins de Saint-Jacques en Gascogne." *R. de Gascogne* 20 (1879): 363–72.

Laville, Abbé. "Notice historique sur l'abbaye royale de Notre-Dame-de-Valsauve." *Mém. Académie de Nîmes* 7 (1884): 139–212, 275–99, 315–18.

Lawrence, C. H. *Medieval Monasticism: Forms of Religious Life in Western Europe in the Middle Ages*. 2nd ed. London: Longman, 1989.

Leblanc, Gratien. "L'église de l'abbaye des moniales de Goujon: étude historique et archéologique." *Mélanges Saint Bernard*, pp. 350–58. Dijon: Assoc. bourguignonne des sociétés savantes, 1954.

———. "La grange cistercienne de Fontcalvi (Aude)." *Fédération historique du Languedoc méditerranéen et du Roussillon*. Sète-Beaucaire: Fédération, 1956–57, pp. 43–57.

———. "La grange Lassale: étude historique et archéologique d'une 'grange' cistercienne." *Fédération des sociétés savantes Languedoc-Pyrénées-Gascogne, Xe congrés: Montauban*, pp. 3–16. Montauban: Fédération, 1954.

———. "La répartition géographique des abbayes cisterciennes du sud-ouest de la

France." *France méridionale et pays ibériques: mélanges géographiques offerts en hommage à M. Daniel Faucher*. 2 vols. Vol. 2, pp. 584–608. Toulouse: Privat, 1949.
Leclercq, Jean. "Une ancienne rédaction des coutumes cisterciennes." *RHE* 47 (1952): 172–76.
———. "Cisterciennes et filles de S. Bernard: à propos des structures variées des monastères de moniales au moyen âge." *Studia Monastica* 32 (1990): 139–56.
———. "Comment vivaient les frères convers." *I laici nella "societas Christiana" dei secoli XI e XII*, pp. 152–82. Milan: Università Cattolicà, 1968.
———. "La date du premier sermon sur le Cantique des Cantiques," *Saint Bernard mystique*, pp. 480–83. Paris: Desclée de Brouwer, 1948.
———. "Les écrits de Geoffroy d'Auxerre." *R. bénédictine* 62 (1952): 274–91.
———. "Epitres d'Alexandre III sur les Cisterciens," *R. bénédictine* 64 (1954): 68–82.
———. "L'érémitisme et les cisterciens." *Eremitismo in occidente nei secoli XI e XII*, pp. 573–80. Milan: Università Cattolica, 1968.
———. "L'identité cistercienne et ses conséquences." *CF 21*, pp. 371–80.
———. "Manuscrits cisterciens dans des bibliothèques d'Italie." *ASOC* 5 (1949): 94–119.
———. "Les manuscrits cisterciens du Portugal." *ASOC* 6 (1950): 131–39.
———. "Monachesimo femminile nei secoli XII e XIII." *Movimento religioso femminile e francescanesimo del secolo XIII: atti del VII convegno internazionale Assisi, 11–13 ottobre 1979*, pp. 63–99. Assisi: La Società, 1980.
———. "The Monastic Crisis of the Eleventh and Twelfth Centuries." *Cluniac Monasticism in the Central Middle Ages*, ed. Noreen Hunt, pp. 215–37. Hamden, Conn.: Archon Books, 1971.
———. "Passage supprimé dans une épitre d'Alexandre III." *R. bénédictine* 62 (1952): 149–51.
———. "La 'paternité' de S. Bernard et les débuts de l'Ordre cistercien." *R. bénédictine* 103 (1993): 445–81.
———. "Recherches dans les manuscrits cisterciens d'Espagne." *ASOC* 5 (1949): 109–19.
———. "Saint Antoine dans la tradition monastique médiévale." *Analecta Anselmiana* 38 (1956): 229–47.
———. "Le témoignage de Geoffrey d'Auxerre sur la vie cistercienne." *Analecta Monastica* 5,2 (1953): 174–201.
———. "Textes cisterciens dans des bibliothèques d'Allemagne." *ASOC* 7 (1951): 46–77.
———. "Textes et manuscrits cisterciens à la bibliothèque Vaticane." *ASOC* 15 (1959): 79–103.
———. "Textes et manuscrits cisterciens en Suède." *ASOC* 6 (1950): 125–30.
———. *Women and Saint Bernard of Clairvaux*. Trans. Marie-Bernard Said. Kalamazoo, Mich.: Cistercian Publications, 1989.
LeClercq, Paulette l'Hermite. *Le monachisme féminin dans la société de son temps: le monastère de La Celle (XIe–début du XVIe siècle)*. Paris: Cujas, 1989.
Leconte, Marie-Laure Crosnier. "Une cousine provinciale dans la France du sud-est: l'architecture de l'Ordre de Chalais." *Mélanges Dimier* 3,5: 65–78.
Lefèvre, J. A. "A propos de la composition des *Instituta generalis capituli apud Cistercium*." *COCR* 16 (1954): 157–82.

———. "A propos de la division des *Instituta Generalis Capituli* en collections séparées, dans le MS Laibach 31." *ASOC* 21 (1965): 110–21.

———. "A propos des sources de la législation primitive de Prémontré." *AP* 30 (1954): 12–19.

———. "A propos d'un nouveau texte de la *Carta Caritatis Prior* dans le MS Metz 1247." *R. bénédictine* 65 (1955): 90–109.

———. "La bulle *Apostolicae sedis* pour Cîteaux avait-elle une souscription longue?" *R. bénédictine* 74 (1964): 111–43.

———. "L'évolution des *Usus Conversorum* de Cîteaux." *COCR* 17 (1955): 65–97.

———. "Pour une nouvelle datation des *Instituta generalis capituli apud Cistercium*." *COCR* 16 (1954): 241–66.

———. "Que savons-nous du Cîteaux primitif?" *RHE* 51 (1956): 5–41.

———. "Saint Robert de Molesme dans l'opinion monastique du XIIe et du XIIIe siècle." *Analecta Bollandiana* 74 (1956): 50–83.

———. "Un texte inconnu de l'*Exordium cistercii* et de la *Summa Cartae Caritatis* dans le ms. Melun 55." *COCR* 17 (1955): 265–71.

———. "Les traditions manuscrites de l'*Exordium Parvum*." *Scriptorium* 10 (1956): 42–46.

———. "Les traditions manuscrites des *Usus Conversorum* de Cîteaux." *COCR* 17 (1955): 11–39.

———. "La véritable constitution cistercienne de 1119." *COCR* 16 (1954): 77–104.

———. "Le vrai récit primitif des origines de Cîteaux est-il l'*Exordium Parvum*?" *Le Moyen Age* 61 (1955): 79–120.

Lefèvre, J. A. and Bernard Lucet. "Les codifications cisterciennes aux XIIe et XIIIe siècles d'après les traditions manuscrites." *ASOC* 15 (1959): 3–22.

Lefèvre, Placide. "A propos de la 'lectio divina' dans la vie monastique et canoniale: essai de critique textuelle et d'originalité." *RHE* 67 (1972): 800–809.

———. "Deux bulles pontificales inédites du XIIe siècle relatives à l'Ordre de Prémontré." *AP* 12 (1936): 67–71.

———. "L'épisode de la conversion de S. Norbert et la tradition hagiographique du 'Vita Norberti.'" *RHE* 56 (1961): 813–26.

Lekai, Louis J. *The Cistercians: Ideals and Reality*. Kent, Ohio: Kent State University Press, 1977.

———. "Le collège St. Bernard au Moyen Age, 1280–1533." *Annales du Midi* 85 (1973): 251–60.

———. "Ideals and Reality in Early Cistercian Life and Legislation." *Cistercian Ideals and Reality*, ed. John R. Sommerfeldt, pp. 4–29. Kalamazoo, Mich.: Cistercian Publications, 1978.

———. "Introduction à l'étude des collèges cisterciens en France avant la Revolution." *ASOC* 25 (1969): 145–79.

———. *The White Monks*. Okauchee, Wis.: Our Lady of Spring Bank Press, 1957.

Lemaître, Jean-Loup. "Les actes transcrits dans les livres liturgiques," *Les cartulaires*, ed. Olivier Guyotjeannin. Paris: Ecole des chartes, 1993.

———. *Bonnaigue: une abbaye cistercienne au pays d'Ussel*. Paris: Boccard, 1993.

Lemarignier, Jean-François. *Etude sur les privilèges d'exemption et de juridiction ecclésiastiques des abbayes normandes depuis les origines jusqu'en 1140*. Paris: Picard, 1937.

Lenglet, Marie-Odile. "La biographie du Bienheureux Géraud de Salles." *Cîteaux* 29 (1978): 7–40.

———. "Notes sur l'histoire de l'abbaye de Bonnevaux." *Mélanges Dimier* 2,4: 700–718.
———. "Les origines de l'abbaye de Mazan: autocritique d'une précédente étude." *Cîteaux* 37 (1986): 76–81.
———. "Un problème d'histoire monastique: la fondation de l'abbaye de Mazan." *Cîteaux* 21 (1970): 5–22.
Lewis, Archibald R. *The Development of Southern French and Catalan Society 718–1050*. Austin: University of Texas Press, 1965.
———. "The Guillems of Montpellier—a Sociological Appraisal." *Viator* 2 (1971): 159–69.
———. "Patterns of Economic Development in Southern France, 1050–1271 A.D." *Studies in Medieval and Renaissance History* 18(1981): 57–83.
Leyser, Henrietta. *Hermits and the New Monasticism: A Study of Religious Communities in Western Europe, 1000–1150*. London: Macmillan, 1984.
Little, Lester K. *Benedictine Maledictions: Liturgical Cursing in Romanesque France*. Ithaca, N.Y.: Cornell University Press, 1993.
———. *Religious Poverty and the Profit Economy in Medieval Europe*. Ithaca, N.Y.: Cornell University Press, 1978.
Locatelli, René. "Frédéric Barberousse et les archévêques de Besançon." *Francia* 15 (1988): 130–47.
———. "Papauté et cisterciens du diocèse de Besançon au XIIe siècle." *L'église de France et la papauté (Xe–XIIIe siècle)*, ed. Rolf Grosse, pp. 304–25. Bonn: Bouvier, 1993.
———. *Sur les chemins de la perfection: moines et chanoines dans le diocèse de Besançon vers 1060–1220*. Saint-Etienne: C.E.R.C.O.R., 1992.
Lucet, Bernard. *Les codifications cisterciennes de 1237 et de 1257*. Paris, 1977.
Lynch, Joseph H. "Cistercians and Underaged Novices." *Cîteaux* 24 (1973): 283–97.
———. *The Medieval Church: A Brief History*. New York: Longman, 1992.
———. *Simoniacal Entry into Religious Life from 1000 to 1260*. Columbus: Ohio State University Press, 1976.
Magnou-Nortier, Elisabeth. "Contribution à l'étude des documents falsifiés: le diplôme de Louis le pieux pour Saint-Julien de Brioude (825) et l'acte de fondation du monastère de Sauxillanges par le duc Acfred (927)." *CCM* 21 (1978): 313–38.
———. "Fidélité et féodalité méridionales d'après les serments de fidélité (Xe–début de XIIe siècle)." *Les structures sociales de l'Aquitaine, du Languedoc, et de l'Espagne au premier âge féodal*, pp. 115–42. Paris: C.N.R.S., 1969.
———. "Formes féminines de vie consacrée dans le pays du Midi jusqu'au début du XIIe siècle." *CF* 23, pp. 193–216.
———. *La société laïque et l'église dans la province ecclésiastique de Narbonne (zone cispyrenéenne) de la fin du VIIIe à la fin du XIe siècle*. Toulouse: Université de Toulouse-le Mirail, 1974.
Mahn, J.-B. *L'Ordre cistercien et son gouvernement des origines au milieu du XIIIe siècle (1098–1265)*. Paris: Boccard, 1945.
Makowski, Elizabeth. *Canon Law and Cloistered Women: "Periculoso" and Its Commentators, 1298–1545*. Washington, D.C.: Catholic University Press, 1997.
Malbois, Emile. "Quelques notes sur l'abbaye du Bouchet." *Bull. Société d'archéologie de la Drôme* 53 (1919): 291–300.
Marboutin, M. R. "L'église de Flaran et l'architecture cistercienne." *Bull. Société archéologique du Gers* 14 (1913): 308–14.
Marilier, Jean. "Le vocable 'Novum Monasterium.'" *CC* 57 (1950): 81–84.

Mariotte, Jean-Yves. "Le schisme de 1159, la légation de Roger de Vico Pisano, et leurs traces diplomatiques à Clairefontaine." *Archiv fur Diplomatik* 18 (1972): 303–41.

McCrank, Lawrence J. "The Cistercians of Poblet as Landlords: Protection, Litigation, and Violence on the Medieval Catalan Frontier." *Cîteaux* 28 (1976): 255–83.

McDonnell, Ernst. *Beguines and Beghards in Medieval Culture, with Special Emphasis on the Belgian Scene*. New Brunswick, N.J.: Rutgers University Press, 1954.

McGuire, Brian Patrick. "The Cistercians and Friendship: An Opening to Women." *Hidden Springs*, vol. 1, pp. 171–200.

———. *The Cistercians in Denmark: Their Attitudes, Roles and Functions in Medieval Society*. Kalamazoo, Mich.: Cistercian Publications, 1982.

———. "The Cistercians and the Rise of the Exemplum in Early Thirteenth-Century France: A Reevaluation of Paris BN MS Latin 15912." *Classica et Mediaevalia* 34 (1983): 211–67.

———. "A Lost Clairvaux Exemplum Collection Found: The *Liber Visionum et Miraculorum* Compiled Under Prior John of Clairvaux (1171–79)." *ASOC* 39 (1983): 26–62.

———. "Who Founded the Order of Cîteaux?" *The Joy of Learning and the Love of God: Essays in Honor of Jean Leclercq*, ed. E. Rozanne Elder, pp. 389–414. Kalamazoo, Mich.: Cistercian Publications, 1995.

McLaughlin, Megan. *Consorting with Saints: Prayers for the Dead in Early Medieval France*. Ithaca, N.Y.: Cornell University Press, 1994.

McNamara, Jo Ann Kay. "The *Herrenfrage*: The Restructuring of the Gender System, 1050–1150." *Medieval Masculinities: Regarding Men in the Middle Ages*, ed. Clare A. Lees, Thelma Fenster, and Jo Ann McNamara, pp. 3–29. Minneapolis: University of Minnesota Press, 1994.

———. *Sisters in Arms: Catholic Nuns Through Two Millennia*. Cambridge, Mass.: Harvard University Press, 1996.

Melville, Gert. "Von der *Regula regularum* zur Stephansregel: Der normative Sonderweg der Grandmontenser bei der Auffächerung der *Vita religiosa* im 12. Jahrhundert." *Vom Kloster zum Klosterverband*, ed. Hagen Keller and Franz Neiske, pp. 342–63. Munich: Wilhelm Fink, 1997.

Menache, Sophia. *The Vox Dei: Communication in the Middle Ages*. New York: Oxford University Press, 1990.

Méras, Mathieu. "L'abbaye cistercienne de Grandselve ressuscitée grace à des fouilles recentes." *Archéologia* 40 (1971): 44–49.

———. "L'abbaye de Grandselve à la fin du XVIIe siècle." *Mém. Société archéologique du Midi de la France* 23 (1965): 95–108.

Mikkers, Edmund. "L'idéal religieux des frères convers dans l'Ordre de Cîteaux aux 12e et 13e siècles." *COCR* 24 (1962): 113–29.

Milis, Ludo. *Angelic Monks and Earthly Men: Monasticism and Its Meaning to Medieval Society*. Woodbridge, Suffolk: Boydell, 1992.

———. "Ermites et chanoines réguliers au XIIe siècle." *CCM* 22 (1979): 39–80.

———. "L'évolution de l'érémitisme au canonicat régulier dans la première moitié du douzième siècle: transition ou trahison?" *Studia Historica Gandensia* 235 (1979): 223–38.

———. *L'ordre des chanoines réguliers d'Arrouaise: son histoire et son organisation de la fondation de l'abbaye-mère (vers 1090) à la fin des Chapitres annuels (1471)*. 2 vols. Bruges: University of Ghent, 1969.

Moore, R. I. "St. Bernard's Mission to the Languedoc in 1145." *Bull. Institute of Historical Research (London)* 47 (1974): 1–14.
Moreau, Marthe. *L'âge d'or des religieuses: monastères féminins du Languedoc méditerranéen au Moyen Âge*. Montpellier: Presses du Languedoc, 1988.
———. "Les moniales du diocèse de Maguelone au XIIIe siècle." *CF 23*, pp. 241–60.
Morin-Sauvade, Hélène. "La filiation de Bonnevaux." *Unanimité et diversité cisterciennes: filiations, réseaux, relectures du XIIe au XVIIe siècle*, ed. Nicole Bouter. Saint-Etienne: Université de Saint-Etienne, 1999.
Mouret, Dominique. "Les moniales cisterciennes en France aux XIIe et XIIIe siècles: la diversité des origines, l'intégration à l'espace, les Cisterciennes et leur temps." Mémoire de Maitrise, Université de Limoges, 1984.
Mousnier, Mireille. "L'abbaye cistercienne de Grandselve du XIIe au debut du XIVe siècle." *Cîteaux* 34 (1983): 53–76, 221–44.
———. "Grandselve et la société de son temps." *CF 21*, pp. 107–26.
———. "Les granges de l'abbaye cistercienne de Grandselve (XIIe–XIVe siècle)." *Annales du Midi* 95 (1983): 7–28.
Moyne, Abbé. *L'abbaye de Sénanque (diocèse d'Avignon): notice historique et archéologique*. Marseille: Laffitte Reprints, 1981.
Müller, Gregor. "Das Beginnenwesen eine Abzweigung von den Cistercienserinnen." *CC* 312 (1915): 33–41.
———. "Generalkapitel der Cistercienserinnen." *CC* 277 (1912): 65–72, 114–19, 152–57.
Mundy, John Hine. "Charity and Social Work in Toulouse, 1100–1250." *Traditio* 22 (1966): 203–87.
———. *Liberty and Political Power in Toulouse, 1050–1230*. New York: Columbia University Press, 1954.
Murray, Alexander. *Reason and Society in the Middle Ages*. Oxford: Clarendon Press, 1978.
———. "Religion Among the Poor in Thirteenth-Century France: The Testimony of Humbert of Romans." *Traditio* 30 (1974): 285–324.
Nadal, Abbé. *Histoire hagiologique ou vies des saints et des bienheureux du diocèse de Valence*. Valence: Aurel, 1855.
Neiske, Franz. "Cisterziensische Generalkapitel und Individuelle Memoria." *Die ordine vitae: Zu Normvorstellungen, Organisationsformen und Schriftgebrauch im mittelalterlichen Ordenswesen*, ed. Gert Melville, pp. 261–83. Münster: Lit, 1996.
———. "Papsttum und Klosterverband." *Vom Kloster zum Klosterverband*, ed. Hagen Keller and Franz Neiske, pp. 252–76. Munich: Wilhelm Fink, 1997.
Newman, Martha. *The Boundaries of Charity: Cistercian Culture and Ecclesiastical Reform, 1098–1180*. Palo Alto, Calif.: Stanford University Press, 1996.
———. "Stephen Harding and the Creation of the Cistercian Community." *R. bénédictine* 107 (1997): 307–29.
Nichols, John A. "Cistercian Nuns in Twelfth- and Thirteenth-Century England," *Hidden Springs*, vol. 1, pp. 49–62.
Nichols, John A. and Lillian Thomas Shank, eds. *Distant Echoes*. Medieval Religious Women 1. Kalamazoo, Mich.: Cistercian Publications, 1984.
———. *Hidden Springs*. 2 vols. Medieval Religious Women 3 and 4. Kalamazoo, Mich.: Cistercian Publications, 1995.
Nicholson, Helen. *Templars, Hospitallers and Teutonic Knights. Images of the Military Orders, 1128–1291*. Leicester: Leicester University Press, 1993.

Niermeyer, J.-F. *Mediae Latinitatis Lexicon Minus*. Leiden: Brill, 1974.
Noschitzka, Canisius. "Die Kirchenrechtliche Stellung des Resignierten Regularabtes unter Besonderer Berücksichtigung der Geschichtlichen Entwicklung im Zisterzienserorden." *ASOC* 13 (1957): 149–78.
Novick, Peter. *That Noble Dream: The "Objectivity Question" and the American Historical Profession*. Cambridge: Cambridge University Press, 1988.
O'Callaghan, Joseph F. "The Affiliation of the Order of Calatrava with the Order of Cîteaux." *ASOC* 15 (1959): 161–93; 16 (1960): 3–59, 255–92.
———. "The Foundation of the Order of Alcàntara, 1176–1218." *Catholic Historical Review* 47 (1962): 471–86.
Oliva, Marilyn. *The Convent and the Community in Late Medieval England: Female Monasteries in the Diocese of Norwich, 1350–1450*. Woodbridge: Boydell, 1998.
Omont, H. "La Collection Doat à la Bibliothèque nationale: documents sur les recherches de Doat dans les archives du sud-ouest de la France de 1663 à 1670." *Bibliothèque de l'Ecole des chartes* 77 (1916): 286–336.
Osheim, Duane J. "Conversion, *Conversi*, and Religious Life in Late Medieval Tuscany." *Speculum* 58 (1983): 368–90.
———. *A Tuscan Monastery and Its Social World: San Michele of Guamo (1156–1348)*. Rome: Herder, 1989.
Ourliac, Paul. *Les pays de Garonne vers l'an mil: la société et le droit*. Toulouse: Privat, 1993.
———. "Les villages de la région toulousaine au XIIe siècle." *Annales* 4 (1949): 268–77.
Pacaut, Marcel. *Alexandre III: étude sur la conception du pouvoir pontifical dans sa pensée et dans son oeuvre*. Paris: J. Vrin, 1956.
———. "La filiation clairvallienne dans la genèse et l'essor de l'Ordre cistercien." *Histoire de Clairvaux: actes du Colloque de Bar-sur-Aube/Clairvaux, 22–23 June, 1990*, pp. 135–47. Bar-sur-Aube: Némont, 1991.
Parat, Lucien. "Les origines de l'abbaye de Mazan." *Revue région* (1987).
Passerat, Georges. "La venue de Saint Bernard à Toulouse et les débuts de l'abbaye de Grandselve." *Bull. de la littérature ecclésiastique (Toulouse, Institut catholique)* 93 (1992): 27–37.
Pasztor, Edith. "Le origini dell'Ordine cisterciense e la riforma monastica." *ASOC* 21 (1965): 112–27.
———. "Studi e problemi relativi alle prime fonti cisterciensi." *Annali della Scuola speciale per archivisti e bibliotecari dell'Università* 4 (1964): 137–44.
Paul, Vivian. "The Abbey Church of Valmagne." *Mélanges Dimier* 3, 6: 639–52.
Perret, Vincent. "Les Cisterciennes des Olieux del Lac." *Bull. Commission archéologique de Narbonne* 31 (1969): 115–24.
Poly, Jean-Pierre. *La Provence et la société féodale, 879–1166: contribution à l'étude des structures dites féodales dans le Midi*. Paris: Bordas, 1976.
Pontus, Paul. *Silvacane Abbey*. Paris: Monuments historiques, 1966.
Porte, J.-B. François and Alphonse Rabbe. "Notice historique sur l'abbaye de N.-D. de Silvacane et ses dépendances." *R. sextienne* 7 (1879): 104–11; 8 (1880): 112–20.
Portela Silva, Ermelindo. *La colonizacion cisterciense en Galicia (1142–1250)*. Santiago: Universidad de Santiago de Compostela, 1981.
Pourtoit, Robert. "Un nouveau texte de la Charte de Charité." *COCR* 8 (1946): 3–9.
Preiss, Martin. *Die politische Tätigkeit und Stellung der Cisterzienser im Schisma von 1159–1177*. Berlin: Emil Ebering, 1934.

Pressouyre, Léon, ed. *Espace cistercien*. Paris: Comité des travaux historiques et scientifiques, 1994.
Pressouyre, Léon. *La rêve cistercien*. Paris, Gallimard, 1990.
Pressouyre, Léon and Terryl N. Kinder, eds. *Saint Bernard et le monde cistercien*. Paris: Monuments historiques, 1990.
Régné, Jean. "L'abbaye de Mazan de 1123 à 1500." *R. Mabillon* 14 (1924): 214–31.
Remensnyder, Amy G. *Remembering Kings Past: Monastic Foundation Legends in Medieval Southern France*. Ithaca, N.Y.: Cornell University Press, 1995.
Reuter, Timothy. "Das Edikt Friedrich Barbarossas gegen die Zisterzienser." *Mitteilungen des Institut fur österreichische Geschichtesforschung* 84 (1976): 328–36.
———. "Zur Anerkennung Papst Innocenz II: eine neue Quelle." *Deutsches Archiv fur Erforschung des Mittelalters* 9 (1983): 395–416.
Reynolds, Susan. *Fief and Vassals: The Medieval Evidence Reinterpreted*. Oxford: Oxford University Press, 1994.
———. *Kingdoms and Communities in Western Europe, 900–1300*. Oxford: Clarendon Press, 1984.
Richard, Jean. "La maison de Clairvaux et le domaine de l'abbaye à Dijon." *Histoire de Clairvaux: actes du Colloque de Bar-sur-Aube/Clairvaux, 22–23 June, 1990*, pp. 149–57. Bar-sur-Aube: Némont, 1991.
Richardot, Hubert. "Le fief routurier à Toulouse aux XIIe et XIIIe siècles." *R. historique du droit* 40 (1935): 307–59.
Rissel, Hiltrude. "Entdeckung einer Inkorporationsurkunde für ein frühes Frauenkloster im 12. Jahrhundert." *Cîteaux* 39 (1988): 43–64.
Robert, A. "L'abbaye cistercienne de Mazan (Ardèche) et ses filles provençales: Sénanque et le Thoronet." *Fédération historique du Languedoc méditerranéen et du Roussillon*. Montpellier: Fédération, 1970, pp. 77–100.
———. "L'abbaye cistercienne de Mercoire en Gévaudan." *R. du Vivarais* 77 (1973): 176–94.
———. "Les abbés du monastère cistercien des Chambons au diocèse de Viviers (1152–1791)." *R. du Vivarais* 72(1968): 119–30; 73 (1969): 30–35.
———. "Deux documents sur les Chambons et la terre de Borne." *R. du Vivarais* 90 (1986): 215–23.
———. "Villeneuve-de-Berg et les moines de Mazan." *R. du Vivarais* 88 (1984): 131–44.
Robinson, Ian Stuart. *The Papacy, 1073–1198: Continuity and Imagination*. Cambridge: Cambridge University Press, 1990.
Roblin, Michel. "L'habitat rural dans la vallée de la Garonne de Boussens à Grenade." *R. géographique des Pyrenées* 8 (1937): 5–72.
Rocca, Emilio Nassali. "La posizione politica dei monasteri cistercensi dell'Alta Italia nei tempi da Frederico I° a Frederico II° di Svevia." *ASOC* 13 (1957): 69–82.
Roehl, Richard. "Plan and Reality in a Medieval Monastic Economy: The Cistercians." *Studies in Medieval and Renaissance History* 9 (1972): 83–113.
Roisin, Simone. "L'efflorescence cistercienne et le courant féminin de piété au treizième siècle."*RHE* 39 (1943): 342–78.
Rosenwein, Barbara H. "Cluny's Immunities in the Tenth and Eleventh Centuries: Images and Narratives." *Die Cluniazenser in ihrem politisch-sozialen Umfeld*, ed. Giles Constable, Gert Melville, and Jörg Oberste, pp. 133–63. Munich, 1998.

———. *To Be the Neighbor of Saint Peter: The Social Meaning of Cluny's Property, 909–1049.* Ithaca, N.Y.: Cornell University Press, 1989.
Rossignol, E. "Une charte d'Aliénor, duchesse d'Aquitaine, de l'an 1172." *R. d'Aquitaine et du Languedoc* 5–6 (1861): 224–28.
———. "Des frères et soeurs donnés dans les établissements religieux au moyen-âge." *R. Historique du Tarn* 2 (1878): 68–71.
Rostan, M. L. "Etude d'archéologie comparée: trois abbayes de l'Ordre de Citeaux: l'abbaye du Thoronet (Var); l'abbaye de Silvacane (Bouches-du-Rhône); l'abbaye de Sénanque (Vaucluse)." *Bull. monumental* 18 (1852): 107–38.
Rouillan-Castex, Sylvette. "Bernard-Aton Trencavel et les carcassonnais." *Carcassonne et sa région: fédération historique du Languedoc méditerranéen et du Roussillon et par la Fédération des Sociétés académiques et savantes de Languedoc — Pyrénées - Gascogne.* Paris, 1970.
Roumejoux, A. de. "Notes sur l'église et l'abbaye de Silvanès." *Bull. monumental* 32 (1866): 793–800.
Rouquette, Daniel. "Note sur la date de fondation et l'emplacement de l'abbaye de Netlieu." *Mélanges Dimier* 3,6: 697–700.
Rudolph, Conrad. "Bernard of Clairvaux's *Apologia* as a Description of Cluny and the Controversy over Monastic Art." *Gesta* 17 (1988): 125–32.
———. "The Scholarship on Bernard of Clairvaux's *Apologia*." *Cîteaux* 40 (1989): 69–111.
———. *The Things of Greater Importance: Bernard of Clairvaux's Apologia and the Medieval Attitude Toward Art.* Philadelphia: University of Pennsylvania Press, 1991.
———. "The 'Principal Founders' and the Early Artistic Legislation of Cîteaux." *Studies in Cistercian Art and Architecture* 3, ed. Meredith Lillich, pp. 1–45. Kalamazoo, Mich.: Cistercian Publications, 1987.
Rumeau, M. R. "Notes sur l'abbaye de Grandselve." *Bull. Société géographie de Toulouse* 19 (1900): 247–85.
Said, Edward W. *Culture and Imperialism.* New York: Vintage Books, 1993.
———. *Orientalism.* New York: Vintage Books, 1978.
Saint-Blanquat, Odon de. "Comment se sont créées les bastides du sud-ouest de la France." *Annales* 3 (1949): 278–89.
Saint-Jean, Robert. "L'abbaye cistercienne de Mazan (Ardêche) et ses filles provençales: Sénanque et le Thoronet." *Fédération historique du Languedoc méditerranéen et du Roussillon.* Montpellier: Fédération, 1970, 77–100.
Saint-Paul, Anthyme. "Bonnefont." *R. de Comminges* 26 (1913): 166–85.
Saurel, Alfred. "L'abbaye de Saint-Pons." *R. de Marseille et de Provence* 9 (1863): 293–307, 348–60.
———. "Géménos-le-Vieux (Castrum de Geminis)." *R. de Marseille et de Provence* 9 (1863): 453–70.
———. *Notice historique sur Saint-Jean-de-Garguier, l'abbaye de St-Pons et Géménos (Bouches-du-Rhône).* Marseille: Olive, 1863.
Sautel, J. "Aiguebelle." *DHGE* 1 (1912): 1122–31.
Sayers, Jane. *Innocent III: Leader of Europe, 1198–1216.* London: Longman, 1994.
———. "The Judicial Activities of the General Chapters." *Journal of Ecclesiastical History* 15 (1964): 18–32, 168–85.
Schimmelpfennig, Bernhard. *The Papacy.* Trans. James Sievert. New York: Columbia University Press, 1992.

Schneider, Bruno. "Cîteaux und die Benediktinische Tradition. Die Quellenfrage des *Liber Usuum* im Lichte der *Consuetudines Monasticae.*" *ASOC* 16 (1960-1): 169-254.
———. "Eine Zeitgenossische Kritik zu Janauscheks *Originum Cisterciensium* Tomus I." *ASOC* 21 (1965) 259-83.
Schneider, Reinhard. *Vom Klosterhaushalt zum Stadt-und Staatshaushalt der Zisterziensische Beitrag*. Stuttgart: Anton Hiersemann, 1994.
Schulenburg, Jane Tibbetts. *Forgetful of Their Sex: Female Sanctity and Society, ca. 500-1100*. Chicago: University of Chicago Press, 1998.
Segondy, Jean. *L'abbaye du Vignogoul*. Montpellier: Impr. de la Charité, 1952.
Sidwell, Keith. *Reading Medieval Latin*. Cambridge: Cambridge University Press, 1995.
Simons, W. "Deux témoins du mouvement canonial du XIIe siècle: les prieurés de Saint-Laurent-au-Bois et Saint-Nicolas de Regny et leurs démêlés avec l'abbaye de Corbie." *Sacris Erudiri* 24 (1980): 203-44.
Sohn, Andreas. "Vom Kanonikerstift zum Kloster und Klosterverband: Saint-Martin-des-Champs in Paris." *Vom Kloster zum Klosterverband*, ed. Hagen Keller and Franz Neiske, pp. 206-38. Munich: Wilhelm Fink, 1997.
Sol, Abbé. "La Lumière-Dieu: abbaye cistercienne de Fabas, en Comminges (1150-1790)." *R. de Comminges* 54 (1941): 65-240.
Somerville, Robert. *Pope Alexander III and the Council of Tours (1163)*. Berkeley: University of California Press, 1977.
Sous la règle de Saint-Benoît: structures monastiques et sociétés en France du Moyen Age à l'époque moderne. Genève: Droz, 1982.
Southern, R. W. *Western Society and the Church in the Middle Ages*. Harmondsworth: Penguin, 1970.
Spahr, Kolumban. "Die Anfänge von Citeaux." *Bernhard von Clairvaux, Mönch und Mystiker, Internationaler Bernhard-Kongress Mainz 1953*, ed. Joseph Lortz, pp. 215-24. Wiesbaden: F. Steiner, 1955.
———. "Zum Freundschaftsbündnis zwischen Cisterciensern und Prämonstratensern." *CC* 73 (1966): 10-17.
Spitzer, Alan B. *Historical Truth and Lies About the Past*. Chapel Hill, N.C.: University of North Carolina Press, 1996.
Spornik, Charles D. G. "The Life and Reign of Pope Eugene III (1145-1153)." Ph.D. dissertation, Notre Dame University, 1988.
Steffen, Stephan. "Heinrich, Kardinalbischof von Albano. Ein Kirchenfurst des zwolften Jahrhunderts." *CC* 21 (1909): 225-36, 267-80, 300-06, 334-43.
Stein, Henri. *Bibliographie générale des cartulaires français*. Paris: Picard, 1907.
Stock, Brian. "Experience, Praxis, Work, and Planning in Bernard of Clairvaux: Observations on the *Sermones in Cantica*." *The Cultural Context of Medieval Learning*, ed. John E. Murdoch and Edith D. Sylla, pp. 219-62. Dordrecht: D. Reidel, 1975.
———. *The Implications of Literacy: Written Language and Models of Interpretation in the Eleventh and Twelfth Centuries*. Princeton, N.J.: Princeton University Press, 1983.
Strayer, J. R. *The Albigensian Crusade*. New York: Dial Press, 1971.
Stroll, Mary. *The Jewish Pope: Ideology and Politics in the Papal Schism of 1130*. Leiden: Brill, 1987.
———. "New Perspectives on the Struggle Between Guy of Vienne and Henry V." *Archivum historiae pontificiae* 3 (1980): 97-115.

Sundt, Richard A. "*Mediocres domos et humiles habeant fratres nostri*: Dominican Legislation on Architecture and Architectural Decoration in the 13th Century." *Journal of the Society of Architectural Historians* 46 (1987): 394–407.
Suydam, Mary. "Origins of the Savigniac Order: Savigny's Role Within Twelfth-Century Monastic Reform." *R. bénédictine* 86 (1976): 94–108.
Swietek, Francis R. and Terrence M. Deneen. "The Episcopal Exemption of Savigny, 1112–1184." *Church History* 52 (1983): 285–98.
———. "Pope Lucius II and Savigny." *ASOC* 39 (1983): 3–25.
Tabacco, Giovanni. "Privilegium amoris: aspetti della spiritualità romualdina." *Il Saggiatore* 4 (1954): 324–43.
Tabuteau, Emily Z. *Transfers of Property in Eleventh-Century Norman Law*. Chapel Hill, N.C.: University of North Carolina Press, 1988.
Talbot, C. H. "The Testament of Gervase of Louth Park." *ASOC* 7 (1951): 32–45.
Tardieu, Joëlle. "Les campagnes de construction de l'église de l'abbaye de Léoncel." *Mélanges Dimier* 3,6: 737–56.
———. "Le cellier de l'abbaye de Léoncel à Beaufort-sur-Gervanne." *R. Drômoise* 83 (1980): 99–106.
Tardieu, Joëlle and Benoît Chauvin. "Léoncel, présentation des archives et bibliographie commentée." *Mélanges Dimier* 2,4: 769–94.
Taupiac, Louis. "L'abbaye de Belleperche." *Bull. Société archéologique de Tarn-et-Garonne* 6 (1878): 89–115.
Taylor-Vaisey, Robert D. "The First Century of Cistercian Legislation: Some Preliminary Investigations." *Cîteaux* 27 (1976): 203–25.
Tellenbach, Gerd. *The Church in Western Europe from the Tenth to the Early Twelfth Century*. Trans. Timothy Reuter. Cambridge: Cambridge University Press, 1993.
Theillière, Abbé. *Monastère de Bellecombe*. Saint-Etienne: Freydier, 1873.
Theurot, Jacky. "L'abbaye de Cîteaux à Dôle (avant 1148–1620)." *Cîteaux* 46 (1995): 5–75.
Thompson, James Westfall. *Economic and Social History of the Middle Ages*. 2 vols. New York: F. Ungar, 1928. Reprint 1959.
Thompson, Sally. "The Problem of the Cistercian Women in the Twelfth and Thirteenth Centuries." *Medieval Women*, ed. Derek Baker, pp.227–52. Oxford: Blackwell, 1978.
———. *Women Religious: The Founding of English Nunneries After the Norman Conquest*. Oxford: Clarendon Press, 1991.
Thouzellier, Christine. *Catharisme et Valdéisme en Languedoc*. Paris: Nauwelaerts, 1969.
———. *Hérésie et hérétiques: Vaudois, Cathares, Patarins, Albigeois*. Rome: Storia et Letteratura, 1969.
Toepfer, Michael. *Die Konversen der Zisterzienser: Untersuchungen über ihren Beitrag zur mittelalterlichen Blüte des Ordens*. Berlin: Duncker and Humblot, 1983.
Toubert, Pierre. *Les structures du Latium médiéval: le Latium méridional et la Sabine du IXe siècle à la fin du XIIe siècle*. 2 vols. Rome: Ecole française, 1973.
Traissac, Elisabeth. "Les abbayes cisterciennes de Fontguilhem et du Rivet et leur rôle cans le défrichement médiévale en Bazadais." *R. historique de Bordeaux* 9 (1960): 141–50.
Trilhe, Robert. "A propos de la fondation de l'abbaye d'Eaunes." *R. de Comminges* 28 (1915): 253–62.

Turk, Joseph. "*Charta Caritatis Prior*." *ASOC* 1 (1945): 11–61.
———. "*Cistercii Statuta Antiquissima*." *ASOC* 4 (1948): 1–149.
Tutsch, Burkhardt. "Texttradition und Praxis von *Consuetudines* und *Statuta* in der *Cluniacensis Ecclesia* (10.–12. Jahrhundert)." *Vom Kloster zum Klosterverband*, ed. Hagen Keller and Franz Neiske, pp. 173–205. Munich: Wilhelm Fink, 1997.
———. "*Cistercium fratrum instituta*." *CC* 52 (1940): 101–7, 118–23, 132–41.
Valvekens, Jean-Baptiste. "Fratres et sorores ad succurrendum." *AP* 37 (1961): 323–28.
Van Damme, J. B. "La Charte de Charité de Chalais." *Cîteaux* 14 (1963): 81–104.
———. "La constitution cistercienne de 1165." *ASOC* 19 (1963): 51–104.
———. "Formation de la constitution cistercienne: esquisse historique." *Studia Monastica* 4 (1962): 111–37.
———. "Genèse des *Instituta Generalis Capituli*." *Cîteaux* 12 (1961): 28–60.
———. "Les origines cisterciennes." *Cîteaux* 18 (1967): 263–65.
———. "Les pouvoirs de l'abbé de Cîteaux aux XIIe et XIIIe siècle." *ASOC* 24 (1968): 47–85.
———. "A la recherche de l'unique vérité sur Cîteaux et ses origines." *Cîteaux* 33 (1982): 304–32.
———. "La *Summa Cartae Caritatis*, source de constitutions canoniales." *Cîteaux* 23 (1972): 5–54.
———. "Les textes cisterciens de 1119." *Cîteaux* 33 (1982): 92–110.
Van den Broeck, G. "De Capitulo Generali in Ordine Praemonstratensi." *AP* 15 (1939): 121–28.
Van der Meer, Frederik, ed. *Atlas de l'Ordre cistercien*. Paris: Séquoia, 1965.
Van Engen, John. "The 'Crisis of Cenobitism' Reconsidered: Benedictine Monasticism in the Years 1050–1150." *Speculum* 61 (1986): 269–304.
Venarde, Bruce. *Women's Monasticism and Medieval Society: Nunneries in France and England, 890–1215*. Ithaca, N.Y.: Cornell University Press, 1997.
Vernet, André. *La bibliothèque de l'abbaye de Clairvaux du XIIe au XVIIIe siècle*. Vol. 1. Paris: C.N.R.S., 1979.
Vidier, Alexandre. "Ermitages orléanais au XIIe siècle: le Gué de l'Orme et Chappes." *Le Moyen Age* 19 (1906): 57–96, 134–56.
Vie, Louis. "L'abbaye de Nizors, notes sur un manuscrit du XVIe siècle." *R. de Comminges* 15 (1900): 33–36.
Voinchet, Bernard. "L'abbaye de l'Escaledieu." *Monuments historiques* 115 (1891): 89–92.
Vongrey, F. and F. Hervay. "Kritische Bemerkungen zum 'Atlas de l'Ordre Cistercien' von Frédéric van der Meer." *ASOC* 22 (1966).
Waddell, Chrysogonus. "The Cistercian Institutions and Their Early Evolution: Granges, Economy, Lay-brothers." *L'espace cistercien*, ed. Léon Pressouyre, pp. 27–38. Paris, Comité des travaux historiques et scientifiques, 1994.
———. "The *Exordium Cistercii* and the *Summa Cartae Caritatis*: A Discussion Continued." *Cistercian Ideals and Reality*, ed. John R. Sommerfeldt, pp. 30–61. Kalamazoo, Mich.: Cistercian Publications, 1978
———. "The *Exordium Cistercii*, Lucan, and Mother Poverty." *Cîteaux* 33 (1982): 378–88.
———. "One Day in the Life of a Savigniac Nun: Jehanne de Deniscourt." *CSQ* 26 (1991): 134–51.

———. "Prelude to a Feast of Freedom: Notes on the Roman Privilege *Desiderium Quod* of October 19, 1110." *Cîteaux* 33 (1982): 247–303.
———. "Simplicity and Ordinariness: The Climate of Early Cistercian Hagiography." *Simplicity and Ordinariness*, ed. John R. Sommerfeldt, pp. 1–47. Kalamazoo, Mich.: Cistercian Publications, 1980.
Waha, M. de. "Aux origines de Cîteaux: rapports entre l'*Exordium Cistercii* et l'*Exordium Parvum*." *Latomus: R. d'études latines* 158 (1978): 152–82.
Wakefield, Walter L. *Heresy, Crusade, and Inquisition in Southern France, 1100–1250*. Berkeley: University of California Press, 1974.
———. "Heretics and Inquisitors: The Case of Le Mas-Saintes-Puelles." *Catholic Historical Review* 69 (1983): 209–26.
Waldman, Thomas A. "Abbot Suger and the Nuns of Argenteuil." *Traditio* 41 (1985): 239–71.
Walker, David. "The Organization of Material in Medieval Cartularies." *The Study of Medieval Records: Essays in Honour of Kathleen Major*, ed. D. A. Bullough and R. L. Storey, pp. 132–50. Oxford: Clarendon Press, 1971.
Wardrop, Joan. *Fountains Abbey and Its Benefactors, 1132–1300*. Kalamazoo, Mich.: Cistercian Publications, 1987.
Weinberger, Stephen. "Les conflits entre clercs et laïcs dans la Provence du XIe siècle." *Annales du Midi* 92 (1980): 269–79.
White, Stephen. *Customs, Kinship, and Gifts to Saints: The Laudatio Parentum in Western France, 1050–1150*. Chapel Hill: University of North Carolina Press, 1986.
Wilkinson, Maire. "Laïcs et convers de l'Ordre de Grandmont au XIIe siècle: la création et la destruction d'une fraternité." *Les mouvances laïques des ordres religieux*, ed. Nicole Bouter, pp. 35–50. Saint-Etienne: C.E.R.C.O.R., 1996.
———. "Stephen of the Auvergne and the Foundation of the Congregation of Muret-Grandmont According to Its Primitive Traditions." *Medieval History* 2 (1992): 45–67.
———. "The *Vita Stephani Muretensis* and the Papal Reconstitution of the Order of Grandmont in 1186 and Thereafter." *Monastic Studies: The Continuity of Tradition*, ed. Judith Loades. Bangor, Gwynned, Wales: Headstart History, 1990.
Winandy, Jacques. "Les origines de Cîteaux et les travaux de M. Lefèvre." *R. bénédictine* 67 (1957): 49–76.
Wolff, Philippe, ed. *Le Diocèse de Toulouse*. Paris: Beauchesne, 1984.
Wollasch, Joachim. "Neue Quellen zur Geschichte der Cistercienser." *Zeitschrift fur Kirchengeschichte* 84 (1973): 188–232.
———. "Parenté noble et monachisme réformateur: observations sur les "conversions" à la vie monastique aux XIe et XIIe siècles." *R. historique* 264 (1980): 3–24.
Zakar, Polycarpe. "Réponse aux 'Quelques à-propos' du Père Van Damme sur les origines cisterciennes: quelques conclusions.'" *ASOC* 21 (1965): 138–66.
Zaluska, Yolanta. *Manuscrits enluminés de Dijon*. Paris: C.N.R.S., 1991.
Zerbi, Piero. *Tra Milano e Cluny: momenti di vita e cultura ecclesiastica nel secolo XII*. Rome: Herder, 1978.
Zerner-Chardavoine, Monique. "L'épouse de Simon de Montfort et la croisade albigeoise." *Femmes, mariages, lignages, XIIe–XIVe siècles: mélanges offerts à Georges Duby*, pp. 449–70. Brussels: De Boeck Université, D.L., 1992.

Index

Abbatis generalis, 271n. 6
Abbot's staff or *virga*, 15
Abbots and abbesses, responsibilities of, 98, 108–9
Acquisitions actively pursued, 165, 172–75, 213, 230
Ad hoc in Apostolicae, attributed to Calixtus II, 87–89, appendix 4, 263n. 6, 284n. 138
Adelaide, wife of Bernard of Saint-Pons, 162
Adelaide, wife of Raymond Peter, 163
Adelaide of Saint-Eulalie, 314n. 143
Adèle of Chartres, manuscript of letters to, 275n. 44
Adelina, at hospital of Saint-Martin, 214–15
Ademar, first abbot of Bonneval, 118
Ademar of Juliac, 183–84, 310n. 77
Ademar of Tosons or Teccos, 308n. 52
Adoption of practices or *ordo*, 42, 56, 68, 73, 93, 162, 223; dating, 220; gradual steps, 85–86, 102–6; by independent houses, 47, 95–97, 98, 101–3, 126, 140, 144, 149–52; at Valmagne, 207–10, 315n. 170
Adrian IV, pope (1154–59), 89
Adult conversion. *See* Conversion, adult
Aelred of Rievaulx, abbot, 146, 302nn. 208, 212
Affiliation. *See* Incorporation
Agde, bishop of, 198; Peter, 316n. 197
Aggressiveness (monastic), 173, 187, 189
Agnes, widow of Peter Blanc, 218
Aicelina, widow of Raymond Talairan, 308n. 40
Aiguebelle, Cistercian abbey for men, dioc. Saint-Paul-Trois-Châteaux, appendix 3, no. 79; 142, 300n. 191
Aiguebelle, grange of Gimont (later bastide of Saint-Lys), 179–80, 184–85, 310n. 64
Aimeric, viscount of Narbonne, 131, 318n. 13
Alamanda, makes gift to Berdoues, 306n. 6
Alazais, wife of William Gac, 162–63
Alazais, wife of Yspanus of Maurencs, 185, 311n. 80

Albergum, 217
Alberic, first abbot of Cîteaux, 5–7
Albert of Finna, monk of Grandselve, 309n. 56
Albi, bishop William granted parish of Beceria to Valmagne, 211
Alexander, bishop of Lincoln, 302n. 207
Alexander III, 10, 12–14, 22–23, 67–68, 70, 73, 76, 79, 82, 89, 91, 151–53, 193, 209–11, appendix 5, 278n. 72, 282n. 120, 285n. 151, 303n. 220, 305n. 252, 313n. 133. *See also Sacrosancta*
Alexander of Cologne, abbot, friend of Bernard of Clairvaux, 73, 128–29, 147–48, 150, 176, 210, 278nn. 80, 81, 287n. 23, 302n. 213. *See also* abbots under Grandselve, Savigny, Cîteaux
Alexandria, daughter of Yspanus of Maurencs, prioress, 185, 311n. 80
Alien brass. *See* Mortgages
Almanarre. *See* Saint-Pierre of l'Almanarre
Alphonse, king of Aragon, 196, 318n. 13
Alvingham, 158
Amada, makes gift to Berdoues, 305n. 6
Amada, makes gift to Valmagne, 205
Amedeus, abbot of Valmagne, 162, 208, 214–15
Anacletian schism. *See* Innocent II
Anastasius, pope (1153–54), 89
Anduze, lords of, 119
Anglo-Norman rulers, 129, 148; charters and cartularies, 146–47; forgeries, 78–79
Animal husbandry. *See* Pastoralism
Annexations. *See* Incorporations
Anti-Cistercian polemic, 266n. 55
Anti-Cluniac polemic, 15
Apostolic gestation, 1, 41, 93, 95, 100, 103–4, 107, 143, 161, 179, 224, 228–29; at Valbonne, 221
Appeals to Rome, 157
Aragon. *See* Alphonse
Arbielle, 181–82
Arbitration of disputes, 86, 180, 195

Archambald, viscount of Comborn, 301n. 203
Architecture (Cistercian). *See* Gothic style; individual churches of Fabas, Fontfroide, Goujon, les Olieux, le Thoronet, le Vignogoul, Saint-Félix, Sénanque, Silvacane, Silvanès, Valmagne
— impressions: aura or spirit, 24, 114; austerity and simplicity, 24; poverty of monks and nuns, 29; unanimity, 23–39; witness to Cistercian mythology, 15, 41
— remains in southern France, fig. 6, 29–39
— support for: gifts for construction, 205, 207, 215; stone quarry given to Valmagne, 209; wooden and stone churches at Cîteaux, 15
— technical details: aisles, 25; barrel-vaults at right angles to nave, 13; cloister location at Fontfroide, 31; flat roofs, 31, 197; fortified aspects, 197–99; light, 25; local construction techniques, 24; nave heights, 113; plans, 24ff; roofs directly on vaults, 133, 201; spolia at Fontfroide, 31; wooden buildings replaced by stone 27–29
Ardorel, Cistercian abbey for men, dioc. Castres, appendix 3, no. 30; 106, 122, 125–26, 143, 205, 207, 293n. 88, 314n. 143, 320n. 43; abbots: Fulk, 205; Peter, 211
Arles, Cistercian hospice, 319n. 30
Arnold, abbot of Morimond, 100
Arnold, prior of Campagnes or Bonnefont, 298n. 182
Arnold Amalric, abbot of Cîteaux, 230, 241, 297n. 151
Arnold Auriolo, husband of Sanchia, 310n. 77
Arnold of Broil, abbot of Gimont (1191–94), 177, 309n. 57
Arnold of Pont, castellan at Pont-de-Camarès, 111, 190–91, 312n. 117
Arnold of Saint-Just, abbot: of Berdoues, 177, 179, 308n. 54, 309nn. 56, 57; of Gimont, 176, 185
Arnold and Centullus of Gironde, 179
Arrivour, Cistercian abbey for men, 280, n. 101
Artigaberd, 140, 299n. 177
Artigue, site for Gimont, 176
Artigues: appropriated by Berdoues in 1152, 108; hermitage became grange of Berdoues, 108, 308n. 52
Assartville, 181
Assets of incorporated houses, 109, 222
Assurances of heavenly favor, 189
Astarac, counts, 137

Atbrandus, *consiliator*, hospice in Montpellier, 209–10, 314n. 158
Ato of Blancafort, donor to Gimont, 179
Ato of Escornabou, 182–83
Auberger, Jean-Baptiste, 98–99
Auch, William, archbishop and papal legate, 137
Augerius, abbot of Bonnefont, 309n. 56
Augerius of Calmont, founder of Boulbonne, 141, 299n. 185
Aula. *See* L'Eule
Austerity, 24, 29, 32, 201
Authority granted medieval voices, 51, 276n. 58
Avarice, 53
Aymeric of Gourdon, Boso and Ebles, viscounts of Brassac, 301n. 203

Balerne, abbey of Cistercian men, 270n. 132
Banols, grange of Grandselve, 128
Barrière, Bernadette, 126, 293n. 95
Bartholomew, abbot of la Ferté, 283n. 131
Bartlett, Robert, 262n. 12
Bastides (new towns), 39, 127, 129–30, 140, 179, 309n. 62
Bearded lay-brothers. *See* Lay-brothers
Beatrix, at hospital of Saint-Martin, 214–15
Beatrix, daughter of count of Bigorre, 138
Beatrix, donor to Silvanès, 168
Beaulieu. *See also* Belloc
Beaulieu-en-Arles, Cistercian abbey for women, dioc. Arles, appendix 3, no. 71; 231
Beaulieu-en-Gard, Cistercian abbey for women, dioc. Nîmes, appendix 3, no. 55
Beaulieu-en-Pamiers or Mirepoix, Cistercian abbey for women, dioc. Mirepoix, appendix 3, no. 18; 36, 300n. 190
Beaumont, parish granted to Grandselve, 128
Beceria, parish granted to Valmagne, 208, 211, 213
Belleaigue, Cistercian abbey for men, abbot William, 301n. 203
Bellecombe, Cistercian abbey for women, mother-house of Nonenque, 40, 117, 189, 193; prioress Elizabeth, 191–93
Belleperche, Cistercian abbey for men, dioc. Montauban, appendix 3, no. 20; 126–29, 157, 320n. 43
Belleperticula, early site of Belleperche, later of bastide of Larrazet, 127
Bellevaux, 270n. 132
Belloc, Cistercian abbey for men, dioc. Rodez,

appendix 3, no. 32; 126–27, 129, 295n. 117, 320n. 43
Benedictine Rule. *See* Rule of Saint Benedict
Benefactions, 169. *See also* Patronage; Patrons
— admission, 71, 217–18, 155; of daughter at Bonnefont, 163; at incorporating house, 227; as lay-brothers, 166, 188
— burial: deathbed promises, 162–63, 185–86, 188; at la Ferté, 76; of women in monastic cemeteries, 20, 70, 188, 191
— cash countergifts, 171, 188
— confraternity, 75, 218
— prayers: anniversary masses, 218; benefits of Cistercian *ordo*, 70; for souls, 163, 185, 188–89, 217, 308n. 42 318n. 13
Berdoues, Cistercian abbey for men, dioc. Auch, appendix 3, no. 2; 108, 137–38, 140–42, 155, 215, 299n. 177, 304n. 237, 320n. 43
— abbot, Arnold, 309n. 56
— adopted Cistercian practices, 73
— charters and cartulary, 73, 136, 174–79, 298n. 182, 307n. 29
— daughter-abbey, Gimont, 176–77
— economic activities, 175, 229
— monks: William Girmon, 309n. 56; William Peter Curta Sola, 309 n.56
— patrons promised: admission, 278n. 71; burial, 305nn. 6, 8
— references to *ordo* in charters, 71–73, table 2
Berengar, archbishop of Narbonne, 316n. 197
Berengar, viscount of Narbonne, 297n. 151
Berengar Rostagnus and his wife Amada, donors, 205
Bernac, grange of Bonnecombe, 131
Bernard, abbot of la Cour-Dieu, 301n. 203
Bernard, abbot of Fontfroide, 225–26
Bernard, abbot of Gimont (1154–67), 178, 308n. 54, 309n. 56
Bernard, count of Astarac, 137
Bernard, hermit founder of l'Escaledieu, 138
Bernard, son of Rostagnus of Popian, educated at Valmagne, 217
Bernard Alcherius, 155
Bernard Bego of Provencos, 212
Bernard Boze, with wife Petronilla and children, 213
Bernard Sicard, to be *conversus*, 166
Bernard William of Montbasen with wife Adelaide gave for Valmagne, 205
Bernard of Badcaina, son of Gassia, nephew of Ademar of Juliac, entered Gimont, 184, 310n. 77

Bernard of Bigorre, claims against Gimont, 180
Bernard of Capraria, 207, 217, 317n. 202
Bernard of Clairvaux. See also *Vita Prima*
— charisma, 96, 99
— charters describe as Dominus not yet *Sanctus*, 283n. 132
— conversion to religious life, 94, 98, 101, 143–45, 148, 156, 303n. 219, 303n. 220
— deposition of Arnold of Morimond, 100, 137
— episcopal appointments, 99
— *exordia* omit, 13–14, 94, 149
— friends. *See* Alexander of Cologne; Eugenius III
— member of textual community, 97
— preacher, 1–2, 94, 96–97, 100, 210; trip to Midi, 31, 227
— stability, 14, 94
— supporter of: Cîteaux's independence from Molesme, 96–97; Fountains, 100; Innocent II and the tithe privilege, 96; nuns at Jully, 96, 232, 286n. 8
— works and ideas, 52, 69, 128; on apostolic poverty, 100; on Desert Fathers, 24, 100; sermons, 225, 286n. 12; on Song of Songs, 274n. 28
Bernard of Cuxa, bishop of Béziers, 196–98
Bernard of la Barthe, abbot of L'Escaledieu, 138
Bernard of Marcellian, donor to Valmagne, 171
Bernard and Raymond of Teccos, 308n. 52, 309n. 61
Bernard-Aton, viscounts (cadet branch of Trencavels). *See* family tree, fig. 47
Bernard-Aton IV, 205
Bernard-Aton V, son of Cecily countess of Provence and Bernard Aton IV, 207, 315n. 184
Bernard-Aton VI, viscount of Nîmes and Agde, 207, 214–16, 218–19, 230; 308n. 38, 316n. 197
Bernarda, daughter of Gassia, sister of Ademar of Juliac, 310n. 77
Bernardo Paganelli. *See* Eugenius III
Bertrand, abbot of Grandselve, 128, 148, 176, 308n. 54
Bertrand of Laurs, 185–86
Bertrand of l'Isle, 140
Beuil, Cistercian abbey for men, 244
Beverly minster, forged charter, 78–79

Béziers, bishop Bernard of Cuxa, 196–98
Biblical commentary by Cistercians, 52, 98
Biddlesden, abbey for Cistercian men, 218n. 105
Bishops, Cistercians become, 99, 149
Blancafort family, patrons of Gimont, 178–80
Blanche of Castile, 43, 230; supports Cistercians, 103, 222, 233
Bona of Toncens, recruit to Artigues (Berdoues), 108
Bondéelle-Souchier, Anne, 235
Bonlieu. *See also* Le Vignogoul
Bonlieu-en-Languedoc (distinct from le Vignogoul), Cistercian abbey for women, dioc. Maguelonne, appendix 3, no. 49
Bonlieu-en-Montélimar, Cistercian abbey for women, dioc. Valence, appendix 3, no. 63; 123, 231, 235, 319n. 32, 321n. 48
Bonlieu-en-Valence, Cistercian abbey for women, dioc. Valence, appendix 3, no. 62
Bonnaigue, Cistercian abbey for monks, 301n. 203
Bonnecombe, Cistercian abbey for men, dioc. Rodez, appendix 3, no. 33; 110, 130–31, 119, 162–63, 195, 278n. 71, 289n. 51, 304n. 237, 320n. 43; abbot, 297n. 144; grange of Vareilles, 308n. 40
Bonnefont, Cistercian abbey for men, dioc. Saint-Bertrand-de-Comminges, appendix 3, no. 12; 136, 138, 140–42, 158–59, 163, 176, 298n. 182, 304n. 237; abbot Augerius, 309n. 56
Bonnefoy, Carthusian house, 304n. 247
Bonneval, Cistercian abbey for men, dioc. Rodez, appendix 3, no. 34; 117–21, 124, 130, 155–56, 158, 195, 304n. 237, 320n. 43; fire destroys archives, 167–68
Bonnevaux, 70, 100, 106, 117, 126, 138–39, 152, 155–56, 158, 189, 205, 207, 211, 287n. 23; 288n. 39; 320n. 43
— abbot, 282n. 120
— congregation in southern France, 27, fig. 30, 119, 121–23
— Calixtus II privilege, 87, 284n. 141, appendix 4
— *Desiderium quod*, 18, 20, 294n. 195
— visited by abbot of Cîteaux, 287n. 34
Book of Gilbert, 145; date, 301, 197
Books returned to Molesme, 17
Bordeaux, salt for Grandselve, 129
Bordesley, abbey for Cistercian men, 281n. 110

Bouchet. *See* Le Bouchet
Bouillas (Portaglonium), Cistercian abbey for men, dioc. Auch, appendix 3, no. 3; 140, 158; abbot Galin, 309n. 56
Bouillas, parish granted to Grandselve, 128
Boulaur, house of nuns of Fontevrault, 126, 295n. 112
Boulbonne, Cistercian abbey for men, dioc. Mirepoix, appendix 3, no. 19; 140–42, 158, 229, 235, 300n. 190, 304n. 245; abbot, 221
Bouton, Jean-de-la-Croix, 264n. 16
Brassac, viscounts of, 301n. 203
Bredero, Adriaan, 150, 237–41, 303nn. 219, 220
Breviter, significance, 7
Broil family, 17778, 184
Brunel, Clovis, 294n. 102, 304n. 245
Buckfast, abbey of Cistercian men (Savigniac) charter, probably forgery, 78
Buildwas, abbey of Cistercian men (Savigniac), 281n. 110
Bullaire of Calixtus II, ed. Ulysse Robert, 87, 284n. 138
Bullaire of Cîteaux. See *Liber privilegiorum*
Burau, grange of Valmagne, 208
Burgundian charter evidence, 75–76
Burgundian Congregation. *See* Congregation, Burgundian
Burgundy: family, 284n. 137; count of, 279n. 90
Bynum, Caroline Walker, 55, 98

Cabana, for cheese-making, 213
Cacian, canons of, 219
Cadouin, 106, 124–26, 138–39, 143–47, 288n. 40, 300n. 193
Cagnotte. *See* Saint-Bernard-de-la-Cagnotte
Cahors, bishop, lord of Calmont-sur-Olt, became founder of Bonneval, 118
Calers, Cistercian abbey for men, dioc. of Rieux, appendix 3, no. 21; 130, 235, 304n. 245, 320n. 43; abbot, 221
Calixtus II (1119–24), 54, 62–63, 67, 100, 121, 143, 270n. 132, 284n. 137, 294n. 136; forged bull *Ad hoc in Apostolicae*, 22–23, 46–47, 56, 59ff, 87–89, appendix 4
Cambridge, Corpus Christi College MS 139, 302n. 208
Campagnes transferred to Villelongue, old site becomes grange, 141
Candeil, Cistercian abbey for men, dioc. Albi, appendix 3, no. 29; 130, 297n. 138, 304n. 237

Canivez, J.-M., 49–50, 206, 302n. 206
Canvern, grange of Valmagne, 71, 73, 122, 208, 211–15, 155, 217, 315nn. 168, 169
Canvernet, mansus of, 212
Capdenier family, 129
Capitula, 49, 56, 275n. 43. *See also* Instituta
Care of souls, 190. *See also* Cura animarum
Caritas. *See* Charity
Carolingian foundations, 79–80
Carta Caritatis Posterior, 9–10, 54, 56, 59–61, 62–63, 103, 139, 263n. 6, 274n. 29, 275n. 43, 276n. 55
Carta Caritatis Prior, 9–10, 54, 56, 59–61, 62–63, 67, 85, 88, 137, 139, 263n. 6, 274n. 29, 275n. 43, 276n. 55
Carthusians, 112, 120, 215
Cartularies: development, 166; evidence from, 169; family, Capdenier, 129; making and women's houses, 14; placement of charters in, 161; Williams of Montpellier, 74
Casale: of Pin, 187; of Saint-Sernin, 185, 311n. 83; of Tresseira, 188
Cash: for provisioning the General Chapter, 75; revenues from endowment at Valmagne, 219
Cassanuéjouls, church given to Nonenque, 193
Castles as index of social power, 184
Cathar or Albigensian heresy
— association with women, 41, 232, 320n. 37
— crusade against, 130–31, 135–36, 268n. 109; Arnold Amalric, leader of, 230; cartulary production as result, 313n. 132; northern houses for nuns support, 319n. 28
— fear of accusations led to concessions to Cistercians; 216, 230–31
CD-ROM searches, 69
Cecily, countess of Provence, wife of Bernard-Aton IV, mother of Ermengardis Trencavella, 205, 207, 293n. 88
Centullus, count of Bigorre, 138
Chaalis, abbey of Cistercian men, papal confirmation of *ordo*, 270n. 132
Chalais, congregation in Provence, 285n. 1
Chambons. *See* Les Chambons
Charismatic leaders: adult converts, 101; Bernard of Clairvaux, 149; congregations, 93; rules and followers, 93; Silvanès chronicle, 114
Charity (*caritas*), 2, 8, 79, 98, 149–51, 154, 224–25, 232, 264n. 28
Charter of Charity, 22, 47–49, 58, 88–87, 94, 99, 152–53, 155, 158, 225, 264n. 16, 283n. 129, 285n. 149. *See also Summa Cartae Caritatis*; *Carta Caritatis Prior*; *Carta Caritatis Posterior*
Charter of Peace with Gilbertines, 158
Charter of Peace with Praemonstratensians, copy from Chaumont, 80, fig. 23, 83–86, 109, 180, 229, 238; attestation clauses, 85; topics covered, 85–86
Charters, 161–75. *See also* Cartularies; Contracts
— appearance of *ordo*, 69, 278n. 77; exceptional cases, 80–87
— document invention of Order, 190, 225
— evidence for: attitudes toward patrons, 172; donors' wishes to enter religious communities, 71; expectations of heavenly rewards, 169; monastic inadvertence, 173; peripheral owners, 225; support for Crusade, 187
— forgery of royal or quasi-royal charters, 78–79
— production: abbreviations, 279n. 84; in scriptoria of earlier centuries, 172–73; witnesses in, 183
— quantitative use, 169, 173, 307 n. 34
— translation, 79
— types of contracts and import, 170–72; formula "Notum sit omnibus," 11–12
— vidimus copy, 83
Chaumont document (Chirograph of Charity), 83, fig. 23, 283nn. 129, 126
Chirograph, 83, 296n. 128
Choisselet and Vernet edition of *Ecclesiastica Officia*, 59, 66, 271n. 3
Churches and tithes. *See* Tithes and churches
Cistercian congregation. *See* Congregation, Burgundian
Cistercian constitutions. *See* Constitutions
Cistercian ideals or principles. *See* Practices, Cistercian
Cistercian Order. *See* Order, Cistercian
Cistercian origins. *See* Origins, Cistercian
Cistercian success. *See* Success, Cistercian
Cistercian Tax Book, 320n. 43
Cîteaux, abbey for Cistercian men, motherhouse of the eventual Order. *See also* Congregations; Order; etc.
— abbots: Alberic (1099–1108), 21; Alexander of Cologne (1168–78), 128–29, 150; Arnold Amalric, 230; Goswin, 279n. 89; John of Ciry (1476–1501), 81; and le Tart chapter, 44, 235; Rainald (1134–51) 85,

Cîteaux (*continued*)
98–99, 279n. 90, 283n. 131, 287n. 23, 301n. 203; Stephen Harding (1108–33), 21, 98–99; visitor for Maubuisson, 222
— Charter of Peace with Praemonstratensians, 83–87
— charters: appearance of *ordo*, 74–79; for Saulier, 284n. 137
— daughter-houses and expansion, 50, 97, 99–100, 143, 146, 159, 222, 318n. 7
— described by Orderic Vitalis and William of Malmesbury, 101; in *exordia*, 5–6, 14–15, 47, 96–97, 220
— detached from Molesme, 96, 286n. 8
— internal chapter, 279n. 89. *See also* General Chapter
— manuscripts. *See* Dijon
— oversight by proto-abbots, 8, 10, 100, 137
— papal privileges, 80–83, 87–92, 301n. 199
Clairvaux, abbey for Cistercian men in Burgundy. *See also* Congregations, Burgundian
— abbots, 14, 67, 126, 149, 157; Bernard, 115–53; Fastrede, 302n. 213; Geoffrey of Auxerre, 145, 150; Girard, 151; Pons of Polignac, 141, 151, 304n. 231; Henry of Marcy, 151; Peter Monocule, 151; and visitation, 103, 288n. 35
— appointments from, 99–100. *See also* Alexander of Cologne; Eugenius III
— benefactions received, 76, 99, 149
— daughter-houses and congregation, 81, 96, 99, 100, 102, 106, 126–29, 143, 149–50, 155, 157, 222, 318n. 7. *See also* Congregation, Burgundian
— *exordia*, 149
— manuscripts. *See* Montpellier H322
— power of the abbey, 96–97, 98–99
— power over Morimond, 137
— success, 136, 149, 150
— textual community at, 96, 98–99
— tithe privilege, 81, 96
Clare, daughter of Pons-William, 142
Clarevallian congregation. *See* Congregations, Burgundian, Clairvaux
Clarevallian flavor of Cistercian history, based on *Exordium Magnum*, 3
Clariana. *See* Le Jau
Clearances at Arbielle, 181–82
Clerical marriage, ecclesiastical legislation against, 102, 164–65
Clermont, bishop, Pons of Polignac (1170–89), 141, 151, 304n. 231

Cluny (Cluniacs), abbey of Benedictine monks in Burgundy: abbot Peter the Venerable, 305n. 251; described in Cistercian terms, 53; priory at Montjoyer and Aiguebelle, 300n. 191
Codicology of Trent MS 1711, 61–62
Colleges, Cistercian, 210
Colonialism, attitudes about expansion among Cistercian reformers, 103–4
Colonization from Burgundy, 1, 95, 107
Comberoger, grange of Grandselve, 128
Commemoration of dead by Cistercians and Praemonstratensians jointly, 86
Competition for property, 109, 156
Congregations:
— Burgundian: becomes an Order, 128–29; early daughter-houses of Cîteaux and Clairvaux act as, 8, 50, 75, 94–100, 102–4, 106, 110–11, 120, 143, 145, 148–51, 153, 158–59
— in Gascony and Spain, fig. 35, 138–40, 142, 176
— at Gimont, 70
— religious reform, 68, 93–94, 99, 106, 128, 149, 285n. 149
Conrad of Eberbach, 2–3; *See also Exordium Magnum*
Consolidation of land, 154, 173–74, 179
Constable, Giles, 157, 273n. 24, 305n. 251
Constitution (Cistercian). *See also Ad hoc in Apostolicae*; *Charter of Charity*; *Sacrosancta*; *Summa Cartae Caritatis*
— development of, 3, 47–48, 50, 54, 87, 89, 91–92, 129, 137, 150, 156
— universal distribution of, 241
Contracts. *See also* Charters
— how many are preserved? 129, 167
— internal aspects: countergifts, 208, 209; fidejussores, mandatores, witnesses, etc., 189, 215, 309n. 61, 310n. 77, 311n. 88; language of donation, 162–66, 168, 171–75; oaths over Gospels, 188
— types: actes-notices, 136; *convenientiae*, 130; disguised sales, 171–72, 308n. 44; new types, 168–70; what do we call them? 171
— understanding of: agency in, 161; invariability, 169–70; to assure gifts, 171
Conversae/conversi See Lay brothers; Lay-sisters
Conversion (adult), 98, 101–2, 110–11, 114, 166, 190; *ad conversionem*, 212–13, 311, n. 88; married couples, 111
Corpus Christianorum, 69
Côte-d'Or archives 11H4, 80–81

Coubirac, grange of Grandselve, 128
Council, Fourth Lateran (1215), 79, 94, 222, 229, 282n. 121
Council of Tours, 240, 303n. 220
Count of Macon, 76
Count of Troyes, 75
Countesses of Flanders, 222
Coyroux, Cistercian abbey for women, associated with Obazine, 40, 123, 144
Creis, grange of Valmagne, 207, 313n. 132, 315n. 184
Criticism of Cistercians, 12–13, 10, 17–18, 23, 148
Crusade, 187–88, 207
Cuelas, grange of Berdoues, murder at, 174–75, 215
Cura animarum or monialium, 190, 233–34
Currency/coinage, Melgueil, Melgorien pennies, Morlaas, pennies, 307n. 32
Customaries for lay-brothers. *See* Lay-brother-treatises

Dalon, abbey for Cistercian men, 124–25, 155–56, 158; cartulary, 294n. 99
Degler-Spengler, Brigitte, 42–43
Delisle, Léopold, 68
Depopulation, 103–4, 112, 174, 215–18
Desert (as ideal site): in *exordia*, 5–6, 11, 14–16, 23–24, 122, 228; as location of abbeys, 41, 102, 209, 215; solitude, 111–12
Desiderium quod, 18, 20, 294n. 105
Dijon, Bibliothèque municipale de la ville, MS 69 (598), *Liber privilegiorum* (Bullaire of Cîteaux), 285n. 147
Dijon, Bibliothèque municipale de la ville, MS 87, *Distinctiones*, Garnerius of Rupeforti, with *Sacrosancta*, 89, fig. 24, 91, 284n. 146
Dijon, Bibliothèque municipale de la ville, MS 114 (once 82), 48, 53, 58, 59, 62, 66, 67, 80, 244, 271n. 3, 274n. 32, 275n. 43, 282n. 122
Dijon, Bibliothèque municipale de la ville, MS 611, chronicle of Pons de Léras, 289n. 49
Dijon, Côte-d'Or archives 11H4, 80–81, 282n. 124
Diplomatic analysis and standard source criticism
—*Ad hoc in Apostolicae*, 87–89
—Charter of Peace with Praemonstratensians, 83–85
—documents embedded in the *Exordium Parvum* or attached to it, 15–23
—*Habitantes in domo*, 80–83

—Roman privilege, *Desiderium quod*, 20, 294n. 105
—*Sacrosancta*, 67–69, 89–92
—specific aspects: attestation clauses, 83; indiction, 85, 89–91; imprecation clauses, 267n. 77; language such as *confirmamus, constitutio, constitutum*, 88, 284n. 139
—statutes, 48–51
Distinctiones of Garnerius of Rupeforti, Dijon MS 87, 89, fig. 24, 91, 284n. 146
Diversity created by expansion, 149
Divielle, or Vielle, 125. *See also* Villedieu
Do, brother of Augerius of Calmont, 299n. 185
Doat Collection, 127, 221, 225, 227, 299n. 182
Documents of Practice. *See* Charters
Domina or Na, 184, 190
Dominican Order, 41, 231
Domus Aimerici. *See* Vajal
Donors to monasteries. *See* Patrons
Double communities, 40, 41, 86, 101–2, 116–17, 123, 175, 196, 203, 205, 228, 232, 293n. 95
Dowries, 188, 215–16
Drayas (transhumance roads), 119
Durandus of Canvern, 212, 315n. 172
Duval-Arnould, edition of Montpellier H322, 66

Eaunes, Cistercian abbey for men, dioc. Toulouse, appendix 3, no. 26; 140; abbot, Sanche, 309n. 56
Ecclesiastica Officia, 47, 48, 56, 59–61, 65–68, 265n. 33. *See also* Choisselet; Vernet
Economic aims, 53, 153, 172
Economic conditions, southern France: Benedictine consolidation by selling off distant cells, 219; Narbonne, being replaced by Montpellier, 196; real estate market, 154, 165
Economic privileges, Cistercian, for Passage rights, exemptions from tolls and tithes, 230
Economy, Cistercian. *See* Acquisitions; Expenditures; Consolidation; Granges; Lay-brothers; Managerial activities; Pastoralism, Tithes; etc.
Education, Cistercian: children at Valmagne, 217–18; new recruits, 23, 98
Eleanor of Aquitaine, 130
Eleanor of Comminges, 268n. 109
Elizabeth, prioress of Bellecombe, 191–93
Encastellation, 316n. 201

Episcopal visitation, papal privileges from, 43, 158
Equality, 53, 93, 149, 154, 159, 167
Eremitical communities. *See* Hermits and eremitical communities
Ermengardis, gave land and was buried at Silvanès, 191
Ermengardis, viscountess of Narbonne, 131, 163, 278n. 81, 318n. 13
Ermengardis Trencavella, married to count of Roussillon, 205è
Ermengardis of Creyssels, countess of Rodez, 190, 316n. 197
Ermengaudis, abbot of Valmagne, 211, 278n. 78
Ermessendis, woman of that name, 205, 217
Escaledieu. *See* L'Escaledieu
Escornabou family, 182–84
Esparrons, son of Yspanus of Maurencs, 185, 311n. 83
Estates, organization under lay-brothers, 20–21
Eudes, duke of Burgundy, 5–6, 15
Eugenius III, Bernardo Pignatelli, monk of Clairvaux, native of Pisa, elected pope 1145 as Eugenius III, usually referred to as first Cistercian pope, 142–48, 151, 153, 207, 238, 279n. 87, 285n. 149, 294n. 105
— bulls issued from Cîteaux, 238–39; to Jully and Bonnevaux, 20; to Molesme, 96, 206n. 8; to Silvanès, 74
— question of 1147 meeting, 142–48
Eule. *See* L'Eule
Exordia: Cîteaux described, 16; contents, 2–3; creation, 12–13, 22–23, 94–95, 110; eyewitness accounts? 23, 46, 53; language, 3–7, 149; legality of Cîteaux's foundation, 10–12; meta-texts, 94–95; Molesme described 16; narratives have been pervasive, 52, 94, 102–3; prefaces to liturgical books, 58; transformative moment, 63. See also *Exordium Cistercii*; *Exordium Magnum*; *Exordium Parvum*
Exordium Cistercii, 94–95, 149, 151, 153–54, 160, 166, 263n. 6
— contents, 3–10
— dating, 21–23, 47, 52–54, 59–61 62–63, 66–67
Exordium Magnum (Great Exordium), written by Conrad of Eberbach, 2–3, 5, 23, 51, 53, 58, 278n. 80, 284n. 138
Exordium Parvum (Little Exordium)

— authenticity of its documents, 10, 12–14, 22
— contents of the text, 9–23; expanded from *Exordium Cistercii*, 10; explains Cistercian success, 23, 94–95; "Instituta monachorum," 20; language of caritas, 149; omissions, 13; rhetoric, 10–15, 17; Roman privilege, 17; use in *Exordium Magnum*, 11, 23
— context in which it is found, 56, 58
— dating, 10–11, 21, 53, 59–63, 67, 107, 139
— relationship to statutes, 47–48, 51
— traditional treatment, 53–54
Expansion, Cistercian, descriptions, 95, 21–22, 110; beyond Burgundy, 95, 106, 159, 222, 237. *See also* Annexation; Apostolic gestation; Incorporation
Expenditures, 191–93, 218, 308n. 40, table 3

Fabas (Lumen Dei), Cistercian abbey for women, dioc. Saint-Bertrand-de-Comminges, appendix 3, no. 13; 36–39, figs. 15, 16, 268n. 109
Falkenstein, Ludwig, 87, 284n. 134
Family monasteries. *See* Double-communities
Farmsteads. *See* Granges
Fastrede, abbot of Clairvaux, 302n. 213
Father-visitors, 147, 233–34. *See also* Internal visitation
Faversham abbey, abbey of Cistercian men, 281n. 110
Ferlet, priory of nuns absorbed by Valmagne, 219
Feuillantines, order growing out of Cistercians, 294n. 103
Feuillants. *See* Les Feuillants
Fevales, 205, 208, 215
Fevum rights, 193
Fezac of Maurencs, 185
Filiation trees, 102–6, fig. 25, 111, 138–39, 152, 155–58, 161, 223–24, 300n. 193, 288n. 40; problems in use of, 103, 136, 154, 228, 288n. 37
Flandrina of Montpezat, 138
Flaran, Cistercian abbey for men, dioc. Auch, appendix 3, no. 4; 140, 158; abbot, William, 299n. 177
Flaxley, Cistercian abbey for men, 281n. 110
Fleurance, bastide of, 140
Foix, counts of, supporters of Boulbonne, 141–42
Following practices of Cistercians, 42, 68, 70–71, 74, 146, 178, 191, 205, 209, 213, 221, 296n. 128, 301n. 203, 316n. 186

Fontcalvy, grange of Fontfroide, 132
Fontdouce, grange of Valmagne, 208–10
Fontevrault, abbey and Order, 41, 123, 128, 159, 203. *See also* Boulaur; Lespinasse
Fontfroide, Cistercian abbey for men, dioc. Narbonne, appendix 3, no. 50; 29–33, 121, 126, 131–36, 140, 142, 163, 219, 221, 227, 320n. 43
— abbots: Vidal, 155, 318n. 13; Bernard, 225–26
— annexations, 127, 131–36, 210, 229
— charters, 133, 225, 268n. 104
— church, 29–33, figs. 7–10
— daughter-houses, 131–36, 221
— foundation and affiliation, 31–33, 128–31
— granges, fig. 31; Fontcalvy, 132; Saint-Hyppolyte, 132–33, 155
— lay-brothers, 133, 136
— preaching against heresy, 127, 135
— site, 29–32
— success, 31–32, 109, 131–36, 230
Fontguillem, Cistercian abbey for men, dioc. Bazas, appendix 3, no. 8; 125
Fontjoncouse, castle, 133
Fonts-de-Rosiers or lès-Alais. *See* Les Fonts-de-Rosiers
Forc, grange of Gimont, 181–83
Foreville, Raymonde, 146
Forqualquier, 26
Forton of Tilh, 299n. 177
Forton of Vic, lay-founder of l'Escaledieu, 137–38
Fortona, niece of Ademar of Juliac, 310n. 77
Fossier, Robert, 263n. 15
Foundation accounts, 95, 100, 124, 137, 175–78
Fountains, Cistercian abbey for men, 77; abbot to visit for Clairvaux in England, 288n. 35; charters, 78–79, 281n. 116; foundation account, 100; manuscript from, 245, 302n. 208; tithe exemption, 303n. 219
Frairesche or joint lordship among brothers, 185, 190
Franciscan nuns, 41
Franquevaux, Cistercian abbey for men, dioc. Nîmes, appendix 3, no. 57; 142, 211, 293n. 90, 300n. 192, 308n. 38
Franqueville, grange of Gimont, 183
Fratres. *See* Lay-brothers
Frederick I, Emperor, 282n. 120
Frègeville, 188
Fulk, abbot of Ardorel, 205

Fulk, count of Anjou, 77–78
Fulk of Marseilles, bishop of Toulouse, 231–32, 294n. 103, 319n. 29
Fundatrix, of Léoncel, 70
Furness, Cistercian abbey for men, 79

Gaillard of Sirac, 181, 183, 296n. 128
Galbraith, V. H., 261n. 4
Galdris, sister of Yspanus of Maurencs, 185, 187, 311n. 83
Galin, abbot of Bouillas, 309n. 56
Gallia christiana, 35, 221, 225, 302n. 210
Garnicia. *See* Vajal
Garonne River, shipping rights for Grandselve for wine and salt, 127, 129
Garrigue of Haute de Vescleran, 155
Garsens, founder of Saint-Pons of Géménos, 231
Garsens of Vintro, *procuratrix* for Nonenque, 193
Garsias, abbot of l'Escaledieu, 309n. 56
Gassia, sister of Ademar of Juliac, 310n. 77
Gassia, sister of Yspanus of Maurencs, married to Odo of Porastron, 185, 311n. 83
Gassia of Juliac, and her son Bernard, 183–84
Gaston de Foix, 268n. 109
Gausbert of Saint-Hyppolyte, 155
Géménos. *See* Saint-Pons-de-Géménos
General Chapter, Cistercian
— as indicator of administrative Order, 93, 102, 222–23
— command, 40, 76, 152, 158, 218
— earliest collections of statutes, 50, 52–53
— earliest meetings, 47, 49, 65, 142–43, 153
— earliest references to, 71, 75–76, 80, 83
— exchange of ideas, 53
— hostility to women, 35
— inventing the Order, 154–58
— legislation. *See* Statuta
— pressures on, 221–22
— travel to, 71, 109, 154–55, 209–10
— was there one in 1147? 142–48
General Chapter, Praemonstratensian, 85
Geoffrey, count of Anjou, 77–78
Geoffrey of Auxerre, abbot of Clairvaux, 145–46, 151, 240, 301n. 201, 303n. 219, 305n. 261
Gerald, abbot of Molesme, 286n. 8
Gerald, abbot of Praemonstratensian Florecensis, 283n. 131
Gerald, count of Roussillon, 314n. 144
Gerald of Broil, 177. *See also* Broil family

Gerald of Salles, 123–24, 127, 143, 223, 300n. 187
Gerits, Trudo, 83
Gerlandus, text of Compotus, 63–65
Gift economy, 170, 189. See also Rosenwein
Gigean. See Saint-Félix-de-Montseau
Gigny, priory, 157, 305n. 251
Gilbert, abbot of Cîteaux, 91–92
Gilbert of Sempringham, 41, 143–46, 148
Gilbertines, 41, 143–47, 158; lay-brothers, 146, 303n. 219
Gimont, Cistercian abbey for men, dioc. Auch, appendix 3, no. 5; 36, 70, 74, 126, 138, 140–41, 152, 157–58, 175–89, 219, 308n. 54, 320n. 43
— abbots: Arnold of Broil, 177; Arnold of Saint-Just, 176, 185; Bernard, 155, 178, 188, 309n. 56
— acquisitions and expenditures, 140–41, 175–89, 192, table 3
— adoption of Cistercian practices, 73–74
— charters and cartulary, 70, 162, 175–89, 298n. 182, 307n. 29, 309n. 59
— congregation, 73–74
— granges: Aiguebelle, 179; Forc, 183, Franqueville, 183; Hour, 180–81, 184; Laurs, 185; Saint-Hyppolyte, 132–33, 155
— other members: grangers, Odo of Maurencs, 185; William of Blancafort, 179; prior, Raymond Vidal, 309n. 56; monks, Ademar of Juliac, 184; Umbertus, 309n. 56; William of Toulouse, 309n. 56; *conversi*, Bernard of Juliac, 184; William of Aspa, 309n. 56
— patrons, 175–89, 278n. 71
Gold, Penny Schine, 159, 305n. 267
Golden age, 2, 40
Golding, Brian, 146, 301n. 194n. 202, 302n. 207
Goliards, 69
Gothic style and Cistercians, 24, 29ff, 124, 127, 196, 203, 313n. 134. See also Architecture
Goujon, Cistercian abbey for women, dioc. Lombez, appendix 3, no. 17; 36–39, figs. 17, 18
Gould, Stephen Jay, 288n. 34
Grandmontines, 120, 303n. 219
Grandselve, Cistercian abbey for men, dioc. Toulouse, appendix 3, no. 27; 31, 73–74, 123, 126–31, 136, 140, 147–48, 155, 157–58, 163, 176, 210, 227, 232
— abbots: Alexander 73, 128, 150, 278n. 81 (*see* Alexander of Cologne); Arnold, 176, 230; Bertrand, 128, 148; 176; Elie Guarin, 230; Pons, 73, 128, 155, 176, 278n. 81, 296n. 128, 309n. 56 (*see* Pons of Polignac)
— adopted Cistercian or Clarevallian practices, 73, 127–29, 152
— bastides founded, 129
— charters and cartularies, 73, 127–29, 148, 296n. 122, 308n. 40; references to *ordo*, 71–73, table 2
— daughter-houses, 129–33; Calers, 129–30; Candeil, 130; Fontfroide, 126–28; Sanctas Cruces in Spain, 129, 210
— granges, 128–29; cultivation dated, 304n. 237; la Terride, 183; Saint-Hyppolyte, 132–33, 155; Saint Jorii, 296n. 128
— hospice in Toulouse, 129
— neighbors: Gimont, 141, 175; Lespinasse, 127, 128
— other monks: Albert of Finna, 309n. 56; Raymond son of William VII of Montpellier, 210; Ugo of Mored, 309n. 56; William VI, lord of Montpellier, 129, 211
— promises of admission, 278n. 71
— viticulture, 129
— women's houses not founded, 127
Granges and grange agriculture of Cistercians, 86, 141, 174; converted to bastides, 130, 309n. 62; cultivation instituted, 267n. 86, 304n. 237; minimum distance between, 141, 180; run by lay-brothers, 8–9, 20–21, 121. See also specific granges under place or abbey names
Great Exordium. See *Exordium Magnum*
Greed. *See* Avarice
Greek ideas about monasticism, 148
Growth, 96, 103–4; by annexation and incorporation, 107–10, 131, 210, 219, 225–27; benefits of annexation, 151; rate, 95
Grundmann, Herbert, 41–42, 269n. 119
Guillelma, daughter of William of Montpesat, entered Bonnefont, 163
Guillelma, daughter of William VI of Montpellier, wife of Bernard-Aton V of Nîmes and Agde, 207, 214–15, 232, 308n. 38, 315n. 184, 316nn. 188, 197
Guillelma Reverdida, at hospital of Saint-Martin, 214–15
Guillelma (Guisla), mother of William of Blancafort, 179–80
Guy Guerrier, son of William VI of Montpellier, conveyed mills, 171, 210, 308n. 42, 314n. 157

Index

Guy of Burgundy, archbishop of Vienne, 100, 121, 284n. 137. *See* Calixtus II

Habitantes in domo, forged tithe privilege, 80–83, 96, 282n. 124
Hagiography, 112, 148
Hautecombe, Cistercian abbey for men, 287n. 23
Hautmont, rights at, 188
Henry, count of Troyes, 157, 305n. 249
Henry, duke of Anjou, 77–78. *See also* Henry II, king of England
Henry, monk from Pontigny sent to be abbot of Cadouin, 143
Henry I, prayers for his soul, 77
Henry II, king of England, 147–8l; for Fountains, interpolated, 281n. 116
Henry of Burgundy, 284n. 137
Henry of France, brother of Louis VII, monk of Clairvaux, bishop of Beauvais, 238–39
Henry of Marcy, abbot of Cîteaux, 151, 241
Heremus. *See* Desert
Herlihy, David, 306n. 12
Herman of Tournai, canon of Laon, 14, 68, 239
Hermits and eremitical communities, 73, 108, 136, 213; clearance and animal husbandry, 175; hunting grounds, 228; joined by priests, 190, 123–24, 285n. 1; seek affiliation, 99, 112; solitude, 111; women, 191. *See also* Arbielle; Artigues; Campagnes; l'Escaledieu; Mazan; Poblet; Silvanès; Western French reformers
Honorius III, pope (1216–27), 231
Hospices or hospitals, 157, 102, 214
— Arles, 319n. 30
— Creis, 207
— Montpellier: for travel to General Chapter, 71, 154–55, 208–10, 314n. 157, 316n. 197; charters conflate with that of Saint-Martin, 316n. 185
— near Montpellier by Guillelma of Montpellier called Saint-Martin, 165, 214, 316nn. 185, 187, 188, 317n. 220
— Nîmes created by abbey of Franquevaux, 308n. 38
— Toulouse for Grandselve, 129
Hospitallers, 138, 195, 277n. 69
Hour, grange of Gimont, 180–84
Hugh, archbishop of Lyons, 5–6, 11–12, 16–17
Hugh, count of Rodez, 316n. 197
Hugh, duke of Burgundy, 279n. 89

Hugh Francigena, monk of Silvanès, wrote chronicle, 110
Hugh of Cévennes, 212
Hugh of Durfort, gift to Villelongue, 141
Hugh of Fleury, 275n. 4
Hugh of Fosse, abbot of Prémontré, 85, 283n. 131

Ideals: of early Cistercians, 50, 56, 153, 222, 224; and reality, 55, 274n. 36
Imitatio cisterciensis, 42
Immunity. *See* Zone of immunity
Impignaverunt, 187. *See* Mortgage
Inadvertence, 175
Incipit, Explicit as used in medieval manuscripts, 275n. 48
Incorporation, 2, 54, 95–97, 100–104, 106–8, 110, 131
— benefits, 106–10, 136, 147–48, 154, 213, 224–25, 229; numerical effects, 107–8
— dating, 104, 154
— literary comments about, 110ff, 145
— reducing men's houses to granges and women's to dependent priories, 135, 142, 229
— strategy for power within Order, 139
Independent reform houses, 95, 108, 151, 205, 223
— adopt Cistercian practices, 2, 47, 95–97, 116, 143, 223
— affiliated with order, 93–95.
— associated with specific reformers, 93
— outside Burgundy, 99–102
— received tithe privileges, 96
Innocent II, pope (1130–43), 96, 157; forged bull *Habitantes in domo*, 80–81
Innocent III, pope (1198–1216), 133
Innocent IV, pope (1243–1254), and Cistercian nuns, 33–35, 233
Instituta, 47, 49–51, 56, 58, 66, 86, 95, 104, 107, 153, 222, 229, 263n. 6
— compared to 1157–61 statutes, 66
— not dated by Trent 1711, 61ff
— published as 1134 Statuta, 275n. 43
Institutions associated with Order, when do they appear? 46
Interactions between religious communities and their neighbors, 172
Interambasaquas. *See* Tramesaigues
Internal chapter of Cîteaux, 67, 270n. 132
Internal visitation, 7, 10, 102–3, 152, 223–24. *See also* References at filiation

International Order, 52, 224
Invention of the Order. *See also* Incorporation, etc.
— caused diversity of practice, 40, 55, 144, 224
— causes, pressures: Clairvaux's excessive power, 46, 69ff, 96–97, 148–50; complaints from outsiders, 154; crisis from growth, 149–50; papal pressure for enforcement of ideals, 93–94, 223; problems of rights and responsibilities beyond individual monasteries, 150
— consequences: 1147 General Chapter a myth, 142–43; cited as model for emulation by Fourth Lateran Council, 94–95; legislation, 48–49, 56, 102; need for *exordia*, 47; for understanding other religious groups, 159–60
— dating difficulty, 223
— inventors, 50, 129, 141, 150–51, 211
— process, 46, 48, 50, 52, 67, 69–71, 73, 92–100, 104, 110, 125, 150–56, 159–60, 184, 220, 222–25, 236
Invention of texts and speeches in medieval chronicles, 265n. 42
Isagogus, Lunar Calendar computations, 63

Jacob of Monsoon's wife gives to Valmagne, 163
Janauschek, Leopoldus, 107, 318n. 7
Jau. *See* Le Jau
Jean Bistan, bourgeois of Narbonne, 133
Jean Homme-de-Dieu, founder of l'Eule, 133
Jean of Cirey, abbot of Cîteaux (1476–1501), and Dijon MS 69 (598) *Liber privilegiorum*, 81, 83, 285n. 147
Jerusalem, to go to, 207
Johanna, gift to Berdoues, 306n. 8
John, abbot of Bonnaigue, 301n. 203
Joint lordship among brothers. See *Frairesche*
Jordana, nun at Nonenque, 191
Judicial procedures, 180
Juliac: family, 183–84; parish, 187
Jully, abbey of nuns attached to Molesme, 14, 39, 96, 99, 196, 232, 277n. 62, 286n. 8

Kings of England, 222. *See also* Henry I; Henry II; Richard; Stephen
King of Majorca, 227
Kirkstead, abbey of Cistercian men, 158
Kiss of peace, used to seal contract, 187
Knights: as patrons, 129, 130, 184, 188; as recruits, 98, 167, 241

Kostanjevica, abbey for Cistercian men, 243
Krenig, Ernst, 41–42

L'Almanarre. *See* Saint-Pierre-de-l'Almanarre
La Bénédiction-Dieu. *See* Nizors
La Cagnotte. *See* Saint-Bernard-de-la-Cagnotte
La Cour-Dieu, Cistercian abbey for men, abbot Bernard, 301n. 203
La Creste, Cistercian abbey for men, 294n. 103
L'Escaledieu, Cistercian abbey for men, dioc. Tarbes, appendix 3, no. 15; 113, 136, 138, 140, 142, 176, 299nn. 177, 178; abbot, Garsias, 309n. 56
L'Eule (Soler), or Aula, Cistercian abbey for women, dioc. Elne, appendix 3, no. 44; 132–33; *filia* of Fontfroide, 133; suppressed, 133
La Falque, Cistercian abbey for women, 191
La Ferté, Cistercian abbey for men, daughterhouse of Cîteaux, 8, 76, 158, 280n. 101, 285n. 149; charters and pancartes, 75–76, 99–100; early abbots, 99–100
La Grande Chartreuse, mother-house of Carthusian Order, 112
La Grasse, Benedictine abbey for men, 298n. 156
La Plan or Plane. *See* Sainte-Madeleine-de-la-Plan
La Peyrouse, Cistercian abbey for women, dioc. Narbonne, appendix 3, no. 53; 132
La Sauve Majeure, Benedictine abbey for men, 289n. 51, 290n. 52
La Serre, grange of Bonneval, 119
La Terride, grange of Grandselve, 183
La Vernaison, Cistercian abbey for women, dioc. Valence, appendix 3, no. 64; 231
Laibach 31. *See* Ljubljana 31
Land: already under cultivation at Silvanès, 111; consolidation, 109; unjustly stolen by patron, 188
Language of charters. *See* Charters, language
Laon, Bibliothèque publique, MS 217, 245
Larrazet, bastide of, 127
Las Huelgas, abbey of Cistercian nuns, 270n. 133
Lateran. *See* Council
Laudatio Parentum, 170, 181
Laurs, grange of Gimont, 185ff; 311n. 78
Lay control of tithes and churches as index of social power, 184
Lay-brother treatises, 3, 47–48, 56, 58, 65, 98, 103, 153, 167; London MS Add. 18, 148, 153, 315 n. 175; not dated by Trent 1711, 61

Lay-brothers, 2, 48, 88, 154; and granges, 8–9; help produce food, 20–21; and monks worked together in fields, 167, 210, 304n. 240; murder at Cuelas, 174; not to be knights, 154; revolts at Fontfroide, 136; treated as equal of monks, 276n. 49
— and lay-sisters, 98, 213–15; at hospital of Saint-Martin, 214–15; at Nonenque, 195; at Sainte-Eugénie, 225
Lay-sisters: Fontfroide and, 131–32; numbers, 165; working as dairymaids, 313n. 128
Le Bouchet (Vauluisant), Cistercian abbey for women, c. 1150 dioc. Saint-Paul-Trois-Châteaux, appendix 3, no. 80; 231, fig. 49
Le Jau (Clariana), Cistercian abbey for men, dioc. Elne, appendix 3, no. 45; 125
Le Lys, Cistercian abbey for women, 222
Le Rivet, Cistercian abbey for men, dioc. Bazas, appendix 3, no. 7; 125, 320n. 4
Le Tart, Cistercian abbey for women in Burgundy, 14, 36, 39, 42, 99, 196, 210, 270n. 132, 277n. 62
— chapter at, 44, 235
— *exordia* do not mention, 13–14
— received *Desiderium quod*, 20, 294n. 105
Le Thoronet, Cistercian abbey for men, dioc. Fréjus, appendix 3, no. 70; 24–27, fig 2, 117–20, 231, 319n. 29, 320n. 43; church, 24ff
Le Tillet, grange of Flaran, 299n. 177
Le Vignogoul (formerly Bonlieu), Cistercian abbey for women, dioc. Maguelonne, appendix 3, no. 48; 39, 122, 195, 201–5, 214, 313nn. 133, 136, 317n. 220; church, 197–203, 201, figs 43–46, frontispiece
Leclercq, Jean, 13, 40, 52, 67
Lefèvre, J.-A., xxi, 54, 65, 273n. 19, 275n. 48
Lekai, Louis J.: Cistercian origins, 1–2; cites 1790 commission, 234; ideals and reality model, 55
Léoncel, Cistercian abbey for men, dioc. Die, appendix 3, no. 60; 70, 74, 121–22
Lepers, 102
Léras, castle of Saint-Nazaire, 315n. 169
Les Baux, lords of, 26
Les Chambons, Cistercian abbey for men, dioc. Viviers, appendix 3, no. 65; 117–18, 120, 320n. 43
Les Feuillants, Cistercian abbey for men, dioc. Rieux, appendix 3, no. 22; 124, 158, 234; and Order of Peace and Faith, 294n. 103
Les Fonts-de-Rosiers, or Fonts-lès-Alais, Cistercian abbey for women, dioc. Nîmes, appendix 3, no. 56; 117
Les Monges. *See* Les Olieux
Les Olieux (les Monges), Cistercian abbey for women, dioc. Narbonne, appendix 3, no. 52; 39, 133–35, 226; church, 133, fig. 33, fig. 34, 135, 298n. 154
Les Olieux (Montsérat), Cistercian abbey for women, dioc. Narbonne, appendix 3, no. 51; Montsérat, 297n. 149
Lespinasse, abbey of nuns of Fontévrault, possible association with Grandselve, 123, 127–28
Levrettes. *See* La Peyrouse
Libellus de diversis ordinibus, 68
Liber Privilegiorum Cistercii, Dijon MS 69 (598), fig. 22, 80–83, 266n. 75, 282n. 124, 285n. 147
Life/Lives. See *Vita/ae*
Lincoln: bishop and chapter, 158; Lincolnshire, 144, 158
Lioujas, villa and grange of Nonenque, 190, 312n. 107
Little Exordium. See *Exordium Parvum*
Liturgical ordines, or Order-books: context for "primitive documents," 47–48, 56, 80, 98, 103; corrected by Stephen Harding, 94, 98; earliest versions, 152–53; extracts in Montpellier MS, 63–65; manuscripts used for sequence of "primitive document" texts, 3, 9, table 1, 58, 275n. 46. See also *Ecclesiastica Officia*
Lives of Desert Fathers, 98, 100
Ljubljana, Laibach, University and State Library, MS 31; 54–59, 62, 80, 243, 264n. 27, 272n. 11, 274n. 33, 275n. 41, 42, 43, fig. 19
Locdieu, Cistercian abbey for men, dioc. Rodez, appendix 3, no. 35; 119, 124, 130, 155, 156, 195, 235, 294n. 102, 304n. 244, 320n. 43
Lodève, Saint-Sauveur, 110, 111, 195, 312n. 109
London, British Library Add. MS 18;148, 153, 245
Longevity, monastic, 187, 229–30
Louis VI, 75, 153
Louis VII, 279n. 89
Louis VIII, 103, 222
Louis IX, 230
Louth Park, Cistercian abbey for men, 158
Lucius II, pope (1144–45), 81

Lucius III, pope (1181–85), 81, 208, 282n. 124
Lumen Dei. *See* Fabas
Lyre, Benedictine abbey for men, 243

Mahn, J.-B., 52
Majorca, king of, 221
Managerial activities, 53, 171
Manrique, Angel, seventeenth-century historian of Cistercians, 49
Mansus at Canvern, 212
Mansus Embacis, given to Silvanès, 168
Mansus Salellis, new site for Silvanès, 193
Manual labor, 2, 48, 229
Manuscripts. *See* Codicology; Dijon; Ljubljana, Montpellier; Paris; Primitive documents; Trent; Statuta; etc.
Marfavius, *conversus*, 306n. 8
Margam, Cistercian abbey for men, 281n. 106
Marian commemoration, 51, 271n. 3, 272n. 11
Marie of Escornabou, 181–84, 232
Marie of Montpellier, 313n. 132
Marilier, Jean, 75
Marrenz, Marrenc, or Marrencs, Cistercian abbey for women, dioc. Rieux, appendix 3, no. 23; 39; founded by counts of Toulouse, 300n. 189
Marsanne, countess of, 231, 319n. 32
Martin, Arnold and Peter of Sotol, hermits at Arbielle, 181–82
Matilda, Empress, contender for rule of England, patron, 147; founder of Margam, 77; rivalry with Stephen, 281n. 106
Matilda of Burgundy, William VII's potential wife, 211
Maubuisson, 222
Maurencs family, 184–89; marriage strategies, 184–85; relationship to Gimont, 186ff; family tree, fig. 37; lordship and castellum, church with own chaplain, rule over knights, 184
Mauvezin, viscounts, 181, 184, 310n. 68
Mazan, Cistercian abbey for men, dioc. Viviers, appendix 3, no. 66; 27, 112, 116–22, 130, 138, 155–56, 158, 190, 195, 291n. 70, 304n. 247, 320n. 43
— abbots, 287n. 23; Peter, 112, 117, 292n. 72
— adopt *ordo*, 152
— congregation, 117–23, fig. 30, 119, 189, 288n. 39
— hermits, 27, 117
— pastoralism, 223

Meaux, England, Cistercian abbey for men, 305n. 252
Mendicants, 41
Mercoire, Cistercian abbey for women, dioc. Mende, appendix 3, no. 31; 117
Mercoire, grange of Valmagne, 208
Merton priory, 305n. 252
Metz, Bibliothèque publique, MS 1247, 62, 91, 153, 244
Mèze, property of Cecily, wife of Bernard-Aton IV, 205, 207
Midi. *See* Southern France
Milis, Ludo, 111–12, 290n. 57
Military-religious orders, 124. *See* Order of Alcantara; Calatrava; etc
Mills: at Paollan on Hérault River given to Valmagne, 171, 208, 308n. 42; at Laurs given to Gimont, 185
Miracle of Cistercian growth explained, 109
Miraculous appearance of food in Silvanès foundation account, 114
Mirepoix, bishop and chapter, 300n. 190
Misogynous elements, 20, 232; increase in later twelfth century, 40, 44; possible for Bernard of Clairvaux, 126–27
Molesme, abbey from which Cîteaux seceded, 39, 41, 159, 173, 196, 270n. 132; double-community, 14–15, 96–97, 286n. 8; *Exordium Parvum* description, 5, 10–12, 16
Mollèges, Cistercian abbey for women, dioc. Avignon, appendix 3, no. 72; 231
Monastic enclosure and stability, 21
Money economy: source of cash for acquisitions, 218; granted to Maurencs and others, 187; for donors moving to towns, 213
Monges. *See* Les Olieux (les-Monges)
Monk and *conversus* members of same family, 184
Monks conducted more consolidation than nuns, 195
Mont-Cornil, Cistercian abbey for women, dioc. Lodève, appendix 3, no. 39; daughter-house of Nonenque, 190–91, 312n. 109
Mont-Sion, Cistercian abbey for women, 1245 dioc. Marseilles, appendix 3, no. 76
Montesquiu, lords, 268n. 109
Montjoyer, Cluniac priory (Aiguebelle), 300n. 191
Montlaurès, priory annexed by Fontfroide, 131–32, 297n. 151
Montpellier, Bibliothèque de la faculté de l'école de médecine, MS H322; 50, 57–59,

63, fig. 21, 65–66, 71, 80, 98, 152–53; from Clairvaux, 242; extracts from earlier liturgical treatise, 66
Montpellier, hospice of Valmagne, 122, 154–55, 157, 209, 214
Montpellier, lords, William VI, 129
Montpezat, castellans, 138
Montreuil, abbey of Cistercian women, 14, 239, 270n. 133
Montsérat. *See* Les Olieux
Montveyre, 133
Morimond, 54, 126, 138–39, 142, 158, 176, 179
— abbots, 56, 137; Arnold, deposed by Bernard, 100, 136; Walter, former prior of Clairvaux, 100, 136–38, 179; Walter II, 73–74
— filiation and daughter-houses in Gascony and Spain, 106, 136–42, 155, 278n. 82
— mission not in 1130s, 137
— poverty, 100, 137
— proto-abbot or not, 8, 76, 85, 100, 137, 139, 142
Mortain, house of Stephen, king of England, grants to Cistercians and Savigniacs, 77, 281n. 103
Mortemer, abbey for Cistercian men, 77–78
Mortgages and pledged land, 130, 149, 185, 187–88, 212, 225, 311n. 90
Mortuary roll for Vidal of Savigny, 68
Mother-abbeys, 106; many ties only in 1180s and later, 102
Mousnier, Mireille, 296n. 133
Murder at Berdoues's grange of Cuelas, 174
Mutual aid, 156
Mystical significance of numbers, 22
Mythology, Cistercian, 1–2, 24, 15, 40–42, 109–10, 143–44, 175. *See also* Foundation accounts

Na or Domina, 184
Narbonne, archbishop, 131, 132, 133; Arnold Amalric, abbot of Cîteaux, 230; Berengar, 316n. 197
Narbonne, viscount, 133; Aimeric, 131, 318n. 13; viscountess Ermengardis, 131, 163, 318n. 13
Narrative accounts for southern France. See *Vita* of Pons de Léras, 110–12
Nazaria, prioress of Nonenque, 193
Negotiations that preceded cartulary making, 166

Netlieu, Cistercian abbey for women, dioc. Agde, appendix 3, no. 40; 205, 317n. 220
New Europe and Cistercians, 110, 228–29
New manuscript findings as irrefutable evidence, 54
New monastery (*Novum monasterium*), 6, 9, 17, 56, 88–89, 264n. 12, 275n. 45
Newman, Martha, 98
Nîmes, hospice of Franquevaux, 142, 155, 196
Nizors, or la Bénédiction-Dieu, Cistercian abbey for men, dioc. Saint-Bertrand-de-Comminges, appendix 3, no. 14; 140
Noble marriage strategies, 164, 184–85
Nonenque, Cistercian abbey for women, dioc. Vabres, appendix 3, no. 37; 40, 112, 116–19, 124, 189–96, 207, 277n. 62, 297n. 145, 315n. 168, 319n. 22
— absorbed hermitages, 108
— charters, 162, 167, 189, 191–93
— daughter-houses, 190
— expenditures and wealth, 190–93, table 3
— grange cultivation, 304n. 237; locations, 194, fig. 38; tithe-free, 193
— members: prioresses, Nazaria, 193, Vitrou, Tiburce of, prioress and abbess, 312n. 118; nuns, Sibilia, 191; chaplain, Raymond of Fraissenel, 315n. 168; procuratrix, Garsens of Vintro, 193
— pastoralism, 194–95
— relationship to Silvanès, 189–90
— secession attempt, 195–96
— size and limited places 191–93
— social status of its nuns, 165, 190
— ties to Bellecombe, 189–90
Norbert of Xanten, 41
Normandy, charter evidence, 77ff
Nos cistercienses in *Exordium Parvum*, 11, 15
Noval lands and tithes (*novalia*), 229
Novitiate, 112
Novum monasterium. See New monastery
Numbers, new abbeys, 154
Nun of Watton, 146, 302n. 208
Nuns, Cistercian, 41–44, 164, 236, 295n. 113, 314n. 140
— architecture, 36, 133. *See also* individual houses
— assumptions about, 13–14, 35–36, 39–45, 144
— economic situation: acquired last and least productive lands, 228; dependence on father-visitors, 43; expended large amounts of cash for blocks of land, 167, 195; found

Nuns, Cistercian (*continued*)
  new houses only rarely, 108; pastoralism an obvious choice, 120; property coveted, 43–44
— history: *exordia* and filiation trees leave out, 14, 103; female/feminine branch a misnomer, 40, 269n. 126; General chapter at le Tart, 44, 235; treated as imitation Cistercians, 40–42
— monks and clerics oppose incorporation, 43
— origins: annexed into Order by men's houses, 108–9, 127, 131–32, 189; in Burgundy, 39ff; foundations by le Thoronet and threat of heresy, 117, 230–31; hermitages and hospitals annexed, 103, 108; independent local foundations, 39–42; patrons, 132, 229, 233; syneisactic communities, 108; recruits, high numbers, 164
— priests and lay-brothers take vows from abbesses, 165
— regularization, 42–45, 122–23, 195, 233, 270n. 136, 297n. 149
— suppression, 123, 234
— treatment: abbess deposed at Nonenque, 118–19, 196; Coyroux and choice of dependency, 320n. 41; la Peyrouse nuns become canonesses, 132; Marrencs, nuns, founded by counts of Toulouse, 300n. 189; few in southwestern France because of Fontevrault, 126
Nuns, Dominican, 41
Nuns, Fontevrault, 41, 126
Nuns, Gilbertine, 41
Nuns, nursing sisters, in reform communities, 102
Nuns, Praemonstratensian, 41
Nuns, Saint-Orient and Saint-Jean, 188, 311n. 80
Nuns, unaffiliated, 39ff, 44–45, 164, 220–33; insufficient spaces, even in twelfth century, 43, 235–36

Obazine, 40, 124, 143–47; charters and cartulary, 145–46, 301n. 203; daughter-houses of Cîteaux in 1165 not 1147, 143–46; double community, 144, 314n. 142
Occitania. *See* Southern France
Octocentenary of Bernard of Clairvaux's death (1953), 42
Odo of Maurencs, 183–85, 311 n. 88
Odo of Porastron, brother-in-law of Maurencs, 311n. 83
Odo of Sirac, nephew of Gaillard, 183
Old Europe and Cistercians, 103, 228–30, 262n. 12, 318n. 11
Olieux. *See* Les Olieux (Montsérat); Les Olieux (les-Monges)
Olive production, 132–33, 140, 155, 218
On the Diverse Orders, 68
Oraison-Dieu (Muret), Cistercian abbey for women, dioc. Toulouse, appendix 3, no. 28; 36
Oraison-Dieu-de-Costejean, Cistercian abbey for women, dioc. Rodez, appendix 3, no. 36
— institution defined by administrative structures: concept of membership in, 195; filiations, 158–59; General Chapter, 156–58; introduction of centralized government, general chapter, internal visitation, written legislation, 69; umbrella group, 47–48, 67, 92, 93, 99
— invention as response to pressures, 93
— traditional definition, 46, 52, 94, 104; denied nuns, 35–44; great and early uniformity enforced, 40, 43, 48, 93; miraculous growth, 1–2, 104, 285n.1; tithe privileges and exemption from episcopal
Order (Cistercian). *See Ordo cisterciensis*
Order of Alcantara, 277n. 69
Order of Calatrava, 277n. 69
Order of Fontevrault, 128
Order of Malta collection, 294n. 102, 304n. 245
Order of Peace and Faith, 294n. 103
Order-differentiation, 85–86
Orderic Vitalis, 68, 101, 238; William of Malmesbury, 101
Orders of society, 68
Ordines, liturgical. *See Ecclesiastica Officia*; Liturgical order-books
Ordo, 88, 91, 116–17, 152, 155–56, 166, 177, 212, 218, 222
— earliest references, 46, 68–69, 80–81, 93; in charters, 68–79; southern France, 70–74; Burgundy, 74–76; Anglo-Norman realm, table 2, 76–79
— meaning, 68–70, 74, 79–80, 112, 223
— non-Cistercian, 215
— our, 68, 71, 217
— possible exceptions in its use, 80–89
Ordo cistellensis, 68, 239; *ordo de Cistel*, 74
Ordo cisterciensis, 43, 68–71, 73, 76–79, 96–97, 103, 112, 116, 140, 154–55, 160, 209, 211–13, 223, 270n. 131, 298n. 182, 313n. 137

Ordo clarevallensis, 96, 150
Ordo clericus, 68
Ordo laicus, 68
Ordo monasticus, 68, 70, 76, 97, 112, 208, 224
Origins, Cistercian as claimed in *exordia*, 3, 10–11, 15, 46
Orthodox religious reform less interesting, 231–32
Ortis, grange of Valmagne, 208
Oxford, Corpus Christi College, MS 209, 245

Paloma, daughter of Yspanus of Maurencs, 185, 311n. 80
Papal bulls issued from Cîteaux, Sept. 1147, only copies exist, 145
Papal confirmations, 42, 46–47, 153; after Calixtus II, 87–91; sought by monastic communities, 42, 77ff, 159, 171; pre-Cistercian Grandselve, 128. See also *Desiderium quod*; *Ad hoc in Apostolicae*; *Sacrosancta*
Papal recommendations of women's houses to General Chapter limited, 43
Papal schism. See Innocent II; Alexander III
Pardieu, winter site for Léoncel, 122, 293n. 86
Paris, Archives nationales document discussed by Gerits, 83
Paris, Bibliothèque nationale, Latin MS 4221, fig. 19, 57–59, 62–63, 275nn. 43, 46, 282n. 122
Paris, B.N. Latin MS 4346, fig. 19, 243, 275nn. 43, 57, 59, 62–63, 67, 284n. 141
Paris, B.N. Latin MS 12169, 275n. 46
Paris, B.N. Latin MS N.A. 430, 59, 62–63, 244, 275n. 43
Paris, Bibliothèque Sainte-Geneviève MS 1207, fig. 19, 57, 63–64, fig. 20, 66, 242, 264n. 12, 275n. 44
Pascal II, pope (1099–1118), bull from *Exordium Parvum (Roman Privilege)*, 17–20, 284n. 141
Passage rights, 147
Pastoralism (and transhumance), 118–19, 120–24, 130, 136, 156, 193, 213, 262n. 13, 298n. 168, 315n. 182, 319n. 22; conflict, 130, 141, 176, 183, 195; economic alternative to lay-brothers and granges, 117–21
Patrologiae Latina, 69
Patronage, 161–65; bourgeois, 129, 132, 219; episcopal, for Cistercian nuns, 270n. 137; for Gimont, Silvanès, Nonenque, and Valmagne, 165–220; mark of silver for General Chapter meeting, 75. See also Benefactions

Patrons, 99, 161–62, 172–74; conflict with, 183, 188; confused notions of what they were supporting, 207; deathbed scenes, 188; kinship ties among those for Gimont, 187–88; liminal state of those about to enter a community, 166, 180; make grudging concessions to Gimont, 181–83; request foundations, 99, 109, 179; resources, 173, 219, 228; temporary gifts, 170ff
Paul, Vivian, 313n. 134
Peace of Paris (1229), 130, 297n. 138
Peace with Praemonstratensians, 83–87
Pensioners at Valmagne, 218
Perpetuity of gifts, 171
Peter, abbot of Ardorel, 211
Peter, abbot of Cluny, 305n. 251
Peter, abbot of Valmagne, 316n. 188
Peter, bishop of Agde, 316n. 197
Peter Gonterius, 316n. 188
Peter Lawrence, husband of Senegundis, 217
Peter Lombard, at hospital of Saint-Martin, 214–15
Peter of Carambad, priest at Arbielle, 181–82
Peter of Castelnau, papal legate, 135–36
Peter of Lerce, founder of Saint-Victor of Montveyre, 101, 133
Peter of Luganio, gave to Pons de Léras, 169
Peter of Pradines, 205
Peter of Vairac, 218
Peter and Pons of Boisedo, 212
Petronilla, prioress of Nonenque, 195
Peyrouse. See La Peyrouse
Pierleoni. See Anacletus II
Pilgrimage, 111, 175
Pioneering, 23–24, 54, 228; and tithe exemption, 229
Plan or Plane. See Sainte-Madeleine-de-la-Plan
Planesylve, 177–78
Poblet, Cistercian abbey for men, daughter-house of Fontfroide, 131, 227, 320n. 43; monk, Arnold Amalric, 230; prior, 318n. 13
Polyculture, mediterranean, 262n. 13
Pons, abbot of Silvanès, 315n. 168
Pons Constantine, recruit to Valmagne, 163
Pons John, at hospital of Saint-Martin, 214–15
Pons Raine, 171
Pons William, donor for Valnègre, 142
Pons William, son of Adelaide and late Bernard of Saint-Pons, 162
Pons of Canvern and Hugh his brother, shepherds for Valmagne, 213

Pons of Léras, 101, 110–12, 117, 166, 190, 279n. 86, 315n. 169, 289n. 51, 290n. 52
Pons (or Pons William) of Polignac, abbot of Grandselve (1158–65), abbot of Clairvaux (1165–69), bishop of Clermont (1170–89), 73, 151, 176, 278n. 81, 308n. 54, 309n. 56
Pontaut, Cistercian abbey for men, dioc. Aire, appendix 3, no. 1; Pontaut, 125, 320n. 43
Pontigny abbey for Cistercian men in Burgundy, 8, 75, 99, 106, 124, 125, 126, 138, 143, 156, 158, 280n. 101, 285n. 149, 303n. 219
— abbots, 99–100
— cartularies, 75, 99–100
— congregation and filiation tree, 124, 143
— foundation narrative, 88–89
— monk Henry went to Cadouin, 143, 288n. 40
Popes of thirteenth century and religious women, 233
Porcelet family and Cistercian nuns, 231
Portaglonium. See Bouillas
Post-Bernard, 159
Practices (Cistercian), 48, 96, 106, 117, 143, 152, 154, 159, 179, 196, 205, 210, 215
Praemonstratensians and Prémontré, 41, 86, 125, 229; abbot, Hugh of Fosse (1128–64), 85; and women, 303n. 219; Charter of Peace with, 109, 215; General Chapter, 83; sisters, 86
Pre-Cistercian and Proto-Cistercian houses and congregations, 97, 102, 106, 121, 136, 138, 140–41, 151, 155, 159, 176, 189, 205, 222, 223; adopt Cistercian *ordo*, 138, 151, 220, 223; associated with women, 126; defined as stage in development of Order, 102
Preaching against heresy in southern France, 135–36, 230
Preaching, Cistercian, 94, 126, 127, 128, 131, 136, 147, 179
Preuilly, 76, 106, 280n. 100
Priests attached to women's houses, 190
Priests' wives, 102–3, 214, 232
Primitive documents, 3, 23, 46–49, 56, 80, 103, 149, 150, 222, 225. See also *Capitula*; *Carta Caritatis Posterior*; *Carta Caritatis Prior*; *Ecclesiastica Officia*; *Exordium Cistercii*; *Exordium Parvum*; *Instituta*; Lay-brother-treatises; *Summa Cartae Caritatis*
— manuscripts: contents, 48–49; dating 46, 56–68; fragments, 63; groupings of texts in, 4, 8

— texts: dated, 59–68; debate, 51–55, 274n. 27; evolution, 62; groupings of primitive documents, 3, figs. 1, 8, 9, 23, 47, 263n. 6; variants and early history of Cistercians, 51–52
Primogeniture, 165
Priories: existing, 108; for women, 42
Pro amore Dei, 178, 298n. 182
Procuratrix, 193, 214
Promises of noninterference by abbot visitors, 224
Protection of smaller houses more effective for monks than nuns, 234
Proto-abbots, 50, 54, 56, 85, 100, 137, 139, 142, 150, 158
Proto-Cistercian. See Pre-Cistercian
Prouille, house of Dominican nuns, 231, 269n. 123, 319n. 29
Provence, Cistercian churches, le Thoronet, Sénanque, Silvacane, 24ff, figs. 2ff
Pseudo-triforium, 203
Puy Bonenque, acquisition of Valmagne, 171

Rainald, abbot of Cîteaux. See Cîteaux, abbots
Raymond, abbot of Saint-Sauveur of Lodève, 195
Raymond, abbot of Verula, 309n. 56
Raymond, prior of Silvanès, 316n. 199. See also Silvanès, priors
Raymond V, Count of Toulouse, 39
Raymond VII, count of Toulouse, 268n. 109; and Candeil, 130, 297n. 138
Raymond Amicus of Provencos, 213
Raymond Beovers, 212
Raymond Gerald, at hospital of Saint-Martin, 214–15
Raymond Roger II Trencavel, 316n. 196
Raymond Sacristan (Porcelet family), 231
Raymond Senex, called abbot of Berdoues, 137
Raymond Vidal, prior of Gimont, 309n. 56
Raymond of Castronovo, donor, 216
Raymond of Fraissenel, chaplain of Nonenque, 315n. 168
Raymond of l'Isle, Crusader, 187–88, 311n. 83
Raymond of Mauvezin, 310n. 68
Raymond of Pereto, 217
Raymond of Portale, 217
Raymonda, at hospital of Saint-Martin, 214–15
Raymonda, wife of Pons Constantine, 163
Ré, Cistercian abbey for men, 75

Real estate market. *See* Economic conditions
Recluse houses and hospitals, 165, 215
Recruits, 184, 218, 306n. 6, 306n. 8
Reform (twelfth-century): aims, 100, 153, 172; and adult conversion, 129, 166; attractions, 17, 94, 97; consequences, 52, 220; language used, 68; stability, 94
Regesta Regum Anglo-Normannorum, 147
Regina, widow of Bernard of Castellione, prioress of Rieunette, 141, 144, 299n. 183
Regularization: Cistercian women's houses in thirteenth century, 44, 94, 108, 195, 233–36 (*see also* Nuns, Cistercian); eremitical communities into cenobitic ones, 111–12. *See also* Hermits
Religio cisterciensis/cistellensis, 68, 75
Religious benefits. *See* Benefactions
Religious communities for women: ephemeral ones, 44–45; Grundmann's categories, 41; lay-sisters, 102. *See also* Nuns, Cistercian
Religious congregations. *See* Congregations, religious
Religious fervor, 213
Religious Order. *See* Order; *Ordo*
Remains, southern French, 268n. 96. *See also* Architecture
Remensnyder, Amy, 79
Resistance to monastic encroachments, 174–75, 220
Responsibilities. *See* Abbots and abbesses, responsibilities
Rhetoric, 17, 209
Rica of Roque, buried at Villelongue, 141
Richard of Saint-Laurent, 155
Rieunette, Cistercian abbey for women, dioc. Narbonne, appendix 3, no. 54; 39, 141
Rievaulx, Cistercian abbey for men, abbot, Aelred, 146; charter from King Stephen, possibly forgery, 78
Rifreddo, Cistercian abbey for women, 44
Riquersella, church granted to Grandselve, 128
Risks for peasants, 129
Rivet. *See* Le Rivet
Robert, Ulysse, 87, 284n. 138
Robert of Arbrissel, 41, 94, 123, 127–28, 223
Robert of Molesme, 5–6, 11–17, 94
Rodez, bishops, 111, 124, 127, 190, 193, 295n. 117
Rodez, countesses, Ermengarde of Creyssels, 190
Rodez, counts, 131, 190; Hugh, 190

Roman privilege, of Pascal II. *See Desiderium quod*
Roman roads, 140, 196
Rosenwein, Barbara, 170, 189
Rostagnus of Popian, 217
Royaumont, abbey of Cistercian men, 103, 222, 230
Rueda, abbey of Cistercian men, 309n. 62
Rule of Saint Benedict, 10–12, 20, 47, 50, 58, 65, 68, 98; on abbot's responsibilities, 100
Rules for affiliation of thirteenth century, 233

Sacristana, daughter of Raymond Sacristan, Porcelet family, 231
Sacrosancta (privilege of Alexander III), 46, 47, 66–69, 89–92, fig. 24, 285n. 149
Saint-Adellan, priory, 219
Saint-Andrew, abbey of Cistercian men, 267n. 93
Saint-Beaulize, parish of, 195, 312n. 109
Saint-Bernard-de-la-Cagnotte, Cistercian abbey for women, dioc. Bayonne, appendix 3, no. 6
Saint-Christophe, new site for l'Escaledieu, 138
Saint-Croix of Orléans, charter, 75
Saint-Etienne of Rogaz, 312n. 109
Saint-Félix of Montseau (Gigean), Cistercian abbey for women, dioc. Maguelonne, appendix 3, no. 47; 32–35, 205, figs. 11–14; stone church reused, 32ff
Saint-Germain, church granted to Grandselve, 128
Saint-Guilhem-du-Désert, 111, 219
Saint-Guillelm gate, Montpellier hospice at, 209
Saint-Hilaire, 308n. 40
Saint-Hyppolyte, shared grange, 155, 176
Saint-Jacques of Compostela, 111
Saint-Jean of Alcapiès, church of Nonenque, 193
Saint-Jean of Gissac, church of Silvanès, 193
Saint-Jean of Olcas, church of Nonenque, 193
Saint-Jorii, parish granted to Grandselve, 296n. 128
Saint-Lys, bastide of Gimont made from Aiguebelle grange, 179
Saint-Martin, hospital, 214, 316n. 188
Saint-Martin of Colons, parish and garrigue, 214
Saint-Martin of Toget, 310n. 77
Saint-Martin of Valnègre, 142

Saint-Mary of Carambad, 181, 182
Saint-Mary of York, 100
Saint-Mary-Magdalene, Grandselve dedication, 128
Saint-Michel of Cuxa, 142
Saint-Michel of la Cluse, 131, 297n. 151
Saint-Paul, grange of Valmagne, 208
Saint-Paul of la Fos, church of Nonenque, 193
Saint-Peter of Beceria, parish granted to Valmagne, 211
Saint-Pierre-de-l'Almanarre, Cistercian abbey for women, 1221, dioc. Saint-Paul-Trois-Châteaux, appendix 3, no. 81; 231
Saint-Pierre-du-Puy, Cistercian abbey for women, c. 1200 dioc. Orange, appendix 3, no. 78; 231
Saint-Pons-de-Géménos, Cistercian abbey for women, c. 1205 dioc. Marseilles, appendix 3, no. 77; 231
Saint-Sauveur of Lodève, 110–11, 195, 312n. 109
Saint-Sernin of Artigues (absorbed by Berdoues), 108
Saint-Sigismond-d'Orthez, Cistercian abbey for women, dioc. Dax, appendix 3, no. 10; 36
Saint-Sulpice-de-la-Pointe, Cistercian priory then abbey for women, dioc. Lavaur, appendix 3, no. 16; 190–91, 297n. 145
Saint-Victor of Marseilles, 26, 133
Saint-Victor of Montveyre, 133
Sainte-Catherine-de-Vaucluse, Cistercian abbey for women, dioc. Avignon, appendix 3, no. 73
Sainte-Claire, Cistercian abbey for women, dioc. Alès, appendix 3, no. 42
Sainte-Croix, Cistercian abbey for women, dioc. Apt, appendix 3, no. 68
Sainte-Eugénie, priory annexed by Fontfroide, 131–33, 225–27, 230; prior, William of Lac, 225
Sainte-Foi of Conques, 216, 219
Sainte-Madeleine-de-la-Plan, Cistercian abbey for women, dioc. Carpentras, appendix 3, no. 74
Salenques, Cistercian abbey for women, dioc. Rieux, appendix 3, no. 24; 36, 268n. 109, 300n. 190
Salvarius, peasant given to Valmagne with his family, 166
Sanche, abbot of Eaunes, 309n. 56
Sanche, count of Astarac, 137

Sanche of las Comères, entered Berdoues, 108
Sanchia, sister of recruit to Gimont, 310n. 77
Sanctas Cruces, abbey of Cistercian men, 129, 210, takes over l'Eule, 133
Sanctimoniales, 190. *See also* Nuns, Cistercian
Sane laborum, 209, 229
Sasena, widow, 308n. 40
Saulier or Sediloci, 88, 284n. 137
Saurimunda, daughter of Raymond of l'Isle and Galdris, married to William Arnold of Bigmont, 187
Sauvelade, Cistercian abbey for men, dioc. Lescar, appendix 3, no. 11; daughter-house of Gimont, 309n. 62
Sauveréal (Ulmet), Cistercian abbey for men, dioc. Nîmes, appendix 3, no. 58; 122–23, 293n. 90, 320n. 43
Savigny, Cistercian abbey for men, 129, 143–48, 158, 301n. 199, 318n. 7
— abbots: Alexander of Cologne, 1158–68, 128, 150, 302n. 213; Vidal, founder, 123; mortuary roll, 68; Serlo, 302n. 214
— congregation, 106, 123, 144, 147, 281n. 103
— incorporation, 143–47
— practices, 144–46
Scandal passed on about rival communities, 146
Scandinavia, Cistercian settlement in, 104
Scholastica, sister of Saint Benedict, 20
Sealing, 170, 265n. 38, 308n. 38; in *Exordium Parvum*, 11–12
Secession, from Molesme, 10; from Order, 235
Seguerius of Saint-Hyppolyte, 155
Sénanque, Cistercian abbey for men, 1148 dioc. Cavaillon, appendix 3, no. 75; 24–27, figs. 2–5; 114
Senegundis, daughter of late Peter William, 217
Sequencing liturgical manuscripts, 57–61, table 1, 274n. 36
Serlo, abbot of Savigny, 147, 302n. 214
Sermons on Song of Songs by Bernard of Clairvaux, 98
Shearing Clairvaux of excessive power, 149
Shift in use of terms, 69, 97, 102, 170
Sibilia, daughter of Ermengardis, nun at Nonenque, 191
Sibilla, daughter of William of Mont-Ferrario, 216
Sicard Alaman, 131, 191, 297n. 145
Silvacane, Cistercian abbey for men, dioc. Aix,

appendix 3, no. 67; 26, 114; church, 24–25, fig. 2, 27
Silvanès, Cistercian abbey for men, dioc. Vabres, appendix 3, no. 38; 40, 71, 74, 110–17, 124, 154, 157, 163, 166, 189–96, 207, 315n. 169, 316n. 188, 319n. 22, 320n. 43
— abbot: as arbitrator for hospice, 209; Pons, 315n. 168
— charters and cartulary, 74, 111, 167, 189–90, 195–96, 209, 278n. 78; references to *ordo*, 71–73, table 2
— chronicle of foundation, 110–12, 114–18, 189, 232, 289n. 49, 315n. 162
— church, 112–16, figs. 26–29
— Cistercian practices, 74, 132, 152, 212, 270n. 132
— expenditures, 191–93, table 3
— granges, fig. 38, 194, 304n. 237
— Montpellier hospice, 209
— Nonenque, 193–96
— patronage and endowment, 111, 190–95
— priors, Raymond, 316n. 199
— promises of admission, 278n. 71
— William VI as witness, 211
Simon de Montfort, 298n. 159
Sincere truth, 11, 51
Single model of monastic practice, even in buildings, 24
Sirac family, 184, 310n. 75
Sites as witness to Cistercian mythology, 23–24, 41, 111, 228
Size limits on communities, 44, 133, 271n. 139, 312n. 116
Social level at Nonenque, 190
Social services at Valmagne, 218
Soler. *See* L'Eule
Solitude. *See* Desert
Sorrow at Cîteaux, according to *exordia*, 17, 21
Source criticism. *See* Diplomatic analysis
Sourden, foundation, 301n. 203
Southern France: cartulary making, 307n. 29; dimensions of term, xvii–xxi, 261n. 11; general, xviii, 262n. 13; heresy over-stressed, 232; pre-Cistercian communities and congregations, 97, 102
Spain, congregations, 131, 138, 140, 176
Spiritual benefits of the Order, 155, 169, 173
Spirituality, Cistercian, 97–98, 102–3; decline, 144
Staffarda, abbey of Cistercian men, 44
Stagnum of Vairac, 217
Statuta, 103, 158, 207, 209, 261n. 2, 263n. 6, 304n. 248. *See also* Filiations; Internal visitation
— criterion for recognition of women's houses, 43, 51
— dated: 1134 and 1152, 48–49; 1152 (items 1 and 6) 51, 275n. 43; dated 1157–61, 49–50, 153
— dating, 48–51, 65–66, 239
— edition by Canivez, 49–50, 56, 238, 301n. 198; manuscript collation for *Statuta*, ed. Canivez, 271n. 6
— as regulations on: conversi and who might be (1188), 154, 166–67; deposition of abbots, 8, 150; expansion, founding new houses, 95, 109, 229; General Chapter and centralized control, 154; limits on abbot-visitors' power over daughter-houses, 7, 10, 93, 103, 149–50, 159; minimum distances between granges and neighbors, 86, 109, 215; prima collectio of 1160s, 50, 238, proto-abbots have oversight of Cîteaux, 100; single abbot or abbey was not to rule, 149; taverns, 275n. 43; treatment of nuns, 232
Stephen, king of England, 77–78, 147–148, 281nn. 103, 105, 106, 110
Stephen Harding, second abbot of Cîteaux, 39, 88, 129, 159, 224, 264n. 16, 279n. 89; as depicted by others, 6, 7, 94, 98, 101; interpretations of reform, 94, 98–99, 100, 287n. 16; death, consequences, 98–99
Stephen of Muret, founder of Grandmont, moved away from women, 120
Stephen of Obazine, 123, 223
Stephana, daughter of Gassia, sister of Ademar of Juliac, 310n. 77
Stiçna manuscripts in Ljubljana, 243
Stock, Brian, 97–98, 286n. 12
Success, Cistercian, 53, 94–96, 102, 109–10, 121–22, 129, 131, 133, 136, 154, 227–28, 230
Summa Cartae Caritatis, 3, 7–9, 50, 53–54, 56, 62–63, 66, 86, 89, 91–93, 137, 139, 149–51, 156, 159, 263n. 6; dating 59–61; place in textual grouping, 7–9
Supra-monastic organization, 48, 151
Swineshead, Cistercian abbey for men, abbot of, 79
Syneisactic or family communities, 101–2, 108, 175–76, 205, 214

Templars, 132, 195, 277n. 69
Tenants, 187–88, 213

Terundo, *mansus* of, 111
Textual community, 97–99
Thomas Becket, 146, 301n. 201, 303n. 219
Thoronet. *See* Le Thoronet
Tithe barns, 52
Tithes
— and churches owned, 144, 154, 207–9, 212, 276n. 56, 305n. 251; at Vairac by Valmagne, 216; by Grandselve, 128; by Nonenque, 193
— Cistercian repurchase, 180, 187
— exemption from, 80–83, 96, 103, 109, 121, 148, 180, 193–94, 228–29; limited to novalia after 1215, 229; related to monastic ideology, 228, 229; treated as denoting Cistercians, 194
— other tithe holders, 121, 229
— ownership and disputes over tithes and churches, 121, 127, 154, 319n. 22
— papal privileges: for Cîteaux and Clairvaux, 76–81; other reform groups, 86–87, 121
— return to the church, 207
— theories of assessment: personal and predial, 121, on labor or land worked by their cattle, 208
— tithe-free agriculture at Nonenque, 193–94
Title deeds, 170
Titled nobles, rarely large benefactors of Cistercians, 184
Tolerance for Cistercian nuns and efforts to limit them, 42
Tortoreria, 205, 209–10, 215, 314n. 143
Tortosa, battle of, 210
Toulouse
— bishop: grants Grandselve two churches, 128; bishop Fulk (1205–31), 231–32, 294n. 103, 319n. 29
— counts: and comital family, 130–31, 261n. 11; count Raymond V, 39, 300n. 189; Raymond VII, 297n. 138
— foundation of Dominicans, 231
— hospice of Grandselve, 129
Tramesaigues, Interambasaquas, 142
Transhumance. *See* Pastoralism
Translation. *See* Charters, translation
Treatise on Accentuation of Latin at Cîteaux in Montpellier H322, 63–65
Tree of Jesse, 104
Trencavel family, 205–6, fig. 47, 215, 313n. 132, 316n. 196
Trent or Trento, bibliotheca communale, MS 1711, fig. 19, 59, 61–65, 66–67, 98, 152–53
Tresseira, *casale*, 188

Tulebras, abbey for Cistercian women, 270n. 133

Ugo of Mored, monk of Grandselve, 309n. 56
Ulmet. *See* Sauveréal
Umbertus, monk of Gimont, 309n. 56
Umbrella group: invented by Cistercians 93–94, 148, 152, 223–24; patronage of larger group, 209, 278n. 78
Unanimity. *See* Uniformity
Uncultivated land, availability, 173–74
Uniformity, 7–9, 52, 55–56, 102, 149, 152, 154, 208, 220; in liturgy, 10; lacking in Cistercian architecture, 24
Urban II, pope, letter in *Exordium Parvum*, 16
Urban hospice, 208–9
Urban centers, 122, 129, 218

Vairac, grange of Valmagne, 208, 214–19, 308n. 40; expenditures, 218; mills at 216–17; villa, 215
Vajal, domus Aimerici, Garnicia, priory of, 142, 299n. 185
Valautre, grange of Valmagne, 208
Valbonne, Cistercian abbey for men, dioc. Elne, appendix 3, no. 46; 221–22, 230
Valcroissant, Cistercian abbey for men, dioc. Die, appendix 3, no. 61; 123, 231, 235, 293n. 92, 321n. 48
Valle de Nutibus, in diocese of Elne, 221
Valmagne, Cistercian abbey for men, dioc. Agde, appendix 3, no. 41; 71, 106, 110, 121, 125, 143, 152, 154, 157, 162, 164, 166, 171, 193, 196–220, 229, 232, 315n. 155n. 168, 320n. 43
— abbots: Amedeus, 162, 208, 215; Ermengaudis, 209, 211; Peter, 171
— adopts Cistercian usages, 122, 207, 209–12
— affiliated by Bonnevaux, 207
— charters and cartulary, 71, 73, 143, 153. 162, 165, 171, 196, 205, 214, 217, 219, 305n. 2, 307n. 29, 313n. 132n. 137; references to ordo, 71–73, table 2
— church; 196–200, figs. 39–42, 313n. 137
— expenditures, 196–205, table 3
— granges, fig. 38, 194, 207–8, 308n. 40; at Canvern, 211–15; at Vairac, 215–20
— hospice in Montpellier, 209–12, 316n. 188
— papal confirmations, 207, 211
— patrons, 196, 205–20
— rents owed to, 217
— women's houses associated with, 122, 203–

5, 317n. 220. *See also* Le Vignogoul; Netlieu; Saint-Félix-de-Montseau; Saint-Martin, Hospital
Valnègre, Cistercian abbey for women, dioc. Rieux, appendix 3, no. 25; 142, 300n. 190; villa of, 142
Valsainte, Cistercian abbey for men, dioc. Apt, appendix 3, no. 69; daughter-house of Silvacane, 26
Valsauve-en-Gard, Cistercian abbey for women, dioc. Uzès, appendix 3, no. 59
Van Damme, J. B., analysis of *Sacrosancta*, 91–92
Vareilles, grange of Bonnecombe, 308n. 40
Vauluisant, Cistercian abbey for men near Sens, charter, 75–76, 241, 274n. 30, 280n. 101
Vauluisant, Cistercian abbey for women in Provence. *See* Le Bouchet
Vergy, 284n. 137
Vernaison. *See* La Vernaison
Veronica, countess of Marsanne, 231
Verula, abbey of, daughter-house of l'Escaledieu in Spain, Raymond, abbot, 309n. 56
Victor IV, pope, 148
Vidal, abbot of Fontfroide, 318n. 13
Vienne, archbishop Guy of Burgundy, became Calixtus II in 1119, 100
Vignogoul. *See* Le Vignogoul
Villa noveta of Vairac (Villeveyrac), 215–18
Villedieu, Divielle, abbey for Cistercian men, dioc. Dax, appendix 3, no. 9
Villelongue, Cistercian abbey for men, dioc. Carcassonne, appendix 3, no. 43; 140–42, 298n. 182; Campagnes hermits, 141; women, 141, 191. *See also* Rieunette
Villers-Bettnach, abbey for Cistercian men, manuscript from, 242
Villeveyrac, 215–18
Vintrou, Garsens of, 193
Vintrou, Tiburce of, prioress and abbess of Nonenque, 312n 118
Violence and murder, 174
Vita Prima of Bernard of Clairvaux, 116, 129, 143–45, 150, 301n. 194, 303nn. 219, 220
Vita of Benedict of Nursia, 20
Vita of Gerald of Salles, 128
Vita of Pons of Léras, founder of Silvanès, 110–11, 289n. 51, 290n. 52
Vita of Stephen of Obazine, 289n. 51; 290n. 52, 291n. 61
Viticulture, 129, 131, 316n. 201

Waddell, Chrysogonus, *Usus conversorum* edition, 275n. 48; proposal regarding liturgical manuscripts, 274n. 36
Walter, abbot of Morimond, 100, 136, 137, 138, 179; Walter I, second abbot of Morimond, former prior of Clairvaux, 100; Walter II, 73–74
Walter, abbot of Praemonstratensian house at Laon, 283n. 131
Walter, bishop of Châlons, 5–6
Warfare in twelfth century, mortality, 164
Watton, Gilbertine nun of, 146, 302n. 208
Wealth, Cistercian, 96, 99, 107, 154; denunciation of, 136, 303n. 219; explanations of, 52, 152; problem of 109–10
Wearing the habit of the Cistercians, 42, 70
Weber, Max, theories of, 14, 305n. 267
Western-French reformers and their congregations in southern France, 123–28; fig. 31, 136, 205
Wettingen MS, 10
Wichard, abbot of Pontigny, 283n. 131
Widow of Humbert of Capraria had him buried at Valmagne, 164
Widows living by alienation of land, 308n. 40
Wife of major donor gets money for her monastic dowry, 217
William, abbot of Belleaigue, 301n. 203
William, lord of Montpellier VI, 74–75, 157, 207, 210–11, 296n. 132, 304n. 233, 308n. 42, 314n. 158, 315n. 160; 315n. 184
William, lord of Montpellier VII, bequests to Valmagne, 75, 219
William, lord of Montpellier VIII, 313n. 132, 316n. 197
William, lord of Montpellier IX, 313n. 132
William Arnold of Bigmont, 187
William Crispin, at hospital of Saint-Martin, 214–15
William Fredo and his wife Ermessendis, 205
William Girmon, monk of Berdoues, 309, n.56
William Peter Curta Sola, monk of Berdoues, 309n. 56
William Raymond of Broil, social position, 309n. 61. *See also* Broil family
William Reverdida, at hospital of Saint-Martin, 214–15
William of Aspa, *conversus* of Gimont, 309n. 56
William of Batcave, *conversus* at Boulaur, 295n. 112
William of Blancafort, monk and administrator for Gimont, 179–80, 185

William of Juliac, 183, 310n. 77
William of Lac, prior of Sainte-Eugénie, 225–27
William of Malmesbury, 68, 101
William of Maurencs, 185, 187–88, 311n. 83
William of Montbazin, 16
William of Saint-Laurent, 155
William of Tortosa, son of William VI of Montpellier, 308n. 42
William of Toulouse, monk of Gimont, 309n. 56
Williams of Montpellier, cartulary, 75, 313n. 132
Women: in southern France, 163–65, 231–32; monastic aversion to, 120 (*see also* Misogyny); religious benefits from monks, 141, 163, 191, 108, 162–63, 163–65, 216, 218
Wooden churches. *See* Architecture
Written customs, 98, 152, 154
Written records, 165

Yspanus of Maurencs, 184–85, 187–89, 311n. 83
Yssingeaux, Bellecombe site, 189
Yvette of Huy, anchoress, 42

Zone of immunity, 70, 86, 109, 135, 215, 218, 230

www.ingramcontent.com/pod-product-compliance
Lightning Source LLC
Chambersburg PA
CBHW030104010526
44116CB00005B/91